www.wadsworth.com

www.wadsworth.com is the World Wide Web site for Thomson Wadsworth and is your direct source to dozens of online resources.

At **www.wadsworth.com** you can find out about supplements, demonstration software, and student resources. You can also send email to many of our authors and preview new publications and exciting new technologies.

www.wadsworth.com
Changing the way the world learns®

The Psychology of Prejudice and Discrimination

BERNARD E. WHITLEY JR. AND MARY E. KITE

THOMSON

WADSWORTH

Australia • Brazil • Canada • Mexico • Singapore • Spain
United Kingdom • United States

The Psychology of Prejudice and Discrimination
Bernard E. Whitley Jr. and Mary E. Kite

Executive Editor: *Michele Sordi*
Assistant Editor: *Jennifer Keever*
Senior Editorial Assistant: *Jessica Kim*
Technology Project Manager: *Erik Fortier*
Marketing Manager: *Chris Caldeira*
Marketing Assistant: *Nicole Morinon*
Senior Marketing Communications Manager: *Tami Strang*
Project Manager, Editorial Production: *Karol Jurado*
Creative Director: *Rob Hugel*
Senior Art Director: *Vernon Boes*

Senior Print Buyer: *Judy Inouye*
Permissions Editor: *Sarah Harkrader*
Production Service: *Sara Dovre Wudali, Buuji, Inc.*
Copy Editor: *Cheryl Hauser*
Illustrator: *Jill Wolf, Buuji, Inc.*
Cover Designer: *Paula Goldstein, Blue Bungalow Design*
Cover Image: *John Fox Images*
Cover Printer: *Transcontinental Printing/Louiseville*
Compositor: *Cadmus*
Printer: *Transcontinental Printing/Louiseville*

Thomson Higher Education
10 Davis Drive
Belmont, CA 94002-3098
USA

For more information about our products, contact us at:
Thomson Learning Academic Resource Center
1-800-423-0563

For permission to use material from this text or product,
submit a request online at **http://www.thomsonrights.com.**
Any additional questions about permissions can be submitted
by e-mail to **thomsonrights@thomson.com.**

Library of Congress Control Number: 2005925112

ISBN 0-534-64271-3

Brief Contents

Contents

Chapter 4

Stereotype Activation and Application   113

Chapter 5

Old-Fashioned and Contemporary Forms of Prejudice   161

Chapter 6

Individual Differences and Prejudice   208

Chapter 7

The Development of Prejudice in Children (Dana B. Narter)   260

Chapter 8

The Social Context of Prejudice   300

Chapter 9

Prejudice Based on Gender, Sexual Orientation, and Age   344

Preface

Throughout our academic careers, we each have had a keen interest in the study of stereotyping and prejudice. It seemed natural, then, that we should teach our department's course on prejudice and discrimination. When we set out to do so for the first time, however, we ran into a surprise: Although there is vast literature on the topic, there were very few textbooks on it. In addition, we found that none of the books struck the balance between empirical rigor and readability that we were looking for. Therefore, as so many before us have done, we decided to write our own book; the result is the book you have before you. Our goal in writing it is to provide students with an overview of what psychological theory and research have to say about the nature, causes, and amelioration of prejudice and discrimination. As a result, the book includes somewhat more detailed discussions of theories and selected research studies than do most other textbooks on the topic. At the same time, we have tried to keep our presentation at a level that is accessible to students whose only previous exposure to psychological theory and research has been in an introductory-level course. Feedback from our reviewers and from students in our courses who used drafts of some chapters as supplemental readings suggests that we have achieved that aim.

Although our book covers the standard topics included in textbooks on prejudice, we also set the goal of covering what we thought were important topics that had been omitted from earlier textbooks. Thus, because of our emphasis on theory and research, we have included a chapter on the research methods psychologists use to study prejudice and discrimination and how research methodology influences the conclusions drawn about the issues studied. Similarly, with one exception, previous textbooks have overlooked the question of how prejudice develops in children. Therefore, with the assistance of Dana Narter, a developmental psychologist, we have included a chapter on the development of prejudice in children. Finally, although psychologists have long understood that attitudes are poor predictors of behavior, previous textbooks have not addressed discrimination as a topic in its own right. We have therefore included a chapter that discusses the nature of discrimination and its relation to prejudice. Other topics we cover that are distinctive to our book include hate group membership, hate crime perpetrators, and prejudice and discrimination in organizations.

Although we have not formally divided the book into parts, the sequence of the chapters represents a progression across several themes. First, we introduce the nature of prejudice and discrimination (including a brief history of research on the topic), followed by our chapter on research methods. The next several chapters address the psychological underpinnings of prejudice: the nature of stereotypes; the conditions under which stereotypes influence responses to other people; contemporary theories of prejudice; individual difference variables related to prejudice; the development of prejudice in children; the social context of prejudice; and prejudice based on gender, sexual orientation, and age. The following two chapters focus on the nature of discrimination and its effects on those who experience it. We conclude with a discussion of prejudice reduction. We realize that every instructor has his or her own outline for how a course should be organized, so we have tried to make each chapter as independent of the others as possible to allow instructors to assign them in the order that best fits their personal goals for the course.

Each chapter begins with an outline to provide students with a cognitive map of its contents, and ends with a summary to provide closure. Within each chapter, key terms are shown in boldface; the index entry for each term also shows in boldface the page on which it is defined. These terms are also included in the glossary. Each chapter also includes boxes that provide supplemental information, additional examples, or other perspectives on issues. A set of questions concludes each chapter. Each set includes factual review questions, designed to integrate topics within the chapter; reflective questions, designed to encourage students to think about how the chapter's contents are relevant to their lives; and more philosophical questions designed to highlight controversies and help students clarify their positions on those issues.

To assist instructors in course development, we have written an Instructor Manual (available in electronic form from the publisher) that provides a list of resources including key readings, Web sites and handbooks of course-related activities. We also provide a list of television shows and films, including both domestic and international feature films specifically addressing psychological concepts, and a note for which chapter they are relevant. For each individual chapter, we provide suggested classroom activities, assignments, and readings for debate or discussion. We also have created a test bank that includes at least 50 multiple-choice questions for each chapter and have provided at least 20 short answer/essay questions for each chapter. Please contact your local Thomson/Wadsworth publishing representative to obtain a copy of the electronic Instructor Manual and Test Bank. We also invite you to explore the Wadsworth Psychology Resource Center at (http://psychology.wadsworth.com) for material relevant to this course.

We welcome any suggestions you have for improving this book. Please send electronic mail to Bernard Whitley at bwhitley@bsu.edu or Mary Kite at mkite@bsu.edu.

Acknowledgments

First, we want to thank Dana Narter for writing the chapter on prejudice in children; her expertise was invaluable. Michele Sordi, our editor at Wadsworth, guided us through the writing process. Her enthusiasm for our book reassured us that we did, in fact, have a good idea and helped us through the many Sloughs of Despond that we encountered along our way. We also thank Ball State University, who granted Bernard Whitley a semester's sabbatical leave to work full time on this book, and the staff of Bracken Library at Ball State University, whose expert assistance advanced our research immeasurably.

A number of people were kind enough to read draft chapters and suggest improvements. Our colleague Linh Nguyen Littleford read and provided feedback on each chapter and directed us to a number of valuable resources. The following people all provided invaluable comments and suggestions for improvement: Von Bakanic, College of Charleston; Charles F. Behling, University of Michigan; Jeff Bryson, San Diego State University; Jane Connor, Binghamton University; Alexandra F. Corning, University of Notre Dame; Peter M. del Rosario, Marist College; Azenett Garza-Caballero, Weber State University; Wind Goodfriend, Boise State University; Jonathan Iuzzini, University of Tennessee, Knoxville; Nancy J. Karlin, University of Northern Colorado; Jeffry S. Kellogg, Marian College; Lois-Ann Kuntz, University of Maine at Machias; Arthur G. Miller, Miami University of Ohio; B. Keith Payne, University of North Carolina at Chapel Hill; Sandra Prince-Madison, Delgado Community College; George E. Schreer, Manhattanville College; Linda Tropp, Boston College; Castellano Turner, University of Massachusetts, Boston; Lisa Wagner, University of San Francisco; and W. Douglas Woody, University of Northern Colorado.

Finally, we must thank the production staff at Wadsworth Publishing Company, both for putting the book into its final form and for their help and patience during the production process.

Introducing the Concepts of Stereotyping, Prejudice, and Discrimination

I have a dream that my four children will one day live in a nation where they will not be judged by the color of their skin but by the content of their character.

—Martin Luther King Jr., August 28, 1963

Surely all parents share Dr. King's dream that their children be viewed as individuals, appreciated for their unique strengths and talents. No one wants their loved ones to be treated differently solely because of their race, or because of their membership in any arbitrary social category. Yet even a cursory review of U.S. history reminds us of how readily people made race-based judgments as the country developed (see, for example, Takaki, 1993). Has there been progress? Looking back over the 40 years since Martin Luther King Jr. delivered his classic "I Have a Dream" speech on the steps of the Lincoln Memorial, it is easy to see the extent to which race relations have improved in the United States. The Jim Crow laws that limited the rights of minority groups have been dismantled and overt racial segregation, such as in restaurants and on public transportation, is a thing of the past.

Today, it is difficult to believe there was a time when White lynching of Blacks took place without serious investigation, let alone punishment. Nonetheless, race is still important to the perceptions of others—particularly those snap decisions people make when they first meet another person. Consider this experience of historian Ronald Takaki (1993):

> I had flown from San Francisco to Norfolk [Virginia] and was riding in a taxi to my hotel. . . . The rearview mirror reflected [the driver,] a white man in his forties. "How long have you been in this country?" he asked. "All my life," I replied, wincing. "I was born in the United States." . . . He remarked, "I was wondering because your English is excellent!" Then, as I had many times before, I explained: "My grandfather came here from Japan in the 1880s. My family has been here, in America, for over a hundred years." He glanced at me in the mirror. Somehow I did not look "American" to him; my eyes and complexion looked foreign. (p. 1)

Takaki's experience illustrates the many research findings that have shown race, sex, and age to be primary categories for organizing information about other people, making them likely to be the first pieces of information people take in about another (Kunda, 1999).

If people move beyond this initial categorization, its effects can be relatively benign. As discussed in Chapters 3 and 4, people can and do move beyond stereotypic judgments under some circumstances. Unfortunately, a person need not look far to see that people do not always do so and that prejudice and discrimination based solely on group membership is alive and well:

> In 1988, in Indianapolis [Indiana], state authorities established a residential treatment center for convicted child molesters in an all-white neighborhood. From the center's opening until mid-1991—a period during which all of the residents of the center were white—neighbors voiced no objection. In June, 1991, however, authorities converted the center into a shelter for approximately forty homeless veterans, twenty-five of whom were black. Soon thereafter trouble erupted as a group of whites . . . loudly proclaimed their opposition to the encroachment of "niggers" and burned a cross and vandalized a car to express their feelings. An all-white cadre of child molesters was evidently acceptable [in the neighborhood], but the presence of blacks made a racially integrated group of homeless *veterans* intolerable! (Kennedy, 2002, p. 27; emphasis in original)

1.1   *The Anti-Muslim Backlash Following September 11, 2001*

- The American-Arab Anti-Discrimination Committee in Washington, DC, reported there had been 270 violent incidents against Arab-Americans, including five murders within about a month after the terrorist attacks (Breslau, 2001). The FBI reported that the number of anti-Muslim hate crimes increased from 28 in 2000 to 281 in 2001, a tenfold increase (cited in Human Rights Watch, 2002).
- Violence against mosques increased dramatically after September 11, including
  - four teenagers burning down a multi-faith worship center in Oswego, New York
  - a self-reported Muslim hater who crashed his pick-up into a mosque in Tallahassee, Florida
  - vandals in Milpitas, California, who broke into a mosque under construction and wrote derogatory remarks
  - firing of 13 to 14 bullet holes in the Islamic Center of Irving, Texas (cited in Human Rights Watch, 2002).

All told, by October 1, 2001, 60 mosques had been attacked (Van Biema, 2001).

- In a CNN/*USA Today*/Gallup poll, conducted in the days shortly after 9/11, respondents were evenly divided as to whether all U.S. Arabs (including U.S. citizens) should be required to carry special ID cards (cited in Van Biema, 2001).
- The majority of Americans supported the idea of profiling Arabs, including those who are U.S. citizens, and subjecting them to special security checks before boarding planes, according to Gallup polls conducted in late September 2001 (Wisby, 2001).
- As late as August 2002, the majority of Americans polled agreed there are too many immigrants from Arab countries in the United States; in March of that year, 60 percent favored reducing the number of Arabs granted admission to the United States (Gallup Organization, 2002).

Clearly, in some situations at least, color still trumps character. As we will see in this book, the more relevant question may not be whether people are prejudiced but whether and under what circumstances people try to override their prejudices and, instead, step back to measure each individual on the content of his or her character.

Recent events also demonstrate how quickly views of other ethnic groups can change. Although, in the United States, attitudes toward Middle Easterners were not necessarily positive prior to the September 11, 2001, terrorist attacks, negative reactions toward individuals from those countries definitely increased after that terrible day. Some examples of those negative reactions are listed in Box 1.1. Looking further back in history to the early 1900s, when the immigration of Irish and Italians reached its high point in the United States, evidence abounds that members of those ethnic groups were the targets of ridicule. Remnants of those strongly held beliefs remain: Most people today can still readily identify the ethnic stereotypes associated with these groups (Peabody, 1985). These days, however, individuals of European descent have relatively few concerns that their ethnic background significantly disadvantages them.

How can it be that 100 years ago, Italians were considered non-White in the United States? If, as most people believe, race and ethnicity are biological categories, marked by differences in skin color, it is not logical that the definitions of who fits a category would change. In fact, there are very few true biological distinctions between what scientists define as racial groups (see Jones, 1997, for an excellent discussion). Moreover, the categories "White" and "non-White" shift with social conventions that, themselves, change over time. Lillian Rubin (1998), writing about the errors in historical memory of immigration in the United States, noted that "being white didn't make 'a big difference' for many [early] immigrants. The dark-skinned Italians and the eastern European Jews who came in the late nineteenth and early twentieth centuries didn't look very white to the fair-skinned Americans who were here then. Indeed, the same people we now call white— Italians, Jews, Irish—were seen as another race at that time" (p. 93). The fact that racial categories are arbitrary and fluid does not dilute their power, however: categorizing people by race and the stereotypes associated with racial groups helps to maintain the White over non-White social hierarchy that gives the dominant group power and control over other groups (see, for example, Jones, 1997; Sidanius & Pratto, 1999). See Box 1.2 for a brief history of the concept of race.

That people hold stereotypic beliefs about other groups seems a given. For as long as psychologists have studied stereotyping and prejudice, there has been no shortage of groups to study, nor a reluctance on the part of individuals to share their knowledge of stereotypes (see, for example, Devine & Elliot, 1995). As we will see, the targets of prejudice differ from culture to culture and across historical time periods. However, although the targets of bias vary between cultures and over time within cultures, the underlying story remains remarkably the same. This book is about why this happens. What is the common thread that runs through all types of stereotypic beliefs? Is there something about human information processing that predisposes people to stereotype? Are these beliefs related to behavior toward others and, if so, in what way? What role does emotion play in this process? We consider all these questions in this book. To begin, we explain some of the terminology used by social scientists who study prejudice and discrimination.

STEREOTYPES, PREJUDICE, AND DISCRIMINATION

In his classic book, *The Nature of Prejudice,* Gordon Allport (1954) argued that an adequate definition of prejudice must include two essential elements: There must be an *attitude* of favor or disfavor and there must be an overgeneralized, erroneous *belief.* This definition captures how most people think of prejudice. Contemporary psychologists take a more fine-grained approach, separating beliefs, or stereotypes, from the evaluation component of those beliefs and from the behavior toward members of the groups about which the beliefs are held.

1.2   *What Is a "Race"?*

If you ask people how they know what race a person is, they will usually tell you that the determining factor is skin color. But why *skin* color rather than some other physical characteristic, such as hair color or eye color? One answer is provided by anthropologist Audrey Smedley (1999) in her book *Race in North America.*

Smedley notes that the word *race* was not used in English to refer to groups of people until the 1600s, and at that time the meaning was very broad, referring to any group of people with common characteristics. For example, one writer referred to "a race of bishops." The meaning of the word *race* slowly narrowed until, in the late 1700s, it took on its present meaning to indicate groups of people sharing common physical characteristics, especially skin color. This narrowing of meaning took place at the same time as Europeans were beginning to colonize and dominate Africa, Asia, and the Americas, areas whose native inhabitants differed in skin color from Europeans. Over time, racial categories based on skin color became a means of differentiating "superior" Europeans from "inferior" others. These categories then became the focus of stereotypes "proving" the inferiority of non-Europeans and justifying European dominance and for race laws limiting the freedom of non-Europeans.

It is important to bear in mind that *race* is a social category, not a biological one. For example, genetic studies find more differences within traditionally defined racial groups than between them (e.g., Zuckerman, 1990). In statistical terms, the differences between races that do exist are trivial relative to the genetic factors common to all people. As Steven Pinker (2002) notes, "The differences in skin color and hair that are so obvious when we look at people of other races are really a trick played on our intuition. Racial differences are largely adaptations to climate. Skin pigment was a sunscreen for the tropics, eyelid folds were goggles for the tundra. The parts of the body that face the elements are also the parts that face the eyes of other people, which fools them into thinking that racial differences run deeper than they really do" (p. 143). In addition, during the period in U.S. history when racial segregation was legal, race was defined by law and people could petition a court to change their racial classifications (Banks & Eberhardt, 1998). If race were a biological fact, it could hardly be changed by court order.

The concept of *race* as we now use it developed, then, not as a set of biological categories but rather as a set of social categories. Its social nature does not diminish the psychological importance of race. It remains a fundamental basis for how people think about and interact with each other (Kunda, 1999).

Stereotypes

In this more contemporary model, beliefs are labeled *stereotypes*, a term Walter Lippman (1922) borrowed from the printing lexicon because it represented a fixed or unchanging process that reproduced exactly the same image every time it was applied (Ashmore & Del Boca, 1981). Writing at the beginning of the last century, Lippman (1922) described stereotypes as "pictures in our heads," noting that "what each [person] does is based not on direct and certain knowledge, but on pictures made by [him or her] self and given to him [or her]" (p. 16). This conceptualization is consistent with how modern social scientists think about stereotypic beliefs. There is no one, universal truth about the social world on which people can all rely. Instead, people's experiences and perspectives color the landscape of their beliefs, for better or worse, and it is this portrait that people use to navigate their social world.

For our purposes, we define **stereotypes** as beliefs and opinions about the characteristics, attributes, and behaviors of members of various groups (Hilton & von Hippel, 1996). There are several key aspects of stereotypes. First, although stereotypes may be pictures in each individual's head, they also come from shared beliefs that are an integral part of culture (see, for example, Jones, 1997). Stereotypes may be refined by each individual, but there is typically group consensus about the content of those beliefs. People learn stereotypes from the media, peers, parents, and even sources such as classic and modern literature. And, of course, people gather information about groups simply by observing the world around them.

A second key aspect of stereotypes is that they can be either accurate or inaccurate. Departing from Allport's (1954) view, most researchers no longer make the assumption that stereotypes are completely erroneous (Ashmore & Del Boca, 1981). Many stereotypes have a *kernel of truth*—they are based to some extent on observations made about the social world. Researchers often assess these observations by asking people to estimate the likelihood or probability that an individual member of a group has a certain characteristic. Men, for example, generally are taller than women, so there is a high probability that a particular man is taller than a particular woman. Hence, raters generally report there is a higher probability or likelihood that a man is tall than that a woman is tall. But it is entirely possible that using this rule will result in an inaccurate description for an individual group member: some women are taller than most men. Thus, a stereotype might be accurate for a group taken as whole, but inaccurate for at least some members of that group. Stereotypes can be inaccurate at the group level also. Think back to many of the beliefs once held about women's abilities, such as the belief that women should play half-court basketball because they were not physically able to do otherwise. And, certainly, many harmful consequences stem from relying on stereotypic beliefs in judgments of and interactions with others, even if that reliance makes it easier to navigate the social world. As discussed in Chapter 4, people face a tension between the need to process information quickly and the desire to treat others fairly, which is not easily resolved.

A third key aspect of stereotypes is that they can be both descriptive and prescriptive. That is, stereotypes of group members can *describe* the characteristics group members are believed to have, but they can also tell us what people believe group members *should be* like. As stereotypes take on more *prescriptive* elements, they put more limits on members of the stereotyped group. For example, it is true that most elementary school teachers are female (a descriptive stereotype), but is there a reason that this *must* be true? If not, should girls and women be encouraged to pursue this occupation while boys and men are discouraged from doing so (a prescriptive stereotype), thereby limiting the career choices of both women and men?

Finally, stereotypic beliefs can be either positive or negative. Think, for example, of the many positive associations with the group "mothers." Although people usually think about stereotyping as a social problem—something to be overcome (Ashmore & Del Boca, 1981), stereotypic beliefs sometimes favor a particular group, even if at the same time they disadvantage another. For example, the belief that women are "better with children" makes it easier for women to get jobs as elementary school teachers while at the same time making it more difficult for men. Even positive stereotypes can have a downside.

Prejudice

From a social science perspective, the affect or emotion a person feels when thinking about or interacting with members of other groups is a separate component from stereotypes, labeled prejudice. We define **prejudice** as an attitude directed toward people because they are members of a specific social group (Brewer & Brown, 1998). Attitudes are considered to be *evaluations* of an entire social group or of individuals because they are members of that group; for example, people may see the group of older adults as positive or negative or an individual older adult as good or bad. In both cases, the evaluations stem from reactions to the general social category. As we saw with stereotypic beliefs, people can hold both negative and positive attitudes toward a social group. However, perhaps because positive associations create relatively fewer problems, the dark side of prejudice is what has captured the imagination of social scientists and lay people alike. For this reason, this textbook focuses primarily on negative attitudes toward social groups. We will, however, also consider positive attitudes about social groups when appropriate. Research on positive attitudes, for example, has focused on bias in favor of one's own group, a topic we discuss in Chapters 3 and 8.

Research suggests that evaluations of social group members are more strongly related to how a person treats those group members than are the beliefs, or stereotypes, he or she holds about them (see Fiske, 1998 for a review). It is important to note that these evaluations may stem from a purely emotional or gut reaction to a social group as a whole or to an individual member of that group (Fiske, 1998; Mackie & Smith, 2002). As we will see in Chapter 4, these gut reactions are often automatic. Indeed, a person may make an emotional decision to like or dislike someone with very little conscious consideration. These emotional reactions also can be positive or negative or a mixture of both (see, for example, Glick & Fiske, 1996; Judd, Park, Ryan, Brauer, & Kraus, 1995). When emotional reactions are mixed, people can have an ambivalent emotional response or their response can be determined by whether the positive or negative feelings are more salient.

Emotional reactions to social groups can originate from several sources. When people perceive that another social group threatens their own group, for example, they may experience fear, anxiety, or hostility (see Fiske, 1998, for a review). Other groups can be threatening if they are perceived to interfere with the goals of one's own group, particularly if those threats take the form of direct competition for resources such as jobs or financial gains. However, other groups also can be seen as threatening simply by having different goals from one's own social group (Fiske & Ruscher, 1993; Smith, 1993).Emotional reactions also can stem from close personal contact with members of other social groups. Some people may feel disgust, for example, when they interact with members of a stigmatized group such as foreigners, persons with disabilities, or gays and lesbians (Fiske, 1998; see Chapter 9). Finally, as we will discuss in Chapter 6, some individuals are chronically intolerant of other social groups. Right-wing authoritarians, for example, tend to be prejudiced against a variety of social groups, especially those condemned by authority figures or those that are perceived to violate traditional values (Altemeyer, 1996). For these individuals, negative emotional reactions stem from their personality traits rather than situational factors.

Even people who consider themselves to be unprejudiced can harbor negative attitudes toward social groups without being aware of it. Although these feelings are generally more along the lines of discomfort, anxiety, and unease rather than hostility or hate, they nevertheless affect people's behavior (Dovidio & Gaertner, 2004). People who feel this way do not want to be prejudiced, hold egalitarian values, and feel ashamed when they become aware of their prejudices. They have nonetheless absorbed a degree of prejudice from the often nonegalitarian culture in which they have grown up and lived (see, for example, Jones, 1997). Finally, people's affective reactions may depend on the contexts in which they deal with members of stereotyped groups (Deaux & Major, 1987; Fiske & Neuberg, 1990). For example, a person may be more accepting of women's assertiveness in a domestic role than in a business setting. We discuss the importance of context in Chapters 4 and 9.

Discrimination

The third factor in the trilogy of concepts is **discrimination,** defined as treating people differently from others based primarily on membership in a social group. As with stereotypes and prejudice, although people tend to think of discrimination in negative terms, it also can result in someone's being treated more positively than he or she otherwise would be based on group membership. Many colleges and universities give a preference in admission to children of alumni, for example. As you might expect, however, the vast majority of the research on discrimination has focused on its negative aspects. When individuals are singled out and treated unfairly because of race, gender, age, sexual orientation, disability status, or any other factor, discrimination has occurred and, as a result, individuals lose opportunities and options. Discrimination can be viewed in terms of individual behavior, institutional policies and practices, and cultural values (Jones, 1997).

Interpersonal discrimination   When one person treats another unfairly because of the person's group membership, **interpersonal discrimination** has occurred. This unfair treatment may result from stereotypic beliefs, evaluations of a group, or a combination of both that results in differential treatment of that person. This discrimination occurs at the individual, or person-to-person level. For example, some people might hold the stereotypic belief that all Irish are alcoholics and feel disgust toward Irish people on that account and so try to prevent Irish people from joining organizations to which they belong. Thus, individual level prejudice leads people to behave in ways that imply that their own group is superior to other groups and that this distinction between groups should be maintained. Much of the research and theory we describe in this book concerns individual level prejudice and discrimination, such as how individuals process information about others, the content of their stereotypes, and individual differences in the tendency to respond in a discriminatory fashion. This perspective assumes that individuals have control over their beliefs and behaviors and that individuals independently choose or do not choose to be prejudiced.

Institutional discrimination   **Institutional discrimination** occurs when institutions or governing bodies sanction beliefs about group superiority. This type of discrimination can occur in subtle ways that are often below the radar in societal consciousness. Institutional discrimination also can be the result of overt practices that give one group an advantage over others by limiting their choices, rights, mobility, or access to information, resources, or other people (Jones, 1997). One of the most striking examples from U.S. history concerns the "separate but equal" school segregation system that was common before the U.S. Supreme Court declared it unconstitutional in the *Brown v. Board of Education* (1954) ruling. Although Chief Justice Warren, writing for the majority, stated that segregated schools deprived students of equal protection under the law, this decision was not universally accepted. In his inaugural address (January 14, 1963), for example, then governor of Alabama George Wallace stated, "I draw the line in the dust and toss the gauntlet before the feet of tyranny and I say segregation now, segregation tomorrow, segregation forever." It was only through government intervention that these schools eventually integrated. The vestiges of this debate remain today; in December 2002, Senator Trent Lott resigned under pressure from his position as Senate Majority Leader after appearing to praise Senator Strom Thurmond's 1948 segregationist presidential bid during a speech celebrating Senator Thurmond's 100th birthday (Waller, 2002).

Cultural discrimination   When, within a culture, one group retains the power to define cultural values as well as the form those values should take, **cultural discrimination** is in evidence (Jones, 1997). The powerful group establishes and maintains its dominance by rewarding those values that correspond to its views and punishing those values that do not. The result is that minority groups and their cultural heritage are marginalized. This marginalization is evidenced in many ways, from the sex stereotypes present in advertising (Kilbourne, 2000) to the skin color of Barbie and GI Joe dolls to the practice on the part of the Boy Scouts to dismiss gay scout leaders—a decision that was upheld by the U.S. Supreme Court (*Boy Scouts of America and Monmouth Council v. James Dale*, 2000). In all cases, the message is that the characteristics and contributions of the dominant group are valued, but those of the minority group are not.

Legislative policy may formally endorse cultural discrimination. At the beginning of the 20th century, for example, the Australian government became concerned with the increasing numbers of so-called half-castes or part-Aboriginal children in that country (Pilkington, 2002; Rowley, 1970). Because officials believed the part-Aboriginal children were more intelligent than full-blood Aborigines, separate institutions were established so that the part-blood children could be reared separately from their culture. On behalf of the Department of Native Affairs, patrol officers were assigned to remove these children from their homes and take them to one of these settlements, which were located as much as 1,000 miles from their families. The goal was to ease these children into White culture and to encourage their eventual inbreeding with Whites so that their Aboriginal ancestry was, in effect, bred out of them. These policies remained in place until the 1970s.

Institutional and cultural discrimination are both difficult to see and sometimes their existence is difficult to accept, especially by those not directly affected by it. To see these forms of discrimination, individuals must sometimes let go of cherished beliefs or deeply held ideas. Some Christians, for example, might have difficulty understanding why groups such as the American Civil Liberties Union (ACLU) have gone to court to prevent the posting of the Ten Commandments in government buildings. From the Christian perspective, there seems little to quibble about; after all, are the commandments not rules by which anyone would want to live? Legally, however, posting only the beliefs of one religion violates the separation of church and state mandated by the U.S. Constitution. And, publicly displaying the beliefs of the dominant group is not psychologically harmless either; the underlying assumption is that everyone should or does hold those beliefs and those who do not are unworthy of consideration by civil authorities.

The Relationships among Stereotyping, Prejudice, and Discrimination

The relationships among stereotyping, prejudice, and discrimination can be complex. Having knowledge of stereotypic beliefs, for example, does not necessarily mean an individual is prejudiced. In a highly influential demonstration of this phenomenon, Patricia Devine (1989) had college students list the characteristics that make up the stereotype of African Americans. She found that high and low prejudiced individuals were equally knowledgeable of the content of the stereotype; the difference was that the low prejudiced people rejected the stereotype but the high prejudiced people accepted it. As we noted earlier, these stereotypes are part of a societal belief system and are learned from many sources, including parents, peers, and the media. It should not surprise you that people have knowledge of these stereotypes, even if they themselves do not accept them.

More troubling, perhaps, is that people can access stereotypic beliefs without awareness and, therefore, such beliefs influence the behavior even of people low in prejudice. To understand this phenomenon, consider the distinction social scientists make between *implicit prejudices*, reactions toward groups or individuals that are outside conscious awareness, and *explicit prejudices*, attitudes that people are aware of and can easily control (Devine, 1989; Greenwald & Banaji, 1995). In Devine's (1989) studies, when stereotypic beliefs were activated at an unconscious level, research participants were unable to control the influence of these stereotypes on their evaluations. Yet, when given the opportunity, low-prejudiced research participants tried and were able to override the influence of their stereotypic beliefs and make unprejudiced responses. That is, people who believe that prejudice is wrong and try to control and eliminate their prejudices can successfully minimize the effects of stereotypes on their behavior.

As we discuss in detail in later chapters, it is not easy to predict when stereotypes lead to prejudice or discrimination or who is most likely to treat people differently based on their group membership. Yet this question is what ultimately interests those involved in social justice, and the answer to this question is the key to reducing prejudice and discrimination.

Isms

One frequently hears words ending in "ism"—such as racism, sexism, and so forth—used as synonyms for *prejudice*. Are prejudices and isms (for want of a better word) the same thing? Probably not, for as Oliver Cox (1948) noted many years ago, "If beliefs, per se, could subjugate a people, the beliefs which Negroes hold about whites should be as effective as those that whites hold about Negroes" (p. 531). What, then, are isms?

Although isms are based in prejudices, they go beyond them to encompass a belief system or ideology based on group superiority and domination and sets of behaviors reflecting that belief system. Isms have several defining characteristics (Jones, 1997; Operario & Fiske, 1998); for the purposes of this discussion we will use racism as an example. Racism is based in the desire to dominate and control members of other racial groups. Therefore, a basic condition for racism is that the group to which racists belong must have the societal power to define racial categories and to establish and enforce race-based social norms and laws. As we noted earlier, racial classifications are arbitrary, so domination and control of other races require a system for classifying people as members of the dominant or a subordinate race. The United States has had a long history of racial classification, often in the forms of laws, and such classifications are still used for census and other purposes, helping to maintain race as an important social category. Similarly, for most of its history, the United States has had laws restricting the freedom of non-Whites, forcing them into subordinate social positions (see, for example, Banks & Eberhardt, 1998).

A second characteristic of racism is a belief in the "natural," usually biologically based, superiority of the group to which racists belong, especially in moral and intellectual terms. This theme is pervasive in the literature and oratory of racist groups (see, for example, Blee, 2002; Ezekiel, 1995). Racists also feel the need to "prove" the superiority of their group and justify racist social policies by citing scientific research. Unfortunately, biologists and social scientists have often contributed to this endeavor, especially in the late 19th and early 20th centuries, by interpreting (and frequently misinterpreting) the results of their research to show non-Whites in a negative light (Richards, 1997; Tucker, 1994). This practice has mostly died out since the mid-1900s, but such **scientific racism** still has its practitioners (Tucker, 1994).

Racism also is reflected in behavior. Although hate crimes spring to mind as examples of racist behavior, racism also is found in everyday behaviors. One behavioral characteristic of racism is the automatic and unthinking rejection and denigration of other groups' cultures, such as their beliefs, customs, language, and arts. Why, for example, is rap music, which is so closely identified with Black culture in the United States, so often condemned? Is it because, as many of its detractors point out, of its violent and sexist lyrics, or is it because it is an expression of Black culture? Carrie Fried (1996) had White adults read a set of violent lyrics from a 1960s folk song, telling some people that the lyrics were from a rap song, others that the lyrics were from a country and western song, and a third group that the lyrics were from a folk song. The song received the most negative ratings when it was labeled a rap song. Fried also found that the song got more negative ratings when people thought it was performed by a Black singer than when they thought it was performed by a White singer. Thus, it was the "race" of the lyrics rather than their content that drove people's reactions to them.

Another behavioral characteristic of racism is behavior on the part of members of the group in power that demeans or harasses members of other groups. Consider, for example, any "joke" beginning "How many Black people does it take to . . . ?" Other unthinking demeaning behaviors include ignoring members of a minority group to focus on members of the majority group, staring at members of minority groups in places where they "don't belong," and avoiding contact with members of a minority group (Mellor, 2003). Harassment can also be carried out under governmental authority, as illustrated by the "crime" of "Driving While Black," discussed in Box 1.3.

Isms, therefore, combine prejudice with a group-centered worldview that emphasizes the "natural" superiority of one's own group over others. This worldview is reflected in laws, social customs, and an attempt to "scientifically" prove its validity. It is enacted in ways that unthinkingly demean members of minority groups and their cultures. It also can, as we will see, be a component of culture.

GROUP PRIVILEGE

Although, as psychologists, we will be focusing on prejudice and discrimination at the individual level, it is important to bear in mind that people live in cultures and that their cultures influence people's behavior, attitudes, beliefs, and other psychological characteristics (Fiske, Kitayama, Markus, & Nisbett, 1998), including those related to prejudice and discrimination (Jones, 1997). As people grow up in a culture, they tend to be unaware of its influence on them until something happens, such as a stay in another culture, that draws some aspect of their culture to their attention (see, for example, Carroll, 1988, for a look at differences between

1.3 *DWB: Driving While Black*

In the movie *Men in Black II,* a car driven by an "autopilot" stops to pick up Agents J and K. Agent K, back from a long hiatus, is impressed with the new technology. Agent J responds that the autopilot used to be Black, but he kept getting pulled over. The concept of Driving While Black (DWB) is not an uncommon reference in the comedy world and was the subject of a compelling advertising campaign, sponsored by the American Civil Liberties Union, that appeared in several national periodicals. Is it really possible that Blacks are more likely to be stopped in their automobiles simply because of their race?

Evidence strongly suggests this is the case. John Lamberth (1998) conducted a census of traffic and traffic violations by race on Interstate 95 in New Jersey, finding that although African American drivers made up 13.5 percent of the drivers on this turnpike (and 15 percent of the speeders), they represented 35 percent of those pulled over. A Black driver, then, was nearly five times more likely to be stopped for a traffic violation than members of other races. Statistics from Illinois suggest that Driving While Hispanic also raises suspicions. Hispanics comprise approximately 30 percent of the motorists stopped by the Illinois State Police, yet they take fewer than 3 percent of the personal vehicle trips in that state (Harris, 1999). Similarly, in Maryland, Black drivers comprise about 17 percent of motorists, but about 70 percent of those stopped and searched on Interstate 95 (Cockburn & St. Clair, 1998).

Why are minorities more likely to be pulled over than Whites? All roads lead to the stereotypic belief that minorities are simply more likely to commit crimes. Heather MacDonald, a writer for the Manhattan Institute's City Journal (quoted in Schencker & Brenner, 2002), thinks targeting Blacks for crimes makes sense because she believes Blacks are more likely to commit certain crimes. As she puts it, "It's not a question of belief, it's a fact." The results of recent court rulings dispute this claim, or at least condemn the behaviors that follow such stereotypic beliefs. In January 2003, the State of New Jersey settled lawsuits brought by the American Civil Liberties Union (2003) by agreeing to pay more than $775,000 to motorists who were stopped because of their ethnicity.

French and American cultures). One way in which the cultural aspect of prejudice and discrimination is expressed is through group privilege.

If you are White, chances are you have not given a lot of thought to your race or ethnicity—chances are, you have had no need to. When individuals are part of the majority, their membership in the dominant group seems normal and natural and is often taken for granted. Researchers have captured this fact of life with the concept of *white privilege.* Simply put, when buying a house or car, driving in an affluent neighborhood, or making a financial transaction, Whites seldom consider the possibility that their race comes into play at all (A. Johnson, 2001; McIntosh, 1989). Members of minority groups, in contrast, are often well aware that even the smallest everyday action can be affected by their race (Williams, 2000). Lena Williams, for example, writes about "the look" Black professionals often get from people who do not expect them to be in such roles. Well-educated Blacks, for example, often hear "*You* went to Harvard?" or "*You're* the *Wall Street Journal* reporter?" from surprised Whites who simply do not expect Blacks to have those credentials.

Group privilege is an unearned favored state conferred simply because of one's race, gender, or sexual orientation (McIntosh, 1989). The concept of group privilege begins with the recognition that there is a corollary to discrimination or undeserved negative treatment based on one's group membership. The corollary is that advantages are granted to people simply because they belong to a particular group. These advantages are typically invisible to the people who hold them, but they nonetheless have frequent and positive influences on everyday life. An important aspect of these advantages are that they are unearned; that is, they are based not on ability, effort, or past success but rather are granted based solely on being a member of the privileged group (A. Johnson, 2006; McIntosh, 1989).

The advantages associated with being a member of a privileged group may, at first glance, seem small and unimportant. However, these seemingly small advantages cumulate and their overall impact can indeed be significant. Every time a Black professional flying first class is asked to show a boarding pass before being allowed to take her seat or every time a well-dressed Black man in a hotel is assumed to be a bell hop, there is an impact on the individual's sense of self (see Williams, 2000). Alvin Poussaint, a noted Harvard psychiatrist, refers to the impact of privilege on the unprivileged as *death by a thousand nicks* (cited in Williams, 2000).

As you might expect, privileges associated with group membership are not limited to race. Paula Caplan (1994) uses the metaphor *lifting a ton of feathers* to describe how subtle prejudice against women and its converse, male privilege, affect their everyday lives. For example, women are much more likely to worry about their personal safety, and with good reason: By one report, approximately half of all women have experienced some form of sexual victimization (Koss, Gidycz, & Wisniewski, 1987). On a more subtle level, men do not have to look far to find heroes or role models of their gender nor do they have to worry about over-paying at the car repair shop because they are male (see, A. Johnson, 2006, for more examples of male privilege). Heterosexuality also has privileges. Heterosexuals, for example, are free to post pictures of their significant others in their offices, or to hold hands or kiss in public, and they can ask for legal recognition of their relationship, options that gay men and lesbians exercise at their own peril, if at all. For an example of group privilege in action, see Box 1.4.

As Allan Johnson (2006) notes, these kinds of privileges make it easy for Whites to see racism as a problem that belongs to people of color, for heterosexuals to see anti-gay prejudice as a problem that belongs to lesbians and gay men, or for men to see sexism as a "woman's problem." In essence, the attitude develops that prejudice and discrimination are someone else's problems, so members of the privileged groups do not have to do anything about them. This perspective, although comforting to the privileged group, ignores a critical piece of the prejudice puzzle: Privilege for one group entails loss for the other group. It is impossible

1.4 *White Privilege = Black Loss*

Law professor Patricia Williams (1997) tells this story of her experience while buying a house:

> Because the house was in a state other than the one where I was living at the time, I obtained my mortgage by telephone. . . . My loan was approved almost immediately.
>
> A little while later, the contract came in the mail. Among the papers the bank forwarded were forms documenting compliance with the Fair Housing Act, which outlaws racial discrimination in the housing market. . . . The act tracks the race of all banking customers to prevent such discrimination.
>
> I should repeat that to this point my entire mortgage transaction had been conducted by telephone. I should also note that I speak a Received Standard English, regionally marked as Northeastern perhaps, but not easily identifiable as black. With my credit history, my job as a law professor, and, no doubt, with my accent, I am not only middle class but apparently match the cultural stereotype of a good white person. It is thus, perhaps, that the loan officer of the bank, whom I had never met, had checked off the box on the fair housing form indicating that I *was* white.
>
> I took a deep breath, crossed out "white" and sent the contract back. . . . A done deal, I assumed. But suddenly the transaction came to a screeching halt. The bank wanted more money, more points, a higher rate of interest. Suddenly I found myself facing great resistance and much more debt. To make a long story short, I threatened to sue [under the Fair Housing Act], the bank quickly backed down and I procured the loan on the original terms. (p. 10)

From "Of Race and Risk" by Patricia William, *The Nation,* Dec. 29, 1997. Reprinted by permission.

to be privileged without withholding the benefits you enjoy as a member of your group from members of other groups. Because group privileges are part of the culture, those who have them take them for granted and are usually unaware of their operation: The privileges are just part of "the way things are." Therefore, unless challenged, privileges perpetuate themselves. However, if prejudice is ever to be eradicated, this "luxury of obliviousness" (A. Johnson, 2006, p. 22) is something society cannot afford. As we consider stereotyping and prejudice throughout this book, keep in mind the two sides of the coin: the disadvantages of experiencing prejudice and discrimination and the advantages of unearned privilege.

THEORIES OF PREJUDICE AND DISCRIMINATION

As students of stereotyping and prejudice, you will read about many theories, all of which seem to explain part of the puzzle of why humans behave in biased ways. You may also find yourself wishing for the one explanation that might lead people to eradicate prejudicial behavior. Psychologists also search for this kind of simplicity. However, to date, finding this single best model of the causes of prejudice has proved elusive. In this regard, the study of prejudice is not unlike the classic tale of the five blind men describing the elephant by touch. Each correctly describes the part he can feel, but the description of the tail, for example, bears little relation to the way an elephant as a whole looks. Similarly, many theories about prejudice do a good job explaining one piece of the puzzle; unfortunately, social scientists have yet to develop an overarching theory that pulls it all together.

To fully understand the reason why theories of stereotyping and prejudice often focus only on certain aspects of these phenomena, it is useful to briefly examine the history of research on prejudice and discrimination and to consider how, over time, the theoretical frameworks and the questions derived from those frameworks have changed. John Duckitt (1994) provides an excellent overview of how historical trends in the United States have influenced the questions psychologists pursue, how social scientists conceptualize prejudice, and the theories that guide the study of prejudice and discrimination.

It is important to recognize that the vast majority of social-psychological work in the last century dealing with prejudice and discrimination was conducted in North America; this situation did not change until the late 1970s when Western European psychologists began to gain prominence in the field. This is not to say that stereotyping, prejudice, and discrimination are unique to the United States; even a cursory survey leaves little doubt that these processes are found in all nations (see, for example, Duckitt, 1994). However, because of the North American predominance, the history of research on stereotyping, prejudice, and discrimination has closely followed societal trends and changes in the United States. As you read the following brief history of research on prejudice and discrimination, think about how researchers from other cultures might have framed their questions. Would the current understanding be different if North American psychology had not been so dominant?

Scientific Racism

Table 1.1 summarizes Duckitt's (1994) history of research on prejudice and discrimination, which we have used as the model for our discussion. Prior to the 1920s, North American and European social scientists nearly all agreed that Whites were superior to people of color. An obvious way to document this superiority, researchers implicitly agreed, was to demonstrate that Whites were more intelligent than Blacks, an endeavor now known as scientific racism (see, for example, Richards, 1997). Prejudice was viewed as a natural response to "backward" peoples; it certainly was not considered to be a social problem. Viewed through a historical lens, such beliefs served to justify White political domination and European colonial rule: Slavery, for example, was justified by the notion that slaves were a lesser class of human being and, as such, appropriately kept in that role. Following the abolition of slavery, the same "logic" was used to justify laws restricting the rights of African Americans and other minority groups (Richards, 1997).

TABLE 1.1   **HISTORICAL TRENDS IN THE STUDY OF PREJUDICE**

Time Period	Social and Historical Context	Social Science Question	View of Prejudice	Predominant Theories
Prior to 1920s	White domination and colonial rule	Identifying deficiencies of "backward peoples"	A natural response to "inferior peoples"	Scientific racism
1920s/1930s	White domination is challenged	Explaining why minority groups are stigmatized; measurement of attitudes and stereotype content	Irrational and unjustified attitudes	Psychodynamic
1930s/1940s	Universality of White racism in the United States	Identifying universal processes underlying racism	An unconscious defense	Psychodynamic
1950s	Legacy of Nazi ideology and the Holocaust	Identifying the prejudice-prone personality	An expression of pathological needs	Psychodynamic
1960s	Black civil rights movement	How social factors influence prejudice	A social norm	Sociocultural
1970s	Persistence of racism in the United States	How prejudice is rooted in social structures	An expression of group interests and intergroup relations	Intergroup relations
1980s to now	Inevitability of prejudice and intergroup conflict	Identifying universal processes underlying intergroup conflict and prejudice	An inevitable outcome of normal thought processes or evolution	Cognitive and evolutionary

Adapted from Duckitt, J. (1994). *The social psychology of prejudice.* Westport, CT: Praeger, Table 4.1, p. 48

Psychodynamic Theory

Although slavery in the United States ended in the mid-19th century, social attitudes did not start to catch up with this political change until the 1920s and 1930s. Accompanying this shift was an influx of immigration into the United States and a Black civil rights movement that challenged White social dominance. Social scientists began to question the notion that prejudice was natural and normal, moving instead to a perspective that prejudice is a social problem stemming from irrational and unjustifiable beliefs and behaviors. Researchers set as their agenda the measurement of Whites' prejudicial attitudes and beliefs. It was during this time period that now well-known measures such as Thurstone and Likert attitude scales were developed (Eagly & Chaiken, 1993) and that Daniel Katz and Kenneth Braly (1933) developed their stereotype checklist, which remained a popular assessment tool for many years. The first public opinion polls also emerged during this period.

If prejudice is indeed irrational and unjustified, why is it so ubiquitous? During the 1930s and 1940s, social scientists turned to this question. The answer, they believed, could be found in psychodynamic theory and, specifically, universal psychological processes such as defense mechanisms. These were the decades that brought the Great Depression in the United States and Europe and the rise of the Nazi party in Germany. These economic and social hardships led to theorizing that people acted out their frustrations in the form of hostility and aggression directed toward minority groups. Researchers proposed, for example, that scapegoating, or symbolically transferring negative behaviors onto others, resulted when chronic social frustration was displaced onto minorities (Miller & Bugelski, 1948).

After World War II, researchers grappled with the aftereffects of the Holocaust in Nazi Germany and the troubling question of how any society could support such heinous crimes. Many scholars adopted a personality-based perspective, drawing on psychoanalytic theory to suggest that certain types of individuals are especially susceptible to prejudice; their research efforts centered on trying to identify those people. In an attempt to explain the influence that Nazism and other fascist political ideologies had had on large numbers of people during the 1930s and 1940s, Theodor Adorno and his colleagues (Adorno, Frenkel-Brunswik, Levinson, & Sanford, 1950) proposed what they called the *authoritarian personality*. People with an authoritarian personality were said to be strongly prone to believe and do whatever authority figures told them, including treating members of derogated groups with contempt. Thus, people high in authoritarianism embraced racism because it was advocated by authority figures such as Adolf Hitler. Adorno and his colleagues proposed that the authoritarian personality, like other psychodynamic concepts, was rooted in early childhood experiences, especially a childhood characterized by strict rules enforced by physical punishment. Although this early work was relatively unsuccessful, more recent endeavors along these lines, such as Bob Altemeyer's (1981) studies of *right-wing authoritarianism*, discussed in Chapter 6, have proved more promising.

The psychodynamic perspective also proposes that prejudice is motivationally based and serves to strengthen one's personal identity and self-esteem. For example, functional attitude theories stress that people can hold similar attitudes for very different reasons (Katz, 1960). Thus, two heterosexuals may both view gay men negatively, but the psychological mechanisms underlying their beliefs can be quite dissimilar. Some heterosexuals' attitudes toward homosexuality are derived from anxiety or the fear of unwanted sexual advances from gay people that, in turn, lead the actor to a defensive prevention of such advances as a means of dealing with this anxiety; these individuals' attitudes serve an ego-defensive function. Others' attitudes stem from the benefits realized through expressing the attitude, such as affirming one's sense of self and increasing self-esteem; these individuals' attitudes serve a social adjustment function (Herek, 1986a).

Sociocultural Theory

Perhaps because the earlier work based on a psychodynamic approach appeared to reach a dead end, the psychological study of stereotyping and prejudice lay dormant from about the mid-1950s until the mid-1960s, when researchers began anew to examine these topics, this time from a sociocultural perspective. Historical events that co-occurred with the rise of this viewpoint include the civil rights movement of the late 1950s and early 1960s. Racism came to be seen as a cultural norm and one that was not easily eradicated. Accordingly, the sociocultural perspective takes the point of view that culture provides stereotypes and that the patterns of these stereotypes are consistently linked to prejudice across time and region of the country.

Ashmore and Del Boca (1981) point to two major models underlying this perspective: the structural-functionalist view and the conflict perspective. In the *structural-functionalist* view, society is characterized as seeking conformity to social norms, including the "proper" attitudes and beliefs people should hold, with little individual deviation in the pattern accepted within the society. In contrast to the psychodynamic approach, this model de-emphasizes individual differences in prejudice, assuming instead that most individuals internalize the culture's stereotypes to gain social acceptance. Classic research designed to determine the content of people's stereotypes reflect this perspective (see, for example, Broverman, Vogel, Broverman, Clarkson, & Rosenkrantz, 1972; Karlins, Coffman, & Walters, 1969). In these studies, a checklist of characteristics was often used; research participants simply indicated agreement or disagreement that the items on the list reflect a stereotypic attribute of a group. The *conflict perspective*, on the other hand, puts forth the notion that society is comprised of groups with different values and interests and that individuals adopt the viewpoint of their particular subgroups. Within a society, then, the conflict perspective allows that attitudes toward a social group may vary considerably.

A recent example of a social-structural theory is social role theory (Eagly, 1987; Eagly, Wood, & Diekman, 2000). This theory proposes that stereotypes emerge from observations about individuals in various social roles; as people make these observations, they come to associate the characteristics of the role with the individuals who occupy it. Because women, for example, are disproportionately represented in roles requiring communal traits, such as kindness and concern for others, observers draw the conclusion that all women are communal. This and similar work from a sociocultural perspective promises to expand psychologists' understanding of how societal norms influence beliefs about social groups. This work also points to the difficulty in changing stereotypes; people are reluctant to let go of ideas that are part of a larger belief system, particularly when society itself discourages a new perspective.

Intergroup Relations Theory

The optimism engendered by the Black civil rights movement of the 1960s dissipated during the 1970s when it became clear that racism persisted in the United States despite the passage of civil rights laws and apparent changes in social norms. In this context, the sociocultural perspective of the 1960s evolved into an intergroup relations perspective. From this point of view, prejudice derives from perceptions of competition with other groups. For example, relative deprivation theory (see, for example, Walker & Smith, 2002) holds that prejudice results from the resentment people feel when they believe that their group has been deprived of some resource that another group receives. Thus, Whites who believe that

Blacks are getting more than a "fair share" of societal resources experience negative emotions toward Blacks, even those White people who are objectively better off than the Black people they dislike.

Although research and theory on stereotyping and prejudice has most often originated in the United States, in the late 1960s European psychologists began to play prominent roles in both theory and research on the topic. Most importantly, the work of Henri Tajfel and John Turner (Tajfel, 1970; Tajfel & Turner, 1986) and their colleagues highlighted the importance of people's own identities in this process. Their social identity theory proposes that people want to have a positive self-identity. Because a large part of this identity is made up of a group identity, people can achieve this goal only by feeling positively about the groups to which they belong. One way to achieve this positive feeling is to find ways to distinguish one's group from others, particularly by seeing one's own group as better (see Smith, 1999, for a recent overview). We discuss intergroup relations theory and social identity theory in more detail in Chapter 8.

Cognitive Theory

Three factors probably influenced social psychologists' move to a cognitive perspective on prejudice and discrimination during the 1980s. The first was a growing belief, fed by worldwide ethnic strife, that prejudice was both universal and inevitable. The second factor was a realization that social structural explanations could not completely account for this fact. The third factor was the so-called cognitive revolution in psychology, in which the two predominant theories of the previous 50 years—psychoanalysis and behaviorism—were overshadowed by an emphasis on the role of thought processes in directing behavior, the ways in which information is stored in and retrieved from memory, and other cognitive factors (see, for example, Hergenhahn, 2005).

Researchers who adopt a cognitive framework view stereotyping as a normal process for reducing a complex stimulus world to a manageable level. From this vantage point, stereotyping is not considered fundamentally different from other cognitive structures or processes. Rather, it is one mechanism individuals use to help them comprehend the huge amount of information that bombards them in everyday life (see Hamilton, 1979, and Taylor, 1981, for early reviews). One such mechanism is to simplify information that is stored in memory, which leads to phenomena such as stereotyping: It is simpler to think of all (or most) members of a group as being similar in their characteristics than it is to think of every person as a complex individual. Because all humans are susceptible to these biases when processing information about people or events, stereotypes are not necessarily thought to be "bad" or invalid. Rather, stereotypes provide a framework through which individuals can comprehend all available information at a given point in time. Cognitive theorists do recognize, however, that there can be negative social consequences to this efficient information processing.

These ideas were not new: As Box 1.5 shows, their roots can be traced back to the writings of Walter Lippman (1922) and Gordon Allport (1954); yet it was not until the 1970s and 1980s that the cognitive revolution led psychologists to give

1.5   *All That Is Old Is New Again*

It may surprise you to learn that one of the most cited writers on prejudice is the journalist Walter Lippman. Lippman is credited for bringing the term *stereotype* into the vocabulary of social science. Perhaps more importantly, Lippman was an astute observer of human failings and foibles. His works anticipated much of the psychological research on stereotyping and prejudice and remain widely read by students of many disciplines.

Our book focuses on theories of stereotyping, prejudice, and discrimination that have been empirically tested. Yet one need not be an empiricist to accurately capture the everyday consequences of prejudice. Journalists, historians, novelists, and philosophers have all written compelling accounts of this human failing. Psychologist Gordon Allport is another author who vividly described the processes involved in stereotyping and prejudice. His writings do not rely heavily on empirical data, but, in his seminal work, *The Nature of Prejudice*, Allport (1954) set the stage for contemporary research on stereotyping and prejudice. Directly or indirectly, Allport's ideas continue to influence psychological thought. Check Allport's book out from your college library; we bet that you will find it is on the shelf, not in the archives, and that, like the copy in our library, it has dog-eared, copiously underlined pages. Read those pages for yourself; you'll find that many of the themes we cover in this book echo Allport's writings.

Here are just a few of the social psychological concepts that appeared in Allport's classic text. We revisit these ideas later in this book:

Prejudice in children. Allport discussed whether prejudice in young children is *adopted* by directly taking on attitudes and stereotypes from their families or cultures or whether it *develops* in an atmosphere that creates suspicions, fears, or hatreds that are later associated with minority groups. Allport also discusses racial awareness and the importance of language in the development of prejudice.

Ingroups and outgroups. Anticipating the development of social identity theory, Allport describes people's need to belong to ingroups and how ingroup loyalty can lead to the rejection of outgroups.

The contact hypothesis. Logically, it would seem that when ingroup members have frequent contact with outgroup members, prejudice and discrimination would be reduced. Allport reviews the conditions under which this may or may not happen.

Re-fencing. This idea, now referred to as subtyping, reflects how people respond to individual outgroup members who do not fit their stereotypic image. As Allport explains, people acknowledge the exceptions, but "the field is hastily fenced in again and not allowed to remain dangerously open" (p. 23), thus allowing the original beliefs about outgroups to stay intact.

them widespread attention. This attention to cognitive factors led to an important shift in thinking from a focus on the specific *content* of stereotypes to the cognitive *processes* that lead to prejudiced thought and action (Devine, 1989; Fiske & Neuberg, 1990). More recent work has considered how emotion and cognition work together to produce prejudiced thoughts and behaviors (Mackie & Smith, 2002).

The many advances that grew out of the shift to a cognitive perspective are the focus of Chapters 3 and 4.

Evolutionary Theory

The belief that prejudice and intergroup conflict were inevitable led to the emergence of evolutionary psychology as a way of explaining universal processes underlying prejudice and discrimination. Evolutionary psychologists have only begun to address prejudice and discrimination in any detail (see, for example, G. R. Johnson, 2001; Kurzban & Leary, 2001). But from an evolutionary viewpoint, the explanation is straightforward: People evolved a suspicion and fear of strangers as a way to protect themselves and their communities from possible harm by outsiders. This harm ranges from seizure of, or damage to, possessions and property, through threats to the social and moral fiber of a community, to genocide. A basic premise of evolutionary psychology is that all behavior derives from psychological mechanisms that evolved to fulfill a function that promotes the transmission of one's genes to future generations (Buss & Kenrick, 1998).

This evolutionary function led to the development of cooperation among relatives and with one's children to ensure mutual survival (called *kin favoritism*). As society developed, cooperative interactions among unrelated people developed as an extension of kin favoritism: Cooperation with nonrelatives, such as in hunting large animals, facilitates the survival of oneself and of one's relatives and children. To support cooperative effort, people developed three cues to allow them to distinguish between others with whom it was or was not safe to cooperate because cooperation with the "wrong" person could result in exploitation or other negative outcomes. These cues include physical similarity to oneself and proximity—how close another person resides to oneself. People who meet such criteria are similar to kin and so it is safe to cooperate with them; people who do not meet the criteria are potentially dangerous. Because members of one's own ethnic group meet the criteria and members of other ethnic groups do not, differences in ethnicity lead to avoidance, competition, and dislike rather than cooperation.

Evidence for the evolutionary point of view can be found in anthropological research that shows that distinguishing between one's own group and other groups, favoritism toward members of one's own group, and *ethnocentrism*— seeing one's group as better than others—are found in all human cultures (Brown, 1991). Similarly, the drive to classify things into discrete categories, one of the cognitive bases of stereotyping, is another of what Donald Brown (1991) has called "human universals." Thus, the psychological underpinnings of prejudice and discrimination might seem to be built into human nature. However, there are two problems with the evolutionary view of prejudice. One is that evolutionary theory holds that people are inherently motivated to protect kin. Yet, as Robert Zajonc (2002) has pointed out during times of extreme ethnic conflict people will kill their spouses and even their children who are "tainted" with descent from the "wrong" ethnic group. Second, Frans de Waal (2002) has noted that although it is easy to claim that a behavior has an evolutionary basis, an effective theory must be able to account for the absence of a supposedly evolved behavior as well as its occurrence. Thus, although evolutionary theory can provide an explanation for prejudice, it provides little in the way of explanation for situations in which prejudice does not occur. For example, although ancient Egypt, classical Greece, and imperial Rome all had frequent contact with Black Africans, there is little evidence of any ethnic or racial prejudice against them; on the contrary, they were admired for their cultural and military achievements (Snowden, 1983). Evolutionary theory cannot explain why racial prejudice is present in some cultures but not in others.

Finally, it is important to note the possibility that prejudice and discrimination have an evolutionary basis, and thus may be part of human nature, does not make them right or even excusable (de Waal, 2002; Pinker, 2002). As evolutionary psychologist Steven Pinker (2002) notes, "The case against bigotry is not a factual claim [rooted in biology]. It is a moral stance that condemns judging an *individual* according to the average traits of certain *groups* to which the individual belongs. Enlightened societies choose to ignore sex, race, and ethnicity in [making decisions about individuals] because the alternative is morally repugnant" (p. 145). And, as Pinker points out, people also may have evolved a sense of morality and fairness as a means of promoting cooperation among people along with the other psychological mechanisms that support interdependent relationships. So, just as ethnocentrism is a human universal, so are the promotion of cooperation and fairness (Brown, 1991). Thus, even if an evolutionary perspective can help psychologists understand why prejudice and discrimination occur and why they seem to be universal and inevitable, taking such a perspective does not excuse them. As Pinker (2002) has written, "As soon as we recognize that there is nothing morally commendable about the products of evolution, we can describe human psychology honestly, without the fear that identifying a 'natural' trait is the same as condoning it. As Katherine Hepburn says to Humphrey Bogart in *The African Queen*, 'Nature, Mr. Allnut, is what we are put in this world to rise above'" (p. 163).

TARGETS OF PREJUDICE

Up to this point, we have been looking at the "big picture" of how people perceive members of other groups and of how social scientists have studied those perceptions. Many of the major theories of prejudice and discrimination, and the research that has tested them, take a broad perspective, assuming, to paraphrase Gertrude Stein, that a prejudice is a prejudice is a prejudice. As we will see, there are, in fact, sets of general processes that describe how people think and react to others. For example, how people categorize race-related information does not differ significantly from how they categorize gender-related information—or information about cars, for that matter. However, prejudice and discrimination also differ in important ways across social groups and a great deal of research has been devoted to understanding reactions to specific targets of prejudice. Let us briefly examine some of those targets.

Race and Ethnicity

When most North Americans hear the word *prejudice* their thoughts almost immediately turn to racial and ethnic prejudice. Such a response is not surprising given the United States' history of stigmatizing racial, ethnic, and immigrant groups (see, for example, Takaki, 1993). Most of the theory and research on racial and ethnic prejudice has focused on White North Americans' prejudice against African Americans, and the theories and research paradigms developed to address that form of prejudice have served as models for more recent studies of White prejudice against Hispanic and Asian Americans (Jones, 1997). Interestingly, the attitudes and behaviors of minority group members toward Whites, and the effects of those attitudes and behaviors on intergroup relations, have been virtually ignored (Shelton, 2000). Indeed, most Whites might be surprised to learn that minority groups *have* prejudicial beliefs about them. Some stereotypic beliefs that Blacks hold about Whites include that Whites do not hug or kiss their children, are packrats, and that wet White hair smells like wet dog (Williams, 2000). Blacks also are puzzled by some Whites' desire to "look Black" by wearing dreadlocks or by excessive tanning (Bowman, personal communication, April 8, 2003). Although the stereotypic beliefs of the minority toward the majority are no more justifiable or accurate than the reverse, the fact remains that they deserve the same empirical attention as their more often studied counterparts.

There are a number of reasons for the emphasis on prejudice and discrimination by Whites against African Americans (Jones, 1997; Pettigrew, 1988). First, of course, was the institution of race-based slavery that Europeans inflicted on Africans. Although Native Americans, Hispanics, and Asians were held in either legal or de facto slavery at various times in U.S. history (Takaki, 1993), this condition lasted longest, and was most severe, for people of African descent. The institution of slavery, and the justifications for it, portrayed Africans as less than human, established a caste system that put African Americans, including free people, at the bottom of the social ladder, a position that continued after the abolition of slavery. This caste system led to what Gunnar Myrdal (1944) called the "American dilemma": the contradiction of a society that professed equality as a basic value while denying equality to a substantial portion of its population. This contradiction led to a series of Black civil rights movements from the 1870s to the 1960s that kept society's (and researchers') attention on anti-Black prejudice and discrimination.

A second factor leading to a focus on anti-Black prejudice is that such prejudice is more pervasive than prejudice against most other groups (Jones, 1997), making it both a larger social problem and of more interest to psychologists who want to understand the roots of prejudice. In addition, Whites' anti-Black attitudes are linked more closely to their attitudes toward race-related social policies such as affirmative action than are their attitudes toward other groups. A third factor focusing attention on anti-Black prejudice was the way it changed from the blatant racism that characterized most of U.S. history to a more subtle form by the 1980s. This change led researchers and theorists to rethink the nature of prejudice and to examine similar changes in prejudice toward other groups.

For these reasons, then, until recently, most of the research on prejudice and discrimination has focused on anti-Black prejudice and discrimination. Therefore, most of the research and theory we cite in this book focuses on that form of prejudice and discrimination. However, we will also point out the ways in which prejudice toward other groups is different from, as well as similar to, anti-Black prejudice.

Religion

Prejudice based on religion has existed for centuries, but has been studied less than racial prejudice in the United States, perhaps because it has been less salient. The early Protestant immigrants to America were not tolerant of other religions: Both anti-Catholic and anti-Semitic (Jewish) prejudice were common until the 1950s (Takaki, 1993) and can still be seen in the rants of hate group leaders (see, for example, Ezekiel, 1995). The Holocaust, in which German Nazis killed some 6 million Jews, made anti-Semitism salient following World War II, leading Gordon Allport (1954) to make it a major theme in his book *The Nature of Prejudice*. Since then, research and theory have focused on race and ethnicity, but the rise of anti-Muslim prejudice, such as that described in Box 1.1, and the increasing influence of religious fundamentalism on all forms on politics (see, for example, Armstrong, 2000) has led to an increasing interest in religious prejudice.

Gender and Sexual Orientation

Prejudice against women has pervaded Western culture since its origins, restricting women's roles in and influence on society (see, for example, Shields & Eyssell, 2001). Gender-based prejudice has both benevolent and hostile components (Glick & Fiske, 1996). The benevolent aspects, including much of the female stereotype, are ostensibly positive, but portray women as weak, vulnerable, and needing protection. Such benevolent beliefs are used as a justification for limiting the social roles permitted to women. Hostile sexist beliefs are derogatory, such as the belief that women demand special privileges and want to control men. Hostile sexist beliefs often have a sexual content that serves as a justification for the sexual exploitation of women. Such beliefs emerge, for example, in sexual harassment, a form of discrimination directed primarily, although not exclusively, toward women.

The term *heterosexism* describes an ideological system that denies, denigrates, and stigmatizes any nonheterosexual form of behavior, identity, relationship, or community (Herek, 1990). Notice that this term reflects a bias in *favor* of a group—heterosexuals; the result of this bias, however, is prejudice and discrimination against people with a homosexual sexual orientation, often labeled *homophobia*. This term, coined by George Weinberg (1972), originally referred to a dread of being in close quarters with homosexuals, although modern researchers often use it to reflect a more general bias.

One of the interesting aspects of heterosexism as a form of prejudice is that it seems to be more socially acceptable to be prejudiced against lesbians and gay men than to be prejudiced against members of other groups. For example, several municipalities have passed laws specifically supporting discrimination against lesbians and gay men, and some states until recently had sodomy laws on the books that make gay male sexuality illegal. The U.S. Supreme Court decision to overturn the Texas sodomy law (*Lawrence v. Texas*, 2003) served as the death knell for these remaining laws just as the once common state laws prohibiting sexual relations between Blacks and Whites all have been overturned. Even so, these laws serve as examples of how institutional discrimination can affect the lives of sexual minorities. And, although these laws were overturned, they have been replaced by others. In the 2004 elections, constitutional amendments prohibiting gay marriage were passed in all 11 states that had them on the ballot, with margins as high as 6–1 in favor of this prohibition (Peterson, 2004).

Age, Ability, and Appearance

Robert Butler (1969) coined the term *ageism* to refer to negative reactions to older people. Although ageism, like gender prejudice, has a benevolent component, such as the doting grandparent image, it also includes negative stereotypes such as lack of competence (Hummert, 1993). Ageism can lead to subtle, almost invisible, forms of discrimination. For example, older people sometimes receive inadequate health care because physicians attribute problems to "old age," based on the assumption that all older adults have physical problems. By doing so, they overlook the role of depression and other psychological problems in older people's illnesses, often allowing them to go untreated (Pasupathi & Löckenhoff, 2002).

An area of growing theoretical and research interest is prejudice against people with physical disabilities (PWD). This kind of prejudice most clearly exemplifies the role that ambivalence, or mixed feelings, can play in prejudice: People generally feel very sympathetic toward PWD, but at the same time feel a great deal of discomfort in their presence (see, for example, Soder, 1990). In addition, the media often portray PWD in a negative light, even to the point of ridicule (Bogdan, Biklen, Shapiro, & Spelkoman, 1990). Perhaps because of the effects of these images on other children, children with disabilities often have difficulty forming and maintaining friendships, leading to low self-esteem and poor social skill development (Gordon, Feldman, & Tantillo, 2003). Finally, even researchers make a number of assumptions about persons with disabilities that affect the way they study prejudice toward them. These assumptions include the idea that PWD are victims and that having a disability is a victimizing experience, the belief that when PWD face a problem it likely stems from the disability, the assumption that having a disability is central to the self-concept of PWD, and that having a disability is synonymous with needing social support (Fine & Asch, 1993).

Finally, physical appearance, especially weight, can be a source of prejudice and discrimination. Christian Crandall (1995), for example, has found that fat people in America are seen in a negative light and are subject to discrimination, at times even by their own parents. Research on anti-fat prejudice illuminates two important bases for negative attitudes toward many groups. First, people who are perceived to have negative traits and who also are seen as responsible for those traits are devalued more than people who are seen as not responsible for them. Thus, people who are prejudiced against fat people often believe that obesity is the fat person's own fault and is due to personal characteristics such as laziness and lack of self-discipline (Crandall, 1994). Second, people tend to dislike others whom they see as violating values they hold dear. One American value that fat people appear to violate is that of self-restraint (Allon, 1982).

WHERE DO WE GO FROM HERE?

This book provides a narrated journey through the social science literature on stereotyping, prejudice, and discrimination. Its 12 chapters cover a wide range of topics, beginning with the general introduction to these topics provided by this chapter. Chapter 2 describes how research on prejudice and discrimination is conducted, with a focus on the process of conducting research and the techniques that have been used to measure stereotypes, prejudice, and discrimination.

Chapters 3 and 4 examine stereotypes, one of the building blocks of prejudice. Chapter 3 explains the basic thought processes that lead to stereotyping, the nature of stereotypes, and the psychological processes that maintain stereotypes and make them resistant to change. Chapter 4 considers the factors that affect people's use of stereotypes, such as their accessibility in memory and individuals' motivation to make accurate judgments. The chapter also examines how situational factors, such as mood and cognitive overload, can affect the use of stereotypes. As we noted earlier, the ways researchers have viewed prejudice have changed over time, in part reflecting societal changes. Chapter 5 examines one of those changes, the transition from old-fashioned (or blatant) prejudice to modern (or subtle) prejudice. It also considers the more recently developed topic of "benevolent" prejudices—beliefs and behaviors that are superficially positive but have the effect of subordinating members of targeted groups. Chapter 6 looks at the question of whether some people are more prone to prejudice than others. The chapter examines the role of individual differences, such as how personality, values, and belief systems influence levels of prejudice.

Chapter 7 examines a relatively under-studied topic, the origins of stereotyping, prejudice, and discrimination in children. Chapter 8 looks at the social context of prejudice—how being members of and identifying with groups leads to favoritism toward those groups and disparagement of other groups. The chapter also examines the factors that lead people to join hate groups.

Social scientists who study stereotyping and prejudice have focused most often on racial prejudice and much of the book focuses on theories about this form of bias. Chapter 9 looks at three other types of prejudice. Gender-based prejudice is a special kind of prejudice, in part because most of us interact with people of the other sex on a daily basis and many people's most intimate relationships are with the other sex. Why, then, would gender-based biases be so prevalent? This chapter addresses that question. Because gender-based beliefs are strongly linked to beliefs about sexual orientation, heterosexism also is included in this chapter. Finally, Chapter 9 concludes with a discussion of ageism, or bias against people simply because of their advanced age.

We also explore the question of discrimination in the textbook. As we noted earlier, the relationship between prejudice and discrimination is not always direct. Chapter 10 explores the topic of when and why prejudice causes discrimination. That chapter addresses the distinction between overt and subtle discrimination. Although the former is easy to identify, the latter often proves difficult to pinpoint; subtle language cues, for example, can convey messages about group members' status in society or a subgroup of society. Historically, work on prejudice and discrimination has focused on the prejudiced person—who is prejudiced, the beliefs he or she holds, and how it affects his or her behavior. Chapter 11 considers the perspective of those on the receiving end. We consider how social stigmas affect the self-perceptions of people who are stigmatized and how minority status, such as being the token member of one's group in a situation, affects self-perceptions.

Given all that we know about prejudice and its role in everyday life, is there hope for reducing or eliminating its negative effects? Chapter 12 discusses the psychology of reducing prejudice and discrimination, focusing on the contact hypotheses and the jigsaw classroom, an intervention for children based on the contact hypothesis. The chapter also discusses educational interventions, such as providing information about groups and affirmative action.

Before U.S. citizens came to accept that no one should be required to sit in the back of the bus, Rosa Parks had to take the enormously courageous action of refusing to do so. But this acceptance also required that millions of others stand up in smaller ways and say "no more." We hope you are one of them. We believe the first step in ending prejudice and discrimination is understanding their nature. With this book, we invite you to explore the contributions of the many social scientists who have offered insights into this topic. By the end of our journey, you will have the understanding you need to make changes in your own life and the lives of those with whom you interact, with the goal of reducing the negative effects of prejudice and discrimination.

Chapter Summary

Social scientists have differentiated between the concepts of stereotypes—organized beliefs about the characteristics of members of various groups, prejudice—attitudes toward group members, and discrimination—behavior toward group members. Typically, there is group consensus about the appropriateness of these beliefs and behaviors; all have a strong cultural component that guides how individuals respond to others. Each of these three concepts also has an individual and a group level basis. Discrimination, for example, can be discussed at either the individual level, based on people's personal beliefs; at the institutional level, based on attitudes and beliefs sanctioned by institutions or governing bodies; or at the cultural level, stemming from the powerful group establishing and maintaining its dominance by rewarding the values that correspond to its views and punishing those that do not. However, as will be discussed in later chapters, the relationships among stereotyping, prejudice, and discrimination are not as straightforward as one might think. People have implicit prejudices, for example, that are difficult to control or describe, and explicit prejudices, that are within an individual's control or awareness. Whether prejudice is implicit or explicit influences how directly it is linked to discrimination.

The study of stereotyping and prejudice, including racism, developed in response to laws and customs in the United States. The concept of scientific racism, defined as researchers trying to demonstrate empirically the superiority of one group over another, was introduced to explain how beliefs were used to justify the status quo. An outgrowth of accepting the status quo is the concept of group privilege, whereby one group has an unearned favored state simply because they are the dominant group. This privilege often goes unrecognized by the majority group, but always comes at a cost to the nonprivileged groups.

Historical events and shifts in societal norms have influenced the development of psychological theory. Historical events such as the Great Depression and the rise of Nazism, for example, formed the basis for psychodynamic theory. This perspective proposes that universal psychological processes account for prejudice; these processes are presumed to be motivationally based and allegedly serve to strengthen one's self-esteem. Sociocultural theories grew out of social scientists' acceptance that stereotyping and prejudice were difficult to eliminate because they were so strongly tied to culture and the structure of society. This shift occurred about the time of the Black civil rights movement in the United States, a time in history when it became clear that progress toward equality would be difficult to achieve. This slow acceptance of change also led to the development of intergroup relations theory, which proposes that competition for scarce resources, and people's resentment that their group might not be getting its fair share, is one basis for prejudice. Cognitive theory developed as prejudice came to be seen as universal and inevitable; at the same time, many social psychologists rejected psychoanalytic theory and behaviorism in favor of cognitive psychology. Stereotyping and prejudice, then, came to be seen as part of normal human information processing. Finally, psychologists have recently explored how evolutionary psychology can explain stereotyping and prejudice; this perspective proposes that these beliefs and behaviors, as does all behavior, stem from psychological mechanisms that evolved to fulfill a function that promotes the transmission of one's genes to future generations.

Social scientists have examined prejudices toward specific groups, such as racism, sexism, and ageism, and, although the overall process might be similar across groups, the study of each offers unique insights and concerns. Many common prejudices toward these subgroups go unrecognized, in part because people have mixed or ambivalent feelings about the group. Chapter 1 concludes with an overview of the textbook, describing how the book is structured and the topics that will be examined in each chapter.

SUGGESTED READINGS

Allport, G. (1954). *The nature of prejudice*. Cambridge, MA: Addison-Wesley.

    Allport anticipated much of current psychological theory on the topics covered in this text and he presents them in a readable, accessible format. His book remains a must-read for any serious student of stereotyping and prejudice.

Duckitt, J. (1994). *The social psychology of prejudice*. New York: Praeger.

    Duckitt provides an excellent review of the social psychological literature on prejudice, with an eye toward the historical factors that have influenced theory development.

Johnson, A. G. (2006). *Privilege, power, and difference* (2nd ed.). Boston: McGraw-Hill.

    This highly readable book reviews the literature on power and privilege, emphasizing the perspective of both dominant and minority groups. Johnson describes both the problem and the solution.

Jones, J. M. (1997). *Prejudice and racism* (2nd ed.). New York: McGraw-Hill.

    This book is a true modern classic. Jones provides a particularly good overview of the social history of prejudice against African Americans and the nature of racism toward this group.

Rothenberg, P. S. (Ed.) (2004). *Race, class and gender in the United States* (6th ed.). New York: Worth.

    This is an outstanding collection of essays and readings addressing stereotyping and prejudice. Readings consider the perspective of many social groups and take many vantage points, including legal and economic perspectives, social constructionist views, and visions for the future.

KEY TERMS

cultural discrimination	interpersonal discrimination
discrimination	prejudice
group privilege	scientific racism
institutional discrimination	stereotypes

QUESTIONS FOR REVIEW AND DISCUSSION

1. The opening quote in this chapter suggests to some that society should be color blind. What would the advantages and disadvantages be of a color-blind society?

2. How do social scientists differentiate between stereotyping, prejudice, and discrimination?

3. Think about the distinction between institutional and individual prejudice. Can one exist without the other? Why or why not?

4. We reviewed how historical events in the United States have influenced the study of stereotyping and prejudice. Think about the recent terrorist attacks, particularly those that have occurred on U.S. soil. How might those events change the research agenda in this literature?

5. Distinguish between the psychodynamic, sociocultural, intergroup relations, cognitive, and evolutionary perspectives on prejudice.
6. Allan Johnson (2006) has suggested that social class influences the extent to which Whites resist giving up their privileged status. If this is true, which social class would you expect to be more resistant to relinquishing these advantages? Explain your answer.
7. Prejudice is most commonly viewed as the dominant group's attitude toward subordinate groups. Can minority groups be prejudiced against the majority? Explain your answer.
8. Why, in the United States, is prejudice generally assumed to refer to White's prejudice against Blacks?
9. Design a study to examine stereotypic beliefs the minority hold about the majority.
10. Describe how stereotyping and prejudice are different for different "isms."
11. Should race be included on the census? What are the advantages and disadvantages of collecting this information?
12. What assumptions do researchers make about persons with disabilities? How might research questions be different if researchers did not make those assumptions?
13. Why has racial prejudice had such an important influence on social science research?
14. Why do you believe legislators find it is acceptable to propose laws that discriminate against gays and lesbians?

HOW PSYCHOLOGISTS STUDY PREJUDICE AND DISCRIMINATION

We can't solve our social problems until we understand how they come about [and] persist. Social science research offers a way to understand the operation of human social affairs. It provides points of view and technical procedures that uncover things that would otherwise escape our awareness.

—Earl Babbie (1999, p. xx)

Why does a book about prejudice and discrimination include a chapter on research? It does because, as Babbie (1999) noted, research informs our understanding of what prejudice and discrimination are, how they come about, and the effects they have on people. Research also offers clues about how to reduce prejudice. Research is the primary source of the information presented in this book, so a full understanding of that information requires an understanding of where it comes from.

Research serves several purposes. First, it provides descriptive information, such as the various characteristics that differentiate people high in prejudice from those low in prejudice. This information can be used to construct theories, such as those described in Chapter 1 and elsewhere in this book, that try to explain why some people are more prejudiced than others. Research then can be used to test those theories, with researchers deriving predictions about behavior from theories and collecting data to see whether those predictions are supported. If necessary, theories are modified in the light of the data. Once psychologists are confident that a theory works well, we can use its principles to design interventions to reduce prejudice. Research is then conducted to see how well those interventions work, and the resulting data can be used to fine-tune both the interventions and the theory on which they are based.

In this chapter we first present an overview of the research process, including the steps involved. That discussion leads to two others: the methods used to collect data and the techniques used to measure stereotypes, prejudice, and discrimination. Researchers can choose from a variety of methods, each of which has its advantages and disadvantages, and often the advantages of one research method compensate for the disadvantages of another. Finally, an important part of research is measurement: If, for example, researchers want to see what factors differentiate people who are high and low in prejudice, they must be able to measure how prejudiced people are.

The Research Process

The goal of research in the behavioral sciences is to develop knowledge about the factors that cause some people to think and behave one way and other people to think and behave in other ways. For example, research can address the question of why some people are more prejudiced than others. Behavioral science research also tries to determine the factors that constrain or limit behavior. For instance, some people act in discriminatory ways whereas others do not. Research can address the question of what circumstances make it easier for people to express their prejudices and what circumstances make it more difficult. The behavioral sciences have developed sets of methods and procedures for collecting data that can provide answers to questions such as those just posed. These procedures are designed to produce data that are as accurate and unbiased as possible (although it is impossible to eliminate *all* inaccuracy and bias). This section provides a broad overview of the procedures that constitute the research process, and subsequent sections discuss specific issues. Figure 2.1 provides a schematic outline of the topics to be discussed.

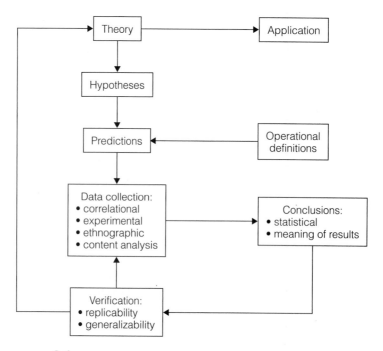

FIGURE **2.1**

THE RESEARCH PROCESS

Researchers derive hypotheses (statements of expected relationships between variables) from theories. When abstract variables are defined in concrete terms (operationally defined), hypotheses become the predictions to be tested in the research. Researchers then collect data using the appropriate research method. Researchers draw two types of conclusions from the data: How likely it is that the results found were due to chance (statistical conclusions) and the meaning of the results. Researchers then verify their results by seeing if the results can be repeated (replicability) and if the results hold up when the hypotheses are tested in different ways and in different settings (generalizability). Once the results are verified, any necessary changes can be made to the theory. Once the theory is well-verified, applications can be developed from it.

Theories and Hypotheses

Where do scientists get the questions that they ask in research? A major source is theories. As noted in Chapter 1, theories organize knowledge by proposing links among variables, such as by proposing possible causes of prejudice. A **variable** is a characteristic on which people differ and so takes on more than one value when it is measured in a group of people; that is, it *varies* across people. For example, prejudice is variable: Some people are high on prejudice, some people are low, and some people fall in between. Biological sex is another example of a variable: Some people are female and others are male. Some variables can also differ for a given person across time or situations. For example, a person's level of prejudice might increase or decrease over time as a result of the person's experiences with members of other groups. Prejudice can also vary as a function of situations: For example, a person is more likely to evaluate another person in terms of group stereotypes in situations in which the evaluator is distracted or busy than in situations in which the evaluator has the time to think carefully about the person's qualifications (see, for example, Gilbert & Hixon, 1991).

In theories, these proposed links among variables are called *postulates.* Theoretical postulates can be based on the results of research, on the theorist's observations and experiences, on speculations about the ways in which variables might be related to one another, or, most commonly, on a combination of all these sources. However, theories are tentative and subject to change because their postulates may or may not be correct. Before researchers can be reasonably certain that theoretical postulates accurately describe the relationships between variables, they must test them. After all, you would not want to spend time and resources using a particular theory to develop ways to reduce prejudice unless you could be confident the theory was accurate; if it were not, your interventions may not be as effective as they otherwise could be. Researchers start the process of testing theories by deriving hypotheses from them.

Hypotheses are derivations of theoretical postulates that can be tested in research. Table 2.1 gives examples of hypotheses that could be derived from some of the theories outlined in Chapter 1. Generally, tests of more specific hypotheses provide data that are more useful than do tests of more general hypotheses. For example, as shown in Table 2.1, a general hypothesis of psychodynamic theory is that prejudices help fulfill psychological needs. However, because this may not be true of all needs, testing the hypothesis in the context of specific needs, such as self-esteem, can provide data that are more useful. If the results of research were to support the self-esteem hypothesis, those results would suggest that finding other ways of bolstering people's self-esteem would help to reduce the amount of prejudice they feel (this suggestion, of course, is itself a hypothesis that would also have to be tested through research).

Hypotheses and Predictions

Hypotheses, such as "People with low self-esteem are more prejudiced than people with high self-esteem," are usually stated in abstract terms. That is, terms such as *self-esteem* and *prejudice* are abstract nouns; the technical term for abstract concepts that are used in theories and studied in research is **hypothetical constructs.** However, researchers must be able to observe variables if they want to collect data about them, and they cannot directly observe abstractions such as self-esteem and prejudice. Therefore, researchers create operational definitions of hypothetical constructs to use in research. **Operational definitions** are directly observable, concrete representations of hypothetical constructs. Scores on questionnaires that assess people's levels of self-esteem and prejudice are examples of operational definitions of those constructs because the scores provide directly observable indexes of people's levels of self-esteem and prejudice. Usually,

TABLE 2.1   **THEORIES AND HYPOTHESES**

The following chart provides possible hypotheses about prejudice that could be derived from some of the theories discussed in Chapter 1:

Theory	Hypothesis
Psychodynamic	Prejudice helps fulfill psychological needs. For example, one might hypothesize that prejudices help people who are low in self-esteem see themselves as superior to the targets of their prejudices.
Sociocultural	Prejudice is based on social norms, so one might hypothesize that anti-Black prejudice would be stronger in areas where prejudice against African Americans is more strongly supported by social norms.
Intergroup relations	Groups compete with one another for resources and people develop a dislike of members of other groups because they are trying to get the things we want. Therefore, one might hypothesize that prejudice would be stronger between competing groups than between cooperating groups.
Cognitive	People have an innate tendency to put people (and things) into categories, such as "my group" and "that other group." One might hypothesize that once these categories are established, they lead to an "us versus them" view of the world.
Evolutionary	People evolved a fear and dislike of strangers to protect themselves against possible aggression, so one might hypothesize that fear of and disliking for strangers would be found in all human cultures.

any one hypothetical construct will have more than one possible operational definition. For example, there are numerous measures of both self-esteem and prejudice, and researchers must choose the operational definitions that best fit the purposes of their research. Later in this chapter we look at some of the ways in which researchers operationally define prejudice and other constructs such as stereotypes and discrimination.

Sometimes researchers manipulate variables rather than measuring them (experimental research such as this will be described in more detail in the next section of this chapter). For example, people have what researchers call worldviews that help them understand events by (among other functions) providing standards for evaluating them as right or wrong, good or bad. Sheldon Solomon, Jeff Greenberg, and Tom Pyszczynski (2000) have hypothesized that challenging people's worldviews makes them anxious because worldviews are closely linked to people's self-concepts, so that challenging those views threatens people's self-esteem, leading to anxiety. People who are threatened in this way might express more prejudice than people who are not because expressing negative attitudes toward others is a way of bolstering self-esteem. (We will discuss this process more fully in Chapter 6.) In a study designed to test these ideas, the researchers would generate anxiety in some people but not in others and compare the levels of prejudice expressed by the people in each group. In this case, the way in which the researchers generated anxiety—by having people think about their own deaths—would constitute the operational definition of anxiety.

Once researchers have chosen their operational definitions, hypotheses become predictions. **Predictions** restate hypotheses in terms of operational definitions. Thus, the hypothesis "People with low self-esteem are more prejudiced than people with high self-esteem" would become the prediction "People with low scores on the Rosenberg (1965) Self-Esteem Scale [one possible operational definition of self-esteem] will have higher scores on the Modern Racism Scale (McConahay, 1986) [one possible operational definition of prejudice] than people with high scores on the Rosenberg Self-Esteem Scale."

Data Collection

When it becomes time to collect data, a number of methods are available, each with its advantages and shortcomings. These methods, which are listed in Figure 2.1, are discussed in the next section. For now, let us move on to the process of drawing conclusions from the data that were collected.

Drawing Conclusions

Although researchers sometimes say that data should speak for themselves, data are often open to multiple interpretations, giving researchers the responsibility to draw conclusions from them. Two important types of conclusions that must be drawn are whether the researchers' hypotheses were supported and what the data mean.

Were the hypotheses supported?
Researchers test hypotheses in their research, so a basic question in research is whether the hypotheses were supported. When the data are quantitative (that is, numerical, such as scores on a prejudice measure), the question is relatively easy to answer. Statistical analysis of the data provides information about how likely it is that a certain outcome occurred by chance as opposed to providing an accurate picture of what is happening. Imagine that researchers tested the hypothesis described earlier about the relationship between self-esteem and prejudice. If the researchers did find a relationship, there are two possible explanations for this outcome. One is that the relationship really exists. The other explanation is that some of the unavoidable errors that occur in research, such as sampling error and measurement error, combined to make it look like a relationship exists when, in fact, there is none. (A detailed examination of the sources of error that can affect research is beyond the scope of this discussion; more information is available in books on research methods such as Stern & Kalof, 1996.) Statistical analyses provide researchers with criteria for deciding whether their results represent true relationships among variables, and so support their hypotheses, or whether those results could have occurred by chance and so cannot be interpreted as supporting the hypotheses.

Qualitative data, such as transcripts of interviews, are narrative rather than numerical. Researchers using qualitative methods analyze their data by looking for patterns of responses or behavior. These patterns might address such questions as, what characteristics and political beliefs do members of hate groups have in common? In what ways are male and female hate group members similar and different? The patterns can be either predicted by theory or, more commonly, emerge from the data. For example, Raphael Ezekiel (1995) found that fear was a common theme running through his interviews with hate group members. Economic fears, such as that of unemployment, were translated into prejudice: I'm unemployed, the thinking goes, because minority group members, aided by government programs that exclude me, are taking all the jobs. Therefore, the way for me to get ahead is to keep minority group members down.

What do the data mean?   Once the data have been analyzed, researchers must decide what the results mean. Consider the common research finding that men have slightly higher prejudice scores than women. The results of research tell us that this difference *exists*, but what does it *mean*? Consider some possibilities:

- Over the course of evolution, people have evolved a fear of strangers because strangers may be a threat to their groups. Because men have historically taken the role of protecting the group (as males of most other primate species do), they have to be sensitive to possible threats and so have evolved a stronger fear of strangers, which is reflected in prejudice.
- Testosterone somehow affects the brain to make people who are higher in testosterone more prejudiced.
- Social norms teach men to be more prejudiced than women.
- Men are more willing to disclose their prejudices to researchers than are women.

Researchers who hold different theoretical orientations are likely to put more faith in interpretations that are consistent with the theories they prefer. An evolutionary psychologist is likely to prefer the first explanation whereas a psychologist who rejects the possibility of an evolved human nature is likely to prefer the third interpretation (Pinker, 2002). Researchers' personal backgrounds can also affect the interpretations they make. Thus, research findings can often have more than one explanation and different people can have different views on which explanation is the correct one.

So which explanation *is* the correct one? Deciding is difficult because some explanations are directly testable whereas others are not. For example, the testosterone explanation implies that higher levels of testosterone should be related to higher levels of prejudice in both women and men, and research could examine this possibility. However, it is sometimes difficult or impossible to directly test an explanation, such as the one that holds that gender differences in prejudice have an evolutionary basis. Finally, it is important to remember that a given phenomenon could have more that one cause; thus it is possible that all four explanations are correct. Multiple causation is a common research finding, so one of the things you will see as you proceed through this book is that because prejudice and discrimination have multiple causes, efforts to reduce prejudice and discrimination have to take more than one route.

Verifying Results

Because, as we noted earlier, the results of any one study may be influenced by chance factors, it is important to verify research results to ensure their accuracy. The verification process has two aspects. One aspect consists of redoing the study using the same research procedures to see if the same results occur. This aspect of research is called *exact replication*. The other aspect of verification consists of redoing the study with changes in the procedures, such as using different measures or research participants with different characteristics (such as college students in one study and older adults in another study). This process is called *conceptual replication* and helps determine whether the results found in the original study generalize (that is, are similar) across variations in research procedures or whether the results are obtained only when the original procedures are used.

Generalizability is an important issue because if a particular psychological principle—such as low self-esteem is related to prejudice—is correct, researchers should find a relationship between low self-esteem and prejudice regardless of how self-esteem and prejudice are measured and regardless of who the research participants are. Conversely, if a study finds that a principle does not generalize well, but instead operates only for some types of people or only under certain circumstances, then the principle only applies to those people and in those circumstances. For example, although positive contact between members of different groups tends to reduce prejudice, contact is more effective in reducing prejudice in some situations, such as work settings, than in others, such as recreational settings (Pettigrew & Tropp, 2000).

Theory and Application

Once researchers are confident about their findings, they return to the theory that guided their research. If the research findings support the theory by confirming the hypotheses derived from it, then all is well and good: The researchers can have confidence in the accuracy of the theory. However, the results of research are sometimes inconsistent with the theory the researchers started with. In that case, the theory must be revised to take the research results into account, such as by noting limitations on the generalizability of the theory's principles. In extreme cases, the theory might have to be abandoned altogether. By their nature, then, theories are dynamic, changing in response to research findings, rather than static.

When researchers feel confident in the correctness of their theories, they can begin to apply those theories in attempts to reduce prejudice and discrimination. Research can be conducted to evaluate the effectiveness of the application to see how well the theory works in the setting in which it is being applied. The information about the effectiveness of the application can also be used to improve the theory: If an application did not work, that failure would indicate that the usefulness of applications based on the theory might be limited to certain situations and the theory would have to be modified to take those limitations into account. Thus, theory leads to research and applications, the outcomes of which feed back into the theory, resulting in a continuing cycle of discovering, integrating, and using knowledge.

RESEARCH STRATEGIES

A research strategy is a general approach to doing research, defined in terms of how data are collected. For example, when using the correlational strategy, researchers measure the variables that interest them and look for relationships among the variables. In contrast, when using the experimental strategy, researchers actively manipulate one (or more) of the variables that interest them to see if changing one variable affects the other variable. This section provides an overview of some of the strategies most commonly used in research on prejudice: correlational studies, experiments, ethnographic studies, and content analysis. Each strategy has its own advantages and disadvantages. At the end of the chapter, we look at how all the methods can be used to study one aspect of prejudice, illustrating how the strengths of one method can offset the limitations of another.

Correlational Studies

In the **correlational research strategy,** researchers measure two or more variables and look for relationships among them. Although correlational studies can take many forms, surveys are perhaps the most common way to conduct correlational research on prejudice.

Survey research   As a college student, you are probably familiar with survey research. Many colleges and universities conduct surveys of their incoming first-year students and if you took an introductory psychology course, you were probably asked (or required) to participate in research, some of which probably used surveys. You also may have received a telephone call at home asking you to participate in a survey, such as one asking about your opinions about public figures or current events. In survey research, respondents answer questions designed to assess their attitudes, beliefs, opinions, behaviors, and personalities. Designing good survey research is a science in itself (see, for example, Babbie, 1990). This section focuses on an issue crucial to the interpretation of the results of survey research: how the researchers find people to answer their questions, a process called *sampling.*

The two types of sampling most commonly used in survey research are probability sampling and convenience sampling. In **probability sampling,** the researchers first define what is called their *research population.* The research population consists of the people to whom the researchers want to apply their results. For example, the research population for a particular study might be the entire population of the United States, the people who live in a certain region of the country, the residents of a particular state or city, or even the students attending a particular college. Because the size of most research populations makes it impossible to administer a survey to all its members, the researchers select from the population a sample of people who will be asked to complete the survey. In probability sampling, the sample is drawn in a way that makes it a small-scale model of research population: All the characteristics of the population—people of different ages, genders, ethnicities, occupations, and so forth—are in the sample in the same proportion they are found in the population. Because the sample so accurately reflects the population, researchers can have strong confidence that any relationships they find in their sample, such as a relationship between level of education and prejudice, exist in much the same degree in the population as a whole.

However, conducting surveys using probability sampling is expensive because of the necessity of contacting people all over the country. In addition, because most probability sample surveys use telephone interviews to collect data, only a limited number of questions can be asked: People do not like to spend a long time answering questions over the telephone. As a result, a considerable amount of survey research on prejudice uses convenience sampling. As its name implies, in **convenience sampling** the research sample consists of people from whom the researchers can easily collect data. Often, a convenience sample consists of students at the college or university where the researchers teach, but it can also be composed of people recruited at shopping malls or other places where people might gather. Convenience sampling allows researchers to collect data relatively quickly and easily, and, especially when "captive" college students comprise the sample, ask a relatively large number of questions. The ability to ask a lot of questions can be important because many of the variables that interest prejudice researchers, such as personality, ideology, and prejudice itself, are best assessed using measures made up of multiple items (see, for example, Whitley, 2002). The major disadvantage of convenience sampling is that there is no way to know how well the sample represents any given population. Consequently, compared to researchers who use probability samples, those who use convenience samples must be more cautious about drawing conclusions about how well the relationships among variables that they find in their samples reflect the relationships that exist in the populations that interest them.

The correlation coefficient   Survey researchers often describe the relationship between two variables using a statistic known as the **correlation coefficient.** The correlation coefficient, abbreviated as r, indicates the strength of the relationship between two variables. So, for example, you might see the relationship between self-esteem and prejudice reported as $r = -.30$. Because we will talk about correlations from time to time in this book, let us look briefly at how to interpret a correlation coefficient.

To interpret a correlation coefficient, you have to break it into two parts, the sign (plus or minus) and the numeric value (.30 in our example). Usually, if the sign is positive, the "+" symbol is left out, so a correlation might appear as $r = .40$ rather than $r = +.40$. The sign of the correlation coefficient indicates the *direction* of the relationship, with a plus sign indicating a positive relationship and a minus sign indicating a negative relationship. In a positive relationship, as the score on one variable increases, the score on the other variable increases. To use a physical example, in the summer there is a positive correlation between outdoor air temperature and electricity consumption: the higher the temperature, the greater the electricity consumption (because people run their air conditioners more). In the context of prejudice research, there is a small positive relationship between age and prejudice: To a minor degree, older people express more ethnic and racial prejudice than younger people (see, for example, Wagner & Zick, 1995).

In a negative relationship, as the score on one variable increases, the score on the other variable decreases. To use another physical example, in cold weather there is a negative correlation between outdoor air temperature and heating fuel consumption: the lower the temperature, the higher the fuel consumption (because people run their furnaces more). In the context of prejudice research, there is a small negative relationship between the amount of education a person has and prejudice: To a minor degree, better educated people express less ethnic and racial prejudice than less well-educated people (see, for example, Wagner & Zick, 1995).

The numeric part of the correlation coefficient indicates the strength of the relationship. The number can range from 0, indicating no relationship at all, up to 1, indicating a perfect relationship. For example, the correlation between people's heights and weights is about $r = .70$, indicating a strong, but not perfect relationship. That is, for the most part, taller people weigh more than shorter people, but there are a lot of exceptions. High correlations between two variables are rarely found in psychological research; as a general guide, correlations with absolute values (that is, ignoring the plus or minus sign) of less than .1 are considered to be trivial, correlations between .1 and .3 are considered to be small, those between .3 and .5 are considered to be moderate, and those greater than .5 are considered to be large (Cohen, 1992).

Correlation and causality   A major limitation of correlational research is that although it can show that two variables are related to each other, it cannot determine whether one of the variables is causing the other. This problem exists because three criteria determine when one can use research results to correctly conclude that one variable is causing another. Correlational research can meet only the first of those criteria, *covariation*, which requires the causal variable to be related to the effect variable. That is, most of the times that the cause is present in a situation the effect must also be present, and most of the times that the cause is absent in a situation the effect must also be absent. In correlational research this relationship is shown by a statistically significant correlation between two variables.

The second criterion for causality is *time precedence of the cause;* that is, the cause must come before the effect. Most of the time correlational research cannot meet this criterion because, as in survey research, all the variables are measured at the same time. So, for example, if survey researchers find a negative correlation between level of education and prejudice, there is no way to distinguish between two possible patterns of causality. On the one hand, prejudiced people may put a low value on education, so that highly prejudiced people stop their schooling earlier than less prejudiced people; on the other hand, education may prevent or reduce prejudice so that more education results in less prejudice. There is no way to know which possibility is correct and, because of the third criterion for causality, both could be wrong.

The third criterion for causality is the *absence of alternative explanations* for the effect. Let us assume that we prefer the possibility that education reduces or prevents prejudice. The question then becomes, is it education itself that is related to lower prejudice, or is it some other characteristic of educated people that makes it look like higher education is related to lower prejudice when in reality it is not? For example, higher socioeconomic status, lower nationalism, and more experience with members of other groups are all associated with both higher education and lower prejudice (Wagner & Zick, 1995). Thus, a person could argue that it is not really education that is related to lower prejudice (and therefore a possible cause of it), but one of the other variables, such as contact with members of other groups. To be able to say that it is really education that is the important variable, researchers would have to be able to show that education is related to lower prejudice even after the influence of those variables has been eliminated (or, in the language researchers use, *controlled*). Such controls are possible, but even if a relationship between education and lower prejudice with the other variables is controlled (as Wagner and Zick, 1995, found), a problems remains: Researchers can only control for variables they included in the study; what if they left one or more out? Therefore, it is almost always impossible to eliminate alternative explanations in correlational research.

The inability of correlational research to establish time precedence of a cause and to eliminate alternative explanations leads to the basic rule for interpreting correlational research: Correlation does not equal causation. That is, *you can never conclude from correlational research that one variable causes another.* Although it is quite appropriate to say on the basis of correlational research that two variables are related, it is not appropriate to say that one of the variables caused the other. However, because two variables must be related if one is causing the other, the lack of a correlation indicates that neither can be causing the other. For example, if researchers hypothesize that a personality trait is a cause of prejudice but their data show no correlation between the trait and prejudice, then they can correctly conclude that the trait is not a cause of prejudice.

Experiments

So, then, how *do* researchers establish causality? They conduct experiments. This section provides an overview of experimental research, first looking at how experiments establish causality and then examining three settings in which experimental research can be conducted: in the laboratory, in the field, and as part of surveys. This section concludes with a caution about interpreting studies that include both experimental and correlational components.

Experimentation and causality   Although the results of correlational research do not permit the conclusion that one variable caused another, the results of experimental research do. This difference exists because in the **experimental research strategy** the researchers take control of the research situation to ensure that the three criteria for causality are met. Experimental research begins with a hypothesis that specifies that one variable causes another. In experimental research, the proposed cause is called the **independent variable** and the proposed effect is called the **dependent variable;** the hypothesis is that the independent variable causes the dependent variable. A defining characteristic of experimental research is that the researchers manipulate the independent variable by creating two or more **conditions,** which are sets of experiences that represent different aspects of the independent variable.

For example, Jennifer Richeson and Nalini Ambady (2003) hypothesized that being put in a position of authority acts as a releaser for prejudiced attitudes, so that White people put in a position of authority over a Black person would show more prejudice than White people put in a subordinate position to a Black person. Richeson and Ambady ensured that their proposed cause came before the effect by manipulating two independent variables, the amount of authority the participants had over a coworker and the race of the coworker. Richeson and Ambady manipulated the authority variable by telling the participants in the research (all of whom were White) that they would be working on a task with another person. The participants in one condition of the authority variable were told that they would be the other person's supervisor and those in the other condition were told that they would be the other person's subordinate. They were then led to believe that the other person was either White or Black, thereby creating the conditions of the other independent variable. Note that Richeson and Ambady have not yet measured their participants' level of prejudice, so in the experiment, the proposed causes of prejudice tested in the experiment—being a supervisor or subordinate and race of the work partner—were able to have an effect on the participants' attitudes before those attitudes were measured. That is, the researchers created a situation in which they knew that the proposed cause came before the proposed effect.

Richeson and Ambady (2003) tried to prevent alternative explanations for any effect of authority from arising in two ways. First, they structured their research situation to ensure that the only factors that could affect the dependent variable were authority and race of the work partner. They did so by making participants' experiences in each condition of the experiment identical except for the events that created that condition of the independent variable. So, for example, regardless of the condition they experienced, all participants took part in the experiment in the same room, interacted with the same experimenter, went through the steps of the experiment in the same order, and had the dependent variable measured in the same way. That is, Richeson and Ambady tried to construct a situation in which the independent variables were the only factors in the research situation that could affect their participants' responses on the dependent variable because they were the only factors that differed from condition to condition in the experiment.

The other way Richeson and Ambady (2003) forestalled alternative explanations was by randomly determining which condition each participant would experience. This procedure ensured that any personal characteristics of the participants that might influence their responses on the dependent variable would be evenly distributed across the conditions of the independent variables. For example, the participants in the experiment probably differed in their levels of preexisting prejudice. If participants are randomly assigned to conditions, probability theory tells us that if a highly prejudiced person is put into the high authority

2.1   *Random Assignment as a Control Procedure in Experiments*

Let us assume that Richeson and Ambady's (2003) hypothesis is correct, and that being in a high authority position rather than a low authority position raises prejudice scores by 15 points on a 100-point scale. Let us also assume that having a high level of preexisting prejudice adds 25 points to a person's prejudice score. In such a case, the outcome for a highly prejudiced person in each condition would look like this:

CONDITION OF INDEPENDENT VARIABLE

	High Authority	Low Authority
Effect of preexisting prejudice:	25	25
Effect of independent variable:	15	0
Total effect:	40	25

When the researchers analyze their data, they will subtract the average prejudice score in the low authority condition from the average score in the high authority condition. In the example, 40 points – 25 points = 15 points, the effect of the independent variable; the effect preexisting

prejudice had in the low authority condition offset the effect it had in the high authority condition.

It is important to note, however, that although random assignment makes it *unlikely* that personal factors such as attitudes and personality traits will balance out across conditions of the independent variable, there is *no guarantee* that it will happen. That is, it is possible, although highly unlikely, that a purely random assignment process would result in most of the highly prejudiced people being in one condition and most of the low prejudiced people in the other condition. If this were to happen, any differences between conditions would look like they occurred because of the effect of the independent variable. However, in fact, they would be due to either the effect of prejudice or a combination of the effects of prejudice and the effects of the independent variable. There is no easy way to prevent such errors of randomization, although probability theory indicates that they would be extremely rare. The possibility of such errors is one reason why researchers conduct replication research, as discussed in the chapter.

condition, another highly prejudiced person will probably be put into the low authority condition. Although preexisting prejudice would have an effect on prejudice as measured in the experiment, the additional amount of prejudice from the highly prejudiced person in the high authority condition would be offset by the additional amount of prejudice from the highly prejudiced person in the low authority condition. When the researchers look at the difference between conditions (which is how the data from experiments are analyzed), the effects created by the two highly prejudiced people cancel each other out, leaving only the difference caused by the effect of the independent variable. Box 2.1 provides a concrete example of this process.

Covariation, the third criterion for causality, is shown in experiments if there is a statistically significant difference between conditions of the independent variable.

For example, Richeson and Ambady (2003) found that participants showed more prejudice when they thought they were going to be a Black person's supervisor than when they thought they were going to be her subordinate. In contrast, having high versus low authority had no effect on prejudice when the other person was White. Any time the two conditions of the independent variable differ significantly, covariation has occurred.

Laboratory experiments   Researchers can conduct experiments in a variety of contexts. In **laboratory experiments,** such as the one Richeson and Ambady (2003) conducted, the research is carried out in a highly controlled environment. This high degree of control lets researchers construct situations that meet all the criteria for causality, but it also entails a high degree of artificiality. For example, the participants in Richeson and Ambady's experiment never met the other person, they only read a biographical summary that had a picture of a White or Black woman attached and prejudice was assessed using a measure presented on a computer. Thus, laboratory experiments provide a high degree of control that allows researchers to draw confident conclusions about causality, but with a loss of naturalism. That is, the controlled conditions of the laboratory can be very different from the free-flowing situations people encounter in everyday life. As a result, the question arises of whether the results found under artificial laboratory conditions hold up under more naturalistic conditions.

Field experiments   One way to achieve greater naturalism is to conduct a field experiment. In **field experiments,** researchers manipulate an independent variable in a natural setting while maintaining as much control as possible over the research situation. For example, Michelle Hebl and her colleagues (Hebl, Foster, Mannix, & Dovidio, 2002) wanted to determine the extent to which lesbians and gay men were subject to discrimination in everyday situations. They conducted their research at a shopping mall in Texas by having research assistants who were supposedly gay or straight go to stores, ask to speak with a manager, and ask the manager for a job application. The gay versus straight independent variable was manipulated by having the research assistants wear a hat with the slogan "Gay and Proud" or one with the slogan "Texan and Proud." To prevent the research assistants from behaving differently based on which hat they were wearing, they were told not to look at the slogan and to avoid mirrors and reflective glass. All the research assistants were dressed in a fashion common to shoppers at the mall and were trained to behave in the same way in each store they entered. The research assistants carried concealed tape recorders to record their conversations. Hebl and her colleagues (2002) used two sets of dependent variables. They assessed formal discrimination by comparing the percentage of "gay" and "straight" job applicants who were told there was a job available, were invited to fill out applications, and who were called back for a job interview. The researchers did not expect differences on these measures, reasoning that social norms forbid formal discrimination. However, they did expect differences on measures of informal discrimination: They expected the managers to spend less time with the "gay" job applicants, to say less to them, and to act in a less friendly manner. All of the researchers' hypotheses were supported.

Although field experiments add a degree of naturalism to experimental research, they can be difficult to conduct. For example, Hebl and her colleagues (2002) used 16 research assistants, all of whom had to be trained and monitored to ensure that they followed their instructions. Also, the researchers had little control over the research setting; for example, they could not always be sure that the person a research assistant talked to had the authority to make hiring decisions. The essential problem is that it is never possible to create a research situation that simultaneously maximizes naturalism and control: To get more naturalism, researchers must give up some control; conversely, to get more control, researchers must give up some naturalism.

Experiments within surveys   One shortcoming of both laboratory and field experiments is that they must use convenience samples. Not only would it be prohibitively expensive to bring a probability sample of participants to a laboratory, it is unlikely that a sufficient number of people would agree to go. Similar expense problems would accompany an attempt to use a probability sample of field settings, such as shopping malls. However, researchers can get probability samples for experiments by conducting experiments as part of surveys—having several versions of the survey, each version representing a different condition of the independent variable.

For example, Mark Peffley, Jon Hurwitz, and Paul Sniderman (1997) wanted to see how much effect racial stereotypes had on people's opinions about women who received welfare payments. Their hypothesis was that personal characteristics of the person being judged, such as whether she was a high school graduate or dropout, would have more influence than race. They created a survey that had four versions, one with a question that asked about a White high school graduate, one that asked about a Black high school graduate, one that asked about a White high school dropout, and one that asked about a Black high school dropout. For example, one version of the question read, "Now think about a black woman in her early twenties. She is a high school graduate . . . and she has been on welfare for the past year. How likely do you think it is that she will try hard to find a job in the next year?" (Peffley et al., 1997, p. 36). The survey (which addressed other issues as well) was administered to a national probability sample of more than 1,600 people. As Peffley and his colleagues had hypothesized, the woman's dropout status had more effect on opinions that did her race: 62 percent of the people asked about the high school graduate thought it very or somewhat likely that she would try hard to find a job compared to 48 percent of the people asked about the high school dropout, but responses to the Black and White woman did not differ significantly within high school completion conditions.

A great advantage of experiments within surveys is that if the surveys use probability samples, the researchers can have a great deal of confidence in their ability to accurately generalize their results to the population as a whole. However, they are limited in that they can only incorporate independent variables that can be manipulated by changing the ways in which questions are asked. In addition, as with laboratory experiments, naturalism is low; for example, the researchers only ask people questions over the telephone, they do not observe people's behavior in its usual context. Once again, there are trade-offs, this time between a gain in generalizability and a loss of naturalism and of the types of independent variables researchers can use.

Individual difference variables within experiments
Although a defining characteristic of experiments is manipulation of independent variables, a study can simultaneously include manipulated experimental variables and nonmanipulated individual difference variables such as personality traits, attitudes, and so forth. It is important to bear in mind the distinction between manipulated and nonmanipulated variables because although it is appropriate to conclude that a manipulated independent variable caused any observed effects on the dependent variable, it is not appropriate to draw such causal conclusions for nonmanipulated variables.

Consider, for example, a study conducted by Jeffrey Bernat and his colleagues (Bernat, Calhoun, Adams, & Zeichner, 2001). The researchers wanted to see if there was a relationship between attitudes toward homosexuality and aggression toward gay men. In a laboratory experiment, they established a situation in which heterosexual male research participants had the opportunity to administer an electric shock to another male research participant who they thought was in a different room but who actually did not exist. The participants were led to believe that the other person was either gay or straight by being randomly assigned to see a videotape of the person. In the "gay" condition, the other person talked about his boyfriend; in the "straight" condition, he talked about his girlfriend. Thus, the sexual orientation of the other person was a manipulated variable. However, a primary concern of Bernat and his colleagues was the participants' attitudes toward homosexuality. This variable had been measured several weeks previously, and the researchers selected 30 men who had scored very high on a measure of negative attitudes and 30 who had scored very low on the measure to participate in the study. Half the men who scored high had the opportunity to administer shocks to the "gay" man and half had the opportunity to administer shocks to the "straight" man; similarly, half the men who scored low had the opportunity to administer shocks to the "gay" man and half had the opportunity to administer shocks to the "straight" man.

One of the dependent variables Bernat and colleagues (2001) used was the percentage of time participants chose to give the most severe shock possible. They found that of the men with highly negative attitudes, 38 percent gave the most severe shock to the "gay" person while 16 percent gave the most severe shock to the "straight" person. The men who scored very low on negative attitudes toward homosexuality chose the most severe shock less than 1 percent of the time regardless of the other person's supposed sexual orientation. What is the most appropriate interpretation of these results? Because sexual orientation of the other person was a manipulated variable, it is correct to say that thinking that a man is gay rather than straight can cause men with highly negative attitudes toward homosexuality to be more aggressive toward the gay man. However, even though the men with highly negative attitudes were more aggressive to both the "gay" and "straight" person, it is not appropriate to say that holding negative attitudes toward homosexuality causes men to be more aggressive overall. It is not appropriate to draw a causal conclusion because the attitude variable was measured rather than manipulated; as a result, that aspect of the research was a correlational study. That is, research participants were not randomly assigned to hold negative or positive attitudes toward homosexuality; they came to the experiment already holding those beliefs. Therefore, all the limitations on drawing causal conclusions from correlational data apply. The moral of this story is that researchers and readers of research reports must carefully examine all aspects of a study to evaluate which aspects are correlational or experimental, and to draw causal conclusions only on the basis of experimental data.

Ethnographic Studies

Ethnographic research uses a variety of qualitative data collection techniques, including participating in events, observing behavior, and conducting interviews, to come to an understanding of how people experience and interpret events in their daily lives. Ethnographic research also emphasizes studying behavior in the context in which it occurs as a way of understanding the influence of context on behavior. In contrast to experimental research, then, ethnographic research emphasizes naturalism over control and understanding events from the research participants' points of view over constructing events (such as research settings, experimental manipulations, and operational definitions of dependent variables) that reflect the researchers' point of view. To some extent, ethnographic research also emphasizes the discovery of new phenomena over the testing of theories, although ethnographic research can test theoretical propositions and the results of ethnographic research can be used to construct theories.

Kathleen Blee (2002) used ethnographic research methods to study women who were members of hate groups such as the Ku Klux Klan. She wanted to understand why women join racist groups, which are also extremely sexist, and how membership in the group affected their daily lives. She also wanted to learn the ways in which group members were similar to and different from women who were not members of such groups. Blee used a variety of techniques, including interviewing women and attending events their groups sponsored. Blee's results are discussed more fully in Chapter 8, but some of her findings include that, contrary to common conceptions about hate group members, most of the women were middle class, well educated, and came from stable families; they were recruited into their groups by friends who were group members; they were motivated by a number of factors, including the belief that American society was deteriorating and that the group provided a mechanism for addressing the societal problems they saw themselves as facing; and that they were not extremely racist when they joined the group, but became so as a result of group membership.

Content Analysis

Like ethnography, content analysis is a way of studying a topic in a naturalistic manner. However, instead of studying people, researchers doing **content analysis** study products people create, such as documents, photographs, and works of art, to identify themes that help the researcher understand the topic being studied.

For example, Megan McDonald (1999) examined the websites of 30 racist groups to examine, among other factors, how they justified their views. She found that 21 percent claimed that Whites were being victimized, 25 percent used cultural symbols such as quotations from famous people, 21 percent used historical references, 11 percent used legal references, and 4 percent claimed scientific support.

Content analysis is not limited to written materials; it can be applied to images as well. This approach is illustrated by Gerry Finn's (1997) analysis of murals painted on the exterior walls of buildings in Northern Ireland by loyalists (those who want to continue to be part of the United Kingdom) and republicans (those who want independence from England and unification with the Republic of Ireland). He wanted to determine the themes the artists used to justify violence as a means of attaining their groups' goals. He concluded that loyalists justified violence by drawing parallels between the use of violence in the original English conquest of Ireland and in suppressing rebellions against England's and loyalist groups' current efforts to maintain that dominance. Republican murals, in contrast, justified violence by portraying it as the only effective response to the Catholic minority's victimization by the British government. However, Finn concluded that, despite their differing content, the murals of both groups had the same goal: to give the impression that the community supports violence as a means to political ends.

Using Multiple Research Strategies

As Table 2.2 shows, the various research strategies have both advantages and limitations. Consequently, when drawing conclusions about the validity of a hypothesis, researchers like to have a body of evidence based on a variety of methodologies that have offsetting strengths and limitations. If the results of research conducted using different methods all point to the same conclusions, researchers can have a great deal of faith in those conclusions.

Consider, for example, the relative deprivation theory of prejudice (see Chapter 8). In its simplest form, the theory proposes that prejudice arises when people believe that a group that is important to them is being deprived of some social benefit that another group is receiving. This perception of being deprived leads to feelings of resentment and prejudice against the other group. Do feelings of relative deprivation, in fact, lead to prejudice?

Ethnographic research suggests that it does. For example, based on her interviews and observations, Blee (2002) noted that "racist groups depict hordes of nonwhite immigrants or welfare recipients as overwhelming the resources of the U.S. economy and taking tax money, jobs, and resources that rightfully belong to whites. . . . Members of racial minorities are seen as threatening white prosperity with their ability to turn the tables, to change from victims into victimizers" (p. 80). Recall also, that McDonald (1999) found that 21 percent of racist Web sites portrayed Whites as victims. Thus, hate groups try to appeal to White people who see themselves as losing out economically to members of minority groups. But how generalizable are these results? Ulrich Wagner and Andreas Zick (1995) conducted a survey using a probability sample of 3,788 residents of four Western European countries. They found a correlation of $r = .25$ between feelings of

TABLE 2.2 **SOME ADVANTAGES AND LIMITATIONS OF VARIOUS RESEARCH STRATEGIES**

Strategy	Advantages	Limitations
Surveys		
Probability sample	Generalizability to population as a whole	Expensive to carry out; can ask only a limited number of questions; usually cannot draw conclusions about causality
Convenience sample	Less expensive; can ask more questions	Low generalizability; usually cannot draw conclusions about causes
Experiments		
Laboratory	High control allows one to draw conclusions about causality	Artificiality of manipulations and measures; low generalizability from convenience samples
Field	Balance between control and naturalism	Can be difficulty to carry out; types of manipulations and measures used are limited
Within survey	High control allows conclusions about causality; high generalizability when probability sample is used	Can only manipulate question content; can ask only a limited number of questions in probability samples
Ethnography	High degree of naturalism	Low control, so cannot draw conclusions about causality; low generalizability because of convenience samples
Content analysis	High degree of naturalism; high generalizability if sampling is done carefully	Limited to what people write or create (may not reflect beliefs)

relative deprivation and prejudice against minority groups. Thus, ethnographic and survey studies show that a relationship exists between relative deprivation and prejudice. But do feelings of relative deprivation *cause* prejudice?

To determine if relative deprivation causes prejudice, Serge Guimond and Michaël Dambrun (2002) conducted a laboratory experiment in which psychology majors were led to feel either deprived or not deprived relative to economics majors. The researchers then measured the students' prejudice against minority groups. As relative deprivation theory predicts, the deprived students expressed significantly more prejudice than did the nondeprived students. Thus, by looking at a variety of studies conducted using different research strategies, we can conclude that feelings of relative deprivation cause prejudice (based on laboratory experimentation), that this effect is probably found throughout the population (based on survey research), and that it operates in everyday life (based on ethnographic and content analysis research).

MEASURING STEREOTYPES, PREJUDICE, AND DISCRIMINATION

To study stereotypes, prejudice, and discrimination, researchers must be able to measure them. Measuring these variables is difficult because researchers cannot assess them directly. That is, although researchers can directly measure what appear to be the effects of prejudice on people's behavior—what they say and what they do—there is no way to look inside people's heads and directly see how prejudiced they are. Because prejudice (and many other psychological variables) can only be measured indirectly, researchers must be confident that the measures they use accurately assess prejudice. Therefore, the first part of this section reviews two essential criteria for accurate measurement, reliability and validity. We then discuss various ways in which stereotypes, prejudice, and discrimination can be measured: self-reports, observations of behavior, assessment of physiological responses, and the use of what are called implicit cognition measures. The section concludes with a brief discussion of the benefits of using more than one measure when studying prejudice.

Reliability and Validity

Two basic criteria for assessing the quality of a measure are reliability and validity. Although the two concepts are related, they deal with different issues.

Reliability   The **reliability** of a measure is its consistency in providing essentially the same result each time it is used with the same person. Researchers expect this kind of consistency, or stability across time, from measures because they assume that the characteristics being measured are relatively stable across time. For example, we assume that although attitudes can change, they usually change slowly, so that if we measure a person's racial attitudes now and do so again a month from now, those attitudes will be pretty much the same both times. Notice that we expect them to be "pretty much the same," not exactly the same. That is because no measure is perfect and there will always be some degree of error.

The reliability of a measure can be assessed in many ways, but the two most common are test-retest and internal consistency. To assess the **test-retest reliability** of a measure, researchers have a group of people complete the measure at two different times. They then compute the correlation coefficient between the time 1 scores and the time 2 scores; the higher the correlation, the more reliable the measure. The internal consistency of a measure can be assessed when the measure consists of multiple items or questions, as do most attitude measures. **Internal consistency** represents the extent to which people respond in the same way to all the items. For example, if people have positive attitudes, they should consistently give high ratings to items that reflect these positive beliefs and low ratings to items that reflect negative beliefs. Researchers assess the internal consistency of a measure by having people complete it once and then using a special statistical technique to examine consistency of response. The resulting statistic looks like a correlation coefficient and can be interpreted the same way: The higher the coefficient, the more reliable the measure is. You are more likely to see internal consistency coefficients than test-retest coefficients in research reports because internal consistency is easier to assess. However, the internal consistency coefficients of measures are correlated with their test-retest coefficients (Schuerger, Zarella, & Hotz, 1989), so a measure that is internally consistent is also likely to be stable across time.

Validity   Although a reliable measure is assessing something consistently, that consistency does not mean that it measures what it is intended to measure; that is, it could be measuring the wrong thing in a consistent manner. The **validity** of a measure refers to its accuracy: A perfectly valid measure assesses the characteristic it is supposed to assess, assesses all aspects of the characteristic, and assesses only that characteristic. Consider racial attitudes. Researchers want a measure of racial attitudes to assess racial attitudes and not something else, such as a person's positive or negative attitudes toward people in general. Because, as we will see shortly, racial attitudes can be made up of many components, a measure of those attitudes should assess all these components. Finally, a measure of racial attitudes should not be assessing something else at the same time, such as a person's tendency to give socially desirable, or so-called politically correct, responses.

Unlike the use of the correlation coefficient in research on reliability, the validity of a measure cannot usually be summarized as a single number. Instead, researchers must collect a variety of research evidence and draw conclusions about the validity of the measure from that evidence. To do this, researchers use two broad categories of evidence, convergent validity evidence and discriminant validity evidence.

Convergent validity refers to the degree to which scores on a measure correlate with scores on measures of the same or related characteristics and with behaviors that are related to the characteristic being measured. For example, Melanie and Todd Morrison (2002) created a measure of attitudes toward homosexuality. They reasoned that scores on their measure should correlate with scores on another measure of attitudes toward homosexuality, but that the correlation would be moderate rather than large because they were assessing subtle forms of prejudice, an aspect of the attitude that other measures did not assess. They also expected scores on their measures to correlate with scores on measures of political conservatism and traditional gender-role beliefs because previous research found correlations between these variables and attitudes toward homosexuality. They further expected people who scored high on their measure to avoid sitting next to a lesbian or gay man when they could do so without appearing to be prejudiced because people with negative attitudes toward homosexuality should want to avoid contact with lesbians and gay men. Research supported all of the hypotheses: Scores on Morrison and Morrison's measure had a correlation of $r = .56$ with another measure of attitudes toward homosexuality and correlations of $r = .50$ with political conservatism and $r = .47$ with traditional gender-role beliefs. They also found that 56 percent of high scorers avoided sitting with a lesbian or gay man, compared to 11 percent of low scorers. Taken as a whole, these results support the convergent validity of Morrison and Morrison's measure.

Discriminant validity refers to the extent to which a measure does not assess characteristics that it is not supposed to assess. One factor researchers do not want their measures to assess is the degree to which people give socially desirable responses. For example, it is not socially desirable to be prejudiced, so if a prejudice measure were assessing respondents' tendencies to give socially desirable responses along with (or instead of) their attitudes, a low score could mean that respondents were trying to "look good" rather than that they had low levels of prejudice. Because there are a number of ways of measuring people's tendency to give socially desirable responses (see, for example, Paulhus, 1991), researchers can determine the extent to which **social desirability response bias** (as it is called) is correlated with scores on their measures.

Self-Report Measures

The most commonly used method of assessing stereotypes and prejudice is **self-report:** asking people about their attitudes, opinions, and behaviors and then recording what they say. Self-reports can be used to assess the stereotypes people hold, their prejudices toward various groups, and their behavior toward those groups.

Assessing stereotypes As we saw in Chapter 1, stereotypes represent shared beliefs and opinions about the characteristics of groups; some measures of stereotypes simply assess the content of those beliefs. One classic, and still widely used, measure is the Katz and Braly (1933) checklist. This measure consists of a list of traits, such as *lazy, hardworking, religious,* and so forth; respondents check off which traits they think describe a given ethnic, racial, or other group. John Dovidio and his colleagues (Dovidio, Brigham, Johnson, & Gaertner, 1996) provide a summary of the stereotypes of White and Black Americans assessed across a 60-year period using the checklist method. One benefit of using a measure consistently is that it allows researchers to see how stereotypes change over time. For example, Dovidio and colleagues' research suggests that the stereotypes of Blacks and Whites have become more similar across time. However, as Patricia Devine and Andrew Elliot (1995) have noted, when using checklists to assess stereotypes, researchers must be careful to avoid two possible sources of error. First, the traits used in the checklist must assess current stereotypes; stereotypes change over time, so checklists can become outdated. Second, as we discuss in Chapter 3, a person can know what the stereotype of a group consists of but not personally accept it as valid. Therefore, researchers must distinguish between social stereotypes (what the culturally shared beliefs are) and personal beliefs (what individuals personally believe) when instructing people what to mark off on the checklist. For example, Devine and Elliot found that whereas the traits people indicated as representing the social stereotype of African Americans were generally negative, the traits they chose as representing their personal beliefs were more positive.

Researchers also assess stereotype content by asking people how likely or unlikely they think it is that group members have various characteristics. Likelihood is often measured as a probability rating (see, for example, Deaux & Lewis, 1984) so that, for example, a person might say that 75 percent of men and

25 percent of women have leadership skills. When these estimates are obtained for more than one group, ratio scores can be computed that indicate the extent to which people believe that members of two or more groups differ from one another (Martin, 1987). In the example just given, men were seen to be three times as likely than women to have leadership skills, a 3 to 1 ratio. Such measures have also been used to assess stereotype accuracy (McCauley & Stitt, 1978). To do this, researchers compare respondents' judgments of the degree to which a group has a characteristic with the average extent to which group members actually have the characteristic as determined by survey research or other methods. We discuss stereotype accuracy in more detail in Chapter 3.

Other researchers have used free response measures, in which respondents make their own lists of characteristics rather than using a list the researchers provide, to assess both stereotyping and prejudice. For example, Alice Eagly, Antonio Mladinic, and Stacy Otto (1994) asked respondents to list five characteristics they associated with men and five characteristics they associated with women; the respondents then rated the extent to which they thought each characteristic they had listed was positive or negative. Thus, Eagly and her colleagues collected information about both the characteristics respondents associated with women and men and the respondents' own views about whether the attributes were positive or negative. These ratings can be combined to produce a measure of prejudice. An advantage of free response measures is that respondents are not influenced by researchers' preconceived ideas about the stereotypes of any particular group; instead, individuals provide their own beliefs about a group's characteristics.

Assessing prejudice   Most prejudice measures take the form of attitude questionnaires, asking respondents to rate the extent to which they agree or disagree with statements about groups. The items on a measure can deal with emotional responses to groups, beliefs about the characteristics of group members or intergroup relations, and often with both (Biernat & Crandall, 1999). Emotional responses can be assessed in several ways. One way is to directly ask people how they feel about a group by having them respond to items such as "Thinking about [group] makes me feel [adjective]." The adjectives would be emotion-related words such as *tense, relaxed,* and so forth. Another approach is to ask people to rate how comfortable they feel when they interact with members of a group. Finally, researchers can have respondents rate the extent to which adjectives apply to a group as a whole. The adjectives are pretested to determine the degree to which people see them as positive or negative, and often represent group stereotypes and their opposites, such as *lazy* and *hardworking.* Thus, this type of measure assesses the extent to which people agree with stereotypes about groups as well as their emotional responses to the groups.

Asking about people's stereotypic beliefs is a rather blatant way of assessing prejudice and can lead to the problem of socially desirable responding. Therefore, researchers have tried to develop measures that assess beliefs that are more subtly related to prejudice. These measures include beliefs indicating resentment toward a group, such as believing that the group is getting more than it deserves from government social policies; beliefs about social policies, such as affirmative action, that aid some groups; and beliefs that members of other groups violate values that respondents see as important (Biernat & Crandall, 1999). Some theorists, such as Thomas Pettigrew and Roel Meertens (1995) have proposed that measures of blatant and subtle prejudice represent different forms of bias; we discuss that distinction in Chapter 5.

Assessing behavior   Self-report measures also can assess how people behave toward members of other groups, or at least how people *say* they behave or would behave. Thus, self-report measures can assess discrimination as well as stereotypes and prejudice. These measures take two forms. On one type of measure, respondents report how often they have performed various behaviors, such as ignoring a member of a given group in a social situation (see, for example, Roderick, McCammon, Long, & Allred, 1998). On the other type of measure, people report how they would respond in various situations. One example of this type is also one of the earliest measures of prejudice and discrimination, Emory Bogardus's (1928) Social Distance Scale. On this scale and similar measures respondents report how closely they would be willing to associate with members of a given group, ranging from the group member's joining the respondent's family by marriage to exclusion from the respondent's country. On other measures of behavior people respond to more specific situations, such as what they would do if they were present when a friend used an insulting term for a minority group (see, for example, Byrnes & Kiger, 1988). As with measures of blatant prejudice, socially desirable responding can be a problem for self-reports of behavior.

Advantages and disadvantages   Self-report measures are popular for a number of reasons. Self-report measures, especially questionnaires on which respondents record their own answers to questions, are easy to administer and efficient in that many people can complete them at the same time. In contrast, many other forms of measurement require that people be assessed individually. Self-report instruments can also cover multiple topics (such as prejudice toward different groups) and about behavior in a variety of situations (such as work, school, and social settings), whereas other types of measures are often limited to assessing one form of prejudice in one situation. In contrast to many other types of measures, self-report does not require special equipment that may be costly to obtain or require extensive training to use properly. Finally, self-report is the only way to find out what people think, such as their reasons for holding certain opinions or for behaving in certain ways.

Although it has many advantages, self-report also has a major disadvantage: It is easy for people to edit what they say and to conceal their true attitudes and opinions. Many factors affect people's willingness to express their true attitudes, especially when it comes to prejudice (Crandall & Eshleman, 2003), and so motivate socially desirable responding. Researchers therefore have developed a number of methods to reduce motivation to give socially desirable responses and to increase motivation to give accurate responses. The simplest way to reduce socially desirable responding on questionnaires is to maintain the anonymity of the respondents: People are more likely to give accurate responses to survey questions when they feel that no one can associate their answers with them personally (Krosnick, 1999). Other ways of reducing socially desirable responding include using unobtrusive and implicit cognition measures so that people do not realize that prejudice is being measured, and assessing responses that are difficult for people to control, such as physiological responses (Maass, Castelli, & Arcuri, 2000).

Unobtrusive Measures

Unobtrusive measures are characterized by subtlety: They give the impression that they have nothing to do with prejudice or that they are unrelated to the research study taking place. Two common forms of unobtrusive measurement used in studies of prejudice involve behavior and judgments.

Behavior In contrast to self-report measures, behavioral measures assess what people do rather than what they say, and so can be used to assess discrimination as well as prejudice. Because people can control and edit their behavior just as they can their self-reports, researchers use behavioral measures that appear to have nothing to do with prejudice or discrimination.

One commonly used behavioral measure is seating distance. For example, Kim Mooney, Ellen Cohn, and Margaret Swift (1992) told the college students who participated in their research that they were going to interview another person. Some participants learned that the interviewee would be an AIDS patient from a local hospital whereas others learned that the interviewee would be a cancer patient. The participant was then asked "to set up two chairs for the interview in any position that would be comfortable for her, and to have a seat" (p. 1446) while the researcher went to the lobby of the building to meet the interviewee. On the average, the participants set the chairs farther apart when they thought they were going to interview an AIDS patient than when they thought they were going to interview a cancer patient.

Researchers also can measure what might be called symbolic distance as well as physical distance. For example, Janet Swim, Melissa Ferguson, and Lauri Hyers (1999) had heterosexual women answer questions as part of a group discussion; the questions had been pretested to determine which answer people were most and least likely to give. Three members of the group (all working for the researchers) answered some questions in the least popular way. A fourth member of the group (also working for the researchers) answered those questions in the most popular way; this dissenter had identified herself as either lesbian or heterosexual based on an answer to an earlier question. Swim and her colleagues found that participants symbolically distanced themselves from the lesbian dissenter by agreeing with her less often than with the heterosexual dissenter. Other behaviors that have been used to assess prejudice include eye contact and leaning toward or away from another person during a conversation, giving and asking for help, and aggression (Maass et al., 2000).

Judgments When research participants evaluate other people in a context that appears to be unrelated to prejudice, they are completing judgmental measures. For example, John Dovidio and Samuel Gaertner (2000) asked people to read résumés of job applicants and decide whether a given person should be hired as a student peer counselor. The résumés included both positive and negative information. In a pretest that excluded information about the applicant's race, 50 percent of the participants recommended the person for the job. Results of the main study showed that when the race of the applicant was implied by information in the résumé, such as membership in student organizations, White participants recommended Black applicants 45 percent of the time, whereas they recommended White applicants 75 percent of the time.

Physiological Measures

Physiological measures assess changes in the body's responses to a stimulus. Physiological measures that have been used in research on prejudice include cardiovascular responses such as heart rate and blood pressure, the electrical conductivity of the skin, voice pitch, small movements of the facial muscles, eye blink rate, electrical activity in certain area of the brain (referred to as *event-related potentials*), and brain imaging (for example, functional magnetic resonance imaging or fMRI). For the most part, these measures can distinguish between positive and negative emotional reactions to a stimulus and can indicate the intensity of the reactions. They cannot, however, distinguish between different types of emotions such as fear, anger, and disgust (Guglielmi, 1999). However, as Sergio Guglielmi (1999) noted, for research on prejudice it is probably sufficient to know how intense a person's reaction to a member of another group is and whether that reaction is positive or negative rather than the specific emotion involved.

The big advantage that physiological measures have over self-report and unobtrusive measures is that most physiological responses are not under voluntary control, and so it is difficult for people to "edit" them. Even with responses that people can try to control, such as facial expression, recording equipment can detect a change even when onlookers cannot (Cacioppo, Petty, Losch, & Kim, 1986). Finally, strong evidence demonstrates the validity of physiological measures as indicators of emotional valence (positive or negative) and intensity (Blascovich, 2000; Guglielmi, 1999). Despite these advantages, since the end of the 1970s, researchers have rarely used physiological measures to study prejudice. Guglielmi (1999) attributes this lack of use to several factors, including an emphasis on the cognitive over the emotional aspects of prejudice that began in the 1980s (see Box 2.2); a lack of training in physiological psychology on the part of researchers, mostly social psychologists, who conduct most of the research on prejudice; and the inherent disadvantages of psychophysiological research, including the cost of the equipment and the need for special training in the operation of that equipment. Nonetheless, some recent research shows the value of physiological measurement of prejudice.

Two studies illustrate the use of these measures. Wendy Mendes and her colleagues (Mendes, Blascovich, Lickel, & Hunter, 2002) measured White college students' cardiovascular responses while interacting with a Black or White student. The particular pattern of responses that Mendes and her colleagues measured assesses feelings of threat as opposed to readiness to take on a challenging

2.2   *The Interplay of Theory and Research Methodology*

Until the 1960s, theorists and researchers conceptualized prejudice in terms of motivation, personality, and emotion (Duckitt, 1994; Fiske, 1998): People were seen as having needs such as those for security and self-esteem, and rejection of outgroup members was seen as a strategy for meeting those needs. In addition, perceived threats of minority groups to majority group members' economic security and traditional values were thought to lead to frustration, which in turn led to feelings of hostility toward those groups. In research that was based on this perspective, one way in which emotional responses to minority group members was assessed was by physiological measures (Guglielmi, 1999).

Then, in 1967, Ulrich Neisser published the first book to bear the title of *Cognitive Psychology*, bringing what has come to be known as the "cognitive revolution" to the attention of psychologists in other fields (see, for example, Hergenhahn, 2005). The primary focus in psychology shifted from factors such as personality, motivation, and emotion to cognition, and from how personality, motives, and emotion affect behavior to how thinking affects behavior. One reason for this change in emphasis was that the older theories were coming to be seen as stale and offering no new insights into human behavior; cognitive theories, in contrast, promised, and provided, useful new insights (S. Taylor, 1998). Research on the personality, motivational, and emotional correlates of prejudice was not abandoned, but those perspectives took a backseat to the cognitive perspective (Fiske, 1998). As a result, the use of physiological measures, which assess emotional responses, fell out of use in prejudice research (Guglielmi, 1999).

The pendulum began to swing back in the other direction in the 1980s, when researchers began to examine how cognition and emotion affected one another (Mackie & Smith, 2002). Spurred both by new theories of emotion and improvements in technology, physiological measures began to make a comeback in the study of prejudice (Guglielmi, 1999). Thus, theories not only provide hypotheses to be tested in research, they can also have a strong influence on the methodology used in the research. In this case, a shift in theoretical emphasis away from emotion to cognition led to the temporary abandonment of physiological measures in the study of prejudice.

but nonthreatening task. The research participants showed threat responses when interacting with a Black student and challenge responses when interacting with a White student. Eric Vanman and his colleagues (Vanman, Paul, Ito, & Miller, 1997) studied facial muscle responses; one pattern of muscle responses indicates a positive emotional reaction to a stimulus, another pattern indicates a negative reaction. Vanman and his colleagues measured their research participants' responses while the participants looked at pictures of Black people or White people. The changes in their muscular activity indicated negative responses to the pictures of Black people and positive responses to the pictures of White people.

An important aspect of these studies was that, in both cases, self-report measures found no evidence of prejudice; on the contrary, the Black task partners in Mendes and colleagues' study and the pictured Black people in Vanman and colleagues' study received more positive ratings than did their White counterparts. Thus, the physiological measures detected a prejudiced response when the self-report measures did not.

An emerging area of psychophysiological research on prejudice uses brain imaging technology such as fMRI. For example, Elizabeth Phelps and her colleagues (2000) used fMRI technology to examine the extent to which one area of the brain, the amygdala, was activated when White research participants looked at pictures of Black and White faces. Phelps and her colleagues focused on amygdala activation because the amygdala is involved in the learning of fear responses and to the expression of learned emotional responses. They found greater amygdala activation in response to pictures of Black faces than to pictures of White faces. In addition, as in the Mendes and colleagues (2002) and Vanman and colleagues (1997) studies, amygdala responses to the pictures of Black versus White faces were unrelated to scores on a self-report measure of prejudice.

Implicit Cognition Measures

Implicit cognition measures assess the degree to which concepts are associated with one another in memory. So, for example, a researcher could compare the strength of the link between *Black* and *pleasant* or *unpleasant* with the strength of the link between *White* and *pleasant* or *unpleasant*. If *Black* were associated more strongly with *unpleasant* compared to *White* and if *White* were associated more strongly with *pleasant* compared to *Black,* then one could conclude that *Black* had a less pleasant meaning than *White* for that person, indicating prejudice against Black people; the stronger the difference in strength of association, the stronger the prejudice. These measures are called *implicit* because they are designed to assess associations without the research participants' being aware of what is being measured. Cognitive psychologists have used implicit measures for a long time to study memory and related processes, but these measures have been adapted to the study of prejudice only fairly recently. The two implicit cognition measures that have been used most often in research on prejudice are priming and the Implicit Association Test (Fazio & Olson, 2003).

In **priming,** exposure to an example of a member of a category, such as a picture of a Black person, activates concepts associated with the category. For example, if a person associates the concept *Black* with the concept *athletic, athletic* becomes activated. Because *athletic* has been activated, it will be easier for the person to recognize the word when he or she sees it. In most cases, a prime (the stimulus that causes priming to occur) activates a large number of associated concepts, preparing people to recognize them. When priming is used to assess prejudice, the primes are things associated with a stigmatized group (such as a picture of a Black person) and things associated with a nonstigmatized group (such as a picture of a White person); the dependent variable is the speed with which people can recognize positive or negative words associated with the primes. A faster

2.3   *Using Priming to Assess Anti-Black Prejudice*

Measurement of prejudice using the priming approach has five steps, illustrated by the following example from the research of Dovidio, Kawakami, Johnson, Johnson, and Howard (1997):

1. Research participants are told the following: A computer will show them a letter, either an H for house or a P for person and then put a word on the screen. The participants' task is to press one key on the keyboard if the word is something associated with the category represented by the letter (that is, *house* or *person*) and a different key if it is not.
2. The computer presents the prime to the research participants. Depending on the condition the participants are in, they see either the face of a Black person or the face of a White person. These pictures flash on the screen so quickly that the participants are not aware that they see them (this is called subliminal priming).

3. The computer then puts an H or a P on the screen
4. The computer shows a word that is either a house word (such as *brick* or *drafty*) or a person word (such as *smart* or *lazy*). Only the participants' responses in the person condition are of interest to researchers; the house condition is used to help disguise the fact that the research deals with prejudice.
5. The computer measures how quickly the participants respond to the word.

Prejudice is scored by combining response times using the following formula: (White prime with positive words – Black prime with positive words) + (Black prime with negative words – White prime with negative words). That is, prejudiced people have stronger associations between Whiteness and positive concepts and stronger associations between Blackness and negative concepts (Dovidio et al., 1997).

response to negative words primed with a Black stimulus combined with a faster response to positive words primed with a White stimulus indicates anti-Black prejudice. Box 2.3 contains a description of the use of priming to assess prejudice.

Priming measures assess prejudice in terms of the extent to which being exposed to one concept (such as a person's race) facilitates recognition of associated concepts (such as racial stereotypes). The **Implicit Association Test** (IAT; Greenwald, McGhee, & Schwartz, 1998) represents the other side of the coin: It assesses the extent to which unassociated concepts makes responding more difficult. To do this, the IAT uses the principle of response competition. Response competition pits two responses against one another, a habitual response and an opposing response. The stronger the habitual response, the longer it takes to make the opposing response. The opposing response is delayed because rather than just making the response, the person has to first suppress the habitual response. The IAT uses the principle of response competition in the following way: White people who are prejudiced against Black people will generally associate positive concepts with Whiteness and negative concepts with Blackness. Consider a situation, then, in which prejudiced White people are shown a series of words and asked to press a key that is under their left hand if a word is either negative or associated with Black people and to press a key under their right hand if the word is either positive or associated with White people. The task will be relatively easy because it requires a habitual response. However, it will be relatively difficult for such people to respond correctly if they are asked to press a key that is under their left hand if a word is either negative or associated with White people and to press a key under their right hand if the word is either positive or associated with Black people: If shown a word associated with Black people, their initial impulse, reflecting their prejudice, will be to press the *negative* key, but that is the wrong response in this case because *negative* is represented by the same key as *White*. Therefore, to make a correct response, they have to stop and think briefly about which key to press, slowing their reaction times. Box 2.4 contains a description of how the IAT is used to assess prejudice.

Implicit cognition measures are useful because they assess prejudice using procedures that make it unlikely that people are aware of what is being studied and that make it difficult for people to consciously control their responses. As a result, their responses are unlikely to be strongly affected by social desirability response bias. However, research using both priming and the IAT requires the use of computer equipment and an environment that minimizes distractions, and so it is usually limited to lab settings. Another characteristic of implicit cognition measures is that scores on them, like scores on physiological measures, tend to have low correlations with scores on self-report measures of prejudice.

Self-Report versus Physiological and Implicit Cognition Measures

One of the notable findings from research on the measurement of prejudice is that there tend to be low correlations between scores on self-report measures and scores on physiological and implicit cognition measures (Dovidio, Kawakami, & Beach, 2001; Fazio & Olson, 2003; Mendes et al., 2002; Vanman et al., 1997). The evidence regarding behavioral measures is inconsistent, with some studies finding little or no correlation between self-report and behavioral measures of prejudice (for example, Mooney et al., 1992) and others finding strong correlations (for example, Sechrist & Stangor, 2001). What do these findings mean given that, as noted in the earlier discussion of validity, measures of the same construct should be related to one another?

One answer lies in the factors that affect how attitudes are expressed. Russell Fazio and Tamara Towles-Schwen (1999) have proposed that people will suppress unpopular attitudes that they hold and control their behavior when they are both motivated and able to do so. In the context of self-report measures, people can be motivated by social desirability concerns to suppress attitudes and behavior that will make them appear in a bad light (such as appearing to be prejudiced) and also are able to control the impression they make by how they respond on the measures. In contrast, physiological responses are so automatic that people have

2.4 Using the Implicit Association Test (IAT) to Assess Anti-Black Prejudice

Measurement of prejudice using the IAT approach has five steps (e.g., Greenwald, McGhee, & Schwartz, 1998):

1. Research participants sitting at a computer are told that a face will be shown on the screen. The face is either one of a Black person or one of a White person. The participants are to press the left of two designated keys on the keyboard if they see a White face and the right key if they see a Black face.
2. Participants are told that a word will be put on the screen. The word will represent either a pleasant concept, such as lucky or honor, or an unpleasant concept, such as poison or grief. They are to press the left key if the word represents a pleasant concept and the right key if the word represents an unpleasant concept.
3. Participants are told that they will see either a face or a word. If they see a White face or a pleasant word, they are to press the left key; if they see a Black face or an unpleasant word, they are to press the right key. For prejudiced people, this should be an easy task because they already associate *Black* with *unpleasant* and *White* with *pleasant* and they make the responses for *Black* and *unpleasant* with the same hand and for *White* and *pleasant* with the same hand.
4. Participants are told that a face will appear on the screen. They are to press the left key if a Black face appears and the right key if a White face appears.
5. Participants are told to press the left key if they see a Black face or a pleasant word and the right key if they see a White face or an unpleasant word. For prejudiced people, this task should be more difficult than the one in step 3 because when they see a Black face, which for them has unpleasant associations, their first impulse is to press the key associated with unpleasant words. However, in this step that is the wrong response because *unpleasant* is indicated by the same key as *White*. Prejudiced participants must therefore stop the automatic response of pressing the right key and then press the left key.

Because the stop-and-restart process in step 5 takes more time than just pressing a key, a person's level of prejudice is indicated by the difference in time it takes to make the step 5 and step 3 responses: the greater the difference, the greater the amount of prejudice.

little ability to control them. The same is true of implicit cognition measures that use the response competition approach, such as the IAT. Implicit cognition measures that use the priming approach are designed so that people are not aware that their prejudices are being assessed, so there is little motivation to control their responses (Maass et al., 2000). Therefore, the low correlations of self-report with physiological and implicit cognition indicators of prejudice are not surprising: To some extent they are measuring different things—the controlled versus uncontrolled (or automatic) expression of attitudes (Guglielmi, 1999).

Maass and her colleagues (2000) point out an interesting implication of the distinction between the automatic and controlled expression of attitudes: Sometimes social desirability response bias is not an issue, so self-reports are good indicators of true attitudes. For example, "If we are interested in the racist attitudes of neo-Nazi groups it may be perfectly superfluous to investigate their implicit beliefs about Blacks through sophisticated [implicit cognition] measures" (Maass et al., 2000, p. 107). Also, some prejudices are more socially acceptable than others, so social desirability concerns will not affect expression of attitudes toward those groups. For example, Francesca Franco and Anne Maass (1999) found that social desirability concerns apparently inhibited expression of explicit negative attitudes toward Jews but did not inhibit expression of negative attitudes toward Islamic fundamentalists (see also Crandall, Eshleman, & O'Brien, 2002).

Using Multiple Measures

Just as it is useful to study prejudice using more than one research strategy, it is useful to use more than one type of measure when studying prejudice. There are several reasons for doing so. As in the case of multiple research strategies, if the results found with different measures all point in the same direction, we can have more confidence in the validity of the results. As shown in Table 2.3, different measures have different strengths and limitations, so if multiple measures are used, the strengths of one can compensate for the limitations of another. Another reason is that prejudice has at least three aspects—the cognitive (such as beliefs and stereotypes), the emotional, and the behavioral—and, as shown in Table 2.4, different types of measures are better for assessing different aspects of prejudice.

A third reason for using multiple measures is that, as also shown in Table 2.4, self-reports assess controllable expressions of prejudice whereas the other types of measures assess relatively uncontrollable expressions of prejudice. Although one might think that the uncontrollable expression of prejudice is what researchers are "really" interested in, it can be useful to know under what circumstances and to what degree people try to exert control over expressions of prejudice. For example, the conflict between people's feelings of prejudice and various factors that inhibit and modify the expression of that prejudice plays a central role in the theories of contemporary prejudice that we discuss in Chapter 5.

Finally, it is important to use measures of both the controllable and uncontrollable expression of prejudice because they are related to different types of behaviors. For example, John Dovidio, Kerry Kawakami, and Samuel Gaertner (2002) conducted a study in which White college students' prejudice was assessed using both a priming measure and a self-report measure. The students later held a conversation with a Black student working with the researchers. Raters who did not know the purpose of the study evaluated the White students' friendliness based on both nonverbal cues, such as eye contact, and verbal cues, such as tone of voice. Dovidio and his colleagues found that prejudice as assessed with the

| TABLE 2.3 | SOME ADVANTAGES AND LIMITATIONS OF MEASUREMENT TECHNIQUES | |

Technique	Advantages	Limitations
Self-report	Easy to use; questionnaires are efficient and require minimal training; can ask about multiple situations; can assess all three aspects of attitudes: emotion, beliefs, and behavior	Artificiality; most susceptible to social desirability response bias (SDRB)
Unobtrusive behavioral	Naturalistic: can be used in field research; in lab research, can be made to appear unrelated to study (e.g., waiting room); some may take place without the person's being aware of it (e.g., leaning toward or away from another person)	Can assess only a limited number of behaviors in a single setting; susceptible to SDRB if people become aware of purpose of study
Judgmental	Good analog of naturalistic behavior in lab research (e.g., evaluation of job applicant); can be made to appear unrelated to prejudice	Can assess only a limited number of judgments; susceptible to SDRB if people become aware of purpose of study
Physiological	Responses occur without conscious control; relatively pure measure of valence (positive or negative) and intensity of emotion	Can only assess emotional response; cannot assess type of response (anger, fear, etc.); equipment required usually restricts research to lab setting; some equipment is very expensive or requires extensive user training
Implicit cognitive	Participants are not aware that prejudice is being measured	Equipment requirements usually restrict research to lab setting; complex procedures can lead research participants to make mistakes

priming measure was related to the White students' nonverbal friendliness during the conversation, $r = .41$, but not to their verbal friendliness, $r = .04$. In contrast, the White students' self-reports of prejudice were related to their verbal friendliness, $r = .40$, but not to their nonverbal friendliness, $r = .02$. That is, the expression of prejudiced attitudes over which the students had little control was related to behaviors over which they had little control, but not to their controllable behaviors; the opposite was true for controllable expression of prejudice and controllable behaviors. Thus, prejudice-related behavior appears to exist at two levels, controllable and uncontrollable, and prejudice-related attitudes can be assessed at the same two levels, with controllable attitudes being better predictors of controllable behaviors and uncontrollable attitudes being better predictors of uncontrollable behaviors.

TABLE 2.4   **USE OF MULTIPLE TYPES OF MEASURES IN RESEARCH ON PREJUDICE**

Aspect of Prejudice Measured	Person's Degree of Conscious Control Over Response	
	Less Control	**More Control**
Cognitive	Implicit cognitive measures such as priming and the IAT; unobtrusive judgmental measures such as ratings of suitability for a job	Self-reports of stereotypes and beliefs
Emotional	Physiological measures, such as cardiovascular and facial muscle responses	Self-reports of emotional responses
Behavioral	Unobtrusive behavioral indicators such as nonverbal cues	Self-reports of behavior

CHAPTER SUMMARY

Research on prejudice and discrimination serves several purposes: It describes the psychological and social processes that underlie prejudice and discrimination, it aids in the development of theories that can point to ways of reducing prejudice and discrimination, and it can test the effectiveness of programs aimed at reducing prejudice and discrimination. The research process has a number of steps. First, researchers derive hypotheses from theories. Hypotheses are turned into predictions that can be tested in research by operationally defining the variables in the hypotheses. Researchers then collect the data to test the predictions and draw conclusions from those data. Two principal questions the researchers want to answer are (1) were the hypotheses supported by the data and (2) what do the data mean? Data are frequently open to more than one interpretation, so researchers who hold different theoretical perspectives may make different interpretations of the same data.

Rather than drawing firm conclusions based on a single study, researchers try to verify their results by conducting further research. This verification process addresses two issues. The first is the extent to which the results of the original study could have resulted from the random errors to which all research is open. The second issue is the extent to which the results generalize across variations in research methods, populations, and procedures. Once researchers have confidence in the accuracy of their results, the results can be used to modify the theory as needed. Once researchers are confident that the theory is accurate, it can be used to design applications. The effectiveness of these applications can then be tested with further research.

Research can be conducted in many ways, each of which has its strengths and limitations. In correlational studies, researchers measure variables and look for relations among them. Surveys are a common way of collecting data for correlational research. Surveys that use probability sampling try to construct a sample of respondents that is an accurate representation of the population of interest and so provide results that can be confidently generalized to the research population. Surveys that use convenience sampling have samples that are drawn from populations that the researchers have easy access to, but which may or may not reflect the characteristics of the population as a whole. Consequently, researchers must be cautious in generalizing results based on convenience samples.

The results of correlational studies are often summarized with a statistic called the correlation coefficient. A positive coefficient indicates that as scores on one variable increase, so do scores on the other variable; a negative coefficient means that as scores on one variable increase, scores on the other variable decrease. Larger coefficients indicate stronger relationships.

The major limitation of correlational research is that it provides no means for determining whether one variable caused another. This limitation derives from the fact that correlational studies are unable to determine the time precedence of the cause or rule out other possible causes for the observed effect. Experimental research overcomes these limitations by constructing situations that meet the criteria for causality. Much experimental research is carried out in laboratory settings, which—although providing the high degree of control needed to draw causal conclusions—are low in naturalism. Field experiments try to increase naturalism by collecting data in natural settings, but entail some loss of control. Researchers can also conduct experiments within surveys by varying the ways in which questions are asked. When probability sampling is used, this procedure allows the results of experimental research to be generalized to the population as a whole. When reading research reports, bear in mind that nonmanipulated variables may be combined with experimental variables as part of the research design. In such cases is it important to draw causal conclusions only about the experimental, manipulated variables but not about the nonmanipulated variables.

Ethnographic methods bring a high degree of naturalism to research by collecting data about people in the context of their everyday lives. Similarly, content analysis focuses on using products people create, such as documents and works of art, to draw conclusions about the factors that affect their behavior. However, these naturalistic methods lack the controls needed to draw causal conclusions. Because each research strategy has its own strengths and limitations, it is best to draw conclusions about the validity of a hypothesis by looking at the findings of a body of research that includes data from studies that have used a variety of methods.

To study stereotypes, prejudice, and discrimination, researchers must be able to measure them. Two essential characteristics of measures are reliability and validity. Reliability refers to the consistency of measurement and can be assessed in terms of test-retest correlations or consistency of response to the items comprising the measure. Validity refers to the accuracy of a measure and is assessed in terms of how well scores on the measure correlated with scores on measures of related traits and behaviors and the extent to which scores on the measure are uncorrelated with scores on measures of unrelated traits and behaviors.

The most commonly used method of assessing stereotypes and prejudice is self-report, asking people to report on their own attitudes, beliefs, and so forth. Stereotypes and prejudice are complex concepts, so researchers have developed a variety of measures for each. Self-reports can also be used to assess behavior toward members of different groups. Self-report measures are easy to administer and allow researchers to efficiently collect a large amount of data from many people in a short period of time. However, they are very susceptible to social desirability response bias, the tendency of people to give responses that make themselves look good. Alternatives to self-report measures include unobtrusive behavioral measures, which assess behaviors that people may not be aware they are performing, and unobtrusive judgmental measures, which assess responses people do not realize are indicators of prejudice. Physiological measures, which assess bodily responses to stimuli, can also be used instead of self-reports because some physiological responses indicate the valence and intensity of emotional responses. However, such measures require costly equipment. Implicit cognition measures assess the degree to which race-related concepts are associated with other positive or negative concepts in memory. People are usually not aware that the responses they make on these measures are related to prejudice, but this approach to measurement requires computer equipment and an environment, such as a laboratory, in which distractions can be kept to a minimum.

A growing body of evidence shows that self-report and other types of measures assess different ways of expressing prejudice. Self-reports assess controllable expressions, that is, what people want others to know about them. The other measures assess uncontrollable expressions of prejudice, that is, expressions that people are unaware that they are making. Not surprisingly then, scores on self-report often have low correlations with scores on other measures. However, scores on self-report measures are also related to different kinds of behaviors than are scores on other types of measures: self-reports are related to controllable behaviors, such as what a person says to a member of another race, whereas scores on other measures are related to less controllable behaviors, such as nonverbal cues. Thus, it can be useful to use a variety of measures when studying prejudice.

Suggested Readings

The Research Process

Pyke, S. W., & Agnew, N. McK. (1991). *The science game* (5th ed.). Englewood Cliffs, NJ: Prentice Hall.

Stern, P. C., & Kalof, L. (1996). *Evaluating social science research* (2nd ed.). New York: Oxford University Press.

Whitley, B. E., Jr. (2002). Validity in research. In M. W. Wiederman & B. E. Whitley Jr. (Eds.), *Handbook for conducting research on human sexuality* (pp. 51–81). Mahwah, NJ: Erlbaum.

Both Pyke and Agnew and Stern and Kalof provide relatively nontechnical introductions to the research process. If you are interested in a more technical approach, a number of excellent research methods books are available; ask your instructor to recommend one. Whitley summarizes the major factors that affect the process of drawing valid conclusions from the results of research.

Research Strategies

Crano, W. D., & Brewer, M. B. (2002). *Principles and methods of social research* (2nd ed.). Mahwah, NJ: Erlbaum.
   Chapters 4 through 7 describe the experimental research strategy and many of its variations. Chapter 8 provides a readable description of the problems and processes involved in correlational research. Chapter 10 discusses sampling and other issues in survey research. Chapter 10 provides an introduction to the process of content analysis.
Finn, G. P. T. (1997). Qualitative analysis of murals in Northern Ireland: Paramilitary justifications for political violence. In N. Hayes (Ed.), *Doing qualitative analysis in psychology* (pp. 143–178). Hove, England: Psychology Press.
   Finn provides an example of a less commonly used form of content analysis, that of visual images.
Mellor, D. (2003). Contemporary racism in Australia: The experiences of Aborigines. *Personality and Social Psychology Bulletin, 29,* 474–486.
   Mellor's study provides a brief example of the use of interviews in ethnographic research.
Miller, P. J., Hengst, J. A., & Wang, S. (2003). Ethnographic methods: Applications from developmental cultural psychology. In P. M. Camic, J. E. Rhodes, & L. Yardley (Eds.), *Qualitative research in psychology: Expanding perspectives in methodology and design* (pp. 219–242). Washington, DC: American Psychological Association.
   Miller and her colleagues present a succinct description of ethnographic research and its use in psychological research.

Measurement

Blascovich, J. (2000). Using physiological indexes of psychological processes in social psychological research. In H. T. Reiss & C. M. Judd (Eds.), *Handbook of research methods in social and personality psychology* (pp. 117–137). New York: Cambridge University Press.
   Blascovich provides an overview of the use of physiological measures, with details on a cardiovascular and a facial muscle measure that show promise for use in research on prejudice.
Brauer, M., Wasel, W., & Niedenthal, P. (2000). Implicit and explicit components of prejudice. *Review of General Psychology, 4,* 79–101.
   Brauer and colleagues compare implicit cognition with self-report measures of prejudice. Brauer and colleagues also provide brief descriptions of a number of implicit cognition measures.
Crano, W. D., & Brewer, M. B. (2002). *Principles and methods of social research* (2nd ed.). Mahwah, NJ: Erlbaum.
   Crano and Brewer's Chapter 3 describes the issues involved in making reliable and valid measurements.
Fazio, R. H., & Olson, M. A. (2003). Implicit measures in social cognition research: Their meaning and use. *Annual Review of Psychology, 54,* 297–327.

Fazio and Olson describe a number of implicit cognition measures and evidence of their reliability and validity.

Guglielmi, R. S. (1999). Psychophysiological assessment of prejudice: Past research, current status, and future directions. *Personality and Social Psychology Review, 3,* 123–157. Guglielmi presents a detailed analysis of the use of physiological measures in prejudice research.

Hoyle, R. H., Harris, M. J., & Judd, C. M. (2002). *Research methods in social relations* (7th ed.). Belmont, CA: Wadsworth. Hoyle and colleagues' Chapter 4 describes the issues involved in making reliable and valid measurements.

Maass, A., Castelli, L., & Arcuri, L. (2000). Measuring prejudice: Implicit versus explicit techniques. In D. Capozza & R. Brown (Eds.), *Social identity processes: Trends in theory and research* (pp. 96–116). Thousand Oaks, CA: Sage. Maass and colleagues discuss the issue of the conditions under which implicit measures are really more useful than simpler-to-use self-report measures.

Phelps, E. A., & Thomas, L. A. (2003). Race, behavior, and the brain: The role of neuroimaging in understanding complex social behaviors. *Political Psychology, 24,* 747–758. Phelps and Thomas discuss the use of brain imaging technologies to explore the neural systems involved in processing information about social groups.

Stone, A. A., Turkkan, J. S., Bachrach, C. A., Jobe, J. B., Kurtzman, H. S., & Cain, V. S. (Eds.). (2000). *The science of self-report: Implications for research and practice.* Mahwah, NJ: Erlbaum. The chapters in this book discuss many of the issues involved in collecting and interpreting self-report data.

Webb, E. J., Campbell, D. T., Schwartz, R. D., & Sechrest, L. (2000). *Unobtrusive measures* (rev. ed.). Thousand Oaks, CA: Sage. (Originally published 1966) This is *the* classic book about unobtrusive measurement. Although the authors do not address prejudice specifically, they do list a wide variety of ways in which behavior can be assessed unobtrusively.

KEY TERMS

conditions of independent variable
content analysis
convenience sampling
convergent validity
correlation coefficient
correlational research strategy
dependent variable
discriminant validity
ethnographic research
experimental research strategy
field experiments
generalizability
hypotheses
hypothetical constructs
Implicit Association Test (IAT)

independent variable
internal consistency
laboratory experiments
operational definitions
predictions
priming
probability sampling
reliability
self-report
social desirability response bias
test-retest reliability
unobtrusive measures
validity
variable

QUESTIONS FOR REVIEW AND DISCUSSION

1. Outline the steps in the research process.
2. Explain the relationships among theoretical postulates, hypotheses, and predictions.
3. Explain the concepts of *hypothetical construct* and *operational definition.*
4. Explain the relationship between the methods used to manipulate and measure variables and the concept of *operational definition.*
5. What is the difference between quantitative and qualitative data? For each type of data, explain how researchers decide if the data support their hypotheses.
6. Describe the factors that affect the ways in which researchers interpret the meaning of their data. Give an example of situation that you know of (perhaps from a previous course) in which different researchers or theorists made different interpretations of the same data. Which interpretation do you agree with? What are your reasons for your choice?
7. What does the term *generalizability* mean? Why is the generalizability of research results important?
8. How are theories in behavioral science related to the applied use of behavioral science knowledge?
9. Explain the differences among correlation, experimentation, ethnography, and content analysis as ways of collecting data. What strengths and limitations does each entail?
10. What is the difference between probability sampling and convenience sampling? What is the relationship between the kind of sampling used in a study and the generalizability of the results of the study?
11. What does it mean if two variables have a correlation of $r = .40$? What does it mean if two variables have a correlation of $r = -.60$? Which of those two correlations represents the stronger relationship?
12. Explain the three criteria for drawing causal conclusions from research data. Based on these criteria, to what extent is it correct to draw causal conclusions from surveys, experiments, ethnographic studies, and content analyses?
13. In experimental research, what roles do the independent and dependent variables play? What does the term *conditions of the independent variable* refer to?
14. Explain the relative strengths and weaknesses of laboratory experiments, field experiments, and experiments within surveys.
15. Suppose a researcher found that men had higher prejudice scores than women. Would it be correct to conclude that being male causes people to be more prejudiced? Explain your answer.
16. Some researchers contend that ethnographic research and content analysis are inherently flawed because they require researchers to get too involved with their research topics and, in the case of ethnographic research, with their research participants, and to make too many subjective judgments. Other researchers contend that such involvement and subjectivity are basic strengths of the methods. Which position do you agree with? Why?

17. Explain the concepts of reliability and validity of measurement. How are reliability and validity related to one another?
18. Explain the concepts of convergent and discriminant validity. Why is it important to demonstrate that a measure has both?
19. Describe the ways in which researchers can use self-reports to assess stereotypes, prejudice, and behavior.
20. What is social desirability response bias? To what extent is it a problem for each of the four types of measures?
21. Explain the relative strengths and weaknesses of self-report, unobtrusive, physiological, and implicit cognition measures of prejudice.
22. Self-report measures assess controllable expressions of prejudice whereas the other measures assess uncontrollable expressions of prejudice. Is this difference a problem or an advantage for research on prejudice? Explain your answer.
23. Choose an aspect of prejudice that interests you. If you were going to conduct a study on that topic, what research strategy would you use and what type (or types) of measure would you use? Explain your choices.

SOCIAL CATEGORIZATION AND STEREOTYPES

For the real environment is altogether too big, too complex, and too fleeting for direct acquaintance. We are not equipped to deal with so much subtlety, so much variety, so many permutations and combinations. And although we have to act in that environment, we have to reconstruct it on a simpler model before we can manage with it.

—*Walter Lippman, 1922 (p. 11)*

It happens in a blink of an eye. You see a person walking in front of you and, before you realize it, you have determined the person's age, race, gender and, depending on other available cues, perhaps her or his occupation or interests. Chances are good that your assessment is correct; people are remarkably adept at this type of information processing. As Lippman (1922) noted nearly a century ago, unless people simplify the world by quickly and efficiently sorting objects and people into categories and think in terms of categories rather than individuals, they will be overwhelmed by the environment. The sheer amount of information people process every day is staggering. Consider, for example, that the average person sees around 3,000 advertisements per day (Kilbourne, 2000); if you add to that figure all the other sources of information people are exposed to, you can quickly appreciate just how efficient people have to be at processing the information the world presents to them.

Unfortunately, this efficiency comes at a cost. Quickly making decisions about people and objects allows perceivers to move ahead, ready to deal with the next piece of information that faces them. But quick decisions also lead people to make snap decisions and to think stereotypically and, perhaps, to make errors of judgment. Careful thought can produce more accurate decisions but prevents them from attending to other information that is demanding attention. The challenge for perceivers is to strike a balance between efficiency and accuracy. When should people strive for careful, considered judgment and when can they safely rely on stereotypes?

To answer this question, we first explain the categorization process and describe the types of categories people use most often in social judgment. Next, we consider the origins of stereotyping: how do people develop the categories they later use for efficient information processing? We then discuss how stereotypes are shared in society through communication between parents and children, between peers, or by the media. The question of whether these stereotypes accurately reflect the characteristics of social groups is then considered. In particular, we focus on the difficulties in assessing accuracy. We next introduce the idea that two different people can hold the same stereotype for very different reasons. This research focuses on the purposes, or functions, that stereotypes sometimes fulfill. The final section of this chapter describes the factors that lead people to maintain or change their stereotypic beliefs.

Social Categorization

To address the complex question of the ways in which efficient cognitive processing can lead to stereotyping and prejudice, we begin with an explanation of how people utilize social information, focusing on the types of social categories they create and use. We then explore the subtypes, or more specific social categories, that perceivers utilize. Our discussion then turns to people's tendency to see the world in two categories, *us* and *them*, and how this tendency perpetuates stereotypic judgment and prejudice.

Why We Categorize

Categorization is the term psychologists use for the process of simplifying the environment by creating categories on the basis of characteristics (such as hair color or athletic ability) that a particular set of people appear to have in common (Macrae & Bodenhausen, 2000). Through this process, people place others (and themselves) into categories called social groups. Once these social groups are created, people develop beliefs about the members of those groups. They then use these beliefs to guide their future interactions with individual social group members. As social psychologists Neil Macrae and Galen Bodenhausen (2000) put it, "knowing what to expect—and exactly where, when, and from whom to expect it—is information that renders the world a meaningful, orderly, and predictable place" (p. 94). That is not to say people always see the world in terms of simple categories and use them to make simplistic judgments about others. Certainly this is not the case. As we will see, people adapt and respond to the demands of the task at hand and, when they are motivated to do so, make thoughtful, complex judgments (Fiske, Lin, & Neuberg, 1999). But people do use categories to make judgments about other people on a daily and perhaps even momentary basis. As a result, understanding the categorization process is fundamental to understanding stereotyping and prejudice.

Stereotypes belong to a class of categories called *schemas*, which are cognitive structures that contain a person's knowledge and beliefs about a particular object or social group. Schemas influence what people pay attention to, how they organize information, and what they later remember (Hamilton, 1981). Hence, stereotypes operate as schemas in that they influence the perceiver's acquisition and interpretation of information about members of social groups (Hamilton, 1979). This acquisition and interpretation, in turn, sets up the expectations for how members of social groups will act.

Two aspects of categorization are relevant to the understanding of prejudice. First is the *content* of people's stereotypic beliefs. What characteristics are associated with particular groups? Is that association consistent across time or group members? If not, what factors might make this content vary? As we saw in Chapter 1, historically, a great deal of research on stereotyping and prejudice has focused on answering these questions. Researchers have explored these questions because these beliefs are the foundation of stereotyping and prejudice; they form the content of schemas. More recently, psychologists have turned to a second critical aspect of categorization: what is the *process* by which people form and use social categories? How are these categories represented in memory? How and when are these representations retrieved and utilized? What motivations and biases influence this process? Do individuals differ in their readiness to rely on categorization? Do established stereotypes change? These questions are the primary focus of this and the following chapter.

To understand the difference between content and process, keep in mind that the human brain is not a digital storage medium—information is not simply recorded and then later retrieved in exactly the same form. For the most part, people remember information in terms of general principles rather than specific individual facts and, when informational gaps exist, people fill in the blanks with what their experiences and beliefs tell them should be there (see, for example, Matlin, 2002). When we factor in the complexity of our social world, it is not surprising that individual biases and situational factors influence how people perceive and remember a person or event (see Box 3.1 for an example of this process from early work in cognitive psychology). Although this point may seem obvious, it was not the perspective taken by most stereotype researchers until relatively recently (see Ashmore & Del Boca, 1981, for a review). As we saw in Chapter 1, for example, researchers in the 1920s and 1930s believed that stereotypes resulted from irrational and unjustifiable beliefs and behaviors. It was not until the early 1980s that researchers began to adopt the perspective that stereotyping is a normal outcome of everyday information processing. This chapter focuses on how this limited information processing capacity affects the learning, retrieval, and utilization of stereotypic information.

Types of Categorization

Think for a moment about the various social groups you come in contact with. A list of those groups would likely include general social groups, such as Blacks and Whites, or more specific groups, such as businesswomen or people who are overweight. Stereotype researchers have found the distinction between general and specific social categories to be important to understanding the categorization process.

Basic social categories   If you are a *Saturday Night Live* fan, you might remember Pat, the character Julia Sweeney played. Pat's gender was purposefully ambiguous; in fact, the skits involving Pat centered around others trying to trick her/him into revealing his/her gender. These skits worked because gender is a **basic social category**, or a category for which a wealth of information is available in memory (Macrae & Bodenhausen, 2000). Race and age also are basic social categories. When people know a person's basic category membership, such as gender, they use that information to draw conclusions about the person's traits, social roles, and physical characteristics (Deaux & Lewis, 1984). When basic category membership cannot be easily determined, people feel off balance; they do not know what assumptions to make or how to begin or continue an interaction. Because information about gender is so tightly woven into the social fabric, for example, the writers of the "Pat" skits had to be extremely creative. Sustaining even a 5-minute interaction without revealing the gender of the protagonist is quite a challenge.

All basic categories have "privileged" status: information about them is readily available to perceivers. Category membership usually is easily observable, and the categories have important cultural meanings (Fiske et al., 1999). Recall from Chapter 1 that, at the societal level, there is generally consensus about the content of stereotypic beliefs. This is especially true for basic social categories. In the absence of a clear motivation to do otherwise, people tend to treat all members of basic social categories similarly, based on the stereotypic knowledge of that social group.

3.1 *Remembering: The War of the Ghosts*

It is easy to think of memory as a recording of facts; when people read stories, hear newscasts or witness events themselves, they usually assume that what they remember closely corresponds to what actually happened. Yet research on human information processing shows this is rarely the case. Consider a Native American story, *The War of the Ghosts*, which Sir Frederic Bartlett (1932) presented to research participants early in the last century:

> One night two young men from Egulac went down to the river to hunt seals, and while they were there it became foggy and calm. Then they heard war-cries and they thought: "Maybe this is a war-party." They escaped to the shore, and hid behind a log. Now canoes came up, and they heard the noise of paddles, and saw one canoe coming up to them. There were five men in the canoe and they said:
>
> > "What do you think? We wish to take you along. We are going up the river to make war on the people." . . .
>
> [O]ne of the young men went, but the other returned home.
>
> And the warriors went on up the river to a town on the other side of Kalama. The people came down to the water, and they began to fight, and many were killed. But presently, the young man heard one of the warriors say: "Quick, let us go home: that Indian has been hit." Now he thought: "Oh, they are ghosts." He did not feel sick, but they said he had been shot.
>
> So the canoes went back to Egulac, and the young man went ashore to his house and made a fire. And he told everybody [what happened]. He told it all, and then he became quiet. When the sun rose, he fell down. Something black came out of his mouth. His face became contorted. The people jumped up and cried.
>
> He was dead. (p. 65)

Bartlett's British research participants each read this story twice. He then asked them to recall the story after 15 minutes, 20 hours, 8 days, or at various intervals up to 6 years later. Over time, the details of the story were shortened; more interestingly, participants changed aspects of the story to bring it closer to their own experience. References to the canoe, for example, were changed to a boat and unusual proper names were forgotten. Moreover, the parts of the story that were difficult to interpret through British culture were changed or embellished. The role of the ghosts, for example, is fairly small in the original story, but it becomes enlarged and embellished in the retelling; the men in the canoe, for example, are often later described as a "ghost clan." Similarly, the "something black" that came out of the dying man's mouth becomes transformed into "escaping breath" or "foaming at the mouth."

Bartlett (1932) conducted experiments using other stories, with similar results, concluding that "accuracy of reproduction . . . is the rare exception and not the rule" (p. 93). Instead, details quickly become stereotyped and, afterward, change very little. Finally, events are recalled more accurately when they fit with the participants' own culture and ideas; those that do not fit become rationalized so that they are more consistent with the recorder's experience. Human memory, then, especially memory for social events, is far from a digital recording and is heavily influenced by preconceptions and experience. Much of the research and theory presented in this chapter echoes the processes Bartlett demonstrated nearly 75 years ago.

Other social categories   Of course, people make decisions about how to interact with others based on other social categories or other types of information as well. Abundant evidence suggests, for example, that physically attractive people are treated differently than physically unattractive people (Eagly, Ashmore, Makjijani, & Longo, 1991). People also are categorized based on their sexual orientation (Simon, 1998), their religion, or specific aspects of their physical appearance, such as weight (Crandall, 1994), disability status (Soder, 1990), or skin tone (Maddox & Gray, 2002). And, of course, people have stereotypes about nationalities (Peabody, 1985). Common stereotypes Americans hold about Germans, for example, include the beliefs that they are always on time, drink in beer gardens, eat bratwurst, and are unfriendly. Germans, in contrast, believe Americans live without restrictions, eat fast food, drive big cars (and drive them fast), and spend most of their time watching television (Below, Molau, & Suchi, 1995).

More generally, people attend to demeanor, making snap judgments based on nonverbal cues such as facial expressions, posture, and gait (Zebrowitz, 1996). Judgments also can be based on something as simple as color; in classic Westerns, the "good guys" wear white and the "bad guys" wear black, implicitly reflecting their moral virtue. Research supports the rationale behind this judgment: athletes wearing black uniforms see themselves, and are seen by others, as more aggressive than athletes wearing uniforms of other colors (Frank & Gilovich, 1988). As is true for basic social categories, classification into many of these other categories is based on physical appearance cues (see Fiske & Taylor, 1991, for a review).

Level of specificity   Evidence suggests that people notice basic category information first. However, in judging others, people tend to give more weight to some social categories than to others. For example, people find knowing another's sex to be more informative than knowing another's race (Stangor, Lynch, Duan, & Glass, 1992). Yet this same research also demonstrated that people recognize that a person can simultaneously be a member of more than one category. That is, when people know both the race and sex of another, they tend to use a single subordinate category, such as *Black woman*, that represents both basic categories simultaneously. This subordinate category is labeled a **subtype**. Subtypes can be formed by a combination of two or more basic category memberships or by combining basic category memberships with role or trait information. People rely on those more specific categories when they need a detailed understanding of another person's underlying characteristics.

All basic categories can have subtypes, but the majority of research on this topic has examined gender and age subtypes. Gender researchers, for example, have identified a set of commonly used subtypes of women and men, such as career woman and businessman, sexy woman and macho man (Deaux, Winton, Crowley, & Lewis, 1985; Vonk & Ashmore, 2003). Similarly, Mary Lee Hummert (1990) has identified both positive and negative subtypes of older adults, such as Golden Ager and Severely Impaired. These subtypes do not negate the broader concepts represented by basic social categories; they do, however, provide additional information, often about the social roles the group member occupies. Knowing that a woman has a career or that an older person is relatively impaired provides clues about the behaviors they are likely to exhibit. When the occasion calls for it, perceivers use this information to make more fine-grained judgments. When older people are described at the subtype level, for example, people's evaluations are more likely to be based on this additional information than on age alone. People are more likely to believe that hearing and memory loss has occurred for members of the Severely Impaired (negative) subtype than for members of the Golden Ager (positive) subtype (Hummert, Garstka, & Shaner, 1995). If perceivers were relying on information about age alone, members of both subtypes would be judged similarly; given the stereotypic belief that older people have poor memory and hearing, if this happened, probably both subtypes would have been judged as deficient.

Ingroups and Outgroups

The Montagues versus the Capulets. The Yankees versus the Red Sox. The British versus the French. Labor versus management. Some rivalries are centuries old, others are more recent. Bets are won and lost based on such rivalries, and often, the emotional loss is more difficult to swallow than the financial loss. One thing is clear: People thrive on dividing themselves into groups. It is a rare college that does not have rivals, in sports or otherwise. And it is indeed a rare "us" that does not have a "them." Social psychologists label "us" the *ingroup* and "them" the *outgroup*. When it comes to stereotyping and prejudice, there is no more basic cognitive distinction than the one made between ingroups and outgroups.

Just how easily ingroups and outgroups can be created may surprise you. Imagine, for a moment, you are a participant in a research study. You are alone in a dark room and are estimating the number of dots on a screen. After you have completed the task, the experimenter explains that some people consistently underestimate the number of dots, whereas others consistently overestimate those numbers. You then find out that you are an underestimator. Now, the experimenter asks you to make judgments about others, both those who are like you (the underestimators) or those who are different from you (the overestimators). You never see or meet members of either group. Do you really feel like part of a unique group? And, if so, will you treat members of your group differently from members of the outgroup?

Many people are surprised to find that the answer to both questions is a resounding yes. The original experiments demonstrating this phenomenon were conducted by Henri Tajfel (1970). Tajfel set out to establish the minimum conditions necessary for a person to distinguish between an ingroup and an outgroup. As Tajfel (1978) described his quest, "we attempted to eliminate from the experimental situations all the variables that normally lead to ingroup favouritism and discrimination against the outgroup. The variables were: face-to-face interaction; conflicts of interest; any possibility of previous hostility between the groups; any 'utilitarian' or instrumental link between the subjects' responses and their self-interest" (p. 77). So, as we have described, participants were alone, and the groups were created based on an unimportant variable, rather than an existing social group about which people had beliefs and feelings. In fact, placement into the "overestimator" or "underestimator" group was done at random, rather than on the participants' actual responses, to ensure that the obtained differences in how the groups were perceived could not possibly have been due to real group differences. This procedure is known as the **minimal group paradigm** because it shows that ingroups and outgroups can be created from the most minimal conditions.

One way Tajfel (1978) explored the differential treatment of ingroup and outgroup members was by asking participants to award payment to two other people. All that the assigners knew about the other individuals was that they had either over- or underestimated the number of dots. The results were strikingly clear: Participants awarded more money to ingroup members than to outgroup members. This happened even though the participants were not allowed to award themselves money, and, as such, never benefited personally from their group favoritism (the self-interest part of Tajfel's design). Based on no information other than knowledge of group membership, participants used the categories "my group" and "other" and, in the process, decided their group was more deserving. This finding, known generally as *ingroup favoritism,* has been replicated many times, in many countries, and is the foundation of a great deal of theorizing and research (Brewer, 2003). We discuss the role group membership plays in prejudice and discrimination in more detail in Chapter 8.

ORIGINS OF STEREOTYPES

Imagine again, for a moment, that you are participating in a research study on the minimal group paradigm. What if the researcher asked you to describe the content of your stereotype about the outgroup (i.e., the overestimators)? Would you have anything to list? Tajfel (1978) did not ask his research participants this question; if he had, chances are they would have had only very sketchy ideas about the outgroup members' characteristics. The minimal group paradigm demonstrates how quickly people can create two groups, us and them, but does not address how people learn the characteristics they associate with ingroups and outgroups. Where do these stereotypes come from? As we saw in Chapter 1, people learn stereotypes from parents, peers, the media, and from their own observations of the world. Psychologists also have looked deeper, exploring the processes by which these stereotypic beliefs become part of people's schemas about social groups. We discuss next three explanations about the process of acquiring these beliefs: the outgroup homogeneity effect, social role theory, and illusory correlations.

The Outgroup Homogeneity Effect

As we noted, the minimal group paradigm can be used to easily create an ingroup and an outgroup, but people probably do not have well-developed stereotypic beliefs about such groups. That does not mean, of course, that they have not developed stereotypes of naturally occurring outgroups. Research shows that not only do people have such stereotypes, they actually see ingroups and outgroups quite differently. People tend to see members of their own group as very different from one another and, at the same time, tend to underestimate the differences between members of other groups (Linville, Fischer, & Salovey, 1989; Park & Judd, 1990). This differential perception is known as the **outgroup homogeneity effect.** To a perceiver, then, members of the outgroup really can "all look alike." Studies of cross-racial identification, for example, show that people have more difficulty recognizing members of a race other than their own (Brigham & Malpass, 1985; Teitelbaum & Geiselman, 1997). But this effect goes beyond physical appearance. People believe outgroup members have similar traits and occupy similar social roles. One consequence of this differential perception is that evaluations of outgroup members tend to be more polarized and extreme than evaluations of ingroup members (Linville & Jones, 1980). We next consider explanations for this cognitive bias.

Reasons for the outgroup homogeneity effect There are a number of reasons why outgroup members all appear similar, but ingroup members do not (Wilder, 1986). These explanations are not mutually exclusive; that is, more than one of them may play a role in perceptions of a particular outgroup. These reasons include:

1. *People simply interact more with members of their own group and, therefore, have more information about them and their unique qualities.* People can readily identify differences between and among members of their own social group. Blacks, for example, are likely to recognize that some Blacks are good at accounting, others at sports, and still others at writing poetry. People's willingness or ability to see these differences comes, in part, from the fact that they have more information about people from their own social group. Whites, for example, are much more likely to spend time with other Whites than they are to spend time with Blacks, and during that time, come to recognize their own group members' individuality. Would spending more time with outgroup members lessen the tendency to see them as all the same? Possibly. For example, the outgroup homogeneity effect emerges less consistently for gender (Brown & Smith, 1989) and age (Harwood, Giles, & Ryan, 1995). Perhaps this is because people know a lot about the other sex, even if they are not a member of that group; many of people's closest relationships, for example, are with a member of the other sex. Similarly, most people have older grandparents, aunts, uncles, or neighbors with whom they regularly interact. As we will see in Chapter 12, however, contact in and of itself does not always reduce stereotyping and prejudice.

2. *The nature of interactions with ingroup members is more familiar, and less affected by social norms.* Because people see ingroup members so frequently, they have more opportunities to notice others' individuality. This is particularly true because this extra time people spend with their own group members gives them a chance to see ingroup members in multiple roles and situations. Students who live in a sorority or a fraternity, for example, see their Greek brothers and sisters studying, socializing, eating, and relaxing.

However, they might see members of other student organizations only in formal settings, when their behavior seems more uniform because of the social norms operating in that situation. As we will see, ingroup biases are related to people's tendency to underestimate the extent to which situational factors affect another's behavior.

3. *People are motivated to see themselves as unique and, therefore, look for ways to distinguish themselves from their group to maintain their individuality.* No one wants to be seen as a complete conformist, with no individual thoughts or actions. Indeed, people are motivated to see themselves as unique individuals and pay attention to the ways in which they are different from the other members of their own group (Brewer, 1991; Brewer & Pickett, 1999). This level of scrutiny is not necessary for outgroups—people already believe outgroups differ from them on important dimensions.

4. *Ingroup versus outgroup comparisons are typically made at the group level.* When people make ingroup and outgroup comparisons, they focus on how the *groups* differ (for example, the Sharks versus the Jets), thereby minimizing within group differences. In contrast, when people look within their own group (how I am doing compared to my classmates?), the focus changes to differences between individuals (Tajfel & Turner, 1986). Republicans, for example, usually are not called on to consider whether individual Democrats might differ in their opinion about a political issue. More typically, political controversies are framed by party lines. For example, a Republican senator hoping to find out whether her party can maintain a filibuster (which can be used to delay a vote on an issue, but requires 60 votes to stop) will consider how individuals within the party might vote, carefully monitoring the differences among ingroup members. In contrast, she may assume that all Democrats will vote in the same way.

The ultimate attribution error   All of the reasons just discussed explain the same result: Members of other social groups are treated stereotypically. As a consequence of seeing people as members of groups rather than as individuals, perceivers often make biased judgments about an outgroup members' actions. One bias, known as the **ultimate attribution error,** occurs when people assume that their own group's negative behavior can be explained by situational factors, but similar negative actions by members of other groups are due to their internal stable characteristics (Pettigrew, 1979). This effect was demonstrated by Birt Duncan (1976), who asked White research participants to watch a video of one man shoving another. When the video depicted a White man shoving another, participants concluded the actor was "horsing around." The picture changed dramatically, however, when the action involved a Black man shoving another. In this case, the cause of the shove was more likely to be deemed "violent behavior" (see Figure 3.1). As the results of this study demonstrate, negative behaviors displayed by an outgroup member are attributed to personal causes—in this case, violent tendencies—whereas negative behaviors by an ingroup member are attributed to situational factors (for example, horsing around). Such assumptions lead to stereotypic beliefs about the outgroups (for example, all Blacks are aggressive).

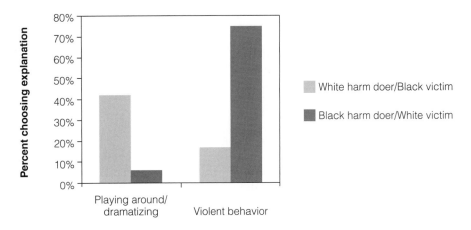

FIGURE 3.1

CLASSIFICATIONS OF HARM DOERS AND VICTIMS FOR CROSS-RACE PAIRINGS

Participants who saw a Black person shoving a White person saw the act as violent, rather than horsing around. When the actor was a White person (shoving another White person), the action was seen as playing around, rather than violent.

Adapted from Duncan, B. L. (1976). Differential social perception and the attribution of intergroup violence. *Journal of Personality and Social Psychology, 34,* 590–598.

If this pattern emerged for positive behaviors or desirable outcomes, the outgroup would actually benefit from the attribution; Whites, for example, would view the academic success of Blacks as due to their inherent intellectual abilities. Interestingly, the ultimate attribution error does not take this form (Pettigrew, 1979). Instead, positive behaviors by an outgroup are likely to be dismissed as due to special advantages (for example, their having benefited from affirmative action), luck, or unusual characteristics of the situation. These same behaviors by an ingroup, in contrast, are attributed to stable personality traits; Whites see their own success as due to their ability, for example. The result, then, is that the favored ingroup benefits from biased thinking whereas the outgroup is negatively labeled. In short, when it comes to pleasing members of another social group, outgroup members cannot win for losing. Evidence suggests the ultimate attribution error can occur in everyday life, such as in sporting events (see Box 3.2). The effect of this bias may be particularly strong, however, when the groups involved have histories of intense conflict (for example, Hindus versus Muslims or Chinese versus Malayans), when the evaluators are highly prejudiced individuals, or when emotions run high (see Hewstone, 1990, for a review).

The behavior of a single minority group member also may significantly influence how members of the entire social group are viewed. Whites who witnessed a Black person responding in a rude manner to a White person were later more likely to avoid sitting next to another Black person, compared with Whites who had witnessed the Black person behaving in a positive way

3.2   *Stereotyping and Prejudice in Sports?*

Americans are fascinated with sports. Discussions of local high school athletics, college, and professional sports are the subject of entire television channels, newspaper coverage, and conversations at the water cooler. But does this relate to stereotyping and prejudice? Evidence suggests that many of the ideas presented in this chapter can be found on the playing field— or at least in people's response to what happens on the playing field. People, for example, show ingroup favoritism by wearing school colors the day following a win (Cialdini et al., 1976) and by being more likely to use "we" language after a successful athletic event (Cialdini & De Nicholas, 1989).

Sports fans also differ in their explanations for the outcomes of sporting events. Joachim Winkler and Shelley Taylor (1979) asked fans to offer explanations for their favorite team's actions in the 1976 Super Bowl. Consistent with research on the ultimate attribution error, results showed that the fans offered more credit to their side for their favorable plays than they did to the other side for similarly positive plays. Participants also predicted what would happen if the play were to be hypothetically repeated. When their team had made a good play, they believed it was more likely to be repeated, compared to when the opposing team had made a good play. Perceptions of the same sporting event are clearly in the eye of the beholder, with the same play being viewed through different lenses depending on where one's loyalties lie.

One only needed to have witnessed the fight that emerged during the 2004 Indiana Pacers/Detroit Pistons basketball game to be assured that emotions run high at sporting events; in anger over Pacer Ron Artest's foul against Piston player Ben Wallace, Detroit fans threw beer, ice, and popcorn at the Pacers. This led to fans and players exchanging punches in the stands and, ultimately, to one of the worst brawls in NBA history (*Motown Melee*, 2004). Nyla Branscombe and Daniel Wann (1991) investigated such emotion in response to an alleged world heavyweight championship match between an American and a Russian. Those individuals who had previously strongly identified with America had more extreme physiological arousal in response to the match than did individuals who did not show strong pride in America. According to the authors, this arousal stems from the threat highly identified participants experienced when faced with the possible loss of a representative of their country. Moreover, this threat led highly identified viewers to derogate the Russian boxer, and Russians in general, more than those low in identification. Strongly identifying with an ingroup produced measurable aggression.

Are sports harmful, then? Probably not. Although one can find evidence of stereotyping and prejudice in sports, the outcomes are mostly all in good fun. One important difference between sports-related prejudice and prejudice against other groups is that people choose the teams they support and can change this support at any time. Obviously, one's race and gender is less mutable. Even so, results such as these demonstrate the generalizability of the processes we describe in this chapter and they do indicate some troubling sports-related aggression. Studying groups such as sports teams is beneficial, too, because it offers the chance to explore research questions without some of the social desirability concerns raised in Chapter 2.

(Henderson-King & Nisbett, 1996, Study One). Such an instance of negative behavior also can affect Whites' overall feelings about Blacks. Research participants who overheard a staged phone conversation about an assault by a Black assailant later rated Blacks as generally more antagonistic than did participants who heard the same conversation about a White assailant. Moreover, those who believed the assailant was Black were more likely to express the belief that Whites have too little power, relative to Blacks, in society (Henderson-King & Nisbett, 1996, Study Three). That is, observing a single instance of a negative behavior involving a member of an outgroup led people to evaluate all members of that group negatively. It also led to protective beliefs about the ingroup—in this case, that Whites were less powerful than they should be.

Social Role Theory

Most humans are people watchers. Observing others is a source of endless fascination, as evidenced by the national obsession with reality TV. It certainly seems logical, then, that beliefs about social groups would stem from watching the world around us. **Social role theory,** developed by Alice Eagly (1987), proposes just that. According to this theory, when people observe others, they pay attention to the *social roles* others occupy, such as their occupations. In doing so, they come to associate the characteristics of the role with the individuals who occupy it. To understand how this works, consider first a basic principle of social psychology, called the *correspondence bias* (Ross, 1977). This bias stems from the tendency to misjudge the demands of the situation: All things being equal, people give relatively little weight to how transient situational factors constrain behavior; instead, they believe another's actions reflect the person's stable personality. People who observe a woman nurse comforting a patient, for example, are more likely to conclude that she is a caring person than they are to conclude that situational factors (such as her job as a caregiver) led to the nurturing act.

Social role theory proposes that this bias leads to the development of stereotypic beliefs. Consider, for example, the widely held stereotypes that women are naturally kind and concerned about others and that men are naturally self-confident and assertive. According to social role theory, these beliefs developed from observations about women and men in the social roles they occupy. Women are traditionally in the homemaker role or in a lower status employee role and men are traditionally in the breadwinner or a higher status employee role. As such, women are disproportionately represented in roles requiring the very traits people associate with women, such as kindness and concern for others, and men are disproportionately represented in roles requiring the very traits people associate with men, such as self-confidence and assertiveness. Because the *situational* factors (in this case, social roles) are not given sufficient weight, gender stereotypic beliefs develop. Perceivers conclude that *all* women are kind and warm and *all* men are assertive and self-confident.

Eagly's research has focused mainly on the development of gender stereotypes, although the theory also has been used to examine age stereotypes, beliefs about nationalities, and perceptions of leadership ability (see Eagly, Wood, & Diekman,

2000, for a review). Yet studying how social roles might help create these widely held stereotypes presents a problem because even young children have stereotypes firmly in place. Curt Hoffman and Nancy Hurst (1990) creatively skirted this problem by asking people to evaluate members of two fictional alien groups, the "Orinthians" and the "Ackminians." These aliens were described as either predominantly city workers or as predominantly child raisers. Because their planet had no female or male sex, the association between human gender stereotypes and these categories was eliminated. Moreover, on their imaginary planet there were no differences between the traits describing city workers and child raisers. Results showed that the correspondence bias influenced responses: City workers were described by characteristics usually associated with that role (such as active and logical) and child raisers were described by characteristics usually associated with that role (such as helpful and patient). That is, people's judgments were based on the role the aliens occupied rather than on their actual traits.

Illusory Correlations

One way to think about stereotypic beliefs is to recognize that they represent a perceived relationship between a group and a characteristic (for example, women are warm, Asians are good at math, college professors are absent-minded). For these perceived relationships to be accurate, however, information about the group and the characteristics must first be encoded, or perceived, correctly (Hamilton, 1981). Unfortunately, accurate encoding can be easily derailed. One way this happens stems from people's tendency to overestimate the relationship between two categories when the information is distinctive, or stands out within the context of the judgment (Chapman, 1967). In doing so, people develop **illusory correlations**—beliefs that incorrectly link two characteristics, such as race and a personality trait. Such beliefs are as firmly held as accurate associations, but nevertheless are based on inaccurate information processing.

In a series of clever experiments, David Hamilton and Robert Gifford (1976) demonstrated how these inaccurate associations can lead to stereotypic beliefs about minority groups. These researchers began with the assumption that majority groups members have infrequent interactions with minority group members. When such interactions do occur, then, they are distinctive. The researchers further reasoned that undesirable behaviors also are relatively unique. What happens, then, when a majority group member observes a minority group member engaging in an undesirable behavior? The co-occurrence between these two distinctive events is given undue weight, leading to the conclusion that minority group members are likely to behave in undesirable ways.

To test their hypothesis, Hamilton and Gifford (1976) asked research participants to read a series of 39 sentences, each of which was associated with either Group A or Group B. The researchers used abstract groups to ensure that prior stereotypic beliefs would not influence their results. Group A represented the majority group; 26 of the 39 sentences were associated with that group. Group B represented the minority group; the remaining 13 sentences were associated with that group. Most of the sentences (27) described positive behaviors; the remaining

TABLE 3.1	DISTRIBUTION OF DESIRABLE AND UNDESIRABLE SENTENCES USED TO CREATE AN ILLUSORY CORRELATION		
	Group A (Majority)	Group B (Minority)	
Behaviors			**Total**
Desirable	18 (69%)	9 (69%)	27
Undesirable	8 (30%)	4 (30%)	12
Total	26	13	39

12 described negative behaviors. As you can see from Table 3.1, each group performed the same proportion of desirable and undesirable behaviors. So, if people's perceptions were accurate, they should have perceived no relationship between group membership and behavior. Results of the study showed that when the behaviors were desirable, and therefore not distinctive, people were in fact reasonably accurate in their associations. However, when the behaviors were undesirable (and therefore distinctive), people overestimated the extent to which the minority group exhibited those behaviors. Research suggests the illusory correlation operates in everyday settings as well. Rupert Brown and Amanda Smith (1989) found that the academic staff of a British university overestimated the number of female, and underestimated the number of male, senior staff on their campus. In other words, respondents inaccurately perceived the relationship between gender and seniority. This bias occurred because female senior staff were few and, therefore, were distinctive. Interestingly, in this case the observance of negative behaviors was not necessary for the creation of the illusory correlation.

What are the implications of this information processing bias? One obvious implication is that many beliefs about minority groups are derived from inaccurate associations (see Box 3.3). These errors are magnified when one group is proportionately smaller than the other (Mullen & Johnson, 1995); the actions of a minority group appear to be under greater scrutiny than similar actions in a majority group. Once these erroneous associations are made, they may be very difficult to change and may set the stage for how additional information is processed (Hamilton & Rose, 1980). Once an expectation is in place, cognitive processing generally works to maintain biases, rather than correct them. Later in this chapter, we will consider in more detail how stereotypes are maintained.

TRANSMISSION OF STEREOTYPIC BELIEFS

As we discussed in Chapter 1, stereotypes exist at the individual level—the pictures in our heads—but there is also an important shared component to stereotype content (Jones, 1997). Recall that much of the research defining the *content* of people's stereotypes focuses on identifying these shared characteristics. But

3.3   *Are Illusory Correlations Perpetuated by the Media?*

"If it bleeds, it leads" the saying goes. Newspapers and television news broadcasts compete for viewers' attention, often by presenting stories about local and national criminals. And why not? After all, crime stories are distinctive and draw in viewers (Klein & Naccarato, 2003). But what if these presentations misrepresent which racial groups are likely to be victims and perpetrators of crime? Travis Dixon and Daniel Linz (2000) examined this question with a content analysis of television news in Los Angeles and Orange counties in California. These researchers found that Whites were more likely to be shown as crime victims than were Blacks. Lawbreakers seen on television news, in contrast, were more likely to be Black than White. When compared with actual crime reports, the portrayals of victims overrepresented Whites; conversely, Blacks were overrepresented as perpetrators. Interestingly, Latinos were largely absent from television news reports, which means they were underrepresented as both crime victims and perpetrators. Studies of the news markets in Chicago and Philadelphia have shown similar results (Klein & Naccarato, 2003). More generally, Roger Klein and Stacy Naccarato (2003) found that 80 percent

of references to Blacks in Pittsburgh's television newscasts were negative, whereas for Whites, fewer than two-thirds were negative.

From an illusory correlation perspective, these findings suggest that the news media is promoting an inaccurate association between Blacks and lawbreaking. Because Blacks are distinctive relative to Whites and because crime is a negative behavior, people may incorrectly assume that more Blacks are criminals than Whites. (Recall from Chapter 1 that the "Driving While Black" statistics support this assumption.) People see the world presented on television as similar to the real world; studies show that the vast majority of people of all ages, from adolescents to older adults, agree that "Local TV news shows me the way the world really is" (cited in Klein & Naccarato, 2003). It is also interesting that the largest ethnic group in Los Angeles and Orange counties, Latinos, also are being inaccurately represented in that market, but in this case, it is an error of omission. How do you think this fits with the illusory correlation model? What conclusions do you think people draw about Latinos as crime victims or perpetrators?

how is this information shared? We next discuss how stereotypes are transmitted in society, beginning with important sources of stereotypic beliefs: parents, peers, and the media.

Sources of Stereotypic Beliefs

Did you grow up in a diverse neighborhood or were most of the children you interacted with of the same race as you? Did you watch Sesame Street, with its ethnically diverse cast, or reruns of Captain Kangaroo, where the main characters were White or male or both? Did your parents provide books about a variety of people and cultures or books mainly about people similar to you? Because children are keen observers of their environment, these subtle and not-so-subtle factors undoubtedly influenced the formation of your stereotypic beliefs.

Parents and peers   It is probably safe to assume that many children learn stereotypic beliefs from their primary caregivers. When children are young, those individuals have a great deal to say about who their children interact with and what they see on television or at the movies. This, in turn, influences what is learned about social groups. Interestingly, parents often teach gender stereotypes both directly and indirectly but appear to impart racial stereotypes primarily through indirect means (P. A. Katz, 2003). That is, parents might tell young children that "trucks are for boys," a direct statement about stereotypes, or they might take away a truck from their daughter, an indirect message about appropriate behavior for her gender. Parents of a White child may not allow her to choose a Black doll at the toy store, indirectly suggesting this doll is inferior because of its color, but they are unlikely to state directly that they believe Blacks are inferior.

As you grew, your peers provided additional information about social groups. In fact, as you got older, parental influence may have lessened and been replaced by peer influence (P. A. Katz, 1987). Peers generally have a significant influence on attitudes and behaviors (see Fishbein, 2002, for a review). Evidence suggests that interacting with peers who are low in prejudice can make highly prejudiced adolescents more accepting of others, for example (Aboud & Fenwick, 1999). And the media probably had an important influence on your stereotype development. One way these influences affect stereotype development is captured by **social learning theory** (Bandura, 1986). According to this perspective, people learn about social behavior either directly (for example, by being rewarded or punished for their actions), or vicariously (for example, by observing the consequences of others' behavior). They retain those beliefs and behaviors for which they are rewarded (or for which they see others being rewarded) and discontinue those beliefs that result in theirs or others' punishment. Children, then, who were encouraged to read books about positive characters from diverse backgrounds would be more likely to develop positive racial stereotypes than children who were discouraged from reading those books.

Stereotype acquisition also is influenced by children's cognitive development. At 2 months, for example, infants can recognize the shift from a male to a female speaker. By the age of 3, children can categorize on the basis of gender; for example, they know which toys are designed for their sex (see Martin, 2000, for a review). This developmental timeline is similar for race-based categorization (P. A. Katz, 2003). As children age, however, their ability to use category-based information becomes more sophisticated. Early on, beliefs about gender are based mainly on biological sex; by about age 9, in contrast, children also consider role information. At a young age, for example, children assume that boys who play with dolls still like trucks; at a later age, children expect that those boys who play with dolls also prefer other feminine activities (Berndt & Heller, 1986). Older children also are able to acknowledge exceptions to the rules (for example, that some males are good cooks). As people develop, then, they are able to make more fine-grained distinctions among group members. We consider the development of children's prejudice, both from a social learning perspective and from a cognitive development perspective, in more detail in Chapter 7.

The media   The media, including film, television, and advertising, are saturated with stereotypes. A recent examination of more than 900 Hollywood films, for example, revealed that Arabs are consistently portrayed as heartless, brutal, uncivilized, and religious fanatics (Shaheen, 2002). These films also conveyed the incorrect message that all Arabs are Muslims and all Muslims are Arabs. Hollywood films also are replete with examples of gender and racial stereotypes (Eschholz, Bufkin, & Long, 2002). Hollywood is not the only source of stereotypic presentations in the media. Major news magazines most often use pictures of Blacks to represent the poor, leading people to the incorrect conclusion that most poor people are Black (Gilens, 1996). Television, too, relies heavily on stereotypic characterizations (Signorielli, 1993). Even when the media depict someone in a nontraditional role (for example, women police officers), the message can still be stereotypic. Media descriptions of female athletes, for example, tend to focus on their attractiveness, whereas descriptions of male athletes usually focus on their ability (Messner, 1988).

Advertisements often portray people in stereotypic roles as well. In television commercials, Whites are shown more frequently than any other ethnic group and they also are portrayed more prominently and are more often seen exercising authority. Whites are also more likely to be portrayed in the parent role or spousal role, whereas Asian Americans are more likely to be shown as children. African American men are more likely to be seen in aggressive roles than Whites. African American women are less likely to be portrayed as sex objects than are White women. Latinos, in contrast, are virtually invisible from commercials, raising the question of whether it is better to be portrayed in a negative light than not portrayed at all (Coltrane & Messineo, 2000). Sex-role stereotyping in advertising also is pervasive. Adrian Furnham and Twiggy Mak (1999) reviewed 14 studies of television commercials that aired in 11 countries over a 25-year period. Their analysis revealed that men were more likely than women to be depicted as authorities; men most often did the voiceovers of commercials (that is, they were the narrators who are heard but not seen), which is portrayed as the literal voice of authority. Men also were more likely to be seen in professional roles whereas women were more likely to be seen in the home, engaged in behaviors that conveyed their dependence. Other research has shown that older women simply appear less frequently in advertisements than do younger women and, when they are featured, it is likely to be in ads for pharmaceuticals, suggesting they are in poor health (Bailey, Harrell, & Anderson, 1993).

It is easy to believe that these stereotypic portrayals do not affect us. Research evidence suggests the contrary, however. Children, for example, learn from the messages conveyed by television: The more television children watch, the more they hold gender and racial stereotypes (Reid, 1979). Children, for example, are well aware that most cartoon characters are boys and they recognize that the actions of these boys are gender stereotypic: For both boys and girls, this recognition correlates with the expectation that they will hold a gender stereotypic job in the

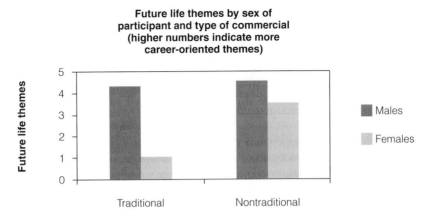

FIGURE **3.2**

FUTURE LIFE THEMES BY SEX OF PARTICIPANT AND TYPE OF COMMERCIAL

Regardless of whether they viewed traditional or nontraditional commercials, men's descriptions of their future life were similar and career oriented. Women's descriptions of their future life were less career oriented when they saw traditional commercials and more career oriented when they saw nontraditional commercials. Higher numbers indicate more career-oriented life themes.

Adapted from Geis, F. L., Brown, V., Jennings (Walstedt), J., & Porter, N. (1984). TV commercials as achievement scripts for women. *Sex Roles, 7/8*, 513–525.

future (Thompson & Zerbinos, 1997). Adults' perceptions also are related to how much media they are exposed to. The more news media people watched during the U.S.-Iraq war, for example, the more likely they were to exhibit implicit prejudice toward Muslims (Martin, Grande, & Crabb, 2004). Watching more television also is related to holding negative stereotypes of older adults. These negative stereotypes may develop because older people who appear on television are portrayed mainly in negative roles: Often older adults are depicted as crime victims, as being betrayed by family members, or in situations in which they are ridiculed (Gerbner, 1997). However, it should be noted that these results are correlational and need to be interpreted with caution (see Chapter 2). In an experimental demonstration of the effects of media depictions on stereotypic beliefs, Lindy Geis and her colleagues (1984) had undergraduates view commercials depicting women and men in traditional or nontraditional roles. The participants then wrote an essay imagining their lives and concerns 10 years in the future. These essays were examined for career achievement versus homemaking themes. Women's essays were highly influenced by the commercials: Those who saw traditional commercials were much more likely to describe their future in terms of the homemaker role than the career role (see Figure 3.2). In contrast, men's essays were not influenced by the type of commercial. The researchers believe these results are due to the ambivalent achievement messages that are part of women's, but not men's, socialization. Taken together, the research results described in this section suggest that stereotypes from the mass media influence both adults and children.

Interpersonal Communication and Social Inference

Another way stereotypes are shared is through language itself, both from person to person and from generation to generation. As Anne Maass and Luciano Arcuri (1996) explain, stereotypes are transmitted through vocabulary. For example, there are about 10 times more expressions describing women's promiscuity than men's, which feeds into acceptance of the sexual double standard (that is, men having many sexual partners is more socially acceptable than women doing so). Speakers also tend to qualify descriptions of people when they occupy nontraditional roles. Think about how often you hear phrases such as "Lady Boilermakers" to describe women's basketball teams. Yet you rarely hear the men's team referred to as the "Gentleman Huskies." Similarly, we talk about "Black" lawyers and "woman" doctors, but do not use qualifiers for the White men who have traditionally occupied these roles. Using qualifiers for the nontraditional groups "marks" them or makes their category membership stand out. Doing so increases the chances that they will be categorized on that basis (see Fiske, 1998, for a review).

Although speakers rarely consider it, many common expressions also convey stereotypes about ethnic groups or nationalities (for example, Jew down a price or Indian giver; Bolinger, 1990). North Americans, for example, often use so-called mock Spanish, especially in creating derogatory terms such as "el stupido" to refer to dumb people, inadvertently creating the perception that Spanish-speaking people are not intelligent. And, when the Terminator says "Hasta la vista baby" right before killing someone, a link between Spanish speakers and violence is suggested. Interestingly, many mock Spanish terms are not actually in the Spanish lexicon. Yet a negative message about Latin Americans (especially Mexicans) is conveyed through their use at the one-on-one level and through mass communication (Hill, 1995). Differential use of foreign accents in movies also can convey negative stereotypes, as we explain in Box 3.4.

Are some stereotypes more likely to be shared through language than others? Recent research suggests that the answer is yes; some stereotypes are more likely to be the subject of conversation than others and, accordingly, are more readily communicated than stereotypes that are less likely to be discussed. In looking at this possibility, Mark Schaller and his colleagues (Schaller, Conway, & Tanchuk, 2002) examined whether the traits that are most often part of everyday conversation are also the ones most likely to persist over time. They began with a list of stereotypes commonly associated with ethnic groups, derived from the classic Daniel Katz and Kenneth Braly (1933) checklist we discussed in Chapter 1 and from more recent research. Results of one study showed that people were more likely to talk about some traits than others—that is, that some traits were more *communicable*. Moreover, people reported that they found discussions of those highly communicable traits more interesting than discussions of less communicable traits. A second study showed that highly communicable traits were more likely to become part of the stereotype of an ethnic group, at least if that group was often the subject of conversation. Results of a third study looked at the persistence of the African American stereotype, based on the five studies that have examined this stereotype over time (see Devine & Elliot, 1995). Results showed

3.4   *Language-Based Stereotypes in Disney Films*

The Walt Disney company is famous for its heartwarming stories and lovable characters. Audiences cheered when Beauty tamed her Beast, Snow White awoke to the handsome prince, and Simba became the Lion King. Of course, gender stereotypes are pervasive in these films. But are there other, less apparent, stereotypes lurking under the surface? Yes, according to Rosina Lippi-Green (1997). Lippi-Green examined 371 characters in 24 Disney films, ranging from Snow White to the Lion King. Confirming the gender stereotypic portrayals, Lippi-Green found that the vast majority of the female characters are never shown outside the home or have traditionally female jobs, such as nurses or waitresses. The male characters, in contrast, are depicted in traditionally male jobs such as doctors, advisors to kings, detectives, and pilots. What is perhaps more interesting, however, is the results of her analysis of the characters' accents. Lippi-Green categorized characters by whether they spoke U.S. English, British English, or foreign-accented English (for example, Stromboli in *Pinnochio*, speaks in a contrived Italian dialect). She further divided characters by their motivations and actions (good, bad, or mixed). Those who spoke U.S. English were mostly likely to have positive (73.5%) rather than mixed (26.5%) motivations and actions. Similarly, those who spoke British English were most likely to have only positive (57.6%) rather than negative or mixed (42.4%) motivations and actions. In contrast, those who spoke foreign-accented English were most likely to have negative or mixed (62.7%) rather than only positive (37%) motivations and actions. One reason we might not notice this pattern is that the characters in Disney films are often animals. Even so, the message to viewers is clear: people who speak standard English are the good guys and people who speak with a foreign accent are the bad guys.

that highly communicable traits were more likely to be retained in the African American stereotype. These results are correlational and, therefore, are subject to the limitations of correlational research discussed in Chapter 2; that is, researchers cannot firmly conclude that the communicability of traits *causes* the obtained effects. Even so, these results suggest that everyday conversations influence how people think about social groups. The power of language in maintaining stereotypes is discussed in more detail later in this chapter.

STEREOTYPE ACCURACY

In movies, you can tell the heroine because she is blonder and thinner than her sidekick. The villainess

is darkest. If a woman is fat,
she is a joke and will probably die.

—Excerpt from "One reason I like opera" by Marge Piercy, 2003*

You do not have to see many movies to recognize the accuracy of this reflection. Not that there are no exceptions. Queen Latifah, a larger Black woman, is the clear heroine in "Bringing Down the House" (Filardi, 2003), for example. But it is certainly much easier to think of instances that fit Piercy's description. On the whole, then, Marge Piercy's analysis seems more accurate than not, at least in describing movie land. Can we conclude, then, that the stereotypes portrayed in this poem reflect reality, at least to some extent?

In everyday life, perceivers are often faced with the question of whether their stereotypes are accurate. A woman walking alone at night must decide whether the man walking nearby is a threat to her safety or is simply another night owl out for a stroll. An employer who is interviewing job candidates wants to know whether his belief that liberal arts majors have good critical thinking skills is accurate. An African American student wonders whether her Caucasian American professor will evaluate her based on her actual performance or her skin color. From a social science perspective, however, the question of whether stereotypic beliefs are accurate is a tricky one. As Gordon Allport (1954) put it: "The distinction between a well-founded generalization and an erroneous generalization is very hard to draw, particularly by the individual who himself harbors the generalization" (p. 20). How, then, to resolve the question of whether members of a social group actually possess the characteristics that are associated with them?

Defining Accuracy

Recall from Chapter 1 that, historically, some researchers have viewed stereotypes as bad and as stemming from biased and faulty information processing. More recent theorists, especially those taking the perspectives discussed in this chapter, have moved toward seeing stereotyping as a natural outgrowth of human information processing that, at least to some extent, reflects a *kernel of truth*— beliefs are not totally unfounded, but have a basis in social reality. How then, does a researcher assess the size of this kernel? This most basic question—"what constitutes accuracy?"—is a slippery one indeed. Surely we can agree that if a belief describes only a few members of a group, it is off the mark. Similarly, we do not expect a trait to describe *all* group members before it is deemed "true." The middle ground, however, is harder to find. Would a stereotype that describes 30 percent of social group members be accurate? How about 50 percent or 75 percent?

To better understand how psychologists have looked at this issue, let us first consider how accuracy is usually measured: by percentage estimates or by measures of dispersion. Percentage estimates are based on whether social group members typically do possess the stereotypic characteristic associated with them. In an early

---

*From *Colors Passing Through Us:* Poems by Mare Piercy. Copyright © 2003 by Middlemarsh, Inc. Used by permission of Alfred A Knopf, a division of Random House, Inc.

use of this measure (McCauley & Stitt, 1978), research participants from various backgrounds estimated the percentage of Black Americans, and Americans in general, who exhibited behaviors stereotypically attributed to Blacks (for example, were illegitimate or on welfare). For each participant, a *diagnostic ratio* was computed by dividing the estimated percentage of Blacks who displayed the behavior by the percentage of all Americans who displayed the behavior. These ratios were compared to similar calculations, based on actual U.S. Census figures for these two groups. Overall, participants' ratings mirrored the census data reasonably well. People were more accurate than not at estimating how many Blacks were on welfare, for example. However, as we will discuss below, this conclusion does not provide unquestionable proof that such beliefs are accurate.

Psychologists also estimate stereotype accuracy by considering the perceived dispersion, or diversity of group members (Ryan, Park, & Judd, 1996). If perceivers believe that most Asians are good at math, for example, they would estimate there was low variability on this trait. But if they believe this ability differs across the Asian population, there would be high variability on this trait. A stereotype might be considered more accurate if it reflects the actual diversity of a characteristic within a group.

Regardless of whether percentage estimates or measures of dispersion are employed, the question is whether people over- or underestimate the group's actual characteristics. To make this judgment, researchers must assume there is an objective way to assess the characteristic of interest, which as we discuss below, is often difficult. Further complicating the picture, these two measures of stereotype accuracy can operate independently. Research participants might be fairly accurate, for example, in their estimates of what percentage of Asians are mathematical, but they might be inaccurate in their estimate of the variability of this characteristic. If perceivers are accurate on one measure, but not the other, does their belief have a kernel of truth? This question is difficult to answer.

The Risks of Assuming Accuracy

To fully understand the complexities of assessing stereotype accuracy, researchers must appreciate the risk of concluding that stereotypes do represent reality. Recall, again from Chapter 1, that stereotypes have been used as justification for maintaining the social status quo. Whites justified their subjugation of racial minority groups in the 1900s, for example, using the belief that minorities were naturally inferior to Whites and that such treatment was therefore appropriate (Duckitt, 1994). It may seem hard to believe now, but that perception *was* deemed accurate at the time. To cite a more recent example, 58 percent of Palestinians approve of suicide bombings inside Israel, presumably because they stereotypically view the Israelis as deserving of such violence (Wolin, 2003). When stereotypes are influenced by societal norms or historical events, the proposition that they might be "accurate" becomes more difficult to support.

Even if less harmful stereotypes are deemed accurate, thus *descriptively* capturing the group as it is today, should these descriptions be used as road maps for the characteristics that individual members of social groups *should* have (that is, should we use them as *prescriptions*)? Consider the belief that all good basketball players are tall. In general, this belief is on the mark. The average height of the 2003–2004 Los Angeles Lakers was 6'6" (National Basketball Association, NBA, 2003). Does this mean a middle or high school coach should discourage shorter players? Of course not. Short players can reach the NBA; Earl Boykins of the Denver Nuggets is 5'5" tall. And, obviously, a person can enjoy playing basketball without making it to the professional ranks. There is another side to prescriptive stereotypes, too. Many tall adolescents can tell you how frustrating it is to have people immediately assume that playing basketball is their dream. Perhaps without meaning to, people do seem to want to prescribe that all tall American boys (and more recently, girls) play basketball. At the group level, then, stereotypes may have a kernel of truth, but relying on them at the individual level may lead to serious judgment errors.

Social psychologists who have grappled with the accuracy issue also recognize that methodological problems stand in their way. Even when they agree, for example, that percentage estimates or measures of group variability are good indicators of stereotype accuracy, other issues arise (see Ryan et al., 1996, for a discussion). For example, how do psychologists assess actual attributes? The first challenge is to find an acceptable operational definition of the characteristic of interest. Objective statistics are available for some things, such as employment rates, income, or physical characteristics, but these data only provide part of the picture; the vast majority of stereotypes are not based on verifiable demographics but on abstract attributes such as *kind* or *lazy* (Stangor, 1995). Another important question is whether it is acceptable to use self-report to assess the match between perceived and actual group characteristics (such as by asking members of stereotyped groups to report their own traits). This procedure has the advantage of letting group members speak for themselves, but, as we saw in Chapter 2, self-report can be inaccurate.

A second methodological concern might be framed "which comparison group?" Imagine researchers are exploring the accuracy of the stereotypic belief that Blacks are more athletic than Whites. Even if researchers agreed on the operational definition of athletic ability, they would still need to determine whose ability to measure. In all probability, this stereotype refers to male athletes. But making this assumption immediately adds another layer of complexity: Is that belief accurate or does a similar stereotypic group difference exist for female athletes? Assuming for the moment that it is most appropriate to focus on men, the researchers still need to find the right sample. Would that be only those men who indicate an interest in athletics or all men? Does it need to be a representative national sample of Blacks and Whites, or can researchers simply ask college students, the respondents in the majority of psychological research? Could the accuracy of this stereotype depend on factors such as the respondents' socioeconomic status or culture (see Ashmore & Longo, 1995, for a discussion)? If you are having difficulty answering these questions, you are not alone. Psychologists who have grappled with the issues find them equally perplexing.

Shifting Standards

The issue of stereotype accuracy is further complicated because perceivers have motivations that affect their responses. If a group feels threatened, for example, its members are probably less accurate perceivers of the characteristics of the threatening group: They will be biased toward forming negative opinions about the outgroup (Tajfel & Turner, 1986). Accuracy also can be influenced by the context in which people make judgments. Monica Biernat and her colleagues (Biernat, Manis, & Nelson, 1991) offer the **shifting standards model,** which proposes that judgments often are influenced by relative comparisons—that is, by the particular yardstick perceivers choose for making judgments in a given situation.

According to the shifting standards model, the language of evaluation and judgment is subjective and perceivers impose their own meaning depending on the group being rated. These meanings are based on within-group reference points: People draw conclusions about an individual based on their beliefs about the group in general (for example, women are compared to women). Assume, for example, that a shove is considered, on average, to be a moderately aggressive act. Note also that people generally believe that men are more aggressive than women. According to the shifting standards model, in deciding whether a woman who shoves another person is aggressive, the perceiver considers the woman's aggression relative to the perceiver's beliefs about the average level of aggression displayed by women. In this example, then, the woman shover would likely be perceived as aggressive. If instead, the judgment was being made about a man who shoved another man, the shover's action would be perceived as average in aggressiveness. This is because the comparison has shifted and the perceiver is now comparing men to men. Moreover, if the man's and woman's aggression are directly compared, the woman's actions would be viewed as more aggressive than the man's.

How do these finding relate to stereotype accuracy? Recall that to determine whether a stereotype is accurate, researchers compare peoples' perceptions of the group to the actual characteristics of the members of that group. In doing so, researchers generally assume that the participants' assessments are stable. But research based on the shifting standards model shows that, instead, assessments are unstable and depend on the reference point the participants adopt when making their evaluations (Biernat, 1994). Rating scales, then, are more subjective than researchers sometimes realize and thus may be inappropriate as estimates of stereotype accuracy. For example, the estimate of men's perceived aggressiveness would differ depending on whether the judgment was made relative to other men or relative to women and it would be impossible to determine which assessment was more "accurate."

Overall, the challenges associated with assessing accuracy are daunting; our asking more questions than we have answered reflects the status of the literature (Lee, Jussim, & McCauley, 1995). Psychologists are divided as to whether stereotype accuracy even should be a focus of research. On the one hand, researchers note that science is best served by empirical research and theory development. Without the ability to assess accuracy, some argue, we will never know if stereotypes do, indeed, have a "kernel of truth" and we will be unable to truly understand the cognitive processes underlying stereotype development and use (Jussim, Clark, & Lee, 1995). On the other hand, it may be impossible to measure stereotype accuracy, particularly because of the difficulties in doing so objectively, as we have discussed (Stangor, 1995). As research continues, researchers are better able to estimate stereotype accuracy and, at the same time, have a better understanding of the limitations of the estimates. It is unlikely that these limitations can be completely overcome, however; it may simply be impossible to know whether a stereotype is "true." For individual social justice researchers, the question may come down to this: how can my research *best* contribute to understanding and eradicating prejudice? For some, the answer will be by trying to assess stereotype accuracy. For others, attention will be directed to different questions. Certainly, this debate will continue, as will research by those who *do* believe the problems can be adequately addressed.

FUNCTIONS OF STEREOTYPES

In most cases prejudice seems to have some "functional significance" for the bearer. Yet this is not always the case. Much prejudice is a matter of blind conformity with prevailing folkways.

—Gordon Allport, 1954 (p. 12)

Most human behavior is driven by motivations and desires, and holding stereotypic beliefs and prejudicial attitudes is no exception. Evidence suggests that these motivations and desires differ among people. Two individuals might have racist attitudes, for example, and might hold those attitudes with equal fervor. But the underlying reason for those beliefs, and the purpose they fulfill, might be very different. The idea that beliefs and evaluations might serve different functions for different people was developed in the 1950s by two researchers, M. Brewster Smith and Daniel Katz, working independently but arriving at similar ideas (see Eagly & Chaiken, 1993, for a review). No set list of functions was ever agreed on, but there are many similarities in the functions that have been studied. We examine three functions stereotypes might serve: the cognitive function, the ego-defensive function, and the social adjustment function (Snyder & Miene, 1994).

Cognitive Function

As we have discussed, one important reason people categorize others is because their cognitive resources are limited and schemas provide useful shortcuts in making decisions about others. Researchers also consider this process to be one of the functions stereotypes might serve for an individual. This cognitive function was labeled a *knowledge* function by Daniel Katz (1960), who theorized that its use stems from the need to maintain a meaningful, stable, and organized view of the world. Although this basic function is critical, and also ubiquitous, it does not capture more complex motives for holding stereotypic beliefs, nor does it address the basic needs that might be served by stereotyping and prejudice. The other remaining two functions better capture these complexities.

Ego-Defensive Function

Beliefs about others can serve an ego-defensive function as well. Such beliefs serve to protect an individual's self-concept against both internal and external threats (Eagly & Chaiken, 1993). As we will see in Chapter 6, people sometimes derogate outgroups as a way to feel better about themselves. One theoretical perspective holds that such derogation can occur because people project their own negative feelings onto members of other groups. Some researchers of anti-gay prejudice take this perspective, assuming, for example, that anxiety concerning the possibility of receiving unwanted sexual advances can result in the defense mechanism of reaction formation. That is, heterosexual men may substitute feelings of anger and resentment toward gay men for the anxiety associated with unwanted sexual advances, perhaps even resorting to violence against gay men as a means of responding to their discomfort (see, for example, Franklin, 1998). Similarly, the results of some research suggest that homophobic men show greater physical arousal to consensual male homosexual activity than do nonhomophobic men, although the self-reported arousal of these individuals does not vary (Adams, Wright, & Lohr, 1996). This difference may occur because homophobic men are repressing their attraction to other men; from a psychodynamic perspective, these repressed feelings could be expressed in the form of a negative stereotype about and prejudice toward gay men (see, for example, Young-Bruehl, 1996).

Social Adjustment Function

Humans are social beings and one of the most fundamental goals they have is fitting in with their social groups. All social groups have norms and expectations and sometimes these expectations direct people how to think and feel about others. Expressing beliefs that are counter to these group norms can be risky and may even result in ostracizatism from the group (Cialdini, Kallgren, & Reno, 1991). Individuals do not have to accept these beliefs to express them, but they nonetheless have a powerful influence over behavior. It is easy to underestimate the power the group has over behavior—the blind conformity Allport referred to. But think about the last time you heard a racist joke that you disapproved of. How did you respond? Did you remain silent and, perhaps, even laugh along with the group? Many people do; they go along to get along because the goal of relationship maintenance can so easily supersede other goals (Eagly & Chaiken, 1993).

An important way that relationships are maintained is through following norms—the rules or customs that groups follow. These norms may be personal, like the more individualized rules or customs that family and friends follow, or they may have the weight of the society behind them. In his influential book on the Holocaust, Daniel Goldhagen (1996) addresses how the power of German society affected the lives of everyday Germans, leading them to participate in perhaps the most inexplicable action of the 20th century, the annihilation of 6 million Jews. Writing about the perpetrators of this event, Goldhagen notes, "[t]hese people were overwhelmingly and most importantly Germans. . . . They were Germans acting in the name of Germany and its highly popular leader, Adolf Hitler. Some were 'Nazis' . . . some were not. The perpetrators killed and made their other genocidal contributions under the auspices of many institutions other than the SS. Their chief common denominator was that they were all Germans pursuing German national political goals—in this case, the genocidal killing of Jews" (pp. 6–7). A major thesis of Goldhagen's book is that killing of this magnitude simply could not have taken place without the consent and participation of vast numbers of people. This consent, he argues, was rooted in the virulent antisemitism that was part and parcel of German culture at that time. As Goldhagen puts it, "[t]he eliminationist antisemitism, with its hurricane force potential, resided ultimately in the heart of German political culture, in German society itself" (p. 428).

Christopher Browning (1992) also points to societal pressures in his study of why members of Reserve Police Battalion 101 willingly participated in the murder of Jews in the Polish town of Józefów in 1942. The commander of this group, Major Wilhelm Trapp, offered the men the opportunity to excuse themselves from participating in the impending mass murder. Yet only a dozen men out of nearly 500 chose to do so. Browning argues that the pressure to conform, which is especially acute for a group of men in uniform, kept the men from bowing out. The evidence he examined suggests that the men strongly believed doing so was a sign of weakness or cowardliness. That anyone would willingly support the goal of eliminating all Jews from Europe remains incomprehensible to most people. Yet at least part of the key undoubtedly lies in understanding the pull of fitting in with the social structure of the day.

STEREOTYPE MAINTENANCE

As Gordon Allport put it, "[p]rejudgments become prejudices only if they are not reversible when exposed to new knowledge" (p. 9). In this chapter, we have examined how the human need for efficient information processing produces stereotypes. Yet, as we will see in the next chapter, human cognition does not always run on autopilot. When people have fewer cognitive resources available, for example, they are less likely to stereotype (e.g., Gilbert & Hixon, 1991). Unfortunately, much of the research we have reviewed in this chapter can also give testimony to people's resistance to stereotype change. We describe next factors that work to maintain stereotypic beliefs, including perception and recall of social information, behavioral confirmation, and linguistic biases. As you read the next section, keep in mind that, as we just explained, understanding the functions stereotypes serve can facilitate change, as can an understanding of the processes we will discuss in upcoming chapters. We close this chapter by considering models of stereotype change.

Perception and Recall of Social Information

Fidelma O'Leary made national news because she was planning a 5-day pilgrimage to Mecca, which all Muslims are expected to do (Mangan, 2003). Why are these, and similar stories, news? The answer stems, at least in part, by people's interest in unique information. People like to learn about exceptions to the rules. In the case of O'Leary, people are interested in why the daughter of an Irish Roman Catholic would convert to Islam. In general, stereotype-inconsistent information surprises people; perhaps because they want to account for this information, they attend to it. Indeed, evidence suggests that people more readily attend to stereotype-inconsistent information than to stereotype-consistent information (Hastie, 1984).

Certain contextual cues capture people's attention. Individuals who are moving, are brightly lit, or are wearing colored clothing grab attention, for example (see Zebrowitz-McArthur, 1981 for a review). Intense or novel events also are likely to be noticed, especially those that are negative, such as crime (e.g., Fiske, 1980). Intuitively, this attention to the unique might seem to impede stereotyping by highlighting the things that make people different rather than the things they have in common. Research suggests that, instead, the consequence of this attention is that people who stand out physically also stand out psychologically. Thus, a solo Black person in a group of Whites is noticed more and is seen in more exaggerated stereotypic terms than the same person in a group of other Blacks (see Fiske & Taylor, 1991, for a review). When this happens, it works to maintain perceivers' stereotypic beliefs. And, as we will see in Chapter 11, there can be long-term negative effects of always standing out in a crowd, for example by being a Black on a predominantly White university campus.

It seems clear that people notice stereotype-inconsistent information. But researchers have long grappled with the question of whether people are better at *remembering* stereotype-inconsistent or stereotype-consistent information. In a now classic study, Claudia Cohen (1981) examined this question. Research participants watched a video of a woman who they believed to be either a waitress or a librarian. In the video, she described her day at work to her husband. While doing so, the woman talked about events or behaved in ways consistent with both the librarian stereotype (for example, she wore glasses and said she liked classical music) or the waitress stereotype (for example, she talked about bowling and said she liked pop music). As expected, participants recalled information that was consistent with their stereotypic expectations much better than the information that was inconsistent with their expectations. Those who believed she was a waitress remembered the things that were consistent with the waitress stereotype and those who believed she was a librarian remembered the things that were consistent with the librarian stereotype. Results of a second study showed that stereotypic expectations affect both what people remember about someone and how they use that remembered information in later judgments. Participants who, in the second study, did not learn about the woman's occupation until *after* they viewed the tape still had better recall for the stereotype-consistent information. That is, when people later discovered that the woman was a librarian or a waitress, they used this knowledge to make sense of what they had already stored in memory about her. Other research supports this result (see, for example, Dijksterhuis & van Knippenberg, 1996; Rothbart, Evans, & Fulero, 1979).

These results, however, do not definitely answer the question of whether memory is better for the unusual or the expected. A review of 54 studies (Stangor & McMillan, 1992) showed that, on balance, people recall information better when it violates their expectations. Yet this review also suggests that a number of factors affect this relationship. People remember information that is expected better when they have strong expectancies (as in the waitress/librarian example described above); when they are engaged in a complex judgment, such as deciding who to hire for a job; when they are asked to recall traits rather than behaviors; and when their goal is to remember specific information, rather than form an overall impression. These factors have an extremely important influence on how people perceive others, as we will see in the next chapter.

Research suggests that people may make different assumptions about the nature of personality and that these assumptions influence how they process and interpret stereotype-consistent and stereotype-inconsistent information (Plaks, Stroessner, Dweck, & Sherman, 2001). Some people are entity theorists; that is, they implicitly believe that personality is fixed and that, for example, regardless of situational factors, an individual's overall moral character is the same. Other people are incremental theorists; that is, they believe that personality is malleable and that, for example, an individual's moral behavior is influenced by the situation. When confronted with new information, entity theorists prefer to focus on stereotype-consistent information whereas incremental theorists pay attention to both stereotype-consistent and stereotype-inconsistent information and, if they do show a preference, it is for stereotype-inconsistent information. These individual differences have implications for stereotype maintenance. That is, because entity theorists decline to consider stereotype-inconsistent information, they also are unlikely to consider changing their stereotypic beliefs about a social group. For example, if they believe priests are always moral, entity theorists would continue to believe that even if an individual priest committed an immoral act. Incremental theorists, in contrast, are likely to consider stereotype-inconsistent information and revise their beliefs accordingly. Even if they initially believe priests are always moral, for example, incremental theorists would still weigh information suggesting otherwise. One way they might do so is by evaluating the circumstances under which a priest might behave immorally and developing a more fine-grained theory about priests' moral behavior that takes these situational factors into account.

Social justice researchers are particularly interested in how information processing influences people's actual judgments or their social interactions with others. One way to evaluate this processing is to consider what information is more likely to be passed along to others. Evidence suggests that people are more likely to share stereotype-consistent information than stereotype-inconsistent information about a group. To demonstrate this, Anthony Lyons and Yoshihisa Kashima (2001) asked Australian university students to read a story about an Australian Rules Football player. Some of his actions were stereotype consistent, others were stereotype inconsistent. The experiment was similar to the telephone game that children play in that the researchers were examining what information was remembered and then shared with others. So, the first group of participants read the story and then recalled it. These participants' reconstruction of the original story was then given to a new group of research participants, a process that was repeated four times. As the story was repeated, more and more stereotype-consistent information was reproduced and more and more stereotype-inconsistent information was lost. These results demonstrate that the tendency to recall information that fits people's beliefs also affects the transmission of stereotypes. Inconsistent information tends to get lost in the retelling.

Stereotype-inconsistent information also tends to get lost when groups discuss their stereotypic beliefs. It is not uncommon for people to discuss stereotyped groups, such as ethnic groups, political groups, or other social groups with others (Thompson, Judd, & Park, 2000). Moreover, research suggests that, as a result of such group discussions, people's beliefs about other social groups become more stereotypic than they were initially (Brauer, Judd, & Jacquelin, 2001). This polarization happens even when most individual group members know that the members of the social group being discussed sometimes behave counterstereotypically. Interestingly, however, if these counterstereotypic behaviors are known to only one member of the discussion group, the effect on group consensus differs. In this case, discussion does not lead to polarized views of the targeted social group. Apparently, when all group members come to the discussion with knowledge of counterstereotypic information, they give that information relatively little weight and it is discussed very little, if at all. When only one group member has counterstereotypic information, however, it is more likely to become part of the group discussion. When that happens, it results in less polarized attitudes toward the social group (see also Burnstein & Vinokur, 1977). Unless there is no voice of dissent about a social group's characteristics, then, people's conversations with others tend to lead them to more stereotypic perceptions.

Behavior Confirmation

> If men describe situations as real, they are real in their consequences.
>
> —William and Dorothy Thomas, 1928 (p. 572)

Stereotypes influence people's behavior in social interactions. When people meet someone for the first time, for example, they direct their conversation toward topics that they believe will be relevant. Especially at first meetings, people's expectations about what topics are relevant might be based on the stereotypes they hold about the groups the other person belongs to. Individuals instructed to learn more about someone whom they believe is an introvert, for example, will ask questions that confirm this introversion such as, "What things do you dislike about loud parties?" (Snyder & Swann, 1978). If the person is, instead, an extrovert, such questions limit her or his ability to demonstrate that trait. After all, extroverts as well as introverts probably dislike some things about loud parties. Leading questions, based on preexisting expectations, then, can take people in the wrong direction. That people search for stereotype confirming information has been demonstrated in a number of studies. Charles Carver and Nora de la Garza (1984), for example, asked people to evaluate an automobile accident and allowed them to ask for the information they needed to do so. Those who believed the driver was 84 years old tended to ask for more information about his physical and mental abilities. Those who believed the driver was 24 years old tended to ask whether he had been drinking or speeding.

Perhaps more troubling, however, is that these expectations, in turn, can influence how others behave toward group members. In a classic demonstration of this effect, Mark Snyder, Elizabeth Tanke, and Ellen Berscheid (1977) asked undergraduate men to talk on the phone with undergraduate women. Each man was provided with a picture of his interaction partner, showing her to be either attractive or unattractive. Based on only this information, the men behaved in ways that led the supposedly attractive women to speak in a friendlier manner than the supposedly unattractive women did. As you might guess, the men's beliefs about the attractiveness of the women with whom they were talking were actually erroneous; the pictures were not of the woman with whom they spoke. Instead, the men had been randomly assigned to see a picture of an attractive or an unattractive woman. These results, then, could not be due to the actual differences in the way attractive and unattractive people behave; instead, the women were responding to the cues the men were sending out.

In a more recent study (Ridge & Reber, 2002), some male participants were led to believe that a female research participant with whom they were going to interact was attracted to them. The other men in the study were given no such expectation and none of the women knew what the men had been told about them. The men who believed a woman was attracted to them behaved in a more flirtatious manner toward her, and received more flirtatious behavior from her, compared with the other men. Interestingly, this effect emerged in an interview about the woman's suitability for a teaching assistantship, not in a dating situation where flirtation might be more germane. Also of interest is that the men believed their behavior to be appropriate and professional in both conditions and that the women who responded in a flirtatious manner seemed unaware of the nature of their behavior. Such self-fulfilling prophecies are not inevitable, however. Individuals who have a goal of being accurate in their perceptions of the other person are less likely to elicit confirmation of their initial beliefs, for example (Deaux & Major, 1987; Snyder, 2001). Nonetheless, abundant evidence does suggest that people see what they believe they will see. Doing so perpetuates their stereotypic beliefs.

Even in the absence of actual interactions, perceptions can confirm preexisting beliefs. For example, John Darley and Paget Gross (1983) found that perceptions of a fourth grader named Hannah were influenced by the setting in which she was depicted: either a depressed urban setting or an affluent suburban setting. Participants watched Hannah complete an oral achievement test. Even though her answers were a balanced mixture of correct and incorrect responses, those who believed that Hannah had upper class roots judged her ability as above grade level, and, when recalling what they saw, inflated the number of questions she answered correctly. Those who believed she came from a lower class background reported that Hannah's ability was below grade level and underestimated the number of questions she actually answered correctly. People's stereotypes led them to see what they expected to see, thus maintaining their stereotypes.

Linguistic Intergroup Bias

Earlier in this chapter, we discussed the role of language in stereotype transmission. We now consider how language facilitates stereotype maintenance through the degree of abstraction speakers use to describe social behaviors. Anne Maass and her colleagues (Maass, Salvi, Arcuri, & Semin, 1989) have proposed that people's

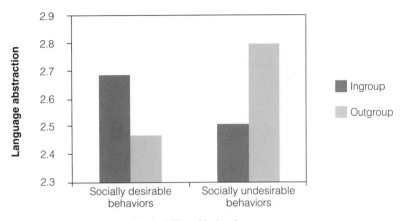

FIGURE **3.3**

LANGUAGE ABSTRACTION AS A FUNCTION OF INGROUP/OUTGROUP MEMBERSHIP AND THE SOCIAL DESIRABILITY OF THE BEHAVIOR

People describe the socially desirable behaviors of their own group and the socially undesirable behaviors of an outgroup using abstract language, but the other groups' positive behaviors and their own negative behaviors using concrete language.

Adapted from Maass, A., Salvi, D., Arcuri, L., & Semin, G. R. (1989). Language use in intergroup contexts: The linguistic intergroup bias. *Journal of Personality and Social Psychology, 57*, 981–993.

descriptions of ingroup and outgroup behaviors vary in their level of abstraction. Abstract terms are general and describe enduring psychological states (for example, Person A is honest, Person B is impulsive) whereas concrete terms are descriptive and observable (for example, Person A visits a friend; Person B kissed a lover). Maass and her colleagues' model of stereotype maintenance, labeled the **linguistic intergroup bias,** proposes that positive descriptions of ingroups and negative descriptions of outgroups tend to be made in abstract terms; in contrast, negative ingroup and positive outgroup actions tend to be described in concrete terms.

In a study testing this possibility, participants were drawn from rival sides of an Italian city during the time of a highly competitive annual horse race (Maass et al., 1989). Competitors in this race represent specific areas of the city and people highly identify with their own neighborhoods, creating natural ingroups and outgroups. Participants saw cartoons depicting either positive behaviors or negative behaviors. Half of the behaviors of each type were supposedly performed by the ingroup and half by the outgroup. The dependent variable was the response participants chose to represent the action. The results were consistent with the linguistic intergroup bias hypothesis: people described their own groups' positive behavior and the other groups' negative behavior in abstract terms (for example, the outgroup is violent) but the other groups' positive behaviors and their own negative behavior in concrete terms (for example, the ingroup member hurt another; see Figure 3.3). Support for this bias has emerged with a wide variety of ingroups and outgroups, including competing schools, nations, women and men, and political interest groups (see Maass & Arcuri, 1996, for a review).

The linguistic intergroup bias helps maintain stereotypes: statements made at a high level of abstraction are more resistant to change than concrete statements because abstract descriptions are difficult to confirm or disconfirm. Seeing Blacks respond to one or two situations in a nonaggressive way, for example, might not convince people who hold the stereotype that the abstract description "Blacks are aggressive" is incorrect. Concrete descriptions, however, can be more easily discounted. A person can more easily see if the description "the Black man shoved the White man" was correct because it is specific and disconfirmable. It is an advantage, then, to describe your own groups' negative behaviors in ways that can be easily proven wrong. People also gain an advantage if they describe their groups' positive behaviors in abstract terms that are hard to disprove. Doing the reverse when describing an outgroups' behavior creates a disadvantage for its members because it works to maintain negative stereotypes.

Stereotype Change

Since the publication of Allport's (1954) classic book on prejudice, researchers have reflected on people's reluctance to change their beliefs. Such change does not come easily. As Allport wrote: "We have fashioned our generalizations as we have because they have worked fairly well. Why change them to accommodate every new bit of evidence? If we are accustomed to one make of automobile and are satisfied, why admit the merits of another make? To do so would only disturb our satisfactory set of habits" (p. 23). At the same time, there are reasons why fixing incorrect beliefs is a good idea. If you think about it, basing decisions on an incorrect belief goes against the very reason beliefs exist in the first place: efficient information processing (Fiske & Taylor, 1991). People cannot be efficient if they are heading down the wrong path. When faced with firm evidence that the available information about a group member contradicts stereotypic beliefs, people have two choices: change the belief or find a way to recategorize the person or persons who do not fit the stereotypic model.

What does it take to make people change stereotypic beliefs? Three answers to this question have been proposed (see Weber & Crocker, 1983). The *bookkeeping model* suggests that change occurs slowly as people add and subtract information from their schema ledger. In this model, both small and large pieces of disconfirming evidence are taken into account, and, over time, the stereotype is adjusted. The *conversion model*, in contrast, is based on the notion that people "see the light" based on undeniably contradictory evidence. In this model, dramatic information has an effect, but less obvious instances of disconfirmation go unnoticed.

The *subtyping model* has received the most empirical support in the psychological literature, perhaps because it is the easiest to test experimentally; for that reason, we discuss this model in some detail. The subtyping model proposes that people rely on a cognitive sleight of hand that allows their beliefs about a group, in general, to remain intact, yet accommodate the discrepant case: that is, they create a special category for the exceptions to the rule. This process, described as *re-fencing* by Allport (1954), occurs when people treat those who do not fit their stereotype as exceptions (Richards & Hewstone, 2001). For example, when people learn that an older man has an excellent memory, which is inconsistent with the stereotype that older people have poor memories, they form a subtype "competent older man." The older person with the good memory is placed in this category, allowing people to retain their stereotypic beliefs about old age and memory.

What process underlies subtype creation? To understand the answer to this question, think about the social group, *women*. Bring to mind, also, that women are stereotypically considered to be unathletic, so that meeting an athletic woman would disconfirm this stereotype (Deaux & Lewis, 1984). Now imagine you meet a very athletic woman, but she is one of the few you have ever met, so she seems to be an exception to the rule. Subtyping researchers label this case *concentrated disconfirmation* (Johnston & Hewstone, 1992) because you know only one athletic woman, all the information that disconfirms the female stereotype is concentrated in this one, seemingly rare example. When disconfirmers are concentrated, perceivers re-fence, or create a new category to account for this unusual person (Weber & Crocker, 1983). What happens, however, if you start to notice that more and more of the women you meet are athletic? Subtyping researchers label this an example of *dispersed disconfirmation* (Johnston & Hewstone, 1992). Here, many women disconfirm the group stereotype. When this happens, it becomes hard to isolate this perception by creating a subtype of exceptions: What might have been seen as an exception is now becoming part of the rule. Therefore, the group stereotype is likely to be changed.

Lucy Johnston and Miles Hewstone (1992) demonstrated this process by asking participants to read about physics students or drama students who either had traits consistent or inconsistent with the stereotype of their group. They also varied whether the inconsistent information was concentrated (applied to two of the eight group members) or dispersed (was spread across six of the eight group members). In each condition, six pieces of inconsistent information were presented. Thus, both groups were given the same amount of disconfirming information but the *percentage of people* to whom the information applied differed by condition: 25 percent of the people in the concentrated condition and 75 percent in the dispersed condition. Greater stereotype change occurred in the dispersed condition—that is, when a greater percentage of the group members exhibited the disconfirming traits. Results also suggested that, in the concentrated condition, the two people who disconfirmed the stereotype were set apart from the group, leaving the stereotype intact. In short, subtypes were created.

Changing Stereotypic Beliefs

Subtyping might be viewed as more of a process for stereotype maintenance, or stereotype revision, than stereotype change (Richards & Hewstone, 2001). Even so, the research described above clearly shows that change in the content of people's schemas can occur. Another possibility for change comes from the research on stereotype functions that we described earlier in this chapter. Functional theorists propose that understanding the purpose being fulfilled by holding stereotypic beliefs is the key to stereotype change. Sometimes this purpose is heavily influenced by situational factors, other times by the personality of the beholder. Evidence suggests that once the function of the belief has been identified, successful strategies can be targeted to change it (see Eagly & Chaiken, 1993, for a review). Gregory Herek (1986a) offers the example of two people who are opposed to a neighborhood treatment facility for the mentally ill. Ms. Wagner opposes the facility because she stereotypically believes the inmates threaten her personal safety, a cognitive function. Mr. Adams opposes the facility because his friends and neighbors oppose it, a social adjustment function. Changing Ms. Wagner's attitude might be accomplished most effectively by convincing her that only a small minority of mentally ill people are violent. Mr. Adams, on the other hand, is likely to change his attitude only if he believes other neighbors or friends actually support the facility. Stereotype change is not a one-size-fits-all endeavor but, by carefully considering the functions the stereotypes are serving, progress can occur. We will discuss changing prejudicial beliefs in more detail in Chapter 12.

CHAPTER SUMMARY

This chapter reviewed the literature on how cognitive processing influences stereotyping. Research on this topic mushroomed in the late 1970s and 1980s, exploring the idea that humans are inherently efficient information processors, and remains an important focus of study today. In reviewing the costs and benefits of processing efficiency, we described the categorization process and its influence on schemas about social groups. When approaching a social interaction, people's first level of analysis relies on basic social categories, such as age, race, and gender. However, perceivers also use more fine-grained social categories and readily recognize that others can belong to more than one basic category at a time. As we saw, one of the most natural cognitive tendencies is to divide the world into two groups—us versus them. The minimal group paradigm demonstrates how little it takes to start this division. By doing so, people set up a world in which they see their own group as both diverse and deserving (ingroup favoritism) and other groups as all alike and less worthy (the outgroup homogeneity effect).

Stereotypes originate from many sources, including parents, peers, and the media. We reviewed these sources and also described theories that outline the process by which these stereotypes form. Social role theory recognizes that people form perceptions from observing the world around them, but acknowledges that their tendency to give too little weight to situational factors tips the balance in these observations. Illusory correlations emerge when people notice that distinctive events are co-occurring with minority status, even if that correlation is erroneously perceived. Messages conveyed through language also influence stereotype formation. Some discourse appears to be more interesting and more communicable. Stereotypes that fit this mold may be more likely to persist. Even so, stereotypes are not all things to all people. In fact, the same stereotype might serve a cognitive, ego-defensive, or social adjustment function to different people. Understanding these differences leads to a better chance for stereotype change.

The seemingly simple question of whether stereotypes are accurate has been perplexingly difficult to answer. Researchers have developed ways to assess accuracy and agree that this assessment should include both measures of central tendency and measures of variability. But the quest for the kernel of truth also has led to considerable discussion of the methodological problems associated with this measurement and even the wisdom of trying to do so. The shifting standards model demonstrates that judgments are subjective and can change with a switch in point of view.

Cognitive processing also influences what people attend to and what they remember. Research suggests that people readily notice stereotype-inconsistent information. What people notice, in turn, influences what they perceive. The issue of whether people recall stereotype-consistent or stereotype-inconsistent information is difficult to answer. In short, it depends on processing goals or other situational factors. Cognitive processes, more often than not, seem to support stereotype maintenance. These processes include behavior confirmation, which leads perceivers to find what they thought they would find, and the linguistic intergroup bias, a process that influences the vocabulary people use to describe ingroups and outgroups. We close the chapter by discussing models of stereotyping change, explaining in detail the model that has received the most empirical support in the literature: the subtyping model. In response to disconfirming evidence, particularly evidence displayed by only a few members of a group, perceivers adjust their schemas by creating subtypes. Subtypes do not replace the group level stereotype, but instead offer a way for perceivers to acknowledge that some individuals do not fit the group stereotype. Limitations of the experimental method make demonstrations of other models of stereotype change, such as the bookkeeping model, difficult. Fortunately, this does not mean such changes do not occur.

SUGGESTED READINGS

Social Categorization

Hamilton, D. L. (1981) (Ed.). *Cognitive processes in stereotyping and intergroup behavior.* Hillsdale, NJ: Erlbaum.

> This classic work includes chapters by prominent researchers whose work became the cornerstones of the modern cognitive approach to stereotyping. The chapters are perhaps more accessible than some more recent explorations and they convey the excitement of this new way of thinking about the topic.

Macrae, C. N., & Bodenhausen, G. V. (2000). Social cognition: Thinking categorically about others. *Annual Review of Psychology, 51,* 93–120.

> Provides an excellent overview of the research on categorization, focusing on (1) when social categories are activated by perceivers, (2) the consequences of this activation, and (3) whether and how perceivers can control this activation.

Tajfel, H. (1969). Cognitive aspects of prejudice. *Journal of Social Issues, 25* (4), 79–97.
This highly influential paper anticipated much of the current work on the cognitive processes involved in stereotyping and prejudice as well as social identity theory, which is discussed in Chapter 8.

Origins of Stereotypes

Eagly, A. H., Wood, W., & Diekman, A. B. (2000). Social role theory of sex differences and similarities: A current appraisal. In T. Eckes (Ed.), *The developmental social psychology of gender* (pp. 123–174). Mahwah, NJ: Erlbaum.
Provides an up-to-date overview of social role theory that has been supported by numerous studies by Eagly and others.

Hamilton, D. L., & Gifford, R. K. (1976). Illusory correlation in interpersonal perception: A cognitive basis of stereotypic judgments. *Journal of Experimental Social Psychology, 12*, 392–407.
Describes Hamilton and Gifford's original study of illusory correlations.

Maass, A., & Arcuri, L. (1996). Language and stereotyping. In C. N. Macrae, C. Stangor & M. Hewstone (Eds.), *Stereotypes & stereotyping* (pp. 193–226). New York: Guilford.
Provides an accessible overview of a relatively neglected area of stereotyping research: the role of language in the development and maintenance of stereotypes. A nice bonus is that many of the examples are from European social groups, testifying to the generalizability of the effects.

Stereotype Accuracy

Biernat, M., Vescio, T. K., & Manis, M. (1998). Judging and behaving toward members of stereotyped groups: A shifting standards perspective. In C. Sedikides, J. Schopler, & C. A. Insko (Eds.), *Intergroup cognition and intergroup behavior* (pp. 151–175). Hillsdale, NJ: Erlbaum.
Provides a comprehensive overview of the research supporting the shifting standards model.

Lee, Y.-T., Jussim, L. J., & McCauley, C. R. (1995). (Eds.). *Stereotype accuracy: Toward appreciating group differences*. Washington, DC: American Psychological Association.
This volume includes a number of highly readable chapters that tackle the complexities of assessing stereotype accuracy. Particularly interesting are the concluding two chapters, one by Charles Stangor, the other by the editors, which provide opposing viewpoints about the benefits and risks of research in this area.

Functions of Stereotypes

Herek, G. M. (1986a). The instrumentality of attitudes: Toward a neofunctional theory. *Journal of Social Issues, 42*(2), 99–114.
Greg Herek can be credited with reviving interest in functional attitude theory, including developing ways to measure attitude function.

Snyder, M., & Miene, P. (1994). On the functions of stereotypes and prejudice. In M. P. Zanna & J. M. Olson (Eds.), *The psychology of prejudice* (pp. 33–54). Hillsdale, NJ: Erlbaum.
Mark Snyder's highly engaging writing style makes this an accessible introduction to the various functions people's stereotypes might serve.

Stereotype Maintenance

Cohen, C. E. (1981). Person categories and social perception: Testing some boundaries of the processing effects of prior knowledge. *Journal of Personality and Social Psychology, 40,* 441–452.
>   The studies reported in this article remain widely cited and provide a good overview of how experimental design can be used to demonstrate cognitive processes.

Maass, A., Salvi, D., Arcuri, L., & Semin, G. R. (1989). Language use in intergroup contexts: The linguistic intergroup bias. *Journal of Personality and Social Psychology, 57,* 981–993.
>   Provides a good introduction to the linguistic intergroup bias. Maass's work is nice because her ingroups and outgroups not ones traditionally seen in the literature.

Weber, R., & Crocker, J. (1983). Cognitive processes in the revision of stereotypic beliefs. *Journal of Personality and Social Psychology, 45,* 961–977.
>   This work remains the classic overview of models of stereotype change.

Encyclopedia Entries

Worell, J. (2001). (Ed.). *Encyclopedia of women and gender: Sex similarities and differences and the impact of society on gender.* San Francisco: Academic Press.
>   Contains excellent summaries of social role theory, expectancy confirmation and self-fulfilling prophecies, and stereotype development. The chapter on gender stereotypes addresses the structure of stereotypes, subtypes, stereotype accuracy, and the shifting standards model.

KEY TERMS

basic social category	shifting standards model
categorization	social learning theory
illusory correlations	social role theory
linguistic intergroup bias	subtypes
minimal group paradigm	ultimate attribution error
outgroup homogeneity effect	

QUESTIONS FOR REVIEW AND DISCUSSION

1. Explain why people categorize.
2. Think of the social categories you use most frequently. Are they at the basic category or the subtype level?
3. Sometimes it is difficult to determine a person's gender by their physical appearance. Based on what you know about categorization, what do you think people do in this situation?
4. Describe the minimal group paradigm.
5. List and describe sources of stereotypic beliefs. Which do you believe are more important?

6. As the media becomes more and more central to our lives, what do you think will happen to stereotypic thought?
7. Do you think people today are more likely to hold stereotypes than those who lived before television and movies? Why or why not?
8. Describe the development of stereotypes about Blacks and Whites using the tenets of social role theory.
9. What are illusory correlations? Specifically, how are they formed and why do they lead to stereotyping?
10. How does language influence the development of stereotyping?
11. Think of some of your favorite songs. Do they contain racial or gender stereotypes? If so, how common do you think this is and what effect does it have on your perceptions of other groups?
12. What is the outgroup homogeneity effect and what are the reasons this effect emerges?
13. Describe the ultimate attribution error.
14. Distinguish between the two measures of stereotype accuracy we described: percentage estimates and perceived dispersion.
15. Do you believe researchers should explore whether stereotypes are accurate? Why or why not?
16. If researchers demonstrate that some stereotypes are accurate, do you think this information could be exploited, for example by members of hate groups? If so, in what way?
17. How accurate is the stereotype that women are better caregivers than men? Base your answer on the shifting standards model.
18. Describe three functions stereotypes might serve.
19. How might you change a stereotype that serves an ego-defensive function?
20. Why would people attend to novel, unique events, but recall stereotype-consistent information about social groups?
21. The quote by William and Dorothy Thomas (1928) that appears at the beginning of the section on behavior confirmation is generally attributed only to William, even though it appeared in a chapter coauthored by the married couple. What stereotypic processes might explain this and what are the consequences of those processes?
22. Explain the difference between abstract and concrete language use. How does this lead to the intergroup linguistic bias?
23. Describe the three models of stereotype change.
24. Distinguish between dispersed and concentrated disconfirmation.
25. Do you believe subtyping is a model of stereotype change or stereotype maintenance? Explain your answer.

STEREOTYPE ACTIVATION AND APPLICATION

It takes no special training to discern sex stereotyping in a description of an aggressive female employee as requiring "a course at charm school." Nor . . . does it require expertise in psychology to know that if an employee's flawed "interpersonal skills" can be corrected by a soft-hued suit or a new shade of lipstick, perhaps it is the employee's sex and not her interpersonal skills that has drawn the criticism.

—United States Supreme Court Justice William J. Brennan, Jr., writing for the majority in Price Waterhouse v. Hopkins, *1989 (p. 256)*

Ann Hopkins, a senior executive at the well-known accounting firm of PricewaterhouseCoopers, was being considered for promotion to partnership status, a very prestigious and important position in the company. The only woman among the 88 candidates for promotion that year, Ms. Hopkins had performed her job in an outstanding manner. She had generated more business for the company than had any of the other candidates and she was popular with her clients. Despite these achievements (and others), she was not promoted; the reason given by the partners making the decision was that she lacked the necessary interpersonal skills, being described as too "macho" and "needing a course in charm school." That is, despite her accomplishments as a member of the firm, Ms. Hopkins was denied promotion because she did not fit the traditional female stereotype. She sued the company for sex discrimination, with the case ultimately being decided by the U.S. Supreme Court. They found in her favor, resulting in the decision by Justice Brennan quoted above.

How do stereotypes lead to outcomes such as Ann Hopkins's being denied a partnership? Several factors are involved. One is *stereotype knowledge,* the extent to which a person is familiar with the content of a stereotype. Stereotype knowledge is widespread in a society, and both prejudiced and unprejudiced people know the content of stereotypes. Thus, for example, both prejudiced and unprejudiced White Americans can describe the American stereotype of African Americans (Devine & Elliot, 1995), both prejudiced and unprejudiced White Britons can describe the British stereotype of West Indians (Lepore & Brown, 1997), and both prejudiced and unprejudiced White Australians can describe the Australian stereotype of Australian Aborigines (Augustinos, Innes, & Ahrens, 1994). **Stereotype endorsement,** in contrast, is the extent to which a person actually agrees with the social stereotype of a group. As we saw in Chapter 1, stereotype endorsement is one component of prejudice.

Before a stereotype can have an effect, it must be activated. **Stereotype activation** is "the extent to which a stereotype is accessible in one's mind" (Kunda & Spencer, 2003, p. 522). Because a stereotype only applies to a given group, it has no function except in relation to its group and so usually lies dormant until activated, such as through an encounter with a member of a stereotyped group. However, stereotypes are not always activated. A precondition for stereotype activation is **categorization:** Based on a person's observable characteristics (such as skin tone, facial features, behavior, and so forth), an onlooker must classify that person as a member of stereotyped group.

Finally, the activated stereotype must be applied to the person. **Stereotype application** is "the extent to which one uses a stereotype to judge a member of the stereotyped group" (Kunda & Spencer, 2003, p. 522). The progression from categorization through stereotype activation to stereotype application is rapid and automatic, with people only rarely being aware that it is happening (Bodenhausen, Macrae, & Sherman, 1999). However, the automatic nature of the process does not mean that its completion is inevitable: Because group membership is not always clear-cut, a number of factors can influence how an onlooker categorizes a person. Similarly, knowledge of a stereotype does not always lead to its activation and activation of a stereotype does not always lead to its application.

This chapter deals with four topics. We first look at the factors that influence how onlookers categorize others. We then consider some of the factors that facilitate and inhibit the activation of stereotypes, following a model developed by Ziva Kunda and Steven Spencer (2003). The third section of the chapter examines the circumstances under which stereotypes are applied, following a model presented by Russell Fazio and Tamara Towles-Schwen (1999). The last section presents some of the effects of stereotype application. Although we discuss categorization, stereotype activation, and stereotype application as discrete processes, in practice each step follows the other so quickly that they can be difficult to separate. While examining the role stereotypes play in how people perceive and interact with others, it is important to bear two factors in mind. First, stereotypes are most likely to be activated and applied to strangers and others whom people do not know very well; the better people know other people, the more likely they are to view those others in terms of their unique characteristics rather than in terms of the stereotypes associated with the social groups they represent (Kunda & Thagard, 1996). Second, as we will see throughout the chapter, when people interact with others, their behavior is driven by goals to be achieved and needs to be fulfilled (Kunda & Spencer, 2003). Some of these motivational factors inhibit the effects of stereotypes and lead people to see others in individualized, rather than stereotypical, terms. However, stereotypes can be very important because they may be the only information people have about others when they first encounter them. Those stereotypes can also shape first impressions of and behavior toward strangers and, as we will see, stereotypes can sometimes influence others' behavior toward us.

CATEGORIZATION

The first step in the stereotype application processes is categorization. Before a stereotype can be activated, an onlooker must categorize a person as a member of a stereotyped group. As we saw in Chapter 3, people tend to classify others into the three basic social categories of gender, race, and age: Simply seeing a person calls attention to his or her group membership in terms of those categories (Fiske, 1998). However, any one person, such as a middle-aged Black woman, falls into all of these categories. Because a person can be placed into more than one category, several processes operate to determine which category gets the most attention and therefore which stereotype is available for activation.

When one person first encounters another, the first category to be noticed is race, quickly followed by gender (Ito & Urland, 2003). Because this process of allocating attention to categories takes only a fraction of a second, no one category necessarily has precedence when the process is complete: As we discussed in Chapter 3, unless other processes intervene, onlookers make use of all three categories to classify a person. This process results in subcategories, such as *young Black woman*, that combine salient social categories (Stangor, Lynch, Duan, & Glass, 1992) and it is the subcategory stereotype that is available for activation.

Prototypicality

One factor that affects the speed and ease of categorization is the **prototypicality** of the person being categorized. A person is prototypical of a social category to the extent that he or she fits the observer's concept of the essential features characteristic of that category. For example, the prototypical African has dark brown skin, dark eyes, tightly curled black hair, a relatively broad nose, and relatively full lips; in contrast, the prototypical European has light-colored skin, light or dark eyes, straight or loosely curled hair that can be either light or dark in color, a relatively narrow nose, and relatively thin lips (Livingston & Brewer, 2002). The more prototypical of a category a person is, the more quickly and easily the person is categorized.

For example, Robert Livingston and Marilynn Brewer (2002) showed people pictures of White Americans and African Americans who had been previously rated as high or low in prototypicality for their respective racial groups and measured how quickly people could correctly categorize the pictures as being of White or Black people. Their research participants categorized the high prototypical pictures about 10 percent faster than the low prototypical pictures. Similarly, Irene Blair and her colleagues (Blair, Judd, Sadler, & Jenkins, 2002) found positive correlations between the prototypicality of pictures of both White and Black people and how quickly they were categorized as White or Black. In addition, using pictures of Black people who varied in skin tone from dark to light, Keith Maddox and Stephanie Gray (2002) found that prototypicality facilitated racial categorization for both Black and White research participants.

Situational Influences

Although categorization is often automatic, situational factors can intervene in the categorization process to emphasize one category over another. Thus, although people spontaneously subcategorize using basic social categories, they may need to be motivated to subcategorize on the basis of other characteristics, such as occupation. For instance, when someone encounters a businesswoman, the salient category will be *woman* because it, and not *businesswoman,* is the basic social category. In the absence of a reason to do otherwise, people use basic categories rather than subcategories (Brewer & Feinstein, 1999; Fiske, Lin, & Neuberg, 1999). For example, Louise Pendry and Neil Macrae (1996) had research participants watch a brief videotape of a woman in an office performing a variety of work-related tasks, such as removing documents from a briefcase and reading reports. Before watching the tape, participants were given one of three goals: to form an accurate impression of the woman, to estimate the woman's height, or to check the clarity of the tape. Pendry and Macrae hypothesized that the participants who were motivated to form an accurate impression would be most likely to use the subcategory *businesswoman* because, for them, this category would provide more information for forming an accurate impression than would the general category of *woman.* The results of the experiment supported the hypothesis, with the accuracy-motivated participants' being more likely to categorize the woman in the videotape as a businesswoman and the other participants' being more likely to categorize her simply as a woman.

The context in which a perceiver encounters another person can also influence categorization. For example, when a person in a group differs in some way from the other members of a group, onlookers pay the most attention to the category in which the person differs from the others (Nelson & Miller, 1995). Thus, Jason Mitchell, Brian Nosek, and Mahzarin Banaji (2003) found that people thought of a Black woman in terms of her gender when she was shown in an otherwise all-male context and in terms of her race when she was shown in an otherwise all-White context. A person's behavior may also draw onlookers' attention to one category over another. Neil Macrae, Galen Bodenhausen, and Alan Milne (1995) found that people thought of an Asian woman in terms of her gender when they saw her putting on makeup but in terms of her race when they saw her eating with chopsticks. In situations such as these, onlookers pay attention to and use the basic social category, such as race or gender, to which the situation draws their attention; other categories are inhibited, which prevents categorization in terms of subcategories (Bodenhausen & Macrae, 1998). As a result, it is the stereotype of the basic category—race or gender depending on the situational cues—that becomes available for activation.

Prejudice

Prejudice does, however, play a role in categorization, because racially prejudiced people tend to pay more attention to race than other characteristics, such as gender, when they see people (Fazio & Dunton, 1997). For example, Charles Stangor and his colleagues (1992) had White research participants watch videotapes of an eight-member discussion group consisting of two Black women, two White women, two Black men, and two White men. Stangor and his colleagues found that participants high on racial prejudice were more likely to categorize discussion participants by race than were low prejudice participants, but that racial prejudice was unrelated to categorization by gender.

Prejudiced people also are biased in the categorizations they make. For example, Michael Quanty, John Keats, and Stephen Harkins (1975) showed research participants who were high or low in anti-Semitism (anti-Jewish prejudice) pictures of people, some of whom were Jewish and some of whom were not. The participants classified the people in the pictures as Jewish or not Jewish. People who were prejudiced against Jews tended to overclassify the people in the pictures as Jewish; that is, they tended to err on the side of classifying Gentiles as Jews rather than err by classifying Jews as Gentiles. More recently, Emanuele Castano and colleagues (Castano, Yzerbyt, Bourguignon, & Seron, 2002) found a similar effect for high versus low ethnocentric Europeans: highly ethnocentric people tended to overclassify others as members of the outgroup whereas low ethnocentric people did not. Jacques-Philippe Leyens and Vincent Yzerbyt (1992) have called this phenomenon *ingroup overexclusion*: prejudiced people want to avoid treating outgroup members as though they were part of the ingroup. It is therefore "safer" for them to misclassify ingroup members as outgroup members (even though it means excluding ingroup members) than to misclassify outgroup members as part of the ingroup (and thus extend ingroup privileges to the "wrong" people). As David Taylor and Fathali Moghaddam (1994) put it, "If we take the case of the prejudiced white person, when grouping black and white others, such a person would identify with the white group, and any racial mixing that took place would, from that person's perspective, negatively affect his or her status. Such a person would try to make sure not to mistakenly place any blacks in the white group" (pp. 68–69).

Exclusion of outgroup members can also be accomplished by accurately classifying people as members of the ingroup or outgroup. Accurate classification can sometimes be difficult, especially when confronted with a person with racially ambiguous characteristics, such as a light-skinned African American or a dark-skinned European American. In such cases, racially prejudiced people may be especially motivated to accurately classify people as Black or White. Therefore, it is not surprising that Jim Blascovich and his colleagues (Blascovich, Wyer, Swart, & Kibler, 1997) found that racially prejudiced White people took longer to categorize racially ambiguous faces as Black or White than did nonprejudiced White people, presumably using the additional time to be more accurate in their classifications. In contrast, prejudiced and nonprejudiced people did not differ on the amount of time they took to classify unambiguous (that is, prototypical) faces.

Prejudiced people may also use group stereotypes to help reduce the ambiguity they face when encountering a person who does not clearly fit into any one category. For example, Kurt Hugenberg and Galen Bodenhausen (2004) created a set of pictures of male faces that combined prototypically White and Black features, half of which had happy expressions and half of which had angry expressions. They showed these pictures to White research participants and found that nonprejudiced participants were equally likely to classify a particular face as White or Black regardless of the emotion it showed. However, prejudiced participants were more likely to classify the angry face as Black, presumably using the stereotype of African American men as hostile as a cue to deciding the race of the person in the picture.

A final factor motivating categorization may be America's historical emphasis on race as an important social category. As Jordan Lite (2001), a young woman of multiracial background recounts in Box 4.1, Americans seem to find it necessary to put her into the "correct" racial category before beginning a closer relationship.

STEREOTYPE ACTIVATION

Once a person has been categorized as a member of a stereotyped group, the stage is set for stereotype activation. In stereotype activation, a dormant stereotype becomes active, ready for use, and capable of influencing a person's thoughts about and behavior toward a member of the stereotyped group. As shown in Figure 4.1, following categorization, two types of stereotype activation processes begin that operate simultaneously and can affect one another. The first type, automatic

4.1   *Please Ask Me Who, Not "What," I Am*

Jordan Lite (2001), a young woman of multiracial descent, wrote the following about her experiences of people trying to categorize her by race by asking, "What are you?"

Each new guy I meet, it seems, is fascinated by my ostensible failure to fall into an obvious racial category. Last year we could opt out of defining ourselves to the Census Bureau, but that option doesn't seem to have carried over into real life. I've lost track of how many flirty men have asked me what I am. . . .

When a potential boyfriend asks me "What are you?" I feel like he wants to instantly categorize me. If he'd only let the answer come out naturally, he'd get a much better sense of what I'm about.

Perhaps acknowledging explicitly that race and ethnicity play a role in determining who we are is just being honest. But I'm not sure that such directness is always well intended. . . . "You're exotic-looking," a man at a party explained when I asked him why he wanted to know. In retrospect, I think he probably meant his remark as a compliment. . . . But if someone wants to get to know me, I wish he would at least pretend it's not because of my looks. . . .

I resent being pressed to explain myself upfront, as if telling a prospective date my ethnicity eliminates his need to participate in a real conversation with me. "What are you?" I am asked, but the background check he's conducting won't show whether we share real interests that would bring us together in a genuine give-and-take.

In a way, I enjoy being unclassifiable. Though there are people who try to peg me to a particular ethnic stereotype, I like to think others take my ambiguous appearance as an opportunity to focus on who I am as a person. So I haven't figured out why being myself should kill any chance of a relationship. Not long ago, a man asked me about my background when we met for a drink.

"Just a Jewish girl from New Jersey," I said truthfully.

I never heard from him again. (p. 9)

From Jordan Lite, Newsweek, July 16, 2001. Reprinted by permission.

processing, is triggered simply by observing stimuli associated with the stereotyped group; the second type, motivated processing, is rooted in people's goals and needs, activating stereotypes when the stereotypes can help fulfill those goals and needs. These motives can arise from either individual difference factors, such as personality, or from situational factors. In addition, activation occurs for motivated stereotypes only if some aspect of the stereotype is relevant to the situation in which the person finds him- or herself. For example, if the person must select someone for a job, stereotypes that include work-related traits such as *lazy* or *hard working* would be activated but stereotypes that do not include work-related traits would not be activated. This section describes the stereotype activation process, looking first at automatic activation processes and then at motivated activation processes. It concludes with a discussion of some characteristics of the activated stereotype.

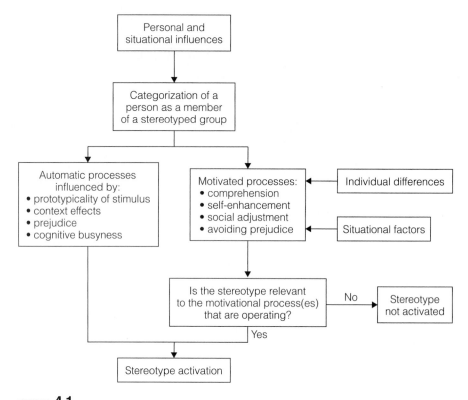

FIGURE **4.1**

STEREOTYPE ACTIVATION

Stereotype activation begins when a person's attention is drawn to a member of a stereotyped group. At that point, two types of processes begin, which operate simultaneously and can affect one another. Automatic processing is triggered by stimuli associated with the stereotyped group. Motivated processing is rooted in people's goals, needs, and motivations, and activates stereotypes when the stereotypes can help fulfill those goals, needs, and motivation. These motives can arise from either individual difference factors, such as personality, or from situational factors. In addition, activation occurs for motivated stereotypes only if some aspect of the stereotype is relevant to the situation in which the person finds him- or herself. (Adapted from Kunda & Spencer, 2003)

Automatic Activation

Categorization paves the way for stereotype activation—the process of making the stereotype accessible in the mind and ready for use. Like categorization, stereotype activation is automatic; that is, it occurs without effort or conscious thought once a person has been categorized as a member of a stereotyped group. The automatic nature of stereotype activation is shown by the fact that even sub-liminal cues—cues presented too quickly to be consciously noted—can activate stereotypes (Bargh, 1999). For example, Steven Spencer and his colleagues (Spencer, Fein, Wolfe, Fong, & Dunn, 1998) had research participants watch a computer screen on which either a Black or White face was shown for less than one-tenth of a second; the participants then completed word stems such as *hos_, wel_, ste_,* and *stu_.* Participants who saw Black faces were more likely to complete the stems with words consistent with the Black stereotype, such as *hostile, welfare, steal,* and *stupid,* whereas those who saw White faces were more likely to complete the stems with nonstereotypic terms, such as *hospital, welcome, step,* and *student.*

Researchers believe that stereotype activation has this automatic and unthinking character because cultural environments establish strong links between a category, such as *Black,* and stereotypes associated with the category, such as *lazy, musical, athletic,* and *hostile.* Because these category-stereotype links are both strong and pervasive in the culture, people learn the links so thoroughly that the stereotype becomes a conditioned, unthinking mental response to the category (Fazio, 2001; Macrae & Bodenhausen, 2000). In one of the first demonstrations of how this process operates in the social world, John Dovidio and his colleagues (Dovidio, Evans, & Tyler, 1984) presented White research participants with the racial categories *Black* and *White* as primes that incidentally activate knowledge structures such as stereotypes (see Bargh, Chen, & Burrows, 1996). After participants were primed by a racial category, they answered "yes" or "no" to the question of whether each stereotypic word could ever be associated with the category. The dependent variable was how quickly people responded, which indicates the strength of the association between the stereotypic word and the racial category. When a White prime was presented, responses were fastest for traits stereotypically associated with Whites and for positive traits. When a Black prime was presented, responses were fastest for traits stereotypically associated with Blacks and for negative traits. People not only accessed a category (Black or White) faster when they were primed, they also accessed the evaluations they associated with that category. The results suggest that Whites saw a stronger connection between White and positive and Black and negative than the reverse. Since Dovidio and colleague's (1984) work, a wealth of evidence has supported the principle that when a category label is presented, people are unable to prevent making the association between the category label and the information they have stored about that category (see Macrae & Bodenhausen, 2000, for a review).

Until recently, most researchers accepted the inevitability of category activation leading to stereotyping (Lepore & Brown, 1999). Testing the alternative—that category activation does not lead to stereotyping—presents a bit of a puzzle because, without a doubt, the relationship between category activation and stereotyping is strong and easily activated. Unlinking them, or separating them experimentally to see if they are independent processes, is difficult. However, although stereotype activation is usually automatic, several factors have been identified that can disrupt the activation process or influence the particular aspect of a stereotype that is activated. These factors include the prototypicality of the stereotyped person, the context in which the person is encountered, the degree of prejudice of the individual encountering the stereotyped person, and the extent to which that individual is cognitively busy.

Prototypicality   Just as the prototypicality of a stimulus person can facilitate the categorization of that person, prototypicality can facilitate activation of stereotypes. For example, Blair and her colleagues (2002) found that White research participants rated a Black person who had more prototypically African facial features as more likely to have behaved in a negative stereotypic way (such as acting aggressively) than a less prototypically appearing Black person. Furthermore, using an implicit cognition measure (see Chapter 2), Livingston and Brewer (2002) found that White research participants associated more negative traits with a more prototypically appearing Black person that with a less prototypically appearing Black person. Thus, Black people who are more prototypically African are seen in more stereotypic terms than Black people who are less prototypically African. In addition to demonstrating the role of prototypicality in stereotype activation, the results of these studies have suggested that categorization may not always be necessary for stereotype activation; see Box 4.2 for more information.

Context   When people encounter others, that encounter takes place within some type of context; for example, a person may see someone on the street, in a classroom, or in church. The context in which a person sees someone can affect the interpretation of what that person is like. Consider the case of stereotypes. Stereotypes can be complex, consisting of both positive and negative components (Judd, Park, Ryan, Brauer, & Kraus, 1995) and both positive and negative subtypes (Devine & Baker, 1991). Therefore, when a stereotype is activated, either the positive or negative component, or both, could be activated. One factor that can influence which aspects of a stereotype become active is the context in which an observer encounters a member of a stereotyped group. For example, you might draw one kind of conclusion about a person lurking up a dark alley but another kind of conclusion if you see the same person praying in church.

Bernd Wittenbrink, Charles Judd, and Bernadette Park (2001) tested the effect of context on stereotype activation by having White research participants watch videotapes or view photographs of Black men in either positive contexts (at a family barbecue or in church) or negative contexts (at a gang meeting or in an urban street scene with graffiti-covered walls). Using an implicit cognition measure, they found more positive associations to the Black men depicted in positive contexts and more negative association to the Black men depicted in negative contexts. Why? Stangor and his colleagues (1992) found that categorization (and therefore stereotype activation) generally occurs at the subtype level (for example, *Black athlete*) rather than the more general category level (such as *Black person*). In the studies Wittenbrink and his colleagues conducted, the different contexts probably led to categorization in terms of different subtypes: *family man* and *churchgoer* versus *gang member* and *ghetto Black* (see Devine & Baker, 1991, for examples of White Americans' subtypes of African Americans). Context can therefore influence which aspect of a stereotype becomes activated.

Prejudice   Just as prejudice can facilitate the categorization process, it can facilitate stereotype activation. For example, several groups of researchers have found positive correlations between level of prejudice and a tendency to attribute

4.2   *Is Categorization Necessary for Stereotype Activation?*

Theorists and researchers have generally assumed that stereotype activation is a three-step process:

- An observer notices characteristics of a target person (such as skin tone, facial features, and so forth) that indicate the target person's membership in a social category (such as *Black person*).
- The observer categorizes the target person on the basis of those characteristics.
- Placing the target person into a category activates the stereotype associated with that category.

However, several groups of researchers (Blair et al., 2002; Livingston & Brewer, 2002; Maddox & Gray, 2002) have recently challenged this assumption, proposing that a target person's characteristics can activate a stereotype independent of categorization. They pointed out that within the category of *African American*, individuals' experiences of prejudice and discrimination vary as function of the prototypicality of their features. For example, compared to more prototypically appearing African Americans their less prototypically appearing peers have better jobs and higher incomes, even given the same level of education and experience (Hill, 2000) and report having had experienced less discrimination (Klonoff & Landrine, 2000). Consistent with the prototypicality hypothesis, these researchers have shown that more prototypically African Black people are negatively stereotyped to a greater degree (Blair et al., 2002; Maddox et al., 2002) and arouse more negative emotion (Livingston & Brewer, 2002). In addition, Blair and her

colleagues showed that prototypicality increased stereotype activation over and above the effects of categorization. Thus, even if the target persons in these studies had not been categorized as *Black*, negative stereotypes and negative emotions would have been activated.

Why do prototypical features activate stereotypes? Researchers have proposed three possible reasons. First, as Blair and her colleagues (2002) note, prototypical characteristics define group membership and are the main bases for categorization. To some extent, the prototype and the category are the same thing: "An African American [the category] is a person with dark skin, coarse hair, and a wide nose [the prototype], and a person with those features is an African American, regardless of actual ancestry" (Blair et al., 2002, p. 6).

Second, Blair and her colleagues (2002) and Livingston and Brewer (2002) suggest that people are conditioned through cultural experiences to associate prototypically African features with negative traits. For example, in the media highly prototypically appearing Black people are likely to be portrayed in negative ways, whereas less prototypically appearing Black people are likely to be portrayed in positive ways (Russell, Wilson, & Hall, 1992). As a result, "dark skin [the prototype] signals not only that a target is African American but also that he or she is likely to be lazy and musical [the stereotype]" (Blair et al., 2002, p. 6). This kind of cultural conditioning may be the reason why, as noted in the text, Maddox and Gray (2002) found that both Black and White research participants associated more stereotypical characteristics with darker-skinned Black people.

(continues)

Is Categorization Necessary for Stereotype Activation? (continued)

Finally, Livingston and Brewer (2002) note that unfamiliarity leads to anxiety and other negative emotions. Because light-colored skin and European facial features are more familiar to White Americans than dark-colored skin and African features, unfamiliarity may lead White Americans to experience negative emotions in response to prototypically African features.

The results of these studies indicate, then, that "when a perceiver makes a judgment on the basis of physical appearance, the target's race-related features may influence that judgment in two ways. First, those features provide the basis for racial categorization, which results in the activation of related stereotypes. Second, those features may directly activate the stereotypic traits. . . . The two processes occur independently and . . . either one is sufficient to result in the attribution of stereotypic traits" (Blair et al., 2002, p. 22).

stereotypic traits to people of African descent (Kawakami, Dion, & Dovidio, 1998; Lepore & Brown, 1997; Wittenbrink, Judd, & Park, 1997). The generality of this tendency is shown by the fact that each of these research groups worked in a different country: Canada, Great Britain, and the United States, respectively. Lorella Lepore and Rupert Brown (1997) also found that compared to people high in prejudice, those low in prejudice were more likely to associate counterstereotypic traits with Black people.

Why does this relationship between level of prejudice and stereotype activation exist? Recall that automatic stereotype activation is believed to occur because of well-learned associations between a category and the stereotypes associated with that category (Fazio, 2001). Kawakami and her colleagues (1998) have suggested that compared to less prejudiced people, more prejudiced people develop stronger associations between stereotypes and categories: "Because high prejudiced people use stereotypes more consistently, engage in repeated activation of stereotypes, and attribute stereotypes more extremely to category members, they may develop associations that are highly accessible [that is, easy to activate] and of sufficient strength to produce automatic activation. . . . Because low prejudiced people engage in less stereotyping in general and attribute stereotypes less extremely to group members, they may develop weaker associations that are less accessible, or even develop [counterstereotypic] associations. . . . These individuals are therefore less likely to activate cultural stereotypes automatically" (p. 414). As Lepore and Brown (1997) put it, "Faced with a member of the stereotyped group . . . people seem to react automatically *according to the representation they have in mind*" (p. 285; emphasis in original). If that representation is negative, negative traits and emotions are activated; if that representation is positive, positive traits and emotions are activated.

Cognitive busyness   Because stereotypes consist of people's mental representations of groups, before they can be used they must be retrieved from long-term memory where they are stored when not in use and brought into working memory. One implication of this process is that if working memory is in use, stereotype activation can be disrupted because little space is left in working memory for stereotypic information (Gilbert & Hixon, 1991; Spencer et al., 1998).

In a classic study of this effect, Daniel Gilbert and Gregory Hixon (1991) had White research participants watch a videotape in which either an Asian or White research assistant showed them a card containing a word with one letter omitted. The participants had 15 seconds to generate as many words as possible based each word fragment. Five of the word fragments could be completed either as words that stereotypically describe Asians or as nonstereotypic words. For example, *RI_E* could be completed as either the stereotypic *rice* or the nonstereotypic *ripe*. Gilbert and Hixon hypothesized that, if participants' working memories were not in use, seeing the Asian assistant would activate the Asian stereotype and lead to more stereotypic word completions; however, if working memory was in use, there would be little room for the stereotype so it would not be activated. Therefore, half the participants who saw each research assistant had their working memory capacity reduced by mentally rehearsing an 8-digit number while watching the videotape (a situation known as *cognitive busyness:* people are busy with one mental task while trying to do another). The researchers found that, of the participants who saw the Asian research assistant, those who were cognitively busy completed fewer words in a stereotypic manner than those who were not. Participants who saw the White research assistant made the same number of stereotypic word completions in both the busy and nonbusy conditions. Thus, seeing the Asian research assistant activated the Asian stereotype for people who were not cognitively busy but not for those who were cognitively busy. In a similar study, Steven Spencer and his colleagues (1998) showed that cognitive busyness can inhibit activation of the Black stereotype as well as the Asian stereotype.

The role of working memory in this process was shown by experiments conducted by Christian Wheeler, Blair Jarvis, and Richard Petty (2001), who found that stereotype activation could disrupt problem solving. They had White research participants write an essay about a day in the life of a college student named either Tyrone (a stereotypically Black name) or Erik (a stereotypically White name). The researchers assessed stereotype activation in terms of whether the essays contained stereotypes of African Americans; 64 percent of the essays by participants who wrote about Tyrone contained stereotypic content, indicating that the Black stereotype had been activated for them, compared to 11 percent of the essays written about Erik. After writing their essays, participants took a difficult math test, a task that requires effective use of working memory. Participants for whom the Black stereotype had been activated solved fewer problems than either those who wrote about Tyrone without having the stereotype activated or those who wrote about Erik. These findings show that stereotype activation uses up working memory capacity; therefore, when working memory is already in use, as in Gilbert and Hixon's (1991) and Spencer and colleagues' (1998) studies, little capacity is left for stereotypes, resulting in a disruption of stereotype activation.

Motivated Activation

Although clear evidence shows that stereotypes are activated automatically, other evidence shows that people's motivations and goals can facilitate or inhibit stereotype activation (Blair, 2002; Kunda & Spencer, 2003). That is, people have goals they want to achieve in various social settings and "when stereotype application can help satisfy such goals, stereotypes are activated for that purpose. But when stereotype application can disrupt goal satisfaction, stereotype activation is inhibited to prevent such application" (Kunda & Spencer, 2003, p. 524). Although a number of motives have the potential to affect stereotype activation (see, for example, Fiske, 2003), we focus on four broad categories (Blair, 2002; Kunda & Spencer, 2003): comprehension goals, self-enhancement goals, social adjustment goals, and motivation to avoid prejudice. These goals can stem from individual differences, situational factors, or both. For example, individual differences in self-enhancement motivation can be seen when one person feels a continuing need to see him- or herself as better than others while another person does not. As an example of situational influences on self-enhancement motivation, people tend to feel a need to enhance their self-images after experiencing failure (see, for example, Fein & Spencer, 1997). It is important to bear in mind that more than one goal may be operating in any situation. As a result, two goals can reinforce each other if both motivate either stereotype activation or inhibition, but can offset each other if one goal motivates stereotype activation while the other motivates stereotype inhibition.

Comprehension   Comprehension goals stem from people's needs to form clear impressions of what others are like and to understand why events happen. Clear understanding of people and events makes the world more predictable, which, in turn, contributes to a feeling of security (see, for example, Kunda, 1999): If one understands how other people will react to events and understands the causes of events, then one can determine how to act effectively to avoid problems and achieve desired ends. Stereotypes contribute to these goals by providing a framework for accomplishing them. For example, in a study conducted by Etsuko Hoshino-Browne and Ziva Kunda (described in Kunda, Davies, Hoshino-Browne, & Jordan, 2003), an Asian confederate who asked questions unrelated to race interviewed White participants. Half of the participants formed an impression of the interviewer's personality and likely career choice; this task set up a comprehension goal—understanding what the other person was like. The other participants focused on the topics the interviewer had asked about; this task should have set no comprehension goals relative to the interviewer. The researchers found that the Asian stereotype was more strongly activated for the participants who had been motivated to understand what the interviewer was like, probably because stereotypic information would help them form an impression of the interviewer.

Another type of comprehension goal is understanding why people behave the way they do. For example, Ziva Kunda and her colleagues (Kunda, Davies, Adams, & Spencer, 2002) had White research participants take part in a simulated jury study in which they decided whether a criminal defendant was guilty or not guilty. They then watched a videotape of a Black student who had supposedly previously taken part in the same study. During the first part of the videotape, the student was interviewed about his impressions of the university where the research took place; the student then gave his opinion of the case, which either agreed or disagreed with that of the participant watching the tape. The participants then took an implicit cognition test of stereotyping. The researchers found that the Black stereotype was more strongly activated for the participants who saw a Black person who disagreed, rather than agreed, with them. Kunda and her colleagues explained that the stereotype was activated more strongly in the first case because people want to understand why others disagree with them. People often assume that members of other groups hold opinions that differ from their own (Miller & Prentice, 1999), so seeing the Black student in terms of his racial group rather than as an individual would help explain the disagreement.

Self-enhancement Self-enhancement goals stem from people's need to see themselves in a positive light. Stereotypes, especially negative stereotypes, can help people achieve this goal because seeing others in a negative light can make oneself look better by comparison (Fein, Hoshino-Browne, Davies, & Spencer, 2003). For example, Lisa Sinclair and Ziva Kunda (1999) had White research participants take what was portrayed as a measure of interpersonal skills. They then received either positive or negative feedback on the test results from either a Black man or a White man. Sinclair and Kunda found that negative stereotypes were activated when the Black man provided negative feedback but not when he provided positive feedback. Similar effects have been found for stereotypes of Asians (Spencer et al., 1998), gay men (Fein et al., 2003), and women (Sinclair & Kunda, 2000). The role of self-enhancement in this process is shown by Sinclair and Kunda's (1999) finding that their participants felt less badly about themselves after receiving negative feedback from the Black evaluator than they did after receiving negative feedback from the White evaluator. Being able to call to mind a stereotype that would make the evaluator look less competent (that is, the negative Black stereotype) seemed to lessen the effect of the negative feedback and so helped the participants maintain a positive self-image.

Based on the idea that stereotyping can help people maintain a positive self-image, Sinclair and Kunda (1999) hypothesized that in addition to activating negative stereotypes, negative feedback would inhibit positive stereotypes; conversely, they hypothesized that positive feedback would activate positive stereotypes and inhibit negative stereotypes. This is the pattern of results they found in a study in which participants received feedback from a Black or White physician: When the Black physician provided negative feedback, the negative Black stereotype was activated and the positive physician stereotype was inhibited; that is, participants tended to think of their evaluator as Black rather than as a physician. However, when the Black physician provided positive feedback, the physician stereotype was activated and the Black stereotype was inhibited; that is, participants tended to think of their evaluator as a physician rather than as a Black man. Sinclair and Kunda suggested that this second effect occurred because thinking of the evaluator in terms of the negative Black stereotype would undercut the value of the praise, whereas thinking of the evaluator in terms of the positive physician stereo-type would enhance the value of the praise.

Social adjustment Social adjustment motives reflect people's desire to adjust their behavior to fit into situations and adhere to the norms or rules of behavior for that setting (Blair, 2002). As a general example, people may behave and speak one way when discussing a topic with their friends but act very differently when discussing the topic with their parents. In the context of prejudice, social adjustment motives can explain the finding that White people are less likely to express preju-diced attitudes to a Black interviewer than to a White interviewer (see, for example, Schuman, Steeh, Bobo, & Krysan, 1997): Because social rules say that one should try to avoid offending others, White people generally moderate their expressed racial attitudes when talking with Black people. Brian Lowery, Curtis Hardin, and Stacey Sinclair (2001) examined whether this kind of motivation affects stereotype activation. Either a Black or a White experimenter asked White research partici-pants to complete implicit cognition measures of stereotyping of African Americans. Lowery and his colleagues found less stereotype activation when the experimenter was a Black woman than when she was a White woman, indicating that the social norm of not offending others is so strong that it can inhibit stereotype activation.

Another type of social adjustment motive is the desire to fit in with one's peers. Fein and his colleagues (2003) showed research participants a videotape of an actual campus panel discussion on gay rights that was edited to give either the impression that most students supported gay rights or that most opposed gay rights. Scores on an implicit cognition measure of stereotype activation indicated that exposure to anti-gay-rights norms activated the gay stereotype, whereas expo-sure to pro-gay-rights norms inhibited the stereotype.

Motivation to avoid prejudice As we discuss in greater detail in Chapter 5, prejudice is generally considered to be a negative trait; as a result, people want to avoid acting in a prejudiced manner. This desire can arise either because prejudice is contrary to their personal values or because they do not want other people to think of them as prejudiced, and is stronger in some people than in others (Dunton & Fazio, 1997; Plant & Devine, 1998). A motivation to avoid prejudice, especially one that is based on personal standards rather than external pressure, can therefore help inhibit the activation of stereotypes. For example, Gordon Moskowitz and his colleagues (Moskowitz, Gollwitzer, Wasel, & Schaal, 1999; Moskowitz, Salomon, & Taylor, 2000) postulated that some people hold strong, long-term beliefs in equality, which they call *chronic egalitarian goals*. Moskowitz and his colleagues reasoned that these goals are constantly, although not always consciously, operating for people who hold them. They further reasoned that because stereotyping others would violate these strong egalitarian standards, people with chronic egalitarian goals should exhibit less stereo-type activation than people without such goals. This outcome is precisely what they found using stereotypes of women and of African Americans. Similarly, Patricia Devine and her colleagues (Devine, Plant, Amodio, Harmon-Jones, & Vance, 2002) found that people who had a motivation to avoid prejudice that was based on strong internal standards showed less stereotype activation than other people. We discuss motivation to avoid prejudice in more detail in Chapter 10.

Stereotype relevance   Although stereotypes can help people fulfill needs such as comprehension and self-enhancement, they can do so only if the content of the stereotype is relevant to the particular goal at hand. That is, even if a need is present while a person is interacting with a member of a stereotyped group, it may not influence stereotype activation or inhibition if the nature of the stereotype does not help to fulfill the need. For example, as Kunda and Spencer (2003) note, people may activate and use the stereotype of Asian Americans as interested in science to predict an Asian student's major because an interest in science is relevant to that goal but are unlikely to use the stereotype of fat people when making the same prediction for a fat student because the stereotype of fat people does not include academic interests.

The Activated Stereotype

Although we have discussed automatic and motivated activation of stereotypes separately, the two processes operate simultaneously and so jointly affect the degree to which a stereotype is activated or inhibited (Kunda & Spencer, 2003). For example, we saw how cognitive busyness can inhibit stereotype activation. However, if a motive is strong enough, it can overcome this automatic inhibition process. Thus, Spencer and his colleagues (1998) found that a self-image threat could activate both the Asian and Black stereotype even when research participants were cognitively busy. Similarly, we saw that prejudice facilitates stereotype activation. However, Sinclair and Kunda (1999) found that an experience that enhanced participants' self-image—praise from a Black physician—inhibited the activation of the Black stereotype even in prejudiced people. Thus, in any situation, multiple motives might be in play whose effects can either reinforce or offset one another (Kunda & Spencer, 2003). One consequence of these multiple simultaneous processes is that in practice it might be very difficult to predict whether a stereotype, or which stereotype, might be activated in any given situation.

One factor that might affect the activated stereotype is the mood a person is in when the stereotype is activated. For example, Victoria Esses and Mark Zanna (1995) found that, compared to people in positive or neutral moods, those in negative moods saw negative stereotypic characteristics as more negative. For example, *aggressive,* when associated with Arabs, was seen as a more negative trait by people in a negative mood than by people in a positive mood. Esses and Zanna concluded that mood affects how people interpret characteristics ascribed to negatively stereotyped groups. "For example, when someone who is in a negative mood says that members of one of these groups are 'religious,' the person might conjure up images of religious wars and fanaticism rather than images of members of the group at prayer" (Esses & Zanna, 1995, p. 1065).

A question that researchers have just begun to ask is once a stereotype is activated, how long does it stay active? Ziva Kunda and her colleagues (2002) found the answer to this question: not very long. The stereotypes they activated dissipated within 12 minutes of activation. They suggest that this decay occurs because during an interaction with a member of a stereotyped group, "as time unfolds, one's attention shifts from the person's category membership to individuating information [which leads one to see other people as individuals rather than in stereotypic terms] or to the demands of the tasks at hand" (Kunda et al., 2002, p. 528). However, Kunda and her colleagues also found that a dissipated stereotype could be reactivated quite easily, such as by a minor disagreement with the other person. Therefore, even though stereotypes can fade over time, incidents might occur during an interaction that reactivate the stereotype.

STEREOTYPE APPLICATION

Once a stereotype has been activated, it is available for use; the more strongly a stereotype has been activated, the more likely it is that it will be used as a lens through which to view members of the stereotyped group (Fein et al., 2003; Sinclair & Kunda, 1999). However, stereotype application is not inevitable; given the right circumstances, people can, consciously or unconsciously, inhibit the application of a stereotype. As shown in Figure 4.2, inhibition of an activated stereotype is a two-step process (Fazio & Towles-Schwen, 1999). The person must first be motivated to inhibit the stereotype. If the person is not motivated to inhibit the stereotype, it will be applied. However, even if a person is so motivated, she or he might not be able to do so. For example, some behaviors, such as verbal behaviors, are easy to control whereas others, such as nonverbal behaviors, are difficult to control. Therefore, a person might be motivated to control the application of stereotype and successfully do so with verbal behavior, such as by speaking politely to a member of a negatively stereotyped group, but not be able to control nonverbal indicators of dislike, such as avoiding eye contact with the other person (see, for example, Dovidio, 2001). Therefore, a person is likely to inhibit the application of a stereotype only if he or she is both motivated to do so *and* is able to do so. Another way of looking at stereotype application is that it is the default option: Unless the person is motivated to inhibit a stereotype and is able to do so, stereotype activation leads to stereotype application (Bodenhausen et al., 1999). Bear in mind, however, that, as shown at the top of Figure 4.2, a stereotype that has not been activated cannot be applied.

Motivation to Inhibit Stereotyping

A number of factors can motivate people to inhibit the application of stereotypes or, conversely, can undermine that motivation. Some of these factors, such as motivation to control prejudice, comprehension goals, and self-enhancement goals are similar to those that influence stereotype activation. Others, such as cognitive style and social power, may be more specific to stereotype application.

Motivation to control prejudice   As we noted while discussing stereotype activation, most people are motivated to avoid acting in a prejudiced manner. This motivation includes a desire not to view or respond to other people on the basis of stereotypes (Darley & Gross, 1983; Yzerbyt, Schadron, Leyens, & Rocher, 1994). Consequently, people try to avoid using stereotypes and experience negative

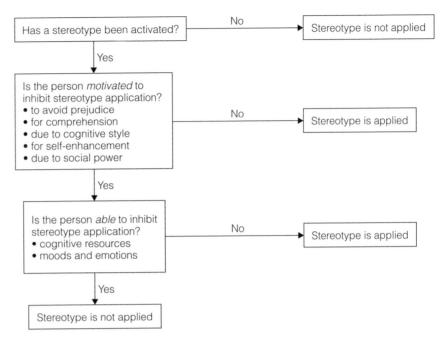

FIGURE **4.2**

STEREOTYPE APPLICATION

Stereotype application is likely to occur automatically after stereotype activation unless both of two conditions apply: The person must be motivated to inhibit the stereotype, and the person must be able to inhibit the stereotype. If either of these conditions is absent, the activated stereotype will be applied. (Adapted from Fazio & Towles-Schwen's, 1999, model of the attitude-behavior relationship)

feelings about themselves when they view others in stereotypic terms (Monteith & Voils, 1998; Monteith, Ashburn-Nardo, Voils, & Czopp, 2002). The more motivated people are to avoid prejudice, the less they use stereotypes. For example, Ashby Plant and Patricia Devine (1998) measured White research participants' personal commitment to avoid prejudice and assessed the extent to which they viewed African Americans in stereotypic terms. They found that personally committed participants were less likely to apply stereotypes not only when they had to respond publicly and so could be exhibiting a social desirability response bias (see Chapter 2) but also when they responded anonymously and so were more likely to be giving their true opinions (see also Plant, Devine, & Brazy, 2003). Not surprisingly, more highly prejudiced people are less motivated to avoid prejudice (Plant & Devine, 1998) and so are more likely to apply stereotypes in their dealings with others (Brown, Croizet, Bohner, Fournet, & Payne, 2003; Kawakami et al., 1998; Lepore & Brown, 1997). Most people are probably motivated to avoid prejudice to some degree, if for no other reason than to avoid the negative feedback from others that prejudiced behavior is likely to entail (Dunton & Fazio, 1997; Plant & Devine,

1998). However, some prejudices (such as those concerning fat people) and their associated stereotypes are more socially acceptable than others (Crandall, Eshleman, & O'Brien, 2002); motivation to control prejudice is less likely to inhibit stereotyping in those cases.

Controlling one's stereotypes requires substantial mental work. For example, during interactions with members of stereotyped groups, people may try to intentionally force stereotypic thoughts from their minds, to seek out more information about the person that goes beyond the content of the stereotype, or to replace a prejudiced response with a nonprejudiced one (Devine & Monteith, 1999). Because of the effort required to control stereotype application, people's attempts to avoid stereotyping can be either helped or hindered by other goals and motives that encourage or discourage engaging in the required mental effort (Kunda & Spencer, 2003).

Comprehension goals   The goals people have when they interact with others also influence stereotype activation. For example, during interactions people are generally motivated to form what they believe to be accurate impressions of those other people. This desire for accuracy exists because having a correct picture of what others are like allows people to interact effectively with them (Kunda, 1999): Without having any idea what the other person was like, people would always be uncertain about how to interact with him or her. For example, a person would constantly have to be concerned about whether she would do or say something that would offend the other person. However, if a person is confident that she knows what the other person is like, she can avoid behaviors she believes to be problematic.

Because of this desire to be accurate, generally people prefer to use **individuating information** when judging others, that is, information that is specific to the person, regardless of whether it is stereotypic to the person's group. For example, "perceivers may expect Tom to be more assertive than Nancy if they know only their names, that is, they apply gender stereotypes to these individuals. However, if they know that Tom and Nancy performed an assertive behavior such as interrupting someone, perceivers view them as equally assertive; they no longer apply the gender stereotypes, basing their judgments instead entirely on the individuals' behavior" (Kunda & Spencer, 2003, p. 538). Ziva Kunda and Paul Thagard (1996) calculated that individuating information carries about four times the weight of stereotypes when people make judgments about others. This preference for individuating information may be one reason why stereotype activation dissipates over the course of an interaction (Kunda et al., 2002): the interaction provides individuating information about the other person that replaces stereotypic information.

However, people do not always seek out individuating information about others. People tend to be, in Shelley Taylor's term, *cognitive misers* (Fiske & Taylor, 1984). That is, unless motivated to do otherwise, people conserve their mental resources and do not exert the cognitive effort required to seek out individuating information about others. One important motivator of individuation is the degree to which the other person is relevant to the perceiver (Brewer & Feinstein, 1999;

Fiske et al., 1999). The more relevant the other person is to the perceiver's life, the more the perceiver is motivated to individuate the person. Thus, people develop very detailed, individualized impressions of people who are close to them, such as family members, close friends, and romantic partners. These individualized impressions facilitate interpersonal relations by allowing people to anticipate how another person will act and how he or she will respond to their actions. People also tend to individuate those who control rewards they desire because an accurate, individualized impression allows them to act in ways that will please the power holder and so induce him or her to reward them. Thus, as we will discuss in more detail shortly, subordinates tend to develop individualized impressions of their supervisors whereas supervisors often do not develop individualized impressions of their subordinates (Goodwin, Gubin, Fiske, & Yzerbyt, 2000; Stevens & Fiske, 2000).

Individuating information does not totally do away with the influence of stereotypes; people still rely on them to some degree (Nelson, Acker, & Manis, 1996). For example, Galen Bodenhausen and Robert Wyer (1985) had research participants read about a crime that was either stereotypic or nonstereotypic of the offender's ethnic group. The case description also included information about the offender's background that could explain his behavior. When participants rated the likelihood of the offender's committing the same offense again, they rated the stereotypic offense to be more likely to be repeated than the nonstereotypic offense. Thus, stereotypes influenced participants' behavior despite the fact that they received information about the offender that bore on his specific likelihood of reoffending.

Stereotypes may continue to function in the face of individuating information for at least two reasons. First, people tend to avoid seeking out new information about members of stereotyped groups and the information they do seek out tends to support the stereotype. For example, Yaacov Trope and Erik Thompson (1997) examined the amount and type of information research participants would seek from an American Jew or a feminist about their views on U.S. support for Israel or support for passage of a constitutional amendment guaranteeing equal rights for women (the ERA). Pretesting showed that support for Israel was stereotypically associated with American Jews but that support for the ERA was not, whereas support for the ERA was stereotypically associated with feminists but not with American Jews. Participants wrote up to five questions that would help them determine someone's attitudes toward a political issue without directly asking. For half the participants the issue was U.S. support for Israel; for the other half it was support for the ERA. The participants then wrote questions about the issue directed to an American Jew and to a feminist. Trope and Thompson found that participants asked fewer questions of the person who was stereotypically associated with the political issue. Apparently, the participants assumed they already knew that person's position and so had no need to ask for more information that would get at the person's individual attitude. Trope and Thompson also found that participants were more likely to ask stereotyped group members stereotype-confirming questions. For example, they were more likely to ask an American Jew a question such as "Do you believe there should be an independent Jewish state?" and more

likely to ask a feminist a question such as "Do you think that current laws sufficiently protect women's rights?"

Second, stereotypes may continue to function despite individuating information because they can affect how people interpret individuating information. For
example, Ziva Kunda and Bonnie Sherman-Williams (1993) gave research participants information about either a construction worker (a group stereotypically high
on aggression) or a housewife (a group stereotypically low on aggression).
Participants were told that the person they read about had engaged in an ambiguously aggressive behavior (hitting someone who had annoyed him or her), an
unambiguously high aggressive behavior (violently hitting someone who had
taunted him or her), or an unambiguously low aggressive behavior (spanking his
or her misbehaving child but then regretting it and comforting the child). Kunda
and Sherman-Williams found that in the high aggression condition, participants
rated both the construction worker and the housewife as being high on aggression
and that in the low aggression condition, participants rated both the construction
worker and the housewife as being low on aggression; that is, the individuating
information overrode the stereotype. However, in the ambiguous aggression condition, the construction worker was rated as being more aggressive than the housewife. That is, the stereotype affected how participants interpreted the
individuating information: an ambiguously aggressive behavior is considered
indicative of generally low aggression if performed by someone stereotypically
low on aggression, but is considered indicative of generally high aggression if performed by someone stereotypically high on aggression. Therefore, one reason
why stereotypes can be influential in the face of individuating information is
because the stereotype can affect the interpretation of that information as being
stereotype consistent (see also Dunning & Sherman, 1997; Kunda, Sinclair, &
Griffin, 1997).

Thus, although people have a general preference for individuating information, they still often rely on stereotypes in making judgments, especially when
they first meet someone or interact with the other person only infrequently
(Brewer & Feinstein, 1999; Fiske et al., 1999). People may need external motivation to ignore stereotypes; accuracy and accountability are two such motives. For
example, simply telling people to make an accurate judgment reduces reliance on
stereotypes (Neuberg, 1989; Neuberg & Fiske, 1987). This reduced reliance on
stereotypes occurs because accuracy motivation leads people to seek out individuating information about the other person (Neuberg, 1989).

Another means of motivating people to make accurate judgments is to hold
them accountable for their decisions. For example, Gifford Weary and her colleagues (Weary, Jacobson, Edwards, & Tobin, 2001) had student research participants judge a case of academic dishonesty in which the accused was either a
member or not a member of a group stereotypically associated with cheating (athletes). Weary and her colleagues found that participants who thought they were
not accountable for their decisions judged the athlete more harshly than the
nonathlete, but that accountable participants were not influenced by the accused's
group membership. Holding people accountable for their decisions probably
motivates a desire for accuracy because people like to see themselves as accurate

judges of what others are like and because making mistakes would lead others to see them as incompetent (Lerner & Tetlock, 1999). In fact, the effect of accountability in inhibiting stereotype use is strong enough to overcome the effects of other factors that facilitate stereotype use (see, for example, Bodenhausen, Kramer, & Süsser, 1994; Bodenhausen, Sheppard & Kramer, 1994). It is important to bear in mind that in many everyday settings, people are accountable for the decisions they make about others, so accountability motivation may attenuate the influence of stereotypes in many situations.

Cognitive style   Individual differences in people's motivation to acquire and use information are called *cognitive styles*. These individual differences can affect stereotype use. For example, people high on the trait of *need for cognition* (Cacioppo, Petty, Feinstein, & Jarvis, 1996) generally like to think about things carefully and consider all options when making a decision even when there is no particular reason to do so. People low on the trait carefully think about things only if they have a reason to do so; otherwise, they prefer to make judgments based on simple rules. Because of this preference for simple rules, people low in need for cognition tend to depend more on stereotypes in making judgments than do people high in need for cognition (Crawford & Skowronski, 1998; Florack, Scarabis, & Bless, 2001); stereotypes present simple ways of judging people without having to exert the mental effort of looking for and thinking about individuating information. In contrast, people high on need for cognition *like* exerting that kind of effort and do so.

Another cognitive style variable is *causal uncertainty* (Weary & Edwards, 1994). The concept of causal uncertainty is based on people's need to accurately understand how the world and other people operate. People low in causal uncertainty feel sure that they have an accurate understanding of the world and other people and so feel little need to look for more information. People high in causal uncertainty have no such feeling of sureness and so are always on the lookout for more information. When dealing with people, this desire for more information leads to a search for individuating information; as a result, people high on causal uncertainty use stereotypes less than do people low on the trait (Weary et al., 2001). Although need for cognition and causal uncertainty both reflect people's orientation toward information (Edwards, Weary, & Reich, 1998), they represent different stages in the information utilization process: Causal uncertainty affects people's search for information whereas need for cognition affects how people use information.

A final type of cognitive style is *need for closure*, also called *need for structure* (Kruglanski & Webster, 1996). People high in need for closure prefer simple, definite answers to questions and dislike ambiguity and uncertainty. Because stereotypes represent simple, definite answers to the question of what people are like, people high on need for closure make more use of stereotypes than do people low on the trait (Dijksterhuis, van Knippenberg, Kruglanski, & Schaper, 1996; Neuberg & Newsom, 1993). Like need for cognition and causal uncertainty, need for closure reflects an orientation toward information, but it is unrelated to the other two (Edwards et al., 1998; Neuberg & Newsom, 1993). Whereas causal uncertainty affects people's search for information and need for cognition affects how people use information, need for closure affects how much information people look for: People high on need for closure stop looking for information when they feel they have an answer to a question (even though it might not be the best answer) and are reluctant to consider new information once they have decided on an answer (Kruglanski & Webster, 1996). Because need for cognition, causal uncertainty, and need for closure have little relation to one another, they operate independently. For example, at the same time that high need for cognition and causal uncertainty are motivating a person to avoid stereotype use, high need for closure could be motivating the same person toward stereotype use. Various combinations of different levels of the traits could therefore either reinforce or offset each other's influence on stereotype use.

Self-enhancement goals   Just as threats to self-esteem can facilitate the *activation* of stereotypes (Spencer et al., 1998), they can facilitate the *application* of stereotypes. For example, Lisa Sinclair and Ziva Kunda (2000) examined college students' reactions to having received a high or low grade from a male or female instructor. Because female college professors are stereotyped as less competent than male instructors (Basow, 1995), Sinclair and Kunda expected students who received a low grade from a female instructor to give more negative (that is, more stereotypical) instructor evaluations than students who received a low grade from a male instructor. The researchers surveyed students about the courses they had taken the previous semester, asking them to report the grade they received in the course and to evaluate the instructor on a scale raging from 0 (*very poor*) to 100 (*excellent*). Not surprisingly, students who received lower grades gave lower instructor evaluations; however, the difference was larger for female instructors. Experimental research has found similar increased stereotyping following negative feedback from women (Sinclair & Kunda, 2000) and gay men (Fein & Spencer, 1997). Furthermore, Steven Fein and Steven Spencer (1997) showed that when participants received negative feedback from a member of a stereotyped group, the amount of stereotyping was correlated with increases in self-esteem. These results indicate that stereotyping functions to maintain self-esteem, probably because seeing an evaluator in negatively stereotyped terms helps one to dismiss the negative evaluation as unimportant: If the evaluator is seen as incompetent, then the evaluation is meaningless and so can be ignored.

If self-image threats facilitate stereotype application, what happens if positive aspects of the self-image are reinforced? Fein and Spencer (1997) examined this question by having some research participants write about a value, such as maintaining good interpersonal relations or pursuit of knowledge, that was important to them personally; other participants wrote about why the value might be important to other people. Fein and Spencer hypothesized that writing about a value that was personally important would reinforce those participants' positive self-images and so reduce their likelihood of using stereotypes. After writing about the value, participants evaluated a job candidate from a group with a strong negative stereotype. Fein and Spencer found that the participants who had had a positive aspect of their self-images reinforced viewed the candidate in less stereotypic terms than did the participants whose positive self-images were not reinforced. Thus, although attacking a person's self-image can facilitate stereotyping, reinforcing a positive self-image can inhibit stereotyping.

Social power   Susan Fiske and her colleagues (Fiske, 1993; Goodwin & Fiske, 1996; Goodwin et al., 2000) have postulated that having power over others, especially the power to control the rewards and punishments that others receive, facilitates stereotyping of the people subject to that power. For example, Stephanie Goodwin and her colleagues (2000) randomly assigned college student research participants to a high or low power role in evaluating a Hispanic high school student applying for a summer program. The researchers found that, compared to the low power participants, those with high power were more likely to view the applicant in stereotypic terms. Other studies have confirmed this power-leads-to-stereotype-use effect in a number of contexts (Goodwin et al., 2000) and for implicit as well as explicit stereotypes (Richeson & Ambady, 2003).

Goodwin and Fiske (1996) have suggested that several factors influence the use of stereotypes by powerful people. First, because of their positions in social hierarchies such as formal organizations, powerful people are entitled to judge others and are often required to. This feeling of entitlement to judge leads to overconfidence in the accuracy of simple belief systems such as stereotypes, and belief in their accuracy leads to their use. Second, powerful people are motivated to maintain the power difference between themselves and those under them because higher power provides benefits such as higher pay and status. Stereotypes of subordinate groups, especially negative stereotypes, help power holders justify their positions in the social structure by portraying subordinates as being suited only to low power positions because they are incapable of doing higher-level work. Finally, people in power may stereotype subordinates because they have no motivation to individuate them. Recall that one factor that motivates individuation is depending on the other person for rewards. However, power holders are in the opposite position: others depend on them for rewards. As a result, power holders do not look for individuating information about subordinates and stereotype them by default, having no motivation to do otherwise. Not surprisingly, then, because low power people depend on high power people for rewards, low power people tend to individuate, rather than stereotype, the people who have power over them (Stevens & Fiske, 2000). As Laura Stevens and Susan Fiske (2000) note, forming individualized (that is, nonstereotypic) impressions of powerful people allows low power people to indirectly control the rewards they get by accurately anticipating what the powerful people want and helping them get it.

However, stereotyping by power holders is not inevitable. For example, Theresa Vescio, Mark Snyder, and David Butz (2003) found that power holders only use stereotypes that are relevant to the decisions they have to make. They hypothesized that, because of either individual differences or situational influences, some power holders are weakness oriented whereas others are strength oriented. Weakness-oriented power holders are motivated to avoid failure and so view subordinates in stereotypic terms when stereotypes indicate that the subordinates might not have the capabilities to do a task. The stereotype is then used as a justification for not allowing the subordinate to attempt the task. In contrast, strength-oriented power holders are motivated to achieve success and so view subordinates in stereotypic terms when stereotypes indicate that the subordinates do have the capabilities to do a task. Vescio and her colleagues had research participants select questions from a list to be used in interviewing female applicants for a stereotypically masculine job. As the researchers had theorized, compared to strength-oriented participants, those with a weakness orientation chose more questions designed to elicit weakness on the task, such as "Tell me about a time you struggled to complete a task involving spatial skills" and fewer questions designed to elicit strengths, such as "Tell me about a time when you completed a challenging mental problem and felt proud of your logic and reasoning skills." Thus, power holders may only stereotype subordinates when those stereotypes are both relevant to the task at hand and consistent with the power holder's strength- or weakness-oriented approach to problem solving.

In addition, power holders can inhibit stereotype use when they are motivated to do so. For example, Vescio and her colleagues (2003) found that power holders' stereotype use disappeared when receiving a reward depended on their subordinates' task performance. Because receiving the reward now depended on accurately assessing subordinate characteristics, power holders focused on individuating information about subordinates rather than stereotypic information regardless of being strength or weakness oriented. Power holders also individuate subordinates when they are motivated to feel responsible for their subordinates' outcomes (Goodwin & Fiske, 1996) or motivated to help subordinates with problems they are having (Overbeck & Park, 2001). Therefore, by appropriately motivating people who are in positions of power, organizations can reduce power holders' use of stereotypes (Goodwin & Fiske, 1996).

Ability to Inhibit Stereotyping

Although a person may be motivated to inhibit stereotype application, he or she may not be able to. A number of factors—including lack of cognitive resources, emotional states, and the low controllability of some behaviors—can interfere with the person's opportunity to inhibit stereotype application.

Cognitive resources   Earlier, we described how Daniel Gilbert and Gregory Hixon (1991) showed that cognitive busyness could prevent the activation of stereotypes by, essentially, filling up working memory so that there was no room for the stereotype. Once a stereotype has been activated and is in working memory, however, cognitive busyness can use up mental resources that could otherwise be used to search for individuating information, thereby preventing stereotype inhibition and facilitating stereotype application. For example, as in their stereotype activation study, Gilbert and Hixon (1991) had White research participants watch a videotape of either a White or Asian research assistant showing cards that contained partial words that could be completed either stereotypically or nonstereotypically. In this study, the participants were not cognitively busy at this point, so the Asian stereotype was activated for the participants who saw the Asian research assistant. The participants then listened to an audiotape of the research assistant describing a day in her life that contained no stereotypic information and formed an impression of her. Half the participants were cognitively busy while listening to the tape; they watched a computer screen on which letters were flashed and had to indicate each time the letter *U* followed the letter *T*. The participants then rated their impression of the research assistant on a set of traits that included Asian-stereotypic terms such as *timid* and *intelligent*. Gilbert and Hixon found that cognitively busy participants gave more stereotypic ratings to the Asian research assistant than did the nonbusy participants; the ratings of the White research assistant did not differ by busyness condition, indicating that cognitive busyness affected only perceptions of a member of a stereotyped group, not perceptions of people in general.

Figure 4.3 illustrates the results of Gilbert and Hixon's (1991) two studies on cognitive busyness. Although the results of those studies might at first glance appear to be contradictory, the contradiction is resolved if you remember that cognitive busyness has opposite effects depending on whether a stereotype is being activated or applied. Cognitive busyness *inhibits stereotype activation* but once a stereotype has been activated, cognitive busyness *facilitates stereotype application*. Although the distinction between stereotype activation and application may seem to be somewhat artificial, Gilbert and Hixon give an example of how the two processes can be separated in everyday life: "A faithful churchgoer who meets a newly arrived Hispanic minister may not experience activation of his or her beliefs about Hispanics because the social demands of the formal encounter may usurp resources that are necessary for the activation of those concepts. . . . If stereotypes are activated prior to a resource consuming social interaction ('Let me take you over and introduce you to Father Gonzales') then the interactants may be especially likely to view each other in stereotypic terms" (p. 515).

Gilbert and Hixon's (1991) research focused on the effect of externally imposed cognitive busyness, but sometimes the task a person is engaged in can generate busyness that can undermine stereotype inhibition. For example, Galen Bodenhausen and Meryl Lichtenstein (1987) found that participants working on a complex task—one that required extensive cognitive resources to complete—were more likely to use stereotypes in making judgments related to the task than were participants working on a simpler version of the task. Bodenhausen and Lichtenstein had research participants read about a criminal trial in which the defendant was either Hispanic or White. Half of the participants expected to rate the aggressiveness of the defendant whereas half expected to determine if the defendant were guilty and, if so, what an appropriate punishment would be. The researchers had tested the two versions of the task and found that people experienced the guilt determination version as more complex than the trait judgment version. As expected, the results of the study showed that the participants carrying out the complex version of the task viewed the Hispanic defendant in more stereotypical terms than did the other participants.

The context in which a task is carried out, as well as the nature of the task, can impose a cognitive load. For example, people who make decisions under time pressure are more likely to use stereotypes in making their judgments (de Dreu,

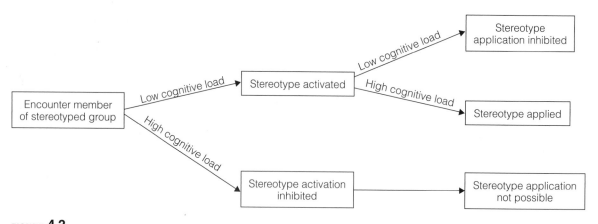

FIGURE **4.3**

COGNITIVE LOAD, STEREOTYPE ACTIVATION, AND STEREOTYPE APPLICATION

When a person encounters a member of a stereotyped group, high cognitive load inhibits activation of the stereotype; there is no stereotype application because an unactivated stereotype cannot be applied. If the person is under a low cognitive load, the stereotype is activated and ready for application because working memory is available for the stereotype. If the person's cognitive load continues to be low, the stereotype is inhibited because the person has the cognitive resources available to prevent stereotype application. However, if the person comes under a high cognitive load after the stereotype has been activated, the stereotype is applied because the person does not have the cognitive resources available to prevent application.

2003; de Dreu, Koole, & Oldersma, 1999; Kruglanski & Freund, 1983). Carsten de Dreu (2003) had student research participants engage in a price negotiation with someone they thought was either a business major or a religion major; in fact, they interacted with a computer program. De Dreu hypothesized that under time pressure to complete a deal, participants would respond to the other person in terms of the stereotype of the other person's group, cooperative in the case of religion majors and competitive in the case of business majors. Because people make less harsh demands of people they see as cooperative, De Dreu expected his participants to settle for less money from the religion student, but only when under time pressure. The results supported this expectation: Participants who were not under time pressure negotiated about the same price from religion and business students, averages of $3,922 and $3,969, respectively. However, participants who were under time pressure asked less of religion students—an average of $3,247—than from business students—an average of $3,999. In essence, religion students received a 17 percent discount when time pressures were operating, presumably because they were being viewed as stereotypical group members rather than as individuals.

Reduced cognitive capacity can result not only from task demands, but also from natural variations in cognitive capacity over the course of a day. Drawing on research that shows that there are morning people who are more effective thinkers early in the day and evening people who are more effective thinkers later in the day, Galen Bodenhausen (1990) hypothesized that people would be more likely to use stereotypes during their "off" periods—early in the day for evening people and late in the day for morning people. Classifying students as morning or evening people based on a standard assessment instrument, Bodenhausen asked them to take part in his research at either 9 A.M., 3 P.M., or 8 P.M. As shown in Figure 4.4, as he had expected, Bodenhausen found more stereotype use by evening people at 9 A.M. and more stereotype use by morning people at 3 P.M. and 8 P.M.

The research that we have considered so far indicates that putting people under cognitive load reduces the ability to inhibit stereotype use. Mark Muraven and Roy Baumeister (2000) have suggested that the ability to inhibit undesired responses is, itself, a mental resource that can be depleted through use. Olesya Govorun and Keith Payne (2004) drew on Muraven and Baumeister's theory to predict that if people carried out a demanding mental task *before* making judgments about stereotyped group members, those people's mental resources would be depleted and they would be unable to inhibit stereotyped judgments. Govorun and Payne had research participants go through a large number of repetitions of a cognitively demanding task, called the *Stroop procedure,* that required them to inhibit a well-learned response—reading the word *red* shown on a computer screen—and to replace it with a different response—naming the color the word is shown in. Because reading a word is an automatic response (try *not* reading a word when you see one), people's immediate tendency is to read the word. However, if the word *red* is shown in a green font, *red* is the incorrect response to the color-naming task; *green,* the color of the font, is the correct response. Therefore, people must inhibit the automatic response of *red* and replace it with the thoughtful response *green.* Govorun and Payne found that, compared to research participants who had undergone relatively few repetitions of the task, those who had undergone many repetitions were more likely to use stereotypes when judging a Black person. These findings indicate that engaging in a mentally demanding task before as well as during the course of evaluating members of a stereotyped group can facilitate stereotype use.

Cognitive load also can undermine an existing motivation to inhibit stereotype use. Recall from our discussion of social power as a motivating factor that depending on another person reduces stereotype use and increases the use of individuating information. Manipulating both dependency and cognitive busyness, Louise Pendry and Neil Macrae (1994) found that cognitively busy research participants made stereotypic judgments regardless of whether they depended on the other person. In contrast, although nonbusy participants made stereotypic judgments when they did not depend on the other person, they made individuated (that is, nonstereotypic) judgments when they did depend on the other person. Pendry and Macrae's study is a good illustration of a point we made earlier: Motivation is not sufficient to inhibit stereotype use; people must also have the ability to exert control over use of the stereotype.

Why does cognitive load facilitate stereotype use? One possibility is that once a stereotype is activated, people pay more attention to stereotypic information as opposed to individuating information when cognitive load is high and show the opposite pattern when cognitive load is low. This difference may occur because stereotype-consistent information is easier to integrate with existing (that is,

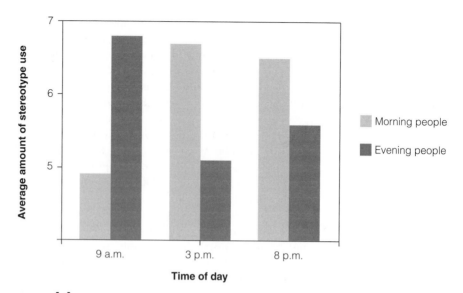

FIGURE **4.4**

CIRCADIAN VARIATIONS IN STEREOTYPE APPLICATION

Because of circadian variations in cognitive efficiency, morning people are more likely to use stereotypes later in the day and evening people are more likely to use stereotypes earlier in the day. (Data from Bodenhausen, 1990, Table 1, p. 321)

stereotypic) information when working memory is limited (Macrae, Hewstone, & Griffiths, 1993). People then use the available information to judge others: stereotypic information when cognitive load is high and individuating information when cognitive load is low.

One factor that is well known to reduce people's cognitive resources is alcohol intoxication. Surprisingly, researchers have only just begun to examine its effects on stereotyping. Not surprisingly, however, the results of such research shows that intoxication leads to stereotype use. For example, Bruce Bartholow, Cheryl Decker, and Marc Sestir (2004) conducted an experiment in which, relative to their body weights, White research participants consumed a high or moderate dose of alcohol or a placebo drink they thought contained alcohol. The researchers found that the more alcohol participants had consumed, the more they stereotyped African Americans. Other measures indicated that the increased stereotyping occurred because the participants who had consumed alcohol had more difficulty inhibiting their stereotypic responses, although they had no problem with nonstereotypic responses. Bartholow and his colleagues were also able to show that although alcohol consumption affects stereotype application, it has no effect on stereotype activation.

Moods and emotions   *Affect* is a general term that includes both mood states and emotions. Research on affect and stereotyping has generally focused on what Galen Bodenhausen and his colleagues (Bodenhausen, Mussweiler, Gabriel, & Moreno,

2002) have called *incidental affect,* affect that is not associated with a given social group but which the person brings to the situation. For example, in most research on affect and stereotyping, an experimental manipulation is used to induce a given affective state in one group of research participants and a different affective state (or a neutral affective state) in another group of participants. The two groups are then compared on the degree of stereotyping they exhibit.

One might think that people's tendency to stereotype would reflect their affective states, so that, for example, happy people would see others in a positive light and so be less likely to stereotype than would sad people. However, one of the most consistent findings in this area of research is that, as shown in the first three bars of Figure 4.5, happy people stereotype to a greater extent than do people in neutral or sad moods (Bodenhausen, Kramer, & Süsser, 1994; Bodenhausen, Sheppard, & Kramer, 1994). Why does this happen? Bodenhausen and his colleagues (2002) suggest that being in a happy mood promotes simplistic thinking by "signaling that 'Everything is fine,' and thus there is little need for careful analysis of the environment. Consequently, happy people may generally prefer to conserve their mental resources [by using stereotypes] rather than engaging in effortful, systematic thinking [by seeking out individuating information about others]. Sad moods, in contrast, suggest to [people] that their environment is problematic and may promote more detail-oriented, careful thinking" (p. 334). One result of happy people's avoidance of careful thought is that, compared to people in sad and neutral mood states, they are more likely to erroneously attribute stereotypic characteristics to others (Park & Banaji, 2000). However, it is important to note that this happy mood effect is not absolute. For example, when happy people are motivated to make accurate judgments, they seek out individuating information (Bodenhausen, Kramer, & Süsser, 1994) and when given clearly counterstereotypic information about others, they rely on that information, not stereotypes, in making judgments (Krauth-Gruber & Ric, 2000).

Other affects, such as anger (Bodenhausen, Sheppard, & Kramer, 1994) and disgust (Tiedens & Linton, 2001), are also associated with stereotyping. For example, as shown in the last bar in Figure 4.5, angry people stereotype to about the same degree as happy people. These findings have led to the hypothesis that "hot" or physiologically arousing emotions facilitate stereotyping by leading people to focus their attention on their emotional state. This internal focus of attention then promotes stereotyping by distracting people from environmental factors, such as individuating information about others, that would otherwise inhibit stereotyping (Wilder & Simon, 2001). This hypothesis is supported by research that shows that any kind of physiological arousal, such as that induced by physical exercise, facilitates stereotype use (Kim & Baron, 1988; Paulhus, Martin, & Murphy, 1992).

However, not all arousing emotions promote stereotyping. For example, Bodenhausen, Kramer, and Süsser (1994) found that both arousing and nonarousing happiness inductions led to the same amount of stereotyping, and Larissa Tiedens and Susan Linton (2001) found that although disgust promoted stereotyping, fear did not. Therefore, although it is clear that some arousing emotions can facilitate stereotyping, it is not clear why they do so. One possible explanation is provided by Paul Rozin and his colleagues (Rozin, Lowery, Imada, & Haidt,

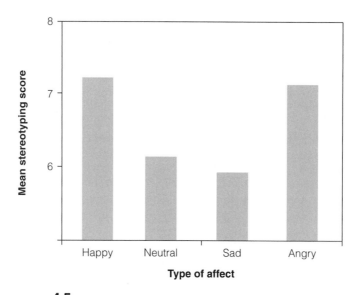

FIGURE **4.5**

AFFECT AND STEREOTYPING

People induced to experience a happy mood stereotype to a greater extent than those in a neutral or sad mood. People induced to feel angry also stereotype to a greater extent than those in a neutral or sad mood and stereotype to about the same degree as people in a happy mood. (Data from Bodenhausen, Kramer, & Süsser, 1994, and Bodenhausen, Sheppard, and Kramer, 1994)

1999) who point out that some emotions, including anger and disgust, are responses to having observed violations of important cultural values, freedom in the case of anger and moral purity in the case of disgust. Because outgroups are often seen as violating important ingroup values (see, for example, Biernat, Vescio, Theno, & Crandall, 1996), experiencing a value-related emotion might reinforce the categorization of a person as a member of an outgroup and so enhance the onlooker's propensity to stereotype the person. However, as Bodenhausen and colleagues (2002) and Wilder and Simon (2001) have noted, the role of affect in stereotyping, especially affects other than happiness and sadness, has not been well explored, so any explanations of how those factors influence stereotyping remain tentative.

CONSEQUENCES OF STEREOTYPE USE

When a stereotype is applied, it influences the person's perceptions of and interactions with members of the stereotyped group. As Bodenhausen and his colleagues (2002) note, "activated stereotypic concepts serve to simplify and structure the process of social perception by providing a readymade framework for conceptualizing [members of stereotyped groups]" (p. 331). In this section, we examine four effects of activated stereotypes: biased interpretation of behavior, biased evaluation of individuals and cultural artifacts, biased memory, and self-fulfilling prophecies. We saw in Chapter 3 that one effect of these processes is that they reinforce stereotypes in people's minds and make them more difficult to change. Here, we look at other effects those processes can have.

Biased Interpretation of Behavior

Stereotypes can act as filters that influence how onlookers interpret the behavior of members of stereotyped groups. In general, ambiguous behaviors—those that can be interpreted in more than one way—are assimilated to the stereotype. That is, onlookers interpret ambiguous behaviors as being stereotype consistent. The classic illustration of the way in which stereotypes can guide the evaluation of individuals' behavior is Birt Duncan's (1976) study, described in Chapter 3, in which White research participants observed a Black or White person giving a slight shove to another person. The onlookers interpreted the behavior as being more aggressive when performed by a Black person than when performed by a White person, consistent with the stereotype of African Americans as more aggressive than White Americans.

Andrew Sagar and Janet Schofield (1980) conducted a study to see whether such biases affect children as well as adults. They showed Black and White 6th graders attending a racially integrated school illustrations of ambiguously aggressive behaviors they had observed in the school, along with a verbal description of the behavior. For example, an illustration showing a boy poking the boy seated in front of him with the eraser end of a pencil was accompanied by the description, "Mark was sitting at his desk, working on his social studies assignment, when David started poking him in the back with the eraser end of his pencil. Mark just kept on working. David kept poking him for a while, and then he finally stopped" (Sagar & Schofield, 1980, p. 593). The perpetrator in each case was either Black or White, as was the victim. An experimenter of their own race tested children individually and asked them to rate how mean and threatening the perpetrator was. Consistent with Duncan's (1976) results, Sagar and Schofield found that both Black and White research participants rated the behavior as more mean and threatening when performed by a Black child, indicating that Black children as well as White children hold the stereotype of African Americans as more aggressive.

Not only racial or ethnic stereotypes affect interpretations. Recall from Chapter 3 John Darley and Paget Gross's (1983) study that focused on Hannah, a child who was described as being from either a low socioeconomic status (SES) background or a high SES background. The participants who had seen the high SES Hannah gave her performance on an academic achievement task a higher rating than those who had seen the low SES Hannah. That is, based on the same behavior, the low SES Hannah was rated as performing one grade level below the high SES Hannah. How did the participants in the different conditions come to different evaluations of Hannah based on the same behavior? Darley and Gross

(1983) found that the participants interpreted the testing situation and Hannah's behavior differently depending on which Hannah they had initially seen. For example, the test was seen as being more difficult for the high SES Hannah than for the low SES Hannah: Participants rated it as assessing 5th grade skills in the high SES condition and 4th grade skills in the low SES condition. Darley and Gross noted that seeing the test as more difficult would justify giving the high SES Hannah a higher performance rating. In addition, participants remembered the high SES Hannah as getting more right answers on the easy and moderately difficult questions (an average of 82 percent) than the low SES Hannah (an average of 66 percent). The participants also gave the high SES Hannah higher ratings on work habits, motivation, and cognitive skills. What happened, then, is that the participants' SES stereotypes led them to interpret Hannah's behaviors as consistent with the stereotype of her SES group.

Stereotypes can also influence the interpretation of even relatively subtle behaviors. For example, Kurt Hugenberg and Galen Bodenhausen (2004) found that people who implicitly endorsed the traditional African American stereotype were more likely to interpret an ambiguous facial expression as indicating anger when the expression was shown on a Black face than when it was shown on a White face. In addition, stereotypes can influence interpretation of physical characteristics: When shown pictures of men and women who were equally tall, people estimate that the man is taller than the woman, consistent with the stereotype (accurate in this case) that men are, on the average, taller than women (Nelson, Biernat, & Manis, 1990). For a harrowing real-life example of the effects of stereotypes on interpretations of behavior, see Box 4.3.

Biased Evaluation

People frequently make evaluations of others, liking them or disliking them, judging their qualifications for employment or political office, deciding on rewards and punishments, and so forth. When a group stereotype is relevant to an evaluation, such as when a particular group is stereotyped as talented in a particular area (as Blacks are in sports) or stereotyped as untalented (as Whites are in sports), the group stereotype can affect the evaluation of a member of the stereotyped group. In addition, group stereotypes can influence the evaluation of cultural artifacts such as music, art, and literature, with artifacts associated with negatively stereotyped groups' being seen in a more negative light.

Individuals   Many of the studies we looked at while discussing the factors that influence the application of stereotypes also dealt with the effect of stereotypes on evaluation. For example, Bodenhausen and Wyer (1985) had research participants read about a case of employee misbehavior on the part of a blue-collar worker. The offense was related to either an aspect of the Arab stereotype—laziness—or an aspect of the American stereotype—lack of cooperation with management (these stereotypes had been elicited from an earlier group of research participants). Each participant read one of four versions of the case; in two versions, the American or Arab employee committed the laziness offense and in the

4.3   *Can Stereotyping Be a Matter of Life or Death?*

Imagine yourself in this situation: You are a police officer searching along a poorly lit street for a suspect you believe to be armed. As you pass a doorway, you see a man resembling the suspect, who begins to lift an object he is holding. Is the object a gun or something harmless? Should you shoot the man to prevent him from shooting you? You have less than a second to make both decisions. A situation similar to this one faced four New York City police officers in February 1999. They thought the man held a gun and shot him. They were mistaken; he was holding his wallet. The man was Amadou Diallo, an immigrant from the African country of Guinea. Were the White police officers predisposed to misperceive the wallet as a gun and to shoot more quickly because Diallo was Black rather than White? Researchers have addressed this question in two ways. The first is by testing the effects of the race of a stimulus person on the perception of objects (Judd, Blair, & Chapleau, 2004; Payne, 2001; Payne, Lambert, & Jacoby, 2002). The second is by having people participate in computerized simulations of situations in which they are shown a person who may or may not be holding a weapon; they must "shoot" at armed stimuli by pressing a button and indicate that they would not shoot at unarmed stimuli by pressing a different button (Correll, Park, Judd, & Wittenbrink, 2002; Greenwald, Oaks, & Hoffman, 2003).

These studies have produced three interesting sets of findings. First, participants were more likely to misperceive a harmless object, such as a pair of pliers, as a gun if they were primed with a picture of a Black person (Judd

et al., 2004; Payne, 2001; Payne et al., 2002) or if they saw a Black person holding the object (Greenwald et al., 2003). This misperception occurred even when the Black person was dressed as a police officer (Greenwald et al., 2003). Participants were also more likely to correctly identify an object as a gun if the object was held by a Black person (Payne, 2001; Payne et al., 2002). Taken together, the results of these studies show that the "he has a gun" response is more likely to occur when the stimulus person is Black, regardless of whether that response is correct or incorrect. Not surprisingly, these kinds of errors increase as time pressure to make a decision increases. For example, Keith Payne and his colleagues (2002) found identification errors to increase from about 5 percent when participants had 0.7 seconds to respond to about 20 percent when they had 0.2 seconds to respond.

The second set of findings suggest that this response is automatic: People make it without thinking about it (Judd et al., 2004; Payne, 2001; Payne et al., 2002). For example, these identification errors occur even when participants are explicitly told "try not to let the race of the [person] influence your decisions" (Payne et al., 2002, p. 388).

The third set of findings deals with how people react once they have identified an object as a weapon. When faced with an *unarmed* stimulus person (that is, when participants had incorrectly identified the object as a weapon), participants made the decision to shoot more quickly if the person was Black (Correll et al., 2002; Greenwald et al., 2003). However, these

(continues)

Can Stereotyping Be a Matter of Life or Death? (continued)

researchers also found that participants were more likely *not* to shoot an *armed* White person. For example, Joshua Correll and his colleagues (2002) found that participants in their simulation shot at 16 percent of the unarmed Black people they saw compared to 12 percent of the unarmed White people they saw, and failed to shoot at 12 percent of the armed White people they saw compared to 7 percent of the armed Black people they saw. That is, participants were more likely to endanger unarmed Black people by mistakenly shooting at them, but were more likely to endanger themselves by not shooting at an armed White person. As with identification errors, shooting errors increased under time pressure. Correll and his colleagues found a similar "shooter bias" in a sample of adults recruited at shopping malls and other public places; they also found that Black and White participants showed an equal degree of shooter bias.

How do stereotypes fit into this problem? Correll and his colleagues (2002) found that the magnitude of shooter bias was correlated with participants' knowledge of the cultural stereotype of Blacks as violent and dangerous. They interpreted their findings as showing that "ethnicity influences the shoot/don't shoot decisions primarily because traits associated with African Americans, namely 'violent' or 'dangerous,' can act as a schema to influence perceptions of an ambiguously threatening target" (p. 1325). They gave two reasons for their conclusion. The first was the correlation they found between shooter

bias and knowledge of stereotypes. The second reason was "the . . . finding that African Americans and Whites, alike, display this bias. . . . It is unlikely that participants in our African American sample held strong prejudice against their own ethnic group . . ., but as members of U.S. society, they are, presumably, aware of the cultural stereotype that African Americans are violent" (p. 1325). Interestingly, people's personal racial attitudes are not related to either weapon misperception or shooter bias (Correll et al., 2002; Payne, 2001).

What can be done about this problem? As Payne (2001) noted, "two requirements must be met to bias participants' error rates. First, stereotypic cues must be present. Second, the opportunity to consider and control one's response must be limited" (p. 190). Therefore, one solution might be to instruct police officers about the shooter bias effect and tell them to try to not let race affect their judgments. However, Payne and his colleagues (2002) showed that this approach might not be effective. Alternatively, one might instruct police officers to stop and think about the situation more carefully before shooting. However, as Payne and his colleagues (2002) note, "Consider urging a police officer to react more slowly during a confrontation with a potentially armed suspect! Speed is obviously important in this situation, and the time pressure immense" (p. 394). The ultimate solution, therefore, may lie in the extremely difficult task of entirely eliminating racial stereotypes from our culture.

other two versions, the American or Arab employee committed the uncooperativeness offense. The participants then recommended a punishment for the offense. Bodenhausen and Wyer found that the more stereotypic offense led to greater recommended punishments. Participants recommended more severe punishment for the American who committed the uncooperativeness offense and the Arab who committed the laziness offense. Other studies also have found that factors that motivate stereotype use also lead to more negative evaluations of members of stereotyped groups in terms of such factors as liking for the person (Fein & Spencer, 1997) and competence ratings (Fein & Spencer, 1997; Sinclair & Kunda, 2000).

Positive stereotypes also can lead to differential evaluation. For example, Jennifer Steele and Nalini Ambady (2004) had research participants interview an Asian woman for a job as a computer technician, a job for which the Asian stereotype is positive but the female stereotype is negative. Information provided prior to the interview either emphasized the interviewee's Asian identity over her female identity, emphasized her female identity over her Asian identity, or put an equal emphasis on both identities. Participants rated the interviewee as better qualified and recommended a higher starting salary when her Asian identity was salient than when her female identity was salient.

Although the role that stereotypes play in evaluation can be straightforward, it also can take complex forms, especially when the evaluation results in the allocation of rewards. In Chapter 3 we noted that one factor that complicates the question of stereotype accuracy is that the standard for accuracy on a particular trait can differ from one social group to another. This **shifting standards model** of stereotyping (Biernat, 2003; Biernat, Manis, & Nelson, 1991) also has implications for the effect stereotypes have on evaluations. In this case, the effect depends on the kind of judgment being made. The basic principle of the model is that if some groups (such as African Americans or women) are seen as less competent than other groups (such as White men), then the standards used to evaluate a person shift depending on the type of decision to be made. When the issue is one of the allocation of a limited resource, such as when only one of many applicants for a job can be hired, then members of the group that are stereotyped as more competent will get the resource even if members of the other group are equally well qualified. However, if a resource is not limited, such as praise for good performance, given equal performance by members of positively and negatively stereotyped groups, members of the negatively stereotyped group will get more of the resource. Why? Because the stereotype leads decision makers to have lower expectations for members of the negatively stereotyped group, so the same level of performance *seems* better relative to the lower standard.

For example, Monica Biernat and Theresa Vescio (2002) had research participants role-play being the manager of a coed softball team. The participants were given photographs of nine men and nine women; the photographs had been pretested to ensure that the men and women appeared to have equal levels of athletic ability. The participants had to choose 13 people for their team and, of those, choose 10 to be starting players; note that team and starting lineup membership were limited resources because not everyone could get those positions.

Participants were more likely to choose men than women for their teams, a difference that was especially large for players who were seen as having moderate (versus low or high) ability, with three men being chosen for every two women. Men also were more likely to be chosen for the starting lineup, again especially among players of moderate ability, where the ratio was three to one. Thus, even though the men and women were matched on ability, members of the group stereotyped as more athletic (men) were more likely to receive the limited resources.

Biernat and Vescio (2002) also investigated the allocation of an unlimited resource, praise for good performance. Their participants indicated, by checking a list of behaviors, how enthusiastically they would respond to each of their players' hitting a single. In this case, female players received more of the resource even though their performance was the same as the men's. That is, members of the group stereotyped as less athletic got more praise because good performance was unexpected. Although giving more praise for performance may sound positive, it is also patronizing (Biernat, 2003): Members of the group stereotyped as less competent get praised for what is seen as routine performance by others, sending the message that the person giving the praise sees the stereotyped group as less competent.

Cultural artifacts   Stereotypes can affect not only evaluations of members of a stereotyped group but also evaluations of aspects of the group's culture. For example, recall from Chapter 1 that Carrie Fried (1996, 1999) examined racial stereotypes as a factor in negative reactions to rap music, a genre associated with urban African American culture. She hypothesized that although rap music is frequently condemned for its content, part of the condemnation on the part of people who are not African American comes from its association with Black American culture. Fried tested this hypothesis by showing people at a shopping mall lyrics taken from a song performed in the early 1960s by an all-White group. The lyrics depicted the protagonist in the story told by the song as being unrepentant over having shot and killed a police officer. The participants were told that the lyrics were from either a rap song or a country and western song. They were then asked to rate the lyrics on dimensions such as offensiveness and the extent to which songs like it were dangerous and a threat to society. Fried found that the lyrics were evaluated more negatively when they were presented as rap lyrics than when they were presented as country and western lyrics. That is, the lyrics were seen as more negative when associated with an aspect of Black culture than with an aspect of White culture.

To further test the role of race in evaluation of the lyrics, Fried (1996) showed the lyrics to another group of research participants without mentioning the type of music they represented. She also showed them a picture of the supposed performer of the song, who was either a young Black man or a young White man. The participants then rated the lyrics on the dimensions used in the first study. Fried found that participants rated the lyrics more negatively when the performer was portrayed as Black than when he was portrayed as White. Thus, negative stereotypes affect not only members of the stereotyped group but also evaluations of the group's culture.

Biased Memory

As we have seen, stereotypes influence how people evaluate others and interpret their behavior. Stereotypes can also affect people's memories about social interactions. One such memory effect is *source confusion,* in which an onlooker incorrectly remembers a behavior performed by Person A as having been performed by Person B because the behavior is more consistent with the stereotype of B's group (Sherman & Bessenoff, 1999; Sherman, Groom, Ehrenberg, & Klauer, 2003). For example, Jeffrey Sherman and Gayle Bessenoff (1999) had research participants memorize a list of behaviors that they had created (List 1); that is, the experimenters were the source of the behaviors. The participants then read another set of behaviors (List 2) that a person named Bob Hamilton had listed as characteristic of himself; Hamilton was the source of these behaviors. Both lists consisted of 10 positive, 10 negative, and 10 neutral behaviors. Participants were also told that Hamilton was either a priest (a group with a positive stereotype) or a skinhead (a group with a negative stereotype) and were asked to form an overall impression of him. The next day, the participants received a list of behaviors and indicated which ones Bob Hamilton had listed as characteristic of himself. During this task, half the participants were put under a cognitive load and half were not. Sherman and Bessenoff found that participants were more likely to incorrectly indicate List 1 behaviors as characteristic of Hamilton when those behaviors were stereotype consistent. That is, participants were more likely to incorrectly remember positive behaviors when Hamilton had been depicted as priest and negative behaviors when he had been depicted as a skinhead. The researchers also found that this effect was stronger for participants who had been under cognitive load during recall. Sherman and Bessenoff suggested that people try to carefully search their memories when asked to recall what a person is like, but when they cannot do so, such as when they are under cognitive load, they rely on stereotypes as memory aids. That is, people reason, perhaps unconsciously, that Person A is an X and Xs typically act this way, so A must have performed this behavior.

Another effect of stereotypes on memory involves *assimilation:* People remember a behavior initially presented to them in general terms as stereotype consistent; that is, the behavior is assimilated to the stereotype. For example, David Dunning and David Sherman (1997) had participants read a set of general statements about behaviors. Some of the behaviors were associated with stereotypic gender differences and were presented as having been performed by either a man or a woman. For instance, they read that either "Laura" or "Luke" had a problem with expressing emotions. Participants later read a list of statements and indicated which they had seen before. In this list, half of the gender-related behaviors were specified as consistent with gender stereotypes, such as "Laura had a problem with expressing her emotions too much" and "Luke had a problem with not expressing his emotions," and half were stereotype inconsistent, such as "Luke had a problem with expressing his emotions too much" and "Laura had a problem with not expressing her emotions." Dunning and Sherman found that participants were more likely to recognize the stereotype-consistent than the stereotype-inconsistent behaviors. Thus, given a general statement about a person's behavior, people may incorrectly remember it as a more specific stereotype-consistent behavior. To give another example, in a separate study, Dunning and Sherman (1997) found that given the statement "Some felt that A's statements were untrue," people remembered A as having lied if he was portrayed as a politician and as having been mistaken if he was portrayed as a physicist.

Self-Fulfilling Prophecies

A **self-fulfilling prophecy** occurs when Person A's stereotype of Person B's group leads Person A to behave in ways that elicit stereotype-consistent behavior, or behavior that Person A interprets to be stereotype consistent, from Person B (Klein & Snyder, 2003). Consider the hypothetical example illustrated in Figure 4.6, in which a White personnel officer interviews a minority applicant for a managerial job. In this example, the interviewer holds negative stereotypes about members of the applicant's group, such as their being hostile toward White people and generally lacking the skills required for the job. These stereotypes lead to expectancies about how the applicant will perform during the job interview. For example, the hostility stereotype leads to an expectancy that the applicant will be unfriendly and the ability stereotype leads to an expectancy that the applicant will have few job-related skills. The interviewer's expectancies lead to two types of behaviors that then elicit stereotype-confirming behaviors from the applicant. First, the interviewer's expectancy of interacting with an unfriendly applicant leads the interviewer to act in a reserved manner, such as making little eye contact, maintaining a greater than normal physical distance, talking in a cold tone of voice, and so forth. Generally, people show *behavioral reciprocation* in their interactions with others, responding in the same way as they are treated (Klein & Snyder, 2003). Therefore, the applicant is likely to respond to the interviewer's behavior in much the same way and to answer questions cautiously and volunteer little information. The second type of interviewer behavior that elicits stereotype-confirming behavior is the interviewer's information-gathering behavior. If the interviewer expects the applicant to have few job-related skills, the interviewer's questions may focus primarily on eliciting information about weaknesses rather than strengths. The applicant answers the interviewer's questions, thereby providing information that confirms the interviewer's stereotypes (Neuberg, 1994; Trope & Thompson, 1997). The applicant's behavior is filtered through the perceiver's perceptual processes, bringing factors such as biased interpretation into play, so that any ambiguous responses the applicant makes are interpreted as confirming the interviewer's expectancies. As an end result of the self-fulfilling prophecy process, the interviewer concludes, *on the basis of the applicant's behavior,* that the applicant is not qualified for the job, and can bolster that conclusion with stereotype-biased memories.

The classic demonstration of a self-fulfilling prophecy in intergroup interaction was provided in a pair of studies conducted by Carl Word, Mark Zanna, and Joel Cooper (1974). In the first study, White undergraduate research participants interviewed both a Black and a White candidate for a position as a member of a decision-making team. Using a set of questions provided by the researchers, the research assistants who acted as applicants were trained to provide answers that

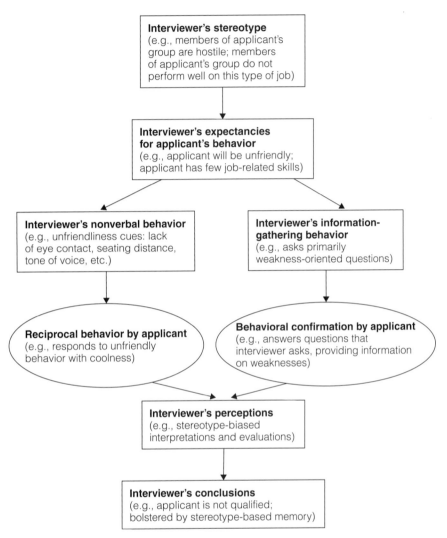

FIGURE **4.6**

THE SELF-FULFILLING PROPHECY

In a self-fulfilling prophecy, a perceiver's stereotypes lead to expectations about another person's characteristics. These expectations lead the perceiver to act in ways that elicit behaviors from the other person that confirm the perceiver's expectations.

showed they were qualified for the job and to behave in similar ways during the interview. The researchers found that the interviewers sat farther away from the Black applicant (62 inches [157 cm]) than the White applicant (58 inches [147 cm]), made more speech errors (a sign of nervousness) when talking with the Black applicant, and held shorter interviews with the Black applicant (an average of 9.4 minutes versus 12.8 minutes). This behavior was not simply a sign of the times in which the research was conducted: Today's White college students respond in similar ways when interacting with African Americans (see, for example, Dovidio et al., 2002; McConnell & Liebold, 2001).

In their second study, Word and his colleagues (1974) examined how people respond to the ways in which the participants in their first study acted toward White people (which we will call *warm* behavior) versus Black people (which we will call *cool* behavior). White research assistants trained to behave in these ways interviewed White research participants; White participants were used so that interracial factors could not affect the results. Compared to participants who were treated warmly, those treated coolly rated the interviewer as less friendly and reciprocated the interviewer's behavior by sitting farther away (by 16 inches [41 cm]) and making more speech errors. The interviewees were videotaped during the interview and judges who did not know the hypothesis of the study rated their behavior. The judges rated the interviewees in the cool treatment condition as more nervous and as having performed more poorly in the interview than those in the warm treatment condition. Taken together, the results of these two studies show that people treat members of stereotyped and nonstereotyped groups differently and that this difference in treatment results in stereotype-confirming behavior on the part of members of the stereotyped groups.

The role of stereotypes in self-fulfilling prophecies was shown in a study conducted by Mark Chen and John Bargh (1997). In the first part of the study, two research participants separately worked on a visual perception task: A random pattern of dots was shown on a computer screen and the participants indicated whether an odd or even number of dots was present. In half of the data-collection sessions, one of the participants was primed with the Black stereotype during this task by having a picture of a Black face subliminally shown on the screen; in the other sessions neither participant was primed. In the second part of the study, the two participants played a word game together and their interaction was audiotaped. The participants then rated each other on a variety of traits, including hostility, which is part of the Black stereotype. Chen and Bargh's hypothesis was that priming of the Black stereotype would lead to behavior consistent with the stereotype (Chen and Bargh focused on hostility) on the part of primed participants toward their game partners, which would elicit reciprocal behavior (that is, hostility) from the partners.

Chen and Bargh (1997) found that judges who listened to the audiotape of the word game rated the primed participants as being more hostile toward their partners than the unprimed participants. The level of hostility was not very high—primed participants received an average rating equivalent to "Subtle signs of frustration. Frequent sighing, increase of voice volume, and terseness of language" and unprimed participants received an average rating equivalent to "Neither nice nor hostile. [Behavior] indicating polite, yet indifferent attitude"—but it was, nonetheless, noticeable to the judges. In addition, primed participants were rated as more hostile by their interaction partners than were unprimed participants, indicating that the partners picked up on the hostility noted by the judges. Finally, the judges rated the interaction partners of primed participants as acting in a more hostile manner than the partners of unprimed participants, showing reciprocity of behavior.

The results of the research conducted by Word and his colleagues (1974) and Chen and Bargh (1997) show that stereotype activation can cause people to act in ways that elicit stereotype-confirming behavior from others. Their research also demonstrated behavioral reciprocity as one mechanism through which this process occurs. The other mechanism—information-gathering behavior—was shown in the study conducted by Vescio and her colleagues (2003) that we described earlier. In that study, weakness-oriented interviewers asked questions that elicited weakness-confirming information from members of a group (in this case, women) stereotyped as having low ability for a task. Research on other types of expectancy confirmation (such as expectancies related to the other person's personality) has also found that people tend to ask questions whose answers will confirm their beliefs about their interaction partners (Neuberg, 1994).

The self-fulfilling prophecy has been found to operate for a variety of stereotypes in addition to race, including those related to gender (Skrypnek & Snyder, 1982; Vescio et al., 2003), obesity (Snyder & Haugen, 1994), mental illness (Sibicky & Dovidio, 1986), and physical attractiveness (Snyder, Tanke, & Berscheid, 1977). However, self-fulfilling prophecy effects are not inevitable. For example, people who are more prejudiced produce stronger effects (Dovidio, 2001), and effects tend to be stronger when the perceiver is cognitively busy (Biesanz, Neuberg, Smith, Asher, & Judice, 2001; Harris & Perkins, 1995) and to be weaker when the perceiver is motivated to form an accurate impression (Biesanz et al., 2001).

Finally, as Olivier Klein and Mark Snyder (2003) point out (see also Neuberg, 1994), the self-fulfilling prophecy requires a kind of cooperation, as it were, from members of stereotyped groups: In response to the perceiver's expectancy-related behavior, they must perform behaviors that either confirm the stereotype or that are sufficiently ambiguous that perceivers can interpret them as confirming the stereotype. Klein and Snyder further note that although the normative demands of many interpersonal interactions (which include such factors as reciprocity of behavior and answering questions that are asked) facilitate expectancy confirmation, some members of stereotyped groups may nonetheless be motivated to behave in ways that disconfirm, rather than confirm, the group stereotype. For example, people who are especially sensitive to their groups' being stereotyped often try to act in ways that contradict the stereotype, and people who want to make a good impression may act in a warm and friendly manner even if faced with cool and unfriendly behavior on the part of the other person. Such stereotype-disconfirming behavior can disrupt the self-filling prophecy process and can serve to motivate the perceiver to view the person in individuated, rather than stereotypic, terms.

CHAPTER SUMMARY

Group stereotypes are problematic because applying them to a member of a stereotyped group can bias interpretation of and memory for the group member's behavior and judgments made about the group member. However, knowledge of the content of stereotypes does not make stereotype application inevitable. Before an onlooker applies a stereotype to a person, three processes must occur. The onlooker must categorize the person as a member of a stereotyped group, the group stereotype must be activated, and the group stereotype must be applied to the person. If categorization does not occur, activation cannot occur; and if activation does not occur, application cannot occur.

People spontaneously categorize others based on the three basic social categories of race, gender, and age, with race categorized first, followed quickly by gender. Categorization frequently occurs in terms of subcategories, such as *young Black woman.* Although categorization is automatic, several factors influence the categorization process. People tend to be categorized on the basis of characteristics that make them stand out from their surroundings, and category-related behavior (such as a woman applying makeup) can draw attention to that category. Individuals whose characteristics are more typical of characteristics that define the group are categorized more quickly. Finally, prejudiced people tend to focus on the categories they are prejudiced against, to overclassify people as members of outgroups, to take more time to categorize people who appear to be ambiguous in terms of category membership, and to use stereotypes as cues for categorization.

Stereotype activation occurs spontaneously after categorization because associations between categories and stereotypes are well learned and therefore strong. Nonetheless, a number of factors can influence the activation process. The context in which activation occurs may favor one stereotypic subcategory over another. More prejudiced people show stronger stereotype activation for groups they are prejudiced against, probably because the category-stereotype link is stronger for them. Finally, cognitive busyness can disrupt stereotype activation by using up the working memory capacity needed by the activated stereotype.

People's motives, needs, and goals also can influence stereotype activation. Stereotypes can aid comprehension by appearing to provide needed information about others and by providing explanations for others' behavior. Negative stereotypes can aid self-enhancement by providing an excuse for ignoring others' criticism of oneself. Stereotypes can aid social adjustment and fitting in with the ingroup by indicating that one shares others' views of outgroups. Finally, most people are motivated to avoid prejudice, and a strong personal motivation not to be prejudiced can inhibit stereotype activation. Although stereotypes can help fulfill motives, needs, and goals, they are activated for that purpose only if their content is relative to the goal at hand.

Automatic and motivated processes jointly influence the activated stereotype. If they operate in the same direction (say, toward activation), they can reinforce each other; if they operate in different directions, one toward activation and the other toward inhibition, they can offset one another. In addition, the strength of the activated stereotype can be influenced by a person's mood; negative characteristics seem more negative to someone who is in a bad mood. Once a stereotype is activated, it may not stay active very long; however, events can occur during an interaction with a member of a stereotyped group that can reactivate a dissipated stereotype.

An activated stereotype will be applied unless the person is both motivated and able to inhibit stereotyping. One motivational factor that acts to inhibit stereotyping is motivation to avoid prejudice. Another factor is comprehension goals: People are generally motivated to form accurate impressions of others and so generally seek out individuating information about them. However, stereotypes may be relied on even when some individuating information is present, and stereotypes can affect how people interpret individuating information. People are especially likely to seek out individuating information when they have an incentive to be accurate. Individual differences in cognitive style also influence stereotype application: People high in need for cognition and causal uncertainty tend to use stereotypes less, whereas people high in need for structure tend to use stereotypes more. Self-enhancement goals may lead people to view others in terms of negative stereotypes when those others threaten their self-images. In contrast, reinforcing people's positive self-images reduces their use of stereotypes. Finally, people who hold power over others tend to stereotype their subordinates because they are generally not motivated to individuate subordinates and as a means of justifying power differentials in hierarchical organizations. However, stereotyping by power holders is not inevitable. They tend to use stereotypes the most when the stereotypes are relevant to the decisions they have to make and tend to inhibit the use of stereotypes when other motives, such as responsibility for subordinates, are salient.

Even when people are motivated to inhibit stereotypes, they may not be able to do so. One factor that facilitates stereotyping is a lack of cognitive resources that could be used to inhibit stereotyping. This lack of resources could arise from cognitive busyness, working on a complex task, time pressure, fatigue, or the effort to control stereotyping itself. In addition, alcohol consumption inhibits people's ability to control their thought processes and therefore to control stereotyping. Some moods, such as happiness, anger, anxiety and disgust, facilitate stereotype use, but others, such as sadness and fear have no effect on stereotyping. It has been proposed that happiness motivates people to avoid the mental effort needed to individuate others and that physiologically arousing emotions distract people from attending to individuating characteristics.

Once a stereotype has been applied, it can have a number of consequences. Stereotypes affect how onlookers interpret others' behavior: Ambiguous behaviors are interpreted to be consistent with group stereotypes. Stereotypes can bias the evaluations people make of members of stereotyped groups and their cultures, with negative stereotypes leading to negative evaluations. Stereotypes also can create shifting standards for evaluation, such that members of stereotyped groups must work harder to be seen as deserving of limited resources but are patronized for good performance, such as by being praised for behavior that would be expected as routine from members of nonstereotyped groups. Stereotypes can bias memory by leading people to incorrectly recall behavior as being performed by a member of a stereotyped group when the behavior is consistent with the group's stereotype and to recall general behaviors as specific to the group stereotype. Finally, stereotypes can lead to self-fulfilling prophecies such that Person A's stereotype of Person B's group leads Person A to act in ways that elicit stereotype-consistent behavior from Person B, or behavior that Person A interprets as stereotype consistent. This process can work to prevent Person B from providing individuating information and to reinforce Person A's stereotype of Person B's group.

Suggested Readings

Stereotype Activation

Bargh, J. A. (1999). The cognitive monster: The case against the controllability of automatic stereotype effects. In S. Chaiken & Y. Trope (Eds.), *Dual-process theories in social psychology* (pp. 361–382). New York: Guilford.

Blair, I. V. (2002). The malleability of automatic stereotypes and prejudice. *Personality and Social Psychology Review, 6*, 242–261.

Kunda, Z., & Spencer, S. J. (2003). When do stereotypes come to mind and when do they color judgment? A goal-based theoretical framework for stereotype activation and application. *Psychological Bulletin, 129*, 522–544.

There is some controversy among researchers over the extent to which stereotype activation is automatic and inevitable versus the extent to which stereotype activation can be influenced by other processes. Bargh presents the case for inevitability; Blair and Kunda and Spencer present evidence for the malleability of automatic stereotypes.

Stereotype Application

Gilbert, D. T., & Hixon, J. G. (1991). The trouble of thinking: Activation and application of stereotypic beliefs. *Journal of Personality and Social Psychology, 60*, 509–517.

Kunda, Z., & Thagard, P. (1996). Forming impressions from stereotypes, traits, and behaviors: A parallel-constraint-satisfaction model. *Psychological Review, 103*, 284–308.

Kunda and Thagard review the research literature on factors that influence the application of stereotypes and present a theory of how those factors operate. Eloquent in its simplicity, Gilbert and Hixon's article provides a highly readable example of how social cognition researchers explore the processes underlying stereotyping and prejudice.

Consequences of Stereotype Use

Klein, O., & Snyder, M. (2003). Stereotypes and behavioral confirmation: From interpersonal to intergroup perspectives. *Advances in Experimental Social Psychology, 35*, 153–234.

Klein and Snyder provide a comprehensive discussion of stereotype-based self-fulfilling prophecies.

Key Terms

categorization	shifting standards model
individuating information	stereotype activation
prototypicality	stereotype application
self-fulfilling prophecy	stereotype endorsement

QUESTIONS FOR REVIEW AND DISCUSSION

1. Draw a diagram of the stereotyping process from categorization through stereotype activation to stereotype application. At each stage, include the factors that affect the process at that point.
2. What happens during the categorization process? Describe the factors that influence how an onlooker categorizes another person.
3. Reread Box 4.1. Do you agree or disagree with Jordan Lite's belief that American society places an undue emphasis on racial categorization as a factor in interpersonal relations? Explain the reasons underlying your answer. If American society does place an undue emphasis on racial categorization, what social and historical factors do you think created that emphasis and operate to maintain it?
4. Why might it be important to try to avoid viewing other people in terms of their social categories, especially in "real world" interactions? Do you think that it is possible to avoid categorization? Why or why not?
5. Stereotype activation is said to be an automatic process. What does that mean? What is it about social categories and stereotypes that makes the activation process automatic?
6. Describe the factors that influence the degree to which stereotypes are activated.
7. What does it mean to say that motives, needs, and goals play a role in stereotype activation? Under what conditions is motivation most likely to affect stereotype activation?
8. Explain how each of the following motives affects stereotype activation: comprehension, self-enhancement, social adjustment, and motivation to avoid prejudice.
9. Explain how the various motives can interact to affect stereotype activation.
10. How do moods affect the activated stereotype?
11. How long does a stereotype stay activated? If stereotypes can dissipate relatively quickly, how is it that they can have an influence during a relatively lengthy interaction?
12. Explain why both motivation and ability are necessary to inhibit the application of an activated stereotype.
13. What does the term *individuating information* mean? What role does it play in stereotyping? Why can stereotypes still have an influence in the face of individuating information?
14. How can people be motivated to seek out individuating information about others?
15. What cognitive style variables are related to stereotype application? What kind of effect does each have?
16. Explain why power holders are likely to stereotype their subordinates. Assume that you are an upper-level manager in an organization. What could you do to reduce stereotyping by power holders? Explain why your solutions would be effective.

17. Describe the various cognitive factors that reduce the opportunity to inhibit stereotyping.
18. Which moods and emotions affect stereotype application? Describe the theories that have been proposed to explain these effects.
19. A factor that pervades the stereotyping process is people's prejudices. Describe how individual differences in levels of prejudice affect each stage of the process and explain why prejudice has the effect it does at that stage.
20. A factor involved in both stereotype activation and application is the availability or unavailability of cognitive resources. Describe the role of cognitive resources in these processes and explain why cognitive resources have the effects they do.
21. Another factor involved in both stereotype activation and application is self-enhancement. Describe its role in these processes and explain why it has the effect it does.
22. Describe how stereotypes can influence the interpretation of behaviors performed by members of stereotyped groups.
23. Describe how stereotypes can influence judgments made about members of stereotyped groups and of the cultures of those groups.
24. Explain how stereotypes result in shifting standards for evaluation of members of stereotyped and nonstereotyped groups. What effects do these shifting standards have? Create an example of shifting standards different from the one given in this chapter.
25. Describe the ways in which stereotypes can bias memory.
26. Describe some ways in which biased interpretation of behavior and biased memory could influence real-life situations in which interpretations and memory are important, such as eyewitness testimony, teachers' grading of students, and supervisors' annual performance ratings of their employees.
27. Explain how a self-fulfilling prophecy operates.
28. What kinds of things can you personally do to prevent stereotypes from affecting the judgments you make about other people?

OLD-FASHIONED AND CONTEMPORARY FORMS OF PREJUDICE

You start out in 1954 by saying "Nigger, nigger, nigger." By 1968 you can't say "nigger"—that hurts you. Backfires. So you say stuff like forced busing, states' rights, and all that stuff. [By 1981] you're getting so abstract [that] you're talking about cutting taxes and all these . . . totally economic things and a by-product of them is that blacks get hurt worse than whites. And subconsciously maybe that is part of it. . . . Obviously sitting around and saying, "We want to cut this," is much more abstract than even the busing thing *and* a hell of a lot more abstract than "Nigger, nigger." [emphasis in original]

—Anonymous member of Ronald Reagan's White House staff
discussing racial politics in an interview with journalist
Alexander Lamis, 1984 (p. 26n)

CHAPTER SUMMARY

SUGGESTED READINGS

KEY TERMS

QUESTIONS FOR REVIEW AND DISCUSSION

If you asked White Americans today if they thought that prejudice is less of a problem now than it was in the past, most would probably agree. For example, 64 percent of White respondents to a 2001 Gallup poll said they were either very satisfied or somewhat satisfied with the ways Blacks were treated in society; 64 percent made the same reply when asked about Hispanics (Gallup, 2002). The results of other research seem to support this perception that prejudice has decreased. For example, Patricia Devine and Andrew Elliot (1995) compared the results of several studies of White college students' stereotypes of African Americans that had been conducted between 1933 and 1995. As shown in Figure 5.1, the stereotypes became less negative over time, changing from very negative to somewhat positive (see also Madon et al., 2001). Survey researchers have found similar changes over time in the general population; for example, 68 percent of Whites supported racially segregated schools in 1942 compared to 4 percent in 1995 (Schuman, Steeh, Bobo, & Krysan, 1997). Jean Twenge (1997b) found that beliefs about women's social roles had become less stereotyped between 1970 and 1995, and Alan Yang (1997) found that attitudes toward lesbians and gay men had become less negative between 1973 and 1996.

But is America truly becoming less prejudiced? Or, as the quotation opening this chapter suggests, has there been less change than appears to be the case, with prejudice becoming more indirect and subtle in recent years compared to the overt and blatant prejudice of the past? This chapter addresses that question. First, we briefly look at some evidence suggesting that prejudice continues to operate despite its apparent decline. We then examine some theories that have been developed to explain this contemporary form of prejudice. We conclude by considering whether prejudice can take the form of positive beliefs; that is, whether positive stereotypes as well negative stereotypes can reflect a prejudiced mind-set.

Before doing so, however, we would like to make three points. The first is that most of the theories of contemporary prejudice that we discuss were specifically developed to explain anti-Black prejudice on the part of White people. Although a few of the theories have been extended beyond racial or ethnic prejudice, as far as we have been able to determine none has been applied to prejudices exhibited by members of minority groups. The second point is related to the first. From time to time in this chapter we use the word *people* to refer to White people. This may make it seem as though this chapter were written for White people about White people. That is not our intention. The occasional use of the terms *White* and *people* interchangeably in this chapter reflects the focus of the theories and a desire to avoid what would otherwise be awkwardly worded sentences.

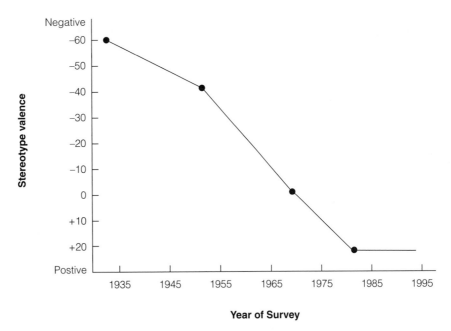

CHANGE IN STEREOTYPES OF AFRICAN AMERICANS OVER TIME

The valence (positivity versus negativity) of U.S. college students' personal stereotypes of African Americans has become less negative over time. (Adapted from Devine & Elliot, 1995, Table 2, p. 1145.)

Because some of the concepts in this chapter are difficult, we want to make it as readable as possible.

The third point concerns an assumption underlying the theories. The theories assume that, because of the historical legacy of racism in American society, all or almost all White people are prejudiced to some degree. This assumption is clearly pessimistic concerning the possibility of eliminating prejudice. However, as Stephen Phillips and Robert Ziller (1997) have noted, theorists and researchers have historically focused on the nature of prejudice and prejudiced people rather than on the nature of nonprejudice and unprejudiced people. As a result, prejudice may appear to be more common than it actually is. As we will see later in this chapter, Phillips and Ziller (1997) and others (for example, Dovidio, 2001; Dunton & Fazio, 1997) have conducted research that indicates that not all White Americans are prejudiced. Also, Chapter 12 will discuss a number of interventions that are effective in reducing prejudice. The bottom line is, despite whatever the situation may appear to be from the perspective of theories of contemporary prejudice, there are people who are accepting of diversity and those who work to be less biased can indeed change their attitudes.

THE TRANSFORMATION OF PREJUDICE

Several lines of evidence suggest that prejudice continues to be alive and well in United States, only in a subtle rather than overt form. In this section, we will review some of that evidence and then consider why prejudice has, so to speak, gone underground.

Prejudice Continues . . .

One source of evidence of continuing prejudice comes from the results of research using a technique called the *bogus pipeline* (Roese & Jamieson, 1993). In **bogus pipeline research,** participants answer questions while their physiological responses are measured by what they believe to be an effective lie detector. The researchers then compare these responses to the participants' earlier responses to the same questions. The theory underlying the technique is that people do not want to be caught lying and so reveal their true attitudes rather than attitudes that are contaminated by social desirability response bias (see Chapter 2). The technique is called the bogus pipeline because, although it is designed to provide a pipeline to participants' true attitudes, the lie detector is bogus: it provides no information at all. Research has consistently found that people express more prejudice under bogus pipeline conditions than when they believe that the truthfulness of their responses cannot be checked (Roese & Jamieson, 1993).

Other evidence comes from physiological and implicit cognition measures of prejudice. As we saw in Chapter 2, some White people whose self-report data indicate low levels of prejudice nonetheless exhibit physiological responses indicative of negative emotions when they interact with African Americans or see pictures of African Americans (see, for example, Guglielmi, 1999). Similarly, some people categorized as low on prejudice by self-report measures unconsciously associate members of minority groups with negative concepts (see, for example, Fazio & Olson, 2003).

Assessments of behavior also indicate that prejudice continues. For example, Kim Gore, Michael Tobiason, and Wesley Kayson (1997) had research assistants make telephone calls to randomly selected people, telling the person who answered the phone that they urgently needed to contact their boyfriend or girlfriend and apologizing for calling the wrong number. The callers said they were at a public telephone and had used the last of their change to make the call. They then asked the person to call their friend and give him or her that number. Both the male and female research assistants asked the person they reached to call either their boyfriend or girlfriend. Thus, half the people called thought they were talking to a lesbian or gay man and half thought they were talking to a heterosexual man or woman. Gore and colleagues found that 82 percent of the people who thought the call came from a heterosexual person passed on the message compared with 48 percent of those who thought the call came from a lesbian or gay man.

Self-reports of behavior indicate that it is close contact with members of minority groups that White people most want to avoid. For example, Donal Muir (1991) surveyed White students at a predominantly White college about their racial attitudes and willingness to interact with Black students. Most of the students said they were willing to interact with Black students in public settings. For example, 92 percent said they would sit next to a Black student in class and 84 percent said that they would eat at the same table as a Black student. The responses for interactions in more intimate settings were different: only 42 percent of the White students said they would be willing to have a Black roommate and only 12 percent said they would be willing to date a Black student. At the same time, these students reported holding positive attitudes toward African Americans: only 15 percent endorsed negative stereotypes of Blacks, 93 percent said Blacks and Whites should be treated equally, and 86 percent said there should not be legal restrictions to keep Blacks and Whites from mixing socially.

Finally, evidence for the continuation of prejudice comes from the day-to-day experience of women and members of minority groups. For example, in the Gallup poll in which 64 percent of White respondents said they were satisfied with the way Blacks and Hispanics were treated, only 39 percent of Blacks and 45 percent of Hispanics said they were very satisfied or somewhat satisfied. These results suggest that White people do not perceive the discrimination that members of minority groups believe exists. In other research, Janet Swim and her colleagues (Swim, Hyers, Cohen, & Ferguson, 2001; Swim, Hyers, Cohen, Fitzgerald, & Bylsma, 2003) had female and Black college students keep records of the sexist and racist behaviors they experienced or directly observed during a 2-week period. Overall, 78 percent of the women and 65 percent of the Black students reported at least one incident, with the women reporting an average of about two incidents per week and the Black students reporting an average of about one incident every other week. As shown in Table 5.1, the incidents reported by women included gender-role stereotyping, demeaning comments, and sexual objectification; Black students reported hostile nonverbal behaviors, verbal expression of prejudice, receiving poor service in stores and restaurants, and various negative interpersonal behaviors, such as rudeness and White people trying to avoid them.

. . . But Only Bad People Are Prejudiced . . .

Why does this apparent contradiction between people's nonprejudiced responses to questions about race, gender, and sexual orientation and their sometimes prejudiced everyday behavior exist? Two social processes seem to be at work. One is the sea change in American racial attitudes that has occurred since World War II (Schuman et al., 1997; Takaki, 1993). Prior to the war, prejudice by the White majority against members of other groups was the social norm. In the domain of race, the prejudice of this era is often referred to as **Jim Crow racism** and had three major components (Sears, Hetts, Sidanius, & Bobo, 2000). One was Whites' acceptance as absolute truth the belief that Whites were inherently superior to other races (and that men were inherently superior to women and that Christians

TABLE 5.1   PERCENTAGE OF WOMEN AND AFRICAN AMERICANS REPORTING HAVING OBSERVED SEXIST OR RACIST BEHAVIOR DURING 2-WEEK PERIODS

Type of Behavior	Examples	Percent Reporting
Sexist Behaviors[a]		
Gender-role stereotyping	Expressions of a double standard for men and women	36
Demeaning comments	Referring to a woman as "bitch" or "chick"	31
Sexual objectification	Staring at breasts, unwanted touches	25
Racist Behaviors[b]		
Nonverbal behavior	Hostile stares, being watched closely in stores	36
Verbal expressions	Racial slurs, prejudiced jokes	24
Bad service	Whites who arrived later seated first in restaurant	18
Interpersonal offense	Rude behavior, avoiding contact	15

[a] From Swim, Hyers, Cohen, & Ferguson (2001)
[b] From Swim, Hyers, Cohen, Fitzgerald, & Bylsma (2003)

were morally superior to adherents of other religions). A second component was a firm belief in the rightness of keeping minorities at a distance through racial segregation; "blacks were supposed to 'stay in their place,' separate and subordinate to whites" (Sears, Hetts et al., 2000, p. 9). The third component was the use of laws and the power of government to establish racially segregated school systems and other forms of discrimination, such as curtailment of voting rights. White people who were not prejudiced were looked on as somewhat strange; to call someone a "nigger lover" was intended as an insult. See Box 5.1 for more about Jim Crow racism.

World War II brought with it the beginnings of a change in those norms, especially in regard to race. As part of its domestic propaganda effort to rally support for the war against Nazi Germany, the U.S. government portrayed the Nazi racist ideology as dangerous and un-American, and the concept of racism as un-American came to be applied to the United States itself. For example, Republican presidential candidate Wendell Wilkie said, "It is becoming increasingly apparent to thoughtful Americans that we cannot fight the forces of imperialism abroad and maintain a form of imperialism at home. . . . Our very proclamations of what we are fighting for have rendered our own inequities self-evident. When we talk of freedom of opportunity for all nations, the mocking paradoxes in our own society become so clear that they can no longer be ignored" (quoted in Takaki, 1993, p. 374).

In the first two decades following the war, a number of events occurred that carried the message that racial prejudice was no longer an acceptable American value. In the immediate postwar years, President Harry Truman ordered the desegregation of the armed forces and proposed legislation (that was not enacted)

5.1   *Who Was Jim Crow?*

The type of racism that was prevalent in the United States until the 1960s is sometimes call *Jim Crow racism.* Jim Crow was a Black character created by the White minstrel show performer Thomas Rice in 1828. Wearing makeup that parodied African facial features, Rice portrayed the stereotypic Black man of the time: a lazy, somewhat stupid, and shiftless but happy-go-lucky person who spoke in an odd dialect and enjoyed singing and dancing (Wormser, 2003). To "protect" White people from such "degenerate" Black people, states passed laws that restricted the freedom of Blacks and other minority groups. Because of the fame of Rice's "Jim Crow" character, Jim Crow became a symbol of the ultra-stereotypic Black person. The laws passed to control and demean Black people then became known as *Jim Crow laws,* and the form of racism represented by those laws and the White attitudes underlying the laws came to be known as *Jim Crow racism.*

What were these laws like? The first Jim Crow laws were enacted in the North prior to the Civil War:

> Blacks . . . were prohibited from voting in all but five New England states. Schools and public accommodations were segregated. Illinois and Oregon barred blacks from entering the state. Blacks in every Northern city were restricted to ghettoes in the most unsanitary and run-down areas and forced to take menial jobs that white men rejected. White supremacy was as much a part of . . . the North as it was [of] the South. (Wormser, 2003, p. xi)

Although Southern states had laws restricting the freedoms of free Black people prior to the Civil War, the most severe laws were enacted after the end of the Reconstruction period when the pre–Civil War White upper class regained political power:

> As punitive and prejudicial as Jim Crow laws were in the North, they never reached the intensity of oppression . . . that they did in the South. A black person could not swim in the same pool, sit in the same public park, bowl, play pool or, in some states, checkers, drink from the same water fountain or use the same bathroom, marry, be treated in the same hospital, use the same schoolbooks, play baseball with, ride in the same taxicab, sit in the same section of a bus or train, be admitted to any private or public institution, teach in the same school, read in the same library, attend the same theater, or sit in the same area with a white person. Blacks had to address white people as Mr. [or] Mrs. . . . while they, in turn, were called by their first names, or by terms used to indicate social inferiority [such as] "boy". . . . Black people, if allowed in a store patronized by whites, had to wait until all the white customers were served first. If they attended a movie, they had to sit in the balcony. . . . They had to give way to whites on a sidewalk, remove their hats as a sign of respect when encountering whites, and enter a white person's house by the back door. . . . And while the degree of these restrictions often varied from state to state and county to county, white supremacy was the law of the South, and the slightest transgression could be punished by death. (Wormser, 2003, pp. xi–xii)

to ensure voting rights and equal employment opportunity for members of minority groups (Schuman et al., 1997). The anticommunist Cold War raised the same issue as Wilkie did during World War II: How could the United States criticize communist governments for violating the civil liberties of their citizens while not granting full equality to all U.S. citizens? For America to be able to influence other nations, its behavior had to be more consistent with its espoused values (Schuman, 2000). Racial equality was formally established as an American norm by the 1954 Supreme Court decision in *Brown v. Board of Education* that made segregated schools illegal and by the Civil Rights Act of 1964.

As these new norms diffused through society and especially as children grew up in a culture that promoted those norms, racism changed from being normal to being bad and racists began to be seen as bad people. Most White Americans came to see themselves as unprejudiced and to define prejudice and racism in terms of extreme behavior such as that associated with the Ku Klux Klan and to view racists as ignorant, crude, hostile, and generally undesirable (Crocker, Major, & Steele, 1998; Feagin & Vera, 1995).

... So "They" Should Stop Complaining

Although a norm of equality has been developing in the United States, it is difficult, if not impossible, to extinguish a cultural legacy of 400 years of racism in only a few decades (McConahay, Hardee, & Batts, 1981). This situation provides the basis for the second social process that contributes to the contradiction between people's nonprejudiced responses to survey questions and their sometimes prejudiced everyday behaviors: learning prejudiced beliefs through socialization. As we saw in Chapter 3, negative racial stereotypes still exist in American culture and Americans still absorb the negative emotions associated with those stereotypes. These negative emotions form part of what are called **implicit prejudices,** prejudices that can be assessed through implicit cognition and some behavioral measures (see Chapter 2), but which people are not aware of having. Despite this lack of conscious awareness, these prejudices affect White people's emotional responses to and behavior toward minority groups (see, for example, Brauer, Wasel, & Niedenthal, 2000; Dovidio, Kawakami, & Beach, 2001). In contrast to old-fashioned prejudice that is reflected in beliefs such as the biological superiority of Whites, support for racial segregation, and opposition to interracial marriage, this new form of prejudice is reflected in beliefs such as that discrimination no longer exists because laws have dealt with the problem and that members of minority groups should stop complaining and just get on with life; if they cannot achieve as much as Whites, that is their problem, not Whites' (McConahay et al., 1981).

As the political advisor quoted at the beginning of the chapter noted, the nature of prejudice has changed from being, in the words of Thomas Pettigrew and Roel Meertens (1995), "hot, close and direct" to being more "cool, distant and indirect" (p. 57). The next section describes some theories that address the nature of this new form of prejudice.

Theories of Contemporary Prejudice

Although, as we will see, there are several theories of this new form of prejudice, all share three propositions. One is that there has been a genuine change in America's social norms since World War II in the direction of belief in the principle of equality for all people. A second proposition is that not everyone has accepted this norm to the same degree. For example, the norm seems to have taken root first among more highly educated and more politically liberal people and to be gradually dispersing through society (Meertens & Pettigrew, 1997). In addition, it seems to be more influential in younger generations than older generations (Schuman et al., 1997). The third proposition is that even those people who have not yet fully accepted the norm are motivated to act in nonprejudiced ways. This motivation exists because these people do accept the norm to some degree and so do not want to think of themselves as being prejudiced and because they know that other people would disapprove of prejudiced behavior on their part (see, for example, Dunton & Fazio, 1997; Plant & Devine, 1998).

As a result, White people who hold contemporary prejudices express those prejudices in ways that can be justified on unprejudiced grounds. In the domain of race, such prejudice could be expressed in such ways as explaining a vote against a Black political candidate not on the grounds that she is Black, but because she is too liberal, and explaining opposition to programs that benefit members of minority groups (such as affirmative action) not as a way to keep minorities down but because such programs violate the American principle of equal treatment for all people. These types of attitudes and behaviors are not necessarily conscious attempts at making oneself look good to others while secretly opposing equality. Rather, they may represent a genuine acceptance of the principle of equality and rejection of traditional prejudice coupled with residual effects of old-fashioned prejudices that have been learned while growing up in an essentially prejudiced society (see, for example, Dovidio & Gaertner, 2004; Pettigrew & Meertens, 1995; Sears & Henry, 2003).

In the following sections, we describe four theories of contemporary prejudice: the theories of modern-symbolic prejudice, subtle prejudice, aversive prejudice, and racial ambivalence. Although most of these theories describe themselves as theories of racism (such as *symbolic racism*), for the most part we will use the term *prejudice* to describe them because many of their principles also apply to other forms of prejudice, such as prejudice based on gender (Swim, Aikin, Hall, & Hunter, 1995; Tougas, Brown, Beaton, & Joly, 1995) and sexual orientation (Morrison & Morrison, 2002). However, most of our examples deal with racial prejudice because the theories were originally developed to address that issue and most of the research inspired by these theories has focused on race.

MODERN-SYMBOLIC PREJUDICE

In the early 1970s, public opinion researchers noticed what appeared to be a contradiction between White Americans' endorsement of racial equality and their support for government interventions that would enforce equality. For example,

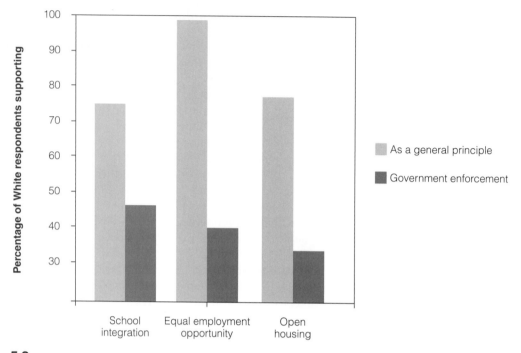

FIGURE **5.2**

INCONSISTENCY OF WHITE OPINION ON RACIAL ISSUES IN THE EARLY 1970S

Although Whites generally supported various aspects of racial equality as general principles, they also generally opposed government intervention to enforce those principles. (Adapted from Schuman, Steeh, Bobo, & Krysan, 1997)

as shown in Figure 5.2, White Americans expressed high levels of support for the principles of school integration, equal employment opportunity, and open housing. However, fewer than half the people surveyed supported government programs designed to put those principles into practice. Findings such as these led David Sears and John McConahay to independently develop the concept originally called *symbolic racism* (McConahay & Hough, 1976; Sears & Kinder, 1971; Sears & McConahay, 1973).

Symbolic racism is a set of beliefs about Black people as an abstract group (as in the anonymous "they" in "if they would only . . .") rather than as concrete individuals. These beliefs portray Black people as morally inferior to White people because Black people supposedly violate traditional (White) American values such as hard work and self-reliance. These beliefs are expressed behaviorally as "acts (voting against black candidates, opposing affirmative action programs, opposing desegregation in housing and education) that are justified (or rationalized) on a nonracial basis but that operate to maintain the racial status quo with its attendant discrimination" (McConahay & Hough, 1976, p. 24). Symbolic racism stands in contrast to **old-fashioned racism,** which is based on belief in the biological inferiority of Black people and the attendant stereotypes of low intelligence, laziness, and so forth; informal discrimination in the form of exclusion from certain jobs and segregated housing and social clubs; and legalized, formal discrimination in the form of racially separate schools and denial of voting rights. Symbolic racism theorists believe that social change has led most White Americans to reject most aspects of old-fashioned racism. However, because symbolic racism is not linked directly to race, but (as we will see) is linked indirectly to race through political and social issues, most White Americans do not see symbolic racist beliefs as prejudice (McConahay et al., 1981).

Although the concept was originally named *symbolic racism,* McConahay changed the name to **modern racism** "to emphasize the contemporary, post-civil-rights-movement nature of the tenets constituting the new ideology or belief system. The change also reflected the realization that both the new racism and the old-fashioned racism are symbolic in the sense that both are group-level abstractions rooted in early racial socialization and not in personal experience" (McConahay, 1986, p. 96). Other researchers also have taken the concept of symbolic or modern racism and given it different names, such as *racial resentment* and *laissez-faire racism.* Despite these differences, all are measured in much the same way and so represent essentially the same concept (Kinder & Mendelberg, 2000); Box 5.2 discusses some of the reasons behind this multiplicity of names. We will use the term *modern-symbolic prejudice* to emphasize that these concepts are essentially identical.

Characteristics of Modern-Symbolic Prejudice

The belief system of modern-symbolic prejudice is characterized by five themes that justify opposition to social policies designed to promote intergroup equality while still endorsing equality as an abstract principle (Henry & Sears, 2002; Sears & Henry, 2003):

- *Racial prejudice and discrimination no longer exist,* or are so rare as to no longer be a major impediment to the success and prosperity of African Americans. For example, people with modern-symbolic prejudice hold that civil rights legislation has eliminated discrimination. They view their own opposition to racially related policy issues such as affirmative action as being based on nonracial grounds such as fairness and therefore as not being a form of prejudice.
- *Any remaining Black-White differences in economic outcomes result from Black people's lack of motivation to work hard enough* to get what they want. Modern-symbolic prejudice is indicated by agreement with survey items such as "Irish, Italian, Jewish, and many other minorities overcame prejudice and worked their way up. Blacks should do the same without any special favors" (Sears & Henry, 2003, p. 275). Thus, inequality is attributed to the characteristics of its victims rather than continued prejudice and discrimination.
- *Because Black people are unwilling to work to get what they want, their continuing anger over inequality is unjustified.* This theme derives from the first two: If discrimination no longer hinders African Americans and if they do not want to work to get ahead, they should stop complaining about inequality.

5.2   *What's in a Name?*

We noted in the text that the terms *symbolic racism, modern racism, racial resentment,* and *laissez-faire racism* all represent essentially the same concept. Why, then, does that concept have so many names? In a workshop he presented as part of the 2003 meeting of the American Psychological Association, statistician Bruce Thompson only half-jokingly remarked that statisticians give the same statistical concept different names to make students think statistics is more difficult than it really is. Although one might be tempted to believe that the same principle is at work among theorists, those who work with the modern racism concept have used different terms because each has wanted to emphasize a different aspect of it.

David Sears and John McConahay (1973) originally chose the term *symbolic racism* to indicate that it was rooted in abstractions, such as cultural stereotypes of Blacks and cultural values, rather than in White people's direct experiences with Black people. As Sears and P. J. Henry (2003) recently wrote, "the term *symbolic* highlights both symbolic racism's targeting Blacks as an abstract collectivity rather than specific Black individuals and its presumed roots in abstract moral values rather than concrete self-interest or personal experience" (p. 260). McConahay renamed the concept *modern racism* "to emphasize the contemporary, post-civil rights movement nature of the beliefs and issues. Modern racism is indeed symbolic, but old-fashioned racism had its symbolic aspects as well—for example, beliefs and stereotypes rooted in socialization and not in personal experience" (McConahay et al., 1981, p. 565n).

Because some people misinterpreted symbolic racism as simply a cover for old-fashioned racism rather than a new form of prejudice, Donald Kinder and Lynn Sanders (1996) chose the term *racial resentment* to emphasize that contemporary racial attitudes are rooted in genuinely felt resentment over Black people's perceived violation of traditional values. Most recently, Lawrence Bobo, James Kluegel, and Ryan Smith (1997) coined the term *laissez-faire racism* to emphasize that modern racism's opposition to government programs designed to increase equality has the effect of keeping race relations essentially the way they were under old-fashioned racism, with Whites as the dominant group. (*Laissez-faire* is a French term that essentially means "let people do what they want" or "let events take their own course.")

- *Rather than working to get ahead, Black people seek special favors* from the government and corporations and are demanding too much from them. Modern-symbolic prejudice portrays policies designed to guarantee equality, such as open housing laws, and policies designed to remedy past discrimination, such as affirmative action, as special favors that minorities could do without if they would only work hard enough.
- *Relative to White people, Black people have been getting more than they deserve economically* because government and private agencies have given in to demands for special favors. Modern-symbolic prejudice portrays life as a

game in which the gains of minority groups must come at the expense of White people; win-win situations are seen as impossible. Thus, modern-symbolic prejudice views White people as being unfairly deprived of jobs, admission to selective colleges, and so forth, so that those resources can be given to members of minority groups who did not earn them.

For an example of how these themes emerge in White people's analyses of their own racial attitudes and how they are absent from Black people's self-analyses of their racial attitudes, see Box 5.3.

Psychological Bases of Modern-Symbolic Prejudice

The theory underlying modern-symbolic prejudice proposes that the themes described above reflect a particular set of interrelated emotions and beliefs (Hughes, 1997; McConahay & Hough, 1976; Sears & Henry, 2003; Sears, Henry, & Kosterman, 2000). The first of these factors is *mild to moderate anti-Black emotions.* Although people with modern-symbolic prejudice genuinely support the principle of racial equality, they nonetheless feel some degree of negative emotion toward African Americans. These emotions are not the strong feelings of hate and hostility experienced by old-fashioned racists, but less intense emotions such as anxiety, dislike, and resentment. Furthermore, unlike the explicit emotions expressed by old-fashioned racists, these emotions are often implicit, so that people may not be consciously aware of them.

People acquire these negative emotions and associated negative stereotypes through socialization. **Socialization** is the process of learning one's culture in childhood by being directly taught what things are important and by observing and imitating adults' behaviors and attitudes. Much of this process usually occurs without conscious awareness, thus facilitating the development of implicit attitudes (see, for example, Katz, 2003). As David Sears and his colleagues (Sears, van Laar, Carillo, & Kosterman, 1997) noted, "For several centuries white Americans have grown up in a socializing culture marked by widespread negative attitudes toward African Americans, a socializing culture that seems unlikely to have been abruptly overturned within the relatively few years since the end of Jim Crow" (p. 18). The effect of this type of socialization is shown by the results of survey research. For example, in 1994, there was virtually no difference in opinion between people born prior to 1936 (and so fully socialized in the culture of old-fashioned racism) and those born after 1962 (and so having grown up in a culture that rejected old-fashioned racism and promoted racial equality) on the extent to which lack of Black success was due to low motivation and not to discrimination (Schuman et al., 1997). Thus, despite an increasing acceptance of racial equality, some racist beliefs persist.

Two lines of research support the role of anti-Black affect in modern-symbolic prejudice. The first is that scores on measures of modern-symbolic prejudice are correlated with scores on measures of anti-Black affect, indicating that anti-Black affect is involved in modern-symbolic prejudice. The second line of research is the analysis of historical trends in survey data that shows that although White people's

5.3   *Modern-Symbolic Prejudice in People's Own Words*

Modern-symbolic prejudice may seem like a rather abstract concept, but it is one that people put into practice on a regular basis. Margo Monteith and Vincent Spicer (2000) asked White and Black college students to write essays about their attitudes toward the other race. As one would expect from the theory of modern-symbolic prejudice, the White students who expressed negative attitudes toward Blacks tended to write about Black people as a group in abstract, symbolic terms, rather than in terms of personal experience, as in this combination of two examples:

I have generally negative attitudes toward Blacks because I feel they follow the "give an inch, take a mile" cliché. Whites have attempted to integrate our society since the Civil War. [a] Although it has been a slow progress, it is to a point now where the civil rights are not really an issue. [b] The problem is, black people are not satisfied with this. They want 50% of everything from corporate positions to baseball coaches. [c] Our society does not work that way, however. People attain jobs or positions because of qualifications and not race now. I believe if you go to school and study, and have goals, you can achieve anything. If [unemployed Black people] wanted a job, they could get one, without blaming their failures on other races. Secondly, I feel that blacks are very guilty of "reverse discrimination." "Black" fraternities, and the "Black" Entertainment Television channel, and the "Black" student union are examples. If that is not segregation and discrimination, I don't know what is. . . . [a] I just think that blacks hold a tremendous chip on

their shoulder for no reason. Slavery is over, and civil rights give them every right and freedom [d] (often more opportunities) than Whites. For example, minority scholarships. (pp. 139–140)

Notice how the essay includes some of the defining elements of modern-symbolic prejudice, such as (a) denial of discrimination, (b) Blacks' making unreasonable demands, (c) appeal to traditional American values, and (d) Black people's gains coming at the expense of Whites.

In contrast, Black students who held negative attitudes toward Whites tended to write in concrete terms based on personal experience, as in this example:

I have generally negative attitudes toward Whites because of my experiences with them as a whole. When I was 10 years old my family moved from . . . an African American neighborhood to a mixed one. The Black kids and White kids would play together, but at school they segregated themselves. I was placed in a high level English class with all the White children. My English teacher, who was White, would give me this stupid grin whenever the subject of race would come up. . . . I heard many comments from my classmates of how stupid, ugly, or inhuman we appeared to them. Any White friend I made would quickly turn against me because their friends or parents didn't approve of me. In high school my best friend was White until I heard her use the "N" word when she described her Black math teacher. I will never fully trust them. (p. 141) attitudes toward the abstract principle of racial equality have become more positive since World War II (as shown by increased support for equal opportunity in housing, education, and employment), their feelings toward Black people have remained essentially unchanged (Schuman et al., 1997). For example, on a 100-point scale, on which higher scores indicate more positive emotion, Whites' feelings toward Blacks averaged 60 in 1964 and 63 in 1996.

A second factor underlying modern-symbolic prejudice is *belief in traditional values.* People with modern-symbolic prejudice also strongly endorse traditional (White) American values such as hard work, individualism, self-reliance, self-restraint, and so forth. However, in modern-symbolic prejudice, these values have become, to use David Sears and P. J. Henry's (2003) term, *racialized.* That is, it is not simple agreement with the abstract values that is implicated in modern-symbolic prejudice. Rather, it is the perception that Black people fail to act in accordance with these values, such as by accepting public assistance, seeking government favors, and acting impulsively, that drive modern-symbolic prejudice. The fact that White people also accept public assistance, seek government favors, and act impulsively is not relevant to people with modern-symbolic prejudice; it is their perception (usually in stereotypic terms) of Black people's behavior they focus on. As Sears and Henry noted, "a White man high in symbolic racism might have only a moderate work ethic himself but might feel that Blacks have reprehensively poor work ethics, which are responsible for many of their problems" (p. 261).

A third factor involved in modern-symbolic prejudice is *low outcome-based egalitarianism.* **Egalitarianism** is a value system that reflects the belief that all people are equal and should be treated identically. An apparent paradox of modern-symbolic prejudice is that people with modern-symbolic prejudice endorse racial equality in principle but oppose policies, such as affirmative action, that could bring it about. Sears and his colleagues (2000) have suggested that this apparent paradox arises because the term *equality* has two somewhat different meanings. One meaning is *equality of opportunity,* the principle that everyone should have an equal, fair chance at success in life and that one function of government is ensuring such equality. People with modern-symbolic prejudice endorse this type of equality.

A second meaning of equality is *equality of outcome,* the belief that government should ensure that everyone, regardless of their personal resources, should receive an equal, or at least a reasonable, share of society's resources. This belief is reflected in support for programs such as government-subsidized health care, housing, child care, and so forth for people who cannot afford them. It is this meaning of *equality* that people with modern-symbolic prejudice reject. They believe that given equal opportunity, success should depend on individuals' talents and effort; people whose talents and effort are equal will have equal outcomes. Therefore, government should not intervene to ensure equality of outcome despite differences in talent and effort; such intervention would be a violation of traditional values and a violation of equality of opportunity. Thus, as was shown in Figure 5.2, people can simultaneously endorse equality of opportunity and reject government intervention to bring about equality of outcome.

A fourth factor implicated in modern-symbolic prejudice is *group self-interest.* The concept of group self-interest reflects the idea that people try to promote the interests of the social groups that are important to them and respond negatively to perceived threats to group welfare. This idea is similar to the concept of *relative deprivation* that we will discuss in Chapter 8. In the context of modern-symbolic prejudice, group self-interest is shown in the perception that social programs designed to benefit minority groups will unfairly deprive Whites as a group of opportunities for jobs, for advancement at work, for education, and so forth. John McConahay and Joseph Hough (1976) noted that "symbolic racism is very much a reaction to the civil rights movement, especially the Northern phase of that movement" (p. 237) that saw the introduction of affirmative action programs.

Finally, people with modern-symbolic prejudice have *little personal knowledge of Black people.* Although racial segregation has decreased in the United States, most White people still live in all-White or predominantly White neighborhoods and most interracial contact occurs in relatively structured settings such as work or school (see, for example, Bonilla-Silva, 2003). Consequently, most White people have little opportunity to get to know Black people as individuals, so the stereotypes that support modern-symbolic prejudice continue to endure.

Historical Roots of Modern-Symbolic Prejudice

Lawrence Bobo, James Kluegel, and Ryan Smith (1997) add a historical perspective to the origins of modern-symbolic prejudice, tracing its roots to the end of the Civil War. They note that old-fashioned or Jim Crow racism functioned to keep Black people, especially those living in the southern United States, in a state of social and economic oppression not substantially different from that which existed when they had been slaves. However, as cultural trends turned away from old-fashioned racism and the social power of Black Americans increased, Jim Crow racism was replaced by what Bobo and colleagues call *laissez-faire racism* (see Box 5.2).

In Bobo and colleagues' analysis, laissez-faire racism frames the cause of Black-White differences in economic success in terms of differences in culture and values rather than in old-fashioned racism's terms of innate, biologically based differences in ability. Yet, laissez-faire racism (or modern-symbolic prejudice) serves the same sociological purpose as old-fashioned prejudice: Modern-symbolic prejudice "legitimates persistent black oppression in the United States, but now in a manner more appropriate to a modern, nationwide, postindustrial free labor economy and [political system]. In effect, a significant segment of white America effectively condones as much black disadvantage and segregation as . . . modern-day free-market forces and informal social mechanisms can reproduce or even exacerbate" (Bobo et al., 1997, pp. 21–22). In this view, modern-symbolic prejudice is motivated by a desire (although not necessarily a conscious one) on the part of many White Americans to retain and justify their traditional privileged position in society and the attendant access to the lion's share of societal resources (such as jobs, educational opportunities, and political power) that they see as threatened by Black economic gain. In Chapter 6, we will examine a more general approach to this attitude called *social dominance orientation.*

Modern-Symbolic Prejudice and Behavior

When it comes to dealing with Black people, White people who experience modern-symbolic prejudice are in a bind. On the one hand, their anti-Black emotions, their resentment over Black peoples' perceived violation of traditional values and the principle that outcomes should result from merit, and their desire to protect White privilege should lead them to behave in ways detrimental to Blacks. On the other hand, people with modern-symbolic prejudice genuinely endorse equality as an abstract principle and so are motivated not to act in ways that could be called prejudiced. In doing so, they hope both to maintain their self-images as unprejudiced people and to appear unprejudiced to others. The solution to this dilemma is to act in ways that are detrimental to Black people only in situations in which the behavior can be attributed to nonracial causes (McConahay, 1983; McConahay et al., 1981). Thus, White people with modern-symbolic prejudice say they oppose affirmative action programs not because they oppose racial equality but because such programs violate the principle of equal opportunity and give an unfair advantage to members of minority groups (see, for example, Sears, Sidanius, & Bobo, 2000).

White people with modern-symbolic prejudice also tend to discriminate against Black people when the discrimination can be justified on nonracial grounds. For example, Arthur Brief and his colleagues (Brief, Dietz, Cohen, Pugh, & Vaslow, 2000) had college students who had completed a measure of modern-symbolic prejudice earlier in the semester evaluate the résumés of 10 job applicants and recommend three for interviews. Of the 10 applicants, three were qualified Blacks, two were qualified Whites, and five were unqualified Whites. The students were also given a copy of a memorandum from the president of the company. For half the students, the memorandum made no mention of race; in the other version of the memorandum, the president wrote that "I feel that it is important that you do not hire anyone who is a member of a minority group" because the person hired would be dealing with coworkers and customers who were White (Brief et al., 2000, p. 80). When no justification had been given for not hiring a Black candidate, students high and low in modern-symbolic prejudice recommended Black candidates at the same rate, 61 percent. However, when discrimination was justified by a business reason given by the company president, 37 percent of the students low in modern-symbolic prejudice recommended a Black applicant compared to 18 percent of the students high in modern-symbolic prejudice. (Note, however, that even students low in modern-symbolic prejudice gave in to pressure from the president, although not to the degree shown by those high in modern-symbolic prejudice.) If Brief and colleagues' research seems too artificial, see Box 5.4 for a real-life example of this process.

5.4   *Modern-Symbolic Prejudice at Work*

Modern-symbolic prejudice tends to operate in subtle ways and be superficially justifiable, as in the story recounted by a business executive:

> I was interviewing a bunch of people for a certain position [at our workplace]. We had a black guy come in who was a supervisor of a division of our type. I ended up hiring an Asian American. Basically, I was weighing in my mind, this [black] guy was really well qualified. But I was also weighing in my mind, well, how would he interact with the people within the group. He was going to be in somewhat of a supervisory role. I was weighing in my mind how people would react to him because he was black. The dilemma was solved for me because I was sitting at home trying to think who would I really like for this position. I said I'd like somebody like this Asian American fellow. (Feagin & Vera, 1995, p. 157).

Notice two characteristics of modern-symbolic prejudice that come out in this story. One is a justification for not hiring the Black applicant that is unrelated to the executive's own racial attitudes: The applicant would not make a good supervisor for this group because, presumably, the people working for him would not accept him. Another is that the executive can maintain his own (and his company's) image as nonprejudiced: After all, he did hire a member of a minority group.

Concluding Comments

By now the theory of modern-symbolic prejudice might seem overwhelming, so Figure 5.3 provides a diagram that ties the pieces together. Modern-symbolic prejudice is rooted in the tension between the genuine belief in racial equality in terms of equal opportunity that has become the American norm since World War II and other emotional and cognitive factors that include implicit anti-Black affect, racialized traditional values, low belief in equality of outcome without equality of effort and ability, group self-interest, and little personal knowledge (as opposed to stereotypic beliefs) about Black people. Modern-symbolic prejudice is reflected in denial of continuing discrimination, the belief that Black people should work harder to achieve success, and the beliefs that claims of continued inequality are unjustified and that Blacks are demanding special favors and receiving undeserved outcomes. Modern-symbolic prejudice is manifested in opposition to equality-enhancing social programs such as affirmative action and individual discrimination when discrimination can be explained in nonracial terms. Although the theory does not address institutional discrimination, the expression of modern-symbolic prejudice by individuals in organizations, as illustrated by the story related in Box 5.4, probably results in institutional discrimination as well. The net result is continuing racial inequality.

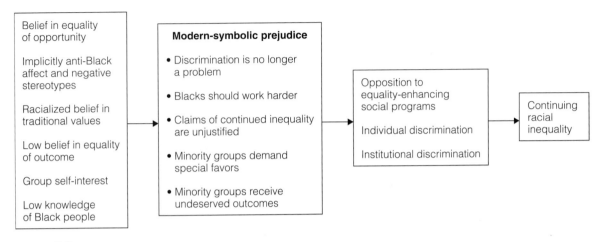

FIGURE **5.3**

MODEL OF MODERN-SYMBOLIC PREJUDICE

Modern-symbolic prejudice is rooted in the tension between belief in equal opportunity and other emotional and cognitive factors that include implicit anti-Black affect, racialized traditional values, low belief in equality of outcome without equality of effort and ability, group self-interest, and little personalized knowledge of Black people. Modern-symbolic prejudice is reflected in denial of continuing discrimination, the belief that Blacks should work harder, and beliefs that claims of continued inequality are unjustified, that Blacks are demanding special favors and receiving undeserved outcomes. Modern-symbolic prejudice is manifested in opposition to equality-enhancing social programs and individual and institutional discrimination when discrimination can be explained in nonracial terms. The net result is continuing racial inequality.

SUBTLE PREJUDICE

Subtle prejudice (Pettigrew & Meertens, 1995; Meertens & Pettigrew, 1997) is an outgrowth of modern-symbolic prejudice. Developed in Europe, where different ethnic groups can be the targets of prejudice in different countries, the concept of subtle prejudice encompasses prejudice toward a variety of groups, in contrast to modern-symbolic prejudice, which is focused on White Americans' prejudice against African Americans. There are also a few conceptual differences. For example, drawing on research that shows that people can have both positive and negative emotional reactions to the same object, the theory of subtle prejudice postulates that members of the majority group feel low positive affect toward members of minority groups. That is, whereas the emotional component of modern-symbolic prejudice consists of mild to moderate negative affect, the emotional component of subtle prejudice is indifference.

Like White people with modern-symbolic prejudice, those with subtle prejudice strongly endorse the traditional values of their cultures. However, Thomas Pettigrew and Roel Meertens (1995) added the concept of exaggeration of cultural differences as a component of subtle prejudice. That is, people with subtle prejudice tend to see differences between majority and minority group cultures as greater than they really are. Thus, subtle prejudice results not only from perceptions that minority groups violate traditional values but also from a perception of a vast gap between cultures. This belief exacerbates the perception of value violation and leads to the belief that minority group members could never adopt or coexist with the majority culture.

Just as scores on measures of old-fashioned and modern-symbolic prejudice are correlated, so are scores on subtle and blatant (as Pettigrew & Meertens, 1995, call it) prejudice. Some critics have suggested that this correlation means that modern-symbolic and subtle prejudice are just old-fashioned prejudice under new names (see, for example, Sniderman & Tetlock, 1986a). However, Pettigrew and Meertens point out that there is a natural overlap between the two concepts because people who endorse old-fashioned prejudice share some beliefs with people who endorse modern-symbolic and subtle prejudice. For example, in addition to beliefs of White superiority and feelings of strong hostility toward minority groups, old-fashioned racists also deny that minority groups are discriminated against, complain about minority groups' not working hard enough to achieve equality, see minority groups as benefiting from special favors to the detriment of Whites, and exaggerate cultural differences between minority groups and the majority group. The difference between old-fashioned racists and people with modern-symbolic and subtle prejudice is that the latter have rejected old-fashioned prejudiced beliefs while retaining contemporary prejudiced beliefs. Truly unprejudiced people reject both old-fashioned and modern-symbolic or subtle prejudiced beliefs.

Aversive Prejudice

Psychoanalyst Joel Kovel (1970) coined the term **aversive racism (or prejudice)** to describe the attitudes of a person who "tries to ignore the existence of black people, tries to avoid contact with them, and at most to be polite, correct, and cold in whatever dealings are necessary between the races" (p. 54). In the 1980s, John Dovidio and Samuel Gaertner began to systematically explore the nature and effects of aversive prejudice (see, for example, Dovidio & Gaertner, 2004).

Characteristics of Aversive Prejudice

Aversive prejudice is similar to modern-symbolic prejudice in that people who experience it truly believe in equality but nonetheless retain implicit negative feelings toward minority groups. As in modern-symbolic prejudice, these negative feelings are usually low key, involving such emotions as discomfort and uneasiness rather than hostility or hatred. As does the theory of modern-symbolic prejudice, the theory of aversive prejudice postulates that White people absorb implicit negative attitudes toward minority groups while they are growing up; indeed, Dovidio and Gaertner (1991) believe that acquiring some degree of racial bias is unavoidable for White children growing up in American culture.

However, aversive prejudice differs from modern-symbolic prejudice in a number of ways (Dovidio & Gaertner, 1998; Gaertner et al., 1997). First, people who experience aversive prejudice generally reject the racialized traditional beliefs that support modern-symbolic prejudice and support equality-enhancing social programs such as affirmative action. Second, people who experience aversive prejudice are more strongly motivated to see themselves as unprejudiced and lack of prejudice is an important aspect of their self-concepts. Finally, despite their strong support for equality and strong motivation to avoid appearing prejudiced, White people experiencing aversive prejudice prefer to avoid most interracial contact because it arouses the negative affect they associate with minority groups.

Aversive prejudice is also reflected in behavior:

- "When interracial interaction is unavoidable, aversive racists experience anxiety and discomfort, and consequently they try to disengage from the interaction as quickly as possible" (Dovidio & Gaertner, 1998, p. 7).
- However, because of their motivation to avoid appearing prejudiced, White people who experience aversive prejudice "strictly adhere to established rules and codes of behavior in the interracial situations they cannot avoid" (Dovidio & Gaertner, 1998, p. 7). "Indeed, they may over-compensate . . . by responding more favorably to blacks than to whites" (Gaertner et al., 1997, p. 169).
- Finally, the negative feelings experienced by White people with aversive prejudice "will get expressed, but in subtle, rationalizable ways that may ultimately disadvantage minorities or unfairly benefit the majority group" (Dovidio & Gaertner, 1998, p. 7). In general, aversive prejudice theory tends to place more emphasis on the pro-White aspect of prejudice, a component that has been largely overlooked until recently in research and theory on prejudice (Gaertner et al., 1997).

Psychological Bases of Aversive Prejudice

Dovidio and Gaertner (1998) propose three psychological underpinnings for aversive prejudice. The first is the human predisposition to cognitive categorization that we discussed in Chapter 3. This predisposition leads people to categorize people into discrete social groups and to contrast the groups to which they belong with other groups. This categorization, in turn, fosters bias because, as we discuss in more detail in Chapter 8, people tend to believe that their own groups are better than other groups. A second factor is motivational: People have a need to control their environments to ensure positive outcomes for themselves and their groups. "In a world of limited resources, one of the ways that people maintain their control or power is by resisting the progress of competing groups" (Dovidio & Gaertner, 1998, p. 6). This motivation is much like the group self-interest factor in modern-symbolic prejudice, but it plays a less direct role in influencing behavior in the theory of aversive prejudice.

The most important psychological component in the theory of aversive prejudice is the socialization of two sets of incompatible values. On the one hand, the theory holds, every White person has been socialized to some extent in the racist traditions that have characterized American history. This socialization process results in implicit prejudice in the form of negative stereotypes and emotions being associated with minority groups. On the other hand, people who experience aversive prejudice have also been socialized to genuinely believe in the American ideals of racial fairness, justice, and equality. The conflict between these inconsistent values leads to conflicting feelings about racial issues and members of minority groups and to inconsistent behavior toward members of those groups: Sometimes people experiencing aversive prejudice will discriminate (reflecting their implicit negative feelings), sometimes not (reflecting their egalitarian beliefs).

It is the characteristics of the situation that determine which behavior aversive prejudice will produce. People experiencing aversive prejudice "will not discriminate in situations in which they recognize that discrimination would be obvious to others and themselves. . . . When people are presented with a situation in which [an egalitarian, nonprejudiced] response is clear, in which right and wrong is clearly defined, aversive racists will not discriminate. . . . [However,] discrimination will occur when appropriate (and thus inappropriate) behavior is not obvious or when an aversive racist can justify or rationalize a negative response on the basis of some factor other than race. Under these circumstances, aversive racists may discriminate, but in a way that insulates them from ever having to believe that their behavior was racially motivated" (Dovidio & Gaertner, 1998, p. 7).

Research on Aversive Prejudice

This focus on the role of situational factors has led researchers who study aversive prejudice to take an approach to research different from that used by researchers working with other theories of prejudice. Most theories of prejudice attempt to identify the prejudiced person by measuring prejudice as a trait and to study prejudice by correlating scores on the prejudice measure with scores on measures of presumed causes of prejudice (such as racialized traditional values in the case of modern-symbolic prejudice) and with discriminatory behaviors. In contrast, Dovidio and Gaertner (1991) note that "the focus of our research has not been on who is biased—we assume that most people, because they are normal, have developed some racial biases. . . . Instead, our focus is on systematically identifying the situational conditions that will prime the egalitarian portion of an aversive racists's attitude and reveal the contexts in which the negative feelings will be manifested" (Dovidio & Gaertner, 1991, p. 131).

One result of this approach to research is that the study of aversive prejudice focuses on interracial interaction, either actual or simulated, and so more on concrete situations in contrast to modern-symbolic prejudice's focus on people's responses to racial groups as abstract collectivities. That is, to a large extent, research on aversive prejudice takes a more personal approach to prejudice, examining, for example, a White person's response to a specific Black person rather than to Black people in general. Another result is that because the theory emphasizes situational factors, there is no measure of aversive prejudice. Instead, the effects of aversive prejudice are inferred from the ways in which people respond to situations that are designed to arouse it.

Aversive Prejudice and Behavior

The theory of aversive prejudice makes a number of rather specific predictions about behavior. The predicted behaviors include avoidance of intergroup contact, overly positive intergroup behavior when situational norms call for polite behavior, a pro-White bias in ambiguous situations, discrimination when the behavior can be justified as unprejudiced, and derogation of members of minority groups who hold higher status positions.

Avoidance of intergroup contact   One characteristic behavior of people experiencing aversive prejudice is avoiding contact with members of minority groups. The results of research suggest that this is especially true for close, personal contact. Recall, for example, the results of Muir's (1991) study of White college students discussed earlier in this chapter. He found that while the vast majority of the students felt comfortable with distant interpersonal contact, such as sitting next to a Black student in a classroom or eating at the same table in the cafeteria, they were less certain about more personal contact. For example, fewer than half said they would be willing to have a Black roommate and only about 10 percent said they would be willing to date a Black student. Results of national surveys lead to the same conclusion about close contact (Schuman et al., 1997): Although 90 percent of White Americans support open housing laws, 43 percent prefer to live in all- or predominantly White neighborhoods; although 87 percent oppose laws forbidding interracial marriage, only 50 percent say they approve of interracial marriage. Sometimes even relatively indirect contact can motivate avoidance; Box 5.5 describes some of the tactics Black homeowners have to use when selling to prevent potential White buyers from avoiding their homes.

The theory of aversive prejudice holds that this kind of avoidance is motivated by feelings of anxiety and discomfort. Several lines of research support this part of the theory. First, using physiological measures, Wendy Mendes and her colleagues (Mendes, Blascovich, Lickel, & Hunter, 2002) found that when interacting with a Black man, White research participants showed cardiovascular responses associated with feelings of threat that were absent when they interacted with a White man. However, the participants' self-reports indicated that they liked the Black man better than the White man. Taking a different approach, Tamara Towles-Schwen and Russell Fazio (2003) asked White college students to imagine themselves in situations of varying degrees of intimacy with either a Black person or someone whose race was not specified. Low intimacy situations included those such as sitting at a library table with the other person; high intimacy situations included those such as sharing a small dorm room with the other person. As in Muir's (1991) survey study, Towles-Schwen and Fazio found that their research participants were more willing to interact with a Black person in low intimacy situations than in high intimacy situations; they also found that the students said they would feel more comfortable with a Black person in a low intimacy situation. Finally, John Dovidio, Kerry Kawakami, and Samuel Gaertner (2002) found behavioral evidence of discomfort in a study in which White college students

5.5   *The Effect of Aversive Prejudice on African Americans: "The Box"*

Aversive prejudice is characterized by a desire to avoid contact with members of other races. This example illustrates not only that even very remote contact can be aversive, but that the aversion also affects the lives of Black people in demeaning ways:

> Some people simply call it "the box." It's usually a large cardboard box found hidden away in a walk-in closet or down in the basement next to the washing machine. It contains diplomas, artwork, books, music, and especially all the family photos—anything that can identify the family as black. If a black family living in a predominantly white neighborhood wants to sell their house, they are often advised by friends or their real estate agent to put everything identifiably black—any vestige of who they are—in the box. Otherwise, white people may not buy the house. . . .

> It happened to a *Wall Street Journal* editor, who, after his house was appraised significantly below market value, decided not only to replace all the family photos with those of his white secretary but asked her and her blond son to be in the house when a new appraiser came by. The strategy worked. Black families are also advised to clear out when prospective white buyers want to see the house. Too many times a white family will drive up to a house, see the black home owner working in the garden or garage, and quickly drive away.
>
> The box is a very small part of the daily commerce between blacks and whites. . . . But as a metaphor for race relations it looms very large, because it shows the lengths to which whites will go to avoid intimate contact with anything black. (Steinhorn & Diggs-Brown, 1999, pp. 29–30)

discussed a race-neutral topic with a Black partner. During the interaction, the White students gave off nonverbal cues, such as avoiding eye contact, that indicate anxiety and discomfort.

Where does this discomfort come from? Walter and Cookie Stephan's (2000; Stephan et al., 2002) theory of intergroup anxiety (discussed in more detail in Chapter 6) proposes several sources: Negative stereotypes and prior negative experiences with members of the other group cause anxiety by leading people to anticipate a negative response from the person with whom they are interacting, and lack of knowledge about the other group makes people uncertain about how to behave in interracial situations. The results of research conducted by Michelle Hebl and Laura Mannix (2003) suggest an additional motive for avoidance and anxiety: concern over stigma by association. Hebl and Mannix found that a man sitting next to an overweight woman was rated more negatively than a man seated next to an average-weight woman. If people believe that others will think less of them for associating with a member of a negatively viewed group, they may try to avoid such associations and feel anxiety when anticipating and during interactions with a member of such a group.

In their study of White college students' comfort with interracial interactions, Towles-Schwen and Fazio (2003) also found that participants expressed a preference for interracial interactions in highly scripted situations. In highly scripted situations, the rules for interaction are clear and accepted by all participants; such situations reduce the likelihood of one person's making a social blunder and inadvertently insulting the other person. It is in these kinds of situations that aversive prejudice motivates White people to adhere to social norms and to act in an unprejudiced manner during interactions with members of minority groups. For example, Dovidio (2001) conducted a study in which White research participants were divided into three groups: traditional prejudice (those who scored high on measures of both explicit and implicit prejudice; see Chapter 2), aversive prejudice (those who scored on low explicit prejudice but on high implicit prejudice), and unprejudiced (those who scored low on both measures). The participants then worked on a problem-solving task with a Black partner. As shown by the lighter bars in Figure 5.4, the participants in the unprejudiced and aversive prejudice groups tried to abide by the norm of the work situation and treat their partners in a friendly (that is, unprejudiced) manner; as would be expected, the participants in the traditional prejudice group made less effort to be friendly. However, as shown by the darker bars, the participants' Black partners perceived those exhibiting both aversive and traditional prejudice to be relatively unfriendly. Even though the aversive prejudice participants were trying to be friendly, their Black partners picked up on their nonverbal expressions of anxiety and interpreted them as indicating unfriendliness, perhaps because those cues contradicted the participants' nonverbal behavior. In contrast, the Black partners of the unprejudiced participants perceived them as friendly because their nonverbal behavior matched their verbal behavior.

Overly positive intergroup behavior   The theory of aversive prejudice also holds that the desire to appear unprejudiced will lead people to overdo their efforts to appear unprejudiced and be unduly positive in their interactions with members of minority groups. An example of this effect appears in a study conducted by Kent Harber (1998). Harber had White students provide written feedback on a poorly written essay that they thought was composed by either a Black or White student. The participants were told that the writer would see the feedback, which, according to the theory of aversive prejudice, should cause the participants to try to be fair in their evaluations because they do not want to appear prejudiced to themselves, the person to whom they are giving feedback, or the experimenter. Because all participants read the same essay, a truly unbiased evaluation would result in the Black and White writers getting the same feedback. However, the Black writer got more positive feedback; their evaluators overcompensated for their aversive prejudice in trying to evaluate the essay fairly. Similarly, Jennifer Crosby and Benoît Monin (2004) found that White college students' being trained as peer counselors were less willing to tell a Black student than a White student that a proposed course load was too difficult. Presumably, the peer counselor trainees were concerned that they would appear prejudiced by implying that a Black student was not capable of handling a heavy academic workload.

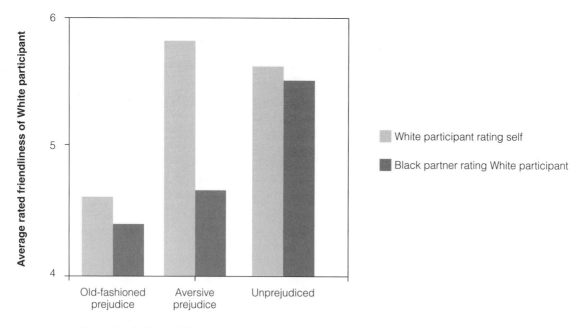

FIGURE 5.4

INTERRACIAL DISCOMFORT IN AVERSIVE PREJUDICE

White research participants who exhibited aversive prejudice (low explicit prejudice but high implicit prejudice) tried to act in a friendly manner, but were perceived to be less friendly because they gave off nonverbal cues indicative of nervousness. In contrast, participants who exhibited traditional prejudice (high on both explicit and implicit prejudice) did not try to act in a friendly manner and were perceived as less friendly and unprejudiced participants (low on both forms of prejudice) tried to act in a friendly manner and were perceived as friendly. (Adapted from Dovidio, 2001, Table 1, p. 845)

Pro-White bias   Although people experiencing aversive prejudice try to be unprejudiced when the situation presents a clearly unprejudiced response to choose, the theory also holds that they will show a pro-White bias in ambiguous situations, when the unprejudiced response is not clearly defined. For example, Dovidio and Gaertner (2000) conducted a study in which White college students were asked to evaluate a candidate for a peer counselor job on the basis of a résumé and the transcript of an interview. The candidate was presented as being either Black or White; in some cases he was well qualified, in some cases he was poorly qualified, and in some cases the qualifications were ambiguous, with the person being well qualified in some ways but poorly qualified in other ways. As shown in Figure 5.5, when the candidate's qualifications were either clearly strong or clearly weak, the participants recommended the Black and White candidates at about the same rate. However, when the ambiguously qualified candidate was presented as White, he was recommended much more often than when he was presented as Black. The pro-White bias in these decisions is shown by the fact that when other research participants evaluated the candidates without being

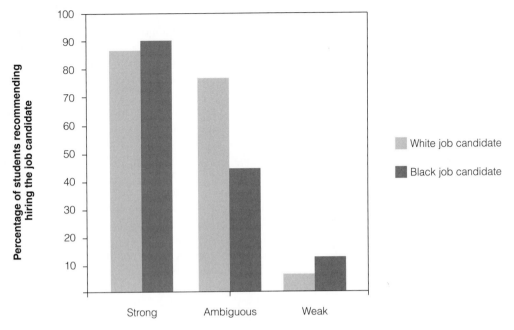

FIGURE **5.5**

PRO-WHITE BIAS IN AVERSIVE PREJUDICE

When the candidate's qualifications were either clearly strong or clearly weak, Black and White applicants were recommended for hire at about the same rate. However, when the candidate's qualifications were ambiguous, the Black candidate was recommended for hire at about the rate that would be expected for an unbiased judgment, but the White candidate was recommended for hire more often than would be expected for an unbiased judgment. (Adapted from Dovidio & Gaertner, 2000, Table 1, p. 317)

given any information about race, the candidate with ambiguous qualifications was recommended about 50 percent of the time. When race was included (Figure 5.5), the Black candidate was recommended 45 percent of the time, indicating an unbiased decision; however, the White candidate was recommended 76 percent of the time, which is much more frequently than would be expected in an unbiased decision. The results of a study conducted by Gordon Hodson, John Dovidio, and Samuel Gaertner (2002) indicated that this difference came about because, when making their decisions, evaluators gave more weight to negative than to positive information about Black applicants. In essence, the White candidate was getting a "benefit of the doubt" that was denied the Black candidate.

Anti-minority discrimination The theory of aversive prejudice also holds that people experiencing aversive prejudice will discriminate against members of other groups when the behavior can be justified as unprejudiced. For example, Dovidio and his colleagues (Dovidio, Smith, Donnella, & Gaertner, 1997) had

White research participants who had previously been classified as high or low on old-fashioned prejudice read a transcript of a murder trial in which either a Black or White defendant was found guilty. Their task was to decide whether the defendant should be sentenced to death or to life in prison without parole. They then saw videotapes of what they thought were five other jurors recommending the death penalty and giving strong reasons for doing so. In one set of tapes all the jurors were White; in the other set one juror was Black. The theory of aversive prejudice would predict that participants low in traditional prejudice (and therefore presumably experiencing aversive prejudice) would not discriminate in recommending the death penalty when only White jurors advocated it because making a stronger recommendation for the Black defendant might make them appear to be prejudiced. However, if a *Black* juror advocated the death penalty, they could justify a death penalty recommendation without appearing to be prejudiced. Because they were following the advice of a Black person who was presumably making a fair recommendation regarding the Black defendant, they would be free to express their prejudice by making a strong death penalty recommendation for the Black defendant. Dovidio and his colleagues found that, as would be expected, participants high in traditional prejudice made stronger recommendations for the death penalty for the Black defendant regardless of whether a Black person advocated it. However, as shown in Figure 5.6, the outcome for participants low in traditional prejudice was consistent with the theory of aversive prejudice: When only White people advocated the death penalty, the White defendant received stronger death penalty recommendation, but when a Black person advocated the death penalty, the Black defendant received stronger death penalty recommendations than the White defendant.

Derogation of higher status minority group members

A final implication of the theory of aversive prejudice is that because one of the implicit attitudes that White people acquire through socialization is a belief in White superiority, the discomfort associated with aversive prejudice should be greater when Black people are in higher status positions. For example, Jennifer Knight and her colleagues (Knight, Hebl, Foster, & Mannix, 2002) had White college students rate the performance of an employee based on a summary of information about the person. The person was either White or Black and in either a supervisory or subordinate job. The research participants gave higher ratings to the White supervisor than the Black supervisor, but rated the Black subordinate higher than the White subordinate. In an earlier study on the effect of status, Dovidio and Gaertner (1981) assigned White research participants to work with either a Black or White partner who was appointed to be either the participant's superior or subordinate and was described as being high or low in ability. During the task the two were working on together, the partner "accidentally" dropped some pencils. Dovidio and Gaertner wanted to see how often the participant helped his partner. They found that the higher status Black partner was helped less often (58 percent) than the lower status Black partner (83 percent), but that the higher status White partner was helped slightly more often (54 percent) than the lower status White partner (41 percent). The researchers also found that the participants

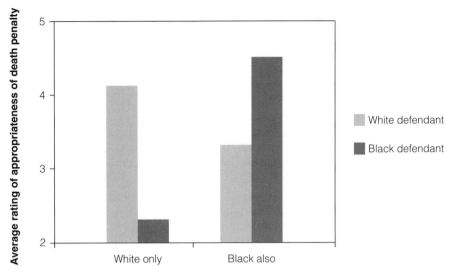

FIGURE **5.6**

ANTI-BLACK BIAS THAT APPEARS UNPREJUDICED

When only White people advocated the death penalty, the White defendant received stronger death penalty recommendations than the Black defendant, but when a Black person advocated the death penalty, the Black defendant received stronger death penalty recommendations than the White defendant. In the first situation, a death penalty recommendation for the Black defendant might look as though it resulted from prejudice, but in the second situation it can be justified as unprejudiced because the participants are making the decision advocated by a Black person, who is presumably not prejudiced against other Black people. (Adapted from Dovidio, Smith, Donnella, & Gaertner, 1997, Figure 1, p. 1478)

thought that the high ability White partner was somewhat more intelligent than themselves, but rated the high ability Black partner as significantly less intelligent than themselves. In a later review of this and similar research, Dovidio and Gaertner (1991) concluded that "although whites may accept that a black person is intelligent on an absolute dimension, [they] are reluctant to accept . . . that a black person is high or equal in intelligence compared to themselves" (p. 140).

AMBIVALENT PREJUDICE

The theories of contemporary prejudice that we have examined thus far have postulated that although contemporary White Americans have, for the most part, adopted the principle of racial equality, some anti-Black emotions and beliefs remain. Like those theories, the theory of **ambivalent prejudice** developed by Irwin Katz and his colleagues (Katz, 1981; Katz & Hass, 1988; Katz, Wackenhut, & Hass, 1986) holds that White Americans genuinely accept the principle of racial equality. However, it

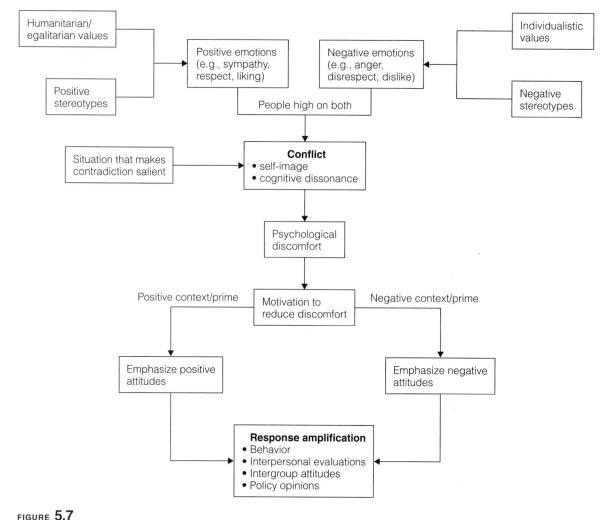

FIGURE 5.7

AMBIVALENT PREJUDICE

People who simultaneously hold contradictory values and beliefs about minority group members experience conflict when they become aware of the contradiction. This conflict generates negative emotional responses that they are motivated to reduce. The discomfort can be reduced by emphasizing one aspect of the attitude over the other; the aspect that is emphasized depends on situational cues. Negative cues lead to overly negative behavior and positive cues lead to overly positive behavior.

also postulates many White Americans have developed genuinely positive attitudes toward Black people that exist along with the lingering negative attitudes. Because these White people see Black people as having both positive and negative characteristics, their attitudes are ambivalent and so is their behavior: sometimes it is positive, sometimes negative. The theory, diagrammed in Figure 5.7, is designed to explain the circumstances that lead to positive or negative behavior.

Ambivalent Attitudes

Two groups of theorists have suggested different, but complementary, sources of ambivalent racial attitudes. Irwin Katz and Glen Hass (1988) postulated that two sets of American values are important to ambivalent prejudice. One set of values centers on *individualism*, emphasizing personal responsibility, hard work as the means to success, self-reliance, and trying to improve one's lot in life. These values are similar to the racialized traditional values of modern-symbolic prejudice, but they are not directly connected to race in the theory of ambivalent prejudice. Katz and Hass (1988) emphasize the value-of-work aspect of the concept, measuring it with items such as "Anyone who is willing and able to work hard has a good chance of succeeding" and "A distaste for hard work usually reflects a weakness of character" (p. 905). The other set of values centers on *egalitarianism* and *humanitarianism,* the beliefs that all people should be treated equally and that people have a responsibility to help others who are disadvantaged. (To keep the terminology simple, we will use the term *egalitarianism* to represent this concept.) This value position is indicated by agreement with items such as "Those who are unable to provide for their basic needs should be helped by others" and "Prosperous nations have a moral obligation to share some of their wealth with poor nations" (Katz & Hass, 1988, p. 905). Note that Katz and Hass's concept of egalitarianism seems to focus on the equality of outcome aspect that people with modern-symbolic prejudice reject.

Two sets of White people's beliefs about Black people also are important to the theory. First, because of Black Americans' history of being the targets of discrimination and exclusion from the mainstream of society, White people perceive Black people as being both deviant and disadvantaged. The deviance aspect comes from a perception that Black Americans' beliefs, customs, and culture lead them to behave in ways that make it difficult for them to fit into "proper" (that is, White) American society. The disadvantaged aspect reflects the reality that Black Americans are, on the average, less well-off economically and socially than White Americans. The theory of ambivalent prejudice holds that these beliefs intersect with people's value orientations. An individualistic orientation leads people to focus on the perception that Black people are deviant and leads to negative feelings, such as aversion; an egalitarian orientation leads people to focus on Black people's state of disadvantage and leads to positive feelings, such as sympathy for Black people and admiration for their ability to cope with and often overcome disadvantage. People who hold both individualistic and egalitarian values therefore experience ambivalence—mixed feelings—toward Black people. As Katz and Hass (1988) note, "Blacks [can be] perceived as deserving help, yet as not doing enough to help themselves; and both attitudes may exist side by side within an individual. . . . Having sympathy for Blacks as innocent targets of discrimination does not necessarily determine how one thinks about what Blacks can and should be doing to help themselves and how well they are doing it" (p. 894). Katz and Hass also note that the belief that innocent victims have a responsibility to help themselves is not limited to racial issues but is also found in other contexts, such as illness.

Tara MacDonald and Mark Zanna (1998) suggest that stereotypes provide another source of ambivalence. MacDonald and Zanna drew on research that shows that two basic evaluations that people make of one another center on the concepts of liking and respect. People tend to like others they perceive to be warm and friendly and to dislike those they perceive to be cold and distant; people tend to respect those who demonstrate intellectual and other achievements and not respect those they perceive as failures. However, feelings of liking and respect are independent of one another: A person can like someone for whom he or she has little respect (the genial klutz) and dislike someone for whom he or she has great respect (the arrogant genius). Similarly, people can have feelings of liking or disliking and respect or disrespect for social groups, based on their beliefs and stereotypes of what members of those groups are like. Thus, people who hold both positive and negative beliefs about a social group can experience conflicting feelings about the group: liking but little respect (for example, that Black people are friendly but lazy) or respect but little liking (e.g., Black people are athletically talented but hostile toward White people). These conflicting feelings are expressed as ambivalent prejudice.

It is important to bear in mind that not all White people are ambivalent toward minority groups. If individualistic values and negative stereotypes are stronger than egalitarian values and positive stereotypes, attitudes and behavior will be consistently negative. Conversely, if egalitarian values and positive stereotypes are stronger than individualistic values and negative stereotypes, attitudes and behavior will be consistently positive. It is only people who *simultaneously* hold individualistic and egalitarian values or positive and negative stereotypes who experience ambivalence. But *can* people simultaneously hold apparently conflicting values and stereotypes? It appears that they can. For example, Katz and Hass (1988) found scores on their measures of individualism and egalitarianism to be essentially uncorrelated and Charles Judd and his colleagues (Judd, Park, Ryan, Brauer, & Kraus, 1995) found that White college students' stereotypes of Blacks contained both strong positive and strong negative elements.

Psychological Conflict

The theory of ambivalent prejudice holds that people's ambivalent attitudes affect their behavior only when they become aware that they have inconsistent feelings toward minority groups. Katz (1981) suggested that interacting with a member of a minority group is sufficient to arouse feelings of ambivalence in White people. Depending on the situation, people might find themselves either feeling sympathy for someone who is down-and-out but doing nothing to help her- or himself, or having negative feelings about someone who is less fortunate. These responses are problematic because the first conflicts with the individualistic value system (one should not have positive feelings toward people who should be helping themselves) whereas the second response conflicts with the egalitarian value system (one should help the less fortunate). Katz believes that such conflicts threaten the person's self-image because, regardless of what the person feels, it implies that the person is not living up to one side or the other of his or her value system.

These feelings of threat cause negative emotions that the person is motivated to reduce. Katz postulates that people reduce the feelings of conflict and threat, and along with them the negative emotions, by behaving in a way that, at least temporarily, makes one value seem to be more important than the other. If one is more important than the other, than the more important value takes precedence and the conflict is resolved.

The theory of cognitive dissonance (Festinger, 1957; Harmon-Jones & Mills, 1999) provides another, and somewhat simpler, way of looking at attitude ambivalence. Cognitive dissonance theory holds that people prefer that all their attitudes, beliefs, behaviors, and so forth adhere to simple, consistent patterns. Any inconsistencies or contradictions lead to a state of unpleasant emotion call *cognitive dissonance,* which people are motivated to reduce. Threats to self-image are not necessary; the awareness of inconsistency is enough to cause psychological discomfort. As does Katz's (1981) theory, the theory of cognitive dissonance holds that one way to reduce negative feelings is to emphasize the relative importance of one of the inconsistent beliefs.

Consistent with both theories, the results of research show that attitude ambivalence is associated with negative self-directed emotions. For example, Margo Monteith (1996) found that White people who scored higher on a measure of ambivalent prejudice reported greater feelings of discomfort and higher levels of negative self-focused moods such as guilt, embarrassment, and disappointment with the self compared to people with lower ambivalence scores. Taking a different approach, Hass and his colleagues (Hass, Katz, Rizzo, Bailey, & Moore, 1992) found that making White people aware of their ambivalent racial attitudes by having them listen to audiotapes of people making both pro- and anti-Black statements led to increased ratings of negative moods such as tenseness, nervousness, and frustration.

Response Amplification

Both the theories of ambivalent prejudice and cognitive dissonance propose that one way to reduce feelings of conflict and the associated negative emotions is to emphasize the importance of one set of values or beliefs over the other. Ambivalence and cognitive dissonance exist only because the two sets of values or beliefs are of equal importance; if one set is perceived as more important, the conflict between the sets is resolved and the negative emotions dissipate. When situational factors no longer force people to confront their conflicting values or beliefs, their importance equalizes again until a new situation arises to bring attention to the inconsistency.

Behaviorally, emphasis on egalitarian values appears in the form of unduly positive behavior directed toward minority group members. Emphasis on individualistic values appears in the form of unduly negative behavior. This pattern of behavior is called **response amplification,** "a behavior toward the stigmatized person that [is] more extreme than behavior toward a nonstigmatized but similar person in the same type of situation" (Katz, 1981, p. 25). Situational cues determine the direction of response amplification. If the situation calls for positive behavior (such as when the other person does something good), the person experiencing ambivalent prejudice acts more positively toward a member of a minority group than toward a White person; if the situation calls for negative behavior (such as when the other person does something bad), the person experiencing ambivalent prejudice acts more negatively toward a member of a minority group. For example, Glen Hass and his colleagues (Hass, Katz, Rizzo, Bailey, & Eisenstadt, 1991) had White students work with either a White or Black student whose behavior caused the pair to either succeed or fail at a task. Asked to evaluate their partners' performance, the research participants rated the Black student more positively than the White student in the success condition but more negatively than the White student in the failure condition. The researchers also found that the degree of response amplification was correlated with the extent to which participants held ambivalent racial attitudes.

Another view of response amplification suggests that amplification can occur even without interaction with a member of a minority group. This view is based on the concept of priming (Bell & Esses, 1997, 2002; MacDonald & Zanna, 1998). A *prime* is a situational factor that sets up people psychologically to respond in ways that are consistent with it—situation primes the behavioral pump, as it were. In the case of ambivalent prejudice, situational factors that make people aware of the positive aspects of their attitudes trigger positive behavior whereas situational factors that made people aware of the negative aspects of their attitudes trigger negative behavior. People with nonambivalent attitudes would not be affected by a prime but would respond consistently with their attitudes. For example, a person with a nonambivalent positive attitudes would have no negative attitudes to be influenced by a prime and so would behave in a consistently positive manner.

The prime itself may have nothing at all to do with the target of the ambivalently prejudiced person's behavior. For example, MacDonald and Zanna (1998) had male students listen to an interview with a male job applicant who exhibited either positive traits (such as competence) or negative traits (such as unfriendliness), which served as primes. They then rated the résumés of several female applicants for a different job, one of whom was described as a feminist. The researchers had previously determined that some of their participants held ambivalent attitudes toward feminists and that others did not. The ambivalent participants who were exposed to the positive prime were more likely to say that they would hire the feminist applicant than those exposed to the negative prime; nonambivalent participants' decisions were not affected by the prime.

Priming also can influence the attitudes people express toward an entire group. David Bell and Victoria Esses (1997) induced positive or negative mood states in Canadian college students by having them listen to different types of music. The participants then completed general measures of attitudes toward Native Canadians and White Canadians and measures of attitudes toward social policies designed to benefit each group. Participants with ambivalent attitudes toward Native people who were in a positive mood expressed more positive attitudes toward them than did the ambivalent participants in a negative mood. Mood had no effect on ambivalent participants' attitudes toward White Canadians and had no effect on any of the ratings of nonambivalent participants. Bell and Esses (2002) found similar effects on intergroup attitudes using a different prime.

A key aspect of the theory of ambivalent prejudice is that response amplification results from a motivation to reduce negative emotions caused by being made aware of one's ambivalent attitudes. Although this tension reduction explanation has not been directly tested, Bell and Esses (2002) showed that response amplification occurs only when people see ambivalence as being negative. Canadian college students with ambivalent attitudes toward Native Canadians were told that ambivalence was either positive because there are advantages to seeing both sides of an issue or that it was negative because there are disadvantages to seeing both sides of an issue. They then received either a positive or negative prime after which their attitudes toward Native people were assessed. Participants who were motivated to see ambivalence as bad exhibited response amplification, whereas those motivated to see ambivalence as good did not. Leading people to see ambivalence as positive presumably removed the negative emotions associated with it and so removed the motive for response amplification.

In contrast to theorists who see response amplification as being unconsciously motivated, Bridget Dunton and Russell Fazio (1997) suggest that positive amplification, at least, is a conscious response. Drawing on a general theory of how people make judgments about others, Dunton and Fazio postulated that people know their attitudes might lead them to respond negatively to members of minority groups. In an attempt to avoid acting in such a way, these people intentionally overcompensate as a way of ensuring that their negative attitudes do not have an adverse impact. Of course, Dunton and Fazio's explanation does not rule out unconscious motivation; positive response amplification could have both conscious and unconscious roots.

One question that might arise at this point is why is it a problem to overcompensate for possible discriminatory behavior? Is it possible to be *too* helpful or accepting? Possibly. If the overcompensation takes the form of overly positive feedback on performance at a task (such as writing an essay), for example, the people receiving the feedback get an incorrect perception of their true level of performance and receive no information on how to perform better in the future. This incorrect perception, which leads them to believe that they are more skillful than they actually are, can set them up for failure the next time they perform the task (Harber, 1998). For example, students who fall behind in math because teachers do not give accurate feedback have difficulty catching up in later grades. In addition, if members of minority groups come to see feedback from Whites as consistently overly positive, they may come to see White people as patronizing and develop a distrust of any feedback they provide (Crocker, Voelkl, Testa, & Major, 1991).

An important aspect of the theory of ambivalent prejudice is that, unlike the other theories we have discussed, it was designed to be a general theory of prejudice, dealing not just with race but with all forms of difference. Thus, response amplification has been found not only in the racial context but also for nondisabled people interacting with people with disabilities (Katz, Hass, & Bailey, 1988), for men's and women's rating of members of the other sex (Kenyon & Hewitt, 1989), and, as noted earlier, for ratings of women described as feminists (MacDonald & Zanna, 1998).

PUTTING THE THEORIES TOGETHER

We have looked at a number of theories of contemporary prejudice, each of which proposes a different source of prejudice. How do they all fit together? Gerard Kleinpenning and Louk Hagendoorn (1993) postulated that the different types of prejudice could be arranged along a continuum of severity as shown in Table 5.2, with old-fashioned prejudice at the most severe end and lack of prejudice at the least severe end. Kleinpenning and Hagendoorn did not include subtle and ambivalent prejudice in their system, so we placed them in the continuum as suggested by Meertens and Pettigrew (1997) for subtle prejudice and Melinda Jones (2002) for ambivalent prejudice. Table 5.2 also summarizes some of the key characteristics of each type of prejudice.

Old-fashioned prejudice is characterized by lack of acceptance of group equality and endorsement of traditional racist beliefs such as the innate superiority of the White race. People with old-fashioned prejudice experience strong negative emotions toward members of minority groups and try to exclude them from society or, failing that, dominate and control them. Modern-symbolic and subtle prejudice are characterized by high acceptance of equality of opportunity for minority groups but rejection of equality of outcome. People with these kinds of prejudice reject most traditional racist beliefs but retain some, such as negative stereotypes. They also strongly endorse the traditional beliefs of their culture, which are racialized in the case of modern-symbolic prejudice. People with modern-symbolic prejudice tend to deny that minority groups still experience discrimination, believe that minority groups demand and receive special favors, and believe that Whites are treated unfairly. They also tend to have mild to moderate negative emotional responses to members of minority groups. People with subtle prejudice tend to exaggerate the differences between their cultures and those of minority groups but their emotional responses tend to be characterized by indifference rather than negativity. People with both types of prejudice tend to oppose social policies that benefit minority groups and show anti-minority bias if the behavior can be justified as unprejudiced.

Aversive prejudice is characterized by acceptance of both aspects of equality. Although people with aversive prejudice see themselves as unprejudiced, they tend to have mildly negative emotional responses toward members of minority groups and experience anxiety during intergroup contact. They try to avoid intergroup contact but are polite during unavoidable interactions. They often show a pro-minority bias to avoid appearing prejudiced, a pro-White bias in ambiguous situations, and an anti-minority bias if it can be justified as unprejudiced. Ambivalent prejudice is also characterized by acceptance of both aspects of equality, but people with ambivalent prejudice also experience conflict between traditional and egalitarian beliefs or between positive and negative stereotypes of minority groups. They tend to have both positive and negative emotional responses to minority groups and to experience discomfort when they become aware of the inconsistency. To reduce the discomfort, they exhibit response amplification, overdoing positive responses when those are called for and negative responses when they are called for.

TABLE 5.2 TYPES OF CONTEMPORARY PREJUDICE

Type of Prejudice	Acceptance of Equality	Rejection of Traditional Racist Beliefs	Other Beliefs	Emotional Response	Behavioral Response
Old-fashioned	Low	Low	Innate superiority of White race	Strong negative, e.g., fear, hatred	Tries to exclude or dominate and control minority groups
Modern-symbolic	High for opportunity; low for outcome	Moderate	Denial of discrimination; racialized traditional values; minorities demand and receive special favors; Whites treated unfairly	Mild to moderate negative, e.g., dislike, resentment, anxiety	Opposes social policies benefiting minorities; anti-minority bias if justifiable as unprejudiced
Subtle	High for opportunity; low for outcome	Moderate	Traditional values; exaggeration of cultural differences	Low positive, e.g., indifference	Same as modern-symbolic prejudice
Aversive	High	High	Sees self as unprejudiced	Mild negative; e.g., discomfort; anxiety concerning intergroup contact	Avoids intergroup interaction; polite during unavoidable interactions; pro-minority bias to avoid appearing prejudiced; pro-White bias in ambiguous situations and/or anti-minority bias if justifiable as unprejudiced
Ambivalent	High	High	Conflict between traditional and egalitarian beliefs, and between positive and negative stereotypes	Both positive (e.g., sympathy) and negative (e.g., aversion); discomfort when aware of ambivalent responses	Response amplification
Lack of prejudice	High	High	Complex social identity; broad scope of moral inclusion; focus on similarities among people rather than differences; positive implicit attitudes	Responds to individual, not group	Responds to individual, not group

Kleinpenning and Hagendoorn (1993) showed that people who hold a more severe type of prejudice endorse beliefs held by people who hold a less severe type, but people who hold a less severe type of prejudice reject the beliefs held by people who hold a more severe type. For example, people holding old-fashioned prejudiced beliefs also agree with beliefs held by people with modern-symbolic prejudice, such as that members of minority groups receive undeserved benefits, and exhibit characteristics associated with aversive prejudice, such as discomfort when interacting with members of minority groups. However, people holding modern prejudice beliefs do not agree with old-fashioned prejudice beliefs, such as the inherent superiority of the majority group.

Although the various forms of prejudice are relatively distinct, their nested nature implies that people can simultaneously exhibit characteristics of more than one type. For example, the results of the response amplification studies (described in the discussion of ambivalent prejudice) may seem to contradict the results of Harber's (1998) study (described in the discussion of aversive prejudice) that White students gave more positive feedback to a poor-performing Black student than to a poor-performing White student. One important difference between the studies, however, is that the participants in Harber's research thought that the person who wrote the essay would see their feedback, whereas in most of the response amplification studies, participants did not expect the person they rated to be informed of the ratings. Knowing that a member of a minority group will see the ratings probably arouses a motive to appear unprejudiced, thereby leading to a more favorable evaluation. This process may explain why, in general, response amplification appears to be stronger for positive responses than for negative responses (Biernat, Vescio, Theno, & Crandall, 1996). Therefore, the processes involved in contemporary forms of prejudice are not necessarily independent and may work together in complex ways to affect behavior.

What about people who are not prejudiced? Interestingly, little research has been conducted on the characteristics of unprejudiced people. They are usually not often studied as a specific group, but rather defined, in contrast to prejudiced people, as being low on characteristics on which prejudiced people are high (Phillips & Ziller, 1997). However, some characteristics of nonprejudiced people can be identified. They are, almost by definition, high on acceptance of both forms of equality. Unprejudiced people also tend to have complex social identities (Roccas & Brewer, 2002). That is, they see themselves as members of many different social groups rather than as members of a single group; Chapter 8 discusses the concept of social identity in more detail. In addition, unprejudiced people tend to focus on similarities among people rather than differences (Phillips & Ziller, 1997) and see differences among people as enriching and interesting rather than disconcerting (see, for example, Thomas, 1996). Unprejudiced people also exhibit a broad scope of moral inclusion, seeing everyone as members of a single group for whose welfare they have a moral responsibility (Opotow, 1995). Too little is known about the nature of nonprejudice; more research is needed on the characteristics of nonprejudiced people and how those characteristics are acquired.

Finally, although this section has focused on contemporary forms of prejudice, it is important to remember that old-fashioned prejudice is not dead. Based on a review of survey results, Dovidio and Gaertner (1998) estimated that 10 percent to 15 percent of White Americans still show old-fashioned prejudice, and Kleinpenning and Hagendoorn (1993) and Pettigrew and Meertens (1995) found similar results in European countries. In addition, the existence and activities of hate groups such as the Ku Klux Klan and the continuing problem of hate crimes show that old-fashioned prejudice still has profound effects on behavior.

BENEVOLENT PREJUDICE

Historically, the study of prejudice has focused on negative beliefs about and negative emotional responses to targets of prejudice. However, in Chapter 3 we saw that stereotypes can be both positive and negative. This duality of stereotypes suggests that there also can be two aspects of prejudice, one involving negative beliefs about the group and the other involving ostensibly positive beliefs. These two types of prejudice have been variously labeled *paternalistic* and *competitive* (van den Berghe, 1967), *benign* and *malevolent* (Wilson, 1996b), and *hostile* and *benevolent* (Glick & Fiske, 1996). Because the last two terms are becoming the ones most often used in psychology, we will also adopt them. **Hostile prejudice,** as the name implies, refers to the traditional form of prejudice, expressed in terms of negative beliefs about and emotional responses to targets of prejudice. **Benevolent prejudice,** in contrast, is expressed in terms of apparently positive beliefs and emotional responses to targets of prejudice. Table 5.3 lists some examples of hostile and benevolent beliefs that are stereotypically held about several groups. Although its tone is superficially positive, benevolent prejudice has the same net effect of hostile prejudice of keeping targets of prejudice in subordinate positions in society.

The idea that groups, on the one hand, can be looked down on but, on the other hand, can be seen as in some ways good is not new. Rudyard Kipling (1899), for example, expressed these sentiments in his poem "White Man's Burden" when he referred to the subjects of English colonialism as "Your sullen, new-caught peoples,/ Half devil and half child" (p. 290) who needed to be reformed from their devilish heathen ways (an expression of hostile prejudice) and protected in their childlike ignorance and naiveté (an expression of benevolent prejudice). Pierre van den Berghe (1967) described the benevolent side of this colonial attitude as viewing the colonized people as "childish, immature, irresponsible, exuberant, improvident, fun-loving, good humored, and happy-go-lucky; in short, as inferior but lovable as long as they stay in 'their place'" (p. 27). Note the overlap with current benevolent stereotypes of African Americans shown in Table 5.3.

The negative side of this apparent benevolence is seen in its use as a justification of the most brutal forms of European colonialism (Hochschild, 1998) and American slavery (Jackman, 1994). For example, one apologist for slavery wrote in 1860 that "slavery . . . is a blessing to this race of people. . . . Our slaves all have homes, are bountifully provided for in health, cared for and kindly nursed in childhood, sickness, and old age; multiply faster, live longer, are free from the corroding ills of poverty and anxious care, labor moderately, enjoy the blessings of

TABLE 5.3   **HOSTILE AND BENEVOLENT PREJUDICE**

Hostile Beliefs	Benevolent Beliefs
African Americans (held by White Americans)	
(Judd, Park, Ryan, Brauer, & Kraus, 1995)	
Hostile	Athletic
Cliquish	Musical
Irresponsible	Religious
Loud	Strong family ties
White Americans (held by Black Americans)	
(Judd et al., 1995)	
Self-centered	Intelligent
Greedy	Financially well-off
Stuffy/uptight	Independent
Sheltered from the real world	Organized
Jews	
(Wilson, 1996)	
Greedy	Intelligent
Dishonest	Hardworking
Uncouth	Ambitious
Loud	Loyal to family
Women	
(Glick & Fiske, 1996)	
When women lose fairly, they claim discrimination	Women should be cherished and protected by men
Women seek power by gaining control over men	Men are incomplete without women
Once a man commits, she puts him on a tight leash	Women have a quality of purity few men possess
Women fail to appreciate all men do for them	Men should sacrifice to provide for women
Men	
(Glick & Fiske, 1999)	
Men will always fight for greater control in society	Woman should take care of man at home, or else he'd fall apart
Even sensitive men want traditional relationships	Women are incomplete without men
Most men are really like children	Men are less likely to fall apart in emergencies
Men have no morals in what they will do to get sex	Men are more willing to risk self to protect others

the gospel, and let alone by wicked men, are contented and happy" (quoted by Jackman, 1994, p. 174).

The most thorough recent analysis of the distinction between hostile and benevolent prejudice lies in Peter Glick and Susan Fiske's (1996, 2001a,b) theory of ambivalent sexism. Glick and Fiske note that two forms of sexism exist. Hostile sexism views women and men as opponents in the so-called battle of the sexes in which women try to control men through marriage, sexual wiles, and demands for attention and material goods, or, more recently, feminist ideology, forcing men to struggle for their independence and maintain their virility. Benevolent sexism, in contrast views women as "pure creatures who ought to be protected, supported, and adored" (Glick & Fiske, 2001a, p. 109), who nurture their children through childhood and their men though adversity and who represent all that is good and pure in humanity. However, benevolent sexism also consigns women to traditional gender roles, portraying them as weak, best suited for the homemaker role, and fit for only a few low status occupational roles outside the home.

But can positive beliefs really be a form of prejudice? Evidence that this is, in fact, the case lies in research results that show positive correlations between measures of hostile and benevolent prejudices. For example, there are correlations between benevolent sexism and hostile sexism (Glick & Fiske, 1996) and between benevolent sexism and negative implicit attitudes toward women (Rudman, Greenwald, & McGhee, 2001; Rudman & Kilianski, 2000). In the domain of race, agreement with positive stereotypes of African Americans is correlated with both agreement with negative stereotypes and with modern-symbolic prejudice (Whitley, 1999). Thus, people who hold benevolent prejudices toward women and African Americans also tend to express negative attitudes toward those groups.

Benevolent prejudices represent an especially insidious form of bias for at least three reasons. First, they provide the prejudiced person with what Monin and Miller (2001) call *moral credentials*. People can express the opinion that women are weak and incompetent or that African Americans do not work hard enough, but can defend against charges of prejudice by pointing to their positive beliefs: Women are more moral than men and mold the characters of their children; African Americans are more family oriented than Whites and more musically and athletically talented. At the same time, the prescriptive aspects of stereotypes (see Chapter 3) imply that women and African Americans are suited *only* for these roles and not for roles that have greater power and social status.

The second insidious impact of benevolent prejudices is that the targets of the prejudices might buy into them. For example, in discussing benevolent sexism, Glick and Fiske (2001a) noted that "women may find its sweet allure difficult to resist. Benevolent sexism, after all, has its rewards; chivalrous men are willing to sacrifice their own well-being to provide for and to protect women" (pp. 114–115). At the same time, "women who reject conventional gender roles or attempt to usurp male power are rejected and punished with hostile sexism" (p. 113). Thus, hostile and benevolent sexism work together to reinforce and maintain the gender-role status quo.

Finally, benevolent prejudices may be difficult to change; as Glick and Fiske (2001a) note, "it does not feel like prejudice to . . . perpetrators (because it is not experienced as antipathy)" (p. 114). That is, because benevolent prejudices are superficially positive, there seems to be nothing to feel guilty about so there may not be much motivation to change.

What determines the type of prejudice that will be directed toward a group? Fiske, Glick, and their colleagues (Fiske, Cuddy, Glick, & Xu, 2002; Glick & Fiske, 2001c) have recently put forth a model proposing that the type of prejudice directed at a group is based on two sets of perceptions of the group. The first set of perceptions concerns how warm or likable the group is seen to be. For example, groups that Americans see as generally warm and likable include the groups they identify with (ingroups) and "nice" outgroups such as older people, people with disabilities, and people with mental retardation. In contrast, groups that Americans see as generally low in warmth and likability include homeless people, people on welfare, and rich people. The second set of perceptions concerns how competent or highly achieving the group is seen to be. For example, groups that Americans see as generally competent and high achieving include Asians, Jews, educated people, and rich people. In contrast, groups that Americans see as generally low in competence and achievement include homeless people, people on welfare, people with disabilities, and older people.

Table 5.4 shows how the two sets of perceptions combine to create different forms of prejudice. High perceived warmth and competence generally characterize attitudes toward one's ingroups, resulting in admiration and a positive prejudice based on respect, admiration, and affection for fellow group members. This attitude is the basis for ingroup biases, such as the pro-White bias we discussed as part of aversive prejudice. High perceived warmth coupled with low perceived competence result in paternalistic (benevolent) prejudice. These perceptions result in positive emotions, but positive emotions such as pity and patronizing affection that are based in a lack of respect for and a feeling of superiority to the group. These attitudes lead the person experiencing benevolent prejudice to feel an obligation to help the groups but at the same time relegate them to low-status social roles and to limit their power and influence in society. For example, Glick and Fiske (2001a) suggest that the positive attitudes that are part of ambivalent prejudice arise because "some liberal Whites may have paternalistic attitudes toward African Americans, characterized by pity and an implicit belief that African Americans are incapable of helping themselves" (p. 116).

The model proposed by Fiske, Glick and their colleagues (Fiske et al., 2002; Glick & Fiske, 2001c) divides hostile prejudice into two forms. Envious prejudice results when a group is perceived as competent but not warm and so represents a potential threat to the ingroup's hold on political and economic power. These perceptions of threat result in feelings of envy, fear, resentment, and hostility toward the targets of prejudice, combined with feelings of respect and admiration for their competence and achievements. These attitudes result in a desire to avoid members of the group and to segregate them into roles that limit their social power. It might also motivate denial of the group's competence, as is found in modern-symbolic prejudice, which attributes minority groups' successes to "special favors"

TABLE 5.4   **GLICK AND FISKE'S TYPOLOGY OF PREJUDICES**

	High Competence	
	High Warmth	**Low Warmth**
Prejudice type	Admiration (Positive Prejudice)	Envious (Hostile) Prejudice
Examples	Ingroups	Jews, Asians, feminists, Black professionals, rich people
Positive emotions	Respect, admiration, affection	Respect, admiration
Negative emotions	None	Envy, fear, resentment, hostility
Behavior	Ingroup bias	Avoidance, exclusion, segregation, denial of competence

	Low Competence	
	High Warmth	**Low Warmth**
Prejudice type	Paternalistic (Benevolent) Prejudice	Contemptuous (Hostile) Prejudice
Examples	Disabled people, housewives, elderly	Poor Whites, poor Blacks, welfare recipients
Positive emotions	Patronizing affection, pity, liking	None
Negative emotions	Disrespect, condescension	Disrespect, resentment, hostility, contempt
Behavior	Personal intimacy but role segregation	Avoidance, exclusion, segregation

Adapted from Peter Glick and Susan T. Fiske. (2001c). Ambivalent stereotypes as legitimizing ideologies: Differentiating paternalistic and envious prejudice. In John T. Jost and Brenda Major (Eds.), *The psychology of legitimacy* (pp. 278–301). New York: Cambridge University Press, Table 12.1, p. 282. Reprinted by permission of Cambridge University Press.

such as affirmative action. The second form of hostile prejudice, contemptuous prejudice, results when a group is perceived as neither competent nor warm and so is also seen an eminently dislikable. This is prejudice as it has traditionally been viewed—characterized by a lack of positive emotions, feelings of contempt, disrespect, resentment, and hostility toward the group, and a desire to avoid the group, exclude it from social power and relegate it to low status social roles.

In closing this section, let us make two points. The first is that the groups shown in the various categories of Table 5.4 are based on the average perceptions of warmth and competence across groups of research participants (Fiske et al., 2002). Because there are individual differences in people's attributions of warmth and competence to different groups, one person might respond with admiration to a group to which another person responds with contempt. Furthermore, the truly unprejudiced person will experience admiration for all groups, making the other categories or prejudice irrelevant to that person. The second point is that Fiske and colleagues' model is relatively new and requires more research to test its validity. Nonetheless, it offers an excellent framework for viewing the several forms that prejudice can take.

CHAPTER SUMMARY

Although overt expressions of prejudice have declined in the United States since the mid-1940s, covert measures of prejudice and some self-report studies of behavior indicate that prejudice continues to exist. In addition, women and members of minority groups continue to experience discrimination. Two factors seem to have contributed to this apparent contradiction. On the one hand, a social norm has developed in the United States that condemns racial prejudice. On the other hand, White Americans, at least, grow up in a culture that still has remnants of prejudice left over from America's history of racism and absorb some of that prejudice through socialization processes. As a result, many White Americans experience a conflict between a genuine belief in equality as a desirable social goal and feelings, often ones that are difficult to articulate, of dislike for and discomfort around members of minority groups. It is this conflict that provides the basis for theories of contemporary prejudice.

Old-fashioned prejudice is characterized by lack of acceptance of group equality, endorsement of traditional racist beliefs such as the innate superiority of the White race, and strong negative emotions toward members of minority groups. Modern-symbolic and subtle prejudice are characterized by high acceptance of equality of opportunity for minority groups but rejection of equality of outcome. People with these kinds of prejudice reject most traditional racist beliefs but retain some, such as negative stereotypes. They also strongly endorse the traditional beliefs of their culture, which are racialized in the case of modern-symbolic prejudice, deny that minority groups still experience discrimination, believe that minority groups demand and receive special favors, and believe that Whites are treated unfairly. They also tend to have mild to moderate negative emotional responses to members of minority groups. People with subtle prejudice tend to exaggerate the differences between their cultures and those of minority groups but their emotional responses tend to be characterized by indifference rather than negativity. People with both types of prejudice tend to oppose social policies that benefit minority groups and show anti-minority bias if the behavior can be justified as unprejudiced.

Aversive prejudice is characterized by acceptance of both equality of opportunity and equality of outcome. Although people with aversive prejudice see themselves as unprejudiced, they tend to have mildly negative emotional responses toward members of minority groups and experience anxiety during intergroup contact and so try to avoid intergroup contact. They often show a pro-minority bias to avoid appearing prejudiced, a pro-White bias in ambiguous situations, and an anti-minority bias if it can be justified as unprejudiced. Ambivalent prejudice is also characterized by acceptance of both aspects of equality, but people with ambivalent prejudice also experience conflict between traditional and egalitarian beliefs or between positive and negative stereotypes of minority groups. They tend to have both positive and negative emotional responses to minority groups and to experience discomfort when they become aware of the inconsistency. To reduce the discomfort, they exhibit response amplification, overdoing positive responses when those are called for and negative responses when they are called for. People who hold a more severe type of prejudice endorse beliefs held by people who hold a less severe type, but people who hold a less severe type of prejudice reject the beliefs held by people who hold a more severe type.

Finally, we considered the possibility that positive beliefs about other groups can reflect prejudice. Although such benevolent prejudice is superficially positive, it has an effect similar to that of hostile prejudice of putting groups in a subordinate position and restricting the social roles group members can hold. Generally, benevolent prejudices are held toward groups that are perceived as likable but incompetent, such as people with disabilities. The envious form of hostile prejudice is held toward groups that are perceived as dislikable but competent, such as Jews, and the contemptuous form of hostile prejudice is held toward groups that are perceived as dislikable and incompetent, such as people on welfare.

Suggested Readings

Theories of Contemporary Prejudice

Dovidio, J. F., & Gaertner, S. L. (2004). Aversive racism. *Advances in Experimental Social Psychology, 36*, 1–52.

Katz, I. (1981). *Stigma: A social psychological analysis.* Hillsdale, NJ: Erlbaum.

Pettigrew, T. F., & Meertens, R. W. (1995). Subtle and blatant prejudice in western Europe. *European Journal of Social Psychology, 25*, 57–75.

Sears, D. O. (1988). Symbolic racism. In P. A. Katz & D. A. Taylor (Eds.), *Eliminating racism: Profiles in controversy* (pp. 53–84). New York: Plenum.

Sears, D. O., & Henry, P. J. (2003). The origins of symbolic racism. *Journal of Personality and Social Psychology, 85*, 259–275.

> Sears's chapter is still an excellent summary of the origins and nature of the theory of modern-symbolic prejudice; Sears and Henry's article addresses some of the problems noted in Sears's chapter. Pettigrew and Meertens's article explains their concept of subtle prejudice. Dovidio and Gaertner's chapter provides an excellent summary of their theory of aversive prejudice. Although old, Katz's short book still provides an excellent overview of ambivalent prejudice.

Benevolent Prejudice

Glick, P., & Fiske, S. T. (2001). An ambivalent alliance: Hostile and benevolent sexism as complementary justifications for gender inequality. *American Psychologist, 56*, 109–118.

Glick, P., & Fiske, S. T. (2001). Ambivalent stereotypes as legitimizing ideologies: Differentiating paternalistic and envious prejudice. In J. T. Jost & B. Major (Eds.), *The psychology of legitimacy* (pp. 278–306). New York: Cambridge University Press.

> The *American Psychologist* article gives a nontechnical presentation of Glick and Fiske's theory of hostile and benevolent sexism. The chapter outlines Fiske's model of four types of prejudice.

KEY TERMS

ambivalent prejudice
aversive racism (or prejudice)
benevolent prejudice
bogus pipeline research
egalitarianism
hostile prejudice
implicit prejudices

Jim Crow racism
modern racism (or prejudice)
old-fashioned racism
response amplification
socialization
subtle prejudice
symbolic racism

QUESTIONS FOR REVIEW AND DISCUSSION

1. The results of research show that, in some ways, White Americans are less prejudiced than they were prior to World War II, but that in other ways prejudice and discrimination continue. What causes have been proposed for this apparent contradiction?
2. Theories of contemporary prejudice are based on the assumptions that most White Americans truly believe in the principle of racial equality but that they have been socialized into being prejudiced to at least some degree by a culture that has historically been racist (and prejudiced in other ways as well). Do you agree or disagree with these assumptions? What are your reasons for agreeing or disagreeing?
3. What is modern-symbolic prejudice? How does it differ from old-fashioned prejudice? In what ways is it similar to old-fashioned prejudice?
4. Describe the five themes that characterize modern-symbolic prejudice.
5. Describe the psychological bases of modern-symbolic prejudice.
6. Explain the two meanings that the term *equality* can have.
7. Describe the behavioral effects of modern-symbolic prejudice.
8. Several criticisms have been made of the concept of modern-symbolic prejudice. These include the following: (a) Modern-symbolic prejudice is not a new form of prejudice; it is just old-fashioned prejudice under a new name. (b) People who express modern-symbolic prejudice do not really believe in equality; they are just hiding their old-fashioned prejudice behind "politically correct" justifications. (c) Many of the themes of modern-symbolic prejudice reflect conservative political values, so calling those beliefs a form of prejudice is just a way for political liberals to discredit conservatives. Do you agree or disagree with these criticisms? What are your reasons for agreeing or disagreeing?
9. In what ways is subtle prejudice similar to modern-symbolic prejudice and in what ways does it differ from it?
10. What is aversive prejudice? Describe its characteristics. What are its psychological bases?
11. Describe the effects that aversive prejudice can have on behavior. Under what circumstances do people with aversive prejudice exhibit positive behavior

toward members of minority groups and under what circumstances do they exhibit negative behavior?

12. Some people say that because it is natural to feel uncomfortable in an unfamiliar situation, such as when a White person interacts with a member of a minority group, that discomfort does not really indicate prejudice. Do you agree or disagree with this point? What are your reasons for agreeing or disagreeing?

13. Bridget Dunton and Russell Fazio (1997) have suggested that some people avoid interracial contact to avoid conflicts that their racial attitudes might cause. Ashby Plant and Patricia Devine (1998) suggest that some people avoid interracial contact to avoid pressure from other people to control their prejudice. Are these types of behavior examples of aversive prejudice? Why or why not?

14. Explain the concept of ambivalent prejudice. What causes ambivalence? What psychological effects does ambivalence have?

15. What does the term *response amplification* mean? Under what circumstances does positive amplification occur and under what circumstances does negative amplification occur? How are these circumstances similar to and different from the circumstances that influence the behavior of people with aversive prejudice?

16. Some researchers think that response amplification is a conscious choice whereas others think it arises from unconscious processes. Which do you think is true? What are your reasons for taking that position?

17. Peter Glick and Susan Fiske (2001a) have suggested that the positive beliefs that people with ambivalent prejudice hold about members of minority groups and the positive emotions they feel toward them might actually represent benevolent prejudice. Do you agree or disagree with their suggestion? What are your reasons for agreeing or disagreeing?

18. Describe Gerard Kleinpenning and Louk Hagendoorn's (1993) continuum of prejudices.

19. What are the characteristics of *unprejudiced* people? Why do you think that so little research has been conducted on nonprejudice compared to the vast amount of research on prejudice? Similarly, why do think that so little research has been conducted on prejudice among members of minority groups?

20. The section on contemporary forms of prejudice provided a number of examples of these prejudices. What other examples can you think of? Which forms of prejudice do your examples represent? Explain how they fit the definition of those forms of prejudice.

21. What is benevolent prejudice? Glick and Fiske (2001a) propose that benevolent prejudice has the same net effect of hostile prejudice of restraining its targets' freedom. Do you agree or disagree? What are your reasons?

22. Have you observed or experienced instances of benevolent prejudice? If so, describe them.

23. Describe the two forms of hostile prejudice that Fiske and her colleagues (2002) have proposed? What factors do they say lead to the different types of prejudice postulated by their model.

INDIVIDUAL DIFFERENCES AND PREJUDICE

[Some people] are so hostile toward so many minorities, they seem to be equal opportunity bigots.

—Bob Altemeyer, 1998 (p. 52)

Are there people who dislike all outgroups equally and so, in Bob Altemeyer's (1998) words quoted above, are "equal opportunity bigots" (p. 52)? That is, are there people who are, as a result of their personalities, belief systems, or other personal characteristics, especially likely to become prejudiced, and become prejudiced toward not just one group, but toward everyone they see as different from themselves? Individual difference researchers address these questions by studying the ways in which people differ from one another and the ways in which these personal characteristics are related to other variables such as prejudice. Individual differences began to become important to the study of prejudice after World War II, when researchers concluded that factors such as realistic intergroup conflict and competition (see Chapter 8) could not explain Nazi anti-Semitism and the Holocaust (Milner, 1981). "Explanations were therefore sought in the disturbed personality, for it was hardly conceivable that these actions could be the actions of normal men" (Milner, 1981, p. 106). This search led to the development of one of the first individual difference theories of prejudice, the theory of the authoritarian personality, which we discuss shortly. A second reason why researchers believe that individual differences play a role in prejudice is that researchers have found that people who score high on prejudice against one group also tend to score high on prejudice against other groups (see, for example, Cunningham, Nezlek, & Banaji, 2004). This similarity of response to different groups suggests that some characteristic of the person may be a common underlying cause of all the prejudices.

This chapter examines the relationships of selected individual difference variables to prejudice. Choosing the variables to discuss was not easy. Researchers have studied more than 25 individual difference variables in relation to prejudice (McFarland, 2001); however, in a set of four studies, Sam McFarland (2001) found that only three of those variables—authoritarianism, social dominance orientation, and empathy—were consistently related to prejudice. This chapter begins, therefore, with those three variables. The second section of this chapter focuses on the role of the self in prejudice, both because of its historical importance and because of some recent theories that connect some self-related variables with prejudice. The third section examines the role of value systems in prejudice, and the last section focuses on two important social ideologies related to prejudice— religion and political orientation.

While reading this chapter, it is important to bear two cautions in mind. First, research on individual differences is, by its nature, correlational. As we discussed in Chapter 2, although correlational research can show that two variables are related to each other, it *cannot* show that one of those variables causes the other. Second, the relationships between individual difference variables and prejudice are far from perfect, so a high score on an individual difference variable that is related to prejudice does not necessarily mean that the person is prejudiced; other factors can offset the effect of any particular variable. Conversely, not all people who score low on an individual difference variable related to prejudice are unprejudiced; other factors can lead the person to be prejudiced.

THE "BIG 3": AUTHORITARIANISM, SOCIAL DOMINANCE ORIENTATION, AND EMPATHY

Authoritarianism, social dominance orientation, and empathy are the individual difference variables most closely associated with prejudice (McFarland, 2001). Although authoritarianism was originally conceptualized as a personality trait and social dominance orientation is frequently referred to as one, John Duckitt (2001) has pointed out that they more closely resemble **ideologies,** sets of attitudes and beliefs that predispose people to view the world in certain ways and to respond in ways consistent with those viewpoints. For example, from an authoritarian perspective, the world is a dangerous place, so people high in authoritarianism seek security by trying to make the world conform to their political and social values. In a similar vein, people high in social dominance orientation see the world as a competitive jungle and respond by trying to prevent people and groups they see as competitors from gaining on them (Duckitt, 2001). Unlike authoritarianism and social dominance orientation, empathy is probably better conceptualized as a personality variable than as a social ideology. As a personality trait, empathy reflects a consistent pattern of emotional responses to factors that affect the welfare of others (Davis, 1994).

Authoritarianism

Theodor Adorno and his colleagues (Adorno, Frenkel-Brunswik, Levinson, & Sanford, 1950) developed the concept of the **authoritarian personality** as a means of explaining the rise of fascism during the 1930s. Fascism is a political philosophy that holds, among other tenets, that those who hold power in a society know what is best for the society, so people should simply do what their government tells them to do. Fascism was quite popular in Europe and the United States during the 1930s; fascist governments were established in Germany, Italy, and Spain, and fascist movements existed in the United States and Great Britain. It was the German fascist (or Nazi) government that directed the systematic annihilation of ethnic and racial minority groups and the mentally and physically handicapped that is known as the Holocaust. As noted earlier, Adorno and his colleagues, along with other researchers, began to look for an explanation for why large numbers of people could become complicit in government-led genocide. These researchers believed that the scope of the Holocaust meant that it could not be explained in terms of intergroup conflict, so the answer must lie within the human mind. They therefore postulated the existence of what they called the *authoritarian personality*, a personality type that is especially susceptible to unthinking obedience to authority.

The authoritarian personality   Adorno and his colleagues (1950) proposed that the authoritarian personality was composed of nine characteristic patterns of thought, five of which are related to prejudice:

Conventionalism. Rigid adherence to conventional, middle-class values.

Authoritarian submission. Submissive uncritical attitude toward idealized moral authorities. . . .

Authoritarian aggression. Tendency to be on the lookout for, and to condemn, reject, and punish people who violate conventional values. . . .

Stereotypy. The . . . disposition to think in rigid categories. . . .

Projectivity. The disposition to believe that wild and dangerous things go on in the world; the projection outwards of unconscious emotional impulses. (p. 228)

Adorno and his colleagues believed that the propensity for rigid adherence to conventional thinking leads people with authoritarian personalities to view the world in stereotypical terms; conventionalism and authoritarian submission combined with authoritarian aggression leads them to be prejudiced against people who violate conventional norms or who are condemned by authority figures; and projectivity leads them to see their own faults in the targets of their prejudice.

Adorno and colleagues (1950) used interviews and questionnaires to examine the relationship of the authoritarian personality to prejudice. One of the questionnaires, the F-Scale, has become a standard measure of authoritarianism (Christie, 1991; Meloen, 1993). Adorno and his colleagues found high correlations between authoritarianism and prejudice against a variety of ethnic groups. Later research using the F-Scale also found support for a relationship between authoritarianism and ethnic and racial prejudice (Brown, 1995; Duckitt, 1994), and scores on the F-Scale also correlate strongly with attitudes toward lesbians and gay men (Whitley & Lee, 2000). Thus, there is good evidence that the authoritarian personality, at least as assessed by the F-Scale, is associated with prejudice.

Despite its early popularity and success, interest in the authoritarian personality began to decline in the 1960s and 1970s. There were several reasons for this change. One was a growing disenchantment among psychologists with psychoanalytic theory on which Adorno and his colleagues (1950) based their theory and a simultaneous growth in interest in the cognitive underpinnings of prejudice (Duckitt, 1994). In addition, a number of flaws were found in the F-Scale, which led to some loss of faith in the original research results; however, subsequent revisions of the F-Scale have corrected those shortcomings (Christie, 1991). A final criticism was that although Adorno and his colleagues conceptualized the authoritarian personality as a characteristic of the political far right-wing, people on the far left could also show some characteristics of the authoritarian personality, such as uncritical acceptance of statements made by authority figures and aggression toward people who do not share their beliefs (Stone & Smith, 1993). This criticism led to attempts to develop measures of generalized authoritarianism that would capture both its right- and left-wing aspects, such as Milton Rokeach's (1960) Dogmatism Scale. However, such attempts have not been very successful (Altemeyer, 1996; Stone & Smith, 1993); for example, although the Dogmatism Scale was designed to be politically neutral, scores on it correlate fairly highly with scores on measures of right-wing authoritarianism, suggesting that the measures assess similar traits (Altemeyer, 1996). Because of problems such as these, recent research has focused on the relationship between what is now called right-wing authoritarianism and prejudice.

TABLE 6.1   SAMPLE QUESTIONNAIRE ITEMS USED TO ASSESS RIGHT-WING AUTHORITARIANISM (RWA)

Authoritarian Submission

It is always better to trust the judgments of the proper authorities in government and religion than to listen to the noisy rabble-rousers in our society who are trying to create doubt in people's minds.

Once our government leaders give us the "go ahead," it will be the duty of every patriotic citizen to help stomp out the rot that is poisoning our country from within.

Authoritarian Aggression

What our country really needs is a strong, determined leader who will crush evil, and take us back to the true path.

The situation in our country is getting so serious, the strongest methods would be justified if they eliminated the troublemakers and get us back to our true path.

Conventionalism

The "old-fashioned way" and "old-fashioned values" still show the best way to live.

Our country *needs* free thinkers who will have the courage to defy traditional ways, even if this upsets many people.*

*Agreement with this item indicates *low* RWA.
From Altemeyer (1998, pp. 49–51)

Right-wing authoritarianism   After languishing during the 1970s, research on authoritarianism was revived by Bob Altemeyer (1981, 1988, 1996), who replaced the concept of the authoritarian personality with that of **right-wing authoritarianism** (RWA). RWA differs somewhat from the original concept of the authoritarian personality; particularly important is that RWA is defined as a set of attitudes rather than as a personality type. Altemeyer defined RWA in terms of three clusters of attitudes that are similar to three of the characteristics Adorno and his colleagues (1950) used to describe the authoritarian personality: "*authoritarian submission*—a high degree of submission to the authorities who are perceived to be established and legitimate in the society in which one lives; *authoritarian aggression*—a general aggressiveness, directed against various persons, that is perceived to be sanctioned by established authorities; *conventionalism*—a high degree of adherence to the social conventions that are perceived to be endorsed by society and its established authorities" (Altemeyer, 1994, p. 133; see Table 6.1 for sample questionnaire items used to assess RWA). If one thinks of prejudice as a form of nonphysical, symbolic aggression, these attitudes lead people high in RWA to be prejudiced against groups that authority figures condemn and that are perceived to violate traditional values.

People high in RWA tend to be prejudiced against a wide variety of groups, including feminists (Duncan, Peterson, & Winter, 1997), lesbians and gay men (Whitley & Lee, 2000), Native Americans (Altemeyer, 1998), Arabs (Webster & Coon, 2004), immigrants (Quinton, Cowan, & Watson, 1996), and fat people

(Crandall, 1994). However, whereas some research shows that people high in RWA are prejudiced against African Americans (for example, Altemeyer, 1998; Rowatt & Franklin, 2004), other research does not (for example, Webster & Coon, 2004; Whitley, 1999). RWA has also been found to be related to prejudice not only in the United States and Canada, but in other countries as well, including Australia (Heaven & St. Quintin, 2003), Belgium (Duriez & Van Hiel, 2002), Germany (Petersen & Dietz, 2000), the Netherlands (Verkuyten & Hagendoorn, 1998), New Zealand (Duckitt, 2001), Russia (McFarland, Ageyev, & Djintcharadze, 1996), and South Africa (Duckitt, Wagner, du Plessis, & Birum, 2002).

Several personal characteristics of people high in RWA may predispose them to prejudice. First, people high in RWA tend to be mentally inflexible. They see the world in simple terms, want definite answers to questions, and have a high need for closure, especially when dealing with issues that are important to them (Altemeyer, 1998; Schultz, Stone, & Christie, 1997; Van Hiel, Pandelaere, & Duriez, 2004). As we saw in Chapter 4, this type of mental inflexibility is associated with a propensity for stereotyping. Perhaps as a reflection of this inflexibility, people high in RWA are uninterested in political issues (Peterson, Duncan, & Pang, 2002) and experiencing new things (Heaven & Bucci, 2001; McCrae, 1996), and so are unlikely to be exposed to views that differ from their own. People high in RWA also tend to see the world as a dangerous and threatening place, leading them to place a high value on security (Duckitt, 2001; Duriez & Van Hiel, 2002). They submit to authority and conform to group norms as a way of finding security in the protection of the group under the guidance of its authority figures (Duckitt, 2001).

In addition, people high in RWA tend to organize their worldviews in terms of ingroups and outgroups (Altemeyer, 1981, 1998). As we discuss in Chapter 8, strong identification with an ingroup promotes prejudice against outgroups, in part by leading people to exaggerate the differences between the ingroup and outgroups. These perceived differences can lead to the belief that outgroups threaten the traditional values embraced by people high in RWA (see the discussion of perceived value differences later in this chapter). By derogating outgroups, people can dismiss them as unimportant and therefore as constituting no real threat to ingroup values. Altemeyer (1981, 1998) also noted that people high in RWA tend to be self-righteous, seeing themselves as more moral than other people and therefore as justified in looking down on anyone authority figures define as less moral than themselves. They may feel especially free to express prejudice against members of outgroups, such as lesbians and gay men, who authority figures condemn as immoral threats to traditional values.

An important aspect of RWA as a theory of prejudice is the role authority figures play. People high in RWA accept as legitimate prejudice against groups authority figures condemn, but not necessarily other forms of prejudice. For example, some studies have found that people high in RWA have negative attitudes toward lesbians and gay men but not toward African Americans (Webster & Coon, 2004; Whitley, 1999). This difference in attitudes is explainable in terms of authority: some religious and political authority figures condemn lesbians and gay men for violating traditional values. However, most religious and political authority figures not only do not condemn African Americans, they actively oppose racial prejudice. Because people high in RWA also tend to hold traditional religious beliefs (see, for example, Spilka, Hood, Hunsberger, & Gorsuch, 2003), they are especially responsive to the directions religious authorities set.

The importance of authority was demonstrated in a study conducted of university students in what had been West Germany before reunification (Petersen & Dietz, 2000). The research consisted of a personnel selection simulation in which the participants had to choose three candidates for a managerial position; half the candidates were from the former West Germany and half were from the former East Germany, a group that was often the target of prejudice by former West Germans. The participants were categorized as high or low in RWA and assigned to one of two experimental conditions. In one condition a memo from the company president indicated that he did not think that hiring a former East German would be a good idea; in the other condition, the memo did not mention the candidates' regional background. Results showed that in making their selections, participants low in RWA did not discriminate on the basis of regional background, nor did participants high in RWA whose memo did not mention regional background. However, participants high in RWA who thought the company president did not want to hire a former East German recommended fewer former East German candidates than did the other participants.

In summary, people high in RWA tend to be prejudiced against a wide variety of groups, especially those that they perceive to violate traditional values and groups that authority figures condemn. A number of psychological characteristics may predispose people high in RWA to prejudice, including mental inflexibility, a disinterest in experiencing new things, a perception of the world as a dangerous place, and a tendency to organize their worldviews in terms of ingroups and outgroups.

Social Dominance Orientation

Social dominance orientation (SDO) is an individual difference variable that reflects "the extent to which one desires that one's in-group dominate and be superior to out-groups" (Pratto, Sidanius, Stallworth, & Malle, 1994, p. 742). It is comprised of two closely related components, group-based dominance and opposition to equality (Jost & Thompson, 2000). Group-based dominance reflects the belief that one's group ought to be at the top of the societal ladder and that other groups ought to be on the bottom; opposition to equality reflects the belief that the groups on the bottom ought to stay there. People high in SDO believe that the groups they identify with, such as racial or ethnic groups, professional groups, socioeconomic status groups, and so forth, should have a superior position in society and control over society's resources and that other groups should "stay in their place" and not ask for more than they have. Thus, people high in SDO prefer a society in which social groups are unequal and their group holds the superior position (Sidanius & Pratto, 1999). See Table 6.2 for sample questionnaire items used to assess SDO.

Not surprisingly, members of groups that hold more power in society exhibit higher levels of social dominance orientation. For example, in the United States, Whites score higher than members of minority groups, men score higher than

TABLE 6.2   **SAMPLE QUESTIONNAIRE ITEMS USED TO ASSESS SOCIAL DOMINANCE ORIENTATION (SDO)**

Group-Based Dominance (GBD)

It's probably a good thing that certain groups are at the top and other groups are at the bottom.

Inferior groups should stay in their place.

Opposition to Equality (OEQ)

We should do what we can to equalize conditions for different groups.*

Increased social equality would be a good thing.*

---

*Agreement with these items indicates *low* OEQ and low SDO.
Note: Items are from Sidanius and Pratto (1999, p. 67); classification of items as GBD and OEQ is from Jost and Thompson (2000, p. 216)

women, heterosexuals score higher than lesbians and gay men, and the wealthy score higher than the less wealthy; similar patterns have been found in other countries (Sidanius & Pratto, 1999). In addition, the longer people are members of a higher-power social group, the higher they score on SDO. For example, Serge Guimond and his colleagues (2003) measured SDO in first-year and upper-year students in a high social power profession—law—and in a low social power profession—psychology. They found that law students' SDO scores increased with years in college whereas psychology students' SDO scores decreased with years in college. In addition, people high in SDO tend to be attracted to high-power professions (Pratto, Stallworth, Sidanius, & Siers, 1997). The link between social status and SDO has been further demonstrated in experiments in which research participants have been randomly assigned to high- or low-power roles. Participants assigned to high-power roles score higher on SDO than do participants assigned to low-power roles (Guimond, Dambrun, Michinov, & Duarte, 2003; Schmitt, Branscombe, & Kappen, 2003). Therefore, social power is not simply correlated with SDO; social power causes people to develop social dominance attitudes. Thus, SDO is related to social power in two ways: People high in SDO are attracted to high-power professions and socialization into the profession increases SDO (Guimond et al., 2003).

Social dominance orientation and prejudice   Given SDO's roots in the desire to maintain social inequality, it is not surprising that people high in SDO are prejudiced against members of groups that challenge the legitimacy of social inequality, including racial or ethnic groups such as African Americans, Asian Americans (Sidanius & Pratto, 1999), Native Americans (Altemeyer, 1998), Arabs (Webster & Coon, 2004), and Australian Aborigines (Heaven & St. Quintin, 2002); immigrants (Esses, Jackson, & Armstrong, 1998); lesbians and gay men (Whitley & Lee, 2000); and feminists (Sidanius & Pratto, 1999). SDO has been found to be related to prejudice not only in the United States, but also in many other countries, including Australia (Heaven & St. Quintin, 2003), Belgium (Duriez & Van Hiel,

2002), China (Pratto et al., 2000), France (Guimond & Dambrun, 2002; Guimond et al., 2003), Israel (Levin & Sidanius, 1999), New Zealand (Duckitt, 2001), South Africa (Duckitt et al., 2002), and Taiwan (Pratto et al., 2000). Thus, like RWA, SDO is related to multiple forms of prejudice in multiple cultural contexts.

Like people high in RWA, those high in SDO have a number of personal characteristics that may predispose them to prejudice. For example, people high in SDO tend to see the world as what John Duckitt (2001) describes as a "competitive jungle characterized by a ruthless and amoral Darwinian struggle for survival, . . . resources and power in which might is right, and winning is everything" (p. 51). In addition, people high in SDO tend to see resources as being in limited supply, so that if someone else gets something, they lose out on it; they have trouble believing that there could be enough for everyone (Esses et al., 1998). Taken together, these characteristics motivate people high in SDO to try to deny resources to members of outgroups and to try to keep outgroups from gaining any power that might force the sharing of resources. People high in SDO are also tough-minded (Duckitt, 2001) and low in empathy (Pratto et al., 1994; McFarland, 2001), sympathy (Heaven & Bucci, 2001), and benevolence (Duriez & Van Hiel, 2002). As we will see shortly, being able to empathize with members of other groups tends to reduce prejudice.

An important aspect of the social dominance theory is the concept of legitimizing myths. **Legitimizing myths** are sets of attitudes and beliefs that people high in SDO can use to justify their dominant position in society (Sidanius & Pratto, 1999). In the context of prejudice, group stereotypes are legitimizing myths that can be used to justify denying equality to other groups despite the fact that prejudice is socially disapproved. For example, the beliefs that members of another group are lazy and of low intelligence could be used to justify denying equal educational opportunity and powerful positions in society to members of the stereotyped group: The logic of social dominance asks, why should society expend precious resources to provide people with opportunities they are inherently unfit to take advantage of? Consequently, being high in SDO leads people to endorse stereotypes of outgroups, especially negative stereotypes, and these negative beliefs then lead to prejudice. For example, Bernard Whitley (1999) found that SDO was positively correlated with endorsement of both positive and negative stereotypes of African Americans. How would positive stereotypes contribute to the goal of keeping other groups down? Recall from Chapter 5 that positive stereotypes can contribute to that goal if they place people in low power roles, such as by stereotyping African Americans as athletes and entertainers rather than as business executives or government leaders. Whitley also found that when endorsement of stereotypes of African Americans and of lesbians and gay men was controlled, the relationship between SDO and other indicators of prejudice was greatly reduced. That is, although people high in SDO are more likely than people low in SDO to endorse legitimizing myths, among people high in SDO, those who endorse legitimizing myths to a greater degree are more prejudiced. These results suggest that legitimizing myths, in the form of stereotypes, are necessary for people high in SDO to justify their other prejudiced responses.

Recall from Chapter 4 that Stephanie Goodwin and her colleagues (Goodwin, Gubin, Fiske, & Yzerbyt, 2000) found that people high in social power tend to use

6.1   *The Motivational Effect of Social Dominance Orientation*

The relationship between social dominance orientation (SDO) and prejudice can take a number of forms. Although we have focused on SDO as a potential cause of prejudice, in one study Henry Danso and Victoria Esses (2001) took a different perspective, viewing SDO as a motive that can be aroused given the right circumstances. They reasoned that if SDO is based on a need to maintain dominance over other groups, people high in SDO should be motivated to prove their group's dominance, even if they are unaware of that motivation.

In their study, Danso and Esses had either a Black or White research assistant individually administer a standardized test of arithmetic ability to White college students. The researchers reasoned that students high in SDO would be motivated to show that Whites are intellectually superior to Blacks and so would do better on the test when it was administered by a Black research assistant; students tested by a White assistant and low SDO students tested by a Black assistant should not differ from one another. Danso and Esses found that the high SDO

students who were tested by a Black research assistant scored an average of about 16 out of 20 possible points on the test, whereas the other groups averaged only about 11.5 points. Although SDO is correlated with prejudice, Danso and Esses reported that in a previous study there was no relationship between level of racial prejudice and performance when tested by a Black or White research assistant. Therefore, the motivational effects found in their study occurred as a result of SDO, not prejudice.

The authors concluded that their findings "may have practical implications for relations between groups for whom there has previously been an unequal distribution of power and resources (e.g., between men and women in managerial positions or between Blacks and Whites in the United States). In such situations, perceived shifts in power balance may represent a threat to the dominance of one group and, as a result, motivate the dominant group members to work to maintain their group dominance, especially if they desire an unequal distribution of resources" (pp. 163–164).

stereotypes to a greater extent than do people low in social power. They attributed this greater stereotype use to people high in power not being motivated to individuate others. In a similar vein, Guimond and his colleagues (2003) have found that power correlates with prejudice: People high in power express more prejudice against a variety of outgroups. Guimond and colleagues explain this finding in terms of SDO: People higher in social power are higher in SDO, which leads to higher levels of prejudice. Social power, then, may potentiate both SDO and stereotyping, with people high in SDO using those stereotypes to justify their prejudices. SDO may also have motivational effects; see, for example, Box 6.1.

Social dominance orientation and authoritarianism   In some ways SDO and authoritarianism sound very similar, both being ideological variables

that predispose people to prejudice, but they are, in fact, different. The most fundamental difference is that authoritarianism focuses on submission to ingroup authority figures regardless of whether they advocate dominance over other groups, whereas SDO focuses on dominance over outgroups regardless of the views of ingroup authority figures. That is, authoritarianism focuses on relations *within groups* (submission to ingroup authority) whereas SDO focuses on relations *between groups* (dominance of the ingroup over outgroups). The intergroup nature of SDO is shown by research that has found that the relationship between SDO and prejudice is higher for people who identify more strongly with their groups (Sidanius, Pratto, & Mitchell, 1994; Wilson & Liu, 2003). Stronger group identity motivates people to make stronger distinctions between their group and other groups, to stereotype members of other groups, and to view other groups less positively than one's own group (see Chapter 8). The importance of ingroup authority in authoritarianism was shown in the study conducted by Petersen and Dietz (2000), described earlier, in which participants high in RWA acted in accordance with an authority figure's hint to discriminate against members of an outgroup whereas participants low in RWA did not.

This difference in the nature of the two constructs is reflected in the low correlations that are often found between scores on measures of SDO and RWA. For example, Duckitt (2001) reported that the average correlation for studies conducted in the United States and Canada was only $r = .18$. However, Duckitt also found that the average correlation was higher for older respondents than for college students; it is also higher for people in Europe, Australia, and New Zealand (see, for example, Duckitt, 2001; Duriez & Van Hiel, 2002; Heaven & St. Quintin, 2003). Duckitt attributes the age difference in correlations to an increasing convergence of attitudes with age: As political attitudes become more firmly set, they tend to become more consistent with one another. Duckitt attributes the geographic differences in correlations to differences in political systems. The countries with the higher correlations tend to make stronger distinctions between the policies of the political left and those of the political right. However, although the correlation between SDO and authoritarianism is higher in some groups than in others, it not very high in any group.

There are also differences in how SDO and authoritarianism relate to different forms of prejudice. For example, SDO is linked to both racial and antigay prejudice, whereas RWA is linked to antigay prejudice but not to racial prejudice (Whitley, 1999, 2001; Whitley & Wilkinson, 2002). This pattern reflects differences in the nature of authoritarianism and SDO (Duckitt, 2001). Authoritarianism focuses on perceived threats and obedience to authority figures' rules as a means of avoiding those threats. Because lesbians and gay men are portrayed by some authority figures as threats to important social values whereas African Americans are not, people high in RWA respond to the purported threat with negative attitudes toward lesbians and gay men but not toward African Americans. Recall that there are two components of SDO, opposition to equality and group based dominance. Because lesbians and gay men are distributed across the socioeconomic spectrum, they do not present a challenge to inequality in the distribution of society's resources—they already have economic parity with heterosexuals. African Americans, in contrast, do challenge inequality. Hence, the opposition to inequality component of SDO is not related to negative attitudes toward lesbians and gay men, but it is related to negative attitudes toward African Americans (Whitley, 2001, 2001b). Group-based dominance is related to negative attitudes toward both lesbians and gay men and African Americans because many heterosexuals classify lesbians and gay men as an outgroup and many White Americans classify African Americans as an outgroup.

In conclusion, then, authoritarianism and SDO represent two separate ideologically based roots of prejudice (Duckitt, 2001; Whitley, 1999). Authoritarianism focuses on seeking security against perceived threats from other groups by conformity to group norms and obedience to authority. SDO focuses on quashing competition for resources from other groups and maintaining the ingroup's dominance in society.

Empathy

The third individual difference variable that McFarland (2001) found to be consistently related to prejudice is empathy. **Empathy** is "an other-oriented emotional response congruent with another's perceived welfare; if the other is oppressed or in need, empathic feelings include sympathy, compassion, tenderness, and the like" (Batson et al., 1997, p. 105). There is a good deal of evidence that the capacity for empathy is an individual difference variable, with some people being more capable of feeling empathy for others (Davis, 1994). Mark Davis (1994) has identified four components of empathy: *Perspective taking* is the "tendency to spontaneously adopt the psychological point of view of others in everyday life," *empathic concern* is "the tendency to experience feelings of sympathy and compassion for unfortunate others," *personal distress* is "the tendency to experience distress and discomfort in response to extreme distress in others," and *fantasy* is "the tendency to imaginatively transpose oneself into fictional situations" (p. 57). Table 6.3 shows some of the questionnaire items that are used to assess empathy.

Although empathy has not played as large a role in prejudice research as have RWA and SDO, several studies have found that more empathic people exhibit less prejudice. For example, empathy has been found to be negatively correlated with a combined measure of several forms of prejudice (McFarland, 2001), with prejudice against African Americans (Whitley & Wilkinson, 2002), and with prejudice against lesbians and gay men (Johnson, Brems, & Alford-Keating, 1997; Whitley & Wilkinson, 2002). Daniel Batson and his colleagues (Batson, Chang, Orr, & Rowland, 2002; Batson et al., 1997) have suggested that empathy affects prejudice through a three-step process: "(a) adopting the perspective of . . . a member of a stigmatized group (i.e., imagining how the individual is affected by his or her situation) leads to increased empathic feelings for this individual; (b) these empathic feelings lead to a perception of increased valuing of this individual's welfare . . .; and (c) assuming that this individual's group membership is a salient component of his or her plight, the increased valuing generalizes to the group as a whole and is reflected in more positive attitudes toward the group" (Batson et al., 2002, p. 1657).

TABLE 6.3	SAMPLE QUESTIONNAIRE ITEMS USED TO ASSESS EMPATHY

Perspective Taking

I sometimes try to understand my friends better by imagining how things look from their perspective.

When I'm upset at someone, I usually try to "put myself in his shoes" for a while.

Empathic Concern

I often have tender, concerned feelings for people less fortunate than me.

I would describe myself as a pretty softhearted person.

Personal Distress

Being in a tense emotional situation scares me.

I sometimes feel helpless when I am in the middle of a very emotional situation.

Fantasy

When I am reading an interesting story or novel, I imagine how *I* would feel if the events in the story were happening to me.

After seeing a play or a movie, I have felt as though I were one of the characters.

Note: From Davis (1994, pp. 56–57).

Of course, correlational research cannot determine causality, but researchers have found that they can manipulate the amount of empathy people feel for another person by having them take that person's perspective on events. For example, Batson and his colleagues (2002) had research participants listen to a tape-recorded interview with a person named Jared Briggs, who was described as a heroin addict and drug dealer serving a sentence in a federal prison. The researchers created a low-empathy condition by instructing participants, "While you are listening to this interview, try to *take an objective perspective toward what is described.* Try not to get caught up in how Jared feels; just remain objective and detached." In the high empathy condition, the instructions were, "While you are listening to this interview, try to *imagine how Jared feels about what has happened and how it has affected his life.* Try to feel the full impact of what Jared has been through and how he feels as a result" (p. 1660; emphases in original). Compared to participants in the objectivity condition, those in the perspective-taking condition not only showed more empathy for the characters described in the manipulations, but also showed less prejudice against the groups the characters represented. Studies using such manipulations have found similar results for drug addicts (Batson et al., 2002); AIDS patients, homeless people, and murderers (Batson et al., 1997); older adults (Galinsky & Moskowitz, 2000); and African Americans (Finlay & Stephen, 2000; Vescio, Sechrist, & Paolucci, 2003). Taken together, these results indicate that empathy can operate as a buffer against prejudice. Being able to see the world from the viewpoint of other groups leads people to see an affinity between themselves and members of those groups, which inhibits the development of prejudice (Galinsky & Moskowitz, 2000).

THE SELF

The *self* represents our awareness of ourselves as living beings who interact with the world and the people in it. This awareness includes our beliefs about what we are like, our characteristic behaviors, our abilities and shortcomings, and so forth. It also includes our evaluation of those characteristics as good or bad, positive or negative. Theorists have related the self to prejudice in two ways. The first is through self-esteem, proposing that people who are low in self-esteem use prejudice to boost their self-images by looking down on others, and that people respond to threats to self-esteem with prejudice as a way of warding off the threat. The second way in which theorists have related the self to prejudice is through the concept of *intergroup anxiety,* the feelings of discomfort many people experience while interacting with or anticipating an interaction with members of outgroups. Although anxiety may not at first glance seem to be related to the self, theories of intergroup anxiety propose that two of its causes are self-related: concern over not knowing how to interact properly with members of outgroups and concern that outgroup members will think that one is prejudiced. We look first at the role of self-esteem in prejudice and then at the role of intergroup anxiety.

Self-Esteem

Self-esteem refers to people's evaluations of their personal characteristics and behavioral patterns. People who evaluate themselves positively are said to have high or positive self-esteem; people who evaluate themselves negatively are said to have low or negative self-esteem. Researchers and theorists have proposed two ways in which self-esteem might be related to prejudice, both of which can operate at the same time (Crocker, Blaine, & Luhtanen, 1993). One role proposed for self-esteem is **self-enhancement:** looking down on others might make one feel better about oneself. The other role is **self-protection:** if one's self-esteem is threatened, looking down on others might again make one feel better about oneself, especially if doing so can directly counteract the threat. For example, if threat comes in the form of criticism from a member of a negatively stereotyped group, viewing that group and its members as incompetent to make a valid criticism can blunt its effect on self-esteem: If criticism comes from someone who is incompetent to judge, it is meaningless and so is no reflection on oneself.

Self-enhancement   Although the self-enhancement role of self-esteem seems to be quite straightforward—one bolsters one's self-image by looking down on others—research on the process is complicated by the fact that the self-enhancement hypothesis can be interpreted in two ways (Aberson, Healy, & Romero, 2000). The traditional interpretation, based on general theories of self-esteem, is that people with low self-esteem should be more prejudiced than people with high self-esteem. It holds that "low self-esteem individuals need to make up for poor self-concept, and therefore they may pick on others to raise deficient self-esteem, whereas high self-esteem individuals do not need to bolster self-esteem"

(Aberson et al., 2000, p. 158). This interpretation postulates a negative correlation between self-esteem and prejudice: People with low self-esteem should be more prejudiced than people with high self-esteem. The alternate interpretation is just the opposite: People with high self-esteem should be more prejudiced than people with low self-esteem because prejudice is one source of self-esteem. As Christopher Aberson, Michael Healy, and Victoria Romero (2000) put it, "bias allows high self-esteem individuals to create, bolster, and maintain positive . . . identities. Low self-esteem individuals have low self-esteem because they do not regularly engage in . . . bias" (p. 158).

Researchers have used two approaches to investigate the self-enhancement hypothesis. In one approach, they create artificial groups in laboratory settings. As we saw in Chapter 3, even arbitrarily assigning people to artificial groups elicits group loyalty that leads them to see their own group in more favorable terms than other groups. Researchers then can use this method to look at the degree to which group members' personal self-esteem is correlated with their ingroup bias. The second approach uses survey research to assess the correlation between people's level of self-esteem and prejudice against minority groups in society. Aberson and his colleagues (2000) reviewed the research using the first approach and found an average correlation of $r = .20$ between self-esteem and intergroup bias. That is, people with high self-esteem showed more bias than people with low self-esteem, but only to a small degree. Survey research has produced inconsistent results: Some studies have found small positive correlations between self-esteem and prejudice (for example, Simoni, 1996; Utsey, McCarthy, Eubanks, & Adrian, 2002; Verkuyten, 1996) but others have found negative correlations (for example, Little, Murry, & Wimbusch, 1998; Valentine, 1998).

What causes these contradictory results? There has been too little research to know for certain, but there are several possibilities. One is that both high and low self-esteem people are prejudiced but that they express their prejudices in different ways (Aberson et al., 2000; Crocker et al., 1993). For example, high self-esteem people may express their prejudice directly, such as by saying negative things about outgroups. Their high self-esteem buffers them against any criticism they may receive from expressing prejudice directly. In contrast, low self-esteem people already have low opinions of themselves and so want to avoid such criticism. They therefore express their prejudice indirectly, such as by giving undeserved low ratings to products created by members of outgroups or by avoiding interaction with them. Because most research has used direct measures of bias, researchers may have overlooked these indirect indicators of prejudice and so may have erroneously concluded that high self-esteem people are more biased.

A second possibility is that self-esteem is related to prejudice, but that the relationship is indirect rather than direct. That is, self-esteem might work through some other variable to influence prejudice. For example, Jane Simoni (1996) found only a small correlation between self-esteem and attitudes toward lesbians and gay men, but larger correlations between both self-esteem and contact with lesbians and gay men and between contact and attitudes toward lesbians and gay men. She showed that higher self-esteem could lead to more contact with lesbians and gay men and that more contact could lead to more positive attitudes (see

Chapter 12 for more discussion of intergroup contact and prejudice). Thus, low self-esteem may make people reluctant to engage in the intergroup contact that could lead to more favorable attitudes.

A final possibility is that there are two kinds of high self-esteem, with one being related to prejudice and the other not. Christian Jordan and his colleagues (Jordan, Spencer, Zanna, Hoshino-Browne, & Correll, 2003) have distinguished between what they call *secure high self-esteem* and *defensive high self-esteem.* People with secure high self-esteem truly have positive opinions of themselves whereas people with defensive high self-esteem act as though they see themselves positively as a way to hide the fact that they really doubt their self-worth. However, both types of people get high scores on traditional measures of self-esteem. Using a measurement strategy that distinguished between the two types of self-esteem, Jordan and his colleagues found that people with defensive high self-esteem expressed more intergroup bias than people with secure high self-esteem. These findings are quite consistent with the self-enhancement role of self-esteem in prejudice: People who are secure in their high self-esteem have no need to be biased, but those who doubt their self-worth use bias as a means of bolstering their self-images.

Self-protection   If prejudice is used to protect self-esteem, then a threat to self-esteem should lead to increases in prejudice. Exhibiting prejudice would reduce the effects of the threat and return self-esteem to its pre-threat level. Unlike the results of research on self-enhancement, those for self-protection have been strongly supportive. We saw some examples of the self-protective role of prejudice in Chapter 4, in which we discussed research on how threats to self-esteem affected stereotype activation and application (Fein & Spencer, 1997; Spencer, Fein, Wolfe, Fong, & Dunn, 1998).

Steven Fein and Steven Spencer (1997) also demonstrated the role of prejudice in self-esteem maintenance. Participants in their study took a bogus intelligence test, after which some were told that they had done poorly (the self-esteem threat condition) and others were told that they had done well (the no threat condition). All participants then completed a self-esteem measure. Then, in what was ostensibly another experiment, they evaluated either an Italian or Jewish job candidate (pretesting had shown that there was a fair amount of anti-Jewish prejudice on the campus where the research was conducted, but not much anti-Italian prejudice). The participants in the self-esteem threat condition made more negative ratings of the Jewish candidate than of the Italian candidate; participants in the no threat condition rated both candidates equally highly. Similarly, Steven Fein and colleagues (Fein, Hoshino-Browne, Davies, & Spencer, 2003) found that male research participants whose self-esteem had been threatened sat farther away from a man they thought was gay than a man they thought was straight; there was no difference in seating distance for participants in a no threat condition. Note that in both of these studies the threat to self-esteem came from the researcher, not from a Jewish person in the first study or a gay man in the second; thus, a threat from any source, not just the target of prejudice, can arouse prejudice.

The results of Fein and Spencer's (1997) research also demonstrated the buffering role of prejudice. They found that participants who rated the Jewish job candidate and whose self-esteem had been threatened showed an increase in self-esteem after making their ratings whereas the self-esteem of the other participants did not change. Putting all their data together, then, Fein and Spencer first showed that the threat to self-esteem caused lower ratings of the Jewish candidate and then showed that those lower ratings were associated with increased self-esteem. That is, expressing prejudice warded off the threat to self-esteem. Examining this issue from a different perspective, Fein and his colleagues (2003) reinforced the self-esteem of some research participants before giving them opportunity to express their opinions about students attending their college and students attending a rival college. The participants whose self-esteem was not reinforced showed the typical ingroup bias, rating students at their college as better than students at the rival college; however, the students whose self-esteem had been reinforced showed no such bias. Thus, reinforcing self-esteem seems to inoculate participants against normal intergroup bias and prevents prejudice.

Finally, it appears that prejudice can have self-protective effects in children as well as adults. Jayne Stake (2003) studied high school students attending a science enrichment program. Focusing on male students, she assessed their self-confidence in their science abilities and their attitudes toward women in science at the beginning of the program and at its end 4 weeks later. Students were exposed to positive information about women in science and to women scientists as role models throughout the program. At the beginning of the program, Stake found that boys with lower science self-confidence tended to have negative attitudes toward women in science. However, boys whose science self-confidence increased over the course of the program had more positive attitudes toward women in science at the end of the program than at the beginning. Apparently, the initial negative attitudes toward women in science functioned to protect the boys' self-esteem as science students. As that self-esteem increased over time, the protection that prejudice provided was no longer needed and their attitudes became more positive.

Intergroup Anxiety

Intergroup anxiety is a term Walter and Cookie Stephan (1985) devised to describe the feelings of discomfort many people experience when interacting with, or anticipating an interaction with, members of other groups. These feelings are caused by expectations that the interaction will have negative consequences; these expectations, in turn, derive from concerns the person has over a number of issues, such as

- the (perhaps implicit) belief that outgroup members are dangerous and potentially harmful;
- the possibility that outgroup members might reject or ridicule the person;
- the possibility that ingroup members might reject or ridicule the person for associating with outgroup members;
- the possibility that the person will embarrass him- or herself by committing a social blunder by not knowing the appropriate norms that apply or behaviors to use when interacting with outgroup members; and

• the possibility that outgroup members will perceive the person as being prejudiced against their group (Klein & Snyder, 2003; Stephan & Stephan, 2001).

The theory postulates these negative expectations exist for one of two reasons: either because the person has had little contact with the outgroup and so sees the outgroup in terms of stereotypes that are often negative or because the person has had negative experiences with members of the outgroup in the past and bases expectations for future interactions on those experiences. Regardless of the reason, intergroup anxiety can lead to avoidance of outgroup members and hostility toward the outgroup. People want to avoid situations that arouse negative emotions, such as anxiety; recall from Chapter 5 that the theory of aversive prejudice is also partly based on discomfort with outgroups, which leads to avoidance of those groups whenever possible. The theory of intergroup anxiety is less clear about anxiety's links to intergroup hostility, but people usually dislike stimuli that arouse negative emotions (Deckers, 2005).

Research conducted to test intergroup anxiety theory has provided strong support for intergroup anxiety's relationship with prejudice, with correlations between measures of intergroup anxiety and prejudice averaging about $r = .40$ (for recent examples, see Plant & Devine, 2003; Stephan et al., 2002; Stephan, Diaz-Loving, & Duran, 2000). In regard to its antecedents, research has found intergroup anxiety to be correlated with low levels of intergroup contact (Islam & Hewstone, 1993; W. G. Stephan et al., 2000), negative intergroup contact (Plant & Devine, 2003; Stephan et al., 2002), and negative stereotypes of outgroup members (Stephan et al., 2002). In addition, Ashby Plant and Patricia Devine (2003) demonstrated that the relationship between negative intergroup contact and intergroup anxiety stems from the expectation that future contact will have negative consequences, which in turn leads to intergroup anxiety. Figure 6.1 summarizes the theory of intergroup anxiety in graphic form.

The relationship of intergroup anxiety to prejudice and negative intergroup attitudes is very robust. The relationship has been found not only for attitudes of White Americans toward minority groups (for example, Plant & Devine, 2003; Stephan et al., 2002; Stephan, Ybarra, & Bachman, 1999), but also for majority group attitudes toward minority groups in other countries, including Bangladesh (Islam & Hewstone, 1993), Israel (Bizman & Yinon, 2001; Stephan, Ybarra, Martínez, Schwarzwald, & Tur-Kaspa, 1998), Italy (Voci & Hewstone, 2003), and Spain (Stephan et al., 1998). Intergroup anxiety is also related to nationality group members' ratings of one another, such as Americans' and Mexicans' ratings of each other (W. G. Stephan et al., 2000; see also Greenland & Brown, 1999). Finally, intergroup anxiety is related to women's attitudes toward men (Stephan, Stephan, Demitrakis, Yamada, & Clason, 2000).

A particular strength of the intergroup anxiety concept is that, unlike many other theories of prejudice, it relates to minority group members' attitudes toward the majority group as well as majority group members' attitudes toward minority groups. For example, intergroup anxiety has been found to be related to African Americans', Asian Americans', and Hispanic Americans' attitudes toward White Americans (Stephan et al., 2002; Stephan & Stephan, 1989) and ratings of the

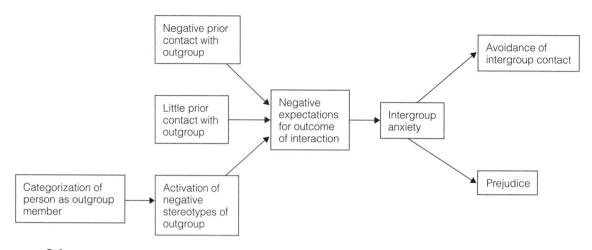

FIGURE **6.1**

INTERGROUP ANXIETY

Intergroup anxiety results from negative expectations about the outcomes of interactions with members of outgroups. These negative expectations derive from negative prior contact with the outgroup, little prior contact, and stereotypes of the outgroup that are activated when the interactant is categorized as a member of an outgroup. Intergroup anxiety leads to avoidance of intergroup contact and prejudice against the outgroup.

Muslim majority by members of the Hindu minority in Bangladesh (Islam & Hewstone, 1993).

Finally, an important implication of the theory of intergroup anxiety is that the relationship between anxiety and prejudice is self-reinforcing. Intergroup anxiety motivates avoidance of outgroup members. However, avoidance of outgroup members lessens the likelihood of having the positive intergroup contacts that can undermine negative expectations and stereotypes. That is, intergroup anxiety promotes behavior that keeps the processes that create the anxiety in operation. People who are higher in prejudice experience greater intergroup anxiety than people lower in prejudice (Blair, Park, & Bachelor, 2003; Boniecki, 2004) and so are particularly motivated to avoid the contact that might reduce their prejudice.

PERSONAL VALUES

Values are the enduring beliefs people hold concerning the relative importance of the goals they aspire to achieve in life and the types of outcomes they should try to avoid (Rokeach, 1973). For example, people who place a higher value on security than on freedom will do all they can to protect themselves and their families from harm, even if it means giving up some freedom. In contrast, people who place a higher value on freedom than on security will do all they can to ensure that others have minimal control over them, even if it means taking risks and therefore giving up some security. In addition to defining goals, values also serve as standards for making evaluative judgments: People and things one perceives to be consistent with one's values are judged to be good and those perceived to be inconsistent with one's values are judged to be bad (Schwartz, 1996).

Psychologists have related values to prejudice in several ways. Some theories, such as Irwin Katz and Glen Hass's (1988) theory of ambivalent prejudice, hold that values are directly related to prejudice: Some values facilitate prejudice whereas other values inhibit prejudice. Other theories, such as Milton Rokeach's (1972) value dissimilarity model and the theory of modern-symbolic prejudice (McConahay, 1986; Sears & Henry, 2003), hold that prejudice arises because outgroup members are perceived as holding values that are incompatible with or threaten those of the ingroup. Finally, the theory of aversive prejudice (Dovidio & Gaertner, 1998) holds that egalitarian values, or beliefs in equality, lead White people to suppress overt prejudice against other groups and to redirect it into more subtle forms, such as avoidance of intergroup contact (see Chapter 5 for discussion of these forms of prejudice). In this section, we first examine the direct relation of values to prejudice and then look at some theories based on perceived value dissimilarity.

Value Orientations

Several theories postulate that two general categories of values are related to prejudice, although different theories give different names to the values (Sampson, 1999). One category, generally referred to as *individualism*, relates to values emphasizing the importance of self-reliance; the other category, generally referred to as *egalitarianism*, emphasizes the importance of all people being treated equally and fairly (Katz & Hass, 1988).

Individualism   **Individualism,** a value that has a long history in America (Kinder & Mendelberg, 2000), places a strong emphasis on self-reliance and independence from others (Biernat, Vescio, Theno, & Crandall, 1996). Donald Kinder and Tali Mendelberg (2000) explain that during the 19th century, individualism came to be associated with hard work as the route to success in life because the wealth obtained through hard work allowed one to be independent of others and to do whatever one chooses. At the same time, idleness came to be seen as a vice. As a result, "in America today, idleness is . . . a moral defect; hard work, in and of itself, a moral virtue; dependence on others, a disreputable condition" (Kinder & Mendelberg, 2000, p. 47). Because of this link between individualism and hard work, most research on individualism defines the concept in terms of what is called the *Protestant ethic* or *Protestant work ethic,* which emphasizes the importance of hard work and perseverance as the way to success in life (Furnham, 1990). Although there are many measures of the Protestant ethic, the scale devised by Katz and Hass (1988) is one of the most commonly used; the first section of Table 6.4 contains some sample items from the scale.

The link between individualism and prejudice is group stereotypes: Groups that are stereotyped as behaving in ways that violate the principles of individualism

---

TABLE **6.4**   SAMPLE QUESTIONNAIRE ITEMS USED TO ASSESS VALUES

Individualism/Protestant Ethic

Respondents rate the extent to which they agree or disagree with each item:

> Most people who don't succeed in life are just plain lazy.
>
> Anyone who is willing and able to work hard has a good chance of succeeding.
>
> If people work hard enough they are likely to make a good life for themselves.
>
> A distaste for hard work usually reflects a weakness of character.

Egalitarianism

Respondents rate the extent to which they agree or disagree with each item:

> There should be equality for everyone—because we are all human beings.
>
> Those who are unable to provide for their basic needs should be helped by others.
>
> Everyone should have an equal chance and an equal say in most things.
>
> Prosperous nations have a moral obligation to share some of their wealth with poor nations.

Source: Katz and Hass (1988, p. 905)

are viewed negatively by those who adhere to these principles (Biernat et al., 1996). Thus, Monica Biernat and her colleagues (1996) found that people who score high on the Protestant ethic hold negative attitudes toward African Americans and fat people, two groups that are stereotyped as lazy, although the correlation is stronger for African Americans as the target group (see Katz & Hass, 1988, and Sears & Henry, 2003, for other examples of racial attitudes and Crandall, 1994, for anti-fat attitudes). Interestingly, Biernat and her colleagues also found a correlation between work ethic scores and negative attitudes toward gay men. This correlation was of about the same magnitude as that for attitudes toward African Americans even though gay men are not stereotyped as lazy. This may be because the Protestant ethic includes values such as self-restraint and avoidance of pleasure seeking and gay men are often stereotyped as hedonistic (Biernat et al., 1996). Not all research supports a link between individualism and prejudice. For example, Margo Monteith and Gina Walters (1998) found essentially no correlation between endorsement of individualism and anti-Black prejudice in a sample of White college students, and Gloria Cowan, Livier Martinez, and Stephanie Mendiola (1997) found that individualism did not correlate with non-Latino college students' attitudes toward illegal Latino immigrants. Thus, the actual link between individualism and prejudice may not be as strong as some theories have proposed.

Egalitarianism   As a value position, **egalitarianism** reflects a strong emphasis on the principles of equal opportunity, equal treatment for all people, and concern for others' well-being (Biernat et al., 1996). The second section of Table 6.4 contains some sample items from the scale most commonly used to assess endorsement of egalitarian values (Katz & Hass, 1988). In contrast to individualism, which is held to facilitate prejudice, theorists propose that egalitarianism inhibits prejudice.

As Biernat and her colleagues (1996) expressed it, White Americans who endorse egalitarian values "either experience feelings of sympathy for Black Americans [as proposed by the theory of ambivalent prejudice] or they work to avoid the threat to self-concept that negative behavior toward Blacks would produce [as proposed by the theory of aversive prejudice]. In either case, egalitarian values work as brakes on racist reactions" (p. 154). In addition, whereas individualism is proposed to affect prejudice only toward groups whose stereotypes include characteristics that are contrary to individualistic values, theorists propose that egalitarianism works to counteract all forms of prejudice: "It represents a form of antiprejudice that is not specific to any particular group or underlying cause of negative affect toward outgroups; it is a 'prejudice antidote'" (Biernat et al., 1996, p. 155).

What, then, is the relationship between egalitarianism and prejudice? Biernat and her colleagues (1996) included egalitarianism as well as individualism in their study of attitudes toward African Americans, lesbians and gay men, and fat people. Endorsement of egalitarian values was negatively correlated with prejudice against each group; that is, greater endorsement of egalitarian values was associated with less prejudice (for other examples, see Cowan et al., 1997; Katz & Hass, 1988; Monteith & Walters, 1998). Biernat and her colleagues also found that egalitarianism was more strongly related to prejudice than was individualism. In addition, using a different measure of values, Lilach Sagiv and Shalom Schwartz (1995) found that endorsement of egalitarian values was positively correlated with Israeli Jews' willingness to interact with Israeli Arabs. Thus, as Biernat and her colleagues (1996) proposed, egalitarianism does appear to be a general antidote to prejudice.

How does egalitarianism have its effects? Recall from Chapter 4 that stereotypes, which in their negative form constitute one aspect of prejudice, must be activated before they can have an effect on people's thoughts about and behavior toward outgroups. Gordon Moskowitz and his colleagues (Moskowitz, Gollwitzer, Wasel, & Schaal, 1999; Moskowitz, Salomon, & Taylor, 2000) have found that stimuli associated with outgroups are less likely to activate stereotypes for people who strongly endorse egalitarian values than for people who are less egalitarian. Thus, egalitarianism may inhibit prejudice by preventing the activation of negative stereotypes.

Perceived Value Differences

Rokeach (1972) proposed that prejudice is, in part, based on the perception that outgroups' value systems differ from one's own. Because values guide judgments of what is good or bad, holding different values implies a lack of goodness in the outgroups. In a sense, this **value difference hypothesis** represents the mirror image of the well-established psychological principle that people like others who are similar to them, especially if they are similar in terms of abstract characteristics such as attitudes and value positions (Berscheid & Reis, 1998). This principle also applies to members of outgroups. For example, several studies have found that people who learn that a gay man holds attitudes similar to their own like him better than people who learn that his attitudes differ from theirs. This finding holds even for people high in prejudice against gay men (Krulewitz & Nash, 1980; Pilkington & Lydon, 1997; Shaffer & Wallace, 1990). Bear in mind, however, that liking one person more than another does not necessarily mean liking that person a lot. These studies also found that expressed liking for a similar gay man was at about the level of that expressed for a dissimilar heterosexual man, and both were liked less than a similar heterosexual man. In this section, we first look at research on the relation of perceived value differences to prejudice. We then present two theoretical explanations for the relation of value differences to prejudice—terror management theory and the attribution-value model.

Value dissimilarity   The value dissimilarity hypothesis holds that one source of prejudice is the belief that members of outgroups do not share the values of one's ingroup. In fact, most people assume that outgroup members' values differ from their own. For example, White Americans believe that Black Americans are less likely to share their important values and less likely to live their lives according to those values than are other White Americans (Biernat et al., 1996); heterosexuals hold similar beliefs about lesbians and gay men (Biernat et al., 1996; Shaffer & Wallace, 1990). Perceptions of group differences in values have also been called **symbolic beliefs** (Haddock, Zanna, & Esses, 1993) and **symbolic threats** (Stephan & Stephan, 2000). However, the last term may be misleading in some cases; although Whites and heterosexuals believe that Blacks and lesbians and gay men do not share their values, they do not always believe that members of those groups violate or disrespect their values (Biernat et al., 1996).

Nonetheless, a perception of a lack of common values seems to be sufficient for prejudice. Perceptions of value differences are correlated with majority group prejudice against minority groups in a number of contexts, including prejudice against African Americans (Biernat et al., 1996; Stephan et al., 2002); Cuban, Mexican, and Asian immigrants to the United States (Stephan et al., 1999); lesbians and gay men (Biernat et al., 1996; Haddock et al., 1993); Native Canadians (Esses, Haddock, & Zanna, 1993; Corenblum & Stephan, 2001); French and Pakistani Canadians (Esses et al., 1993); Russian immigrants to Israel (Bizman & Yinon, 2001); and fat people (Biernat et al., 1996). As with intergroup anxiety, Stephan and Stephan (2000) propose that perception of value differences is a two-way street: It should be related to minority group members' attitudes toward the majority group as well as for majority group attitudes toward minority groups. This pattern has been found for ratings of White Americans by African Americans (Stephan et al., 2002), of White Canadians by Native Canadians (Corenblum & Stephan, 2001), and of men by women (C. W. Stephan et al., 2000).

Most of the research cited above has measured value differences in general terms, examining the extent to which outgroup attitudes are perceived to be different from one's own. The value dissimilarity hypothesis also holds that because specific groups are sometimes stereotyped as violating specific values, prejudice against those groups should be higher among people who endorse those values. Supporting this idea, Biernat and her colleagues (1996) found that the extent to which people gave *beauty* a high rating as a value was correlated with prejudice against fat people. Perhaps the best known example of a values-prejudice relationship is that of using family values as a justification for discrimination against lesbians and gay men; see Box 6.2.

6.2   *Family Values and Prejudice*

Since the 1992 presidential election, the concept of family values has played a major role in political debates in the United States, especially in debates about the civil rights of lesbians and gay men (see, for example, Cloud, 1998). Although the concept of family values is poorly defined (Cloud, 1998), lesbians and gay men are stereotyped as violating those values, being perceived as incapable of maintaining stable relationships, being bad parents, corrupting children, and violating traditional gender roles that some people view as fundamental to family life (Vescio & Biernat, 2003). Because of this perceived conflict between the gay/lesbian stereotype and the stereotype of the traditional family (see, for example, McLeod & Crawford, 1988), one would expect that endorsement of the traditional family would be related to attitudes toward lesbians and gay men.

Surprisingly little research has been conducted on this topic, but what research there is supports the hypothesis. For example, Gregory Herek (1988) found negative attitudes toward lesbians and gay men to be correlated with scores on a measure of traditional family ideology that focused primarily on parents as the authority in the family and traditional husband-wife and other gender roles. More recently, Theresa Vescio and Monica Biernat (2003) examined college students' evaluations of a gay or heterosexual man who was portrayed as either a good father or a bad father. Participants who rated family security as an important value evaluated the heterosexual father more favorably than the gay father; participants who rated the value as less important evaluated the two fathers equally favorably. Interestingly, whether the men's parenting behavior was consistent or inconsistent with traditional family values had little effect on the ratings. That is, even when the gay father's

behavior demonstrated support for one aspect of traditional family values, effective parenting, participants who said they valued the family highly gave him a lower rating than a heterosexual father who behaved in the same way.

Family values are also associated with attitudes toward homosexuality in some non-Western cultures. For example, Ming-Hui Hsu and Judith Waters (2001) assessed the relationship between filial piety and attitudes toward lesbians and gay men among Chinese college students. *Filial piety* refers to "the highest virtue within Confucian doctrine, . . . the production of male offspring to maintain the family name [and] offer sacrifices after death" (Hsu & Waters, 2001, p. 3). Hsu and Waters found that greater endorsement of filial piety was associated with more negative attitudes toward both lesbians and gay men for both male and female students. Thus, as the value dissimilarity model would predict, people who strongly endorse a variety of beliefs that can be categorized as family values hold negative attitudes toward lesbians and gay men, a group stereotyped as violating those values.

Finally, Dana Cloud (1998) reports an interesting sidelight on the family values issue. She notes that its first political use was in the context of race, not sexual orientation. It occurred when, in May 1992, then Vice President Dan Quayle said that racial unrest then taking place "is directly related to the breakdown of family structure" (quoted in Cloud, 1998, p. 395). In fact, Cloud found that in political discourse from December 1992 to July 1996, family values were mentioned almost three times more often in a racial context than in a sexual orientation context. Despite this difference in use, there appears to be no research on the relationship between endorsement of family values and racial attitudes.

Terror management theory   Jeff Greenberg, Sheldon Solomon, and Tom Pyszczynski (1997; Pyszczynski, Solomon, & Greenberg, 2003) developed **terror management theory** to explain (among other issues) how people's desire to promote and defend their belief and value systems results in prejudice. Their explanation is rooted in two human characteristics—the instinct for self-preservation and the contrasting knowledge that one's death is inevitable. Greenberg and his colleagues propose that the coexistence of the self-preservation instinct and the knowledge of one's vulnerability to death leads to terror because the self-preservation instinct motivates people to try to avoid the unavoidable, death. As a species, one way in which humanity has dealt with this terror is by developing cultural institutions and worldviews that promise immortality. The promised immortality can take two forms. It can be literal, in the form of religious beliefs in an immortal soul that lives on after physical death. Immortality can also be symbolic, in the form of identification with time- and death-transcending social institutions such as the family and the nation and of tangible reminders of continuity such as children and culturally valued achievements that carry on one's reputation after death.

Because culture and its values provide a buffer against the terror created by death, people are motivated to defend their culture against perceived challenges to its validity, such as those posed by different cultural worldviews. If such challenges were to succeed, they would undermine the protective cultural worldview and leave people open to the terror created by the knowledge of death. The theory therefore proposes that if people are made aware of the inevitability of their own deaths they will experience a need to reinforce their faith in their culture. One form this reinforcement takes is the rejection of people who challenge the culture's beliefs and values or who represent other cultures: "The mere existence of alternative [worldviews] will be psychologically unsettling, because granting their validity either explicitly or implicitly undermines absolute faith in one's own worldview. . . . The most common response is to simply derogate either the alternative worldview or the people who hold that view. By dismissing other worldviews as inaccurate, or the people who hold such views as ignorant savages who would share our perspectives if they were sufficiently intelligent or properly educated, the threat to one's own point of view is minimized" (Greenberg et al., 1997, p. 70).

Terror management theory researchers test the effects of awareness of one's future death by using an experimental manipulation to induce what they call *mortality salience*. As part of what is presented to them as a projective personality test, participants in the mortality salience condition write a brief paragraph about what they think will happen to them when they die and the emotions they feel while thinking about their own deaths. Participants in the control condition typically write about a negative experience that does not imply death, such as dental pain. Although this manipulation may sound somewhat minimal, there is a substantial body of research attesting to its effectiveness (Greenberg et al., 1997). After participants write their paragraphs, researchers administer other manipulations and measure the dependent variables, such as by having participants evaluate a person who either does or does not challenge their worldviews.

Most research on terror management theory has focused on responses to people who directly challenge participants' worldviews and cultural values, such as someone who has written an essay challenging some aspect of traditional American values (Greenberg et al., 1997); much less research has focused on reactions to ethnic groups or other targets of societal prejudice. In one study that did so (Greenberg et al., 1990), research participants who identified themselves as Christians underwent a mortality salience manipulation, after which they read what they were told were self-descriptions written by two other students at their university, one of whom was depicted as a Christian and the other as Jewish. Participants in the mortality salience condition rated the Christian student more positively than the Jewish student; the religion of the students being rated did not affect the evaluations of the participants in the control condition. Taking a different approach to the assessment of prejudice, Lori Nelson and her colleagues (Nelson, Moore, Olivetti, & Scott, 1997) manipulated mortality salience and then had research participants read the case of a man who had been seriously injured when his car crashed. The victim was suing the car's manufacturer, alleging that a manufacturing defect caused the accident; in one condition of the experiment, the car manufacturer was American, in the other condition the manufacturer was Japanese. Participants rated the extent to which they thought the car manufacturer was to blame for the accident. Those in the mortality salience condition assigned more blame to the Japanese manufacturer than to the American manufacturer; there was no difference in the control condition.

Finally, Jeff Schimel and his colleagues (1999) examined the effects of mortality salience on stereotyping. They hypothesized that because outgroup stereotypes are components of cultural worldviews, participants experiencing mortality salience would respond favorably to an outgroup member who acted consistently with the group stereotype (because such behavior would be consistent with their worldview) and would respond unfavorably to an outgroup member who acted inconsistently with the group stereotype (because such behavior would contradict with their worldview). After undergoing a mortality salience manipulation, White research participants read one of three essays purportedly written by a Black student about his summer activities. In the stereotype-consistent condition, the student reported engaging in such activities as "splitting to L.A., serious hoop, slammin' night life, cruisin' for honeys, clubbing, getting stupid, a few run-ins, drinking forties" (Schimel et al., 1999, p. 914). In the stereotype-inconsistent condition, the writer used formal language and told about taking summer engineering classes, working for a software company, and reading two novels about World War II. A stereotype-neutral essay told about the student's traveling to San Francisco for sightseeing, to Ohio to visit family, and to New Orleans for a friend's wedding; he could afford the trips because his mother worked for an airline. As shown in Figure 6.2, in the mortality salience condition, liking for the Black student decreased as his behavior became less stereotype consistent; the opposite pattern was found in the control condition. Another way of looking at these results is that for control participants, liking increased with apparent value similarity, which is consistent with the belief similarity effect discussed earlier; however, for mortality salient participants, liking decreased with apparent value similarity because that similarity contradicted the participants' worldviews.

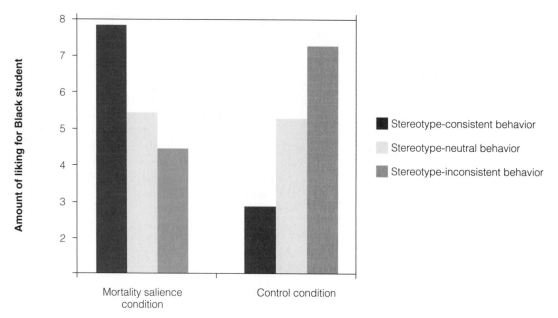

FIGURE **6.2**

MORTALITY SALIENCE AND STEREOTYPING

Under mortality salience conditions, White research participants liked a Black student more as his behavior became more stereotypical. Under control conditions, White research participants liked a Black student less as his behavior became more stereotypical.

(Adapted from Schimel et al., 1999, Table 3, p. 914)

Taken together, the results of these studies indicate that mortality salience leads to increased prejudice. What psychological mechanism underlies this effect? From a terror management theory perspective, prejudice and stereotyping of outgroup members reinforces people's cultural worldviews. It does so by emphasizing the negative characteristics of the outgroup that is challenging their worldview. The presence of these negative characteristics implies that any challenge the group makes is defective and therefore no real threat to the worldview. Mortality salience also increases people's feelings of identification with their ingroup (Castano, Yzerbyt, Paladino, & Sacchi, 2002); as we discuss in Chapter 8, strong ingroup identification tends to lead to prejudice. This increased identification with the ingroup can result in a kind of "My group, right or wrong!" mentality, leading people to tolerate negative behaviors by ingroup members they would otherwise condemn. See Box 6.3 for an example.

The attribution-value model The **attribution-value model** (Crandall et al., 2001) proposes that prejudice begins with the perception that members of minority groups have characteristics that are contrary to majority group values. Thus, fat people are seen as lazy and unable to exercise restraint in eating, and lesbians and

6.3   *Mortality Salience and Tolerance for Racism*

Two of the effects of mortality salience are a motivation to defend one's cultural worldview by derogating other groups (Greenberg et al., 1997) and increased identification with the ingroup (Castano et al., 2002). As two studies have shown, the combination of these factors can lead people to tolerate acts of racism that they would otherwise condemn. Jeff Greenberg and his colleagues (Greenberg, Schimel, Martens, Solomon, & Pyszczynski, 2001) had White research participants undergo a mortality salience manipulation after which they read an employment discrimination case in which the plaintiff alleged that he was repeatedly passed over for promotion because of his race. In one version of the case, the employee was Black and the manager who had allegedly blocked his promotion was White; in the other version, these roles were reversed. Participants rated the extent to which they thought the manager was guilty of discrimination. Participants in the mortality salience condition rated the White manager as less guilty of discrimination and the Black manager as more guilty of discrimination compared to participants in the control condition. Thus, mortality salience functioned to lessen the perceived guilt of an ingroup member who harmed an outgroup member and to increase the perceived guilt of an outgroup member who harmed an ingroup member.

Joel Lieberman and his colleagues (Lieberman, Arndt, Personius, & Cook, 2001) examined a more extreme situation, that of hate crimes. Following a mortality salience manipulation, research participants read a summary of a crime in which two young men attacked a man who had just left what was described as a "Jewish Pride rally," a "Gay Pride rally," or just "a rally." The first two versions of the crime were clearly hate crimes because witnesses reported that the attackers shouted aggressive anti-Jewish or antigay insults as they beat their victim; in the control condition, nonspecific insults were used. The victim had to be hospitalized because of the injuries he received. After reading the case, participants recommended the amount of bail that one of the alleged perpetrators should be required to post. Participants in the control condition recommended higher bail amounts for the hate crimes than for the other assault; in the mortality salience condition, lower bail was recommended for the alleged hate crime perpetrator. As in the job discrimination study, mortality salience lessened the perceived guilt of an ingroup member who harmed an outgroup member.

gay men are seen as violating family values. Coupled to that perception is the belief that members of those groups are responsible for their undesirable characteristics. Because people who are seen as responsible for their negative characteristics arouse negative emotions in others (Weiner, 1995), prejudice results when groups are perceived to be responsible for their negative stereotypic characteristics. Thus, studies conducted in a number of countries have found that dislike of fat people is correlated with the belief that fatness is a matter of choice: If fat people would only choose not to eat so much, they would not be fat (Crandall, 1994;

Crandall et al., 2001; Crandall & Martinez, 1996). Similarly, researchers have found that less negative attitudes toward homosexuality are held by people who believe that homosexuality is a matter of biology rather than choice (for example, Ernulf, Innala, & Whitam, 1989; Matchinsky & Iverson, 1996) or, more generally, that homosexuality is not something that is changeable or under a person's control (for example, Haslam, Rothschild, & Ernst, 2002; Herek & Capitanio, 1995; Whitley, 1990).

The research just cited was correlational and so could not show that attributions of responsibility cause prejudice. However, some experimental research has been conducted to examine whether manipulating people's perceptions of the cause of a negative characteristic results in differing evaluations of people with that characteristic. For example, William DeJong (1980) had research participants give their impressions of a young woman who was portrayed, through photographs and information in a fact sheet, as overweight. The fact sheet told some participants that the woman's overweight was due to a medical condition; the fact sheet read by other participants provided no cause for the overweight, implying that it was due to overeating. A third group of participants rated an average weight woman. The woman who was overweight due to a medical condition was rated more favorably than the overweight woman without a medical condition and equally favorably as the average weight woman. Therefore, leading people to believe that a negative characteristic was caused by something not under the person's control led to more favorable ratings of the person. Similar results have been found for ratings of a person whose offensive body odor was attributed either to a medical condition or to not bathing (Levine & McBurney, 1977) and for attitudes toward lesbians and gay men after participants read about homosexuality being either a matter of biology or an undetermined cause (Piskur & Degelman, 1992).

Although strong evidence shows that the attributions for the cause of obesity and homosexuality are related to attitudes toward those groups, the attribution-value model might not apply equally well to all forms of prejudice. For example, Nick Haslam and his colleagues (2002) found that beliefs about whether a group's characteristics are changeable were related to attitudes toward gay men but not to racial or gender attitudes. This difference may exist because of two dimensions people use to classify social groups (Haslam et al., 2000). One dimension is *naturalness*, the extent to which group membership is seen as biologically based. If a group is seen as highly natural, group members cannot leave their group for another; for example, a woman cannot change into a man. However, members of low-naturalness groups can change their membership; for example, a Republican could become a Democrat. The other dimension is *entitativity*, the extent to which group members are seen as being similar to each other, to which knowing that a person is a member of the group provides useful information about the person, and to which group membership is exclusive (the person either clearly belongs to the group or not; there is no in-between state). For example, all members of a political party are assumed to hold the same political views, people assume that knowing a person's party affiliation provides information about those views, and a person is either a Republican or a Democrat, not both at the same time.

Some groups, such as racial and gender groups, are seen as being high on both dimensions. Femaleness, for example, is seen as both natural in a biological sense and as entitative: all women are perceived to share certain characteristics, knowing that a person is a woman rather than a man supposedly provides useful information about her, and (most people believe) a person must be either a man or a woman: there is nothing in between. Other groups, such as lesbians and gay men, are seen as high on entitativity but low on naturalness. That is, they are seen as coherent social groups, but not as natural or biological in nature, and so people can change from one group to another (for example, from homosexual to heterosexual). Therefore, being gay or lesbian is seen as a matter of choice, just as one can choose to be a Republican or a Democrat (political groups are also seen as low on naturalness but high on entitativity). Haslam and his colleagues (2002) therefore suggest that attributional models of prejudice apply only to groups that are seen as high on entitativity and low on naturalness: "Categories that are represented as unambiguous natural kinds—such as races and genders—cannot be understood in terms of personal control and choice. Their members cannot be held responsible for belonging to them if membership is a matter of immutable biology. . . . By this account, prejudice towards [lesbians and] gay men is more strongly associated with [entitativity] than are sexism and racism because the culture's prevailing belief that homosexuality is not a natural kind allows a particular form of stigmatizing" based on attributions of responsibility for violating cultural values (pp. 96–97).

SOCIAL IDEOLOGIES

As we noted earlier, ideologies are sets of attitudes and beliefs that predispose people to view the world in certain ways and to respond in ways consistent with those viewpoints. As John Jost and colleagues (Jost, Glaser, Kruglanski, & Sulloway, 2003) explain, ideologies are psychologically important for two reasons. First, "people adopt ideological belief systems . . . to satisfy their psychological needs and motives" (p. 341). For example, authoritarianism appeals to people with strong needs for structure and certainty; authority figures can provide both (see, for example, Altemeyer, 1996). Second, "people embrace ideological belief systems at least in part because they inspire conviction and purpose" (p. 351); that is, they give people goals to strive for. Two important social ideologies that have been studied in relation to prejudice are religion and political orientation.

Religion

More than half a century ago, Gordon Allport (1954) wrote that "the role of religion [in prejudice] is paradoxical. It makes prejudice and it unmakes prejudice. . . . The sublimity of religious ideals is offset by the horrors of persecution in the name of these same ideals" (p. 444). The situation has not changed much since then: as we will see, some forms of religiosity (ways of being religious) are positively correlated with prejudice and other forms of religiosity are negatively correlated with prejudice. We first examine the relationship of degree of religious involvement to prejudice, continue with the concept of religious orientation, take a bit of a detour to look at the concepts of proscribed and permitted prejudices, and conclude with religious fundamentalism.

As you read this section, there are two cautions to bear in mind. First, almost all the research on the relationship between religion and prejudice has been conducted in North America and most of the participants in the research have been White, middle-class Christians (Batson, Schoenrade, & Ventis, 1993; Duckitt, 1994). Therefore, little is known about the relationship of religious faith to prejudice among believers in other religions such as Buddhism, Hinduism, Islam, and Judaism, to name only a few of the world's other large religions. Second, because most of the focus of researchers has been on the degree or nature of research participants' religiosity, nonreligious people have rarely been included in the research (Batson & Burris, 1994). Consequently, we know relatively little about the ways in which nonreligious people differ from religious people and how those differences relate to prejudice.

Religious involvement   Because almost all religions teach intergroup tolerance, one would expect that people who are more involved in their religions, and so presumably believe their religion's teachings more strongly, would show less prejudice. However, based on a review of 38 studies conducted from 1940 to 1990, Daniel Batson and his colleagues (1993) found that religious involvement was consistently correlated with a variety of forms of prejudice. Research conducted since 1990, which has focused largely on attitudes toward homosexuality, has found a similar pattern of results (for example, Agnew, Thompson, Smith, Gramzow, & Currey, 1993; Fisher, Derison, Polley, Cadman, & Johnston, 1994). Thus, it appears that, as Batson and his colleagues (1993) wrote, "religion is not associated with increased love and acceptance but with increased intolerance, prejudice, and bigotry" (p. 302).

Intrinsic and extrinsic religious orientation   These findings were not received well by religious leaders and researchers interested in the psychology of religion, who had expected that there would be a negative correlation between religious involvement and prejudice (Batson et al., 1993). As a result, the focus of research shifted from the degree to which people are religious to the way in which they are religious, that is, from *quantity* of religious involvement to *quality* of religious involvement. This shift is consistent with a distinction Allport (1954) had made some years earlier: "belonging to a church because it is a safe, powerful, superior in-group is likely to be the mark of an authoritarian character and to be linked with prejudice. Belonging to a church because its basic creed of brotherhood expresses the ideals one sincerely believes in, is associated with tolerance" (pp. 452–453). These ideas evolved into the concepts of *intrinsic* and *extrinsic religious orientation* (Allport & Ross, 1967).

People with an **intrinsic religious orientation** truly believe in their religions' teachings and try to live their lives according to them. They "find their master motive in religion. . . . Having embraced a creed the individual endeavors to internalize it and follow it fully. It is in this sense that he *lives* his religion" (Allport & Ross, 1967, p. 434, emphasis in original). People with a strong internal orientation should be unprejudiced to the extent that their religions teach intergroup tolerance. In contrast, people with an **extrinsic religious orientation** use religion as a way to achieve nonreligious goals, "to provide security and solace, sociability and distraction, status and self-justification. The embraced creed is lightly held or else selectively shaped to fit [nonreligious] needs" (Allport & Ross, 1967, p. 434). People high in extrinsic orientation are hypothesized to pay little attention to religious teachings and so to accept and express their societies' prejudices even when those prejudices run counter to their religions' teachings (Herek, 1987; Duck & Hunsberger, 1999). The first two sections of Table 6.5 present some sample questionnaire items

---

TABLE 6.5 | **SAMPLE QUESTIONNAIRE ITEMS USED TO ASSESS RELIGIOUS ORIENTATIONS**

Intrinsic[a]

It is important to me to spend periods of time in private religious thoughts and meditation.

I try hard to carry my religion over into all my other dealings in life.

Quite often I have been keenly aware of the presence of God or the Divine Being.

Religion is especially important to me because it answers questions about the meaning of life.

Extrinsic[a]

Although I believe in my religion, I feel there are many more important things in life.

The church is most important as a place to formulate good social relationships.

I pray chiefly because I have been taught to pray.

Occasionally, I find it necessary to compromise my religious beliefs in order to protect my social and economic well-being.

Quest[b]

As I grow and change, I expect my religion also to grow and change.

It might be said that I value my religious doubts and uncertainties.

I was not very interested in religion until I began to ask questions about the meaning and purpose of my life.

Questions are far more central to my religious experience than are answers.

Fundamentalism[c]

God has given mankind a complete, unfailing guide to happiness and salvation, which must be totally followed.

The long-established traditions in religion show the best way to honor and serve God, and should never be compromised.

Whenever science and sacred scripture conflict, science must be wrong.

To lead the best, most meaningful life, one must belong to the one, true religion.

---

[a]From Allport and Ross (1967), reproduced in Batson, Schoenrade, and Ventis (1993, p. 162)
[b]From Batson, Schoenrade, and Ventis (1993, p. 170)
[c] From Altemeyer (1996, pp. 158–159)

used to assess intrinsic and extrinsic religious orientation. Research findings have generally supported the hypothesis that an extrinsic orientation is positively related to prejudice, although the correlations are often small. The results for intrinsic religiosity are less clear, but studies have generally found either a small negative correlation with prejudice or no correlation (Batson et al., 1993).

The findings that sincere religious belief, defined in terms of an intrinsic religious orientation, was negatively correlated with prejudice were more satisfying to researchers than the finding that religious involvement was positively correlated with prejudice. However, Batson and colleagues became concerned that intrinsically religious people might not really be low in prejudice, but instead were simply motivated not to *appear* prejudiced (Batson, Flink, Schoenrade, Fultz, & Pych, 1986; Batson, Naifeh, & Pate, 1978). That is, because their religions tell them they should be unprejudiced, intrinsically religious people give socially desirable—that is, unprejudiced—responses on self-report measures. As Daniel Batson and Christopher Burris (1994) put it, "every major [religious] denomination is on record opposing racial prejudice and discrimination. Yet we are given pause when we see a headline that reads, 'Sunday morning at 11 remains most segregated hour of the week' (*Atlanta Constitution,* August 9, 1987, p. 11-A). We suspect that in many cases the intrinsic believer, attending to the practice of the religious community as well as the preaching, is [learning] a very different, more pharisaical norm: The truly religious can't look racist" (p. 167).

Batson and his colleagues (1978, 1986) tested this hypothesis in two studies. In the 1978 study, they found a negative correlation between intrinsic religiosity and a self-report measure of anti-Black prejudice among White research participants; however, using a covert measure of prejudice—participants' preference for being interviewed by a Black or White research assistant—they found a small positive correlation between intrinsic religiosity and prejudice. In the 1986 experiment, Batson and his colleagues told White research participants that they and another student would watch and evaluate a short movie in one of two two-person "theaters." When participants arrived at the theaters, they found a Black student waiting in one and a White student waiting in the other. There were two experimental conditions. In the overt prejudice condition, the same movie was being shown in each theater, so choosing to sit with the White confederate might make participants appear to be prejudiced, because the race of the other person was the only factor that differentiated the two theaters. In the covert prejudice condition, different movies were being shown in each theater, so choosing to sit with the White confederate could be attributed to a factor other than prejudice—the movie. Batson and his colleagues reasoned that if social desirability influenced the racial attitudes of internally religious people, they would choose to sit with the Black person in the overt prejudice condition as a way of demonstrating their lack of prejudice, but would choose to sit with the White person when that choice could be attributed to movie preference rather than prejudice. A lack of prejudice would be indicated if an equal number of participants chose to sit with the Black student and the White student. The researchers' results partially supported their expectation: In the overt prejudice condition, 75 percent of the intrinsically religious participants chose to sit with the Black student compared to 46 percent of the intrinsically religious participants in the covert prejudice condition. Note that although the intrinsically religious participants exhibited a social desirability response bias by favoring the Black student over the White student, they made unprejudiced choices in the covert condition, sitting with the Black and White students at about the same rate. Thus, although intrinsically religious people do appear to be influenced by social desirability concerns, they also appear to be unprejudiced, at least in regard to race. Contrary to the theory underlying the concept of religious orientation, extrinsic religiosity was unrelated to prejudice in either study.

Quest orientation   Based on his study of theology and the results of his psychological research, Batson (1976) proposed a third type of religious orientation, which he named **quest.** Quest reflects a view of religiosity as a search, or quest, for answers to questions about the meaning of life. "An individual who approaches religion in this way recognizes that he or she does not know, and probably never will know, the final truth about such matters. Still, the questions are deemed important and, however tentative and subject to change, answers are sought" (Batson & Burris, 1994, p. 157). The third section of Table 6.5 shows some sample questionnaire items used to assess quest orientation. Quest orientation is only minimally correlated with intrinsic and extrinsic orientation (for recent examples, see Duck & Hunsberger, 1999; Rowatt & Franklin, 2004; Wilkinson, 2004) and so constitutes a third dimension of religious orientation that Batson (1976) described as a "more . . . flexible type of religiosity than the other two" (p. 207).

Because quest orientation reflects an open-mindedness and willingness to change that would include tolerance for members of other social groups, researchers have hypothesized that it would be negatively correlated with prejudice (Hunsberger, 1995; McFarland, 1989). With few exceptions, research has supported that hypothesis and also has found that quest is more strongly related to prejudice than either intrinsic or extrinsic orientation. In addition, the relationship between quest and low prejudice seems to be unaffected by social desirability concerns. For example, in Batson and colleagues' (1986) "movie theater" study described earlier, about half of research participants high on quest orientation chose to sit with the Black student in both the overt (44 percent) and covert (54 percent) prejudice conditions, indicating a lack of prejudice. Thus, quest initially appeared to be the source of "universal love and compassion" sought by psychology of religion researchers (Batson, Floyd, Meyer, & Winner, 1999).

Proscribed versus permitted prejudices   Theorists have pointed out that although most religions teach tolerance toward outgroups, some outgroups may be tolerated more than others (Batson et al., 1993; Duck & Hunsberger, 1999; Herek, 1987). That is, although some religions proscribe (that is, forbid) some forms of prejudice, such as racism, they may at the same time permit prejudice against people, such as lesbians and gay men, who are perceived to violate the religion's values. Because intrinsically religious people believe strongly in their religions' teachings (see, for example, Rowatt & Franklin, 2004; Wilkinson, 2004), researchers hypothesized that they would follow their religions' teachings regarding proscribed and permitted prejudices. That is, researchers expected that intrinsic religiosity would be negatively correlated with proscribed prejudices and positively correlated with permitted prejudices. In contrast, researchers hypothesized that quest orientation would be negatively correlated with both types of prejudice because of the generalized tolerance it engenders (Batson et al., 1993). Extrinsic religiosity has not received much attention in this research because extrinsically religious people are hypothesized to be more influenced by societal norms than by religious norms (Herek, 1987). Because societal norms may or may not coincide with religious norms, it is not possible to formulate clear hypotheses about the influence of religious norms on extrinsically religious people.

One approach has been to examine the correlations of religious orientations to proscribed and permitted prejudices, using racism as the proscribed prejudice and anti-gay attitudes as the permitted prejudice (Duck & Hunsberger, 1999; Kirkpatrick, 1993; McFarland, 1989). The correlations that have been found for the relationship of intrinsic orientation with both forms of prejudice have been small. Nonetheless, as hypothesized, researchers have found intrinsic religiosity to be negatively correlated with racism and positively correlated with anti-gay attitudes. The results for quest orientation have not been as clear: Although researchers have found quest to have a negative correlation with anti-gay attitudes, they have also found it to have no correlation with racism.

Another approach to testing the hypotheses is experimental, studying people's reactions to individuals who are presented to them as violating or not violating their values. For example Batson and his colleagues (1999) gave college student research participants who were high on intrinsic religiosity the opportunity to help another student earn some money. The other student was portrayed as either heterosexual and needing the money to visit his or her grandparents, as gay and needing the money to visit his or her grandparents, or as gay and needing the money to attend a gay rights rally. Although levels of helping were high in all three conditions, participants were more likely to help the student portrayed as heterosexual than the student portrayed as gay, regardless of why the student needed help. Thus, intrinsically religious students were reluctant to help someone who violated their religious values even when the help would promote a value-consistent behavior (visiting grandparents) rather than value-violating behavior (attending a gay rights rally).

In contrast to these results for intrinsic religiosity, Batson and his colleagues (1999) found that participants high on quest religiosity were equally willing to help the other student regardless of experimental condition. Thus, students high on quest were willing to help someone who violated their religious values even when the help would promote a value-violating behavior. However, Batson and colleagues (Batson et al., 1999; Batson, Eidelman, Higley & Russell, 2001) noted that people high on quest might value the openness and tolerance that characterizes their approach to religion more than any particular religious doctrine, such as the prohibition against homosexuality. People high on quest, therefore might be tolerant of people who violate religious principles but might dislike prejudiced people. To test this possibility, Batson and his colleagues (2001) conducted an experiment similar to the one just described, except that the student the participants could help was either tolerant of homosexuality and needed money to visit his or her grandparents, intolerant of homosexuality and needed money to visit his or her grandparents, or intolerant of homosexuality and needed money to attend an anti-gay-rights rally. The researchers found that although participants high on quest were equally willing to help both the tolerant and intolerant student visit grandparents, almost none of them were willing to help the intolerant student to attend the anti-gay-rights rally. That is, people high on quest were tolerant of someone whose religious beliefs were different than their own, but would not support behavior that was contrary to their beliefs.

Although these findings shed a positive light on people high on quest, Jerry Goldfried and Maureen Miner (2002) proposed that this tolerance may be limited. They suggested that whereas people high on quest may be tolerant of *attitudes* that differed from their own, they may not be tolerant of a *religious style* that ran contrary to theirs, such as fundamentalism. Using a research design similar to Batson and colleagues (2001), Goldfried and Miner found that people high on quest were unwilling to help a person who expressed a fundamentalist religious orientation even when the help would not promote fundamentalist religious goals. Thus, people high on quest appear to be tolerant of prejudiced people (Batson et al., 2001), but not of intolerant behavior or people whose religious style is inconsistent with their own open-minded orientation. Thus, there appears to be no universally tolerant religious orientation: Intrinsic and quest orientation are each related to some form of prejudice.

Religious fundamentalism   **Religious fundamentalism** is "the belief that there is one set of religious teachings that clearly contain the fundamental, basic, intrinsic, essential, inerrant truth about humanity and deity; that this essential truth is fundamentally opposed by forces of evil which must be vigorously fought; that this truth must be followed today according to the fundamental, unchangeable practices of the past; and that those who believe and follow these fundamental teachings have a special relationship with the deity" (Altemeyer & Hunsberger, 1992, p. 118). Religious fundamentalists also are committed to using their belief system as a guide for understanding and interacting with the secular world (Kirkpatrick, Hood, & Hartz, 1991). Fundamentalist movements sharing these characteristics are found among Christians, Jews, and Muslims (Armstrong, 2000). The last section of Table 6.5 shows some sample questionnaire items used to assess religious fundamentalism. Not surprisingly, given its nature, fundamentalism is highly correlated with an intrinsic religious orientation and somewhat negatively correlated with quest orientation (Kirkpatrick, 1993; McFarland, 1989; Rowatt & Franklin, 2004). These correlations reflect fundamentalists' adherence to religion and to living their religion in their everyday lives on the one hand and, on the other, the contrast between questers' search for answers to theological question and fundamentalists' confidence that their religion already provides those answers.

Research on religious fundamentalism has found it to be consistently associated with prejudice (Spilka et al., 2003). For example, across eight studies published between 1989 and 2003, fundamentalism had an average correlation of $r = .46$ with negative attitudes toward homosexuality and an average correlation of $r = .18$ with negative racial attitudes. Note that, as with intrinsic religious orientation, the correlation is stronger for a permitted prejudice (against homosexuality) than for a proscribed prejudice (racism). However, whereas intrinsic orientation has a negative correlation with proscribed prejudice, fundamentalism has a positive, albeit small, correlation. In addition, Aubyn Fulton, Richard Gorsuch, and Elizabeth Maynard (1999) concluded that "the homosexual antipathy of fundamentalism is in excess of what is required by their [sic] religious ideology" (p. 20). They came to this conclusion based on two of their research findings. First, although fundamentalists' religious values require them to reject homosexuality on moral grounds, they did so on nonmoral grounds as well, thereby going beyond the requirements of their religion. Second, Fulton and colleagues (1999) found that fundamentalists expressed prejudice against celibate as well as sexually active gay men, even though the former group "are not in violation of the perceived biblical injunctions [against homosexual behavior]" (p. 20).

Conclusions   Given the complexity of the relationship between religion and prejudice, what can we conclude? Three factors stand out. First, almost all religions teach acceptance and tolerance of all people, including people belonging to different racial and ethnic groups. Second, in practice, this acceptance and tolerance can be limited to those who are perceived to share one's religious values; prejudice may be permitted against those who are perceived to violate those values. Note, however, that permitting a prejudice is not the same as requiring it. That is, people are allowed to adhere to permitted prejudices, but are not required to do so; as a result, people may or may not exhibit a permitted prejudice based on other factors that influence their beliefs. Finally, it is essential to bear in mind that all the data relating religiosity to prejudice are correlational, so one should not come to the conclusion that religion causes prejudice. Although that might be true in some cases, in other cases people might be using religious doctrine as a justification for their preexisting prejudices. As Allport (1954) noted more than 50 years ago, "Piety may . . . be a convenient mask for prejudices which . . . have nothing to do with religion" (p. 447).

Political Orientation

Political orientation is one of the most controversial topics addressed by those who study the psychology of prejudice. The controversy arises from research that has consistently found a correlation between endorsement of conservative political beliefs and prejudice (for reviews, see, Duckitt, 1994; Jones, 2002). As a result, some writers have objected that conservatives have become what might be called the "designated villains" of prejudice. For example, Paul Sniderman and Philip Tetlock (1986a) have suggested that the typical portrayal is that "Racists . . . are by definition conservatives; and conservatives, again by definition, are racists" (p. 181). The symbolic prejudice approach (see Chapter 5) has been particularly singled out for criticism in this regard because it defines prejudice partly in terms of some of the traditional American values that conservatives endorse (see, for example, Sniderman & Tetlock, 1986a, 1986b; Tetlock, 1994; for a reply, see Sears, 1994).

In this section, we examine some of the recent research on the relation of political orientation to prejudice, looking first at prejudice itself and then at attitudes toward social policies, such as affirmative action, that are intended to relieve some of the effects of prejudice and discrimination. While reading this section, it is important to bear in mind that there has been little consensus on how to define *liberal* and *conservative*, the two key terms of political orientation, either conceptually or operationally (Knight, 1999). As a result, direct comparison of the results of different studies can be difficult.

Conservatism and prejudice   As was the case for older research, more recent studies have found a relationship between endorsement of conservative beliefs and prejudice. The correlations average $r = .30$ for racial prejudice (for example, Agnew, Thompson, & Gaines, 2000; Federico & Sidanius, 2002; Lambert & Chasteen, 1997; Sidanius, Pratto, & Bobo, 1996) and $r = .45$ for prejudice against lesbians and gay men (for example, Agnew et al., 2000; Heaven & Oxman, 1999; Morrison & Morrison, 2002; Whitley & Lee, 2000). However, as Duckitt (1994) noted, the more important question is not *whether* a relationship exists between conservatism and prejudice, but *why* it exists. Two principal explanations have been proposed, both rooted in concepts we discussed earlier in this chapter.

One explanation draws on the concepts of social dominance orientation (SDO) and right-wing authoritarianism (RWA). Endorsement of conservative beliefs is correlated with both SDO (for example, Federico & Sidanius, 2002; Sidanius et al., 1996; Whitley & Lee, 2000) and RWA (for example, Chirumbolo, 2002; Crowson, Thoma, & Hestevold, 2003; Whitley & Lee, 2000), which are themselves related to prejudice. Together, RWA and SDO account for a large proportion of variance in conservatism (Van Hiel & Mervielde, 2002) and when SDO and RWA are controlled, the correlation between conservatism and prejudice is greatly reduced (Federico & Sidanius, 2002; Sidanius et al., 1996; Whitley & Lee, 2000). From the perspective of social dominance theory, these results suggest that prejudice is really caused by SDO and RWA rather than a conservative belief system: The correlation between conservatism and prejudice arises because conservative beliefs constitute one form of legitimizing myths that people high in SDO can use to justify their prejudice (Sidanius, Singh, Hetts, & Federico, 2000; Federico & Sidanius, 2002). That is, conservatism does not cause prejudice; rather, some prejudiced people use the conservative belief system as a means of justifying their prejudices.

Another explanation for the relationship between conservatism and prejudice draws on the attribution-value model of prejudice. Researchers have found that, compared to liberals, conservatives are more likely to see people as being responsible for negative outcomes they experience, such as poverty and unemployment (for a review, see Skitka, Mullen, Griffin, Hutchinson, & Chamberlin, 2002). Therefore, when one group experiences a negative outcome, such as unemployment, to a greater degree than another group, conservatives are likely to attribute the outcome to a factor under group members' control, such as laziness (especially if laziness is part of the group stereotype). In contrast, liberals are more likely to attribute the outcome to factors beyond individuals' control, such as poor economic conditions. These different perceptions make conservatives more likely to be prejudiced because, in terms of the attribution-value model, they are more likely to perceive others as violating an important social value (hard work in our example) and dislike them for it.

This principle is illustrated by research conducted by Alan Lambert and Alison Chasteen (1997), who examined prejudice against African Americans and older adults. Lambert and Chasteen chose these groups because, although both are perceived to be economically disadvantaged, African Americans are stereotypically blamed for their economic situation because they are seen as violating the work ethic, but older people are not blamed for their situation because they are seen as victims of circumstance. The researchers hypothesized that liberalism would be correlated with positive attitudes toward both groups because liberals tend to attribute disadvantage to situational factors regardless of value issues. In contrast, they hypothesized that conservatism would be correlated with negative attitudes toward African Americans because they are perceived as value violators, but with positive attitudes toward older people because they are not. Lambert and Chasteen's research is unusual in that they assessed liberalism and conservatism separately, so each research participant received a score on each ideological dimension. That is, rather than assuming that people are either liberal or conservative, they assumed that people can have a mixture of liberal and conservative beliefs. This approach allowed them to examine individual differences in both liberalism and conservatism. Lambert and Chasteen's results supported their hypotheses: liberalism was correlated with positive attitudes toward both African Americans and older adults, whereas conservatism was correlated with negative attitudes toward African Americans but with positive attitudes toward older people (see also, Agnew et al., 2000).

If at least some of the relation between conservatism and prejudice comes from attributional differences between liberals and conservatives, where do these differences come from? Linda Skitka and her colleagues (2002) found that the answer lies in liberalism rather than conservatism. Using an approach that classified people as either liberal or conservative, they found that both liberals and conservatives initially attributed responsibility for negative outcomes to the person experiencing the outcome. They had expected this finding because personal responsibility is an American value that both liberals and conservatives have internalized. However, liberals were more likely than conservatives to change their attribution to a situational one (that is, one that fit their value system) when given an opportunity to elaborate on their responses. Because an attribution of personal responsibility is consistent with conservative values, conservatives have no need to change their attribution. Therefore, what is typically viewed as the conservative reaction—attributions of personal responsibility for value-violating outcomes that lead to blame that in turn lead to prejudice—is the "default option" for both liberals and conservatives.

Liberalism and prejudice   John Dovidio and Samuel Gaertner (1998) have suggested that both liberals and conservatives can be prejudiced, but that prejudice takes different forms in the two groups. Conservatives, they proposed, exhibit modern-symbolic prejudice whereas liberals exhibit aversive prejudice (see Chapter 5). Paul Nail, Helen Harton, and Brian Decker (2003) tested this possibility by having White research participants who had classified themselves as liberal, moderate, or conservative read a summary of a legal case in which a police officer had assaulted a motorist. In one condition of the experiment the police officer was White and the motorist was Black; in the other condition, the police officer was Black and the motorist was White. In both conditions, the officer was acquitted of assault charges in state court despite strong evidence against him (for example, the assault had been videotaped by a witness) but later was found guilty of violating the motorist's civil rights in federal court. After reading the case, the participants rated the extent to which they thought the police officer was being exposed to double jeopardy; that is, being tried twice for the same offense.

Nail and his colleagues (2003) hypothesized that if modern-symbolic prejudice is associated with conservatism, then conservatives would rate double jeopardy exposure as being lower for the Black police officer because doing so would allow them to express their prejudice subtly, in that the double-jeopardy rating does not directly criticize the Black officer. In contrast, they hypothesized that if liberalism is associated with aversive prejudice, liberals would rate double jeopardy as higher for the Black police officer because they would feel guilty over their residual negative racial feelings and overcompensate for their guilt by being more sympathetic to the Black officer. The researchers proposed no hypotheses concerning moderates because neither theory of prejudice addresses that situation. Figure 6.3 illustrates the results of the research. As predicted, liberals favored the Black police officer and conservatives favored the White police officer; that is, both liberals and conservatives were prejudiced but in different ways. In contrast, moderates, who had no political ideology that might bias their responses, treated both police officers equally.

Social policy attitudes Generally, people with conservative political beliefs hold more negative attitudes toward social policies intended to increase intergroup equality than do people with liberal political beliefs (for example, Sidanius et al., 2000; Sniderman, Crosby, & Howell, 2000). Perhaps the best known and most controversial of these programs is affirmative action. Three explanations can be offered to explain why conservatives are more opposed to affirmative action than are liberals. One is that because conservatism is correlated with prejudice, conservatives oppose such programs because they are prejudiced. The second explanation parallels the first, holding that because conservatism is correlated with SDO, conservatives oppose the programs because they are anti-egalitarian. The third explanation has been variously labeled *principled conservatism* (Sidanius et al., 1996), *principled objections* (Federico & Sidanius, 2002), and *principled politics* (Sidanius et al., 2000). This hypothesis proposes that conservatives oppose affirmative action because they sincerely believe in certain principles—such as fairness, individual merit, and minimal government—that they see as being inherently inconsistent with programs that favor one group over another, especially when these programs are mandated or carried out by the government. While reading our summary of the research evidence bearing on these hypotheses, keep in mind that interpretation of

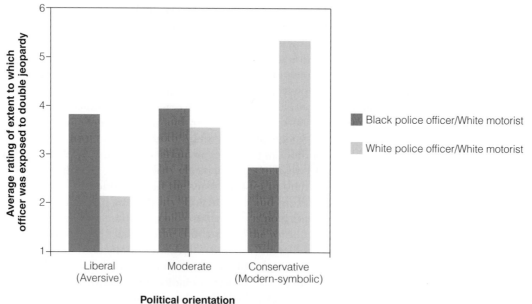

FIGURE **6.3**

Pro-Black Bias in Aversive Prejudice

Politically liberal participants (presumably experiencing aversive prejudice) rated the Black police officer to be experiencing double jeopardy to a greater extent than the White police officer, politically conservative participants (presumably experiencing modern-symbolic prejudice) showed the opposite pattern of response, while politically moderate participants made similar ratings for Black and White officers.

(Adapted from Nail, Harton, & Decker, 2003, Figures 1, 2, and 3, pp. 758, 760, and 761)

the research is complicated by the facts that the term *affirmative action* can have many meanings and that people's attitudes toward affirmative action vary as a function of the meaning they apply to it. For example, although most people think affirmative action means giving preferential treatment to women and members of minority groups, such an approach is only legal if an organization is making up for past discrimination. In its most accurate sense, *affirmative action* means establishing policies and procedures that ensure equal opportunity for women and members of minority groups (Crosby, Iyer, Clayton, & Downing, 2003).

The prejudice explanation of conservative opposition to affirmative action implies that if levels of prejudice are controlled, there should no longer be a relationship between conservatism and opposition. In this context *controlling* means using statistical procedures that show what a relationship between two variables, such as political orientation and opposition to affirmative action, would look like if everyone had similar scores on a third variable that is correlated with the other two, such as prejudice. In this case, controlling for prejudice means asking what the correlation between political orientation and opposition to affirmative action would look like if both liberals and conservatives had similar scores on a measure of prejudice. The results of such research show that when prejudice is controlled, there is only a small reduction in the relationship between conservatism and opposition to affirmative action (Federico & Sidanius, 2002; Sidanius et al., 1996). These results indicate that there is more to the relationship between conservatism and opposition to affirmative action than prejudice.

The anti-egalitarianism explanation of conservative opposition to affirmative action implies that if SDO is controlled, there should no longer be a relationship between conservatism and opposition. However, as with prejudice, controlling for SDO reduces the conservatism-opposition relationship only slightly (Federico & Sidanius, 2002; Sidanius et al., 1996, 2000). Therefore, conservative opposition to affirmation action cannot be explained entirely in terms of anti-egalitarianism.

The principled objections explanation is more difficult to evaluate than the other two because a number of principles are at issue and no research has systematically investigated all of them. We focus on two of the principles, fairness and minimal government. One conservative objection to affirmative action is that it is inherently unfair because it favors one group over another. One implication of this position is that conservatives should be less opposed to affirmative action programs that do not violate the principle of fairness or merit (such as by offering the same professional development programs to members of both majority and minority groups) than to those that do. Research shows that people who believe in the principle that rewards should be based on qualifications (the *merit principle*) also support such equal treatment programs but do not support programs that give members of one group preference over members of other groups (Bobocel, Son Hing, Davey, Stanley, & Zanna, 1998). People who support the merit principle are also less likely to oppose preferential treatment programs that are instituted as a remedy for discrimination (Son Hing, Bobocel, & Zanna, 2002). Because discrimination is itself an unfair impediment to application of the merit principle, in such a case affirmative action would promote fairness.

One complication to fairness as a principled objection to affirmative action is that perceptions of fairness are themselves related to prejudice and SDO: Prejudiced people and those high in SDO are more likely to endorse unfairness as an objection to affirmative action than are less prejudiced people and those low in SDO (Bobocel et al., 1998; Federico & Sidanius, 2002), perhaps as a means of justifying their prejudice. A second complication is that the fairness objection should apply equally to all groups, but conservatives are more opposed to affirmative action for African Americans than for women (Reyna, Henry, Korfmacher, & Tucker, 2004; Sidanius et al., 2000; Sniderman et al., 2000). (Sniderman et al. also found that liberals' attitudes differed in the same way.) Christine Reyna and her colleagues (2004) found that this difference was related to an aspect of fairness—deservingness. Women are seen as more deserving of the help provided by affirmative action, perhaps because of the laziness component of the Black stereotype. Reyna and her colleagues found that when attributions of deservingness were controlled, there was no difference in approval of race- and gender-based affirmative action programs. These results also suggest that fairness as a principled objection is somewhat contaminated by prejudice.

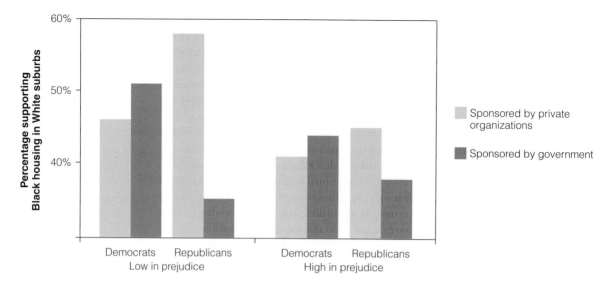

FIGURE **6.4**

SUPPORT FOR OPEN HOUSING BY POLITICAL PARTY AFFILIATION, PREJUDICE, AND PROGRAM SPONSORSHIP

Respondents high in prejudice showed low support for open housing regardless of party affiliation or program sponsor. Among respondents low in prejudice, Democrats were equally supportive of open housing regardless of sponsorship, but Republicans were much more supportive of a privately sponsored program than of a government-sponsored program, reflecting the conservative principle of minimal government. In addition, low-prejudice Republicans were more favorable to a privately sponsored program than low-prejudice Democrats were to a program from either sponsor.

(Data from Carmines & Layman, 1998, Table 5.4, p. 115.)

A second principled objection is that of minimal government. That is, conservatives argue that because government programs create expensive and inefficient bureaucracies, if action needs to be taken to reduce societal inequalities, private interests should do it, not government. This position implies that conservatives should favor privately sponsored antidiscrimination programs and oppose government programs. Carmines and Layman (1998) tested this hypothesis by asking respondents to a national survey whether they supported a program to help African Americans buy houses in White suburbs. Some of the respondents were asked about a program sponsored by religious and business groups; others were asked about a government program. As shown in Figure 6.4, unprejudiced Republicans favored the private program more than the government program, and favored it to a greater extent than unprejudiced Democrats favored either program. Both programs received low levels of support from prejudiced respondents regardless of their party affiliation.

Conclusions   What can we conclude about the relationship of political orientation to prejudice? First, the research does indicate a moderate correlation between conservatism and prejudice, but the research also indicates that SDO and RWA can account for the relationship. That is, some conservatives are prejudiced and some are not, and those who are prejudiced tend to be high on SDO or RWA.

Second, liberals as well as conservatives can be prejudiced, but it appears that liberals are more likely to exhibit aversive prejudice and that conservatives are more likely to exhibit modern-symbolic prejudice. Finally, some evidence shows that the objections many conservatives make to programs such as affirmative action are based on principle rather than prejudice. However, prejudiced people may use those principles to justify objections that actually stem from prejudice.

CHAPTER SUMMARY

Individual difference researchers study the ways in which people's personal characteristics relate to other variables such as prejudice. The three individual difference variables that have been most consistently linked with prejudice are right-wing authoritarianism (RWA), social dominance orientation (SDO), and empathy. The study of authoritarianism as a factor in prejudice began after World War II. The research initially focused on what was called the authoritarian personality, a personality type that was postulated to be especially susceptible to unthinking obedience to authority and to prejudice. Recent research has focused on RWA, a refined version of the original concept. People high in RWA are prejudiced against a wide variety of groups, especially groups that are perceived to violate traditional values and groups that authority figures condemn. A number of psychological characteristics may predispose people high in RWA to prejudice, including mental inflexibility, a disinterest in experiencing new things, a perception of the world as a dangerous place, and a tendency to organize their worldviews in terms of ingroups and outgroups.

SDO is a belief system that leads people to want their ingroup to dominate in society and be superior to outgroups. It is composed of group-based dominance, the belief than one's ingroup should dominate in society, and opposition to equality, the belief that societies should be structured so that one group dominates others. Generally, members of groups that hold more power in a society exhibit higher levels of SDO. People high in SDO are prejudiced against a variety of groups, especially those that challenge the legitimacy of social inequality. Psychological characteristics that might predispose people high in SDO to prejudice include seeing the world in competitive terms, belief that other groups' successes necessarily come at their ingroup's expense, and low empathy. People high in SDO justify their prejudices with legitimizing myths, or belief systems, such as group stereotypes that portray outgroups as inferior to the ingroup. Although SDO may appear to be similar to RWA, the two concepts differ in a number of ways. For example, SDO emphasizes relations between ingroups and outgroups whereas RWA emphasizes obedience to ingroup authority; scores on measures of SDO and RWA are only slightly correlated; and the two constructs have different patterns of relationships to some forms of prejudice.

Empathy is the ability to feel the emotions that others experience as a result of being able to see the world from their point of view. Although empathy has been much less studied in relation to prejudice than have RWA and SDO, researchers have consistently found that people high on empathy are low on prejudice.

The self represents our awareness of ourselves as living beings who interact with the world and the people in it. Two aspects of the self that have been found to be related to prejudice are self-esteem and intergroup anxiety. Self-esteem refers to a person's self-evaluation as positive or negative and theorists have proposed that prejudice can both enhance and protect self-esteem. Prejudice enhances self-esteem by providing people with groups they can feel superior to. Although one might expect that it would be people low in self-esteem who are more prejudiced, research has found a small positive correlation between self-esteem and prejudice. Three explanations have been proposed for why it has been high rather than low self-esteem that has been linked to prejudice. One is that people both low and high in self-esteem are prejudiced, but in different ways; however, because researchers have not focused on the ways in which low self-esteem people express prejudice, it looks like people high in self-esteem are the more prejudiced. The second explanation that has been offered is that the relationship between low self-esteem and prejudice is indirect; that is, that low self-esteem results in behaviors, such as avoidance of intergroup contact, that can lead to prejudice. The third explanation is that there are two kinds of high self-esteem, secure and defensive; people with defensive high self-esteem do not really value themselves and so bolster their self-images by looking down on others. Prejudice also protects self-esteem by deflecting criticism: If the person making the criticism is a member of a devalued group, the criticism can be shrugged off as meaningless because members of that group are not qualified to make valid judgments. Thus, researchers have found that being the recipient of criticism increases prejudice. Conversely, if a person's self-esteem is reinforced, the person will exhibit less prejudice.

Intergroup anxiety refers to the feelings of discomfort many people feel when interacting with members of other groups; the anxiety derives from the expectation that intergroup interactions will have unpleasant outcomes. People with high levels of intergroup anxiety tend to be prejudiced against the groups that arouse their anxiety. A particular strength of the intergroup anxiety concept is that it encompasses minority group members' attitudes toward the majority group as well as majority group members' attitudes toward minority groups; that is, intergroup anxiety is related to intergroup attitudes for members of both majority and minority groups. The relationship between intergroup anxiety and prejudice is self-reinforcing: The anxiety motivates avoidance of outgroup members, but avoidance of outgroup members lessens the likelihood of having the positive intergroup contacts that can undermine negative expectations and stereotypes.

Values are beliefs people hold concerning the relative importance of the goals they aspire to achieve in life and the types of outcomes they should try to avoid. Two value orientations have been related to prejudice. Individualism emphasizes the importance of self-reliance, and egalitarianism emphasizes the importance of all people being treated equally and fairly. The link between individualism and prejudice is group stereotypes: Groups that are stereotyped as behaving in ways that violate the principles of individualism are viewed negatively. In contrast, egalitarianism appears to be negatively correlated with all forms of prejudice. Egalitarianism may have its effects by suppressing stereotype activation.

Although some value orientations appear to be directly related to prejudice, prejudice is also related to the perception that outgroups' value systems differ from one's own: Because values guide judgments of what is good or bad, holding different values implies a lack of goodness in the outgroups. Research has shown that people generally believe that members of outgroups hold values that differ from their own, and research has also shown that perceptions of value difference are related to prejudice. One explanation for the values-prejudice relationship comes from terror management theory, which holds that awareness of one's mortality increases one's adherence to the ingroup's cultural values; people who are aware of their mortality express prejudice against groups they see as challenging those views as a way of deflecting that challenge. The attribution-value model holds that groups that are seen as violating values are disliked because they are seen as choosing to violate those values, and so are responsible for their negative (that is, value-violating) behavior. In general, people who are seen as responsible for their negative behaviors and outcomes are liked less than people who are seen as not responsible, their behaviors and outcomes being due to factors they cannot control, such as biology or economic circumstances.

Social ideologies are sets of attitudes and beliefs that predispose people to view the world in certain ways and to respond in ways consistent with those viewpoints. Two important social ideologies that have been studied in relation to prejudice are religion and political orientation. Early research on the relationship between religion and prejudice focused on religious involvement and found that involvement was positively correlated with prejudice. Researchers then examined ways of being religious, and found that intrinsic religious orientation, which views faith as an end in itself, had a small negative correlation with prejudice whereas extrinsic orientation, which views religion as a means for achieving other goals, had a small positive correlation with prejudice. However, other research suggested that some of intrinsic orientation's negative relation to prejudice might have resulted from people's desire to appear unprejudiced rather than from a true lack of prejudice. A third orientation, quest, views religion as a process of seeking answers to life's important questions, and is negatively correlated with prejudice.

A more recent approach to studying the religion-prejudice relationship has focused on the contrast between prejudices that religions proscribe, such as racial prejudice, and prejudices that some religions permit, such as anti-gay prejudice. Generally, intrinsic religiosity has been found to have positive correlations with permitted prejudices and small negative correlations with proscribed prejudices. The results for extrinsic and quest orientations have not been as clear: Although researchers have found extrinsic orientation to have a positive correlation with racial prejudice, it has had no correlation with anti-gay attitudes, and although quest has been found to have a negative correlation with anti-gay attitudes, it has had no correlation with racial prejudice. However, people high on quest do appear to be prejudiced against people, such as religious fundamentalists, whose style of religious belief runs counter to their own.

Religious fundamentalism itself has been found to be positively correlated with both anti-gay prejudice and racial prejudice, although the latter correlation is much smaller. As a psychological trait, fundamentalism is composed, in part, of

RWA and a strong adherence to orthodox religious beliefs. Thus, religious orthodoxy triggers hostility toward targets of permitted prejudice that is supplemented by hostility arising from compliance with religious authority figures' condemnation of those groups.

Researchers have generally found a positive correlation between endorsement of a conservative political orientation and prejudice. One reason for this relationship may lie in the positive correlation between conservatism and SDO: With SDO controlled, the conservatism-prejudice correlation is greatly reduced. From this perspective, conservative beliefs constitute one form of legitimizing myths that people high in SDO can use to justify their prejudice. That is, conservatism does not cause prejudice; rather, some prejudiced people use the conservative belief system as a means of justifying their prejudices. A second explanation for the relationship lies in the attribution-value model of prejudice. Compared to liberals, conservatives are more likely to see people as being responsible for negative outcomes they experience, such as poverty and unemployment. Therefore, when one group experiences a negative outcome to a greater degree than another group, conservatives are likely to attribute the outcome to a factor under group members' control. In contrast, liberals are more likely to attribute the outcome to factors beyond individuals' control. These different perceptions make conservatives more likely to be prejudiced because they are more likely to perceive others as violating an important social value and dislike them for it. However, the correlation between conservatism and prejudice does not mean that liberals are necessarily unprejudiced. Some research suggests that whereas conservatives experience modern-symbolic prejudice, liberals experience aversive prejudice.

People with conservative political beliefs tend to hold more negative attitudes toward social policies intended to increase intergroup equality, such as affirmative action, than do people with liberal political beliefs. Three explanations have been offered for this difference. Two of those explanations, that the relationship is due to conservatives' being more prejudiced and that it is due to conservatives' being high on SDO, have not found much research support. The third explanation, that conservative opposition is rooted in race-neutral political principles, has found some support. However, there is also evidence that support for at least some of these principles is correlated with prejudice. It is therefore possible that those principles are used by prejudiced people to justify objections that stem from prejudice rather than principle.

Suggested Readings

Authoritarianism

Adorno, T. W., Frenkel-Brunswik, E., Levinson, D. J., & Sanford, R. N. (1950). *The authoritarian personality.* New York: Harper & Row.

Altemeyer, B. (1996). *The authoritarian specter.* Cambridge, MA: Harvard University Press.

Stone, W. F., Lederer, G., & Christie, R. (Eds.). (1993). *Strength and weakness: The authoritarian personality today.* New York: Springer-Verlag.

Adorno and colleagues' *The authoritarian personality* is the classic original exposition of the theory of authoritarianism. The chapters in Stone and colleagues' book summarize much of the research that has been conducted on the theory. Altemeyer's book summarizes his revision of the original theory and presents some of his research on his theory.

Social Dominance Orientation

Altemeyer, B. (1998). The other "authoritarian personality." *Advances in Experimental Social Psychology, 30,* 47–92.

Sidanius, J., & Pratto, F. (1999). *Social dominance: An intergroup theory of social hierarchy and oppression.* New York: Cambridge University Press.

Sidanius and Pratto's book presents the theory underlying the concept of social dominance orientation (SDO) and much of the research that has been conducted on it. Altemeyer's chapter compares SDO and right-wing authoritarianism.

Empathy

Stephan, W. G., & Finlay, K. (1999). The role of empathy in improving intergroup relations. *Journal of Social Issues, 55,* 729–743.

Stephan and Finlay provide an overview of the role empathy plays in prejudice and discrimination.

Self-Esteem

Crocker, J., Blaine, B., & Luhtanen, R. (1993). Prejudice, intergroup behaviour and self-esteem: Enhancement and protection motives. In M. A. Hogg & D. Abrams (Eds.), *Group motivation: Social psychological perspectives* (pp. 52–67). New York: Harvester Wheatsheaf.

Crocker and her colleagues provide an overview of theories that relate self-esteem to prejudice.

Intergroup Anxiety

Plant, E. A., & Devine, P. G. (2003). The antecedents and implications of interracial anxiety. *Personality and Social Psychology Bulletin, 29,* 790–801.

Plant and Devine briefly review theories of intergroup anxiety and propose and test a model of its origins and relationship to prejudice.

Personal Values

Biernat, M., Vescio, T. K., Theno, S. A., & Crandall, C. S. (1996). Values and prejudice: Toward understanding the impact of American values on outgroup attitudes. In C. Seligman, J. M. Olson, & M. P. Zanna (Eds.), *The psychology of values* (pp. 153–189). Mahwah, NJ: Erlbaum.

This chapter provides an overview of the relationship of values to prejudice, including the roles values play in theories of contemporary prejudice.

Terror Management Theory

Greenberg, J., Solomon, S., & Pyszczynski, T. (1997). Terror management theory of self-esteem and cultural worldviews: Empirical assessments and conceptual refinements. *Advances in Experimental Social Psychology, 29,* 61–139.

Pyszczynski, T., Solomon, S., & Greenberg, J. (2003). *In the wake of 9/11: The psychology of terror.* Washington, DC: American Psychological Association.

Solomon, S., Greenberg, J., & Pyszczynski, T. (2000). Pride and prejudice: Fear of death and social behavior. *Current Directions in Psychological Science, 9,* 200–204.

The chapter by Greenberg and colleagues provides a detailed explanation of terror management theory. The article by Solomon and colleagues presents a succinct overview of the theory focusing on prejudice, and the book by Pyszczynski and colleagues interprets the September 11, 2001, terrorist attacks on the United States in light of their theory.

Attribution-Value Model

Crandall, C. S., D'Anello, S., Sakalli, N., Lazarus, E., Wieczorkowska, G., & Feather, N. T. (2001). An attribution-value model of prejudice: Anti-fat attitudes in six nations. *Personality and Social Psychology Bulletin, 27,* 30–37.

Weiner, B. (1995). *Judgments of responsibility: A foundation for a theory of social conduct.* New York: Guilford.

The article by Crandall and his colleagues outlines the attribution-value model. Weiner's book presents the theory on which the model is based.

Religion

Batson, C. D., Schoenrade, P., & Ventis, W. L. (1993). *Religion and the individual: A social-psychological perspective.* New York: Oxford University Press.

Spilka, B., Hood, R. W., Jr., Hunsberger, B., & Gorsuch, R. (2003). *The psychology of religion: An empirical approach* (3rd ed.). New York: Guilford.

Batson and colleagues' Chapter 9 provides an overview of research and theory on the relations of religion to prejudice, which Spilka and colleagues update in their Chapter 14.

Political Orientation

Nail, P. R., Harton, H. C., & Decker, B. P. (2003). Political orientation and modern versus aversive racism: Tests of Dovidio and Gaertner's (1998) integrated model. *Journal of Personality and Social Psychology, 84,* 754–770.

Sidanius, J., Singh, P., Hetts, J. J., & Federico, C. (2000). It's not affirmative action, it's the Blacks: The continuing relevance of race in American politics. In D. O. Sears, J. Sidanius, & L. Bobo (Eds.), *Racialized politics: The debate about racism in America* (pp. 191–235). Chicago: University of Chicago Press.

Sniderman, P. M., Crosby, G. C., & Howell, W. G. (2000). The politics of race. In D. O. Sears, J. Sidanius, & L. Bobo (Eds.), *Racialized politics: The debate about racism in America* (pp. 236–279). Chicago: University of Chicago Press.

Nail and his colleagues present evidence that both liberals and conservatives are prejudiced, but in different ways. Sidanius and his colleagues and Sniderman and his colleagues present different sides of the principled objections debate.

KEY TERMS

attribution-value model
authoritarian personality
egalitarianism
empathy
extrinsic religious orientation
ideologies
individualism
intergroup anxiety
intrinsic religious orientation
legitimizing myths

quest religious orientation
religious fundamentalism
right-wing authoritarianism (RWA)
self-enhancement
self-protection
social dominance orientation (SDO)
symbolic beliefs
symbolic threats
terror management theory
value difference hypothesis

QUESTIONS FOR REVIEW AND DISCUSSION

1. Explain *authoritarianism* as conceptualized by Adorno and his colleagues (1950) and by Altemeyer (1981). In what ways are those conceptualizations similar and in what ways do they differ?
2. Describe the characteristics of people high in right-wing authoritarianism (RWA) that may predispose them to prejudice. How are these characteristics related to the ones described in Chapter 4 that are associated with a propensity for stereotyping?
3. Explain the role authority figures play in shaping the prejudices of people high in RWA.
4. What is social dominance orientation (SDO)? In what ways is it similar to RWA and it what ways does it differ from RWA?
5. Describe the characteristics of people high in SDO that may predispose them to prejudice. How are these characteristics related to the ones described in Chapter 4 that are associated with a propensity for stereotyping?
6. Explain the concept of *legitimizing myths* as it is used in social dominance theory.
7. Think back to Chapter 5. Do any of the theories of contemporary prejudice postulate that people use what social dominance theory calls *legitimizing myths* to justify their prejudices? If so, what are those myths?
8. What is empathy? Describe how it is related to prejudice.
9. Explain the distinction between self-esteem enhancement and self-esteem protection as motives for prejudice. How are these motives related to the ones described in Chapter 4 that are associated with a propensity for stereotyping?
10. What are the two hypotheses that can be derived from the self-enhancement view of the role self-esteem plays in prejudice? What has research on these hypotheses found? What explanations have been offered to account for these findings?
11. What has research on the relationship between self-esteem protection motives and prejudice found?

12. What is intergroup anxiety? What causes it? Explain the process by which intergroup anxiety leads to prejudice.

13. Debate the following proposition: The consequences of intergroup anxiety should not be considered to be prejudice because it is normal for people to feel anxious when they are in a new situation, such as when interacting with members of groups they are not familiar with.

14. What are values? Describe the value orientations that have been studied in relation to prejudice. How is each related to prejudice? What processes have linked each value orientation to prejudice?

15. Explain how the perception of value dissimilarity can lead to prejudice. What individual difference variables are related to this process?

16. Describe the terror management theory explanation for the role played by perceived value dissimilarity in prejudice.

17. Describe the attribution-value explanation for the role played by perceived value dissimilarity in prejudice. How are perceptions of a group's naturalness and entitativity related to this process?

18. What are social ideologies? In what ways do religion and political orientation fit the definition of an ideology? In what ways do they not fit that definition?

19. Allport (1954) wrote that religion "makes prejudice and it unmakes prejudice" (p. 444). What did he mean by that? What light has subsequent research shed on his statement?

20. Describe the relationship of religious involvement to prejudice. Why were religious leaders and psychology of religion researchers displeased by these findings? What new approach did researchers take?

21. Explain the concepts of intrinsic and extrinsic religious orientation. In theory, how should each be related to prejudice? What has research shown about how each is related to prejudice?

22. Debate the following proposition: Intrinsically religious people are no less prejudiced than anyone else; they are just more motivated to give socially desirable responses to questions about prejudice.

23. Explain the concept of quest as a religious orientation. How is it related to prejudice?

24. What is meant by proscribed and permitted prejudices? We used racial prejudice as an example of a proscribed prejudice and anti-gay attitudes as an example of a permitted prejudice. What other examples can you think of for each category? Is the concept of proscribed versus permitted prejudices unique to the religious context or does it apply to society in general?

25. Describe how each of the three religious orientations is related to proscribed and permitted prejudices.

26. Define *religious fundamentalism.* How is it related to prejudice? What seem to be its major psychological components? How might each of these components contribute to fundamentalism's relationship to prejudice?

27. Allport (1954) wrote that "piety may . . . be a convenient mask for prejudices which . . . have nothing to do with religion" (p. 447). What did he mean?

28. Researchers generally find a positive correlation between political conservatism and prejudice. What explanations have been offered to account for that relationship?
29. Describe the relationship between political liberalism and prejudice.
30. Researchers generally find a positive correlation between political conservatism and attitudes toward social policies, such as affirmative action, that are intended to increase intergroup equality. What explanations have been offered to account for that relationship? Which explanation do you think is best supported by the research evidence? Explain the reasons for your answer.
31. Debate the following proposition: Political conservatism may be a convenient mask for prejudices that have nothing to do with politics.

THE DEVELOPMENT OF PREJUDICE IN CHILDREN

DANA B. NARTER
Ball State University

We lived in a neighborhood that was, I guess, about a mile and a half from a black neighborhood. So I can remember early on, during my youth, we had a black park . . . I used to enjoy [going] there, and the idea was that it was somehow dangerous now to go there. We had a swimming lake there, and I was ten or eleven, and blacks were allowed then to go to that park. It was just overnight that, "Well son, you're not allowed to go there because there are black people swimming there now." Basically we had to go twenty miles out to a different lake to go swimming. They just said, "You don't want to go there because it's dangerous. Black people are there. You never can tell what they might do to you."

—Anonymous White research participant
quoted by Joe Feagin and Hernán Vera, 1995 (p. 158)

The opening quotation describes the childhood experience of one White American adult. If you refer back to the quote, you will notice that this person's notion of Black people's being dangerous was not based on his personal experiences with Black people, but rather it was based on other people's stereotypes. In fact, as a boy, he probably never had the opportunity to get to know many Black people personally because he was segregated from them. Thus, he learned about members of other races indirectly, from parents, teachers, friends, and the media. Most people can probably come up with at least one similar experience that they had as children—either being taught prejudice like the person in the opening quotation, being warned about others' prejudice, or being the target of prejudice. Of course, not all childhood exposure to prejudice and discrimination is based on race; it also can be based on gender, religion, age, or a multitude of other social categories.

The ease with which prejudice can be fostered in children was demonstrated in a classroom exercise developed by elementary school teacher Jane Elliott following Dr. Martin Luther King's assassination. She wanted her students to experience firsthand what it felt like to be targets of discrimination, so she divided her class into groups based on eye color. On the first day, blue-eyed children were designated the "superior" group and brown-eyed students were designated the "inferior" group. The brown-eyed children wore collars so that they would easily be identified as the low status group. Elliott gave her blue-eyed students special privileges such as having extra time at recess and being permitted to go back for seconds in the cafeteria at lunch. Furthermore, she encouraged the blue-eyed children to discriminate against their brown-eyed classmates by convincing the blue-eyed children that they were smarter, better, cleaner, and more civilized. On the next day, Elliott reversed the children's roles.

The results of this exercise were astounding (Peters, 1970). According to Elliott, the "superior" group (whether brown-eyed or blue-eyed) became mean and nasty while the "inferior" group felt isolated and hopeless. Elliott even noted changes in academic performance based on group membership. When the students were perceived as "inferior" their school performance suffered, whereas when they were the "superior" group their performance was enhanced. At the end of the day, the "inferior" students were allowed to remove their collars and throw them away. One boy in the class tried to rip his cloth collar before throwing it away because he did not like how it made him feel and how others treated him when he wore the collar. One girl started to cry because she was happy to be back with all of her friends again. Other students seemed relieved and eager to remove the collars, so that they were no longer marked as the low status group. (For more information on Elliott's brown eyes/blue eyes exercise, see Box 7.1.)

Although Elliott's lesson on discrimination was not an empirical study, it was a bold attempt to illustrate the devastating effects of prejudice and discrimination in a classroom setting. This chapter describes theory and research on the development of prejudice in children. The first section covers children's awareness of social categories. It is important to note that categorical distinctions based on race, gender, and other characteristics do not necessarily lead to prejudice in

7.1   *More on Jane Elliott's Brown Eyes/Blue Eyes Exercise*

A documentary film entitled *Eye of the Storm* (Peters, 1970) about Jane Elliott's lesson on prejudice and discrimination was produced in 1970. In the movie, Elliott was filmed while she conducted the exercise with 3rd graders in Riceville, Iowa. The results were truly shocking. Elliott watched what she called "marvelous, cooperative, wonderful, thoughtful children turn into nasty, vicious, discriminating, little third graders" (Peters, 1970). The initial impact that the exercise had on her students was even more amazing. One student said, "Yeah, I felt like I was—like a king, like I ruled them brown-eyes, like I was better than them, happy."

In 1985, a second documentary on Elliott's exercise was made, entitled *A Class Divided* (Peters & Cobb, 1985). The second film combined original footage from *Eye of the Storm* with a reunion of the 3rd graders from the original film, who were now young adults. *A Class Divided* showed these individuals as they discussed the impact that Elliott's lesson had on them. One man who had participated in the exercise as a child said, "It made everything a lot different than what it was. . . . It was hard on you; when you have your best friend one day and then he's your enemy the next, it brings it out real

quick in you." Everyone agreed that Elliott's exercise opened their eyes to how awful prejudice and discrimination can feel, especially when you are the target. Some of the students also acknowledged that they felt powerful when they were the "superior" group. Clearly, Elliott's exercise had a long-lasting impact on these individuals. Many of the people at the reunion mentioned talking with their children about the important lessons that Elliott's exercise taught them, and most agreed that similar exercises should be implemented in other elementary schools.

A Class Divided also showed Elliott using a modified version of the brown eyes/blue eyes lesson with adult employees in Iowa's prison system. Interestingly, the adults' reactions to the exercise were quite similar to those of children. One man who was assigned to the lower status group said, "I think I learned from the experience a feeling like I was in a glass cage and I was powerless, there was a sense of hopelessness, I was angry, I wanted to speak up and yet I—at times I knew if I spoke up, I'd be back in a powerless situation, I'd be attacked, a sense of hopelessness. Depression." Hence, this exercise appears to have a powerful impact on adults as well as children.

children; however, they provide the foundation for preferences, attitudes, and behaviors toward members of other social groups. The second section highlights research on the development of prejudice in children and is organized in terms of the two social dimensions that have been studied most often, race and gender. The final section ties everything together by presenting three types of theories of prejudice: social learning theories, inner state theories, and cognitive developmental theories.

AWARENESS OF SOCIAL CATEGORIES

As we saw in Chapter 3, adults use categories to help them organize, simplify, and make sense of the world around them. Some categories and their underlying concepts refer to particular social groups (such as conservatives, athletes, and Jews), whereas other categories are nonsocial in nature (such as tables, flowers, and snakes). Adults classify people, objects, and events based on shared characteristics, and children form categories on the same basis and for the same reasons that adults do, such as simplifying a complex world. However, children have an even greater need to simplify their worlds through categorization because of their more limited mental abilities (Friedman, Putnam, Hamberger, & Berman, 1992). Categorization allows children to free up some of their mental resources so that they can use those resources for other tasks. It would be difficult to imagine exactly what life would be like if we did not form categories. However, the environment would be quite complicated, unorganized, and chaotic if we did not group people, objects, and events together. To illustrate, suppose that children did not possess the concept "woman." Each time children saw an adult female, they would think to themselves, "What is that?" Clearly, this process would be counterproductive and inefficient in terms of functioning adaptively in the world. Thus, categorization is helpful in simplifying the complexities of our physical and social environment.

Categorization also helps children develop an accurate picture of their social world. People differ—whether in hair, eye, or skin color, in size, or in gender—and it is appropriate for children to notice these differences. By doing so, children are forming a more accurate perception of what the world around them is like. If they did not notice these real differences, then their views of reality would be distorted or inaccurate. Some children who demonstrate awareness of social categories will be prejudiced, whereas others will not. Prejudiced children will respond negatively to the distinctions they note; nonprejudiced children will not (Zargarpour, 2002). The last section of this chapter discusses some of the factors that theorists have proposed as being important to the development of prejudice in children.

When researchers study children's awareness of social categories, they divide awareness into two types: implicit and explicit awareness (see, for example, Zimmerman, 2002). *Explicit awareness* of social categories is conscious awareness of particular social groups. For example, a child who points at a picture of a woman in a magazine advertisement and says, "She's tall!" has demonstrated explicit awareness of a social category based on height. However, children may be aware of certain social categories before they begin using language to place labels on those groups. In other words, it is possible that preverbal children have an *implicit awareness* of social categories.

This section reviews some of the research on the awareness of social categories in infants and children. We cover implicit awareness first because it emerges earlier in development, during infancy, before children have acquired language. Then, we discuss explicit awareness of social categories in verbal children.

Implicit Awareness of Social Categories

Even before children begin to produce words such as "boy," "pretty," and "old," evidence shows that they have an awareness of basic social categories such as gender, attractiveness, and age. That is, children implicitly recognize differences between or among basic social categories without being able to verbalize those differences explicitly. Even infants display this ability. For example, Joseph Fagan and Lynn Singer (1979) used what is known as an *habituation paradigm* with 5- to 6-month-old infants to investigate whether babies could discriminate pictures on the basis of gender, age, and race. In an habituation paradigm, an infant is presented with a photograph of a person repeatedly until she has gotten used to the picture. Then, the original photo and a new photo are presented simultaneously, and an observer measures the amount of time the baby spends looking at each photo. Looking time is commonly used as an index of infants' awareness of difference, novelty, or change. The logic is that if the baby looks reliably longer at the new picture, then she has discriminated between the two photographs and prefers the new one over the old one because it represents something new in her environment.

Fagan and Singer's (1979) experiment had two conditions. In one condition, the babies first saw a picture of a person who was a member of a particular basic social category, such as sex, age, or race, and then they saw a picture of another person who fell into the same category. For example, if the first picture was of a boy, then so was the second picture. In the other condition, the second picture was a different subcategory of the same social category. For example, if the first picture was of a boy, then the second picture was of a girl. Fagan and Singer matched the photographs on a number of facial features such as thickness of lips, hair length and texture, and separation of the eyes; this procedure was used so that the infants would not simply respond to surface physical differences between the people in the photos but to deeper conceptual differences. The researchers found that infants spent significantly more time looking at a new photograph when it was of a different gender or age than when it was of the same gender or age as the old photo. This finding suggests that gender and age were meaningful categories for the infants. However, these infants did not differentiate between pictures of a White woman and a Black woman, suggesting that race was not a meaningful category for them.

Infants also differentiate between people based on physical attractiveness, preferring attractive faces over unattractive ones long before socialization from parents, peers, and the media could affect these preferences. Judith Langlois and her colleagues (1987) examined this possibility with two groups of infants: a younger group (2- to 3-month-olds) and an older group (6- to 8-month-olds). Infants were shown color slides of White women's faces; half of the faces were rated as attractive by adult judges and half were rated as unattractive. When an attractive and an unattractive face were presented side by side, both groups of infants spent significantly longer looking at the attractive faces than the unattractive ones, suggesting that the infants preferred the attractive faces. In a subsequent set of experiments, Langlois and her colleagues (Langlois, Ritter, Roggman, & Vaughn,

1991) extended the original research by varying the gender, race, and age of the individuals in the photographs. Again, infants (6-month-olds in this experiment) looked longer at photos of attractive people regardless of whether they were of men or women, Blacks or Whites, or adults or infants.

More recently, researchers have suggested an attractiveness bias in infants as young as 2 months of age (Game, Carchon, & Vital-Durand, 2003) and perhaps in newborns under 1 week of age (Slater et al., 1998). This early preference for attractive faces could exist either because infants have a built-in mechanism that responds to faces or because infants learn about faces relatively soon after birth. It is possible that this early preference for attractive faces underlies the "beauty is good" stereotype, which is the perception that people who are physically attractive also have positive psychological characteristics, such as intelligence or kindness (Langlois et al., 2000).

Taken together, the results from these studies indicate that infants are implicitly aware of social categories based on gender, age, and physical attractiveness by 6 months of age or perhaps even earlier. However, infants of this age do not show an awareness of race. Infants' early awareness of their social environment suggests that their ability to form social categories is not something that is influenced by adults, but rather reflects an innate propensity to organize their social world in meaningful ways.

Explicit Awareness of Social Categories

When do children first demonstrate explicit or conscious awareness of social categories? I can recall a humorous conversation I had with my then 2½-year-old son Max that illustrates explicit awareness of social categories. The dialogue went something like this:

Mom: *"Are you a girl or a boy?"*
Max: *"I'm a boy, silly!"*
Mom: *"Are mommies women or men?"*
Max: *"Mommies are women . . . they're girls."*
Mom: *"Is daddy a man or a woman?"*
Max: *"He's a man."*
Mom: *"Is Elliot [Max's 6-month-old baby brother] a boy or a girl?"*
Max: *"He's not a boy or a girl. He's a baby"*

This conversation demonstrates that Max had accurate and explicit knowledge of some social categories such as "boy," "woman," and "man." However, he seemed to think that his little brother was neither a boy nor a girl, but a baby. Eventually Max came to realize that his little brother was both a baby and a boy, and that the two categories are not mutually exclusive.

When researchers examine explicit awareness of social categories, they generally require the child to apply a label correctly or to identify which person goes with a particular label by presenting the child with pictures or dolls. For example, in one study of children's awareness of gender as a social category, Spencer Thompson (1975) showed young children photographs of people and asked them to classify the photos as being pictures of males or females. He found that 75 percent of the 2-year-olds in his study could correctly identify males and females, and that by 3 years of age 90 percent displayed this ability. Findings from other studies confirm that by 2½ or 3 years of age, children are using gender labels appropriately (Yee & Brown, 1994).

Other researchers have used more open-ended tasks to examine children's early awareness of gender and racial categories. In one such task, children are given a set of photographs and are asked to group the ones that "look alike" or "belong together." Sometimes children are allowed to use only a preset number of categories; other times they are free to create as many categories as they would like. The photographs usually vary on several dimensions such as age, sex, and ethnicity. In one study that used this procedure, 7- to 10-year-old White children primarily used the dimension of ethnicity to sort the photos and seldom used gender (Davey, 1983). However, when given more specific instructions, such as to match two pairs of photographs to play together, the results were different. Children used gender as the category of choice; for example, children were more likely to match a Black boy and a White boy together than a boy and a girl of the same race. Thus, the context in which children were asked to sort the photographs influenced the way in which children categorized them. When children were asked to simply sort the photos, they focused on ethnicity; however, when the task was extended to the broader cultural context (in this case, playmate choice), then they did not focus on race. Such results suggest intergroup attitudes and intergroup behaviors may develop along multiple pathways.

Kenneth and Mamie Clark (1947) pioneered the study of children's racial category awareness, and their **doll technique** is still used today. In this paradigm, the child is presented with two (or more) dolls. In the simplest scenario using only two dolls, one of the dolls is White with blond hair, and the other doll is Black with black hair. Then the child is asked, "Which looks like a White (or Black) child?" When the doll technique is used with 3-year-olds, fewer than 25 percent of them can point to the correct doll (or, in some research, picture of a doll) when provided with the labels *Black* and *White*. However, by 4 or 5 years of age, accuracy increases to 75 percent or higher regardless of their own ethnicity (see, for example, Williams & Morland, 1976). Thus, it appears that the preschool years are critical in the development of awareness of social groups based on race.

Interestingly, children's differentiation of Native Americans, Chinese, and Latinos comes at a later age, perhaps because the features that differentiate these groups are less perceptually obvious than the features that distinguish Whites and Blacks. David Fox and Valerie Jordan (1973) found that between 5 and 7 years of age, White and Chinese American children are able to identify Chinese people as a separate category. Similarly, identifying Latinos proved to be more of a challenge for both White and Latino children, but their accuracy improved between 4 and 9 years (Rice, Ruiz, & Padilla, 1974; Weiland & Coughlin, 1979). Along the same lines, researchers have discovered that White and Native American children's identification of Native Americans is fairly well developed by 6 years of age but continues to improve until age 9 (George & Hoppe, 1979; Hunsberger, 1978). Note that awareness of one's own ethnicity parallels awareness of others' ethnicities.

It thus appears that explicit awareness of social categories develops by approximately 3 years of age for gender-based categories, by 4 or 5 years of age for the racial categories Black and White, and between 5 and 9 years for other racial groups such as Native Americans, Chinese, and Latinos. But *how* do children develop awareness of racial categories in early childhood given that they are not part of infants' repertoire of social categories?

In his book entitled *Race in the Making: Cognition, Culture, and the Child's Construction of Human Kinds,* Lawrence Hirschfeld (1996) uses a developmental perspective to explain how racial categories are formed. Hirschfeld is not interested in which racial groups children like better, but rather he is concerned with how children acquire knowledge about the existence of racial groups and the boundaries between groups. He asserts that to be able to think about different kinds of people, individuals must sort others into meaningful groups based on behavioral, appearance-based, and emotional characteristics. Thus, race becomes an essential dimension of humankind that encompasses common underlying features of groups. Race is a natural category, and like other natural categories, such as vegetables and birds, it has fuzzy boundaries and a graded structure (i.e., some people are more prototypical examples of a particular racial group than others). Hirschfeld states that racial categories are not simply based on skin color, but that perhaps skin color serves as a cue to deeper properties that underlie race.

Based on a set of studies in which children were randomly assigned to be members of artificial groups, Rebecca Bigler and her colleagues (Bigler, Spears-Brown, & Markell, 2001; Brown & Bigler, 2002) suggest that children become aware of racial categories because they see adults distinguishing between people on the basis of race. That is, because children see adults respond differently to people of different races, children begin to categorize people along those lines. Differences among people that adults do not emphasize, such as eye color, do not become salient categories for children.

It is clear, then, that children can make many social-group-based categorical distinctions during the preschool years. But does making these sorts of distinctions lead to prejudice? Not always. Some children will go on to become prejudiced, whereas others will not. The next section describes the course of development of prejudice in children.

THE DEVELOPMENT OF PREJUDICE

Just because children demonstrate awareness of various social categories does not necessarily mean that they value some categories more than others. The literature on how children add values to social categories has been described using several terms, including category preference, prejudice, and discrimination. The term *category preference* means that children select or prefer one group over another; however it does not necessarily imply a derogation of the nonselected group or groups. For example, suppose a child prefers playing with Asian children on the playground at recess. This does not necessarily mean that the child has negative attitudes about children who are not Asian, although it could mean that. Instead, it might suggest that the child has neutral attitudes about non-Asian children or that she has positive attitudes about non-Asian children but those attitudes are not as positive as her attitudes about Asian children. Moreover, it is not always clear whether attitudes underlie children's preferences or whether preferences for one group over another are based on some other social, emotional, or cognitive process. Recall that the way in which children categorized other children varied as a function of the reason for category formation: categories in general or categories of playmates.

As we saw in Chapter 1, the term *prejudice* refers to an evaluative response toward the members of some group, based solely on their membership in that group. Although prejudicial reactions can be positive, negative, or mixed, most research on prejudice focuses on the negative attitudes toward particular social groups. As also noted in Chapter 1, the term *discrimination* refers to behaviors directed toward social groups who are the object of prejudice. Again, the emphasis is usually on negative behaviors, but it can also refer to positive behaviors. Although children might engage in what appears to be discrimination by excluding other children from activities based on their social group membership, it is difficult to determine whether negative attitudes underlie exclusionary behavior in children, especially in young children with limited verbal abilities. Therefore, we discuss the development of prejudice as encompassing the various age-related changes that occur as children add value judgments to social categories, including preferences, attitudes, and behaviors. Although it may appear that we are mixing apples and oranges in taking this approach, researchers often have used very similar operational definitions for what they have variously referred to as preference, prejudice, and discrimination (see, for example, Aboud, 1988; Brown, 1995; Fishbein, 2002). On that basis, then, this section examines what we know about the development of racial and gender prejudice in children.

The Development of Racial Prejudice

Because it is challenging to find ways to tap into children's racial attitudes, this section first addresses some of the methodological issues faced by researchers who study the development of racial attitudes. After an overview of the methods used, we summarize the research literature on racial attitudes in children, with the primary focus on Black and White children because that has been the major emphasis in the research literature.

Methodological issues   John Williams and J. Kenneth Morland (1976) first created the methods and materials most commonly used to examine children's attitudes about race, and these techniques have had a profound influence on subsequent research in this area. Williams and Morland developed two tasks, the Color Meaning Test (CMT) and the Preschool Racial Attitude Measure, Second Version (PRAM II). Both tests assess the development of racial prejudice using a **forced choice method,** in which the participant must choose one of two options presented. During the CMT, the child is presented with a picture that displays drawings of two animals that are identical except that one is black and one is white. Next, the child is told a story about the animals and is asked to identify the animal described. For example, one story reads: "Here are two lambs. One of them is a good lamb. She does what her mother tells her to. Which is the good lamb?" Half of the stories contain positive adjectives (such as good, pretty, smart), and half contain negative adjectives (such as naughty, stupid, mean). A child is said to have a color bias if she consistently associates one color with the positive adjectives and the other color with the negative adjectives.

In the PRAM II, children are presented with photographs of two very similar drawings of humans; the only difference is that one of the individuals in the drawing has pinkish-tan skin and the other has medium-brown skin. Then, children hear short stories about the two people and are asked a question. For example, the children are told: "Here are two little boys. One of them is a naughty little boy. People do not like to play with him. Which is the naughty little boy?" Again, half the stories contain positive adjectives and half contain negative ones. If a child reliably associates one color with the positive adjectives and the other color with negative adjectives, then racial bias is presumed to exist.

A problem with this method is that although consistently choosing a picture of a White child over a picture of a Black child indicates a preference, it does not automatically mean a rejection of Black children. For example, consider a situation in which a child is presented with pictures of two children, one of a child who is overweight and the other of a child of average weight. The child indicates her preference about who she would rather have as a friend by pointing to a picture. What we do not know is the child's attitudes about the two individuals in the photos. Perhaps the child favored one photo over the other for some other reason that has nothing to do with the body types of the children pictured. For example, if a participant says, "I chose that child because he has friendlier eyes than the other child," then this does not give us any information about the child's attitudes based on body type. Furthermore, choosing one child over another does not necessarily mean that the participant disliked the unchosen child; rather, it tells us that the participant liked the chosen child more than the unchosen child. In fact, the participant might actually have positive feelings toward both children, with one set of feelings being more positive than the other. If that is the case, then the participant is not prejudiced against either child. Conversely, if a participant says, "I wouldn't want that child as my friend because he's pudgy," then that gives us information about the participant's prejudices about children who are overweight.

Using a **continuous measure** of prejudice, in which children are not forced to choose one child or the other, can help to overcome this problem. One example of a continuous measure is the social distance scale, which can be used with older children to assess complex attitudinal judgments. In this scale participants answer questions such as "Would you feel comfortable living next door to a Black family?" There are five options for a response, ranging from *Yes, definitely* to *No, definitely*. Thus, continuous measures of prejudice allow researchers to make finer-grained distinctions. In a similar vein, Frances Aboud and Frank Mitchell (1977) asked 6- and 8-year-old White children to indicate how much they liked (or disliked) their own ethnic group and other ethnic groups on a continuous scale.

Overall, the White children liked their own ethnic group the best; however, they liked their own ethnic group only slightly more than their next preferred group, and they gave the least liked group a neutral rating. Therefore, having positive attitudes about their own ethnic group does not necessarily mean that children have negative attitudes about other ethnic groups.

Researchers have several other ways to assess prejudice in children. These measures are based on the assumption that children do not interact with those they dislike. In one method, researchers observe the extent to which children interact with children of their own and different races on the playground, in the classroom, or in the school cafeteria at lunch. A second method is to collect self-reports from children about their interactions with others. For example, children might report how frequently they socialize with members of different ethnic groups or members of the other sex. A third method is to use **sociometric ratings.** There are two types of sociometric procedures: the best friends procedure and the roster and rating procedure. In the best friends procedure, children are provided with the names of all their classmates and asked to identify their best friends. The researcher then notes the race and gender of those listed as friends. One problem with the best friends technique is that not being named as a "best friend" is not the same as being disliked. The roster and rating procedure does not have this limitation because children are given all of their classmates' names and are asked to use a continuous scale to rate how much they like to interact (play or work) with each student.

In sum, forced choice methods, such as the CMT and the PRAM II, have some methodological shortcomings. However, by using continuous measures of prejudice, some of these difficulties can be overcome. Observations of behavioral interactions, self-reports of behavioral interactions, and sociometric ratings such as the best friends procedure and the roster and rating procedure have also been used to assess prejudice in children. However, it is important to note that different methods sometimes yield different results. Typically, self-reports and behavioral observations yield similar results, whereas the results from the two sociometric procedures, best friends and roster and rating, have tended to be similar to one another, but different from the result of self-reports and behavioral observations. Thus, findings must be interpreted carefully.

Now that we have discussed some of the methodologies used to study the development of racial prejudice in children, we look at the research findings using these methods and others. One important distinction to be aware of when reading the research on racial attitudes is that children's attitudes toward their own ethnic group are not always measured independently of children's outgroup attitudes; as we noted earlier, if a child expresses a preference for his own group, it may not be possible to tell whether his attitudes toward the other group are positive, negative, or neutral. However, some researchers have developed ways in which they can partially separate ingroup favoritism from outgroup dislike (see, for example, Aboud, 2003; Kowalski, 2003). Because the development of racial attitudes depends, in part, on the child's own ethnic group membership, we review the research findings in this area separately according to the ethnic status of the child.

White children's attitudes When considering the development of White children's racial attitudes, the first question you might ask is "At what age do White children first exhibit a pro-White bias and prejudice toward ethnic minorities?" Research has shown that White children develop racial attitudes, both positive and negative ones, as early as 3 years (Katz & Kofkin, 1997) and definitely by 4 years (Aboud, 2003). Frances Aboud (2003) used a measure that partially separates ingroup favoritism from outgroup prejudice. Using this measure with two samples of 4- to 7-year-old White children, Aboud found that ingroup favoritism emerged first and reached significant levels at 5 years of age. Outgroup prejudice also emerged at age 5, but was comparatively weaker than ingroup favoritism across age. Aboud concluded that ingroup and outgroup attitudes were distinct sets of attitudes. Her findings have important implications for the way in which prejudice is measured in children, suggesting that when measures of prejudice are used that do not allow a separation of children's ingroup and outgroup attitudes, positive attitudes toward the ingroup may be mistaken for outgroup prejudice, given that ingroup favoritism appears earlier in development and is stronger.

Do racial attitudes in White children change with age or do they stay relatively constant as children get older? It appears that racial prejudice reaches its highest levels around 4 or 5 years of age. Rebecca Bigler and Lynn Liben (1993) had 4- to 9-year-old White children complete a measure of racial stereotyping, in which they assigned positive and negative traits (such as, clean, smart, ugly, and sick) to "only Black people," to "only White people," or to "both Black and White people." Participants' responses were classified into one of three types: stereotyped responses (assigning positive traits to "only White people" and negative traits to "only Black people"), counterstereotyped responses (assigning positive traits to "only Black people" and negative traits to "only White people"), and nonstereotyped responses (traits assigned to "both White and Black people"). The youngest children, 4- and 5-year-olds, gave the most stereotyped responses, the fewest counterstereotyped responses, and the fewest nonstereotyped responses, suggesting that they had the highest degrees of racial stereotyping. The oldest children in the study, 8- and 9-year-olds, had the lowest degrees of racial stereotyping, indicating that prejudice declined between 4 and 9 years of age.

In line with Bigler and Liben's (1993) findings, Anna Beth Doyle and Frances Aboud (1995) found that by the age of 7, more than half of White children show a substantial decline in racial prejudice. Doyle and Aboud examined longitudinal changes in White children's prejudice toward ethnic minorities in kindergarten and again in 3rd grade, and they found that prejudice declined as children got older. For example, 85 percent of kindergartners were biased against Black people, whereas only about half of 3rd graders held this bias. On a measure that distinguished between ingroup bias and outgroup prejudice, kindergartners held more positive attitudes toward White people and more negative attitudes toward Black people and Native Americans. By 3rd grade, however, the children's positive and negative evaluations did not differ among the three races. Thus, a decline in racial prejudice occurred sometime between 6 and 9 years of age. Furthermore, it appears that the decrease in prejudice continues until age 12 and perhaps beyond (see, for example, Kalin, 1979).

Black children's attitudes   Black children, like White children, begin to develop racial attitudes at 3 or 4 years of age. For example, Phyllis Katz and Jennifer Kofkin (1997) tested Black children and their families longitudinally during the first 5 years of the children's lives, and found that 3-year-old Black children's attitudes were initially either pro-Black or unbiased.

However, in contrast to White children, no typical ethnic attitudinal patterns have been found for 5- to 7-year-old Black children. In a comprehensive review of 36 studies on Black children's attitudes toward their own and other ethnic groups, Frances Aboud (1988) found that some Black children in those studies held pro-Black attitudes, some held pro-White attitudes, and some were unbiased. For example, Margaret Spencer (1982) found that Black preschoolers and kindergartners scored at the midpoint on the PRAM, indicating that children assigned negative and positive qualities to Black targets and White targets equally. Researchers who use the doll technique also find a lack of consensus among the children (see, for example, Morland & Suthers, 1980).

Other studies find pro-Black attitudes between 5 and 7 years of age (for example, Burnett & Sisson, 1995; O'Connor, Brooks-Gunn, & Graber, 2000). Myra Burnett and Kimberly Sisson (1995) used the doll technique with 6- to 9-year-old Black children and found that pro-Black attitudes were most prevalent. In addition, pro-Black attitudes increased with age in this sample. However, other studies show just the opposite—a pro-White bias. For example, Mary Newman and her colleagues (Newman, Liss, & Sherman, 1983) studied Black kindergartners' attitudes about Whites, Blacks, and Latinos by showing the children drawings of children their own age from three ethnic groups (Blacks, Whites, and Latinos) in pairs and asking them to select which one they would like as a friend. They found that Black children preferred Whites and Latinos equally over Blacks. When a Black child was shown paired with a child of another race, the research participants chose the Black child less than half the time.

Between 7 and 10 years of age, pro-White bias disappears, and Black children typically either express more pro-Black attitudes or do not exhibit any bias (for example, Aboud & Doyle, 1995; Averhart & Bigler, 1997). When researchers have examined Black children's attitudes toward Blacks and their attitudes toward Whites independently of one another, they have found that a preference for Blacks does not necessarily mean a rejection of Whites. In fact, it appears that Black children become neutral, rather than negative toward Whites (for example, Aboud, 1980; Davey, 1983). Black children's attitudes between 7 to 10 years probably reflect their earlier attitudes. Those who had been pro-White become racially neutral, those who were neutral become pro-Black, and those who were already pro-Black become more pro-Black. For instance, when Aboud and Doyle (1995) examined differences in Black children's racial attitudes in kindergarten and 3rd grade, they found that 3rd graders were more pro-Black than kindergartners. They also found that pro-Black attitudes were stronger in children with higher Black self-identification.

Thus, it appears that Black children show less stability than White children in their racial preference patterns. One explanation for these mixed results is that Black children, being members of a nondominant group, simply have a more complicated developmental pattern in terms of their attitudes. Some Black children prefer other Black children, perhaps because of similar appearances, whereas other Black children prefer White children possibly because White children are the high status group. Black children who did not exhibit any racial preferences might be in a transitional stage and might not have solidified their preferences yet.

Attitudes of children from other groups   Most research on racial attitudes has focused on Black and White children. However, the research literature extends beyond these groups to include other ethnic groups as well. This research indicates that the preference patterns for children of other races are less consistent than they are for White children.

To illustrate, both Mexican American and Asian children show attitudinal patterns similar to those displayed by Black children, characterized by heterogeneity in attitudes between 5 and 7 years. That is, some studies find a pro-White bias, some find a pro-ingroup bias, and some find neutral attitudes (see, for example, Bernal, Knight, Ocampo, Garza, & Cota, 1993; Morland & Hwang, 1981). Between 7 and 10 years, any pro-White bias shown previously by Mexican American or Asian children has disappeared, and children either express a pro-ingroup bias or no bias at all (Bernal et al., 1993; Boulton & Smith, 1996). Again, this pattern is similar to that found for Black children. For example, Michael Boulton and Peter Smith (1996) examined racial preferences in 8- to 10-year-old White and Asian children and found that all children, regardless of race, preferred classmates who were of their own race over classmates of a different race.

Native American children's racial attitudes, however, are different from those for Black, Asian, and Latino children. Native American children are largely pro-White from 4 years on (see, for example, Corenblum & Annis, 1987, 1994). However, Native American children have expressed positive attitudes toward their own ethnic group when their attitudes toward several racial groups were examined (Aboud, 1977; Aboud & Mitchell, 1977). In these studies, Native American children held positive attitudes toward their own and other racial groups, and they also held negative attitudes toward other racial groups. Perhaps Native American children's negative racial attitudes toward White individuals might be the result of negative interactions with White people.

Finally, it is interesting to consider the ethnic attitudes for biracial children—children whose parents are of different races. Given the findings noted earlier on Black and White children's preferences, one might expect that biracial children would have racial attitudes that fall somewhere in between those of Black and White children because they are members of and presumably identify with both racial groups. In a study that tested this idea with Black-White biracial preschoolers, Deborah Johnson (1992) found that biracial children did not differ significantly from Black children or White children in their racial attitudes, although Black children and White children differed significantly from one another. That is, because biracial children identify with both ethnic groups, their ethnic attitudes also seemed to reflect both of their ethnicities.

In conclusion, all children, regardless of their race, acquire racial preferences and attitudes between 3 and 5 years of age. It is during this time that children express negative attitudes toward certain ethnic group members. Whom the negativity is directed toward depends in part on the child's own ethnicity. White children are consistently prejudiced against members of other racial groups. Black, Latino, and Asian children are more heterogeneous in their attitudes, with some children initially showing negativity toward members of their own ethnic group. Only Native Americans seem to hold more negative attitudes about other Native Americans than about Whites.

Let us note that prejudice is not a phenomenon found only in the United States; it can be found almost anywhere. For example, the Arab-Israeli conflict has generated a great deal of prejudice on both sides. A group of researchers at Tel-Aviv University in Israel have been investigating the development of prejudice against Arabs in Israeli Jewish children (Bar-Tal, 1996). See Box 7.2 for a summary of this research.

Intergroup behavior   If you have spent time with young children, you are probably aware that it is sometimes difficult to get specific information from them verbally. Perhaps they are distracted by someone or something more interesting than you, they just do not want to answer your questions at that particular moment, they would prefer to answer questions about something else, or they do not yet have the language skills to respond in an appropriate manner. Given these difficulties, some researchers have opted to observe children's behavior rather than assess their attitudes directly.

Sometimes children's attitudes and their behaviors seem inconsistent with one another. For example, Harold Fishbein and Satomi Imai (1993) observed Black, White, and Asian preschoolers during free play. They found that girls of all three races preferred to play with girls of their own race, but boys of all three races preferred to play with White boys. That is, girls showed a same-race preference but boys showed a pro-White preference. Note that these results are inconsistent with what we saw previously about the development of racial attitudes in children. Recall that all preschoolers, regardless of their gender, typically say that they prefer to play with a White child. However, the preschool-aged girls in Fishbein and Imai's study played with girls of their own race at recess. Thus, girls' behavior seems to be inconsistent with their attitudes. How might this finding be explained? One simple explanation is that perhaps there is not a one-to-one correspondence between children's attitudes and their behavior. If you consider your own attitudes and behaviors, you will see that they do not always correspond with one another. For example, you might disagree with something your college professor says in class, but when she asks if anyone disagrees you do not raise your hand or speak up. The same might hold true for children. If you consider the socialization process that people go through, it is socially adaptable for people to not always show how they feel.

When using sociometric methods, roster and rating measures typically indicate much less prejudice than best friends measures. To illustrate, Olga Jarrett and Lorene Quay (1984) used both roster and rating and best friends techniques to examine kindergartners' and 1st graders' playmate preferences. Best friends methods yield no same-race preferences for kindergartners, but shows that 1st graders display same-race preferences. However, the roster and rating method indicates that both White and Black kindergartners and 1st graders preferred White peers

7.2   *The Arab-Israeli Conflict in Children*

Ethnicity is an important distinction for people living in Israel, including children. For Israeli Jews, Arabs are probably the most significant outgroup. Daniel Bar-Tal (1996) notes that Israeli children begin to use the word "Arab" between 2 and 2½ years of age. Between 2½ and 3 years, Jewish children can identify Arabs and tell you something about them, which suggests that they have acquired the concept of *Arabs*. Children in this age range understand that Arabs are people who are different from Jews, and they can draw a picture of an Arab man. The traits Jewish children use to describe Jews and Arabs indicate that older children (5½ -to 6½-year-olds) evaluate "the Arab" more negatively than younger children (2½- to 3½-year-olds). Moreover, both groups evaluated "the Arab" more negatively than "the Jew." Between 10 and 12 years of age, the concept of "Arab" becomes more multifaceted, and both positive and negative attributes of Arabs are mentioned.

The general pattern of Bar-Tal's findings are similar to what you might expect to find if you conducted the same research project in the United States with White children as participants, and you presented them with the same sorts of items about Black and White people. However, some differences between the political and social situations in Israel and the United States may account for any differences between the two groups. For example, Jews and Arabs live in close proximity to one another in the midst of continuing tension between the two groups. Therefore, it is essential for both Jewish and Arab children to learn the differences between these groups very early and perhaps to develop attitudes about the groups at an earlier age than might be found in the United States. However, acknowledging individual differences in Israeli children and children in the United States should by no means overshadow the commonalities that emphasize the universality of the development of prejudice.

and rejected Black peers. The researchers found no significant correlation between children's responses on the two measures. However, it is clear that, starting in 1st grade, both Black and White children designate best friends on the basis of race.

Between kindergarten and 8th grade, observations conducted in nonclassroom settings indicate that children prefer interacting with same-race, same-sex peers (Finkelstein & Haskins, 1983; Schofield & Francis, 1982). However, when observed in classroom settings, the results are different, with females interacting with same-race peers and males showing little or no racial segregation (see, for example, Schofield & Francis, 1982). Racial segregation increases between 6 and 8 years of age (Singleton & Asher, 1977), then levels off or declines until the age of 12 (Schofield & Francis, 1982).

It seems that racial segregation, or best friend choice, is at its peak in 6th to 8th grades, with few students naming peers of another race in these three grades

(Shrum & Cheek, 1987). Moreover, from 6th grade on, Black children are more likely to list other-race best friends than are White children (Shrum, Cheek, & Hunter, 1988). When roster and rating procedures are used, a somewhat different developmental story unfolds. In kindergarten and 1st grade, both Black and White children preferred Whites (Jarrett & Quay, 1984). In 3rd through 8th grades, there was some same-race preference, but this was overshadowed by a same-sex preference (Singleton & Asher, 1979). Perhaps teachers' gender and racial stereotype expectations influenced this finding. However, there are no data for high school students using the roster and rating method.

To fill this gap in the high school literature, Martin Patchen (1982) used interviews and questionnaires to examine high school students' racial attitudes. Both Black and White students reported that they avoid sitting or walking near, talking to, or standing with students of other races. There were no race differences in terms of interracial avoidance: Black students avoided White students as much as White students avoided Black students. Although the majority of students reported that there were friendly cross-racial contacts at school (such as greeting, walking with, and talking with), only half the students reported friendly cross-racial contacts off campus (such as interracial dating and visiting the home of cross-racial peers). There were large racial differences in reports of unfriendly cross-racial interactions. Significantly more White students than Black students reported being called names, being threatened, and being physically blocked from passing. However, these differences were much smaller in other categories, such as interracial arguments, pushing, and fighting.

Beverly Daniel Tatum (1997) has written an interesting book on the topic of racial segregation in children and adolescents, in which she explains why all the Black students sit together in the cafeteria at lunch. See Box 7.3 for more information on this book.

In sum, children's intergroup behavior, like adults', is not always consistent with their attitudes. During preschool, there appears to be either an own-race or a pro-White bias. However, by 1st grade both Black and White children show an own-race bias that increases with age and is at its highest level during 6th to 8th grades. In high school, it seems that the majority of students reported having positive cross-race interactions at school, but less than half of students reported having positive cross-race experiences outside of school.

The Development of Gender-Based Prejudice

If you think back to your own childhood, you might remember holding negative attitudes toward members of the other sex. You might recall hearing little girls saying that they had "boy germs" because a boy had touched them on the playground or little boys talking about getting "cooties" from girls. How do these negative attitudes toward members of the other sex develop?

The origins   We begin in toddlerhood, where the roots of gender-based prejudice emerge. Ironically, toddlers begin to form gender stereotypes before they can even say the words "boy" and "girl." For example, some evidence shows that even infants younger than 2 years of age have visual preferences for and knowledge of

"Why Are All the Black Kids Sitting Together in the Cafeteria?" *and Other Conversations About Race* by Beverly Daniel Tatum

If you walk into the cafeteria at a racially mixed high school, you will most likely see Black students all seated together in the cafeteria. Beverly Tatum (1997), a clinical psychologist, posed the question: "Why are all the Black kids sitting together in the cafeteria?" Tatum begins by pointing out that in racially diverse elementary schools it is quite common to see children of different ethnicities working, playing, and eating together. However, by the time these children are in 6th or 7th grade, this racial segregation has begun. Why? Tatum believes that when children enter adolescence, they begin to search for a personal identity.

An especially important aspect of personal identity for Black teens is racial identity. Why is race so important to Black adolescents? Probably because everyone else thinks of them in racial terms. Resisting Black stereotypes, such as that Blacks are not as smart as Whites or that all Black people love to dance, and defining themselves in other ways is a major task for Black teens. So perhaps it is Black children's experiences with racism that lead them to self-segregate in the cafeteria. Associating only with other Black teens would protect them from the racism that they may experience in other contexts. Moreover, Black teens turn to other Blacks for social support because other Black students are more likely to understand how they feel than are White teens. To make matters worse, White teens are generally not very supportive when Black teens want to talk to them about racism.

Sometimes Black adolescents develop an oppositional identity in which they want everyone to be aware of their Blackness. When a group of Black teens are together, this oppositional group may be perceived as threatening.

Unfortunately, getting good grades in school is not considered part of most Black teens' identities. In fact, if a Black adolescent achieves academically, then some of her peers might say that she is trying to become White. Black teens avoid situations that will distinguish them from their peers, such as participating in a gifted program. But how do Black students who do well in school find acceptance among White students? It seems that Blacks downplay or de-emphasize their racial identity, but they do not reject it.

Getting back to the original question: Why are all the Black kids sitting together in the cafeteria? According to Tatum, sitting at the Black table is a way to express their identity. The results from two studies of college students suggest another reason for self-segregation by both Blacks and Whites. Nicole Shelton and Jennifer Richeson (2005) and Linda Tropp and Rebecca Anderson (2004) found that both Black and White students were interested in becoming better acquainted with members of the other race, but both also thought that any overtures they might make would be rejected. Thus, both Black and White students were reluctant to initiate interracial contact because of a misperception of disinterest on the part of the other group.

What about the Black children who choose not to sit at the Black table in the cafeteria? Lawrence Graham (1995) was one of those Black children who did not even consider sitting at the Black table in the cafeteria. He recollects that he avoided the Black table because he was afraid that by sitting at that table he would lose his White friends. To Graham, sitting at the Black table would make a racist or anti-White statement.

gender-stereotyped toys. To illustrate, Lisa Serbin and her colleagues (Serbin, Poulin-Dubois, Colburne, Sen, & Eichstedt, 2001) tested 12-, 18-, and 24-month-old infants' preferences for photos of vehicles or dolls. They found that by 18 months, infants showed preferences for gender-stereotyped toys, with the girls preferring the dolls and the boys preferring the vehicles. Serbin and her colleagues also wanted to determine whether infants would associate gender-stereotyped toys with the faces and voices of male and female children. By 18 months of age, girls "matched" the gender-stereotyped toys with girls' and boys' faces, although boys did not do so until 24 months.

By around 2½ or 3 years of age, children know something about their own gender and the gender of others ("I'm a girl, and he's a boy."). However, this awareness does not necessarily mean that they have a complete understanding of gender identity. For example, although over 90 percent of 2- to 5-year-old children know their own gender (Slaby & Frey, 1975), they seem unclear on some other aspects of gender such as **gender constancy:** the understanding that gender is permanent despite superficial changes in hairstyle, clothing, behavior, or age. That is, young children have some basic knowledge about their own gender and the gender of others, but their gender identity is not fully developed. Moreover, there is a relationship between children's level of gender constancy and their preference for attending to (that is, looking at) same-sex adults. For example, Ronald Slaby and Karin Frey (1975) found that children who had a more advanced level of gender constancy attended more to the individuals of their own sex who were shown in brief video clips.

Similarly, young children do not use gender-role stereotypes as readily as adults do, but rather are more likely to base judgments strictly on biological sex. That is, they are not as adept at distinguishing biological differences between the sexes from differences based on socially derived gender roles. For example, boys described as having feminine interests, such as playing with dolls or playing dress-up, are still thought to prefer boys' activities by other children (Martin, 1990). By around age 9, children begin to associate gender roles, rather than biological sex, with activities and interests. Yet even young children are well aware of gender-associated expectations and make judgments based on those assumptions. Thus, children as young as 2 years can readily identify which toys are appropriate for their sex (Blakemore, LaRue, & Olejnik, 1979), and they know which activities are stereotypically associated with women and men (Levy & Fivush, 1993). Children assume that if they like a gender-neutral toy, then other members of their sex will also like it but that children of the other sex will not. Moreover, children say they like very attractive toys less if they learn these toys are designed for the other sex and assume their peers will hold the same belief (Martin, Eisenbud, & Rose, 1995).

Within most Western cultures, children first exhibit same-sex preferences around 3 or 4 years of age (LaFreniere, Strayer, & Gauthier, 1984; Jacklin & Maccoby, 1978). However, same-sex preferences emerge either earlier or later in cultures with different family and social structures. For example, in a rural Kenyan community, same-sex preference does not develop until 6 to 9 years of age (Harkness & Super, 1985). This later emergence of preference compared with children from Western cultures might be due to the increased interactions that

Kenyan children have in mixed-sex groups. Given the significant family and economic responsibilities involving mixed-sex groups, such as helping with child care and supervising cattle, it makes sense that Kenyan children might not exhibit the same-sex preference as early as children in other cultures because they have more experience with members of the other sex. These findings highlight the importance of the environment on gender preferences. In cultures where mixed-sex groups are more common, **homosociality,** or the tendency to interact socially only with members of one's own sex, occurs later in development.

Gender-based prejudice emerges by age 3 and is quite strong by 4 years of age (Bussey & Bandura, 1992; Martin, 1989). Researchers have consistently found that, overall, boys like boys and men better than girls and women, whereas for girls the opposite is true. Therefore, prejudice on the basis of gender is initially symmetrical and bidirectional, with boys holding negative attitudes about girls and girls holding equally negative attitudes about boys.

Older children's attitudes   An interesting shift occurs in children's gender-based attitudes between 4 and 8 years, in which the process becomes more lopsided or asymmetrical. To illustrate, Carol Martin (1989) showed 4½- and 8½-year-old children pictures of boys and girls and also read descriptions of the target children's interests and friends. The following types of descriptions of gender characteristics were presented: gender neutral characteristics, same-sex stereotyped interests, other-sex stereotyped interests, a boy labeled as a sissy, and a girl labeled as a tomboy. When asked how much they liked the target children, 4½-year-old children disliked tomboys more than all of the other groups, whereas 8½-year-old children disliked sissies the most. The age-related shift from disliking tomboys to disliking sissies might be explained by the fact that older children value male characteristics more than female characteristics in both sexes (Smetana, 1986); thus, older children would have the most negative attitudes toward children thought to be sissies because they devalue feminine characteristics. It is important to note that Martin (1989) found no significant differences for the other three groups: gender neutral, gender-stereotyped, or counterstereotyped interests. Taken together, these findings suggest that labels were more important than behaviors for these children's preferences.

Other-sex prejudice increases until about age 8, then declines somewhat between 8 and 10 years of age (Zalk & Katz, 1978). The decline may be due to increases in gender-role flexibility and the beginning of heterosexual interest. Eight- to 10-year-old boys and girls both increasingly value masculine characteristics, but now boys want to be involved with masculine girls, and girls want to be involved with masculine boys. Therefore, girls in this age group value masculine characteristics but boys of the same age do not value feminine characteristics.

During preadolescence, the findings are somewhat murky, but the consistent trend is that both boys and girls like gender-role traditional girls the most. For example, Thalma Lobel and her colleagues (Lobel, Bempechat, Gewirtz, Shoken-Topaz, & Bashe, 1993) showed 10- and 12-year old Israeli children one of four videotapes. In these videotapes, a target child was shown playing a gender-appropriate game (soccer for boys and jump rope for girls) with members of the same sex or a gender-inappropriate game (jump rope for boys and soccer for girls) with members of the other sex. After watching the videotape, participants rated the target child on several dimensions. Based on masculine and feminine trait ratings, both the boy and girl targets who played soccer were rated as more masculine than feminine. Conversely, the boy and girl targets who jumped rope were rated as more feminine than masculine. In terms of perceived popularity with their peers, the least liked child was the boy who played jump rope with girls, while the likability of all other targets was the same. In terms of how much participants personally liked the target child, traditionally sex-typed girls were liked the most. In other words, both boys and girls personally most liked girls who played with other girls. In terms of willingness to engage in activities with the target, boys preferred to engage in other activities with the girl who played soccer with the boys, whereas girls preferred to engage in other activities with the boys who played soccer with other boys. Again, this finding suggests that both boys and girls highly value masculine characteristics.

When considering Lobel and her colleagues' (1993) findings, it is important to note that the research was conducted with Israeli preteens—not American preteens; consequently, their findings may or may not generalize to American children. For example, in both Lobel and her colleagues' and Martin's (1989) studies, children disliked sissies the most. However, all children in Lobel and her colleagues' study liked girls who played with other girls the most, whereas in Martin's study boys liked boys who played with other boys, and girls liked girls who played with other girls.

It appears, then, that other-sex prejudice emerges by age 3 and is in full force by age 4. This early prejudice is bidirectional, with girls having negative attitudes about boys and vice versa. Between 4 and 8 years of age an asymmetry emerges, with both boys and girls rejecting "sissies." After 8 years of age, other-sex prejudice declines slightly, perhaps due to heterosexual interest. In other words, perhaps prejudice toward the other sex becomes less prevalent as children become romantically interested in one another.

Intergroup behavior   As we have mentioned previously, holding a negative attitude about someone based on social group membership does not always result in discriminatory behavior against that person. As with race, even if children's behavior indicates segregation based on gender group, we cannot be sure that this behavior is arising from prejudice. For example, if a girl chooses to play four-square with other girls on the playground at recess, does this necessarily mean that she holds negative attitudes about boys and is discriminating against them? Perhaps it simply means that she likes playing four-square and so do several other girls in her class.

To examine whether younger children discriminate against members of the other sex, researchers generally use behavioral observations. In one such study, Peter LaFreniere, Floyd Strayer, and Roger Gauthier (1984) observed 15 groups of 1- to 6-year-olds over a 3-year period to determine how frequently they displayed positive behaviors toward same- and other-sex peers. The 1-year-olds did not exhibit any sex-based preferences. By 2 years of age, girls showed same-sex preferences but boys did not. At 3 years, both boys and girls held same-sex preferences, directing twice as many positive social initiatives to same-sex peers. By 5 years of age, girls were still directing twice as many initiatives toward other girls, but that ratio had increased to 3-to-1 for boys. In another observational study of young children, Eleanor Maccoby and Carol Jacklin (1987) studied 4½ - and 6½ -year-olds. The younger group was in preschool and the older group was in kindergarten. The researchers found that younger children were 2½ times more likely to be playing with a same-sex peer than an other-sex peer; the older children were 11 times more likely to be playing with a same-sex friend. It is evident that there is a dramatic increase in other-sex discrimination between preschool and kindergarten. Thus, the development of attitudes and behaviors based on gender are consistent with one another. Same-sex attitudinal and behavioral preferences can be seen by 2½ years of age and are stable until 4½ years. At this time, both attitudes and behaviors become stronger and more prevalent. By 6½ years, other-sex discrimination is in full swing.

To study other-sex discrimination in older children, researchers typically use a form of the roster and rating method. For example, Laura Hayden-Thomson, Kenneth Rubin, and Shelley Hymel (1987) gave children a photo of every child in their class and asked them to sort the photos into three groups: "like a lot," "sort of like," and "don't like." Children of all ages rated same-sex peers higher in likability than opposite-sex peers. From kindergarten through 3rd grade, children had a negative bias toward other-sex classmates, and this other-sex negativity increased with age. From 3rd grade through 6th grade, no particular trends were noted. Therefore, other-sex discrimination increased from kindergarten to 3rd grade, then remained stable from 3rd grade to 6th grade.

Wesley Shrum and Neil Cheek (1987) studied 3rd through 12th graders in a racially integrated school located in the South. Participants were asked, "Who from school are your best friends?" To understand how gender, race, and age influenced social networks in the schools, they examined three social categories: isolates, liaisons, and groups. An isolate is someone who has either zero or one reciprocal friendships. A liaison is someone who has reciprocal friendships with several others, but is not part of a particular group. Finally, a group is a set of three or more people who are friends. Shrum and Cheek found that from 3rd to 6th grade only 17 percent of groups were composed of both boys and girls, compared with 66 percent of groups at 7th and 8th grades, and 100 percent at 12th grade. Thus, the gender segregation that is seen in early elementary school changes during junior high school. This change might be due to an increased romantic interest in members of the other sex for the majority of junior high school students.

In related research, Shrum and his colleagues (1988) analyzed other-sex friendships (but not group membership) in two ways: segregation and preference. Their goal was to examine the extent to which gender friendships, both same and other sex, occur relative to chance. If there is no sex discrimination, then the proportion of various gender friendships (male-male, female-male, female-female) should be directly linked to the proportions of males and females in the school. Both segregation and preference measures yielded similar results. Shrum and colleagues found that mixed-gender friendships were very infrequent from 3rd to 12th grade, although frequency increased a little during junior high through high school. For boys, same-sex preferences peaked at grades 3 and 6. Same-sex preferences were highest for girls at 7th grade. Students in all grades reported that they had, on average, at least five times as many same-sex friends as other-sex friends. Thus, it appears that children exhibit other-sex prejudice quite early in development and this is apparent in children's self-segregating behavior. This self-segregation seems to continue during elementary school, middle school, and high school, with reductions in other-sex prejudice being associated with heterosexual interest.

As heterosexual interest emerges, it also seems to affect adolescents' attitudes toward gay and lesbian individuals. For example, Janet Baker and Harold Fishbein (1998) presented White, suburban students in the 7th, 9th, and 11th grades with a measure of anti-gay prejudice. They found that males were more prejudiced than females, and this gender difference was greater toward gay males than toward lesbians. Additionally, same-sex prejudice was greater than other-sex prejudice. Interestingly, these findings parallel those found with adult participants (see Chapter 9). Additionally, prejudice increased between grades 7 and 9 for both males and females. However, from grades 9 to 11, prejudice decreased for females and increased for males. To explain this, the researchers proposed that males were feeling increasingly vulnerable as a result of experiencing defensive reactions in response to the prospect of intimate relationships. Thus, although other-sex prejudice declines with age, antigay and lesbian prejudice does not.

THEORIES OF PREJUDICE DEVELOPMENT

Now that we have reviewed the research findings on the development of racial and gender prejudice in children, let us look at some of the ways in which theorists have attempted to explain how prejudice develops. Some theories of prejudice emphasize the role of the environment, whereas others emphasize that prejudice comes from within. This section discusses three current types of theories of how prejudice develops in children: social learning theory, inner state theories, and cognitive developmental theories.

Social Learning Theory

Social learning theory (Bandura, 1977, 1986) provides a comprehensive explanation for many aspects of social development, including the development of prejudice, in terms of three learning processes: direct teaching, modeling and imitation, and vicarious learning. Direct teaching occurs when an individual is rewarded for behaving in a certain way. In this case, a White child might receive a smile from a parent for avoiding children of color on the playground. Bandura's theory also holds that children can be taught indirectly through observational learning. Observational learning sometimes involves imitating the attitudes or behavior of a live model, such as a parent or peer, but observational learning can also occur through symbolic modeling, such as reading a book or watching a television show. Vicarious learning occurs when the child observes someone else being reinforced for a particular attitude or behavior. For example, if one boy sees another boy being applauded by his same-sex peers for calling a girl a mean name, then the first child might learn vicariously, or indirectly, that it is a good idea to call girls mean names. As we saw in Chapter 3, some researchers believe that stereotypes are learned through observational or vicarious learning.

Direct teaching   Although Gordon Allport (1954) believed that explicit or direct teaching of prejudice is not very common, it does occur in some situations. For example, children whose parents are members of hate groups are likely to be exposed to direct teaching of prejudice. Based on interviews with women active in organized racist groups, Kathleen Blee (2002) discovered that children of group members are explicitly taught religious and racial hatred at a very early age. Sentiments from parents such as "stay away from nigger children," "Jews are inhuman," and "nonwhites should be called 'mud people'" were not uncommon. Additionally, Blee found that Klan members' homes were filled with racist drawings, flyers, pamphlets, books, and videos. The explicit teaching of prejudice happens not only in the home, but also in the racist organizations themselves. Blee reported that the Ku Klux Klan has a special group for children called the "Klan Kid Korp" to prepare children to become racists. Children dressed in miniature Klan robes hold imitation torches and guns as they run or dance around burning crosses with adults. Sometimes children are given tasks in racist groups such as folding pamphlets and delivering them. Blee noted that schooling is another method of direct transmission of prejudice to the children of hate group members, with some children attending "Aryan-only" schools and others being homeschooled to prevent their being "corrupted" by exposure to minority children and egalitarian beliefs. In addition, children are encouraged to have pen pals in other racist groups to strengthen their racist attitudes.

Indirect teaching   Although direct teaching of prejudice has been known to occur in extremely racist families, Phyllis Katz (2003) suggests that most teaching of racial prejudice is indirect, occurring through processes such as modeling, imitation, and vicarious learning. Sources of indirect learning include parents, peers, cultural background, media, and school programs. For example, Joe Feagin and Hernan Vera (1995) interviewed a White woman in her 20s who described an incident from her childhood illustrating the indirect role that other people play in the development of prejudice. The woman recalled:

> I'm playing with my black paper dolls, having a good time. Then somebody comes to visit my parents, and they saw these dolls. And they say, "Oh, you let her play with nigger paper dolls? You let her do that?" Later, when this person leaves, my parents come over, and it's "She bought nigger paper dolls! What's with her?" And they took my paper dolls away. To this day there's this little something in me that, I want those paper dolls back. Because that just wasn't where my head was at, I wasn't about being black or white, I just wanted those paper dolls. (p. 159)

By taking her paper dolls away, this child's parents were giving her an indirect message that Black paper dolls were not appropriate for her to play with. Presumably, her parents' message also implied that it was not appropriate for her to play with Black children either.

Allport (1954) considered indirect teaching of prejudice by parents, such as the words and associated emotions that parents attach to particular social groups, as one way in which children are socialized to become prejudiced. For example, if children hear their parents use derogatory language, such as "fags," to refer to particular social groups, then they might imitate those words. According to Allport, at first children imitate these words without attaching them to a referent (in this case, gay men). Eventually, children will attach these terms and negative emotions to their referent. By adolescence, these emotions have been internalized and are part of the teen's personality.

The most straightforward way to show that parents influence the acquisition of prejudice is to examine the correlation of children's attitudes with their parents' attitudes. Some studies have found a small correlation (see, for example, Carlson & Iovini, 1985), but others have found no correlation (see, for example, Aboud & Doyle, 1996b), suggesting that parental influences on prejudice may be slight. Bear in mind, however, that as we saw in Chapter 5, most Americans see prejudice as a negative trait, so parents may try to inhibit their prejudiced reactions in front of their children, giving them little to imitate. However, parents' prejudice may have other effects. For example, Tamara Towles-Schwen and Russell Fazio (2001) found that college students' perceptions of their parents' degree of prejudice were positively correlated with avoiding negative feedback from others as a motive for controlling their own prejudiced reactions. That is, children of prejudiced parents may learn their parents' prejudices but may also learn from their parents how to control the expression of prejudice (see Chapter 10 for a discussion of motivation to control prejudice).

Another reason for a low correlation between children's prejudice and that of their parents is that the effect of parental prejudice may be indirect, operating through other factors. For example, Christopher Agnew, Vaida Thompson, and Stanley Gaines (2000) found no direct link between family factors and prejudice in college students, but did find that family factors were related to direct predictors of prejudice, such as level of tolerance and political beliefs. Thus, parents may influence their children's level of prejudice indirectly through the values they teach their children rather than by directly teaching them to be prejudiced.

Peers also can influence the development of prejudice. For example, Frances Aboud and Anna Beth Doyle (1996a) examined how children's racial attitudes were influenced by talking about their attitudes with a peer whose level of prejudice differed from their own. White 3rd and 4th graders were classified as being either high- or low-prejudiced, based on their scores on a measure of racial attitudes. Next, Aboud and Doyle paired high-prejudice children with low-prejudice children in dyads, and the children were asked to discuss one positive item and one negative item from the racial attitudes measure administered earlier. Children were instructed to talk about how the children in the items, who were of three different racial groups (White, Black, and Chinese), should be evaluated and to provide a rationale for their evaluation. Following the discussions, each child was retested individually on the same racial attitudes measure they had completed at the beginning of the study. The researchers found that high-prejudice children subsequently adopted less prejudiced attitudes, and the changes were the greatest when the low-prejudice partner made more comments about the similarities among people of different races coupled with more positive Black evaluations and negative White evaluations. However, low-prejudice children did not become more prejudiced.

Symbolic models of prejudice include images and words that children see or hear about in the media. As we saw in Chapter 3, children can indirectly learn about stereotypes through what they read in books, magazines, and newspapers, and what they watch on television, video, or in a movie theater (see, for example, Diekman, 2004; Lott & Maluso, 2001).

For example, to examine gender and racial minority roles in daily newspaper comics, Jack Glascock and Catherine Preston-Schreck (2004) sampled 50 comic strips from four daily newspapers during a month-long period. Overall, male characters (69 percent) appeared more frequently than female characters (31 percent) and characters were gender stereotyped in a number of ways. For example, women characters were more likely than men characters to be married and have children and not as likely to have a job outside the home. When women characters did work outside the home, they had a lower job status than did male characters. In terms of activities and behaviors, female characters did more domestic work, such as household chores and child care, and male characters participated in more yard work. Female characters were portrayed as exhibiting more verbal aggression, whereas male characters displayed more physical aggression. Ninety-six percent of the characters in the comics were White, indicating that racial minorities are underrepresented.

In addition, the absence of certain social groups from the media can give children an indirect message about the relative value of that social group. Many social groups rarely appear in the media, and when they are seen they are depicted in a negative light (Klein & Naccarato, 2003). Similarly, a child whose book collection is dominated by White characters learns indirectly that people of color and their cultures are not valued.

Finally, children's awareness of race as a social category may derive from social learning. As we saw earlier, awareness of categories such as age and gender arises so early that it might be innate. However, awareness of racial categories arises later in childhood and so might be a function of social learning. In this regard, recall that Rebecca Bigler and her colleagues (Bigler et al., 2001; Brown & Bigler, 2002) have found that children establish social categories based on how adults treat members of different groups—race becomes a salient social category for children, and therefore a potential basis for prejudice—because of the emphasis adults (and probably also the media) place on race. It is also important to note that heterosexism is directly and indirectly taught to children, which might help explain the disproportionately high suicide rates for gay and lesbian adolescents.

Inner State Theories

Inner state theories are essentially theories of individual differences, such as those discussed in Chapter 6. Aboud (1988) has labeled them inner state theories because the theories propose that prejudice is caused by something inside the person, such as personality. Although most of the theories we examined in Chapter 6 do not address developmental issues, one of the earliest theories—authoritarianism—does, and various theorists have considered its development in terms of personality, genetics, and social learning. The development of social dominance orientation has also been addressed.

Personality　　As you will recall from Chapter 6, Theodor Adorno and his colleagues (Adorno, Frenkel-Brunswik, Levinson, & Sanford, 1950) developed the concept of the authoritarian personality to explain the popularity of fascism during the 1930s. They proposed that a certain type of person—one with an authoritarian personality—was especially susceptible to the appeal of authoritarian political parties. In addition to describing the characteristics of the authoritarian personality, Adorno and his colleagues drew on psychoanalytic theory to propose a model of how that personality developed.

As with other psychoanalytic theorists, Adorno and his colleagues (1950) placed the origin of authoritarianism in early childhood experience—specifically in child-rearing practices. According to this theory, adults who are high in authoritarianism had parents who set strict rules and used punishment to enforce those rules, especially rules dealing with obedience. As a result of these punitive experiences, the child experiences psychological conflict. On the one hand, the child feels resentment and hostility toward the parents stemming from the punishments the parents inflict; on the other hand, the child must repress all desires and impulses toward expressing that resentment because it would be futile to attack the more powerful parents and because the child has learned (through punishment) to obey the parents' authority. Unless these feelings of conflict are resolved, they generalize to all authority figures and continue on into adulthood.

This conflict gives rise to the authoritarian personality. As we saw in Chapter 6, this personality type includes characteristics such as rigid adherence to conventional values, a submissive attitude toward authority, a tendency toward aggression against people who violate conventional values, a tendency toward using rigid cognitive categories, and a tendency to project one's emotional impulses onto others. This personality type is linked to prejudice through stereotypic thinking, prejudice against people who violate conventional norms (that is, people who are different from oneself) or who are condemned by authority figures, and a tendency to see one's own faults in the targets of prejudice. (See Forbes, 1985, for a more detailed description of the psychoanalytic underpinnings of the authoritarian personality.)

Unfortunately, there has not been much research on the relationship of child-rearing practices to either authoritarianism or prejudice, and what research exists has provided inconsistent results (Hopf, 1993). On the one hand, research using paper-and-pencil measures of authoritarianism and people's memories of how their parents treated them as children has generally found little support for a relationship. Bob Altemeyer (1981), for example, examined the correlation between several measures of punitive child-rearing practices and found that the measures were not highly correlated with one another. On the other hand, Christel Hopf (1993) noted that studies using qualitative techniques, such as personal interviews, have tended to find such a relationship.

Does this disparity in results simply reflect differences in research methods? Perhaps not. John Duckitt (2001) has suggested that child-rearing practices do play a role in the development of authoritarianism, but that other factors intervene, obscuring their role. As shown in the left half of Table 7.1, Duckitt proposes that punitive child-rearing practices lead to a conforming personality (because nonconformity is punished), and this experience with punishment causes the child to see the world as a threatening and dangerous place. These perceived threats motivate the child (and later, the adult) to seek security and to seek control over the environment as a means of minimizing those threats. Because authoritarian political and social ideologies advocate controlling the environment, the person embraces those kinds of ideologies and the prejudices that accompany them. In contrast, tolerant child-rearing practices lead to an independent personality that perceives the world as safe and secure. This perception causes the person to be motivated by personal freedom and to adopt social and political ideologies that also emphasize personal freedom.

As shown in the right half of Table 7.1, Duckitt (2001) has proposed a similar model for the development of social dominance orientation. In this model, cold, unaffectionate child-rearing practices lead to a tough-minded personality (because that is how the parents behave), and tough-mindedness causes the child to see the

TABLE 7.1   **DUCKITT'S MODEL OF THE DEVELOPMENT OF AUTHORITARIANISM AND SOCIAL DOMINANCE ORIENTATION**

| | Adult Outcomes | | | |
| | Authoritarianism | | Social Dominance Orientation | |
	High	Low	High	Low
Childhood experience	Punitive	Tolerant	Unaffectionate	Affectionate
Personality	Conforming	Independent	Tough-minded	Tender-minded
Worldview	Threatening and dangerous	Safe and secure	Competitive	Cooperative
Motivation	Social control and security	Personal freedom	Superiority	Concern for others
Social ideology	Authoritarianism	Freedom	Social dominance	Equality

Note: The order of development is from top to bottom. Adapted from John Duckitt. (2001). A dual-process cognitive-motivational theory of ideology and prejudice. *Advances in Experimental Social Psychology, 33,* 41–113, Table 4, p. 53.

world as a competitive jungle in which each person must look out for him- or herself first. This worldview leads the child (and later, the adult) to want to attain superiority over others and thus promotes a social dominance orientation. In contrast, warm, affectionate child-rearing practices lead to a tender-minded personality that sees the world as cooperative. This worldview promotes concern for others and an orientation toward social equality rather than social dominance. Duckitt has found support for his models in studies conducted in the United States, New Zealand, and South Africa (Duckitt, 2001; Duckitt, Wagner, du Plessis, & Birum, 2002). Both Adorno and colleagues' (1950) and Duckitt's (2001) models hold that authoritarianism (and, for Duckitt, social dominance orientation) are based in personality characteristics that are formed by child-rearing practices. However, note that the models differ in their views of *how* child-rearing practices affect personality. For Adorno and his colleagues, improper child-rearing instigates intrapsychic conflict that is not properly resolved; for Duckitt, parental behavior teaches the child to view the world in certain ways.

Genetic influences   Although Adorno and colleagues' (1950) and Duckitt's (2001) models emphasize the influence of child rearing on personality development, recent research has shown that a fair amount of personality is inherited (see, for example, Larsen & Buss, 2002). It is therefore interesting to note that the two personality traits in Duckitt's models, conformity and tough-mindedness, reflect moderate degrees of genetic influence (Bouchard et al., 2003; Jang, McCrae, Angleitner, Riemann, & Livesley, 1998). Consequently, inherited predispositions, as well as childhood experience, may play a role in the eventual development of authoritarianism, social dominance orientation, and prejudice.

Social learning   Bob Altemeyer (1981, 1988, 1996) rejects the roles of both early childhood experience and genetics in the development of authoritarianism and its associated prejudices. Instead, he proposes a social learning model that holds that authoritarian beliefs are acquired through socialization. Altemeyer believes that this learning begins in adolescence because it is only at that stage of cognitive development that children reach a point at which they can understand the kinds of social and political issues on which authoritarianism is based. Although Altemeyer does not address social dominance orientation in his books, the idea that the same process is at work there is consistent with his perspective.

Altemeyer (1988, 1996) proposes two main sources of social learning. The first, not surprisingly, is parents. Altemeyer points out that one of the first things parents teach their children is obedience to themselves; later, parents also teach obedience to authority figures outside the home, such as teachers, police officers, and so forth. Other adults with whom children interact, such as day-care staff, grandparents, and teachers also teach obedience. In addition, to some extent, children pick up their parents' attitudes; Altemeyer has found a positive correlation between the authoritarianism scores of college students and their parents. The second source of authoritarian attitudes is personal experience. Altemeyer had people complete a questionnaire about personal experiences related to authoritarian attitudes; for example, one item on the questionnaire read, "The people I have known who are unpatriotic and disrespectful toward authority have seemed to me to be ignorant troublemakers" (Altemeyer, 1988, p. 76). Altemeyer found a strong positive correlation between personal experience and authoritarianism, making it the strongest of the predictors he studied. Altemeyer also points out that the kinds of experiences that affect authoritarian attitudes continue throughout life, not just in childhood. Thus, Altemeyer found that students' average authoritarianism scores decreased while they were at college and continued to decrease after graduation.

Cognitive Developmental Theories

Some developmental theorists were not satisfied with how social learning theory and inner state theories accounted for developmental aspects of prejudice, which led to the emergence of **cognitive developmental theories** to explain the development of prejudice (Aboud, 1988). These theories emphasize the ongoing interplay between children's mental development and their environments, accounting for social-cognitive processes such as prejudice in terms of both nature (natural developmental changes) and nurture (experience). These theories hold that prejudice would be qualitatively different across stages of development as a result of the reorganization of underlying cognitive structures that occurs as children grow older. In other words, the development of prejudice involves discontinuous, or abrupt, shifts that correspond to cognitive stages. These theories imply that although prejudice is unavoidable at certain stages of development, it is probably not permanent and will decrease or disappear entirely as the child advances cognitively.

Piaget's theory   Jean Piaget was a pioneer in the study of children's cognitive development, and his theory is still influential today. Piaget (1932) proposed that cognitive development occurs in four stages: the sensorimotor stage (birth to age 2), the preoperational stage (2 to 7 years), the concrete operations stage (7 to 11 or 12 years), and the formal operations stage (11 or 12 years to adulthood).

The sensorimotor stage is not relevant to the development of prejudice because thought is not representational or symbolic during most of this stage. If infants cannot internally represent people and objects in the world, then they cannot hold attitudes (either positive or negative) about them. During the preoperational stage (2 to 7 years) children's thinking is described as being egocentric. **Egocentrism** is a focus on oneself as the center of everything coupled with the inability to take the perspective of another person. Another element of preoperational thought is **centration,** the tendency to focus on a single piece of information when multiple pieces of information are relevant. For example, a 4-year-old child might centrate on skin color or gender because they are perceptually obvious when deciding who to play with on the playground, even though other factors, such as having similar interests, should come into play when choosing playmates. At around 7 years of age, children's thinking becomes concrete operational, which means that thought is now logical and systematic, but it is limited to concrete, as opposed to abstract, objects and events. According to Piagetian theory, prejudice that is seen before 7 years of age is qualitatively distinct from prejudice observed after 7 years because of the cognitive reorganization that occurs around that time.

One hypothesis of Piaget's theory of prejudice is that changes in cognitive processes underlie changes in prejudice. Thus, prejudice develops in three cognitive stages: the egocentric stage, the sociocentric stage, and the reciprocal stage (Piaget & Weil, 1951). From 4 to 7 years of age, thought is *egocentric*. Children do not notice differences in people because they assume that everyone experiences the world the way they do. Any social group preferences displayed before 7 years are considered random and different for each child. From 7 to 10 years of age, thought is *sociocentric*. Children no longer focus only on themselves, but on their own social group. Focusing on your own social group (for example, people of the same religion, race, or gender) makes it difficult to understand the perspectives of other social groups. Other social groups are conceptualized in terms of how they differ from the child's own social group. For example, a White, Christian child might consider other White, Christian people as the "template" for comparison. Thus, she compares all other social groups to her own social group. Preferences will change accordingly, with children having positive attitudes about their own social group and negative attitudes about other groups. Between 10 and 15 years of age, children's tendency to centrate continues to decline, which allows them to distinguishing among other social groups. In addition, they begin to apply the principle of *reciprocity* to those groups. Reciprocity refers to give-and-take or bidirectional symmetry in a relationship. In terms of prejudice, it means that children believe that outgroup members' beliefs about them reflect their beliefs about the outgroup. Piaget did not clearly describe this last stage, so whether he would predict prejudice would remain high or diminish between 10 and 15 years is uncertain. Table 7.2 describes the characteristics of children's thought as related to prejudice in each of the four stages.

Piaget's theory of prejudice seems inconsistent with some of the findings presented earlier in this chapter on children's attitudes based on race and gender. First, research shows that the onset of prejudice on racial- or gender-based prejudice occurs between 3 and 4 years of age. However, Piaget claimed that during his preoperational stage (2 to 7 years), children's thought is egocentric, which prevents them from having systematic attitudes such as those based on race or gender. Instead, Piaget's theory would predict that between 2 and 7 years of age, children's attitudes are random because they are not aware of various social groups, presumably due to their focus on the self during the preoperational stage. Second, Piaget's theory suggests that prejudice would reach its highest levels during the concrete operational period (7 to 12 years). However, research findings indicate that racial prejudice reaches its highest levels at around 5 years and declines by 7 years. Similarly, gender-based prejudice increases until 8 years then declines. Both of these findings suggest that prejudice is already beginning to decline by 7 or 8 years of age, which is contradictory to Piaget's theory. Finally, based on Piaget's theory, it is not clear what happens to prejudice during the formal operational stage (12 years and older). Prejudice might decline or it might stay at the same levels as it was during the concrete operational stage. As we saw earlier, results from research show a decline in prejudice before the age of 12.

TABLE 7.2	PIAGET'S THEORY OF COGNITIVE DEVELOPMENT AS IT RELATES TO PREJUDICE	

Stage	Age	Characterization of thought and prejudice
Sensorimotor	Birth to 2 years	No representational thought
		No prejudice
Preoperational	2 to 7 years	Thought is representational, but not logical
		Prejudice is *egocentric* (Children are unaware of groups and so social preferences are idiosyncratic.)
Concrete Operational	7 to 12 years	Can reason logically about concrete objects and events
		Prejudice is *sociocentric* (Children focus on how their own group differs from others, and thus attitudes become more positive toward their own group and more negative toward other groups.)
Formal Operational	12 years and up	Can reason logically about abstractions and hypothetical situations
		Prejudice is *reciprocal* (Children distinguish among other groups, but it is not clear whether prejudice would remain at the same levels or decline.)

This is not necessarily contradictory to Piaget's theory, but he did not clearly specify what would happen after 12 years.

In addition Aboud (1988) noted two conceptual weaknesses in Piaget's theory. First, Piaget suggested that decentration refers only to children's noticing group differences. However, it seems that the decentration process also includes children's awareness of individual differences within these groups. In other words, Piaget said that the group was the child's point of reference for reciprocity, but it is possible that children actually make a shift to individual reciprocity. For example, a child may reason, "I am a smart child according to my social group, and he is a smart child according to his social group. Thus, he may have some smart qualities like I do." Second, Piaget's explanation of early preferences is somewhat vague. He did not clearly specify the processes that underlie preferences during the egocentric stage. Instead, Piaget assumed that the processes are random and therefore different for each child. This explanation is contradictory to the empirical findings demonstrating that ethnic preferences, for example, are quite similar and systematic in egocentric children.

Aboud's theory Using Piaget's theory as a foundation, Aboud (1988) created her own theory of the development of racial attitudes. In this theory, Aboud describes two waves or sequences of development: the process sequence and the attention sequence. The **process sequence** proceeds from emotional states to perceptions to cognitions. The **attention sequence** overlaps with the process sequence. As the name suggests, the attention sequence involves the shift of attention from the self to groups to individuals. According to Aboud, at any given age a child's attitudes about racial groups will be determined by where he or she is in terms of these sequences at that particular time. Thus, certain steps in these two sequences dominate at different times in development, and the child will be most influenced by information that is consistent with his or her present level of development. Table 7.3 summarizes Aboud's theory.

Given that the process sequence and the attention sequence are overlapping process, it makes sense to discuss them chronologically as the child develops. Note, however, that Aboud (1988) does not specify the age at which each step begins and ends. In the first step of the process sequence, racial preferences are determined by emotional responses toward individuals, such as fear and happiness, but they are not influenced by the child's identifying with her own ethnic group. Therefore, emotional information rather than information about social group membership is most important at this time. For example, if you have ever spent time with an infant 9 to 12 months of age, you might have noticed that the baby displayed stranger distress, a wariness of strangers. During infancy, this fear applies to anyone who looks different than people the child knows well. For example, infants whose parents have blond hair and blue eyes sometimes get more upset when they see a stranger with dark hair and dark eyes than when they see a stranger who looks more like their parents. Wariness of strangers continues into toddlerhood but changes occur. During toddlerhood, children may only fear those strangers whose behavior is unpredictable. For example, they may only fear the stranger who approaches the toddler too quickly then immediately picks up the child. Early attitudes are also shaped by positive emotions such as happiness, but they are not directly relevant to the development of prejudice.

TABLE 7.3   ABOUD'S (1988) THEORY OF THE DEVELOPMENT OF RACIAL PREJUDICE

	Step 1[a]	Step 2	Step 3
Process Sequence Prejudice determined by	emotions	perceptions of similarity/dissimilarity between self and others	cognitive understanding of ethnicity
Attention Sequence Emphasis on	the self	differences between ingroups and outgroups people as	individuals
Nature of Prejudice Based on	fear and the assumption that others feel the same way	exaggerating differences between ingroups and outgroups; prejudice peaks	a conceptual understanding of people as individuals; prejudice declines

[a] Aboud (1988) does not specify the ages encompassed by each step.

During the first step of the attention sequence, egocentric children are most aware of themselves, and they pay attention to their own preferences and perceptions. Egocentrism has been well documented in a variety of domains. Simply stated, children under the age of 7 are of a single mind. In other words, they are under the assumption that everyone sees the world the same way they do. For example, a preschooler might be looking at a book so you cannot see what the child is reading. Then the child says, "Look at this picture!" He makes no attempt to turn the book toward you because he assumes that because he can see the picture in the book then you can see it, too. This type of egocentrism is often called perceptual egocentrism; however, egocentrism can also be cognitive. For example, suppose you receive a doll from your 5-year-old niece for your birthday. Assuming that you are like most adults, this gift probably was not one of the items on your birthday wish list. However, this particular niece would love a doll for her birthday, so she assumes that you would like one as well. Applied to prejudice, this means that if you do not value or devalue social groups in the same way the child does, then you are wrong.

Thus, during the first step of both sequences, the nature of children's prejudice is dominated by emotions and a focus on the self. Aboud (1988) is not suggesting that prejudice does not exist before the age of 7, but rather that prejudice is qualitatively different in the initial step than it will be in the second step. Before the age of 7, children cannot take another individual's perceptual or cognitive perspective, so children's prejudice in this step is somewhat irrational or illogical. Based on research findings on children's prejudice, we know that preschoolers exhibit prejudice on the basis of race and gender, which is consistent with Aboud's theory. However, the basis of early prejudice is not clearly described in the research literature.

In the second step of the process sequence, perceptions of other people develop relative to oneself, with children noting perceptual similarities and dissimilarities between themselves and others in terms of race. Children overemphasize obvious perceptual differences, such as differences in skin color, hair texture, and language, and they underemphasize or perhaps entirely ignore the deeper, underlying similarities between people. Based on these perceptions, children form the foundation for racial self-identification. Children identify with the racial group to which they look most similar. For example, a Japanese child will identify with other Japanese children because they share perceptual features such as hair color and texture, eye shape, nose shape, language, and skin tone. Conversely, the same Japanese child will notice and possibly overemphasize the perceptual differences between herself and White children in terms of the same characteristics mentioned previously.

In the second step of the attention sequence, children begin to categorize people according to social group membership, which is much like Piaget's sociocentric stage. Following from this, prejudice develops out of an overly enhanced focus on groups. During this step, children note the difference between their own social group and other social groups. At first, children exaggerate the contrast between their own and other social groups to aid in their understanding of the groups. However, this exaggeration may lead to dichotomous attitudes—sort of an "us versus them" mentality. Eventually children become aware of the similarities and differences between their own and other groups, which reflects that they are becoming more cognitively flexible. Thus, any declines seen in prejudice might be explained by this increased cognitive flexibility.

Taken together, prejudice in the second step is characterized by perceptions of dissimilarity between the self (as a member of the ingroup) and others (as outgroup members). These differences are observable, such as differences in skin color, but do not include deeper, more conceptual differences between groups or individuals. Initially the dissimilarities are exaggerated, which may account for high levels of prejudice during the second step. However, Aboud's (1988) theory seems inconsistent with research findings indicating that racial prejudice begins to decline by 7 years.

In the third step of the process sequence, a cognitive or conceptual understanding develops. Therefore, categorizing or classifying people is no longer just based on perceptual similarities and differences, but it now involves looking at people's internal qualities as well. Now children categorize people based on both social group membership and their individual qualities. It is at this level in which children realize that people do not choose their ethnicity, and it is not something that people can change like clothing, but rather it is a permanent characteristic that gets inherited. According to Aboud, ethnic prejudice declines between 8 and 10 years of age, and this time is when children would be most responsive to interventions to reduce prejudice.

During the final step of the attention sequence, children attend to people as individuals. Thus, one should expect reduced levels of prejudice during this step, as children judge people in terms of their personal qualities rather than the qualities of their ethnic group. This is not to say that all individuals will be judged positively, but the criterion for making judgments about others will not be based on ethnic group membership.

During the final step of Aboud's (1988) theory, a cognitive understanding of ethnicity underlies racial prejudice. Children now understand the deeper, more conceptual differences between individuals of different races. Coupled with a deeper understanding of ethnicity is the notion that race is permanent and cannot be changed. Given that Aboud is not explicit about the general ages associated with each step, it is difficult to ascertain that age at which children reach the third step. Her prediction is that racial prejudice would be reduced in the third step, and the research literature clearly shows a decline in prejudice with age. However, it seems that the decline at approximately 7 years in the research literature might not map onto a presumably later onset of decline Aboud suggests.

So Where Does Prejudice Come From?

Does prejudice originate in social learning, inner states, or cognitive development? The answer probably is, to some extent, all of the above. Each person is born with a unique genetic heritage that contributes to the personality factors, or inner states, that are related to prejudice. However, inner states are also influenced by experience, and social learning teaches children which social categories are important, the characteristics stereotypically associated with those categories, and whether those characteristics are good or bad. In addition, information does not simply take root in a child's mind, but is influenced by stages of cognitive development. For example, prejudice in the adult sense may not begin to emerge until children grasp the concepts of ingroups and outgroups during preschool and might not be fully formed until late elementary school when they begin to understand the potential impact their attitudes have on other people and the abstract, social meanings of those attitudes (Sears & Vallentino, 1997). During the latter part of the developmental sequence, children also begin to learn that prejudice is bad and to control its expression.

The bottom line is, we do not have a good understanding of how children turn into either prejudiced or nonprejudiced adults (Aboud & Amato, 2001). One reason for this lack of understanding is that, traditionally, the study of prejudice has been the domain of social psychologists and the study of cognitive and social development has been the domain of developmental psychologists, and the two groups have rarely collaborated to study the development of prejudice (Levy, 2004). That situation is changing (Levy, 2004), so the future should bring a better understanding of how prejudice develops.

CHAPTER SUMMARY

There is a natural human tendency to organize and simplify the world around us. One way that we do this is to form categories. There is some evidence that even infants have implicit awareness of social categories such as age sex, and physical attractiveness, although not race. However, because infants cannot talk, we cannot explicitly ask them to tell us about the sorts of categorical distinctions they make. Explicit awareness of racial categories such as Black and White emerges at 4 or 5 years of age, but awareness of other racial categories such as Native Americans, Asians, and Latinos arises a few years later. Explicit awareness of social categories based on gender is present slightly earlier in development, by 3 years of age. It is important to remember that children's awareness of differences between social groups does not mean that they prefer or value one group over another.

When value judgments are added to children's distinctions between social groups, then positive and negative attitudes (in other words, prejudices) are formed. The research methods used to examine the development of prejudice have included both forced choice and continuous measures. Furthermore, researchers have used observations of behavioral interactions, self-reports of behavioral interactions, and sociometric ratings to examine children's racial attitudes.

Both Black and White children first exhibit prejudice toward other ethnic groups by 3 or 4 years of age. For White children, racial prejudice reaches its highest levels at about 5 years, and by 7 years a decline in prejudice is seen. However, the pattern for Black children is not as straightforward. For Black children, there is no typical racial attitudinal pattern. Some Black children hold pro-Black attitudes, some hold pro-White attitudes, and still others hold neutral attitudes between 5 and 7 years. Between 7 and 10 years, any pro-White bias has disappeared and Black children tend to express either pro-Black attitudes or unbiased attitudes.

The pattern of development of racial attitudes for Latino and Asian children is similar to the patterns seen in Black children. However, Native American children tend to be pro-White from age 4 on. Biracial children's attitudes fall between the two races of which they are members, suggesting that biracial children identify with both races.

When researchers look at children's intergroup behavior (for example, observations, self-report, or sociometric methods) to assess their racial attitudes, they sometimes find that children's attitudes and behavior seem inconsistent with one another. This finding is not unusual, given that adults' behaviors and attitudes do not always match up either. During preschool, behavior suggests an own-race or pro-White bias. However, by 1st grade both Black and White children show an own-race bias that increases with age, peaking at around the 7th grade. During high school, students report having positive cross-race interactions at school, but had few positive cross-race interactions outside of school.

The foundation for gender-based prejudice appears during toddlerhood, as children start to show preferences for gender-stereotyped toys. By 3 years, children know their own gender and the gender of other people, but their gender identity is not fully developed. Within most Western cultures, gender-based prejudice first emerges during preschool and increases until about 8 years of age. Between 8 and 10 years, gender-based prejudice declines slightly, possibly due to romantic interest in the opposite sex. When researchers look at children's intergroup behavior, they find that by 3 years of age both boys and girls displayed more positive behaviors to members of their own sex than to members of the other sex. In terms of segregation on the basis of gender, both preschoolers and kindergartners exhibit this behavior, but it is even more common in kindergartners than in preschoolers. When peer nominations are used with kindergartners through 3rd graders, other-sex negativity increases with age. From 3rd to 6th grade, very few friendship groups are composed of both boys and girls. However, by 7th grade more than half of groups are composed of children of both sexes, and by 12th grade all groups are mixed in terms of gender composition.

Three types of theories have been used to explain the development of prejudice in children. Social learning theories explain prejudice in terms of direct reinforcement, modeling and imitation, and vicarious learning. Direct teaching of prejudice is not very common; indirect teaching of prejudice from live models (for example, family members, peers, and teachers) and symbolic models in the media are primarily responsible for the learning of prejudiced attitudes.

Inner state theories focus on the development of prejudice in terms of age-related changes in personality and other individual-difference variables. The genetic and environmental contributions to personality development may also be important when explaining the development of prejudice.

Cognitive developmental theories, such as those proposed by Piaget and Aboud, suggest that changes in prejudice are the result of cognitive growth. Piaget adapts his model of cognitive development to explain the development of prejudice. He describes the development of prejudice as shifts from egocentric to sociocentric to reciprocal thought. According to Piaget, as the nature of children's thinking changes in each stage, so does the way in which they conceptualize prejudice. Using

Piaget's model as a springboard, Aboud proposes a model of the development of prejudice with two overlapping sequences: a process sequence and an attention sequence. The process sequence proceeds from emotions, to perceptions to cognitions, whereas during the attention sequence, attention shifts from the self, to groups, to individuals.

So where *does* prejudice come from? Each of the three theories mentioned have some merit and seem at least somewhat consistent with the findings on the development of children's prejudice. The answer is that we do not yet have a complete understanding of how prejudice develops in children.

SUGGESTED READINGS

Aboud, F. (1988). *Children and prejudice*. New York: Basil Blackwell.
   This book is a comprehensive review of research and theories on racial prejudice in children.
Fishbein, H. D. (2002). *Peer prejudice and discrimination: The origins of prejudice* (2nd ed.). Mahwah, NJ: Erlbaum.
   This recent book has chapters on the development of racial and opposite-sex prejudice, but it also covers prejudice and discrimination toward persons who are deaf and mentally retarded.
Helwig, C. C. (2002). Is it ever OK to exclude on the basis of race or gender?: The role of context, stereotypes, and historical change. *Monographs of the Society for Research in Child Development, 67*, 120–129.
   This is a commentary on Killen and colleagues' (2002) research (see below) on racial and gender exclusion.
Killen, M., Lee-Kim, J., McGlothin, H., & Stangor, C. (2002). How children and adolescents evaluate gender and racial exclusion. *Monographs of the Society for Research in Child Development, 67*, 1–119.
   This recent monograph is a detailed description of research on children's (4th graders) and adolescents' (7th and 10th graders) social reasoning about exclusion based on gender or race.
Williams, J. E., & Morland, J. K. (1976). *Race, color, and the young child*. Chapel Hill: The University of North Carolina Press.
   A classic on the development of racial prejudice.

KEY TERMS

attention sequence
centration
cognitive developmental theories
continuous measure
doll technique
egocentrism
forced choice method

gender constancy
homosociality
inner state theories
process sequence
social learning theory
sociometric ratings

QUESTIONS FOR REVIEW AND DISCUSSION

1. The chapter opens with an excerpt from an interview with a White research participant. In what ways were your own childhood experiences with prejudice similar to or different from this person's experiences?
2. Jane Elliott's brown eyes/blue eyes exercise was first conducted in the late 1960s. Do you think that this exercise would have the same impact on children today? Explain why or why not.
3. Explain why it is useful for children to categorize people, objects, and events in their environments.
4. Based on the research literature, provide evidence that infants have implicit awareness of certain social categories.
5. Explain how the doll technique is used to study children's explicit awareness of social categories. What have researchers found out about children's category awareness using this technique?
6. Describe the differences between implicit and explicit awareness of social categories. Do you think the two are related? Explain why or why not.
7. Explain the distinction between social categorization and prejudice.
8. Do you think that there is a distinction between preference and prejudice? Explain why or why not.
9. Describe the methodological difference between forced choice and continuous measures of prejudice and provide an example of each.
10. What is sociometrics? Discuss the two types of sociometric techniques used to study racial prejudice in children.
11. Describe the patterns of racial attitudes for White and Black children. Are they the same or different? Are Black children's racial attitudes similar to those of other racial minority groups?
12. Describe the difference between ingroup favoritism and outgroup prejudice. Why is it important for researchers to be able to separate these attitudes from one another?
13. What is the relationship between children's intergroup attitudes and their intergroup behavior?
14. Describe the origins of gender-based prejudice during toddlerhood.
15. Explain how gender constancy relates to developing a gender identity. How do you think gender constancy relates to the development of other-sex prejudice?
16. What roles do experience, environment, and culture play in the development of gender preferences?
17. According to social learning theories of prejudice, children can be taught prejudice directly and indirectly. Give one example of direct teaching of prejudice and one example of indirect teaching of prejudice. Which type of teaching do you think is more influential in the development of prejudice? Explain the reasons for your answer.
18. Explain how the development of personality influences the development of prejudice.

19. Use Duckitt's (2001) model to explain how child-rearing practices affect personality.
20. Discuss the role that genetic influences might play in the development of personality and subsequently the development of prejudice.
21. Do you think that authoritarian beliefs can be learned? Explain why or why not.
22. Compare and contrast Piaget's and Aboud's stage models in explaining the development of prejudice.
23. Briefly describe the three theories about how children become prejudiced. Based on your own experiences, which theory makes the most sense to you? Why?

CHAPTER

THE SOCIAL CONTEXT OF PREJUDICE

8

Human relationships always occur in an organized social environment—in a family, in a group, in a community, in a nation—that has developed techniques, categories, rules and values that are relevant to human interaction. Hence the understanding of the psychological events that occur in human interactions requires comprehension of the interplay of these events with the social context in which they occur. . . . The social psychologist must be able to characterize the relevant features of the social environment in order to understand or predict human interaction.

—*Morton Deutsch and Robert Krauss, 1965 (pp. 2–3)*

The theories and research presented prior to this chapter have generally focused on people as individuals in isolation from any social context. This chapter takes a different perspective. Rather than considering people in isolation from others, it focuses on the social context of prejudice and the influence other people have on individuals' attitudes and beliefs. As Deutsch and Krause (1965) pointed out in the quotation that opened this chapter, people do not operate in a vacuum; rather, they operate in an environment—a social context—made up of other people and other social groups.

The first four sections of this chapter describe theories that deal with the ways in which relationships between groups—intergroup processes—can contribute to prejudice. The intergroup process perspective focuses on what happens when people think of themselves and others in terms of the social groups to which they belong instead of thinking of themselves and others as individuals. For example, the first theory we discuss, realistic conflict theory, holds that people come to dislike members of other groups because they see those groups as competing with their own group for resources that they and their group need. From this perspective, it is not the individual group members' stereotypes and ideologies that influence their attitudes, but the nature of the relationship—competitive or cooperative—between the groups: People dislike members of competing groups and like members of cooperating groups. Following realistic conflict theory, we describe two other intergroup theories of prejudice, social identity theory and relative deprivation theory. We then present integrated threat theory, a perspective that helps to show how the other theories are related to each other. The final section of the chapter takes a look at hate groups, groups whose very existence is predicated on prejudice, and the kinds of people who are attracted to those types of groups.

REALISTIC CONFLICT THEORY

Realistic conflict theory (Bobo, 1988; LeVine & Campbell, 1972; Sherif, 1966) is the earliest intergroup theory of prejudice, tracing its roots back to the beginning of the 20th century. In 1906 William Sumner wrote that "the insiders in a we-group are in a relation of peace, order, law, government, and industry, to each other. Their relation to all outsiders, or other-groups, is one of war and plunder. . . . [Attitudes] are produced to correspond. Loyalty to the group, sacrifice for it, hatred and contempt for outsiders, brotherhood within, warlikeness without—all grow together, common products of the same situation" (p. 12). In contemporary terms, realistic conflict theory proposes that people dislike members of outgroups because their ingroup is competing with the outgroup for resources, resulting in Sumner's "war and plunder."

Realistic conflict theory views people as being motivated by a desire to maximize the rewards they receive in life, even if that means taking those rewards away from other people (Taylor & Moghaddam, 1994). Thus, people join groups to make it easier to get rewards through cooperation with ingroup members. However, different groups are frequently in pursuit of the same resources, and so end up competing for them. According to realistic conflict theory, this competition leads to conflict between groups; one result of this conflict is a disliking for, or prejudice against, members of competing groups.

The Work of Muzafer Sherif

The research of Muzafer Sherif (1966) provides what is perhaps the most famous demonstration of the principles of realistic conflict theory. From 1949 through 1954, Sherif conducted a series of studies on intergroup conflict, the best known of which is the "Robbers Cave" study carried out at Robbers Cave State Park in southeastern Oklahoma. (Robbers Cave got its name because Jesse James and other outlaws had supposedly used it as a hideout.) The participants in these studies were 11- and 12-year-old boys who thought they were simply attending a summer camp; the researchers were part of the camp staff so they could observe the boys without arousing their suspicions. The boys were carefully selected so that they had similar socioeconomic backgrounds, were strangers to each other before they arrived at the camp, and showed no evidence of mental or emotional problems. They were assigned to two groups that were similar in terms of average physical strength, athletics skills, and other characteristics of the members. Sherif wanted to be sure that none of the research results could be attributed to systematic differences among the boys or between the groups.

Group members were given time to get to know one another and to permit the emergence of natural leaders within the groups. During this period the groups devised names for themselves and group members worked together on tasks designed to build group cohesion, but the two groups did not yet interact. The researchers then brought the groups together and introduced an element of competition by setting up a series of games—such as baseball, football, and a treasure hunt—in which prizes were awarded to the members of the winning group. Box 8.1 provides Sherif's description of the outcome: derogation of and aggression toward the outgroup. (Sherif ended each of the studies with activities that restored good relations between the groups.) Sherif (1966) concluded that "the *sufficient condition* for the rise of hostile and aggressive deeds and for . . . derogatory images of the outgroup [is] the existence of two groups competing for goals that only one of the groups could attain" (p. 85; italics in original).

Although Sherif's (1966) research was conducted more than 50 years ago and used a very restricted participant sample (White, middle-class, Protestant boys), his findings have stood the test of time. Rupert Brown (1995), for example, noted that evidence supporting realistic conflict theory has been found in both laboratory and field research in Europe, Australia, Israel, and Africa as well as the United States.

John Duckitt's Extension of Realistic Conflict Theory

Realistic conflict theory is a relatively straightforward approach to prejudice: competition leads to conflict that leads to prejudice. However, John Duckitt (1994) has pointed out that most tests of realistic conflict theory have been limited to one

8.1   *Groups in Competition: The Robbers Cave Study*

The tournament started in a spirit of good sportsmanship, but as it progressed good feeling began to evaporate. The "good sportsmanship" cheer customarily given after a game, "2-4-6-8-who do we appreciate," followed by the name of the other group, turned into "2-4-6-8-who do we appreci-*hate*." Soon, members of each group began to call their rivals "stinkers," "sneaks," and "cheats." . . . The rival groups made threatening posters and planned raids, collecting secret hoards of green apples as ammunition.

The Eagles, after defeat in a game, burned a banner left behind by the Rattlers. The next morning the Rattlers seized the Eagles' flag when they arrived on the athletic field. From that time on, name-calling, scuffling, and raids were the rule of the day. A large proportion of the boys in each group gave negative ratings to the character of *all* boys in the other. When the tournament was over, they refused to have anything more to do with members of the other group. . . .

Near the end of this stage [of the study], the members of each group found the other group and its members so distasteful that they expressed strong preferences to have no further contact with them at all. In fact, they were subsequently reluctant even to be in pleasant situations (eating, movies, entertainments), if they knew that the other group would be in the vicinity.

From Muzafer Sherif. (1966). *In common predicament: Social psychology of intergroup conflict and cooperation.* Boston: Houghton Mifflin, pp. 82–83. (Italics in original)

type of competition, competition between groups of equal status and power. He went on to note that conflict often arises between groups of unequal power and status, such as when a majority group in a society dominates one or more minority groups. Also, in some of these cases, although the majority group denies the minority groups the full benefit of the society's material and social rewards, open conflict often fails to materialize. To account for these situations, Duckitt developed a typology of types of realistic conflicts and the resulting patterns of prejudice. Table 8.1 shows a portion of his typology.

Two types of conflict in Duckitt's (1994) scheme are based on direct intergroup competition. Realistic conflict theory addresses the first type, in which the ingroup sees the outgroup as a threat to the ingroup's ability to acquire some resource. This perceived threat leads the ingroup members to feel hostility toward the outgroup. These feelings of hostility provide the motivation for the group to engage in a conflict with the outgroup as a way to acquire the resource. But, Duckitt asks, what happens if one group wins the conflict? In that case, the result often is that the winning group dominates and exploits the losing group. For example, domination and exploitation have historically characterized the relationships of the White majority in the United States to minority groups and

TABLE 8.1 TYPES OF REALISTIC CONFLICT AND RESULTING PATTERNS OF PREJUDICE

Nature of conflict	Image of Outgroup	Orientation to Outgroup	Function for Ingroup
Intergroup Competition			
Competition with equal group	Threatening	Hostility	Mobilizes group members for conflict
Domination of outgroup by ingroup	Inferior	Derogation	Justifies dominance and oppression
Responses to Domination by Outgroup			
Stable oppression of ingroup by outgroup	Superior	Submission	Avoids conflict
Unstable oppression of ingroup by outgroup	Oppressive	Hostility	Mobilizes group members to challenge oppression
Responses to Challenges to Ingroup Dominance			
Ingroup sees challenge as unjustified	Inferior and threatening	Hostility and derogation	Justifies suppressing the challenge and mobilizes group members for conflict
Ingroup sees challenges as justified	Powerful	Appearance of tolerance	Avoids conflict

Note: Adapted from Table 6.1, p. 109, in John Duckitt. (1994). *The social psychology of prejudice*. Westport, CT: Praeger, 1994. Reprinted by permission of Greenwood Publishing Group, Inc.

the relationships of colonial powers to the people whose lands they colonized. In such cases, members of the dominant group generally see members of the subordinated group as inferior and derogate them by stereotyping them in negative ways or in positive ways that connote low power and status. This positive stereotyping reflects the "benevolent" form of prejudice discussed in Chapter 5. The dominant group then uses these stereotypes as what social dominance theory (Sidanius & Pratto, 1999; discussed in Chapter 6) calls legitimizing myths to justify their dominance and oppression. For example, these myths include the assertion that the "negative" qualities of the subordinated group must be controlled for the protection of both groups and that members of the subordinated group must not be given too much responsibility or power because they are incapable of handling it.

How does a subordinated group respond to the dominating group? Duckitt (1994) proposes that either of two processes can occur. In *stable oppression*, the subordinated group accepts the dominating group's view that it is superior to them and submits to that group to avoid conflict. Members of the subordinated group may also take on the dominating group's value system, rejecting their own group's values in the process. This acceptance of the dominant group's values is sometimes referred to as **false consciousness,** "the holding of false or inaccurate beliefs that are contrary to one's own social interest and which thereby contribute to [maintaining] the disadvantaged position of . . . the group" (Jost, 1995, p. 400). False consciousness leads "members of a subordinate group to believe that they are inferior, deserving of their plight, or incapable of taking action against the causes of their subordination" (Jost, 1995, p. 400), which makes them unwilling to challenge the dominant group's position. In the second process, *unstable oppression,* the subordinated group rejects the subordinating stereotypes and lower status assigned to it by the dominating group and sees the dominating group as oppressive. The realization that they are oppressed leads members of the subordinated group to develop hostility toward the dominating group. These feelings of hostility provide the motivation for members of the subordinated group to challenge the other group's dominance and oppression.

Duckitt's (1994) final question is how does the dominating group respond to the subordinated group's challenge? If the dominating group sees the subordinated group's challenge as unjustified, the dominating group views the subordinated group as threatening as well as inferior. The dominating group then responds with hostility to the perceived threat and with increased derogation to reinforce their view that the subordinated group is inferior. These attitudes justify suppression of the challenge and motivate members of the dominating group to take whatever action is necessary to maintain the status quo. However, in some cases the dominating group comes to see the subordinated group's challenge as justified. For example, Duckitt (1994) noted that the U.S. civil rights movement began to become successful in the 1960s because of "the perception by many whites that the black struggle is one that cannot legitimately be denied on the basis of important social values such as democracy and equality of opportunity" (p. 107). Acceptance of the legitimacy of the subordinated group's challenge by the dominating group gives the subordinated group the power to demand change. The perception of the subordinated group as powerful leads the dominating group to treat the subordinated group with tolerance; this may be true tolerance, but in many cases is only the superficial appearance of tolerance. For example, as was discussed in Chapter 5, overt prejudice in the United States has been supplanted by more subtle forms of prejudice that have been described as modern, symbolic, or aversive. This tolerance, whether real or superficial, provides a means of avoiding overt conflict between the groups.

Realistic conflict theory holds that prejudice and discrimination arise as a result of real competition between groups for resources that both groups want. These resources may be either material, such as money, goods, or land, or social, such as status or power. One implication of realistic conflict theory, then, is that if groups are not in competition, then there should be no prejudice or discrimination. However, the next theory to be considered, social identity theory, holds that intergroup competition is not a prerequisite for prejudice and discrimination; rather, the mere existence of social groups is all that is necessary.

Social Identity Theory

Following Sherif's (1966) work on intergroup conflict and prejudice, research on intergroup behavior virtually disappeared in the United States (Turner, 1996), replaced by an emphasis on individual-level cognitive processes (E. E. Jones, 1998). Social identity theory was developed in Europe by psychologists who believed that American psychology was putting too much emphasis on the individual and not paying sufficient attention to the role social group membership plays in influencing attitudes and behavior (Turner, 1996). Foremost among these theorists was Henri Tajfel. Tajfel noted that realistic conflict theory was correct in holding that competition for resources leads to intergroup conflict; however, he wondered if such competition was *necessary* for conflict and proposed that group membership "can, *on its own,* determine . . . intergroup behavior" (Tajfel, Billig, Bundy, & Flament, 1971, p. 153; emphasis in original).

Social identity theory is based on the concept of **social identity,** the part of a person's self-concept that derives from membership in groups that are important to the person. Such groups can include one's family, college, nation, and so forth. When identifying with a group, the person feels that what happens to the group is happening to him or her as well (Augoustinos & Walker, 1995). For example, if someone praises your college, you feel good about it; if someone disparages your college, you feel upset. Why do you, as the saying goes, "take it personally?" Because your college is part of your social identity, so how people see your college *does* reflect on you personally; your college is, to some extent, part of you, a part that links you to similar people, such as other students who attend your college, and differentiates you from other people, such as students at other colleges. People have multiple social identities (Deaux, 1996), such as being a male New Yorker who is a student at the University of Alabama; the particular identity or identities that are active or salient at any one time depends on a number of factors that we discuss shortly. Social identity theory also holds that people are motivated to develop and maintain social identities that clearly set their groups apart from other groups and that are positive. That is, people want to see their groups as distinct from other groups in ways that make their groups better than other groups: They want their group to be number 1.

Social Identity and Intergroup Bias

Tajfel and his colleagues (Tajfel, 1969; Tajfel et al., 1971) proposed that when people identify with an ingroup and view other people as members of an outgroup, they would perceive members of the ingroup in more positive terms than members of the outgroup. Tajfel and his colleagues demonstrated this phenomenon in a series of experiments using what is known as the **minimal group paradigm.** A *paradigm* is a standard set of procedures for conducting research on a topic; studies using the same paradigm to study a phenomenon all use very similar sets of research procedures. Social identity theory's research paradigm is called the minimal group paradigm because research participants are assigned to groups based on very minimal, even trivial, criteria.

In his first study using this paradigm, Tajfel (1970) had participants estimate the number of dots that were projected on a screen for a brief period. Based on random selection, Tajfel told half of the participants that they were "overestimators" who consistently overestimated the number of dots and told the other participants they were "underestimators" who consistently underestimated the number of dots. Then, in what was ostensibly another experiment, Tajfel had his participants allocate rewards to members of both their own group and the other group. He found that people tended to give higher rewards to members of their own group; that is, people showed a bias in favor of members of their own group. This **ingroup bias** occurred even though the groups were artificially constructed on the basis of a trivial criterion that was unrelated to the task on which the rewards were based. Although the amount of ingroup bias found in this kind of research is often small, the effect is consistent, having been repeatedly replicated in the decades since Tajfel's original research (Mullen, Brown, & Smith, 1992).

Social identity theorists have proposed two hypotheses to explain the ingroup bias effect. These hypotheses are the *categorization-competition hypothesis* and *self-esteem hypothesis,* and the processes they describe can operate either separately or in tandem.

The categorization-competition hypothesis

The categorization-competition hypothesis holds that categorizing oneself and others into an ingroup and an outgroup is sufficient to generate intergroup competition. When a particular social identity is activated, an **outgroup homogeneity effect** (Ostrom & Sedikides, 1992) occurs: People perceive members of the outgroup as more similar to each other than they actually are, while seeing members of the ingroup as distinct individuals. As a result, people believe differences between the ingroup and the outgroup to be greater than they really are. For example, many Americans who are not of Latin American descent tend to see "Latinos" or "Hispanics" as a single cultural group, all of whose members share similar values, customs, food preferences, and so forth. In contrast, Cuban Americans, Mexican Americans, Puerto Ricans, and people whose ancestors came from other Latin American countries see themselves as distinct groups and can point to significant cultural and language differences that set them apart from one another (Huddy & Virtanen, 1995). When a social identity is activated, then, people place themselves and others into sharply distinct and contrasting categories.

This categorization process results in people taking an "us versus them" perspective on the ingroup and outgroup (Hartstone & Augoustinos, 1995). North American culture (among others) teaches that relations between groups are naturally competitive, and so one should not trust other groups because those groups are out to get the resources "our" group needs (Insko & Schopler, 1987). Categorizing people into ingroups and outgroups therefore arouses feelings of competition and a desire to win. These competitive feelings then lead to an ingroup favoritism effect: People favor their own group to protect their group's interest against the competition (Tajfel & Turner, 1986). On a larger scale, perceptions of competition can lead people to think of outgroups as causing society's problems and to want to avoid contact with them (Jackson, 2002). One implication of this competition arousal hypothesis is that intergroup bias should be strongest when people see their group in relation to just one other group. Intergroup bias should decrease as the number of other groups increases, because people's feelings of competition are diluted across more outgroups. Thus, the ingroup bias is found in research when participants are divided into two groups, which arouses the competitive motive, but not when people are divided into three groups, which dilutes that motive (Hartstone & Augoustinos, 1995; Spielman, 2000).

The self-esteem hypothesis   Although the categorization-competition hypothesis provides one explanation for intergroup bias, perhaps the most studied explanation has been the self-esteem hypothesis (Aberson, Healy, & Romero, 2000; Rubin & Hewstone, 1998). Social identity theory proposes that people are motivated to achieve and maintain positive social identities. Because people's social identities interact with their personal identities, having a positive social identity leads to positive self-esteem: When a group we identify with does well, we also feel good about ourselves. For example, people who identify with their colleges often enhance their self-esteem by basking in the reflected glory of successful athletic teams, enthusing about how *"we* won" and *"we're* number 1" (Cialdini et al., 1976).

Michael Hogg and Dominic Abrams (1990) proposed that self-esteem plays three roles in intergroup bias. First, intergroup bias results in an increase in positive social identity by demonstrating that the ingroup is better than the outgroup; this increase in positive social identity is reflected in an increase in self-esteem. Second, because engaging in intergroup bias can raise self-esteem, people with low self-esteem will engage in intergroup bias to raise their self-esteem. Third, when an event threatens people's self-esteem, especially an event linked to an important social identity, they can defend their self-esteem through intergroup bias.

As we saw in Chapter 6, considerable research has been conducted on the self-esteem hypothesis. Although the results of the studies have not always been consistent with one another, research using the minimal group paradigm has generally supported Hogg and Abrams' (1990) three propositions (Aberson et al., 2000; Rubin & Hewstone, 1998). Thus, in line with the first proposition, researchers have found small but consistent positive correlations between self-esteem and intergroup bias, with higher self-esteem being associated with more bias. Although this finding might seem to contradict the second proposition, that low self-esteem leads to bias, Christopher Aberson and his colleagues (2000) noted that people with low self-esteem do engage in intergroup bias but use different tactics than people with high self-esteem. People with high self-esteem are more likely to engage in direct bias, such as by overrewarding members of their groups, whereas people with low self-esteem tend to show bias indirectly, such as by expressing a desire for greater separation from the outgroup. Finally, the results of research on the effects of self-esteem threat have generally supported the third proposition, that threats to self-esteem motivate intergroup bias.

Factors that Influence Social Identity

Not surprisingly, intergroup bias effects are greater for people who identify more strongly with their groups (Perreault & Bourhis, 1999). People have multiple potential social identities—such as student, friend, sorority member, woman, child-care worker—each of which is available for activation at any one time. What factors, then, affect which social identity or identities are active in a person and the strength of those social identities? Four factors appear to be important: self-categorization, a need for optimal distinctiveness, chronic social identities, and individual differences.

Self-categorization   Research using the minimal group paradigm randomly assigns people to artificial groups; that is, research participants are categorized into groups by the researchers. However, people are more likely to accept a social identity and that identity is likely to be stronger if they categorize themselves (Perreault & Bourhis, 1999). Several factors influence self-categorization.

Self-categorization theory (Turner & Oakes, 1989), proposes that categorizing oneself as a group member becomes more likely as the perceived difference between the ingroup and an outgroup increases. One way of looking at this process is in terms of *distinctiveness,* the extent to which a person feels that he or she differs along some dimension from other people in a situation (Sampson, 1999). The greater the perceived difference, the more likely a person is to self-categorize on the differentiating dimension and take on the social identity associated with that dimension. For example, members of racial and ethnic minority groups are more likely to identify with those groups when most of the people around them are White (McGuire & McGuire, 1988). Also, women and men are more likely to think of themselves in terms of their genders when assigned to groups in which the other sex are in the majority compared to groups in which their own sex is in the majority (Swan & Wyer, 1997).

The particular identity self-categorization activates depends on factors that change from situation to situation; as a result, social identity can change from situation to situation. For example, social identity as a sorority member might be low for Miranda when she attends a meeting of her sorority. In this setting, she sees herself and her sorority sisters as individuals with unique personalities and there are no women from other sororities present to create a perception of difference from other groups. However, at a meeting of the Panhellenic Council, Miranda may be the only member of her sorority present, so the contrast between herself as member of her sorority and the other women present as members of their sororities becomes more salient, leading Miranda to feel greater social identification with her sorority. If Miranda goes from the Panhellenic Council meeting to a meeting at which she is the only woman, her social identity as a sorority member may fade into the background as her social identity as a woman becomes more salient; now the contrast is based on gender rather than sorority membership. Box 8.2 provides a real-life example of how feelings of distinctiveness can lead to prejudice.

One result of self-categorization is that as social identity increases and personal identity decreases, group identity, group goals, and the influence of other

8.2 *Residential Integration and White Prejudice*

Social identity theory holds that increased feelings of social identity lead to prejudice because of perceptions of intergroup competition and as a way of maintaining self-esteem. One factor that increases social identity is an increase in distinctiveness, which can be brought about by the presence of members of other groups. Consequently, as members of other groups become more salient to people, their feelings of prejudice should increase.

This process is illustrated by the results of a study conducted by Marylee Taylor (1998). She used national survey data to examine the relationship between the proportion of Black residents in neighborhoods and anti-Black prejudice among White residents of those neighborhoods. As Figure Box 8.2 shows, the distinctiveness-prejudice hypothesis

was partially supported: White prejudice increased as the percentage of Black residents increased to around 20 percent. Taylor also found, as would be predicted by social identity theory, that White residents' feelings of competition with Blacks, indicated by feelings of economic and political threat, were correlated with both the percentage of Black residents in their neighborhoods and their degree of prejudice.

Note that prejudice peaked when the proportion of Black residents was about 20 percent and then decreased as the Black population increased. This finding reflects the principle that, under certain conditions, intergroup contact can reduce prejudice (Pettigrew, 1998a). The role of intergroup contact in reducing prejudice is discussed in Chapter 12.

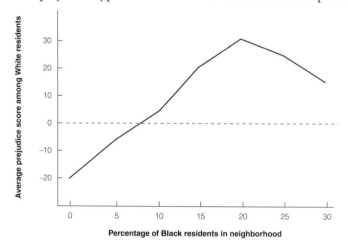

WHITE PREJUDICE AS A FUNCTION OF PERCENTAGE OF BLACK RESIDENTS IN THEIR NEIGHBORHOODS

As the percentage of Black residents increases from zero to 20 percent, prejudice increases and then begins to decrease. Scores are standardized, which means that zero represents the average prejudice score of all the White respondents; negative numbers indicate less than average prejudice and positive numbers indicate greater than average prejudice.

(Adapted from Taylor, 1998, Figure 1, p. 526.)

group members become more important than personal identity, personal goals, and personal motives in guiding beliefs and behavior (Oakes, Haslam, & Turner, 1994). Self-categorization theory calls this process **self-stereotyping:** group members view themselves in terms of the (usually positive) stereotypes they have of their group so that the self becomes one with the group and the positive view of the group is reflected in a positive view of the self.

Differentiation from outgroups, then, is one factor that motivates self-categorization. A second factor is a need for certainty or correctness. Michael Hogg and Barbara Mullin (1999) pointed out that there is a long history of research in psychology that shows that people have a strong need to believe that their attitudes, beliefs, and perceptions are correct. Uncertainty about what to believe or how to act is unpleasant because it implies that one has little control over one's life; consequently, people are motivated to reduce uncertainty by verifying the correctness of their beliefs. However, the problem with determining whether one's beliefs are correct is that there is no concrete standard for judging abstract beliefs. People therefore seek verification of their beliefs by comparing what they believe with what other, similar people believe. If the beliefs match, this consensus is taken as evidence of correctness, and the more people who agree, the more correct the beliefs are assumed to be.

Hogg and Mullin (1999) proposed that one way to achieve this kind of validation is by identifying with a group that provides clear norms for structuring beliefs and guiding behavior. Because the self-stereotyping effect leads people to substitute the group identity for their personal identities, group beliefs on which everyone agrees replace less certain personal beliefs. Because reducing uncertainty removes an aversive state, people experience the process as a pleasant one, which reinforces self-categorization and group identification. Research that has manipulated how certain people feel about the norms in a particular situation (for example, Grieve & Hogg, 1999) has confirmed that people who feel uncertain are more likely to identify with groups that provide information and that reduces feelings of uncertainty.

Self-categorization theory assumes that seeing oneself as different from others and the need for certainty are unconscious processes that lead people to categorize themselves in terms of group identity. Researchers have also studied conscious processes as precursors of self-categorization; one of those processes is making a choice to identify with a group. Not surprisingly, people who choose to join a group have a stronger social identity for that group than people who are assigned to a group (Perreault & Bourhis, 1999). There are at least two reasons why this happens. First, people tend to join groups composed of others who have attitudes and values similar to their own (Forsyth, 2006), so a strong basis for mutual identification already exists. Second, once people make a choice, they tend to be committed to that choice and to see it in positive terms. To do otherwise would be to admit to having made a mistake, which most people are reluctant to do (Markus & Zajonc, 1985).

Optimal distinctiveness   Self-categorization theory holds that people are motivated to identify with groups that provide them with distinct positive social identities and that fulfill their needs for certainty. One result of this process is self-stereotyping, in which people replace their personal identities with the group identity. One shortcoming of the self-stereotyping hypothesis is that people have a countervailing need to experience themselves as unique individuals who are different from other people (Brewer, 1991; Brewer & Pickett, 1999). Marilynn Brewer (1991) therefore proposed a modification to self-categorization theory, which she calls optimal distinctiveness theory. Optimal distinctiveness theory holds that people are most likely to identify with groups that provide the most satisfying balance between personal identity and group identity. Consider the earlier example of Miranda, the young woman who represented her sorority at the Panhellenic Council meeting. As we saw, self-categorization theory says that she will identify with her sorority because of the contrast she sees between her sorority and the other sororities represented at the meeting. Optimal distinctiveness theory agrees that that kind of contrast motivates group identification, but adds that Miranda's identification with her sorority is also motivated by her being able to feel that while being a member of the sorority she can still be her own person. If the sorority tried to force Miranda to completely replace her personal identity and values with those of the sorority, her level of group identification would be reduced.

Threat to the group   Events that threaten the well-being of the group generate stronger identification with the group. For example, Sophia Moskalenko, Clark McCauley, and Paul Rozin (2004) found that U.S. college students' ratings in response to the question "How important to you is your country?" increased following the September 11, 2001, terrorist attacks on the United States compared to ratings made 6 months previously. Eighteen months later, their ratings had decreased to the pre-attack level. However, reminders of threat can cause ingroup identification to increase once more. For example, Mark Landau and his colleagues (2004) found that having U.S. college students think back to the events of September 11, 2001, increased their favorability ratings of President George W. Bush (an indicator of ingroup identification) compared to ratings made by students in a control condition. Interestingly, Landau and his colleagues found that the approval ratings increased for both students who had characterized themselves as politically liberal and those who had characterized themselves as politically conservative.

Chronic social identities   Although social identity theory emphasizes the role that the social context plays in eliciting social identities that can change from situation to situation, Steven Sherman and his colleagues (Sherman, Hamilton, & Lewis, 1999) remind us that people also have **chronic identities** that influence their behavior. Chronic identities are ones that are always with us, regardless of how much the situation changes. As Sherman and his colleagues (1999) note, "A ballplayer on the playing field will obviously self-categorize in terms of that athletic category, but may also think of himself as 'a black ballplayer.' A physician will self-categorize as a member of the medical profession, but if female, may often think of herself as 'the woman doctor'" (p. 92). Chronic identities may be especially important for members of minority groups, whose minority status makes them distinctive in any intergroup situation regardless of any other identities that situational factors activate.

Individual differences   Just as chronic identities can influence social identity, so can other chronic personal characteristics, such as personality and ideology. Although, as we saw in Chapter 6, researchers have studied the relationships between individual difference variables and prejudice for a long time, social identity theory researchers have just begun to look for links between these variables and social identity. For example, Stéphane Perreault and Richard Bourhis (1999) studied the relationship of ethnocentrism, the tendency to favor one's own ethnic and nationality groups over other such groups, to social identification. Using the minimal group paradigm, they found that people high in ethnocentrism were more likely to identify with their assigned groups than were people low in ethnocentrism. Thus, some people may have a predisposition to identify more strongly with the groups to which they belong independent of any situational factors that might be operating.

Issues in Social Identity Theory

Although social identity theory has proven to be a useful framework for studying prejudice, a few issues require more research. These issues include whether social identity processes can lead to outgroup derogation as well as ingroup favoritism, the relation between social identity and intergroup tolerance, and the relative importance of social identity and personal motives in prejudice.

Ingroup favoritism versus outgroup derogation   Generally, research on social identity theory has found that although people show favoritism toward members of their ingroups, they do not necessarily penalize members of outgroups (Brewer, 1979, 1999; Mummendey & Wenzel, 1999). Instead, they treat outgroup members in a neutral manner. For example, John Dovidio and Samuel Gaertner (2000) conducted a study in which White students were asked to make hiring recommendations for either a Black or White job applicant. Based on the applicants' objective qualifications, each should have been recommended for hiring 50 percent of the time. However, 75 percent of the White research participants recommended hiring the White applicant whereas 45 percent recommended hiring the Black applicant. That is, the participants overbenefitted the applicant who was a member of their (White) ingroup and treated the (Black) outgroup member in a neutral, apparently fair, manner consistent with his objective qualifications. Nonetheless, in a real situation, three White people would have been hired for every two Black people despite the fact that, based on their qualifications, they should have been hired at equal rates. Other research has found that ingroup bias and affective ratings (such as liking versus disliking) of outgroup members are generally uncorrelated (Brown, 1995). That is, ingroup bias is usually accompanied by feelings of indifference toward members of the outgroup.

Despite these research findings, by looking at the world around us, it is easy to see that ingroup favoritism is often accompanied by harmful discrimination and hostile attitudes toward outgroups. Amélie Mummendey and Michael Wenzel (1999) have suggested that activation of a social identity leads to such negative outcomes only after two conditions have been met. First, members of the ingroup must believe that a common set of norms and values apply to both themselves and to members of the outgroup. Second, the ingroup must see its values as the *only* acceptable values, so that their values trump those of the outgroup and are the ones that should guide both themselves and the outgroup. The combination of these two factors leads the ingroup to perceive members of the outgroup as deviant, morally inferior, and a potential threat to ingroup values because the ingroup believes that outgroup members do not adhere to those values. This perception of being morally superior to and threatened by the outgroup activates hostile attitudes toward the outgroup and provides a justification for discrimination: The outgroup must be controlled to protect ingroup values from the outgroup's corrupting influence. For example, many people believe that the only acceptable form of sexual expression is heterosexuality. Because lesbians and gay men violate this norm, these people develop hostile attitudes toward lesbians and gay men and want to restrict their behavior, both sexually and by excluding them from certain social roles such as parenthood, teaching, and military service (Kite & Whitley, 1998).

Social identity and intergroup tolerance   Although social identity theory has focused on the negative intergroup effects of social identity, researchers and theorists have begun to address how social identity relates to intergroup tolerance. One approach to this issue focuses on conditions for tolerance and another on the complexity of social identity.

Mummendey and Wenzel (1999) note that their model of the relation of ingroup identification to hostility also implies conditions for tolerance: If the ingroup either does not believe that it and the outgroup should share a common set of values or does not see their own values as more valid than those of the outgroup, then there will be no hostility. They illustrate their point with the case of Germans' attitudes toward Turks: "Many Germans, although on the one hand generally having negative attitudes towards Turks living in Germany, on the other hand love to spend their holidays in Turkey. Because during their holidays they are on Turkish territory and in the Turkish culture, they may to a lesser extent represent Turks and themselves as [being governed by the same set of values] and thus experience strange habits and customs as less of a norm violation or deviance" (p. 169).

Noting that people have many potential social identities, Sonia Roccas and Marilynn Brewer (2002; see also Brewer & Pierce, 2005) have proposed that the more complex a person's social identity is, the more tolerant of other groups that person will be. A person with a complex social identity is aware of having multiple identities and sees people who share any of those identities as part of his or her ingroup. In contrast, a person with a simple social identity focuses on only one identity and sees only people who share that one identity as part of the ingroup. Consider, for example, a woman who is Black and a lawyer. If she has a complex social identity, she will view all women, all Black people, and all lawyers as members of her ingroup; if she has a simple social identity that focuses on her profession, she will view all lawyers as members of her ingroup, but exclude anyone who is not a lawyer, even women and Black people who are not lawyers. Roccas and

Brewer (2002) postulate that a complex social identity leads people to be more tolerant of group differences because a complex identity reduces the motivation to self-categorize as a member of any one group. For example, having multiple concurrent social identities reduces feelings of distinctiveness—the person sees him- or herself as fitting in with many groups—and low distinctiveness leads to a lower likelihood of self-categorization. In addition, Roccas and Brewer suggest that a complex social identity protects people from threats to social identity that can lead to ingroup bias: If people have more than one social identity, a threat to one identity can be offset by focusing on a more positive identity until the threat has passed.

Personal motives versus social identity motives   If you think back to Chapter 6, which dealt with individual differences and prejudice, you might see some commonalities that some of the theories discussed there have with the social identity theory view. For example, social identity theory's categorization-leads-to-competition hypothesis and Mummendey and Wenzel's (1999) value threat hypothesis both tie in nicely with John Duckitt's (2001) model of individual difference variables and prejudice. As you will recall, Duckitt proposed that perceptions of competition from other groups arouse social dominance motives and that perceptions of threat arouse authoritarian motives; these motives, in turn, lead to prejudice. Despite these similarities, it is important to bear in mind that personal motives for prejudice are based on seeing oneself as an individual whereas social identity motives are based on replacing those personal motives with group motives through self-categorization. So, for example, when Maykel Verkuyten and Louk Hagendoorn (1998) had people focus on themselves as individuals, authoritarianism (a personal motive) was related to prejudice but positive perceptions of the ingroup (a social identity motive) were not. In contrast, when they had people focus on group identity, perceptions of the ingroup were related to prejudice but authoritarianism was not. Thus, different psychological factors can motivate prejudice in different situations.

Looking Back at Social Identity Theory

We have spent a lot of time discussing social identity theory because it is one of the most important theories of intergroup relations and so has developed in a complex and multifaceted way. Therefore, let's take a moment to put it all together. Figure 8.1 summarizes social identity theory in diagrammatic form. At the center of the theory, of course, is social identity: the part of one's self-concept that comes from membership in groups. Social identity derives from both temporary, situational factors such as self-categorization and the need for optimal distinctiveness, and from long-term factors such as chronic identities and individual difference variables. Self-categorization, in turn, derives from feelings of distinctiveness, need for certainty, and choosing one's identities. Taking on a social identity leads to feelings of competition with contrasting outgroups and a motivation to maintain a positive social identity. These factors lead to ingroup bias, which promotes a positive social identity and self-esteem, thereby reinforcing the social identity.

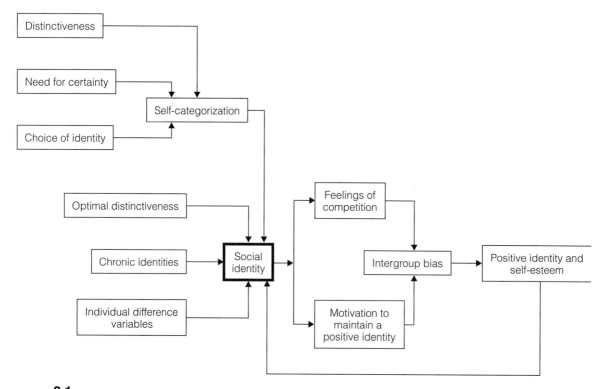

FIGURE **8.1**

SOCIAL IDENTITY THEORY

Social identity derives from both situational factors such as self-categorization and the need for optimal distinctiveness and from long-term factors such as chronic identities and individual difference variables. Self-categorization derives from feelings of distinctiveness, need for certainty, and choosing one's identities. Taking on a social identity leads to feelings of competition with outgroups and a motivation to maintain a positive social identity. These factors lead to ingroup bias, which promotes a positive social identity and self-esteem, thereby reinforcing the social identity.

RELATIVE DEPRIVATION THEORY

Relative deprivation theory (Crosby, 1976; Davis, 1959; Gurr, 1970; Runciman, 1966) addresses the questions of how people become dissatisfied with some aspect of their lives and how they react to that dissatisfaction. The theory holds that people become dissatisfied if they either compare their current situation to similar situations they had experienced in the past or compare themselves to other people currently in their situation and as a result decide that they lack some resource that they deserve to have. They are not necessarily deprived in absolute terms; in fact, their objective situation might be quite good (Tyler & Smith, 1998). Rather, they *feel* deprived *relative to* what they had in the past or *relative to* people who have the resource they believe they deserve, giving rise to the term **relative deprivation.** Relative deprivation's relation to prejudice comes in how people respond to feelings of deprivation: If people blame another group for causing the deprivation, they come to dislike that group and its members.

The concept of relative deprivation originated in research conducted with American soldiers during World War II. One aspect of that research dealt with soldiers' levels of satisfaction (or perhaps more accurately, dissatisfaction) with army life. There were a number of unexpected findings, among which was that soldiers in the air corps expressed more dissatisfaction than soldiers in the military police. This finding was unexpected because promotions and the consequent raises in pay and other benefits came much faster in the air corps than in the military police (Stouffer, Suchman, DeVinney, Star, & Williams, 1949). The researchers explained these findings in terms of relative deprivation: Because airmen saw many fellow soldiers promoted quickly, they felt deprived when they were not promoted; in contrast, because military policemen saw few people being promoted quickly, they did not feel deprived relative to their colleagues and as a result felt more satisfied with the promotion system.

Since World War II there has been a vast amount of research conducted on relative deprivation theory in a wide variety of contexts (see Walker & Smith, 2002, for a history of this research). Here, of course, we focus on its relationship to prejudice and intergroup relations. After describing how the theory proposes that dissatisfaction arises and how people respond to dissatisfaction, this section looks at research on the relation of relative deprivation to prejudice and at the related concepts of relative gratification and scapegoating.

Relative Deprivation, Dissatisfaction, and Resentment

Relative deprivation theory holds that people become dissatisfied when they compare their current outcomes with some standard. If they see that they are getting less than the standard, they then feel deprived. As shown in Figure 8.2, the standard can be based either on personal experience or from comparing one's own situation to another person's situation (social comparison). James Davies (1969) proposed that personal experience can cause feelings of relative deprivation when reality fails to meet people's expectations. Davies noted that people's expectations for future outcomes tend to increase over time as their actual outcomes get better. For example, in the United States the overall standard of living increased from World War II until the 1980s; people got used to this steady increase and expected it to continue, and children came to expect to do better economically than their parents did. According to Davies's model, people are satisfied as long as their outcomes are a good match for their expectations. However, if outcomes begin to decline, as when the United States began to lose jobs because of increasing competition from other parts of the world, an increasingly large gap forms between expectations and outcomes. When the size of the gap becomes too large, people feel deprived relative to their past experience.

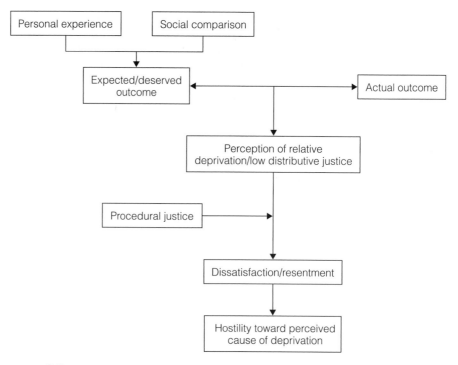

FIGURE **8.2**

RELATIVE DEPRIVATION AS A SOURCE OF DISSATISFACTION AND RESENTMENT

People compare the outcomes they receive to what they expect and believe that they deserve to receive. This expectation is based on what they received in the past and on what other people are receiving. If they see their outcomes as being less than they deserve, feelings of relative deprivation and low distributive justice (unfairness) ensue. These emotions lead to feelings of dissatisfaction and resentment, which are intensified if people believe that the outcomes are distributed using unfair procedures (low procedural justice) as well as being too low. Resentment of deprivation leads to hostility toward the perceived cause of the deprivation.

This process is illustrated by Michael Kimmel's (2002) description of men who join White supremacist groups:

> They are the sons of skilled workers in industries like textiles and tobacco, the sons of owners of small farms, shops, and grocery stores. Buffeted by global political and economic forces, the sons have inherited little of their fathers' legacies. The family farms have been lost to foreclosure, the small shops squeezed out by Wal-Marts and malls. These young men face a spiral of downward mobility and economic uncertainty. They complain that they are squeezed between the omnivorous jaws of global capital concentration and a federal bureaucracy that is at best indifferent to their plight and at worst complicit in their demise. (p. B11)

That is, these people feel deprived relative to what they had come to expect to receive based on their parents' successes.

The second source of feelings of relative deprivation is social comparison: People see that others have something and want it; not having it leads them to feel deprived relative to the comparison other. This was the process that was operating among the air corps soldiers during World War II (Stouffer et al., 1949).

Thus, feelings of relative deprivation are similar to feelings of unfairness, or what is known as low **distributive justice** (Greenberg, 1996): the perception that outcomes are not being distributed on the expected basis that people who deserve more get more, but on some other, unfair basis, such as ingroup favoritism. As shown in Figure 8.2, this perception of relative deprivation or unfairness leads to feelings of dissatisfaction and resentment. Robert Folger (1987) points out that the negative feelings are exacerbated if people believe that **procedural justice**—the fairness of the process by which rewards are distributed (Greenberg, 1996)—is also low. For example, a student might feel deprived and upset if she sees that someone got an A on a test on which she got a C; she'd feel even more upset if she thought the other person got the A unfairly, such as by cheating. Conversely, John Jost (1995) has proposed that convincing people that procedural justice is high when distributive is low can reduce feelings of dissatisfaction and resentment. Thus, Brenda Major (1994) has suggested that one reason many women are willing to accept less pay than men is that they believe that they do not deserve more money. That is, these women may believe that their outcomes are unfair (low distributive justice), but also believe that the difference in salaries between women and men is appropriate, so dissatisfaction is low (high procedural justice). In situations in which feelings of dissatisfaction and resentment are aroused, they lead to hostility toward the group perceived to be benefiting at one's expense. One way these feelings of hostility can be expressed is in the form of prejudice (Duckitt & Mphuthing, 2002; Taylor, 2002).

Relative Deprivation and Prejudice

Relative deprivation researchers make a distinction between personal and group relative deprivation (Runciman, 1966). **Personal (or egoistic) relative deprivation** refers to the degree to which a person feels deprived as an individual. In contrast, **group (or fraternal) relative deprivation** refers to the degree to which a person feels that a group he or she identifies with has been deprived of some benefit, independent of the amount of relative deprivation experienced. This distinction is important because, generally, group relative deprivation has been found to be related to prejudice whereas personal relative deprivation has not.

The classic study of the relationship of relative deprivation to prejudice was conducted by Reeve Vanneman and Thomas Pettigrew (1972). Using survey data of White respondents from four northern cities, Vanneman and Pettigrew classified respondents as personally deprived if they saw their economic gains over the prior 5 years as being less than those of other White people and as experiencing group deprivation if they saw their gains as being less than those of Black people. Vanneman and Pettigrew were therefore able to construct four groups of respondents: (1) those high in both personal and group relative deprivation, (2) those low in both, (3) those high in personal relative deprivation but low in group relative deprivation, and (4) those high in group deprivation but low in personal relative deprivation. They found a modest relationship between group relative deprivation and prejudice: 54 percent of the White people high in group relative deprivation expressed negative attitudes toward Black people compared to 42 percent of Whites who were low in group relative deprivation. In contrast, personal relative deprivation was unrelated to prejudice, with 48 percent of the members of both the high and low groups expressing negative attitudes. Note the importance of the relativity of the feelings of deprivation: Although the White respondents in these surveys were *objectively* better off than their African American contemporaries, 42 percent of them thought they were losing out *relative to* African Americans, and it was they who expressed the most prejudice.

Ursula Dibble (1981) found similar results in data from a survey of African Americans that was conducted at about the same time as Vanneman and Pettigrew's (1972) survey. Dibble studied relative deprivation in terms of job discrimination: People who had themselves experienced job discrimination were classified as personally deprived and those who had not experienced it as not deprived. Group relative deprivation was assessed in terms of how much job discrimination Blacks in general experienced. Dibble used a measure of hostility as her dependent variable: advocating violence as a means of gaining civil rights. Her results paralleled those of Vanneman and Pettigrew's study of Whites: 28 percent of those high in group relative deprivation advocated violence compared to 13 percent of those low in group relative deprivation. In addition, those high in both forms of relative deprivation were the most likely to express hostility. In Dibble's study, personal relative deprivation may have resulted in additional hostility because it was defined in very personal terms—direct experience of job discrimination—whereas Vanneman and Pettigrew defined it more broadly in terms of general economic gains.

In the years since Dibble (1981) and Vanneman and Pettigrew (1972) conducted their studies, research has continued to show a relationship between group relative deprivation and factors such as prejudice and hostility toward outgroups, both in the United States and in other countries (Brewer & Brown, 1998; Taylor & Moghaddam, 1994). Although most of this research has been correlational in nature, experiments in which participants' feelings of group relative deprivation are manipulated indicate that relative deprivation causes feelings of prejudice and hostility. For example, Peter Grant and Rupert Brown (1995) created groups that either received an expected reward from an outgroup or were deprived of the reward by the outgroup on the basis of their group membership. Participants who experienced group relative deprivation made more negative ratings of the outgroup and made twice as many derogatory remarks about the outgroup compared to nondeprived participants. In addition, Grant and Brown found that it was the participants' emotional responses to deprivation—feelings of discontent, dissatisfaction, and of being treated unfairly—that led to their prejudiced reactions. Furthermore, Serge Guimond and Michaël Dambrun (2002) found that relative deprivation led to prejudice and hostility toward a minority group even when that group did not cause the deprivation.

Clearly, then, feelings of relative deprivation and the associated resentment play a role in intergroup prejudice. Also, as Tom Tyler and Heather Smith (1998) point out, it is one of the few theories of prejudice that can explain why some objectively well-off people explain their prejudices as arising from their victimization by less well-off groups.

Relative Gratification

As Guimond and Dambrun (2002) have pointed out, the concept of relative deprivation implies that people can also experience **relative gratification.** People experience relative gratification when they perceive things to be getting better, in contrast to relative deprivation, in which people perceive things to be getting worse. Bernard Grofman and Edward Muller (1973) first proposed a relationship between relative gratification and feelings of resentment and discontent. Using survey data, they divided respondents into three groups: those who thought their economic situation would be worse in the future than in the past (relative deprivation), those who thought their economic situation would be better in the future than in the past (relative gratification), and those who thought things would stay the same. Grofman and Muller assessed resentment and discontent in terms of endorsement of political violence as a way to bring about change. They found that both people who thought things would get better and those who thought things would get worse were more willing to endorse political violence than those who saw no change ahead for themselves. More recently, Guimond and Dambrun (2002) replicated Grofman and Muller's (1973) results experimentally, using a measure of ethnic prejudice as their dependent variable. They found that both people who had experienced relative gratification and those who had experienced relative deprivation expressed more prejudice than members of a control group.

Why do both deprivation and gratification lead to prejudice? Guimond and Dambrun (2002) suggest that it is because people define their self-interest differently in the two situations. People who are relatively deprived focus on their perceived losses and experience resentment and hostility toward those whom they blame for those losses. In contrast, people who are relatively gratified focus on their group's superior position relative to outgroups. As proposed by social dominance theory (Sidanius & Pratto, 1999; discussed in Chapter 6), they hold negative beliefs about outgroups as a means of justifying their relatively advantaged position. People who see themselves as neither deprived nor gratified relative to outgroups—that is, people who perceive their ingroups and outgroups as having equivalent outcomes—have neither the need to ascribe blame for loss nor the need to justify their greater outcomes as motives for prejudice.

Scapegoating

One aspect of Guimond and Dambrun's (2002) findings that you may have noticed is that the participants in their research expressed prejudice against members of a group who played no role in their relative deprivation. This process of blaming (and sometimes punishing) an innocent outgroup for the misfortunes of one's ingroup is called **scapegoating.** Perhaps the most infamous example of scapegoating was the Nazis' blaming the Jewish people for all the economic and social problems that beset Germany following World War I. The Nazis then used the Jews' supposed guilt as a justification for murdering 6 million Jews.

Blaming an outgroup for the ingroup's problems is not a new phenomenon. For example, Gordon Allport (1954) quoted the 3rd century Roman writer Tertullian as having observed that "[the Roman people] take the Christians to be the cause of every disaster to the state, of every misfortune to the people. If the Tiber reaches the wall, if the Nile does not reach the fields, if the sky does not move or if the earth does, if there is a famine, or if there is a plague, the cry is at once, 'The Christians to the lions'" (p. 243). In essence, then, scapegoating provides what might be called a "designated villain" to explain the deprivation and frustration caused by social and economic problems.

Two theories have been proposed to explain scapegoating, frustration-aggression-displacement theory and Glick's (2002) ideological theory. Both theories view scapegoating as a response to frustration; however, they differ in their explanations of the psychological processes that lead from perceived deprivation to intergroup hostility.

Frustration-aggression-displacement theory   Frustration-aggression-displacement theory was one of the first theories proposed to explain scapegoating (Allport, 1954). This theory is based on the frustration theory of aggression, which John Dollard and his colleagues derived from the psychoanalytic theory of aggression (Dollard, Doob, Miller, Mowrer, & Sears, 1939; see Berkowitz, 1993, for a more recent account of the theory). The frustration theory of aggression holds that frustration causes aggression. The preferred target of that aggression is the cause of the frustration, but if it is not possible to be aggressive toward the source of the frustration, aggression will be displaced onto a more readily available target. For example, a person who is treated unfairly by her boss might feel like taking aggressive action either physically or verbally, but may do nothing out of concern for losing her job. However, she vents her frustration when she gets home by yelling at her dog; that is, she displaces her aggression from her boss to her dog. Post–World War I Germany faced a host of social and economic problems, including hyperinflation of the currency, high crime rates, and political riots. Because there were no clear causes for these problems, the Nazis exploited the situation by blaming the problems on a Jewish conspiracy to undermine Germany.

Although the frustration-aggression-displacement theory of scapegoating has been around for a long time, it has a number of shortcomings. One of the biggest is that more than 60 years of research have failed to provide strong support for it (Duckitt, 1994; Glick, 2002). Even the study most commonly cited in support of the theory, Carl Hovland and Robert Sears' (1940) study of the relation between deteriorating economic conditions and racial lynchings in the United States, has been shown to be problematic. Hovland and Sears postulated that White Americans would scapegoat African Americans during economic downturns and provided historical data that appeared to show a correlation between negative economic indicators and lynchings. However, using more modern statistical tools,

Donald Green and his colleagues (Green, Glaser, & Rich, 1998) showed that the correlation did not really exist. In addition, they were not able to find correlations between economic downturns and hate crimes directed at other minority groups.

Another problem is that frustration-aggression theory is, at heart, a theory of individual, not group, behavior: The theory cannot explain why individual frustration should result in scapegoating of groups and in group action against the scapegoated group (Glick, 2002). Even at the individual level, support for the theory is weak. For example, compared to nonprejudiced people, prejudiced people who are frustrated show more aggression toward members of groups against whom they hold prejudices. However, prejudiced individuals also show more aggression toward people against whom they are *not* prejudiced. Thus, prejudiced people seem to be aggressive against everyone, not just the targets of their prejudices as the theory would predict (Duckitt, 1994). Finally, the frustration-aggression-displacement theory cannot explain why some outgroups are chosen as scapegoats while others are not (Duckitt, 1994), a problem Allport noted in 1954. However, a more recent theory of scapegoating, Peter Glick's (2002) ideological theory, does explain how scapegoats are chosen.

Ideological theory   Figure 8.3 shows Glick's (2002) ideological theory of scapegoating. The theory starts with a perception of group relative deprivation. If there is no clear cause for the deprivation, people search for one. If an ideology (such as Nazism) exists that provides a scapegoat to explain their predicament, people take up that ideology because it fulfills their need to understand the cause of their deprivation. The ideology can also fulfill other needs, such as having a positive social identity, by providing a common outgroup for people to contrast themselves with, and by showing that the predicament is the outgroup's fault, so ingroup members should not feel bad about themselves.

Several factors increase a group's vulnerability to becoming a scapegoat (Duckitt, 1994; Glick, 2002). Scapegoats should have little power so that they cannot effectively resist or retaliate for any actions taken against them. They should be visible enough in society to be salient to the ingroup. Visibility can take a number of forms, including physical characteristics such as skin color or well-publicized deviance from social norms as in the case of a political group. They should be disliked and already stereotyped in ways that make them believable as the cause of the group's deprivation. For example, in describing the German Nazis' scapegoating of Jews, Ervin Staub (2002) noted that "there had been a long history of anti-Semitism, with periods of intense mistreatment of Jews. . . . In addition to early Christian anti-Semitism . . . , the intense anti-Semitism of Luther . . ., who described Jews in language similar to that later used by Hitler, was an important influence. Centuries of discrimination and persecution further enhanced anti-Semitism and made it part of German culture" (p. 15). Finally, the scapegoated group should be seen as a threat to the ingroup, a theme that is usually strongly emphasized in ideological propaganda.

Commitment to the ideology leads to hostile action against the scapegoated group. Because people need to feel justified in taking such action, the action both reinforces and enhances the negative stereotypes of the scapegoat: People reason

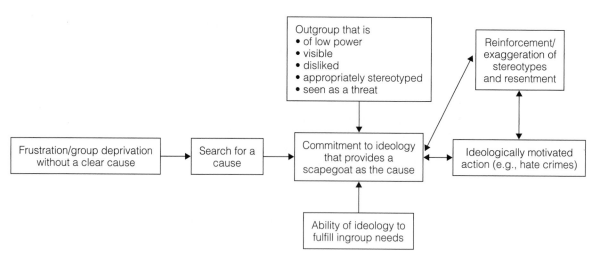

FIGURE **8.3**

PETER GLICK'S (2002) IDEOLOGICAL MODEL OF SCAPEGOATING

Group relative deprivation without a clear causal agent leads to a search for a cause of the deprivation. If an ideology (such as Nazism) exists that provides a causal scapegoat, people adhere to the ideology because it fulfills their need to understand the cause of their deprivation. The ideology can also fulfill other needs, such as social identity and collective self-esteem. Outgroups are chosen as scapegoats if they have little power, are visible, are disliked, are stereotyped in ways that make them appropriate as the cause of the deprivation, and are seen as a threat to the ingroup. Commitment to the ideology leads to action against the scapegoated group. The action both reinforces the stereotypes and commitment to the ideology. The reinforced stereotypes lend additional apparent validity to the ideology and help justify the actions taken against the scapegoated group. Adapted from Peter Glick. (2002). Sacrificial lambs dressed in wolves' clothing: Envious prejudice, ideology, and the scapegoating of Jews.

Adapted from Peter Glick. (2002). "Sacrificial lambs dressed in wolves' clothing: Envious prejudice, ideology, and the scapegoating of Jews." In *Understanding Genocide: The Social Psychology of the Holocaust*, ed. by Newman and Erber. Reprinted by permission of Oxford University Press, Inc.

that the outgroup must in fact be bad to deserve what we did to them. Taking action in support of the ideology also tends to increase commitment to the ideology. The reinforced stereotypes lend additional verisimilitude to the ideology.

Glick's (2002) ideological theory is very new and as yet has not been tested with research. However, it does an excellent job of explaining the process of scapegoating and so holds great promise.

INTEGRATED THREAT THEORY

Although we have discussed realistic conflict theory, social identity theory, and relative deprivation theory separately, they are, in fact, closely linked. Walter and Cookie Stephan's (2000; Stephan et al., 2002) integrated threat theory of prejudice, illustrated in Figure 8.4, provides one way of showing how the theories relate to one another. Stephan and Stephan propose that prejudice derives from three types of perceived threat to one's ingroup: intergroup anxiety, perceptions of realistic threats, and perceptions of symbolic threats. Intergroup

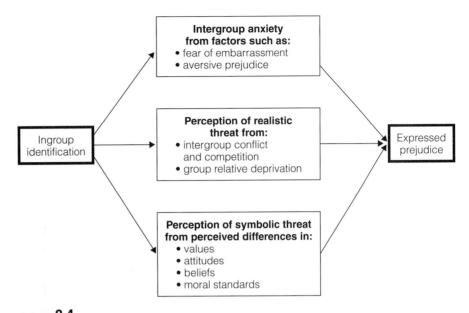

FIGURE **8.4**

WALTER AND COOKIE STEPHAN'S (2000) INTEGRATED THREAT THEORY OF PREJUDICE

Greater identification with the ingroup leads to more perceived realistic and symbolic threats and more intergroup anxiety. Higher levels of these factors lead to more prejudice. Adapted from Walter G. Stephan and Cookie W. Stephan. (2000). An integrated threat theory of prejudice.

In S. Oskamp (Ed.), *Reducing prejudice and discrimination* (pp. 23–46). Mahwah, NJ: Erlbaum. Figure 2.4, p. 37. Reprinted by permission of Lawrence Erlbaum Associates, Inc.

anxiety, discussed in Chapter 6, consists of factors that make people feel anxious or nervous in the presence of members of other groups. These factors include such things as fear of being embarrassed by saying or doing the wrong thing, aversive prejudices, and so forth.

Perceptions of realistic threat derive from intergroup conflict and competition, and from feelings of group relative deprivation. As noted earlier, sometimes groups really are in competition for resources and so constitute threats to each other and, as research using the minimal group paradigm has found, simply putting people into groups can create ingroup favoritism which, in turn, can stimulate competition. Feelings of relative deprivation may or may not stem from real deprivation, but, as we saw earlier, in either case blaming another group for the deprivation creates hostility toward that group. In addition, feelings of group relative deprivation can lead to feelings of competitiveness with the outgroup (Mummendey, Kessler, Klink, & Mielke, 1999).

Symbolic threats come from perceptions that the outgroup differs from the ingroup in terms of values, attitudes, beliefs, moral standards, and other symbolic, as opposed to material, factors. Perceptions of such differences are often associated with the belief that the outgroup is trying to undermine those factors, especially values, and destroy the ingroup by destroying its cultural underpinnings (Biernat, Vescio, Theno, & Crandall, 1996).

Identification with the ingroup is associated with all three types of threat. As shown earlier in Figure 8.1, increases in ingroup identification lead to increases in feelings of competitiveness with the outgroup, and increased social identity has been found to be associated with perceptions of greater group relative deprivation in both correlational research (Mummendey et al., 1999; Tropp & Wright, 1999) and experimental research (Grant & Brown, 1995). Furthermore, stronger identification with the ingroup reflects stronger investment in group values, moral standards, and so forth. Therefore, people strongly identified with the ingroup are more sensitive to seeing ingroup-outgroup differences in values as threatening (Stephan et al., 2002). Stephan and his colleagues (2002) also found stronger ingroup identification to be associated with higher intergroup anxiety. Thus, social identity ties intergroup conflict and competition, relative deprivation, and other factors into a package of perceptions that potentiates prejudice.

HATE GROUP MEMBERSHIP

Hate groups represent an extreme form of social identity. A **hate group** is an organization whose central principles include hostility toward racial, ethnic, and religious minority groups. Most hate groups also espouse White racial supremacy and advocate the segregation or deportation of minority groups, or, in a few cases, the annihilation of those groups. Some hate groups, such as the one called Christian Identity, claim to be religions or churches; others, such as the Ku Klux Klan do not claim religious status but do assert that Christianity is one of their guiding principles. A number of hate groups, such as the Ku Klux Klan, are fairly well organized with a national structure, whereas others, such as racist skinheads, are loose coalitions of local groups.

Hate groups engage in a variety of activities, including holding membership meetings, rallies, and bring-the-family social events; engaging in protests and demonstrations; distributing pamphlets; producing television shows for public access cable channels; running World Wide Web sites; and producing and distributing recordings of racist music. Interestingly, despite the violent rhetoric hate group leaders often use in their speeches and literature, with a few exceptions (such as racist skinheads) the groups rarely initiate violent activities and often disown members who engage in violence (Levin & McDevitt, 2002). The groups operate this way because they want to project an image of normalcy, an image of people who prefer to disagree peacefully with government racial policy but who are also willing to engage in armed defense of what they see as their rights (Blee, 2002; Ezekiel, 1995).

The purpose of this section is to examine the psychological factors that predispose people to join hate groups, the way in which hate groups recruit new members, how the groups socialize recruits into becoming "good" group members, and factors that motivate people to leave the groups. Space does not permit a discussion of the historical, political, and sociological factors that have led to the rise and continuation of hate groups in the United States. Betty Dobratz and Stephanie Shanks-Meile (2000), among others, have done an excellent job of covering this complex topic.

Most of the information about hate group members comes from ethnographic studies of current and former members, especially those conducted by James Aho (1988, 1990), Tore Bjørgo (1998), Kathleen Blee (2002), and Raphael Ezekiel (1995, 2002). As Blee (2002) notes, one must be careful when evaluating people's reports of their motivations because autobiographical memory is constructive; that is, people, usually unconsciously, select and interpret past events in terms of their current belief systems to help them justify those beliefs. Nonetheless, the consistencies in the findings of the research conducted by Aho, Blee, Ezekiel (who worked in different parts of the United States at different times), and Bjørgo (who worked in Europe) provide support for the generality of the motivational themes and group processes they identified.

Why People Join Hate Groups

There is no one reason why people join hate groups. Rather, there seem to be a set of factors that, in various combinations, lead people to see joining a hate group as something reasonable to do when the opportunity arises. Among these factors are the person's racial attitudes, being in search of solutions to problems and questions that have arisen in the person's life, youthful rebellion, the allure of violence, and being male.

Racial attitudes   Clearly, racial attitudes play a role in hate group membership: No one who holds nonracist attitudes is likely to join such a group. However, although rabid racism might characterize a few people at the time they join hate groups, most new recruits do not hold extreme racist attitudes (Aho, 1990; Bjørgo, 1998; Blee, 2002). Rather, as Blee (2002) noted, they are characterized by what Philomena Essed (1991) called **everyday racism** or what James Jones (1997) called **cultural racism.** Everyday racism and cultural racism reflect the assumption inherent in much of American culture that the only correct social and cultural values are European Christian values. This assumption, in turn, promotes negative, stereotyped views of people, such as members of minority groups, whose values are presumed to differ from the European Christian norm (Biernat et al., 1996). Everyday racism is the process that, for example, lets people laugh at racist jokes and leads them to feel uncomfortable in the presence of minority group members, even though they see themselves as unprejudiced and would not intentionally act in a racist manner.

Everyday racism does not by itself lead people into hate groups, but it does provide a foundation on which hate group recruiters can build when trying to persuade people to join their groups. As we will see, once people are recruited into hate groups the process of organizational socialization converts everyday racism into extreme racism, or in Blee's (2002) term, **extraordinary racism.** Aho (1988), for example, noted that "It is not uncommon to meet presently dedicated neo-Nazis who, when they first read or heard its doctrines were either shocked by them, morally revolted, or simply amused by what they took to be its patent absurdities" (p. 161).

A search for solutions   Stephen Worchel (1999) has suggested that throughout their lives people are on a search for solutions to the philosophical and practical problems that inevitably confront them. They are trying to decide what things are important in life. When bad things happen, people want to understand the causes so they can put things right. People want the sense of comradeship and community that comes from associating with like-minded people. People want to make the world a better place for themselves and their children. Hate groups can appeal to some people because the groups seem to provide the answers to their questions and solutions to their problems.

As Worchel (1999) noted, people want their lives to have meaning and purpose, they want to know that they are having an impact on the world and on other people, they want to have sense of pride and self-value. Membership in hate groups can help fulfill such needs. Based on his interviews with young members of racist groups, Ezekiel (1995) concluded that participating in the groups "brings a sense of meaning—at least for a while. . . . To struggle in a cause that transcends the individual lends meaning to a life, no matter how ill-founded or narrowing the cause. For young men in the neo-Nazi group that I had studied in Detroit, membership was an alternative to atomization and drift; within the group they worked for a cause and took direct risks in the company of comrades" (p. 32). Pride and self-image may also play a role in the appeal of hate groups. Bjørgo (1998) concluded that pride "perhaps is the most important factor involved when youths join racist groups. . . . Individuals who have failed to establish a positive identity and status in relation to school, work, sports, or other social activities sometimes try to win respect by joining groups with a dangerous and intimidating image" (pp. 235–236). Other people, especially young people, may simply be drifting, looking for something to give purpose and direction to their lives (Bjørgo, 1998). For example, Aho (1990) reported that while observing a paramilitary training exercise being conduced by a hate group, "I spoke to a young man garbed in jungle fatigues carrying an automatic rifle. . . . Behind the mosquito face-net I discovered a bored . . . high school student who became animated only when conversation shifted to his 'real' interests in art, drama, and wrestling" (p. 32). Thus, one neo-Nazi recruiting manual urges members to "recruit . . . disaffected white kids who feel 'left out,' isolated, unpopular, or on the fringe or margins of things at school (outsiders, loners). . . . Working with Nazi skinheads will give them a sense of accomplishment, success, and belonging. In recruiting, proceed from such 'outsiders' inwards toward the mainstream, conventional, average students" (quoted in Blazak, 2001, p. 988).

One propaganda tool that hate groups use to attract high school and college students who are searching for direction and meaning in their lives is racist rock music (Blee, 2002; Lööw, 1998). Racist rock bands write and perform songs that disparage and dehumanize members of racial and religious minority groups while extolling the superiority of the White race. Blee (2002) quotes one neo-Nazi leader as saying that "music has the potential to get through to the kids like noth-ing else. The great thing about music is, if a kid likes it, he will dub copies for his friends, and they will dub copies for their friends, and so on. This has the poten-tial to become a grassroots, underground type movement" (p. 161). This approach can be effective. Blee (2002) goes on to describe one young woman who told her: "How I really started believing, thinking in that white separatist sense and then got all white separatist, it was really through the music. There's a whole other genre of music out there that no one ever hears about, and it's real powerful, espe-cially at that awkward stage where no one knows exactly who they are. It gives you an identity, it says you're special, you know, because you're white" (p. 162).

Many members of hate groups have grievances and want to set them right. For example, they may believe that the government and other powerful groups whose actions they cannot control, such as employers, are treating them unfairly. In some cases, this sense of grievance might be a reaction to the loss of White priv-ilege brought about by civil rights legislation. No longer, for example, does a White job applicant get automatic preference over minority applicants (Turpin-Petrosino, 2002). Exploiting the principle of group relative deprivation, hate group recruiters frame this situation as one of minority group members unfairly taking jobs away from more deserving White applicants. In other cases, personal grievances might lead to feelings of deprivation. Ezekiel (1995), for example, suggested that a sense of grievance might be especially characteristic of poor Whites who feel their plight is being ignored because news media reports and government officials' speeches focus on minority group poverty. This attention paid to minority group poverty may also lead poor Whites to feel shortchanged on social services (Bjørgo, 1998). Similar processes might also be at work among the middle class (Kimmel, 2002). Thus, one hate group recruiter told sociologist Randy Blazak (2001), "The easiest place to recruit is around some big layoff. . . . You wait for things to get bad and you go to the kids, not the parents and say, 'You know why your dad got laid off? It's because the money hungry Jews sent his job to China. They care more about the . . . Chinese than they do about White workers" (p. 992).

In addition, Ezekiel noted that the poor White hate group members he inter-viewed "were people who at a deep level felt terror that they were about to be extinguished. They felt that their lives might disappear at any moment. They felt that they might be blown away by the next wind" (p. 156). Their fear came from being born in poverty and from a lack of hope that things would get better. Hate groups try to recruit new members by claiming to provide a means for White peo-ple to unite and fight for what the groups present as rightfully theirs.

People also need to feel a sense of community. Bjørgo (1998) and Ezekiel (1995) reported that the young hate group members they interviewed usually had few strong social ties outside the group. The groups therefore provided friendship and support networks not otherwise available to their members. In addition, most of the members had few close family ties and often did not have a father figure in the home. For these young men, older group members served as father figures and role models, providing advice and guidance.

Finally, in his study of hate group members, Aho (1990) noted that one impor-tant motivation was to make the world a better place. Most of Aho's interviewees were Christian religious fundamentalists who saw a strong conflict between their religious standards and the corruption and immorality rife in the United States and the world at large. For these people, the hate groups provided a set of scapegoats to blame for the perceived corruption and immorality—religious and racial minority groups—and a solution—wresting control of the country from those groups and putting it in the hands of right-minded White Christians. See Box 8.3 for more on religion and hate groups.

Youthful rebellion   Some young people may join hate groups as a way of expressing rebellion against established authority, especially when they feel disenchanted with and alienated from the political process. Bjørgo (1998) noted that youthful rebellion moves counter to whatever the current establishment political doctrine is. Young rebels turned to leftist politics in the 1960s because the political establishment was then conservative; a more liberal political establishment pushes rebellion toward the political right. For example, Bjørgo (1998) quoted one former member of a European hate group as saying, "If you really want to provoke society these days, you have to become either a National Socialist [Nazi] or a Satanist" (p. 235). Similarly, Ezekiel (1995) found that the young hate group members he interviewed in Detroit "feel strongly the urge to be shocking and to scandalize the Establishment, and nothing serves the purpose easier [sic] than the swastika" (p. 157).

The allure of violence   Some people, especially young men, find hate groups attractive because of the violent images the groups project (Bjørgo, 1998). Because most groups rarely engage in violent activities but do indulge in violent rhetoric, membership provides a feeling of machismo, excitement, and danger without much real risk. Many groups also provide paramilitary training, so that members can feel empowered by the use of weapons but do not have to undergo the rigors and discipline of military training.

Gender   Most hate group members are men (Aho, 1990; Blee, 2002; Ezekiel, 1995), perhaps because the groups' violent images repel women while attracting men. In addition, most hate groups promote traditional gender roles and male leadership and dominance in all activities. For the most part, male hate group members' attitudes toward White women are benevolently sexist: women's proper roles are raising children and housework while men provide women with the protection they need to carry out their roles (Blee, 2002). In contrast, hate group members tend to be hostilely sexist toward minority group women, portraying them as sources of moral corruption. Despite these sexist organizational attitudes, many hate groups have a significant number of female members, and the groups target women for recruitment, perhaps in an effort to soften their images (Blee, 2002).

Myths concerning hate group members   Although there is a stereotype that portrays hate group members as being poor and uneducated (Aho, 1990; Blee, 2002), that is not always the case. Although Ezekiel (1995) focused his research on hate group members in poor White neighborhoods, most of the people Aho (1990) and Blee (2002) interviewed were middle-class and reasonably

8.3   *Religion and Racism*

Although it may seem like a contradiction, some hate groups claim to be religions. Betty Dobratz (2001) and Jonathan White (2001) identify three principal racist religions: Christian Identity, Creatorism, and Odinism (The World Church of the Creator). Christian Identity has three central beliefs (Barkun, 1997): that European Whites, not Jews, are the chosen people of God, and as such should have dominance over all other peoples; that Jews are the children of the devil, born from the liaison between Satan and Eve; and that "Aryans" must battle a Jewish conspiracy to prevent the Second Coming of Christ. Creatorism is a form of racist deism that holds that the Creator set the universe in motion and established laws of nature to govern it; people must work things out on their own within the strictures of these natural laws. According to Creatorism, racial primacy and purity are essential to human survival because "nature does not approve of miscegenation or mongrelization of the races" (Dobratz, 2001, p. 290). Creatorism claims no scriptural base for its racism, but holds that "Our religion is our race" (quoted in White, 2001, p. 940). Finally, Odinism is a resurrection of ancient Norse mythology in the service of racism. It claims that Northern European "Aryans" are a separate race that is superior to all other races and so must be kept racially pure. The best way to ensure purity is through the separation of the races (Dobratz, 2001).

Although racist religions, especially those that claim a Christian basis, focus their recruiting efforts on people whom White (2001) refers to as mainstream fundamentalists (Dobratz, 2001), there are important differences between mainstream Christian fundamentalism and racist religion (White, 2001). Although we present those differences in terms of end points of a continuum, any one person's beliefs could fall somewhere between those points:

- Although both mainstream fundamentalism and racist religion favor a literal interpretation of the Bible, mainstream fundamentalists embrace its call for universal love. In contrast, racist religion "accepts the idea of love [only] for one's own kind [and] is defined by hate. One does not simply love, one loves in conjunction with hate. For example, one loves Christians because one hates everyone who is not a Christian. One loves Whites because one hates everyone who is not White" (White, 2001, p. 945).
- Racist religion claims that the Bible can be interpreted to support racism; mainstream fundamentalists reject such claims.
- In the United States, mainstream fundamentalist belief is not linked to one's race or ethnicity, whereas race is a central feature of racist religion, which claims that God favors the White race and God's love (and by extension, believers' love) applies only to Whites.
- Mainstream fundamentalists believe that they must prepare for the Second Coming of Christ, which will take place in accordance with Biblical prophecies yet to be fulfilled, through religious observance. Racist religions believe that the prophecies have already been fulfilled and that they must fight to create conditions conducive to the Second Coming. They believe that they must "give history a push" (Lacqueur, 1996, p. 32).

(continues)

Religion and Racism (continued)

- Both mainstream fundamentalism and racist religion view evil as an active, important force on the world that must be countered. However, mainstream fundamentalists attribute evil to the work of Satan, which must be countered through religious adherence, whereas racist religion attributes evil to secular conspiracies, especially Jewish conspiracies, which must be physically destroyed.

  Racist groups present themselves as religions because religion can unify people who might actually hold disparate racial beliefs, provide a justification for those beliefs, and, as noted earlier, be a recruiting tool (Dobratz, 2001; White, 2001). For example, Dobratz (2001)

quotes the leader of one group as saying, "Christianity provides us with the moral framework of our groups, as well as, the spiritual outlet" (p. 293). In addition, different religious visions—such as Christianity, deism, and paganism—permit appeals to different kinds of people (Dobratz, 2001). For example, someone who rejects Christianity might be attracted to a deist or pagan version of racism. Dobratz also notes, however, that religion can create tensions between groups whose religious visions are fundamentally opposed. In addition, some racists groups, such as White Aryan Resistance, reject religion entirely. As a result, many hate groups downplay religion, considering it to be a personal matter that is irrelevant to the group's goals.

well educated. In fact, as described in Box 8.4, Blee was particularly struck by the ordinariness of the women she interviewed. Of the 278 hate group members Aho interviewed, 50 percent had completed college or had had some post-high-school education and 39 percent had completed high school or had obtained a General Educational Development (GED) certificate; only 11 percent were high school dropouts. Currently, many hate groups are focusing their recruiting efforts on the better-educated segment of the population, especially those in high school and college (Turpin-Petrosino, 2002).

The psychological functions of group membership People can be attracted to hate groups because they are searching for answers and solutions to life's questions and problems, because they feel a need to rebel, because they find the violent images of the hate groups appealing, or from a combination of these factors. Especially for people searching for answers, their everyday racist attitudes can provide a source of answers: Being faced with the contrast of living in poverty when others have more leads to a search for someone to blame; racism's answer is that there is a minority group conspiracy to keep you down (Ezekiel, 1995). When faced with a conflict between one's religious principles and a degenerate secular world in which one must live, racism's answer is to remove the corrupting

8.4   *The Ordinariness of Extraordinary Racists*

Kathleen Blee (2002) described the women she interviewed as being extraordinary in terms of their degree of racism. Nonetheless, she noted that almost all lived rather ordinary lives and would not stand out in a crowd of everyday working- and middle-class people. Consider two of the women she talked with, who could be almost anyone's mother or grandmother:

> Among the women I interviewed there was no single racist *type*. The media depict unkempt, surly women in faded T-shirts, but the reality is different. One of my first interviews was with Mary, a vivacious [Ku Klux] Klanswoman who met me at her door with a big smile and ushered me into her large, inviting kitchen. Her blond hair was pulled back into a long ponytail and tied with a large green bow. She wore dangling gold hoop earrings, blue jeans, a modest flowered blouse, and no visible tattoos or other racist insignia. Her only other jewelry was a simple gold-colored necklace. Perhaps sensing my surprise at her unremarkable appearance, she joked that her suburban appearance was her "undercover uniform."
>
> Trudy, an elderly Nazi activist I interviewed somewhat later, lived in a one-story, almost shabby ranch house on a lower-middle-class street in a small town in the Midwest. Her house was furnished plainly. Moving cautiously with the aid of a walker, she brought out tea and cookies prepared for my visit.

From Kathleen Blee. (2002). *Inside organized racism: Women in the hate movement.* Berkeley: University of California Press, pp. 7–8.

influence by removing religious and racial minority groups (Aho, 1990). When faced with a decline in traditional White dominance, racism's answer is to restore White entitlement (Turpin-Petrosino, 2002).

As Ezekiel (1995) wrote of the people he interviewed, "Most were members in this extreme racist group because the membership served a function, not because they had to enact their racism. Given another format in which they could have relieved their fears, given an alternative group that offered comradeship, reassuring activities, glamour, and excitement, they could easily have switched their allegiances. They would have remained racist—like their neighbors who hadn't joined a group—but they would not have needed to carry out racist actions in a group setting" (p. 159).

Recruiting Hate Group Members

Why is it that some people who are psychologically predisposed to join hate groups do so while others do not? Having a psychological predisposition to joining a hate group is not sufficient. Potential new members must be recruited into the group; those who are not recruited are likely to find more constructive ways of resolving their personal searches for answers, such as through church work, neighborhood associations, or traditional political activities (Aho, 1990).

Most people who join hate groups do not seek the groups out; instead, current group members recruit them into the groups (Aho, 1990; Blee, 2002). The recruiting is usually done by someone the recruit knows; as Blee (2002) noted, "It is a mistake to assume that the process of recruitment into racist groups differs markedly from that through which individuals enter churches, neighborhood associations, or bowling leagues—they join because of contacts with current members and, in some cases, a particular receptivity to the group's ideas" (p. 188). Thus, Aho found that 55 percent of the hate group members he interviewed had been recruited by friends or family members, 17 percent by other personal acquaintances such as coworkers, and 18 percent by people encountered at political meetings. Only 10 percent sought membership after reading literature produced by a group. As one of Aho's (1990) interviewees explained, "It was my friends that started to convince me that blacks weren't my equal" (p. 188).

The recruiter is someone the recruit trusts and respects, either because the recruiter is a family member or friend, or because the recruiter has gained the recruit's trust and respect by acting as mentor and role model in an activity important in the recruit's life. For example, Aho (1990) told of a group of young railroad employees who developed strong feelings of respect for an older work group leader who was also a racist: "His [personality] first attracts the younger men to him, not his beliefs. Only after strong bonds are established does he open to them his prolific library of radical literature" (p. 189).

As this example shows, recruitment into a hate group is usually a gradual process (Aho, 1990; Blee, 2002). After gaining the trust of potential recruits, the recruiter guides conversations toward political issues of general interest, such as crime, unemployment, education, and government policies. While doing so, the recruiter feels out the potential new group members for receptivity to the group's ideology. A recruiter might, for example, interpret crime statistics in racial terms by blaming members of minority groups to see how potential recruits react. If they appear to be receptive to the group's ideology, the recruiter can guide them to draw on their everyday racism to make such interpretations for themselves, encouraging their commitment to the group's belief system. Finally, the recruiter will invite recruits to a group function to meet other people who think the same way.

Many group functions are rather innocuous events, such as bring-the-family picnics, giving the group an appearance of normalcy. For example, "A flyer advertising a neo-Nazi event promises a day of fellowship and racist learning, along with a social time of music and meals at a local banquet hall" (Blee, 2002, p. 131). This normalcy reassures the recruits that these people, at least, do not meet the stereotype of rabid racist maniacs, but are "just plain folk" who, like the recruits, are trying to raise their families in a difficult world. Blee (2002), for example, reported that "a neo-Nazi recalled being surprised to find that a racist event was 'kind of like a big powwow or something. There was no cross burnings or screaming'" (pp. 130–131). Thus, one step at a time, recruits are drawn into full group membership.

Group Socialization

Socialization is the process by which new members of a group learn a group's values and learn how to be good group members. This section discusses the process of socialization in hate groups and some of the social and psychological outcomes of that socialization process.

The socialization process   Like other groups and organizations, hate groups socialize new members by means of formal and informal education and through participation in rituals. In addition, hate groups try to reinforce the socialization process by isolating members from opposing viewpoints.

Formal education of both new and old group members uses lectures and speeches by leaders, books and pamphlets about the group's ideology, and video and audio recordings of speeches of propaganda disguised as documentary presentations. However, Blee (2002) suggested that these efforts may not be very effective because members tend to "tune out" the speeches and the printed, audio, and video materials are usually poorly written and produced, and boring. For example, she reported that "[a]t a neo-Nazi gathering I attended, most people paid only sporadic attention to long, boring speeches [on the topic of Jews and African Americans as racial enemies] by the group's self-proclaimed leaders. Even a livelier (at least to me) presentation by two younger members . . . had no more success in sustaining the interest of the audience, many of whom left early or spent time conspicuously reading the newspaper" (Blee, 2002, p. 76).

In contrast, Blee (2002) found that "much more animated discussions of racial enemies occurred in informal conversations held in the food line, in the queue for bathrooms, or in small groups clustered at the outskirts of the tent where speeches were given" (p. 77). That is, discussions with peers and other people in the group whom members respect personally is a much stronger source of information than formal presentations. Such face-to-face indoctrination is especially effective because the discussions can address issues of special concern to the person being socialized and the indoctrinator can exploit this concern to lead the person into more extreme beliefs and greater commitment to the group's ideology.

Participation in rituals is an important part of the socialization process for hate groups. These rituals include group singing of racists songs, parades and marches, dressing in ritual clothing such as Ku Klux Klan robes and neo-Nazi uniforms, and ceremonies such as formal initiation into group membership and cross-burnings (Aho, 1990; Blee, 2002). These rituals serve two purposes. First, they promote group unity and cohesiveness. Doing things together and dressing alike increase members' identification with the group and their feelings of oneness with other members. The second purpose rituals serve is increasing members' commitment to the group. Taking action on behalf of a group, especially public action, increases one's psychological investment in the group (see, for example, Forsyth, 2006). Putting effort and psychological energy into the group's activities means that a person has more to lose by leaving the group: The act of leaving essentially says that the time and effort given to the group were wasted resources that cannot be recovered.

As new members become more committed to the group, they spend more time with other group members and less time with family, friends, and acquaintances who are not members of the group. This change in the new members' social networks has two effects (Aho, 1990; Bjørgo, 1998; Blee, 2002). First, by associating with people who share their beliefs, group members receive support for those beliefs and reassurance that the beliefs they hold are correct. Second, increased association with group members isolates people from information that contradicts the group's ideology and provides the group with the opportunity to rebut any contradictory information members might encounter. As one of Bjørgo's (1998) interviewees noted, "In the past, when I had an opinion, I could discuss it with people who disagreed with me. Now I can only discuss with people who already agree with me completely. What if I am wrong?" (p. 240). To maximize isolation from information that contradicts the group's ideology and to increase dependence on the group for social support, many hate groups encourage new members to sever ties with nonracist family members and friends and to replace them with the "family" of the group (Bjørgo, 1998; Blee, 2002).

The outcomes of socialization

Blee (2002) noted that "[r]acist groups change people. Most of the women I interviewed were changed profoundly by being in a racist group. . . . They went from holding racist attitudes to being racial activists, from racial apathy to racial zeal" (p. 188). These changes involve members' social networks, their self-concepts, and the way they think about the world.

Hate group members tend to let their social relationships with nonmembers wither away and create new relationships with other group members. As noted earlier, the groups encourage this change to isolate members from the information that contradicts the group's ideology. However, the members often find the new relationships rewarding (Aho, 1990; Blee, 2002). Aho (1990), for example, noted that "while they rarely mention this as a motive for joining [the racist] movement, most [members] appear to have benefited personally from their affiliations by sustaining rewarding relationships with their recruiting agents" (p. 76). This restructuring of social networks is accelerated and made easier when, as often happens, the new members' families and friends shun them for joining a hate group (Aho, 1988; Blee, 2002). As a result, the group becomes the center of members' social lives.

Because the group members live in a social environment that emphasizes race and supposed racial differences, being White becomes more central to members' social identities, intensifying the effects of social identity described in the discussion of social identity theory. For example, one woman member of the Ku Klux Klan told Blee (2002), "It is not so much that I am in the Klan, it is the fact that the Klan is in me. By the Klan being in me I have no choice other than to remain, I can't walk away from myself" (p. 32).

In groups that advocate violence, the social environment makes violence seem to be acceptable and proper, and members become more tolerant of violence toward minority groups and of taking part in such violence. For example, one member of a violent hate group explained her experience this way: "It is remarkable how fast I have shifted my boundaries regarding violence. I used to be against violence, but now it does not cost me a penny to beat and take out all my aggression against someone who represents what I hate. . . . From being stunned and scared by seeing and experiencing violence, I have come to enjoy it" (quoted by Bjørgo, 1998, p. 239).

Hand in hand with changes in the self-concept come changes in how members think about the world. Because of the groups' emphasis on race, members begin to interpret events, especially negative events, in racial terms (Aho, 1990; Blee, 2002; Ezekiel, 1995). When bad things happen, people want to understand why. The ideology of hate groups provides the answer for their members: It is because religious and ethnic minority groups have conspired to make them happen. Similarly, group members come to redefine their self-interest in racial terms, believing that keeping members of minority groups from improving their lives will make life better for the hate group members and their families. Finally, racial attitudes become more extreme and more solidified, with everyday racism being transformed into extraordinary racism, so that "being prejudiced against Jews [becomes] believing that there is a Jewish conspiracy that determines the fate of individual Aryans [the term used by racist groups for people of Northern European descent], or . . . thinking that African Americans are inferior to whites [becomes] seeing African Americans as an imminent threat to the white race" (Blee, 2002, pp. 75–76).

Leaving the Group

Although most hate groups have a core of dedicated members, for the most part, hate group membership is very unstable: People continuously come and go between various groups and move into and out of the racist movement as a whole. "In the words of one [Ku Klux] Klan chief, the movement is a revolving door" (Ezekiel, 1995, p. xxii). Why do people leave racist groups? Two factors seem to be the most important: disenchantment with the group's ideology or tactics (such as violence) and the pull of social relationships outside the group.

Disenchantment with the group   Disenchantment with the group can stem from a number of sources (Bjørgo,1998). These sources include negative effects on members' lives, loss of faith in the group's ideology, and concern over group extremism.

As noted earlier, joining a hate group can generate disapproval from the member's family and friends, sometimes resulting in ostracism. If these social relationships are important to the person, he or she may give up the group to preserve those relationships. In addition, group membership can affect members' work and careers. Being very active in the movement can take time away from a job, resulting in poorer job performance and risk of being fired. In addition, because having hate group members working for them may adversely affect the reputations of their businesses, employers may fire employees who are known to be members of hate groups and refuse to hire known members. Finally, for members who take an active part in demonstrations and engage in violent activities, there is the possibility of arrest and prosecution, and the resulting adverse publicity.

Many people join hate groups because the groups and their ideology appeal to members' real need for meaning in their lives and answers to their problems. However, as Ezekiel (1995) has noted, very often the main thing the groups provide is "a particular kind of theater. The movement lives on demonstrations, rallies, and counterrallies; on marches and countermarches; on rabid speeches at twilight; on cross-burnings with Gothic ritual by moonlight. By their nature those actions guarantee failure [because they] bear little relation to the issues of [the members'] lives" (p. 32). Even when groups have an ideology that provides answers, if those answers prove unsatisfactory, or if people come to see the answers as incorrect, they will be motivated to leave the group (Aho, 1988, 1990; Blee, 2002).

Although many hate groups advocate, and some engage in, violence against their "enemies," very often they prefer to downplay the violent aspects of their ideologies to make themselves more appealing to potential new members. Bjørgo (1998) suggested that people who are attracted to racist ideology but reject violence as a means of achieving racist goals will leave groups when the violent aspect of their ideology becomes apparent. However, Ezekiel (1995) noted that concern over violence may also result from fear for personal safety: Groups "lose the greater part of their followers as dangerous confrontations multiply; the less intense followers decide after a few such experiences that there are better ways to spend time" (p. 102).

Relationships outside the group

Because hate group members often sever their ties with family members and friends who are not group members, they become dependent on the group for meeting their needs for affiliation, status, and respect. Consequently, even when people become disenchanted with a group's ideology they may not leave if they cannot satisfy their social needs outside the group. Therefore, establishing or renewing a rewarding relationship with a person who is not a group member is the key to defection from the group (Aho, 1988, 1990; Bjørgo, 1998; Blee, 2002; Ezekiel, 1995). A person is most likely to leave a hate group if he or she does not find group membership to be rewarding but does have a rewarding relationship outside the group. For example, "Getting a girlfriend who is not involved with the [racist] movement is probably the most common circumstance that motivates boys to leave and remain outside. . . . However, if the relationship breaks up, chances are high that they will return to the group" (Bjørgo, 1998, p. 317). The more extensive and rewarding a social network a defector from a hate group has, the less likely the person is to return to the hate group movement if one relationship ends.

Therefore, rather than shunning a family member or friend who joins a hate group, one should maintain contact as a way of encouraging the person to leave the group. This encouragement should take two forms. One is finding out the needs that group membership fulfills and providing alternative, constructive ways for the person to meet those needs. Simultaneously, one should work to counter the group propaganda aimed at solidifying the attitudes that support the person's membership in the group.

CHAPTER SUMMARY

This chapter examined two aspects of the social context of prejudice: intergroup processes and hate group membership. Realistic conflict theory is the oldest intergroup theory of prejudice. The theory holds that people dislike members of outgroups because the ingroup is competing with the ingroup for resources. Because this competition threatens the survival of the ingroup, outgroup members are seen in negative terms. If one group wins the competition and gains dominance over the other group, the dominating group justifies its position by viewing the subjugated group as inferior and stereotypes them in negative ways or in positive ways that emphasize their low power and status. The subjugated group, in turn, can avoid conflict by accepting the dominating group's definition of their position; conversely, viewing the dominating group as oppressive can mobilize members of the subjugated group to challenge the dominating group's position. The dominating group can respond to this challenge by defining the subjugated group as threatening as well as inferior as a way of preparing to suppress the challenge; conversely, the dominating group can avoid conflict by being more tolerant of the subjugated group's desire for equality.

Social identity theory explains prejudice in terms of the link between people's self-concepts and their membership in groups that are important to them. Because people see these groups as part of themselves, they try to ensure the status of these groups by favoring ingroup members over outgroup members when allocating resources. This ingroup bias arises from feelings of competition that arise when people think of their group relative to other groups and from a need to enhance their own self-esteem by enhancing the position of their group relative to other groups. An important factor influencing people's level of identification with a group is self-categorization: seeing oneself in group rather than individual terms. Self-categorization increases when situational factors emphasize one's group membership, when one looks to the group as a source of information on important topics, and when one has chosen to join the group. Other factors influencing identification with the group are a need to balance group and personal identity, the chronic identities one always experiences, threats to the group, and attitudes and values that emphasize the group over the individual. Although social identity can lead to prejudice, it can also lead to tolerance if ingroup members do not see their values as conflicting with those of the outgroup or if a person has a complex social identity.

Relative deprivation theory explains prejudice as a reaction to feelings of being treated unfairly: If people blame a group for their unfair treatment, they develop negative feelings toward members of that group. These feelings of unfair treatment can be either personal or people can see their group as the collective victim of unfair treatment. Feelings of group deprivation are more closely related to prejudice than are feelings of personal deprivation. Feelings of being more highly benefited than other groups can also cause prejudice: rather than feeling angry because the other group has deprived them of something, people derogate the other group to justify being better off. Feelings of relative deprivation can result in scapegoating: choosing a group to be the "designated villain" who caused the deprivation. Frustration-aggression-displacement theory explains scapegoating as a way of shifting blame for deprivation from one's own group to the designated group. Glick's (2002) ideological theory explains scapegoating as a way of fulfilling people's need to understand why the deprivation exists. Groups chosen as scapegoats tend to have little power, be salient to members of the ingroup, be disliked, be stereotyped in ways that make them believable as causes of the deprivation, and be seen as a threat to the ingroup.

Integrated threat theory brings realistic conflict theory, social identity theory, and relative deprivation theory together using the concept of threat. Perceptions of realistic threat can derive from intergroup conflict and feelings of group relative deprivation, and perceptions of symbolic threat can derive from social identity processes.

Hate groups are organizations whose central principles include hostility toward racial, ethnic, and religious minority groups. People attracted to hate groups tend to have negative racial attitudes, to be searching for solutions to problems and questions that have arisen in the person's life, to be young and rebellious, and to be attracted to violence. Contrary to the stereotype of hate group members, many are reasonably well-educated members of the middle class. Most hate group members are recruited by friends or relatives and undergo socialization processes that make their racial attitudes more extreme. Socialization tactics include education, isolation from opposing viewpoints, and participation in rituals. This process tends to reduce members' social networks to only other group members, provides them with a greater sense of social identity as White people, and leads them to see the world as dangerous and threatening. People who leave hate groups generally do so because they become disenchanted with the group's ideology and establish social ties outside the group that meet their psychological needs.

SUGGESTED READINGS

Realistic Conflict Theory

Duckitt, J. (1994). *The social psychology of prejudice.* Westport, CT: Praeger.
   Chapter 6 includes a complete description of Duckitt's extension of realistic conflict theory.

Sherif, M. (1966). *In common predicament: Social psychology of intergroup conflict and cooperation.* Boston: Houghton Mifflin.
   Sherif's book contains a detailed description of the Robbers Cave study and related research.

Taylor, D. M., & Moghaddam, F. M. (1994). *Theories of intergroup relations: International social psychological perspectives* (2nd ed.). Westport, CT: Praeger.
   Chapter 3 provides an overview of the current status of realistic conflict theory.

Social Identity Theory

Brewer, M. B. (1999). The psychology of prejudice: Ingroup love or outgroup hate? *Journal of Social Issues, 55,* 429–444.

In this article Brewer provides an excellent discussion of the distinction between ingroup favoritism and outgroup derogation.

Brewer, M. B., & Pickett, C. L. (1999). Distinctiveness motives as a source of the social self. In T. Tyler, R. Kramer, & O. John (Eds.), *The psychology of the social self* (pp. 71–87). Mahwah, NJ: Erlbaum.

This chapter provides a recent overview of optimal distinctiveness theory.

Brown, R. (2000). Social identity theory: Past achievements, current problems and future challenges. *European Journal of Social Psychology, 30,* 745–778.

Brown provides an overview of the current status of social identity theory.

Roccas, S., & Brewer, M. B. (2002). Social identity complexity. *Personality and Social Psychology Review, 6,* 88–106.

Roccas and Brewer discuss the implications of having a complex versus simple social identity.

Relative Deprivation Theory

Glick, P. (2002). Sacrificial lambs dressed in wolves' clothing: Envious prejudice, ideology, and the scapegoating of Jews. In L. S. Newman & R. Erber (Eds.), *Understanding genocide: The social psychology of the Holocaust* (pp. 113–142). New York: Oxford University Press.

Glick provides an excellent explanation of the psychological underpinnings of scapegoating.

Guimond, S., & Dambrun, M. (2002). When prosperity breeds intergroup hostility: The effects of relative deprivation and relative gratification on prejudice. *Personality and Social Psychology Bulletin, 28,* 900–912.

Guimond and Dambrun discuss the counterintuitive finding that relative gratification, as well as relative deprivation, can lead to prejudice.

Walker, I., & Smith, H. J. (2002). Fifty years of relative deprivation research. In I. Walker & H. J. Smith (Eds.), *Relative deprivation: Specification, development, and integration* (pp. 1–9). New York: Cambridge University Press.

This chapter provides a historical overview of relative deprivation theory. Other chapters in the book discuss the current status of theory, including its application to prejudice and discrimination.

Integrated Threat Theory

Stephan, W. G., & Stephan, C. W. (2000). An integrated threat theory of prejudice. In S. Oskamp (Ed.), *Reducing prejudice and discrimination* (pp. 23–46). Mahwah, NJ: Erlbaum.

This chapter provides a comprehensive overview of Stephan and Stephan's theory.

Hate Group Membership

Blee, K. M. (2002). *Inside organized racism: Women in the hate movement.* Berkeley: University of California Press.

Ezekiel, R. S. (1995). *The racist mind: Portraits of American neo-Nazis and Klansmen.* New York: Penguin.

Ezekiel, R. S. (2002). An ethnographer looks at neo-Nazi and Klan groups: *The Racist Mind* revisited. *American Behavioral Scientist, 46,* 51–71.

Blee and Ezekiel (1995) are excellent ethnographic studies of hate group members that provide a good "feel" for what the people are like. Ezekiel (2002) summarizes his 1995 findings and ties them in with more recent research.

KEY TERMS

chronic identities
cultural racism
distributive justice
everyday racism
extraordinary racism
false consciousness
group (or fraternal) relative
  deprivation
hate group
ingroup bias

minimal group paradigm
outgroup homogeneity effect
personal (or egoistic) relative
  deprivation
procedural justice
relative deprivation
relative gratification
scapegoating
self-stereotyping
social identity

QUESTIONS FOR REVIEW AND DISCUSSION

1. Describe the realistic conflict theory of prejudice.
2. Using Table 8.1 as a guide, describe how intergroup conflicts now taking place in various parts of the world fit Duckitt's model.
3. Describe the processes by which social identity can lead to prejudice on the one hand or to tolerance on the other hand. Illustrate your explanation with examples from your own experience.
4. Describe the factors that influence the degree of identification one feels with a group.
5. Explain the factors that influence self-categorization. In what ways is self-categorization similar to and different from the social categorization of others discussed in Chapter 4?
6. Explain optimal distinctiveness theory. What shortcomings of self-categorization theory does it address?
7. What are chronic social identities? Which of your social identities would you describe as chronic?
8. Explain the difference between ingroup favoritism and outgroup derogation. Why is this distinction important?
9. Describe the relative deprivation theory of prejudice.
10. How can feelings of relative gratification cause prejudice?
11. Think back to the theory of modern-symbolic prejudice described in Chapter 5. How are feelings of relative deprivation related to that form of prejudice?
12. What is scapegoating? Describe the frustration-aggression-displacement and ideological theories of scapegoating. What characteristics make a group vulnerable to scapegoating?

13. Describe some current examples of scapegoating. How well do the scapegoated groups fit the profile of vulnerability to scapegoating? Which theory better explains each example?
14. Explain how integrated threat theory links realistic conflict theory, social identity theory, and relative deprivation theory. How are these theories related to social dominance theory, described in Chapter 6?
15. What are hate groups? What psychological functions does hate group membership have?
16. How are hate group members recruited? What factors make a person vulnerable to recruitment by hate groups?
17. Describe the process of socializing a hate group member. What are the outcomes of the socialization process?
18. What factors motivate people to leave hate groups?
19. Describe how hate groups exploit the processes described earlier in the chapter (such as realistic group conflict, social identity, relative deprivation, and so forth) to recruit and socialize new members.

PREJUDICE BASED ON GENDER, SEXUAL ORIENTATION, AND AGE

We have stopped on this journey; when my father says to
we will go on, leaving this paradise, leaving
the family place. We have my father's job.
Like him, I will be strong all my life.
We are men. If we squint our eyes in the sun
we will see far. I'm ready. It's good, this resolve.

—Excerpts from A Farewell, Age 10, by William Stafford, 1998[*]

Female students feel that they have to conform to traditional ideals of femininity while also accomplishing the highest level of academic success. They need to be attractive, but not too attractive, smart, but not too smart. The ideals affect, among other things, how women dress, eat, study, date, and show initiative.

—Kate Dube, 2004, commenting on the expectation that Duke University women undergraduates achieve "effortless perfection" (p. 45)

The quotes at the beginning of this chapter, reprinted from two very different sources, share an important commonality: They both illustrate the prescriptive nature of gender stereotypes. Recall from Chapter 1 that stereotypes often have both a descriptive component (what is) and a prescriptive component (what should be). William Stafford's poem conveys a definite message about what the boy believes he should be like as a man; Kate Dube's quote focuses on what Duke University undergraduate women, and probably many other undergraduate women, believe is expected of them. In the United States and most other cultures, one need not look far to find communications that convey the prescriptive nature of gender stereotypes. If you doubt this, pick up a magazine or flip through the television channels to see how long it takes to find messages about the appropriate social roles for the sexes. Chances are it will not take long. Or, take a trip to the baby section of any department store; you will readily see that children's clothing is gender segregated and gender stereotypic. In North America, boys' clothing has trucks, tools, and balls whereas girls' clothing has dolls, hearts, and flowers—early life messages that tell children the kinds of people they "should" become.

The focus of the first section of this chapter is research documenting the content of those gender-associated messages and the consequences of adhering or refusing to adhere to them. Beliefs about what constitute appropriate roles for women and men also influence beliefs about sexual orientation. These beliefs result in a strong cultural bias toward *heterosexism,* or the ideological system that prescribes heterosexuality and denies, denigrates, and stigmatizes any nonheterosexual form of behavior, identity, relationship, or community (Herek, 1990). Research on the nature of this cultural bias and its relationship to anti-gay prejudice and discrimination also is summarized in the second part of this chapter. In the final section of this chapter, we explore another group for which there are strong prescriptive stereotypes—older adults. There are cultural expectations that aging involves both physical and mental decline and these expectations form the core of ageist beliefs (Hummert, 1999; Kite & Wagner, 2002). These beliefs, too, have consequences; our behavior toward older adults, for example, is affected by our expectations about what they should be like. Gender roles influence these expectations as well, although the relationship between gender and aging is not as well established as the relationship between gender and heterosexism.

GENDER-BASED STEREOTYPES, PREJUDICE, AND DISCRIMINATION

American culture, as do all cultures, has an established set of beliefs about men and women and the traits and roles they should possess and occupy (Deaux & LaFrance, 1998). Kay Deaux and Mary Kite (1987) describe these sets of beliefs as a *gender belief system* that includes both descriptive and prescriptive elements. These elements influence both people's self-concept and their perceptions of others. As with information about other social groups, the content of this belief system is conveyed through the media, and through parental and peer influence among other sources

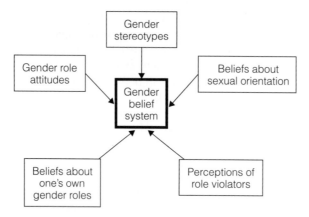

FIGURE **9.1**

THE GENDER BELIEF SYSTEM

This figure illustrates the components of the gender belief system including beliefs about gender roles, gender-associated stereotypes, attitudes toward women's and men's gender roles, and perceptions of those who violate those roles, including violations based on sexual orientation.

Source: Author.

(see Chapters 3 and 7). As we saw in previous chapters, learning about gender begins early in life and continues throughout the life span. The information contained in the gender belief system encompasses stereotype content, attitudes toward the appropriate roles for women and men, and perceptions of those who violate gender-based expectations (see Figure 9.1). We begin by summarizing research on gender stereotypes, which Kay Deaux and Marianne LaFrance (1998) argue is the most fundamental aspect of the gender belief system.

Gender Stereotypes

Early work exploring the content of gender stereotypes was conducted in the late 1960s and early 1970s by Paul Rosenkrantz, Inge Broverman, and their colleagues (Broverman, Vogel, Broverman, Clarkson, & Rosenkrantz, 1972; Rosenkrantz, Vogel, Bee, Broverman, & Broverman, 1968). These and many subsequent studies identified two constellations of traits, one associated with men and the other associated with women, which represent a core component of gender-based stereotypes (see Deaux & LaFrance, 1998, for a review). Stereotypes about men's traits are represented by a competence cluster that includes characteristics such as independent, strong, and self-confident. Researchers label this cluster *agentic* or *instrumental*. Stereotypes about women's traits are represented by a warmth-expressiveness cluster that includes characteristics such as emotional, helpful, and kind. Researchers label this cluster *communal* or *expressive*. Table 9.1 contains a list of the gender-associated characteristics contained in these clusters.

TABLE 9.1   **THE CONTENT OF GENDER STEREOTYPES**

	Beliefs about Women	Beliefs about Men
Traits	Able to devote self to others	Active
	Aware of others' feelings	Can make decisions easily
	Emotional	Competitive
	Helpful	Feels superior
	Gentle	Independent
	Kind	Never gives up easily
	Understanding	Self-confident
	Warm	Stands up well under pressure
Roles	Cooks the meals	Assumes financial obligations
	Does the household shopping	Head of household
	Does laundry	Financial provider
	Is fashion conscious	Leader
	Source of emotional support	Responsible for household repairs
	Takes care of children	Takes initiative in sexual relations
	Tends the house	Watches sports on television
Physical Characteristics	Beautiful	Athletic
	Cute	Brawny
	Dainty	Broad-shouldered
	Gorgeous	Burly
	Graceful	Muscular
	Petite	Physically strong
	Pretty	Physically vigorous
	Sexy	Rugged
	Soft voice	Tall
Cognitive Abilities	Artistic	Analytical
	Creative	Exact
	Expressive	Good at abstractions
	Imaginative	Good at numbers
	Intuitive	Good at problem solving
	Perceptive	Good with reasoning
	Tasteful	Mathematical
	Verbally skilled	Quantitatively skilled

Reprinted from: Kite, M. E. (2001). Gender stereotypes. In J. Worell (Ed.). *Encyclopedia of Women and Gender: Sex similarities and differences and the impact of society on gender* (Vol. 1, p. 563). New York: Academic Press.

The traits associated with women and men have been widely researched for many years; indeed countless studies have replicated the basic pattern described above. More recently, researchers have noted that gender-associated beliefs are multidimensional, encompassing ideas about women's and men's physical characteristics, roles, cognitive abilities, and emotions in addition to their traits (see Table 9.1). Men, for example, are assumed to be the head of the household and are believed to enjoy watching sports on television, whereas women are assumed to be fashion conscious and perceived as the caretakers of the house (Cejka & Eagly, 1999; Deaux & Lewis, 1984). Moreover, men are thought to be good at abstract thinking and problem solving whereas women are thought to be artistically and verbally skilled (Cejka & Eagly, 1999).

Women's and men's physical characteristics also figure prominently in people's gender belief system. Women are viewed as dainty and pretty for example, whereas men are viewed as muscular and rugged (Cejka & Eagly, 1999). Evidence suggests that women's and men's facial characteristics affect other gender-stereotypic beliefs. The male face is typically dominated by a prominent browridge and noseridge, a larger jaw, and thicker eyebrows—an overall more mature-looking face. The female face is more likely to have full cheeks, a small jaw, and large eyes—an overall more babyish appearance. Research on perceptions of these typical faces has revealed that men with the typical male face are believed to be more powerful, dominant, and shrewd and that women with the typical female face are believed to be weaker, submissive, and naive. Note that these assumptions map onto the personally traits generally associated with the sexes. When researchers created faces that softened the prominence of these gender-linked physical characteristics, the associated gender stereotypes also were eliminated (Friedman & Zebrowitz, 1992), suggesting that at least some of the traits associated with men and women come from differences in physical appearance.

Our gender belief system also encompasses ideas about the appropriate emotions for the sexes. Ashby Plant and her colleagues (Plant, Hyde, Keltner, & Devine, 2000) studied 19 emotions, including guilt, sadness, fear, and sympathy. Women were perceived as more likely than men to both experience and express the majority of those emotions; men were perceived as more likely to experience and express only anger and pride. Moreover, results of a second study by Plant and her colleagues (2000) showed that the actor's gender influenced interpretation of emotional displays. Men's expression of anger was interpreted as representing only anger, but the same expression by a woman was interpreted as a combination of anger and sadness, perhaps because it is less socially acceptable for women to show anger. Although both women and men are viewed unfavorably when their emotional responses to an event suggest an overreaction, these judgments are more severe when the emotional response was gender stereotypic. For example, Sarah Huston-Comeauz and Janice Kelly (2002) found that people viewed men more negatively when their overreaction was in response to an anger-arousing event but viewed women more negatively when their overreaction was in response to a happy event.

Some other dimensions of gender-stereotypic beliefs merit attention. First, people's beliefs reflect **gender polarization,** the assumption that gender-associated characteristics are bipolar (Bem, 1993); that is, people believe that what is masculine is not feminine and that what is feminine is not masculine. A corollary of this belief is that people expect a person who is masculine (or feminine) on one gender-stereotypic dimension to be masculine (or feminine) on other dimensions. People expect, for example, that a man who occupies a stereotypically masculine social role also will have stereotypically masculine physical characteristics and personality traits (Deaux & Lewis, 1984). Conversely, people do not expect a woman with stereotypically feminine physical characteristics to have stereotypically masculine personality traits. Second, as we discuss later in this chapter, gender polarized beliefs influence assumptions about an individual's sexual orientation. When asked to make a prediction about an individual's sexual orientation, people estimate that men who have feminine characteristics are likely to be gay and that women who have masculine characteristics are likely to be lesbian (Deaux & Lewis, 1984). However, people are more certain that men's femininity indicates a gay sexual orientation than they are that women's masculinity indicates a lesbian sexual orientation (McCreary, 1994). Finally, judgments about power and status are associated with gender stereotypes. High-status individuals are believed to have stereotypically male traits and low status individuals are believed to have stereotypically female traits (Conway, Mount, & Pizzamiglio, 1996). In general, the male gender role has higher power and status that the female gender role (Deaux & LaFrance, 1998).

How widespread are gender-stereotypic beliefs? Psychologists often are criticized for their reliance on college students as research participants and their failure to explore the beliefs and attitudes of other groups. However, research exploring the sexes' perceived agency and communion does not follow this pattern. Indeed, these beliefs have been examined in many groups and one of the remarkable aspects of this research is the similarity of the results across respondent age, geographic region, and, with some exceptions we discuss below, across time. Similar constellations of gender-associated traits, for example, have been found in a variety of populations, including not only college students, but also the general populations of the United States and of 30 other countries (J. Williams & Best, 1990). Moreover, research conducted in the 1990s found basically the same set of gender-associated traits as research published 20 years earlier (A. C. Harris, 1994; Lueptow, Garovich, & Lueptow, 1995). Gender-stereotypic traits, then, appear to have a remarkable universality and stability. Other gender-associated beliefs also have been replicated cross-culturally (see, for example, Glick et al., 2000).

Despite this consistency, a word of caution is in order. This research, although extensive, does have an important limitation; it is usually based on studies that, either implicitly or explicitly, assess the perceptions of middle class White women and men or, in the case of the cross-cultural studies, on the perceptions of the majority groups in the respective countries. Results of the few U.S. studies that have examined whether perceptions vary by social class or ethnicity suggest a complexity that remains poorly understood. When the ethnicity of the person being rated is taken into account, for example, free-response assessments show that White women and men are described differently than Black and Asian women and men (Niemann, Jennings, Rozelle, Baxter, & Sullivan, 1994). Hope Landrine (1985), for example, examined gender-associated stereotypes by race and social class. Her results showed that Black women are seen as less feminine than White women. And, although these characteristics are not gender associated, her results further showed that lower-class women were rated as more confused, dirty, hostile, inconsiderate, and irresponsible than middle-class women. These studies, although few in number, testify to the gaps in current understanding of how gender stereotypes are affected by knowledge of other social group member-ships. Correction of this limitation in future research is critical (Howard & Hollander, 1997). Similarly, researchers have relied heavily on the perceptions of White respondents and too little on the perceptions of people of color, a situation that also needs to be remedied. These criticisms apply equally to the research on anti-gay prejudice and ageism, described later in this chapter. As you read about the research described in this chapter, keep these shortcomings in mind.

Accuracy of gender-associated beliefs

How well do gender stereotypes map onto the actual characteristics of women and men? One way to answer this question is simply to see whether women and men possess the characteristics associated with their social group (see Chapter 3). The available research shows that, on average, stereotypic beliefs mirror the characteristics women and men use to describe their own traits—that is, men are more likely than women to describe themselves as independent and competitive and women are more likely than men to describe themselves as gentle and helpful (see Lippa, 2005, for a review). These findings suggest that, at the group level, people are reasonably accurate observers of women's and men's characteristics (see also Swim, 1994).

Yet this accuracy comes at a cost. The knowledge that gender stereotypes are generally accurate at the group level can easily lead to erroneous conclusions about *individual* women and men. Such inaccurate conclusions are often rooted in the belief that there is no overlap between the sexes in the distribution of gender-associated traits—for example, a belief that all women are kinder than all men. In fact, some men are higher in communion, or in female-associated traits, than are most women and some women are higher in agency, or male-associated traits, than are most men. Within each sex, then, there is considerable variability on these constellations of traits. Therefore, it may well be inaccurate to conclude that a particular man is agentic or that a particular woman is not. Another problem with making assumptions about what women and men *are* like is that it also sometimes moves gender-stereotypic beliefs from descriptive to prescriptive—that is, it leads to assumptions about what women and men *should be* like. When that happens, gender-based stereotyping and prejudice can result, perhaps especially toward those who do not fit with expectations. For example, the assumption that all men are assertive and that, therefore, every man should be assertive, could lead to negative perceptions of men who are not assertive.

Change over time

It is interesting to note that the degree of agency associated with women and men has changed over time, indicating the socially based

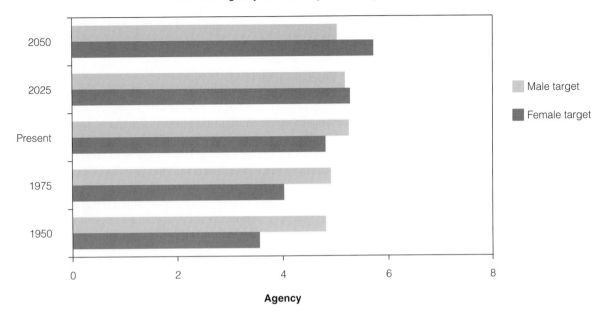

FIGURE **9.2**

PERCEIVED AGENCY OVER TIME BY SEX OF TARGET

People believe that women's and men's agency is more similar in the present than in the past; they also believe that in the future, women and men will become increasingly similar on this dimension.

(Adapted from Diekman, A. B. & Eagly, A. H. (2000). Stereotypes as dynamic constructs: Women and men of the past, present and future. *Personality and Social Psychology Bulletin, 15*, 543–558.)

nature of gender stereotypes (see Chapter 3). For example, Jean Twenge (1997a) found that today's women are significantly more likely to report having agentic characteristics compared to women of 20 years ago. However, over the same time period, women's self-endorsement of communal traits has not changed, nor has men's self-endorsement of either agentic or communal traits. (Which is not to say there will be no change on these characteristics during the next 20 years.) Interestingly, these changes have not gone unnoticed. When Amanda Diekman and Alice Eagly (2000) asked people to describe the gender-associated characteristics of women and men in the past (1950s), present, and future (2050), they found that, across all time periods, people believed women were more communal than men and that men were more agentic than women. However, mirroring Twenge's (1997a) findings about changes in self-perceptions over time, people believed that women's and men's agency is more similar today than in the past; this change is due to the perception that women today are more agentic than in the past, but that men's agency has not changed over time. They also predicted this pattern of change would continue into the future (see Figure 9.2). Men's and women's communion was predicted to be comparatively more stable over time. Stereotypic gender beliefs, then, reflect the dynamic changes women and men perceive in their own gender roles and that perception has led people to expect more change in the future.

Attitudes toward Women and Men

As you look at the list of gender-associated stereotypes in Table 9.1, you can read-ily see that the characteristics are, overall, quite positive. Do these generally posi-tive stereotypes relate to *liking* of women and men? Recall from Chapter 1 that stereotypes provide information about a group but do not necessarily represent the affect associated with that group; affect, you will recall, reflects the *evaluative* dimension of attitudes toward social groups. Based on the higher social status accorded to men (Conway et al., 1996), you might expect that men also would be liked better than women. However, research exploring the affect people associate with the social categories "women" and "men" actually shows a bias in favor of women, or what Alice Eagly and Antonio Mladinic (1994) have dubbed the *women are wonderful effect*. Their work shows that the global category "women" is viewed more positively than the global category "men" on traditional evaluative mea-sures. This finding has been widely replicated and is supported by earlier research on attitudes toward the sexes (see Eagly , Mladinic, & Otto, 1991, for a review), although, interestingly, the pattern went unnoticed for many years. This pattern also emerges in measures of implicit attitudes toward women and men. Laurie Rudman and Stephanie Goodwin (2004) found that positive words, such as good, happy, and paradise, are associated more often with women than with men, a pref-erence that was particularly strong for women participants.

As you might know from your own experiences, however, being liked does not automatically lead to being treated fairly. Gender-based prejudice is wide-spread and well documented and, more often than not, affects women more neg-atively than men. Consider, for example, the gender wage gap: in 2000, U.S. White women earned 72.2 percent of what White men earned. This gap was even larger for Black and Hispanic women, who that year earned 64.6 percent and 52.8 per-cent, respectively, of what White men earned (National Committee on Pay Equity, 2004). Moreover, such discrimination is not limited to the United States. Across the 15 member countries in the European Union, women earn 87 percent of what men earn (Broughton, 2002). Even larger wage gaps are present in Asian, Middle Eastern, and South American countries (Nierenberg, 2002). Box 9.1 describes a recent example—the pay equity dispute between two major corporations and their female employees.

Sometimes the discrimination women face is more subtle, as demonstrated by research on gender differences in the prices paid for new cars. Ian Ayres and Peter Siegelman (1995) had male and female Black and White research assistants visit new car dealers in the Chicago area and use identical negotiating strategies to determine a price for a new car. Even when these equivalent strategies were used, White females paid, on average $94 more for a car and Black females paid, on average, $411 more for a car than did White males. (This subtle discrimination

9.1   *"Rife with Discrimination"*

On June 22, 2004, federal judge Martin Jenkins certified a lawsuit by six current and former Wal-Mart employees as a class action affecting more than 1.6 million women who have worked at Wal-Mart stores since December 1998. With this ruling, the case became the largest work-place-bias lawsuit in the United States (Green-house & Hays, 2004). What is this dispute about? According to Brad Seligman, a lawyer for the plaintiffs, "Wal-Mart is rife with discrim-ination" (Armour, 2004, p. B3). The complaint alleges that although the hourly sales workforce at Wal-Mart is predominantly female, men are disproportionately assigned to some depart-ments such as hardware, electronics, and sport-ing goods, areas that offer better pay and greater chance for advancement. And, although women are the majority of employees at the lower ranks, they comprise less than 10 percent of all store managers and approximately 4 per-cent of district managers—numbers substan-tially lower than found in Wal-Mart's top competitors. Moreover, according to the plain-tiffs' lawyers, women store managers earned an average of $89,280 in 2001, compared to male store managers' earnings of $105,682; at the district manager level, the gap was even wider ($239,519 for men versus $177,149 for women).

The effects of this alleged discrimination are more vividly illustrated in the plaintiff's personal stories. Plaintiff Melissa Howard was expected to attend monthly sales meetings at a Hooters restaurant and was pressured to enter a strip club on a business trip. When Stephanie Odle complained that a less experienced male manager was earning $20,000 more than she, she was told the man was a single father with children to support; Kim McLamb received a similar reply when she questioned women's lower salaries (Armour, 2004). Angela Horton believes her career was damaged by subtle sexism, but was reluctant to complain after hearing managers refer to other women com-plainants as "whiners" (Cummins, 2004).

That the case will be heard as a class-action suit does not mean, however, that Wal-Mart is guilty; such a determination depends on the outcome of the upcoming trial. Yet echoes of this case can be seen in the recently settled case against Morgan Stanley, brought by the U.S. Equal Employment Opportunity Commission. The lead plaintiff for this case, Allison Schieffe-lin, claimed she was denied a promotion even though less qualified men were granted one, and that her complaint about this situation led to her firing (Ackman, 2004). News reports suggest the settlement was reached, at least in part, to avoid testimony from witnesses who claimed they were groped sexually and were the recipients of lewd comments. Moreover, witnesses claimed clients were taken to men-only strip club outings (McClam, 2004). For now, both cases are mak-ing headlines and, in the Wal-Mart case, some analysts predict the backlash may be "felt across the workplace landscape" (Arisa Lieberwitz, quoted in Joyce, 2004, p. 1) as other companies consider their policies and practices and other women weigh their own situations.

especially affected Black males who paid, on average, $1,100 more for a car than White males.) Other examples of less obvious discrimination against women are discussed later in this chapter and in Chapter 10.

What explains the paradox between the generally positive view of women and the overwhelming evidence that gender-based discrimination exists? To begin our explanation of this *discrimination-affection paradox* (Eckes, 2002), we must first distinguish between women as a social group and women as occupants of social roles. As we saw above, affective responses to the social group "women" are generally positive. Yet much of the work on attitudes toward women does not focus on this larger social group but, instead, examines attitudes toward women in particular social roles and, in particular, women who occupy nontraditional roles.

Subtypes of Women and Men

Women and men work and play together frequently and in a variety of contexts and, often, our closest and most intimate relationships are with members of the other sex. Because of this, having and using detailed information about the other sex plays an important role in our navigation of the social world (see Chapter 4). As we discussed in Chapter 3, one strategy people use to handle such complex information is to create **subtypes,** or categories that are subordinate to the more basic categories of sex, race, and age. Abundant evidence shows this to be a common practice for gender-related categorization. Indeed, over 200 gender-associated subtypes have been identified (Vonk & Ashmore, 2003; see also Deaux, Winton, Crowley, & Lewis, 1985; Eckes, 1994). Research further shows, however, that these many subtypes can be grouped into major categories such as occupations (career woman, secretary), family roles (housewife, family man), ideologies (bourgeois, feminist), physical features (athletic woman, athletic man), and sexuality-related subtypes (sexy woman, macho man; Carpenter & Trentman, 1998). Roos Vonk and Richard Ashmore (2003) explored how subtypes were categorized by examining the perceived similarities and differences among them. Results suggested that people first categorized the subtypes by their gender (that is, they created separate groups for male and female subtypes); this was evidenced by the presence of a strong masculine and feminine dimension that distinguished the subtypes. People also categorized the subtypes as traditional (for example, housewives and family men) or modern (for example, businesswomen and eternal bachelors). Finally, people divided gender-based subtypes by age, with younger subtypes including "adolescent" and "prissy girl" and older subtypes including "granddad" and "old maid."

As Vonk and Ashmore's (2003) analysis suggests, the characteristics people associate with male and female subtypes vary; research shows that evaluations of the subtypes also vary. Subtypes defined as traditional are preferred to subtypes defined as modern (Haddock & Zanna, 1994; Kite & Branscombe, 1998). Subtypes reflecting sexuality (macho men and sexy women) also receive relatively low evaluations (Kite & Branscombe, 1998). Research examining the sometimes puzzling response to the nontraditional category "feminist" is presented in Box 9.2. Susan Fiske and her colleagues (Fiske, Xu, Cuddy, & Glick, 1999) have suggested

9.2   *What Is Feminism, Anyway?*

"Feminism is the radical notion that women are people" reads a button available from the National Organization of Women (NOW, http://www.now.org, 2004). This idea has been promoted by women's movements since the work of Elizabeth Cady Stanton, Susan B. Anthony, and their colleagues finally resulted in the ratification of the 19th amendment, giving women the right to vote. Rush Limbaugh (2004), in contrast, refers to "feminazis" (with Hillary Rodham Clinton as the representative example) and contends that feminists wrongly encourage women to have a career and, in the process, give up traditional roles that are actually more important to them.

Research on stereotypic perceptions of feminists reveals evidence of both viewpoints. On the one hand, Jean Twenge and Alyssa Zucker (1999) found that feminists are seen as serious, intelligent, knowledgeable, productive, and modern; on the other hand, they were rated as stubborn, angry, and nontraditional. Moreover, feminists were believed to be assertive and career oriented, opinionated, active, and outspoken, with left-leaning political beliefs, but not "anti-male." Interestingly, feminists were thought to be only somewhat more likely to be female than male and the stereotype that "feminists are lesbians" was not supported by the data. Even so, Twenge and Zucker found their respondents were generally reluctant to identify as "feminist" (25 percent reported being somewhat or definitely feminist). Moreover, when asked to write a story about a female or male feminist, a sizable number (36 percent) included negative statements. Some statements about the female feminist were extremely negative ("she probably worships Satan" or she "decided to stop caring for her feminine hygiene") as were statements

about the male feminist (suggesting he was a cross-dresser or had denounced his manhood).

As the authors note, these perceptions may prevent even those who hold feminists beliefs from adopting that label. Research supports this claim, showing that self-identified feminists responded more favorably to a feminist message when it was presented by a feminine-looking, rather than a masculine-looking speaker (Bullock & Fernald, 2003; responses of nonfeminists were not affected by speaker appearance). Similarly, Kate Dube's (2004) less formal survey of her students' attitudes toward feminists showed that women who answered "no" to the question "Are you a feminist?" often followed that response by "but," as in "but I believe in women's rights." Interestingly, research suggests that the title "Ms."—introduced in the 1960s as a courtesy title for women that did not indicate martial status—is now evaluated more positively than in the past; evaluation of this title is similar to that of other women's courtesy titles, such as Mrs. and Miss (Crawford, Stark, & Renner, 1998). Even so, Carol Lawton and her colleagues (Lawton, Blakemore, & Vartanian, 2003) found that people (and especially younger people) associate the title "Ms." with unmarried women, and particularly those who are too old to use the title "Miss." This finding suggests that the title is no longer clearly associated with a neutral marital status. As Mary Crawford and her colleagues (1998) note, it is possible that "Ms." has lost its association with feminism and, for that reason, is viewed more positively by today's college students. Whether the title "feminist" loses or gains status over time remains to be seen, but for now, it seems, both the Rush Limbaugh and the NOW perspective are represented in people's perceptions.

that, when evaluating others, people appear to distinguish between *liking* and *respect* and make relatively independent judgments on these two dimensions. That is, people may like housewives, but not respect them and, conversely, may respect successful businessmen, but not like them. Notice that the *liking* dimension is related to the communal stereotype associated with women (e.g., warmth and kindness) whereas the *respect* dimension is reflected in the agentic stereotype associated with men (e.g., independent, self-confident). Supporting the idea that people distinguish between these dimensions, Thomas Eckes (2002) found that subtypes such as "housewife" and "senior citizen" were rated high on warmth but rated low on competence, but the reverse held for subtypes such as "feminist" and "manager" (see also Fiske et al., 1999). Moreover, subtypes rated as high on competence were viewed as having higher status than those low on competence whereas subtypes rated as high on warmth were perceived as being more cooperative than those rated low on warmth (Eckes, 2002). One answer to the question of whether women and men are liked, then, depends on the roles occupied by the person being evaluated. People who fill roles requiring male-associated characteristics, such as competence, are not necessarily liked and people who fill roles requiring the female-associated characteristics, such as warmth, are not necessarily respected.

Attitudes toward women's rights and responsibilities   As we have seen, attitudes toward the social category "woman" are positive, but attitudes toward particular subtypes of women may or may not be positive. Some of the most disliked subtypes represent women in nontraditional roles. Research also has focused specifically on attitudes toward those nontraditional roles. One of the instruments most commonly used to assess these attitudes is the Attitudes toward Women Scale (AWS; Spence & Helmreich, 1972); this instrument and others like it focus on explicit beliefs about women's rights and responsibilities. Sample items from the AWS are presented in Table 9.2. Individuals agreeing with these and similar items are labeled traditional in their gender role attitudes; those disagreeing are labeled nontraditional. These measures assess blatant prejudice toward women's rights and responsibilities (see Chapter 5).

Early research using measures such as the AWS showed that a significant proportion of the population expressed negative attitudes toward nontraditional women's roles (Spence & Hahn, 1997; Spence & Helmreich, 1972). However, this research also showed that women typically held more egalitarian views, overall, than did men (Twenge, 1997b). In recent years, however, this distribution has changed; researchers now generally find both women and men reporting greater acceptance of women's rights and responsibilities on these types of instruments (Spence & Hahn, 1997; Twenge, 1997b). As we saw in Chapter 5, these findings suggest that people today are less likely to directly express blatant prejudice than they were in the past.

Yet, as we also saw in Chapter 5, this does not mean that gender-based prejudice has disappeared. Research using measures of subtle sexism, such as the Modern Sexism Scale (Swim, Aikin, Hall, & Hunter, 1995), the Neosexism Scale (Tougas, Brown, Beaton, & Joly, 1995) and the Ambivalent Sexism Inventory (Glick & Fiske, 1996, 1997) shows that gender-based prejudice today is expressed

TABLE 9.2   SAMPLE ITEMS FROM MEASURES OF ATTITUDES TOWARD WOMEN AND MEN

Attitudes toward Women Scale (AWS; Spence & Helmreich, 1972)

Women should worry less about their rights and more about becoming good wives and mothers.

The intellectual leadership of a community should be largely in the hands of men.

In general, the father should have greater authority than the mother in the bringing up of children.

Modern Sexism Scale (Swim, Aiken, Hall, & Hunter, 1995)

Discrimination against women is no longer a problem in the United States.

It is rare to see women treated in a sexist manner on television.

Women often miss out on good jobs due to sexual discrimination.

Neosexism Scale (Tougas, Brown, Beaton, & Joly, 1995)

Women's requests in terms of equality between the sexes are simply exaggerated.

Women shouldn't push themselves where they are not wanted.

Over the past few years, women have gotten more from the government than they deserve.

Ambivalent Sexism Inventory (Glick & Fiske, 1996)

Benevolent Sexism

Many women have a quality of purity that few men possess.

Every man ought to have a woman whom he adores.

A good woman should be set on a pedestal by her man.

Hostile Sexism

Once a woman gets a man to commit to her, she usually tries to put him on a tight leash.

Many women are actually seeking special favors, such as hiring policies that favor them over men, under the guise of asking for "equality."

Women are too easily offended.

Ambivalence toward Men Inventory (Glick & Fiske, 1999)

Benevolence toward Men

Even if both work, woman should take care of man at home.

Men are more willing to risk self to protect others.

Women are incomplete without men.

Hostility toward Men

Most men are really like children.

Even sensitive men want traditional relationships.

When men "help" women it is to prove they are better.

in less direct ways. Items from these measures are presented in Table 9.2. Modern sexists, for example, believe that gender-based job segregation can be explained by biological differences between the sexes, and they are less likely to believe this segregation is due to discrimination against women (Swim et al., 1995). Modern sexists also hold negative attitudes toward feminism and the women's movement

(Campbell, Schellenberg, & Senn, 1997). Finally, modern sexists believe that is it important to stay the course and maintain current gender roles, and so do not support policies such as affirmative action that might reduce gender inequality (Tougas et al. 1995). As we saw with traditional gender role attitudes, modern sexist beliefs often are directed toward women in nontraditional roles.

Hostile and benevolent sexism   Peter Glick and Susan Fiske (1996, 1997) have proposed there are actually two separate, but related, dimensions of modern sexism: hostile and benevolent sexist beliefs. Hostile sexist beliefs are derogatory, such as the beliefs that women demand special privileges and want to control men through marriage and their sexual wiles. Benevolent sexist beliefs are more positive, such as the beliefs that women are more nuturant and morally pure than men and deserve adoration. It is both possible and common for people to hold both sets of beliefs, even though doing so means holding two contradictory attitudes toward women at the same time. The ambivalence this creates can result in oscillation between these two attitudes, such as loving and hating women at the same time (Glick & Fiske, 2001a). This ambivalence, which is an important component of Ambivalent Sexism Theory, provides another possible explanation for the affect-discrimination paradox.

Benevolent sexist beliefs result in the *women are wonderful effect* described earlier—the affection part of the paradox. Those holding these beliefs view women who occupy traditional roles, such as homemaker and mother, in positive terms. Because these roles are those associated with the general social category "women" (Eagly, 1987; Glick & Fiske, 2001a), such benevolent sexist beliefs lead to women in general being seen in positive terms. Thus, women (or at least traditional women) are wonderful because of their nurturance and purity. From the viewpoint of the benevolent sexist, keeping women in these traditional roles shields them from the stress of high status roles, such as those traditionally occupied by men; to benevolent sexists, this shielding is a form of chivalry and male self-sacrifice. However, in doing so, they also are discriminating against women by excluding them from roles that afford more prestige in society. As a result, women are the targets of discrimination (by being locked into a limited set of social roles) at the same time that they are the recipients of liking and admiration. This combination of affect and discrimination, then, also serves as justification for men's greater power and privilege (see Chapter 1 and Glick & Fiske, 2001a; Glick et al., 2000). Men have to take on the "tough jobs" from which women must be protected.

What about women who embrace nontraditional roles? Attitudes toward these women account for the discrimination part of the paradox, and it is here that hostile sexist beliefs become important. People endorsing hostile sexist beliefs view some women, such as those who occupy nontraditional roles, as a direct threat to male status and power and they dislike those women because of it. According to Glick and Fiske (2001a) it is the coupling of negative reactions toward nontraditional women (hostile sexist beliefs) with positive reactions toward traditional women (benevolent sexist beliefs) that helps maintain the status quo. That is, these reactions produce the dual strategies of rewarding "appropriate" behavior and punishing "inappropriate" behavior. As these authors put it, under this arrangement "women receive special privileges, as long as they stay in line" (Fiske et al., 1999, p. 484). Staying in line means maintaining prescribed gender roles, not competing with men in their traditional gender role domain, and seeking intimacy through heterosexual interactions. Interestingly, across 19 countries, both men's benevolent and men's hostile sexist beliefs were negatively correlated with measures of gender equality in that society (Glick et al., 2000). For example, the higher men's benevolent sexism scores in a country were, the less likely it was that the women in that country were represented in high-status jobs in business and government. These results are correlational and do not demonstrate that men's sexism *causes* gender inequality. Even so, these results suggest that individually held beliefs do relate to women's welfare at the national level.

Men's gender roles   The common thread running though all the research on gender role attitudes is that societal beliefs strain and constrain both women and men. Theories of modern sexism, for example, such as Ambivalent Sexism Theory (Glick & Fiske, 1997, 2001a), point to the importance of societal roles in understanding prejudice and discrimination against women, a topic we turn to shortly. But before doing so we want to point out that men's gender roles and people's attitudes toward them also can be limiting. Research supports the existence of a masculine ideology that stems from cultural constraints on the male gender role. As we saw in the poem that opened this chapter, men are expected to be strong and in control. Boys and men are discouraged from exhibiting feminine characteristics, but are encouraged to exhibit an aura of toughness and violence. Indeed, people see men as threatening and intimidating and this association may be related to their general preference for women (Rudman & Goodwin, 2004). Moreover, men are expected to strive for power and success and to stand on their own two feet (Fischer & Good, 1998; Fischer, Tokar, Good, & Snell, 1998). Evidence suggests that the strain of trying to meet these expectations can have a variety of negative consequences for some men, including low self-esteem, increased probability of drug use and suspension from school, and other unhealthy behaviors (Pleck, Sonenstein, & Ku, 1993). And, as we will see later in this chapter, acceptance of the traditional male gender role is also strongly associated with anti-gay prejudice (Pleck, Sonenstein, & Ku, 1994). Interestingly, recent research suggests that, like attitudes toward women, attitudes toward men can have both benevolent and hostile components (see Table 9.2 for example items from a measure of these attitudes). Benevolent sexist attitudes toward men reflect the belief that men must be protected and nurtured whereas hostile sexist attitudes toward men reflect a resentment of their higher status and power (Glick & Fiske, 1999).

Face-Ism

Sexism can exist right under our eyes, but is often out of our awareness. Imagine, for example, two separate billboards, one depicting a male and the other a female model. What is the focus of each billboard? Would you be surprised if, for the man, the face was more prominent than for the woman? According to Dane Archer and his colleagues (Archer, Iritani, Kimes, & Barrios, 1983), you should not be. Moreover, these authors believe that "[i]f media depiction of men and women differ in terms of facial prominence, these differences may (wittingly or not) communicate something important about the relative importance for each sex of the mind and body. Because the face and head are the centers of mental life—intellect, personality, identity, and character—the relative prominence of this part of the anatomy may be symbolically consequential" (p. 72). By making the male face prominent, they argue, the conveyed message is that men's essence resides in the head and face more so than does women's. Women's essence, in contrast, is conveyed by the more frequent depiction of her body.

Archer and colleagues (1983) tested these ideas by comparing the relative size of male and female faces in a variety of photographs and drawings, a measure they refer to as *face-ism*. For example, the researchers coded 1,750 published photographs in five prominent U.S. magazines. Results showed a strong tendency for men to be represented by their faces and for women to be represented by their bodies. A second study replicated this pattern for major periodicals from 12 societies within Europe, the Far East, Africa, and South America. Yet another study found similar results in a study of artwork produced between the 15th and the 20th centuries. Finally, the same pattern emerged when undergraduates drew a woman or a man on a blank piece of paper. These artists were more likely to fill in men's facial features, but to omit this detail in drawings of women. Does face-ism affect person perception? Evaluation data suggest it does; Archer and his colleagues (1993) found that respondents saw high prominence faces as more intelligent and ambitious than low prominence faces.

The results of these studies are striking for a number of reasons. First, the authors replicated their basic findings across medium, culture, and time. Second, the creators of the photographs and artwork could not have known their work would be part of a research project, so this could not have affected the images they produced. And it is unlikely that the students asked to draw women and men could have guessed the experimenter's purpose. These differential portrayals, then, are part of everyday life. And, chances are, unless you had read about this research previously, you were unaware of them. Does that mean that these depictions do not affect perceptions of women and men and their appropriate roles? You decide.

Women in Leadership Roles

A Dilbert cartoon depicts a female supervisor asking a male subordinate to kill a mouse in her office. He remarks that after 20 years of the women's movement, nothing has changed—to which she responds that if he does not remove the mouse, he is fired. He concedes that *that* part *has* changed. This interaction reflects a fundamental conflict. Women's roles have changed and there are many models of successful women in all arenas. Even so, expectations about what women are like have not kept pace with women's changing roles. Women in non-traditional roles are still expected to behave like women. In this section, we address how this conflict affects women's advancement.

To begin our discussion, we focus first on some basic statistics about women in the workforce and at the entry point to high level jobs: higher education. Although room for improvement remains, women are present in increasing numbers in higher education and in the workplace. Today, the majority of U.S. undergraduates are women (U. S. Department of Education, 2003) and these women are more likely to earn a baccalaureate degree and a graduate degree than are men (National Opinion Research Center, 2003; Syverson, 2003). In the United States, 47 percent of all workers are women (U.S. Bureau of Labor Statistics, 2002a), and women are achieving ever higher levels in the workplace; 51 percent of people with executive, administrative, and managerial positions are women, up from 41 percent in 1983 (U.S. Bureau of Labor Statistics, 2002b). The numbers, then, are changing and women's presence is being felt.

Even so, many jobs remain gender segregated. Occupations such as secretary, speech therapist, and elementary school teacher are predominated by women whereas occupations such as engineer, dentist, and physician are predominated by men (see Matlin, 2004). For women, this job segregation often leads to a *sticky floor* because many of the traditionally female occupations do not offer avenues for promotion or advancement and, as such, are dead-end jobs (Gutek, 2001). At the highest professional levels, White men are, without question, dominant. As of the mid-1990s, men comprised 85 percent of tenured professors, 89 percent of the membership in the U.S. House of Representatives, 90 percent of the U.S. Senate, 95 percent of *Fortune 500* corporate executive officers, and 99.9 percent of athletic team owners (see Fassinger, 2001). These numbers support the claim that even women who gain entry into professional jobs often reach what is known as the *glass ceiling*, an invisible barrier that prevents women (and minorities) from reaching the highest levels of an organization (Gutek, 2001; Thomas 2005). Evidence suggests that men have an advantage even in careers where women outnumber them. These men often ride what is known as the *glass escalator.* That is, men who work in female dominated professions enjoy a fast track to management positions. Research shows that the higher the percentage of women in a profession, the more likely it is that men will be promoted. Women, in contrast, are *less* likely to be promoted in female-dominated professions than they are in male-dominated professions (Maume, 1999).

Role congruity theory

What are the factors that prohibit women's entry into professional positions and further limit the success of those women who do gain entry? Alice Eagly and Steven Karau (2002) have proposed that two types of prejudice prevent women from pursuing high level positions or succeeding when they do obtain such positions. Their theory focuses on women leaders, but their predictions can be generalized to other high achievement settings. According to their role congruity theory, one form of prejudice stems from the belief that women are less likely than men to be successful in a leadership role. This belief can prevent women from seeking high level jobs and from being selected for them when they do seek them. Where does this belief come from? Recall from Chapter 3 that people observe women and men in their social roles and, from these observations, draw conclusions about the characteristics the sexes have. This prediction, based on social role theory (Eagly, 1987), explains why men are perceived to be agentic. Specifically, men, more than women, tend to be observed in the higher status, breadwinner role, which requires those characteristics. From the observation of men in those roles, people conclude that men have the agentic attributes associated with that role. Women, in contrast, tend to be observed in lower-status roles that require communal attributes; people, then, conclude that women are communal. Because people observe that the leadership role requires agentic traits and is typically occupied by men, they conclude men are best suited to be leaders.

Research shows this theory can account for who is selected to be a leader. Alice Eagly and Steven Karau (1991), for example, reviewed 58 studies on leader emergence and found that, consistent with role congruity theory, men were consistently more likely to emerge as leaders than were women. Research also shows that who emerges as a leader depends on both the leaders' characteristics and the task at hand. Barbara Ritter and Jan Yoder (2004) paired individuals high and low in dominance and assigned them to work on identifying the steps involved in either a masculine task (playing a football game), a feminine task (planning a wedding), or a gender-neutral task (planting a garden). Some dyads were same sex (that is, two men or two women); others were mixed sex (one man and one woman). In the same-sex dyads, for whom gender-based expectations did not matter, the dominant individual consistently emerged as the leader, regardless of the task. In mixed-sex dyads, however, the man more often emerged as the leader when the task was masculine or gender neutral, regardless of his dominance level. Often, this happened because the dominant woman actually appointed the low dominance man to be leader. As Ritter and Yoder note, even when women are better equipped to serve as leader, they acquiesce to the man when the task is masculine (that is, gender role incongruent for them). Only when the woman was dominant and the task was feminine (gender role congruent) was she more likely to emerge as leader in mixed-sex dyads.

What happens when women overcome this first form of prejudice and assume a leadership role? Role congruity theory (Eagly & Karau, 2002) predicts that the second form of prejudice now comes into play. According to this theory, these women face a higher probability of negative evaluations than do men in a similar role. This is because those women leaders occupy a role that violates expectations in two ways. First, it violates the expectation about what leaders should be like (high status males). Second, it violates expectations of what women should be like (communal; recall that the leadership role requires agentic traits). For women leaders, these expectations are at odds, but for male leaders, they are not because the role of male and leader are thought to overlap.

Women in faculty roles   Consider the experiences of female faculty members at a college or university. As with many other types of women professionals, these women face a double bind because the stereotypic perception of a faculty member is similar to the male gender role—faculty are expected to be directive, assertive, and knowledgeable, for example—but dissimilar to the female gender role requiring nurturance, warmth, and supportiveness (Caplan, 1994). The effects of this double bind emerge in a number of ways. One consequence is that women are sometimes held to a different standard than are men. Women who choose a less-structured classroom style, for example, report more negative student reactions than do men who choose a similar classroom style (Statham, Richardson, & Cook, 1991). And, to receive high ratings, women are expected to interact socially with students outside of class, yet men are not expected to do so (Kierstead, D'Agostino, & Dill, 1988). Student evaluations of teaching also have been shown to be gender biased, particularly for women in traditionally male-dominated fields such as chemistry (Basow, 1995; Basow & Silberg, 1987). And, women and men students may have opposing expectations that put women faculty in an unresolvable bind. One study found that female students preferred women who used an affiliative lecture style that encouraged discussion and interaction but that male students preferred women who used an instrumental lecture style that focused on providing information; ratings of male faculty were not influenced by their lecture style (Winocur, Schoen, & Sirowatka, 1989). These outcomes are consistent with role congruity theory. Women faculty are believed to have characteristics that are at odds with the professor role and this perceived role conflict leads to different expectations about and negative evaluations of their performance.

Although women can and do successfully meet the demands of the leadership role (Heilman, Block, & Martell, 1995), resolving this double bind is not easy. As the studies above suggest, being perceived as similar to a male colleague can actually work to a woman's disadvantage because, by doing so, she violates the expectations of her own gender role. This can lead to unfavorable evaluations, even for successful women, as Madeline Heilman and her colleagues (Heilman, Wallen, Fuchs, & Tamkins, 2004) showed. These researchers had students review the educational history and career trajectory of two hypothetical employees, one male and one female. When that performance was ambiguous, the male employee was rated as more competent than was the female employee, but both were seen as likeable. And, the successful man was liked *and* seen as competent. The successful woman, however, earned high marks for competence but lost out in pleasantness. Characteristics associated with these women included selfish, manipulative, and untrustworthy. Consistent with role congruity theory, a second study showed these effects were limited to employment areas that are typically male dominated. Negative labeling of competent women is not uncommon. Eagly and Karau (2002) cite several examples of nicknames applied to some very successful women, including the labeling of the former British Prime Minister Margaret Thatcher as "Iron Lady" and the more general tendency to refer to powerful women by terms such as "dragon lady" and "battle ax."

Factors that improve women's chances for success   Although research shows that women face prejudice when entering and filling leadership roles, a number of factors improve their chances for success (see Eagly and Karau, 2002, for a review). One factor is that not all leadership roles are perceived as equally masculine. Some, for example, require skills that are associated with women, such as cooperation and affiliation. Accordingly, Eagly and Karau (2002) propose that when roles are less masculine, the tendency to view women as less qualified should disappear or weaken. Teaching evaluations for women English professors, for example, are less likely to be gender biased than are teaching evaluations for women chemistry professors (Basow, 1995; Basow & Silberg, 1987), perhaps because people see less incongruity between "English professor" and "woman" than between "chemistry professor" and "woman." Moreover, not everyone exhibits gender bias to the same extent. Evaluator sex, for example, may also influence perceptions; supporting this idea, research shows that women generally give higher ratings to female professors than do men (Basow, 1995). Similarly, women tend to have less gender-stereotypic views of managerial roles and, therefore, may be less biased toward women leaders than men are (Eagly & Karau, 2002). How much the leader, herself, deviates from her prescribed gender role might also affect how she is perceived. Women who behave in particularly assertive, directive, or self-promoting ways violate traditional gender roles more clearly than women who bring a more communal approach to their leadership style. Supporting this premise, a review of the literature found that, across 61 studies, women who had a particularly autocratic leadership style were evaluated more harshly than males using a similar style (Eagly, Makhijani, & Klonsky, 1992). Those who merge the agentic and communal role may be viewed more favorably (Eagly & Karau, 2002).

This is not to say that only women who occupy nontraditional roles experience discrimination. To bring us back full circle to the beginning of this chapter, evidence of gender-stereotypic beliefs and gender-based prejudice abound. We now turn to a discussion of how gender-associated beliefs result in anti-gay prejudice.

HETEROSEXISM AND ANTI-GAY PREJUDICE

"If they don't have the guts, I call them girlie men."

—California Governor Arnold Schwarzenegger, July 19, 2004

Regardless of what you know about the events leading up to this quote, which happened to be a battle over the California budget, Governor Schwarzenegger's message is clear. Men without courage are feminine and that is not a good thing. As we discussed earlier in this chapter, men are expected to be masculine, strong, and tough (Fisher et al., 1998). Children learn the importance of conforming to these expectations at an early age and there are many messengers, including parents, teachers, peers, and the media. Boys, especially, are given this message early and often. Even very young children make it clear to boys that feminine behavior is unacceptable (Fagot, 1985). The more feminine a boy is perceived to be, the more unpopular he is expected to be; these predictions are especially strong when made by other boys (Berndt & Heller, 1986; Zucker, Wilson-Smith, Kurita, & Stern, 1995). People also expect that boys' femininity is permanent (Martin, 1990). When girls behave like tomboys, in contrast, it is likely to be ignored (Fagot, 1985), perhaps because people assume they will outgrow their boyish behavior (Martin, 1990). People have similar reactions to adults; faults associated with feminine men include poor career adjustment, emotional difficulty, including psychiatric problems, and both relationship and sexual problems. In contrast, masculine women are seen as generally well adjusted (Tilby & Kalin, 1980).

Stereotypes of Lesbians and Gay Men

These gender-role expectations are echoed in stereotypes about gay men and lesbians. When people are asked to list characteristics associated with gay men, for example, the most frequently noted characteristics are feminine, has feminine qualities, high-pitched voice, and feminine walk, mannerisms, or clothing (Kite & Deaux, 1987). Lesbians are most frequently described as masculine, with short hair, a masculine appearance, and masculine clothing (Eliason, Donelan, & Randall, 1992; Kite & Deaux, 1987). A similar pattern emerges when people evaluate gays and lesbians on specific gender-associated characteristics such as those listed in Table 9.1 Gay men are rated as more similar to heterosexual females than to heterosexual males, especially on the components reflecting physical characteristics and social roles. Lesbians, too, are seen as more similar to heterosexual men than to heterosexual women on these gender-associated components (Kite & Deaux, 1987; Weakland & Kite, 1999). People also believe that lesbian couples have one masculine person who fulfills the dominant role and one feminine person who fulfills the submissive role (Corley & Pollack, 1996). Apparently, even in relationships involving two women, people expect the traditional heterosexual gender roles to be present.

Although both lesbians and gay men are presumed to have the gender-associated characteristics of the other sex, evidence also suggests that the relationship is stronger for gay men than for lesbians. To account for this difference, Donald McCreary (1994) has proposed the **sexual orientation hypothesis**—the prediction that people are more likely to believe feminine men are gay than to believe that masculine women are lesbian. Results of several studies support this hypothesis. First, as we noted above, people presume that men with feminine characteristics are gay and, although they also predict that masculine women are lesbian, their estimates of this likelihood are not as high (Deaux & Lewis, 1984; Martin, 1990; McCreary, 1994). Men's use of feminine language is seen as an indication of a homosexual orientation, but women's use of masculine language is not seen as evidence of lesbianism (Rasmussen & Moely, 1986). Finally, the belief that lesbian women are similar to heterosexual men is not as firmly held as the belief that gay men are similar to heterosexual women (Kite & Deaux, 1987). We return to this discrepancy when we discuss sex differences in anti-gay prejudice.

More generally, gays and lesbians are stereotypically perceived as "different." As Greg Herek (2003) states, "*homosexual* has been defined as a counterpart to the *normal person*" (p. 277, italics in original). It was not so long ago that homosexuality was classified as a mental illness; this designation was removed from the *Diagnostic and Statistical Manual* of the American Psychiatric Association in 1973 (see Bayer, 1987). A significant portion of the U.S. population continues to view homosexuality as unnatural and lesbians and gay men as generally deviant (Herek &

Capitanio, 1996). Other common stereotypes are that gays and lesbians have domineering mothers, are cross-dressers, and are child molesters (Gilman, 1985; Eliason et al., 1992; LaMar & Kite, 1996). Many of these beliefs are more strongly held about gay men than about lesbians (Herek, 2002). Gay men also are likely to be seen as hypersexual (Gilman, 1985). However, it is important to note that, historically, researchers have focused on stereotypes about and attitudes toward gay men, perhaps because gay men's sexuality is viewed as more serious than lesbians' or, more generally, because lesbian sexuality has been generally invisible in Western societies (Blackwood & Wieringa, 2003). As a result, measures developed for gay men often are simply altered to assess perceptions of lesbians (see Herek, 2002). The stereotypes people typically are queried about, then, may simply be more applicable to gay men than to lesbians. An exception is Mary Amanda Dew's (1985) work, which demonstrated that lesbians were stereotypically perceived as unattractive, especially by those who were less tolerant of both homosexuality and women's rights. In any case, research conducted to date shows that stereotypes of both lesbians and gay men are generally negative.

Attitudes toward Lesbians and Gay Men

Public opinion toward gay men and lesbians is changing and people are more likely to be accepting of gays and lesbians than in previous decades. Compared with the 1970s, for example, when about two-thirds of the general population believed homosexuality was always wrong, by the 1990s 56 percent expressed this belief (Yang, 1997). Notice, however, that the majority of the population still holds a negative opinion about homosexuality. People also have negative emotional reactions to gays and lesbians (Herek, 2002); such negative reactions have even been used as justification, albeit unsuccessfully, for the murder of a lesbian who was seen having sexual relations with her partner (see Box 9.3). Despite these negative perceptions, a higher percentage of people are willing to grant gays and lesbians basic civil rights, such as equal access to housing and employment (Yang, 1997).

As we saw in Chapter 6, however, a number of individual difference variables influence people's attitudes toward gays and lesbians. Those with the most negative attitudes, for example, tend to be high on right-wing authoritarianism and social dominance orientation. They also are likely to hold fundamentalist religious beliefs (Herek, 2000). Findings such as these support the idea, presented in Chapter 3, that people have different motivations for holding heterosexist beliefs. For some, heterosexism stems from conformity to authority, for others from a desire to conform to the expectations of one's social group, and for others from a strong belief that homosexuality is immoral (Herek, 1986a). People also may hold more positive attitudes toward individual gay men and lesbians than toward lesbians and gay men as a social group (Laner & Laner, 1979; Lord, Lepper, & Mackie, 1980; see Chapter 4 for a discussion of individuation and its effect on attitudes toward social groups). Another important individual difference variable is whether a person knows a lesbian or gay man personally; those who do are much less likely to hold negative attitudes toward that individual,

9.3   *Eight Bullets*

On May 13, 1988, Claudia Brenner was on the second day of a backpacking trip with her partner, Rebecca Wight. On their hike, they met a stranger who, it was later learned, was named Stephen Carr. Little did they know that he altered his path so that they would once again meet—although he would stay hidden. After watching Brenner and Wight make love, Stephen Carr shot the couple eight times and left them for dead. Claudia Brenner escaped to safety, miraculously surviving five bullet wounds. She knew if she did not leave the scene, she would not live and her perpetrator would likely not be apprehended. She also knew that Rebecca Wight would not survive even if she stayed.

Stephen Carr was arrested, brought to trial, and convicted of first degree murder.

During the trial, Carr claimed he was provoked to murder by the disgust he experienced witnessing their sexual relations, which he claimed "produced a reaction of overwhelming revulsion that led to the crime" (Nussbaum, 2004, p. B6). Claudia Brenner's (1992) survivor's story is one of many thousands, albeit one of the more brutal. Their experiences compelled researchers and social activists to successfully push for the passing of the Hate Crimes Statistics Act of 1990, which requires the Justice Department to collect data on crimes that stem from prejudice based on race, religion, sexual orientation, or ethnicity—the first federal law ever to include sexual orientation (Herek & Berrill, 1992).

especially if the relationship is a close one (Herek & Capitanio, 1996). Keep in mind, however, that correlation is not causality. Individuals who are more accepting of gays and lesbians are more likely to report such close relationships, suggesting that they are open to knowing about and accepting another's sexual orientation. "Coming out" to intolerant individuals who are not so accepting may not improve their attitude and carries considerable risk, as we will see later (Herek, 2003).

Sex differences in anti-gay prejudice   One of the most consistent individual differences in attitudes toward homosexuality is that heterosexual men have greater intolerance of homosexuality than do heterosexual women. Mary Kite and Bernard Whitley (1996, 1998) reviewed 112 studies examining men's and women's attitudes toward homosexuality and found that, overall, men were more negative than women were. This greater negativity was particularly strong when the person being rated was a gay man; indeed, the sexes held similar attitudes toward lesbians (see also Herek, 2002). This pattern is found in studies of both college students' attitudes and national survey samples (Herek, 2002; Kite & Whitley, 1996). Men also hold more negative attitudes toward homosexual *behavior* than do women, although this sex difference is smaller than that found for attitudes toward gays and lesbians as a social group (Kite & Whitley, 1996, 1998). This is noteworthy because men are generally more permissive toward sexual behavior than are women (Oliver & Hyde, 1993); apparently this permissiveness does not extend to homosexual acts.

Why would men be more negative toward homosexuality, especially gay male homosexuality, than would women? Kite and Whitley (1996, 1998) have theorized that the gender belief system model described earlier in this chapter can explain this pattern. As noted earlier, people clearly associate homosexuality with other-sex gender roles and these associations appear to be more firmly held for gay men than for lesbians. These beliefs are part of the larger gender-based norms dictating that men should be masculine and should eschew femininity (Bem, 1993; Hort, Fagot, & Leinbach, 1990). These norms prescribe that any action or feeling that violates this expectation, especially one associated with femininity, should not and will not be tolerated (Herek, 1986b). Not only are men expected to reject their own femininity, they are expected to reject others' femininity as well. Because gay men are seen as feminine, then, they would be among those rejected. Indeed, rejecting homosexuality is a straightforward way to show compliance with this social norm. Supporting this idea, Frances Shen and colleagues (Shen, Longo, Ernst, Reeder, & Pryor, 2004) provide evidence that men are motivated to follow this norm: their research showed that threatening men's masculinity by telling them they scored poorly on a test of masculine knowledge resulted in defensiveness toward homosexuality and expression of more anti-gay attitudes. More generally, this perspective explains why gay men are rejected, especially by heterosexual men.

Why would women be excused from this rejection of homosexuality? One answer stems from the relatively higher status of the male gender role (Bem, 1993; Conway et al., 1996). Men have more to lose when they step outside their gender roles, including the status associated with that role (but see McCreary, 1994, for another viewpoint). Women, however, can follow a cultural gender script that offers greater flexibility and, accordingly, does not dictate that homosexuality be rejected. In short, women are allowed to accept homosexuality whereas men are not, in part because lesbianism (or behaving similarly to the male gender role) does not result in a loss of status. In fact, women taking on traditional men's roles might be seen as a step up (Tilby & Kalin, 1980). Following this reasoning, women need not reject either gay men or lesbians because failing to do so will not affect their social standing; men also need not reject lesbians because those women are not violating the male gender role.

If the gender belief system model can explain attitudes toward homosexuality, then there should be a relationship between anti-gay prejudice and gender-role attitudes; research indicates that this is the case. Bernard Whitley (2001a) reviewed the results of 42 studies and found that people who endorsed traditional gender role attitudes also tended to have negative attitudes toward homosexuality. Moreover, consistent with the finding that men, more than women, are expected to reject gender role violators, Whitley found that the relationship between gender-role attitudes and attitudes toward homosexuality was stronger for men than for women. These findings support the hypothesis that gender role beliefs are related to anti-gay attitudes.

Civil rights attitudes   The work described above reviews sex differences in affective responses to lesbians and gay men, but these attitudes do not necessarily reflect how the sexes feel about gay and lesbian civil rights. Research suggests that people have a complicated set of reactions to this issue. Women and men respond similarly to measures of global civil rights, such as "gay men should have the same civil rights as anyone else" (Davies, 2004). And, a review of 12 studies showed that women and men had similar attitudes toward gays and lesbians' right to free speech (Kite & Whitley, 1996). However, for other civil rights, such as discrimination in employment and housing, male respondents have been found to be less open-minded than female respondents (Herek, 2002; LaMar & Kite, 1996). In addition, men have indicated less acceptance for gays in the military than have women (Harris & Vanderhoof, 1995).

The results summarized so far tell us whether women and men agree on these issues, but do not speak to overall acceptance of gay rights. National opinion poll data show relatively high support for equal employment rights, but less support for passing laws to ensure those rights (Herek, 2002). This same survey showed that the majority of U.S. citizens oppose gay marriage, gay domestic partnerships, and permitting adoption by gay and lesbian couples. These latter attitudes may be due to the belief, strongly held by many, that marriage is between a man and a woman ("Law and Civil Rights," 2004). Finally, although the sexes appear to have similar attitudes toward gay and lesbian civil rights, other individual difference variables do predict attitudes toward those civil rights. Specifically, people who believe homosexuality is a lifestyle choice are less accepting of gay rights than those who believe sexual orientation has a biological basis. Those who are politically conservative, have little contact with gays, and hold more fundamental religious beliefs are also more likely to oppose gay rights (Wood & Bartkowski, 2004). Finally, people with positive attitudes toward feminism are more accepting of gay civil rights, but attitudes toward male toughness and hostile sexism are unrelated to those attitudes (Davies, 2004).

Attitudes toward bisexuals   So far, we have focused on heterosexism and its relationship to anti-gay prejudice. However, recall that heterosexist attitudes deny and degrade any nonheterosexual behavior. Bisexuals, too, then, should be viewed as unacceptable from this perspective. Unfortunately, little research has been conducted on stereotypes about and attitudes toward bisexuality. As MacDonald (1981) noted, historically researchers have not differentiated between bisexuals, gay men, and lesbians, implying that they believe "bisexuals are really homosexuals who are engaging in homosexual denial" (p. 99). He argues that bisexuality is seen as more of a transitory stage or an act of curiosity than a clear sexual preference. Another criticism of bisexuals is that they are sitting on the fence and, by doing so, are taking advantage of heterosexual privilege (Strong, DeVault, Sayad, & Yarber, 2005).

The available research suggests that heterosexuals, gay men, and lesbians all hold relatively negative attitudes toward bisexuality (Eliason, 1997; Mohr & Rochlen, 1999; Rust, 1995) and that gays and lesbians often exclude bisexuals from their communities (Bohan, 1996). That gays and lesbians reject bisexuals in both attitudes and actions suggests that they see them as an outgroup and treat them as such, although this possibility needs to be researched further. In general, beliefs about bisexuals often center around sexuality and relationships. One common belief is that bisexuals are promiscuous (Ochs, 1996). Leah Spalding and Letitia Peplau (1997), for example, asked heterosexuals to evaluate a dating couple who was described as either bisexual, heterosexual, or homosexual. Respondents thought bisexuals were less likely to be monogamous and, therefore, expected them to more readily cheat on their partner than would heterosexuals. They also believed bisexuals were more likely to give their partner a sexually transmitted disease. But they also thought bisexuals were superior sexual performers, believing that bisexuals would be more likely to satisfy their partner in bed than would heterosexuals, gays or lesbians. Interestingly, people rated male and female bisexuals similarly and were not more positive toward bisexuals currently dating an other-sex partner—even though by doing so they were conforming to heterosexual norms. However, people believed a bisexual was more likely to cheat on a heterosexual partner than a gay or lesbian partner. They also thought bisexuals could more easily please an other-sex partner sexually than they could a same-sex partner.

Taken together, the available research, although limited, suggests that heterosexism is operating and that bisexuals are not viewed positively. Finally, we mention briefly that even less is known about attitudes toward transgendered people—those whose biological sex does not match their own gender role self-concept (Bolin, 1997). However, because a common misconception is that gay men and lesbians want to be members of the other sex (Kite & Deaux, 1986) and, more generally, because these individuals also violate traditional gender roles, it is likely that attitudes toward the transgendered would be similar to those toward gays and lesbians and that they would also be negative.

Heterosexism in the Workplace

Regardless of whether the general public is accepting of gays and lesbians or their civil rights, the fact remains that discrimination based on sexual orientation is legal in much of the United States. Gays and lesbians face myriad forms of discrimination that, similar to gender-based discrimination, can affect their physical health, as when gays and lesbians experience violence, or their pocketbooks. We discuss violence against gays and lesbians in the context of hate crimes in Chapter 10 and some mental and physical health consequences of being a sexual minority in Chapter 11. Here, we focus on workplace discrimination.

On a positive note, an increasing number of organizations, including colleges and universities, are denouncing such discrimination and even have written policies prohibiting it (van der Meide, 2000). On the downside, however, significant numbers of gays and lesbians report workplace discrimination; estimates across samples vary from 25 percent to 66 percent of gay and lesbian employees (Croteau, 1996). One important factor sets this type of discrimination apart from workplace discrimination based on race or gender: Gay men and lesbians usually have a choice as to whether to reveal their sexual orientation. Evidence from the workplace (Ragins & Cornwell, 2001) suggests that around 12 percent of gays and lesbians do stay completely in the closet; others (around 37 percent) choose to disclose to only a few people. Approximately 25 percent of gays and lesbians report being "out" to most people and approximately 26 percent report being "out" to everyone in the workplace (see also Schneider, 1987). As we will discuss more fully in Chapter 11, gays and lesbians can have this choice because homosexuality is a concealable stigma. That is, unlike with race or gender, you cannot tell a person's sexual orientation by looking at them. You would not have this information unless a gay or lesbian told you directly or you learned it from a third party.

How do gay men and lesbians decide whether to disclose their sexual orientation? The answer is not simple. To understand the complexity of this decision, first keep in mind that heterosexuals are free to openly discuss their intimate relationships (Herek, 2003). Heterosexuals, for example, can display a picture of the person they are dating in their office or dorm room. Or they can talk about plans for the weekend with their spouse or greet her or him with a kiss in front of friends. These acts are part of a larger *heterosexual privilege* this is taken for granted; such privileges are not extended to gays and lesbians (Johnson, 2006; see Chapter 1). Not disclosing a gay or lesbian sexual orientation, then, means that even casual details about one's intimate relationships must be kept secret. One way heterosexual privilege is evidenced can be seen by the questions posed in Box 9.4; these represent queries heterosexuals never have to answer in practice, but are often posed to gays and lesbians who openly discuss their sexual orientation.

The disclosure of one's heterosexuality, then, can be done casually, but disclosure of a homosexual orientation is not taken so lightly. As Gregory Herek (2003) notes, this is because disclosing a homosexual orientation leads to assumptions about the individual's personality and lifestyle. A heterosexual orientation is not viewed this simplistically because a heterosexual's orientation is not considered to be the single defining factor in her or his life (Herek, 2003; Johnson, 2006). Put another way, most people do not have strong stereotypes of heterosexuals, so knowing that another is heterosexual does not lead to conclusions about what the person is like. However, people do have definite stereotypes of gays and lesbians and, therefore, believe knowing a person is gay or lesbian provides a lot of information about her or him (Deaux & Lewis, 1984; Kite & Deaux, 1987). Heterosexuals, then, can make casual conversation about their intimate relationships without being stereotyped but gays and lesbians do not have this luxury.

The problem this creates is related to another issue Herek (2003) discusses: In our society, self-disclosure is generally expected to be reciprocal; if a new friend tells you something personal, you are likely to respond with a similarly personal anecdote. Yet if disclosing something as simple as your partner's name can lead to rejection, reciprocity between heterosexuals and gays can be problematic; without coming out, gays and lesbians cannot match the intimacy level of many personal conversations. Finally, choosing not to self-disclose carries another risk; that is, failing to let another know you are gay or lesbian early in the relationship can create distrust or *discrediting* (Goffman, 1963) when the information is finally shared; even people who are accepting of gays and lesbians may

9.4   *The Heterosexual Questionnaire*

Martin Rochlin (1977) developed a set of questions for heterosexuals that are similar to those gays and lesbians are often asked about when discussing their sexual orientation, but that heterosexuals are rarely asked. Some of the questions he poses are:

- What do you think caused your heterosexuality?
- When and how did you decide you were heterosexual?
- It is possible that your heterosexuality is just a phase that you may grow out of?
- Is it possible that your heterosexuality stems from a fear or dislike of others that are the same gender as you?
- If you've never slept with a person of the same sex, is it is possible that all you need is a good gay lover?
- Do your parents know you're straight? Do your friends and/or roommate know? How did they react?
- Why do you insist on flaunting your heterosexuality? Can't you just be who you are and keep it quiet?

- Why do heterosexuals place so much emphasis on sex?
- A disproportionate majority of child molesters are heterosexual. Do you consider it safe to expose children to heterosexual teachers?
- Just what do women and men do in bed together? How can they truly know how to please each other, being so anatomically different?

That heterosexuals are rarely asked these questions reflects a form of privilege, especially the freedom to talk about personal relationships openly without seeming to flaunt one's sexuality, the knowledge that one's heterosexuality will not be used to undermine achievement, and the assurance that one's hiring, promotion, or firing are unrelated to sexual orientation (Johnson, 2006). If you are a heterosexual, how would you answer such queries?

wonder why they were not told sooner. They might also believe they were lied to unnecessarily. In a workplace setting, misstepping in the self-disclosure process can lead to negative job evaluations or loss of opportunity. At the extreme, it can lead to termination.

Is it safer to self-disclose in some workplaces than in others? According to Belle Rose Ragins and John Cornwell (2001), the answer is yes; a number of factors make a workplace less heterosexist. These researchers documented these factors in a national survey sample of members of U.S. gay rights organizations who described their job satisfaction and workplace experiences and reported whether they had come out to their coworkers. One important factor is the presence of other gays in the workplace, either as a supervisor or as a coworker; when other gays were present, self-disclosure was more likely and job satisfaction was higher. A second factor was whether the organization had gay-friendly policies—if it did, the work environment was better and people felt freer to come out. Moreover, these researchers showed that the most gay-friendly policy is one that openly welcomes gay partners at social functions; as they put it, these organizations "walk the talk" (p. 1256). A third factor is whether the place of employment is in a locale where legislation does prohibit discrimination against gays. Again, if so, gays and lesbians fared better. Organizations that were gay friendly on these factors also provided better environments for those who chose not to come out. Moreover, the positive effects of these environments extended to overall career attitudes; gays and lesbians who worked in such environments felt better about their career and were more committed to it. Another study showed these experiences were similar for women and men and for White people and people of color (Ragins, Cornwell, & Miller, 2003).

At the individual level, no one factor accounts for anti-gay prejudice. Gender-associated beliefs matter, but so do individual differences factors such as social dominance orientation and religious beliefs (Kite & Whitley, 1998; Herek, 2002). Some evidence suggests that heterosexism springs from the same well as sexism and racism and, indeed, these factors are correlated (see Cunningham, Nezlek, & Banaji, 2004, for a review). Yet elements of anti-gay prejudice strongly suggest its uniqueness. That is, this prejudice is based on the combined effects of gender role expectations, religious beliefs, and a general tendency to reject those who are different from oneself. Moreover, for no other group is sexuality so strongly linked to perceptions and attitudes (Herek, 2004).

AGEISM

When thinking about **ageism,** or evaluative judgments about persons made simply due to their advanced age (Butler, 1969), a logical first question is "When does old age begin?" If you were to answer this question based on the content of greeting cards, you would conclude that anyone over the age of 40 is past her or his prime. These individuals can expect birthday parties decorated with black crepe paper and cardboard tombstones reading "over the hill." The message that youth is valued over old age is conveyed in this and many other ways. Yet the reality is that even though most people slow down with age—at least compared to when they were in their 20s—many also find reaching middle and old age brings stability and happiness (see Erber, 2005, for a review). Older adults with good health and strong social support networks report higher levels of satisfaction and have fewer complaints than their younger counterparts (Morgan, 1992). Moreover, evidence suggests that older adults are more likely to experience positive affect than their younger peers (Diener, Sandvik, & Larsen, 1985; M. P. Lawton, Kleban, Rajagopal, & Dean, 1992). Box 9.5 describes other advantages of aging. As we discuss, these advantages are not necessarily represented in people's beliefs or in how they treat older adults.

9.5   *The Advantages of Aging*

Although "old age" and "decline" might be synonyms for many, this need not be reality. Erdman Palmore (1979, 1999) has identified the ways growing old benefits both society and the individual, all of which are supported by empirical research. Society benefits because older adults are more law abiding and are more likely to vote or otherwise participate in the political process. Moreover, older adults are the core of many volunteer organizations. And, those who continue to work tend to be as good or better at their jobs, compared to younger people. At a personal level, people over the age of 65 are less likely to be crime victims and have a lower accident rate than younger people. Many, but not all, older adults have sufficient economic resources to allow them to retire and live a comfortable life, in part because their taxes are lower and they receive many free or reduced-rate services. They are also less likely to experience mental illness, alcoholism, or drug abuse. Finally, older adults are free to be eccentric. As Jenny Joseph (2001) warns, "When I am an old woman, I shall wear purple with a red hat that doesn't [match]. . . and I shall sit down on the pavement when I am tired . . . and press alarm bells . . . and make up for the sobriety of my youth" (pp. 29–30).

When Does Old Age Begin?

Researchers often think of age in terms of broad categories, such as young, middle aged, and older adult (Kite & Wagner, 2002). The "older adult" category is sometimes further subdivided into the "young-old" and the "old-old" (Neugarten, 1975) to capture the trend toward more negative attitudes toward the oldest individuals (Hummert, Garstka, & Shaner, 1997; Kogan, 1979). Sometimes researchers assign specific ages to these categories; in these cases, the typical pattern is to label adults in their 20s and early 30s as young, those between 35 and 60 as middle-aged, those between 60 and 75 as young-old, and those older than 75 as old-old (see Erber, 2005, for a review). When research participants list the specific ages associated with general age-based categories, their estimates correspond fairly well to those of the researchers, although, as we will see, the general population tends to believe women reach the categories "middle-aged" and "old" at a younger age than do men (Zepelin, Sills, & Heath, 1986). As we will also see, however, specific age categories have less influence over age-related prejudice than does other information about the people being evaluated. Respondents, for example, report that deciding whether a person has reached old age depends on factors such as whether she or he is "senile" or "useless." As Erdman Palmore (1999) points out, there is a contradiction between using the term "old" to refer to chronological age and using "old" to mean worn out, useless, or debilitated. The former need not bring to mind negative beliefs and attitudes, but the latter certainly does.

It is also worth noting that as people age, they often report feeling younger then their actual age (Montepare & Lachman, 1989). Even people as old as 75 deny that they are old, probably because of the term's negative connotations (see Palmore, 1999). As this reluctance suggests, our attitudes toward aging are a bit paradoxical—we dread aging and but also eschew the alternative: death. After all, if you are not aging, you are no longer living. Interestingly, Jeff Greenberg and his colleagues (Greenberg, Schimel, & Martens, 2002) have argued that it is precisely the fear of death that makes aging threatening. As they put it, "[t]he elderly represent the threat to the young of their own fate: the prospects of diminishing beauty, health, sensation, and, ultimately, death" (p. 29). This premise, based on terror management theory (Greenberg, Solomon, & Pyszczynski, 1997, see Chapter 6), leads to the prediction that younger people cope with this threat by physically distancing themselves from older adults—for example, by avoiding places that older adults frequent or by keeping them out of the workplace. Another coping strategy is to use psychological distancing—for example, viewing older adults as an outgroup (see Chapters 3 and 8) and exaggerating the differences between their own group and "older people." Older adults may cope with this threat by using strategies that promote a positive self-image. They may, for example, find negative examples of aging and then demonstrate that "that's not me." Relatedly, they may associate with positive groups, such as the Older Women's League and the American Association of Retired Persons. Another strategy is to use positive language, referring to themselves as "older adults" rather than "senior citizens" (Harwood, Giles, & Ryan, 1995).

Beliefs about Older Adults

Recall from Chapter 3 that age is a basic social category and, as such, is one of the first things people notice about others. As was true for the other basic categories, people generally know what characteristics are associated with old age in their society, even if they, personally, reject the negative aspects of those beliefs. Neale Chumbler (1995) surveyed college students about their age-related stereotypes and found the stereotypes could be classified in terms of four factors: intolerance, health, personality, and activity. Others have found similar factors, including a negative physical appearance factor that is similar to the health factor, and a sociable factor or isolation factor, similar to the activity factor (Kite, Deaux, & Miele, 1991; Palmore, 1999). Other research suggests that age-associated beliefs also are represented by a dejected factor (Palmore, 1999). Representative characteristics for each factor are presented in Table 9.3. As you look at this table, notice that many age-related stereotypic beliefs are negative, but that positive beliefs about older adults also are represented.

Amy Cuddy and Susan Fiske (2002) suggest that age-based stereotypes, like gender stereotypes, also can be captured by warmth and competence clusters. (Note that the competence cluster overlaps with the activity cluster described in Table 9.3.) Recall from our discussion of gender stereotypes that people tend to perceive outgroups as being characterized by one of these clusters but not both; that perception holds for ageist beliefs as well. Cuddy and Fiske (2002) compared

TABLE 9.3   THE CONTENT OF AGE-BASED STEREOTYPES

Factor

Intolerance	Health/Physical Appearance	Personality	Dejected	Activity/ Sociability
Get upset easily	Have health problems	Are set in their ways	Poor	Unproductive
Talk to themselves	Never fully recover from illness	Meddlesome	Hopeless	Not optimistic
Grouchy	Walk slowly	Old-fashioned	Unhappy	Physically inactive
Intolerant/Impatient	Wrinkled	Think about good old days	Lonely	Active outside home
Rigid	Talks slowly	Give good advice	Insecure	Has lots of friends
Critical	Hard of hearing	Interesting to meet	Complains a lot	Has hobbies
Miserly		Good companion		
		Likeable		
		Interesting		
		Experienced		

the perceived warmth and competence of 24 groups, including older people, people with disabilities, the educated, the poor, and five ethnic minorities. Older adults were rated as less competent than 75 percent of the groups they studied, but were rated as warmer than 92 percent of those groups. Mary Kite and her colleagues (Kite, Stockdale, Whitley, & Johnson, 2005) provide evidence supporting these findings. Their review of 75 studies showed that older adults were rated as less competent than younger adults. An additional review of 46 studies showed that older adults were viewed as significantly less agentic (that is, self-confident, independent, and strong) than were younger adults (Kite, Stockdale, & Whitley, 2002). However, a review of 15 studies showed that older and younger adults' communion (that is, warmth and kindness) were viewed similarly (Kite, Stockdale, & Whitley, 2004). Perceivers, then, see older adults as lacking competence and activity, relative to other groups, but generally see them as having communal traits.

Another stereotypic belief is that older adults are less physically attractive than younger adults. Observers, even children as young as preschool age, can readily identify the physical changes that accompany aging, such as wrinkling, sagging, and the presence of a double chin (see Zebrowitz, 1996, for a review). Such changes are not viewed positively. Consider the number of terms used for older adults that reflect unattractiveness, such as crone, fossil, goat, hag, witch, withered, wizened, and wrinkled (see Palmore, 1999). Moreover, Mary Lee Hummert

(1994) found that as the perceived age of a person increased so did the number of negative stereotypes about that person. This pattern was particularly strong for older women. Wernick and Manaster (1984) also found that unattractive faces were perceived to be older than attractive faces, but only by younger raters; older raters' age estimates did not depend on facial attractiveness. Perceivers also judge others based on their gait, associating a youthful walking style with greater movement and a bouncy rhythm, compared to an older walking style (Montepare & Zebrowitz-McArthur, 1988). Moreover, people walking with a youthful gait were seen as more powerful, sexier, and happier than those walking with an older gait. Interesting, these perceptions held even when observers knew the age and sex of the walker—that is, older adults walking with a youthful style created the same positive impression as younger adults who conveyed this exuberance.

> A man, even an ugly man, can remain eligible [for marriage] well into old age. He is an acceptable mate for a young, attractive woman. Women, even good looking women, become ineligible (except as partners of very old men) at a much younger age.
>
> —Susan Sontag, 1979 (p. 465)

Is there a double standard of aging?   The above quotation is from a well-known essay on the double standard of aging—the idea that aging occurs at an earlier age and has more serious consequences for women than for men. Susan Sontag's essay focused largely how changes in women's physical appearance affect perceptions of them, especially the idea that they are less sexually desirable than younger women. Does research support the existence of this double standard? Yes, under some conditions. But, as we will see, not always.

Recall our earlier discussion of the chronological ages perceivers believe define age-based categories such as "young" and "old." As we noted, research shows that women are believed to enter both middle and old age at a younger age than men; women are thought to reach middle age approximately 2 years ahead of men and old age and the "prime of life" approximately 5 years earlier than men (Seccombe & Ishii Kuntz, 1991; Zepelin et al., 1986). Similarly, Francine Deutsch and her colleagues (1986) found that both men's and women's perceived physical attractiveness declined with age, but that the decline for women was perceived as greater. It was not until old age that men's unattractiveness was perceived to exceed women's. This double standard extended to women's perceived femininity as well; older women's femininity was thought to diminish as they aged. Perceptions of men's masculinity, however, did not vary by the age of the person being rated.

Research conducted by Mary Harris (1994) also supports the idea that age-related physical changes affect perceptions of women more than men. Respondents in her study found the physical changes associated with aging to be unattractive, especially for women. Interestingly, however, she also found characteristics typically associated with male aging, such as balding, to be unattractive. Moreover, her findings indicated that women are thought more likely than men to conceal signs of aging, such as by coloring gray hair or using wrinkle cream. These beliefs were supported by women's and men's reports of their actual attempts at age concealment (M. B. Harris, 1994). Women were much more likely to report coloring their hair (67 percent) than were men (23 percent). Women also reported having plastic surgery (38 percent) more often than men (17 percent) and they more frequently reported using wrinkle cream (75 percent of women compared to 13 percent of men). The stereotypical perception that women lie about their age also was confirmed: 52 percent of women reported doing so, compared with 34 percent of men. Despite these findings, the benefits of being more attractive than one's peers (see Chapter 3) do not disappear for older adults. Douglas Johnson and John Pittenger (1984) found that attractive people between the ages of 60 and 93 were judged to have a more favorable personality, to have more successful life experiences, and to have greater occupational achievements than less attractive people of the same age.

Does the double standard of aging affect other age stereotypes besides physical appearance? Mary Kite and her colleagues (2005) explored this question by reviewing studies examining how women and men are viewed on three age-related dimensions: evaluation, behavior/behavioral intentions, and competence. In Chapter 1, we explained that evaluations reflect affective responses to groups, as indexed by items such as "good/bad" or "positive/negative" and that behaviors reflect discrimination toward a group; behavioral intentions reflect how people believe they will act. The competence dimension represents the stereotypic belief that older adults are less able than are younger people. To make the relevant comparisons, Kite and colleagues computed the average size of the *difference* in, for example, evaluations of older and younger men. This average difference was compared to the size of the *difference* between evaluations of older and younger women. A double standard of aging would be in evidence if people saw larger differences between younger and older women than between younger and older men. These researchers made similar comparisons for behaviors/behavioral intentions, and judgments of competence.

On the evaluation dimension, Kite and colleagues (2005) found that perceived age differences were larger for women than for men, although the absolute size of this difference was not large (see the first pair of bars, Figure 9.3). So, evidence shows that a double standard of aging favoring men exists on this dimension, but the size of the difference is not compelling. As shown in the second pair of bars in Figure 9.3, on the behavior/behavioral intentions dimension, there were larger differences in the treatment of younger and older women than in the treatment of younger and older men, providing evidence of a double standard favoring men on that dimension. Finally, as shown in the third pair of bars in Figure 9.3, for measures of competence, the double standard of aging was reversed; people saw larger differences in the competence of younger and older men than in the competence of younger and older women. Interestingly, this pattern is consistent with the stereotype that men are agentic; as we explained, competence is an important component of that trait cluster. Other research has shown that men's, but not women's, aging is associated with a loss on that dimension of their masculinity (Kite, 1996).

Additional research has shown that specifically stating that the older person is "mentally healthy, mature, and socially competent" results in no double standard

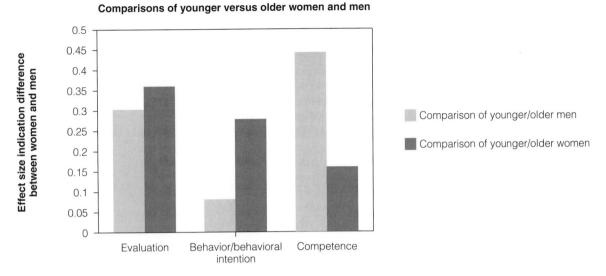

FIGURE 9.3

COMPARISONS OF YOUNGER AND OLDER WOMEN AND MEN BY TYPE OF DEPENDENT MEASURE

Supporting the double standard of aging, there are larger differences between how older and younger women are evaluated and treated than between how older and younger men are evaluated and treated. However, this double standard appears to reverse for competence ratings; here people see larger differences between younger and older men's competence than between younger and older women's competence.

Adapted from Kite, M. E., Stockdale, G. M., Whitley, B. E., Jr. & Johnson, B. T. (2005). Attitudes toward older and younger adults: An updated meta-analysis. *Journal of Social Issues.*

of aging, but describing the older person as "typical" does produce a double standard (Canetto, Kaminski, & Felicio, 1995). The double standard of aging, then, appears to have a "now you see it, now you don't" quality. It may be that the double standard applies to women's physical appearance, but not their competence; for men, the reverse may be true. And, the double standard may have less to do with liking of older women, compared to men, than with how they are treated. Finally, some evidence suggests that the double standard may simply disappear at a certain age. Agnes O'Connell and Naomi Rotter (1979) found that women's and men's effectiveness and autonomy were perceived similarly at age 75, but at earlier ages, men were seen as more likely to possess these characteristics than were women. As these findings suggest, the relationship between gender and aging is quite complex and, before firm conclusions can be drawn, additional research and a new perspective on these comparisons is needed.

Subtypes of older adults   As we noted first in Chapter 3 and again earlier in this chapter, people use basic category membership as a first pass in their judgments of others. Research suggests that, at this basic level, bias against older adults is evident. As we have discussed, people have clearly defined stereotypes of older adults and they see older people as less desirable than younger people. Overall, bias against the basic category "older adults" is quite consistent, as demonstrated by a recent review of 100 studies examining global evaluations of older and younger adults (Kite et al., 2005). As we saw in Chapters 3 and 4, however, when people are asked to make detailed judgments of others, they go beyond basic categorization and often turn to subtypes of that category. Research shows that people also have a well-defined set of subtypes about older adults and that they use these in their evaluations of that group.

In extensive research on subtypes of older adults, Mary Lee Hummert and her colleagues (Hummert, 1990; Hummert, Garstka, Shaner, & Strahm, 1994) have identified a set of subtypes—some positive and some negative—that reflect shared stereotypes of older adults (see also Schmidt & Boland, 1986). Negative subtypes include Severely Impaired, Shrew/Curmudgeon, Despondent, and Recluse. Positive subtypes include John Wayne Conservative, Golden Ager, and Perfect Grandparent. These subtypes are shared by young, middle-aged, and older adults. Members of these latter two groups identified additional subtypes, such as Small Town Neighbor, which appear to result from their more fine-grained subtyping of the more general categories (Hummert et al., 1994). People, then, appear to make greater distinctions among categories as they become actual members of them.

In general, negative beliefs about older adults appear to be limited to individuals in the negatively subtyped groups (Brewer, Dull, & Lui, 1981; Schmidt & Boland, 1986). Moreover, as we saw in our discussion of gender-based prejudice, this pattern points to the importance of contextual or role information in understanding stereotyping and prejudice. Research suggests that when more detailed information is available, people evaluate older adults based on their subtype rather than their actual age (Hummert, Garstka, Shaner, & Strahm, 1995; Schmidt & Boland, 1986). Memory problems, for example, are perceived to be more prevalent for the Despondent subtype than for others, such as the Golden Ager (Hummert, Garstka, & Shaner, 1997). Negative attitudes diminish even when the contextual information provided is fairly minimal—for example, if the person is described simply as healthy or employed (see Kite et al., 2005, for a review). Moreover, when the information is extensive, the influence of age on the evaluation of the person can disappear or even be reversed. Individuals described as healthy, for example, are rated more positively than unhealthy targets, regardless of their age (Gekoski & Knox, 1990), and David Ross and his colleagues (Ross, Dunning, Toglia, & Ceci, 1990) found that a 74-year-old witness who testified competently was evaluated as more credible than a 21-year-old witness of similar competence. Indeed, across 24 studies, Kite and her colleagues (2005) found that differences in evaluations of older and younger adults were minimal when extensive information was provided about the people being rated. Kite and colleagues also found smaller perceived differences in the competence of older and younger adults when extensive information was available and, similarly, people were more likely to treat older and younger adults the same when they had more information about them.

The forgetfulness stereotype   It happens to all of us. We walk into the next room and suddenly cannot remember our reason for doing so. Or, we go to the grocery and forget the one item we needed the most. Yet, for those middle aged and older, such actions are labeled "Senior moments" whereas for younger people, they are seen as a sign of busyness or stress. Indeed the existing literature documents that people firmly believe that memory declines with age, and does so precipitously after age 40 (Hertzog, Lineweaver, & McGuire, 1999). Of course, not all memory failures are viewed as equally serious. Forgetting the name of a new acquaintance is not as significant as forgetting the name of a lifelong friend. Joan Erber (1989) has documented these differential perceptions of everyday forgetfulness and has shown that people do recognize that certain types of memory failures are more significant than others. Even so, she found that younger people also saw identical acts of forgetfulness as more troublesome for 70-year-olds than for 30-year-olds. Older perceivers were more even-handed, seeing little difference in the seriousness of memory failure due to the actor's age. In fact, older adults saw forgetting as less serious, overall, than did younger people. Even so, research shows older adults also are more likely to *predict* a decline in memory than are younger adults (Ryan, 1992). Older perceivers, then, may be more likely to recognize memory decline, but also may be more understanding of forgetfulness when it occurs than are younger perceivers.

Other research shows that memory failure is viewed as more worrisome and less controllable when exhibited by older rather than younger targets (Bieman-Copland & Ryan, 1998) and people are more likely to recommend medical evaluation for older people who forget things (Erber & Rotherberg, 1991). In contrast, people believe that younger people's forgetfulness can be explained by their lack of attention (Erber, Szuchman, & Rothberg, 1990). Finally, making excuses for memory failure can add humor to the situation, but may actually lead to more negative perceptions of the failure, including the prediction that the person's memory will fail in the future (Ryan, Bieman-Copland, Kwong See, Ellis, & Anas, 2002).

In the research described so far, perceivers had only minimal information about the person they were rating. What happens when more extensive information is provided, such as whether the person is often or seldom forgetful? Consistent with what you now know about the role of individuating information in stereotype application, this more detailed information played an important role in judgment. Specifically, respondents stated that they would be more likely to rely on a person who was less forgetful when they needed help with a memory-related task, regardless of that person's age (Erber, Szuchman, & Etheart, 1993). Interestingly, an unexpected finding emerged: When choosing between the older and younger person, raters preferred the older adult overall, regardless of level of forgetfulness. Results of a second study (Erber et al., 1993) suggested that this was because people did not associate dependability with forgetfulness for older targets, but they did see a relationship between those two variables for younger targets. That is, they saw the older adults as dependable regardless of their foibles, and were therefore forgiving of their errors. Younger people's forgetfulness was seen as due to unreliability. Other research showed that people assigned tasks to volunteers based on their level of forgetfulness rather than their age (Erber,

Etheart, & Szuchman, 1992). And, as before, participants had a higher opinion of the older adults' memory, regardless of whether or not they were forgetful. These findings generalize to the employment setting as well; Joan Erber and Debra Danker (1995) found that attributions about memory failures did not differ by employee age. If the situation was high pressure, on the other hand, perceivers did expect those problems to be more likely to continue in older rather than younger employees and, relatedly, were less likely to recommend training as a remedy when the older employees failed, perhaps because they saw the situation as unchangeable. Having additional information, then, can reduce but not eliminate the stereotype that older people have memory problems.

It is interesting that, in many cases, when researchers provide extensive detail, the information often violates the stereotype of older adults. Note, for example, that being described as healthy, competent, or not forgetful violates age-related stereotypes. In our discussion of gender and sexual orientation, we noted that stereotype violation had a negative effect on perceptions of women and men, a pattern that does not appear to hold for older adults. Instead, as Erber and colleagues' (1993) research shows, this role violation can sometimes lead to a preference for the role-violating older adult. As far as we know, researchers have not explored this difference in perceptions about role violation for different basic category members. As we will see in the Chapter 11, however, people have definite expectations about how members of minority groups should behave and these expectations have a strong impact on the lives of those group members. For now, it seems that portraying older adults positively can lead to better perceptions of them. We consider next whether people take advantage of one venue ripe for such positive portrayals, the media.

How do the media portray older adults?   If people are generally positive toward older adults who are competent, happy, and successful, one question to consider is whether the older adults in the media have these characteristics. In Chapter 3, we explained that the media have a powerful influence on beliefs about and attitudes toward social groups. One way to look at the question of whether the media influence age-related perceptions is to simply ask how often older adults *appear* in the media. The answer is, not very often. Evidence suggests that older adults appear relatively rarely in both print media (Palmore, 1999) or on television (Robinson & Skill, 1995). On prime-time television, for example, only about 3 percent of the characters are over the age of 65 and, of those, less than 10 percent occupy a major role (Robinson & Skill, 1995). Psychologists themselves are often no better about bringing forward issues relevant to older people; the majority of psychology textbooks give only minimal attention to such topics. When they do so, they often send negative or mixed messages, such as by positioning a picture of a decrepit older adult next to text describing an optimistic view of aging (Whitbourne & Hulicka, 1990).

Older adults are also relatively invisible in magazine advertisements, a situation that appears to have changed little since the 1950s. Patricia Miller and her colleagues (Miller, Miller, McKibbin, & Pettys, 1999) found that in magazines such as *Better Homes and Gardens* and *Popular Mechanics* older adults were represented in an average of 9.8 percent of advertisements depicting people. And, even though those depictions generally reflected positive subtypes, the percentage representing negative subtypes has increased over time to its current level of 25 percent. Even in a magazine written specifically for people over the age of 50, *Modern Maturity*, only 42 percent of the advertisements included an older adult (Baker & Goggin, 1994). Interestingly, the majority of the older adults depicted were male (60 percent) even though women outnumber men in this age group. The relative absence of older adults in *Modern Maturity* was especially noteworthy when the advertisements were for clothing, automobiles, and drugs. In fact, virtually none of the clothing advertisements featured older adults. Imagine, in contrast, a magazine such as *Seventeen* or *Cosmopolitan* failing to use models representative of their target audience. Similarly, William Bailey and his colleagues (Bailey, Harrell, & Anderson, 1993) found that in publications such as *Good Housekeeping, Time,* and the *Journal of the American Medical Association*, older women were most frequently seen in ads for pharmaceuticals. Younger women, in contrast, were most frequently depicted in advertising for self-care products.

Older adults remain startlingly underrepresented in televisions commercials, appearing in approximately 7 percent of the advertisements (Roy & Harwood, 1997). And, as Baker and Goggin (1994) found for printed advertisements, women were particularly underrepresented for their actual numbers, comprising only 38 percent of older characters even though they constitute the majority of the older adult population. Yet Abhik Roy and Jake Harwood (1997) found approximately 95 percent of the older adults who appeared in television commercials took strong, active, or happy roles. Older adults in family oriented television also are portrayed fairly positively and are even seen somewhat frequently. Paula Dail (1988) identified 193 characters portraying older adults during 30 hours of prime-time programming (although she did not report the comparative number of younger characters portrayed). She further categorized these portrayals as positive or negative; overall, portrayals were generally positive, although this was more true for depictions of older males and depictions of characters over the age of 55. There appear to be bright spots, then, in how the media portray older adults. Even so, it seems there is room for improvement, especially in the area of advertising. And, when older adults are portrayed in the news or in documentaries, the focus is usually on a negative event or a problem (Atchley, 1997). At the very least, the size of the older population is inaccurately depicted in the media; older adults are clearly underrepresented relative to their numbers (Vasil & Wass, 1993). Given the well-documented influence of the media on stereotypes, advancement toward more, and more positive, representation can only improve how older adults are perceived.

Age-Based Discrimination

As we will see in Chapter 10, discrimination against less powerful groups is a fact of life. We discuss here three areas in which discrimination toward older adults is particularly acute. One area where older adults experience discrimination is in the workplace; such discriminatory acts have been documented in both the job-seeking process and in the evaluation of their performance. The second is in the language people use in conversation with older people. The third is in the way older adults are evaluated and treated in the healthcare system.

Workplace discrimination   Workplace discrimination against older people has interested gerontologists for over half a century (Tuckman & Lorge, 1953a; 1953b). Such discrimination has been illegal since 1967, when President Lyndon Johnson signed the Age Discrimination in Employment Act (ADEA), prohibiting age discrimination in the workplace for individuals over 40. The passing of this legislation, however, did not stem the tide. Research shows that the number of lawsuits alleging age discrimination has continued to increase, not decrease (Grosch, Roberts, & Grubb, 2004). This trend may reflect greater awareness and reporting of age-based employment discrimination. And, also on a positive note, many of these lawsuits have been won (see McCann & Giles, 2002, and Erber, 2005 for reviews).

Palmore (1999) calls workplace discrimination the most common type of economic discrimination against older people. The case is particularly easy to see for older workers who lose their jobs; they often have difficulty securing a new one and, when successful, often take a greater earnings loss than younger workers in the same situation (U.S. Senate Special Committee on Aging, 1986). This difficulty was documented by a clever study on age discrimination in the hiring process. Marc Bendick and his colleagues (Bendick, Brown, & Wall, 1999) trained four teams of testers, each of which had a younger and older member, in résumé preparation and interviewing. These pairs then interviewed for jobs in Washington, DC, and the surrounding area. Overall, the young applicant was much more likely to receive a favorable response to a résumé. Moreover, even when interviews were obtained, the applicants were treated differently. Older applicants waited longer before the interview, had shorter interviews, were less likely to be called by their first name, and were more likely to be perceived as overqualified. In short, as the authors concluded, the job search process is far from age blind, but instead is influenced by employers' age-based expectations.

Things are not much better once an employee is hired. Lisa Finkelstein and her colleagues (1995) reviewed the literature on age discrimination in real and simulated employment settings. In the typical study they examined, respondents made employment decisions, such as hiring or promoting an individual, or evaluated the candidate's employment-related skills, such as their potential for development or interpersonal skills. Results of those studies examining job qualifications showed that younger evaluators showed a bias in favor of workers their own age, but older evaluators were more even handed. On the other dependent variables, the available research was limited to younger people's evaluations; results of these studies also showed that younger raters favored younger workers. Yet consistent with our earlier discussion of the effects of individuating information on attitudes and behavior, when the worker was presented in a positive light, younger raters' preference for younger workers was decreased compared to when no additional information was available.

Evidence abounds that discrimination in the workplace is rooted in inaccurate beliefs. Employers believe that workers over the age of 55 are unable to meet the physical demands of the workplace, even though today only a small percentage of

9.6 *People First Language*

"People first" language refers to a manner of speaking that focuses on individuals and not their social category or, especially, their limitations. The point of this language is to emphasize who the person is and avoid the association of that person with negative stereotypes. People first language is most commonly recommended when describing people with disabilities. For example, statements such as "a person who is blind" is preferred, rather than "a blind person" (Life Span Institute, 2004). However, people first language also applies to older adults. Terms such as *elderly* and *aged* have taken on negative connotations and may be considered disparaging. For this reason, two of the major journals within the field of gerontology, *Journal of Gerontology* and *Gerontologist,* both have an editorial policy that terms such as *elderly* and *aged* may not be used as nouns, although they are permitted as adjectives. Instead, the Gerontological Society of America recommends the following terms: *older people,*

older adults, older persons, or *elders* (see also American Psychological Association [APA], 2001). APA also recommends the use of *dementia* rather than *senility* to describe age-related decrements in cognitive functioning. Similarly, the APA (2001) believes the term *homosexual* reflects bias and recommends that the term not be used as a noun. Preferred terms are *lesbian* and *gay.*

People sometimes feel frustrated with changes in language and have difficulty adjusting to new terminology. You may be one of them. However, over time, such changes become second nature. As you become aware of what might seem to be subtle differences in terminology, you will also notice that major news organizations such as the Associated Press (Goldstein, 1992) have adopted the use of this terminology. And you will find that those individuals who benefit from "people first" language will sincerely appreciate your efforts.

jobs involve manual labor (Mirvis, 1993). Furthermore, older workers are believed to have high rates of absenteeism, even though these beliefs are not supported by attendance data (see McCann & Giles, 2002, for a review). Even in physically demanding jobs, there is little evidence for age-related decline in actual performance. For example, Frank Landy (1996) found that police officers and firefighters over the age of 50 were less likely to die of catastrophic illness or injury than were their younger counterparts. Similarly, although employers generally believe that work productivity declines with age (Munk, 1999), evidence suggests that older workers may actually be more productive than their younger counterparts (Forteza & Prieto, 1994). In short, evidence suggests that, because of stereotypic beliefs, older workers have difficulty changing jobs or getting a fair shake in the job they hold. And, while on the job, they often endure ageists comments, such as "old and tired," "too long on the job," or "we need young blood around here" (see McCann & Giles, 2002, for a review). Box 9.6 describes more appropriate ways to refer to older adults.

Communication with older adults   Think about the last time you had a conversation with an older person. Was your conversational style different than it might have been if discussing the same topic with a younger person? Did you believe, for example, that you had to explain things in more detail or did you keep the conversation at a superficial level? Research suggests that these kinds of changes are not uncommon. In interactions with older adults, younger people often use **patronizing speech,** or change their conversational strategies in ways that reflect age stereotypic beliefs (Hummert & Ryan, 1996; Ryan, Giles, Bartolucci, & Henwood, 1986). Examples of patronizing speech include simplifying one's speech, such as by speaking more slowly or using simple vocabulary; using clarification strategies, such as by making an effort to speak especially clearly; using a demeaning emotional tone, such as by being bossy or overly familiar; or by keeping the conversation at a superficial level. An extreme form of patronizing talk is *elderspeak,* or the tendency to use baby talk in conversations with older people (Kemper & Harden, 1999). Elderspeak is reflected in a higher voice pitch, slow speech rate, and shorter utterances (Harwood, Giles, & Ryan, 1995). Interestingly, listeners are able to discern whether speakers are talking to an older or a younger person just by hearing such voice cues (Montepare, Steinberg, & Rosenberg, 1992).

Speakers have been found to use patronizing talk in a variety of settings, including nursing homes (Caporael & Culbertson, 1996), interactions between strangers (Coupland, Coupland, Giles, Henwood, & Wiemann, 1988), and interactions between family members (Montepare, Steinberg, & Rosenberg, 1992). Evidence suggests that use of elderspeak and other forms of patronizing speech are rooted in negative stereotypes of older adults and the mistaken assumption that older adults have memory or hearing problems (Hummert, Garstka, & Shaner, 1995; Hummert 1999). In other words, younger people appear to use these forms of speech to accommodate what they believe to be the needs of older adults. For example, in a classic study demonstrating these effects, Kenneth Rubin and Ian Brown (1975) asked undergraduates to explain a game to a same-aged partner or an older adult. Participants used less complex speech with an older adult than with a peer. Evidence suggests, however, that patronizing speech is used less frequently when the older adult is positively stereotyped, compared to when he or she is negatively stereotyped or no information is given (Thimm, Rademacher, & Kruse, 1998). Yet even with this positive information, speech patterns still differed toward older and younger conversational partners.

It is important to note that observers find patronizing speech to be disrespectful and demeaning (Ryan, Meredith, & Shantz, 1994); however, the relationship with the speaker matters as well. Older adults tend to associate elderspeak from friends with warmth, compared with elderspeak from service workers, which they associate with a condescending attitude (O'Connor & St. Pierre, 2004). Even so, older adults are less likely to use elderspeak when talking to other older people (Kemper & Kemtes, 2000), perhaps because they realize it has negative connotations. This is not to say that older adults require no accommodations in the way a message is presented. Elderspeak can, for example, improve recall of medical information (McGuire, Morian, Codding, & Smyer, 2002). However, individuals who are appropriately trained can reduce their use of elderspeak while still retaining quality care (K. Williams, Kemper, & Hummert, 2003). Before assuming at the outset that patronizing speech is appropriate, keep in mind the power of the self-fulfilling prophecy, discussed in Chapter 4. Treating older adults as if they can not understand may actually reduce their ability to do so.

Health care for older adults   One of the strongest stereotypes about older adults is that illness is normal and, perhaps, irreversible (see Palmore, 1999). Unfortunately, evidence suggests that health care providers are just as likely to hold these stereotypic beliefs as are members of the general population (Greene, Adelman, Charon, & Hoffman, 1986; Reuben, Fullerton, Tschann, & Croughan-Minihane, 1995). Do these beliefs affect the quality of care older people receive?

The evidence is mixed. Research shows that older adults are sometimes treated unfairly. David Reuben and his colleagues (1995), for example, surveyed beginning medical students across the five campuses of the University of California schools of medicine and found that they saw 70-year-old patients as more ineffective, dependent, and personally unacceptable than a comparable 35-year-old patient. Moreover, when evaluating a hypothetical case of an acutely ill patient, they indicated they would be significantly less likely to pursue aggressive treatment when the person was 85 years old rather than 10 years old. Other research shows that therapeutic recreation majors prefer to work with younger clients (MacNeil, Hawkins, Barber, & Winslow, 1990). Michele Greene and her colleagues (1986) also found age-related bias in actual interviews between physicians and patients. Although interviews with people of different ages did not differ in length, the topics covered varied. For example, physicians covered fewer medical and psychosocial issues when the clients were older and provided better information and support to younger clients. Finally, physicians were more engaged, patient, and respectful of younger clients. Interestingly, when doctors primarily treat older patients with a chronic illness, they may come to hold more stereotypic beliefs about older adults (Revenson, 1989).

Even psychiatrists specializing in geriatrics can be biased; for example, in reviewing a hypothetical case history, these physicians were less likely to take a sexual history or recommend appropriate treatment of an older man with sexual dysfunction than a middle-aged man with the same presenting problem (Bouman & Arcelus, 2001). Moreover, evidence suggests that emotional problems may be masked by symptoms associated with the "normal" aging process and, hence, overlooked (Katz, Curlick, & Nemetz, 1988). However, treatment is not always biased: Eric Hillerbrand and Darlene Shaw (1990) reviewed medical records of older and younger patients and found that, in general, psychological evaluation and assessment, recommendations for follow-up, and behavioral interventions did not differ by patient age; however, in the areas of suicide ideation, orientation, and attention, evaluations were less complete for older patients. Lilian-Jean Reekie and Finy Hansen (1992) found that social workers evaluated depressed clients similarly, regardless of their age. Similarly, undergraduates' evaluations of a client depicted in a mock intake interview did not differ by client age (Matyi & Drevenstedt, 1989).

Findings based on hypothetical cases may not be representative of older adults' real experiences. Another factor to consider is that, as Monisha Pasupathi and Corinna Löckenhoff (2002) have noted, some observed treatment differences may be rooted in real differences between older patients and younger patients. For one thing, older people are more likely to visit a physician over the course of the year, in part because they are more likely to suffer from chronic health problems (see Erber, 2005, for a review). Moreover, older people are likely to want their physician to take control of their health. Some of the observed treatment differences, then, may be due to the real expectations and demands of older patients. This does not mean, however, that cognitive biases are not operating, perhaps exacerbating real differences. And, if cognitive biases are present, they may prevent older adults from getting treatment that would improve their condition (Grant, 1996).

Finally, differences in the extent to which people accept age stereotypes as applicable to themselves can affect their health and well-being. Research conducted by Becca Levy and her colleagues (Levy, Slade, Kunkel, & Kasl, 2002) showed that individuals who, at a younger age, had disagreed with the statement "when you get older, you are less useful" lived on average 7.5 years longer than those who had agreed with the statement. This survival advantage remained even when baseline data, such as age, gender, and functional health, were taken into account. In another study, Levy (1996) found that older individuals primed with positive age stereotypes performed better on a later memory test than those primed with negative stereotypes (see Chapter 2 for a description of how priming works). Exposure to positive stereotypes also has been shown to increase older adults' walking speed (Hausdorff, Levy, & Wei, 1999). Unfortunately, activation of negative stereotypes about older adults can begin in childhood and continue throughout the life cycle and is, therefore, difficult to counteract in the long term (Levy, 2003; Levy & Banaji, 2002). Hence, regardless of whether negative stereotypes are held by the young, the old, or both, research shows they can have detrimental effects as people enter old age, often resulting in harmful, discriminatory acts against older adults.

CHAPTER SUMMARY

The gender belief system includes stereotypes about and attitudes toward women and men and the roles deemed appropriate for them in society. Gender stereotypes are multidimensional and include male-associated traits represented by the agentic cluster and female-associated traits represented by the communal cluster. They also include beliefs about men's and women's appropriate social roles, their cognitive abilities, their physical characteristics, and the emotions deemed appropriate for them. These components of the gender belief system are gender polarized—that is, people believe what is masculine is not feminine and vice versa. Research has documented that these beliefs are highly stable across time, respondent age, and culture; even so, differences due to the social class and ethnicity of the people being rated remain poorly understood.

Researchers have looked at attitudes toward women and men in two ways. First, they have explored attitudes toward the social groups "women" and "men." This research shows that women are wonderful—that people like the typical woman more than they like the typical man. But the second way researchers explore these attitudes tells a different story. This research looks at particular sub-types of women and men. People have many gender-associated subtypes that can be grouped into major categories such as occupations, ideologies, physical features, and sexuality. Research shows that people have more positive attitudes toward individuals who occupy traditional subtypes compared with individuals who occupy nontraditional subtypes.

Researchers also have focused on attitudes towards women's rights and responsibilities. These studies show that people hold less traditional attitudes toward women's rights than they did in the past. However, research on modern sexism shows that people are still willing to indirectly express negative attitudes toward women in nontraditional roles. There is, then, a discrimination-affection paradox; people like women as a social group, but still discriminate against them. Ambivalent sexism theory suggests that the concepts of benevolent and hostile sexism help to explain this paradox. Benevolent sexism rewards traditional women whereas hostile sexism punishes nontraditional women. Together, these two attitudes work to maintain the status quo. Prejudice against women can emerge in subtle ways, as illustrated by the research on face-ism. This research suggests that portrayals of men typically focus on their face, suggesting they are intelligent and of high character whereas portrayals of women typically focus on the body, suggesting this is their most important feature.

Maintaining the status quo means keeping women out of leadership roles. According to role congruity theory, two forms of prejudice keep women from such positions. The first form of prejudice stems from the belief that women do not possess the characteristics needed for leadership; this belief discourages women from pursuing it in the first place. Yet even when women do pursue and land leadership positions, they face a double bind created by expectations of what women are like and what leaders should be like—that is, a man. Because women cannot meet both sets of expectations, they may face negative performance evaluations. However, this situation can be modified by a number of factors, including how masculine the leadership role is, the woman's own characteristics, and who the evaluator is.

The male gender role also is limiting; people expect men to be strong and tough. These expectations have negative consequences for men and boys and sometimes can lead to negative behaviors such as drug abuse, low self-esteem, and anti-gay prejudice. These expectations for men also are part of the gender belief system. Such beliefs are linked to stereotypes about gay men and lesbians, which includes the belief that they have the characteristics of the other sex. However, research also supports the sexual orientation hypothesis that people are more likely to believe feminine men are gay than to believe that masculine women are lesbian. Anti-gay attitudes are linked to the gender belief system. Men, for example, hold especially negative attitudes toward homosexuality, perhaps because they believe they are expected to conform to the male gender role and reject anything associated with femininity generally and gay men specifically. Failing to do so can result in a loss of status. Women, in contrast, are not so clearly expected to reject either gay men or lesbians, perhaps because they occupy a lower status social role; for women, then, accepting homosexuality does not result in a loss of status. More generally, gays and lesbians are stereotypically viewed as violating what is "normal."

Over time, people have become more accepting of homosexuality, and people today are particularly willing to grant gay men and lesbians civil rights. However, this change is limited to equal rights in employment and housing; the majority of U.S. citizens reject the idea of gay marriage or allowing gays to adopt children. Women and men hold similar views on gay civil rights. Attitudes toward bisexuals have received little research attention, but the available data suggest they also are viewed negatively; stereotypes about these individuals focus on their sexuality and, especially, their promiscuity. Finally, a number of individual difference variables are related to anti-gay prejudice. For example, those who are high on social dominance and right-wing authoritarianism are particularly negative, as are those who hold fundamentalist religious beliefs. People who know a gay or lesbian personally tend to be more accepting.

A number of factors affect whether gays and lesbians choose to "come out." Although heterosexuals take for granted that they are free to talk about their relationships, gays and lesbians do not have the option of casual self-disclosure. This is because a heterosexual orientation is not presumed to be the single defining factor in one's life, but a homosexual orientation often is. Because of this, gays and lesbians may choose not to talk about their relationships at all. Even if a gay man or lesbian later concludes it is safe to discuss her or his sexual orientation, it can have negative repercussions. For example, they might be distrusted for not sharing this information sooner, and the other person may feel hurt that they were not told at the beginning. Self-disclosure in the workplace is an important issue for gays and lesbians as revealing one's sexual orientation can lead to negative job evaluations or termination, regardless of performance. Some workplace environments make gays and lesbians feel more welcome, and they are more likely to thrive in those more friendly settings.

Ageism occurs when people are judged negatively simply because of their advanced ages. Both lay people and researchers agree that old age begins around 65, but many people have trouble accepting this label when they themselves reach that age. Five factors capture age-related stereotypes: intolerance, health, personality, dejection, and activity. As with gender stereotypes, physical appearance provides important cues that affect evaluations of older adults; those viewed as less attractive are more readily devalued. As was true for gender stereotypes, older women and men are evaluated at the subtype level and a set of both negative and positive subtypes exist.

There appears to be a double standard of aging—that is, people seem to believe women reach middle and old age sooner than men; evidence suggests physical decline is thought to occur at a younger age for women than men, too. Yet the double standard of aging is not universal; differences in evaluations of younger and older women and men are relatively small. And for judgments of competence, it is men who are perceived to decline at a younger age. More generally, forgetfulness and aging are viewed as going hand in hand, but people are sometimes more forgiving of forgetfulness in older people. Stereotypic portrayals of older adults in the media reflect such negative beliefs. Even so, older adults are largely absent from television, print media, and advertisements.

Age-based discrimination is a significant problem for older adults. In the workplace, for example, older adults have an uphill battle, both in seeking a job and in being accepted at their current job. Age-based discrimination also can lead to patronizing speech or elderspeak. That is, people use different voice tones and rates of speech when talking to older people. This may have positive benefits; nevertheless, it is generally viewed as demeaning. Finally, stereotypic expectations may affect the health care older adults receive. All types of discrimination can be harmful and this applies to all the groups examined in this chapter.

SUGGESTED READINGS

Gender

Deaux, K., & LaFrance, M. (1998). Gender. In D. T. Gilbert, S. T. Fiske & G. Lindzey (Eds.), *The handbook of social psychology* (4th ed., Vol. 1, pp. 788–827). Boston: McGraw-Hill.
This comprehensive chapter reviews the whole of social psychological knowledge about gender, including gender-associated stereotypes, attitudes, and the important role context plays in gender-based interactions.

Frieze, I. H. & McHugh, M. C. (Eds.) (1997). Measuring beliefs about appropriate roles for women and men. *Psychology of Women Quarterly, 21.*
This special issue includes a number of relevant articles on blatant and modern sexism. Other influential articles, by Glick and Fiske, are noted in the Suggested Readings for Chapter 5.

Unger, R. K. (Ed.) (2001). *Handbook on the psychology of women and gender.* New York: Wiley.
This edited volume is another excellent resource. Part II includes chapters on men and masculinity, gender roles, gender and language, gender and social interaction, and sexualities.

Worrell, J. (Ed.) (2001). *The encyclopedia of women and gender: Sex similarities and differences and the impact of society and gender.* New York: Academic Press.
This is a highly accessible resource, with entries covering many relevant topics including gender stereotypes, men and masculinity, prejudice, women in nontraditional work fields, and working environments.

Heterosexism and Anti-Gay Prejudice

Garnets, L. D. & Kimmel, D. C. (Eds.) (2003). *Psychological perspectives on lesbian, gay, and bisexual experiences.* New York: Columbia University Press.
Section Two of this book focuses on sexual prejudice, discrimination, and violence and includes chapters on sexual prejudice and the mental health consequences of anti-gay violence.

Herek, G. M. (2004). Beyond "homophobia": Thinking about sexual prejudice and stigma in the twenty-first century. *Sexuality Research and Social Policy, 1*, 6–24.
   Provides both a historical and a current overview of the literature on heterosexism and anti-gay prejudice, including a discussion of the term *homophobia*. This critique is thoughtful and suggests avenues for future research.

Ragins, B. R. & Cornwell, J. M. (2001). Pink triangles: Antecedents and consequences of perceived workplace discrimination. *Journal of Applied Psychology, 86*, 1244–1261.
   This award-winning paper provides an excellent review of workplace discrimination and its effects on the experiences of gays and lesbians.

Ageism

Erber, J. T. & Prager, I G. (1999). Age and memory: Perceptions of forgetful younger and older adults. In T. M. Hess & F. Blanchard-Fields (Eds.), *Social cognition and aging* (pp. 198–217). San Diego, CA: Academic Press.
   Summarizes the work of Joan Erber and her colleagues (and others) on attributions about forgetfulness in older adults.

Hummert, M. L. (1999). A social cognitive perspective on age stereotypes. In T. M. Hess & F. Blanchard-Fields (Eds.), *Social cognition and aging* (pp. 175–196). San Diego, CA: Academic Press.
   Reviews Hummert's highly influential work on stereotypes about and subtypes of older adults. Also summaries her work and others' on age-related communication, including patronizing speech.

Nelson, T. D. (Ed.), *Ageism: Stereotyping and prejudice against older persons*. Cambridge, MA: MIT Press.
   This groundbreaking book on the social psychology of aging has chapters on many important topics, including stereotypes, terror management theory, implicit ageism, attitudes, ageism in the workplace, and ageist behavior.

Palmore, E. B. (1999). *Ageism: Negative and positive*. New York: Springer.
   This highly readable book covers ageist attitudes, stereotypes, and prejudice and includes a discussion of institutional influences on ageism.

KEY TERMS

ageism
gender polarization
patronizing speech

sexual orientation hypothesis
subtypes

QUESTIONS FOR REVIEW AND DISCUSSION

1. List the components of the gender belief system and give an example of each.
2. Kay Deaux and Marianne LaFrance (1998) argue that gender stereotypes are the most fundamental aspect of the gender belief system. Do you agree or disagree and why?

3. List the two constellations of traits that are associated with women and men. What characteristics comprise these two constellations?

4. Which emotions are stereotypically associated with women and which are associated with men? Do you think this affects the emotions women and men display? If so, how?

5. What is gender polarization? Do you believe that this belief accurately reflects men's and women's actual characteristics?

6. Provide evidence supporting and refuting the accuracy of gender stereotypes.

7. What is the *women are wonderful effect*? Does this effect apply to all women? Why or why not?

8. List three major ways women are discriminated against in the United States and around the world. Why do you think these patterns are similar cross-culturally?

9. Is modern sexism more or less harmful than blatant sexism? Defend your answer.

10. Describe how blatant sexist attitudes have changed over time. Do you believe modern sexist attitudes will also change? Why or why not?

11. What is the discrimination-affection paradox? How does ambivalent sexism theory account for it?

12. Describe ways in which the male role is prescriptive. Do you believe these prescriptions affect men's lives in important or minor ways or both?

13. List the dimensions people use to categorize subtypes of women and men. What dimension distinguishes subtypes that are liked and disliked?

14. How do you feel about feminists? Why do you believe attitudes toward feminists are polarized?

15. Explain how hostile and benevolent sexist attitudes work in tandem to "keep women in their place."

16. What is face-ism? Find examples from the media, magazines, or art. Then see if you can find counterexamples.

17. According to role congruity theory, what two forms of prejudice combine to limit women's entry into and success in leadership roles?

18. Think of an example of a highly successful woman. Does her experience encourage or discourage you? Why? Use the theories described in this chapter to explain your viewpoint.

19. Research shows the worst insult directed toward a man, but not toward a woman, is "homosexual"(Preston & Stanley, 1987). Explain this result in terms of the sexual orientation hypothesis.

20. What stereotypes are associated with lesbians and gay men?

21. Researchers are more likely to study stereotypes about and attitudes toward gay men than toward lesbians. Why do you think this might be the case?

22. Use the gender belief system model to explain why men, compared with women, are more intolerant of gay men.

23. Speculate what might happen to the greater acceptance of lesbianism as women gain power and status in U.S. society.

24. Which civil rights are people most willing to grant gays and lesbians? Why do you think people are willing to grant some rights and not others?

25. Based on your knowledge of ingroups and outgroups, why would gays and lesbians be intolerant of bisexuals?

26. According to Greg Herek (2003), what factors influence whether a lesbian is likely to disclose her sexual orientation to a coworker? Would a gay person in your class be likely to come out? Why or why not?

27. List the factors that affect whether gays and lesbians experience workplace discrimination.

28. What ages delineate the categories "young," "middle aged," and "old?" When are researchers' and participants' estimates similar and different?

29. How does terror management theory explain ageism? Do you think this theory is more applicable for some age groups than others? Why or why not?

30. Why do you think physical appearance is such an important component of age-related stereotypes?

31. Explain the double standard of aging. On what dimensions is it most likely to emerge?

32. List the major subtypes of the category "older adults."

33. Under what circumstances might a younger person's forgetfulness lead to negative evaluations?

34. Describe a television advertisement that would depict older people in a positive light.

35. Is it important or unimportant that older adults are largely absent in the media? Explain your reasoning.

36. Give examples of age-related stereotypes that affect older people in the workplace.

37. If you were an employer interested in reducing age-related bias in your hiring practices, what training would you provide? As this same employer, what would you do to reduce ageism on the job site?

38. What is patronizing speech? Give examples. When is it likely to be used? Is it ever helpful? Explain why or why not.

39. If you were taking an older adult to a doctor's appointment, what would you do to ensure he or she was treated fairly?

40. How might a medical intake interview differ for an older and younger patient? What are the implications of those differences for treatment?

FROM PREJUDICE TO DISCRIMINATION

Rush hour on board a bus or train. . . . The flood of incoming passengers begins to solidify. . . . I am sitting next to a window, my eyes half-closed. . . . Dressed conservatively in a tweed jacket and tastefully bold tie, I am an unremarkable man . . ., as unnoticed as any other commuter. Except for one thing: amid the growing crush, the seat beside me remains empty. At stop after stop, . . . a succession of seemingly random individual decisions coalesces into a glaring pattern of unoccupied spaces next to black males—including me. Soon the seats beside us are the only ones left. Other passengers remain standing, leaving only these seemingly quarantined seats.

—Bruce Jacobs, 1999 (pp. 15–16)

Prejudice, which has been the main focus up to this point in the book, is an attitude; it deals with how people think and feel about members of other groups. Discrimination, in contrast, is behavior; it deals with how people act toward members of other groups. **Discrimination** consists of behaving differently toward people based solely or primarily on their membership in a social group. The term is usually used to refer to acting in an unfair or demeaning manner, but it can also refer to giving someone an undeserved advantage. Bruce Jacobs's (1999) experience cited above illustrates one aspect of the ongoing problem of discrimination in modern American society: Many White people avoid contact with members of minority groups, even when the avoidant behaviors cause inconvenience for themselves. Although discrimination against members of minority groups is not always as blatant as it was prior to the civil rights movement of the 1960s, it still occurs. As we discuss the research on discriminatory behavior you might be tempted to say, "Well, it's obvious: Prejudiced people discriminate," but, as we will see, there is only a moderate correlation between people's degree of prejudice and their propensity to engage in discriminatory behavior. That is, not all prejudiced people discriminate every time they have an opportunity, and some nonprejudiced people discriminate in some situations. In presenting what psychologists know about discrimination, we first look at the nature of discrimination and then focus on the two forms most often studied by psychologists, interpersonal discrimination and organizational discrimination. We conclude with a brief examination of the most severe form of discrimination, hate crimes.

While reading this chapter, bear in mind a point we made in Chapter 6 concerning prejudice: some forms, such as racial prejudice, are socially proscribed whereas other forms, such as anti-gay prejudice, are more socially permissible. The same principle applies to discrimination. For example, David Schneider (2004) noted the following forms of socially acceptable discrimination: "Most of us would fight having a group home for convicted rapists placed next door to our home, no matter how 'cleaned up' or 'ex-' the rapists claimed to be. Most church groups do not invite homeless people to share their potluck dinners. . . . Many women prefer their gynecologists to be female, and most males discriminate against males as their sexual partners. That's the kind of discrimination we all know and generally approve. So it is not the fact of discrimination that is controversial, but its application to specific groups" (p. 291). For example, Christian Crandall, Amy Eshleman, and Laurie O'Brien (2002) had college students rate the acceptability of prejudice and discrimination directed at various groups. Table 10.1 shows the groups for which prejudice and discrimination had the highest and lowest approval ratings.

WHAT IS DISCRIMINATION?

Discrimination can manifest itself in many ways, both verbally and behaviorally, and in many settings. For example, David Mellor (2003) interviewed members of the Koori people, a group of urbanized Australian Aborigines, about their experiences with discrimination. Common experiences included being spoken to in demeaning

TABLE 10.1   SOCIALLY APPROVED AND DISAPPROVED PREJUDICES

Approved Prejudices	Percent Approving	Disapproved Prejudices	Percent Approving
Rapists	98	Mentally retarded people	3
Child abusers	98	Native Americans	6
Child molesters	97	Black Americans	6
Wife beaters	97	Jews	6
Terrorists	95	Catholics	6
Racists	92	Whites	7
Members of the Ku Klux Klan	91	Hispanics	7
Drunk drivers	91	Asian Americans	7
Members of the American Nazi Party	90	Canadians	7
		Ugly people	10
Pregnant women who drink alcohol	89	Interracial couples	11
Men who refuse to pay child support	89	People with AIDS	11
		Fat people	11
Negligent parents	86		
People who cheat on their spouses	82		

Note: From Crandall, Eshleman, and O'Brien (2002, Table 1, p. 362).

terms, such as "nigger" and "coon," and hearing both direct and indirect derogatory comments about their people. One woman recounted that, while reporting her rape to police, "I had one female copper stare at me in the face, and she told me that I loved it, and that . . ., and I quote, 'being Black, I asked for it.'" (p. 477). Comments also took the form of jokes, intentionally hurtful remarks, intimidating comments, and direct threats. Respondents experienced behaviors ranging from being ignored and refused service in shops and hotels to physical assaults by police. This section describes the forms that discrimination can take and the social levels, from the individual to the cultural, at which it occurs. The boundaries between forms and between levels are not always clear-cut, as these distinctions represent areas along a continuum rather than hard-and-fast categories: As a result, they overlap to some degree.

Forms of Discrimination

Given the many forms that discrimination can take, it is useful to have a system for classifying forms of discrimination to show how they relate to one another. Nijole Benokraitis and Joe Feagin (1995) developed one such system, based on three forms of discrimination—blatant, subtle, and covert—that can be found at four levels of social interaction—interpersonal, institutional, organizational, and cultural. Although Benokraitis and Feagin developed their typology in the context of sexism, it applies to other forms of discrimination as well. Let us begin by looking at the three forms of discrimination.

Blatant discrimination   **Blatant discrimination** consists of "unequal and harmful treatment . . . that is typically intentional, quite visible, and easily documented" (Benokraitis & Feagin, 1995, p. 39). Extreme cases of blatant discrimination, such as the murder of Matthew Shepard, a gay man who was beaten and left to die on a fence in Wyoming (*Laramie Project Archives,* 2002), and the murder of James Byrd, a Black man who was chained to the back of a truck and dragged along a road in Texas until he died (Texas NAACP, 1999), often receive national attention. However, blatant discrimination occurs in everyday contexts as well. For example, a Black college student interviewed by Janet Swim and her colleagues (Swim, Hyers, Cohen, Fitzgerald, & Bylsma, 2003) told of how "a man at a party addressed her by a racist label and ordered her to perform a menial task" (p. 52).

Some forms of blatant discrimination against some groups are illegal and generally condemned, such as racial discrimination at work, in school, and in public accommodations. However, other forms, such as discrimination against lesbians and gay men, are often legal and are accepted as "normal" by many people. Consider, for example, a website on which visitors can find a picture of Matthew Shepard burning in hell, along with a record of how many days he has been there. Visitors are invited to click on his picture and hear him scream as he endures the flames of hell.

Subtle discrimination   **Subtle discrimination** consists of "unequal and harmful treatment . . . that is typically less visible and obvious than blatant discrimination. It is often not noticed because people have internalized subtle [discriminatory] behaviors as 'normal,' 'natural,' or customary" (Benokraitis & Feagin, 1995, p. 41). Subtle discrimination tends to be harder to document than blatant discrimination, but it can often be done. Unlike the other forms of discrimination, which are often intentional, subtle discrimination is often unintentional. For example, Claude Steele (1992) related a story told by a friend of his who

> noticed over many visits [to her son's third-grade classroom] that the extraordinary art work of a small black boy named Jerome was ignored—or, more accurately perhaps, its significance [as a sign of artistic talent] was ignored. As genuine art talent has a way of doing—even in the third grade—his stood out. Yet the teacher seemed hardly to notice. Moreover, Jerome's reputation, as it was passed along from one grade to the next, included only the slightest mention of his talent. . . . Had Jerome had a reading problem, which fits [American society's stereotypic image of black children], it might have been accepted as characteristic of him more readily than his extraordinary art work, which contradicts [that image]. (p. 72)

Thus, subtle prejudice had the effect of directing teachers' attention away from Jerome's artistic talent because, by society's definition, Black children do not have that particular talent. Subtle prejudice also can be manifested in everyday speech, as described in Box 10.1.

10.1 *The Language of Prejudice*

Some of the most common examples of subtle prejudice can be found in everyday speech. Examples include:

- *Hostile humor* calls attention to the negative stereotypes associated with outgroups, such as low intelligence, selfishness, stinginess, and alleged bad habits such as drunkenness (Ruscher, 2001). People are often tolerant of outgroup disparagement that is presented as joke because the humor context implies that listeners should not take the speaker's remarks seriously (Ford & Ferguson, 2004). Humor can therefore also function as a justification for derogatory speech. How often have you heard someone who has just been confronted for making a prejudiced remark reply with "Hey, it was only a joke"?
- *Patronizing speech* implies that outgroups are less competent than members of the speaker's ingroup. Patronizing speech can take two forms (Ruscher, 2001). *Baby talk* is often directed at the elderly, implying that they have regressed cognitively to the level of infants (see Chapter 9). Although baby talk is usually well intentioned—speakers view it as comforting—recipients find it insulting. *Controlling talk* is directed at members of groups the speaker views as having lower social status and "functions to keep low-status individuals 'in their place'" by controlling the direction of the conversation (Ruscher, 2001, p. 88). For example, when talking to women, men are more likely to interrupt and to give commands than when talking to other men (Ruscher, 2001).

- *Vanishing* uses linguistic devices to make outgroups disappear. A common way of doing so is to replace the active voice of a verb (for example, "Bill hit the ball") with the passive voice ("The ball was hit"). As Thomas Greenfield (1975) noted, this rhetorical device makes "the creator or instigator of action totally disappear from a reader's [or listener's] perception" (p. 146; see also Chapter 3). For example, Greenfield (1975) recounted his experiences on a guided tour of Thomas Jefferson's home at Monticello, Virginia. He noted that the tour guide always referred to Jefferson in the active voice but always referred to the work of Jefferson's slaves in the passive voice. For example, while describing a set of interior doors with a complex operating mechanism that had required no repair in the 166 years since Jefferson's slaves had built and installed them, the guide said, "Mr. Jefferson designed these doors" (p. 147). In contrast, the guide said, "These doors *were installed* originally in 1809" (p. 147, emphasis in original), making the enslaved carpenters whose skilled work had created the remarkable doors effectively disappear from history.
- *Abnormalization* involves describing outgroup members in ways that emphasize their lack of compliance with ingroup norms. For example, Maykel Verkuyten (2001) conducted focus groups in which Dutch residents of Rotterdam were asked to discuss life in their neighborhoods. The participants were chosen because they lived in areas in which large numbers of immigrants also lived. She found that when immigrants were mentioned,

The Language of Prejudice (continued)

participants almost always described them in ways that emphasized their differences from the Dutch norm, often using extreme examples to illustrate a point. For example, one participant supported his view that immigrants from India were ignorant and crazy by citing a case of a family that had built a cooking fire on the floor of their apartment.

Linguistic devices such as these serve several functions. Hostile humor and abnor-malization indicate ways in which the ingroup is superior to the outgroup and patronizing speech reinforces the higher status and power of the ingroup (Ruscher, 2001). Vanishing denigrates the skills of outgroup members and denies their contributions to society, implying that progress comes only through the efforts of the ingroup (Greenfield, 1975). All forms of prejudiced speech serve to draw clear boundaries that separate the "good" ingroup from the "bad" outgroup.

Covert discrimination   **Covert discrimination** consists of "unequal and harmful treatment . . . that is hidden, purposeful, and, often, maliciously motivated. . . . [It is] behavior that consciously attempts to ensure . . . failure, as in hiring or other employment situations" (Benokraitis & Feagin, 1995, p. 42). Covert discrimination tends to be very difficult to document. Examples in the employment context include tokenism, hiring one or a few members of a group as evidence that an organization does not discriminate; containment, restricting members of a group to a limited number of job categories; and sabotage, arranging for members of a group to fail, such as by assigning them low volume sales territories but setting their sales quotas at levels similar to those of salespeople with better territories (Benokraitis & Feagin, 1995). As an example of containment, consider the results of Sharon Collins's (1997) interviews with Black executives in large White-owned corporations. She found that 63 percent had been career-tracked into jobs designed to "mediate the social pressures related to black protest for civil rights, [such as] affirmative action or urban affairs manager" (p. 327). Often, the only "qualification" these executives had was their race: Professionals with advanced degrees in fields such as accounting, engineering, and chemistry were put into these positions despite the fact that they had no training or previous experience in the field. These managers were moved from their chosen career fields based solely on a stereotype—that members of minority groups make better diversity managers simply because of their group membership. Furthermore, such jobs tend to be "dead-end" positions, slowing the incumbent's career progression (James, 2000). Lower-level employees may be segregated not by job, but by supervisor. For example, Joel Lefokowitz (1994) found that clerical workers who had supervisors of a race different than their own tended to move to jobs supervised by a member of their own race, usually within the first 5 months of their employment.

Levels of Discrimination

Each type of discrimination can occur at any of four levels of society: interpersonal, institutional, organizational, and cultural (Benokraitis & Feagin, 1995). Because psychologists have focused their attention primarily on interpersonal and organizational discrimination, we examine discrimination at those levels later in this chapter. For now, let us briefly describe the nature of discrimination at each level.

Interpersonal discrimination   **Interpersonal discrimination** consists of the behaviors individuals direct at other individuals. These behaviors can be passive, such as when White commuters avoid sitting next to Black riders on public transportation (Jacobs, 1999) or when restaurant personnel ignore Black patrons to give priority to White patrons. Interpersonal discrimination can also be active, ranging in intensity from hostile stares (Swim et al., 2003) through demeaning remarks and commands (Swim, Hyers, Cohen, & Ferguson, 2001; Swim et al., 2003) and men touching women inappropriately (Swim et al., 2001) to hate crimes, including murder (Levin & McDevitt, 2002).

Institutional discrimination   **Institutional discrimination** occurs when the norms, policies, and practices associated with a social institution such as the family, religious institutions, the educational system, and the criminal justice system, result in different outcomes for members of different groups (Benokraitis & Feagin, 1995). Institutional discrimination often results from decisions that are neutral in regard to race, gender, and sexual orientation, but end up having a disparate impact on members of a group. Myron Rothbart and Robert Mauro (1996) give the example of the behavioral profile that police officers use to identify potential drug couriers. They noted that a study Mauro had conducted in Oregon found that, of motorists stopped because they fit the profile, 48 percent were Hispanic, whereas only 27 percent were non-Hispanic Whites. However, searches found drugs in only 20 percent of the cases in which Hispanic motorists were stopped compared to 30 percent of the cases in which non-Hispanic White motorists were stopped. Why were Hispanic drivers more likely to be stopped even though they were less likely to be transporting drugs? "A clue can be found in the content of the profile. . . . In the study area, many of [the items in the profile]—such as traveling to or from a source area for illicit drugs (such as Los Angeles or Mexico) and being extremely nervous when contacted by the police—are correlated with being Hispanic" (Rothbart & Mauro, 1996, p. 155). Thus, although the drug courier profile is itself race neutral, Hispanics were more likely to fit the profile, leading some police officers to "treat 'Hispanic' as if it were an additional profile item. This caused them to spend hours engaged in fruitless searches. In fact, had the officers ignored race and relied solely on the factors in the drug courier profile (and used a moderately conservative decision rule), they could have made hundreds more successful searches" (Rothbart & Mauro, 1996, p. 156).

Organizational discrimination   **Organizational discrimination** is the manifestation of institutional discrimination in the context of a particular organization. It occurs when "the practices, rules, and policies of formal organizations, such as corporations or government agencies" have discriminatory outcomes (Benokraitis & Feagin, 1995, p. 44). Much of people's lives are lived within organizations, especially work organizations, so we have made discrimination within organizations one of the major focuses of this chapter. However, organizational discrimination does not always take place within the work context; it can influence other aspects of people's everyday lives as well. For example, the effects of organizational discrimination can emerge in situations in which the average person would never expect them—in the supermarket. Richard Topolski, Kimberly Boyd-Bowman, and Heather Ferguson (2003) purchased fruit from stores in one of three neighborhoods in a large city: low socioeconomic status (SES), middle class, and upper class. Independent raters evaluated the quality of the fruit for taste and appearance. Raters, who were unaware of where the fruit had been purchased, found the fruit from low SES neighborhoods to appear and taste less fresh than fruit from higher SES neighborhoods, with ratings for fruit from the middle class neighborhoods falling between those for fruit purchased in the other two areas. In addition, participants were significantly more likely to refuse to even taste the fruit from stores located in lower SES neighborhoods. These results provide evidence of discrimination on the basis of social class and race: Census data showed that the low SES neighborhoods included in the study had a higher percentage of minority residents than did the middle class or high SES neighborhoods.

The implications of these findings go beyond just how well or poorly food tastes. As Topolski and his colleagues (2003) note, "all available evidence indicates that individuals in lower SES neighborhoods receive fewer options and lower quality of perishable groceries. In the absence of . . . quality perishable goods, such individuals may resort to purchasing nutritionally inferior grocery items such as processed or junk foods. . . . As a result, they will have reduced intake of vitamins and minerals considered essential for maximally healthy development" (p. 117).

Cultural discrimination   **Cultural discrimination** consists of "discrimination and inequality . . . built into our literature, art, music, language, morals, customs, beliefs, and ideology . . . [to such a degree that they] define a generally agreed-upon way of life" (Benokraitis & Feagin, 1995, p. 49; see also Jones, 1997). For example, modern American culture has a Eurocentric standard of beauty: The more European one's physical features are, the more beautiful one is considered to be. Whites are not the only group to adhere to this standard. Mark Hill (2002) analyzed data from a national survey of Black Americans as part of which Black interviewers rated the skin color and physical attractiveness of the people they interviewed. Hill found that lighter skin was associated with higher attractiveness ratings of both male and female interviewees, although the relationship was stronger for women. Lighter skin color is also associated with higher self-ratings of attractiveness among African Americans and Puerto Ricans (Hall, 1998, 2002).

INTERPERSONAL DISCRIMINATION

Interpersonal discrimination refers to individual, person-to-person discrimination: one person treating another unfairly because of the person's group membership. This section addresses four aspects of interpersonal discrimination. The first deals with the relationship between prejudice and discrimination and the circumstances under which prejudice is more or less likely to predict discriminatory behavior. The second section examines an important factor affecting interpersonal discrimination, people's motivation to control their prejudiced feelings and discriminatory behavior. The third section discusses factors that can undermine motivation to control prejudice and allow discriminatory behavior to occur. The final section examines how people react to having acted in a prejudiced manner.

The Relation between Prejudice and Discrimination

As we noted earlier, when asked what causes interpersonal discrimination, most people would probably reply "prejudice." If that were the case, one would expect to find a strong correlation between people's prejudiced attitudes and their propensity to engage in discriminatory behavior. However, when John Dovidio and his colleagues (Dovidio, Brigham, Johnson, & Gaertner, 1996) reviewed the results of 23 studies of the prejudice discrimination relationship, they found an average of correlation of $r = .32$. Even when researchers find fairly high correlations between prejudice and discrimination, about 30 percent of the participants in those studies exhibited behavior that was inconsistent with their attitudes (Duckitt, 1994). Although results such as these might seem discouraging, they are, in fact, consistent with the results of research on the relationship between attitudes and behavior in general. For example, Stephen Kraus (1995) found an average correlation of $r = .38$ between attitudes and behavior across a wide variety of domains. As it turns out, attitudes are related to behavior, but the relationship is not a simple one: A number of factors influence that strength of the attitude-behavior relationship (Eagly & Chaikin, 1998). Some of the factors that influence the prejudice-discrimination relationship are personal stereotypes, attitude-behavior correspondence, and perceived social support for the attitude.

Personal stereotypes   Recall from Chapter 3 that stereotypes can exist at two levels. Social stereotypes are characteristics of groups that most people in a society agree on and personal stereotypes are individuals' beliefs about group characteristics. Personal stereotypes usually overlap with social stereotypes, but some of their content may be different. Prejudiced people are more likely to discriminate against outgroup members who fit their personal stereotype of the outgroup than against those who do not. In a study of this process, Shawna Ramsey and her colleagues (Ramsey, Lord, Wallace, & Pugh, 1994) assessed college students' personal stereotypes of former mental patients. Several weeks later, the students read about a former mental patient who either closely matched their personal stereotype or who was very different from their stereotype but matched other students' stereotype.

For example, some students stereotyped former mental patients in terms of schizophrenic symptoms whereas others stereotyped them in terms of depressive symptoms. The students then chose from a list of activities those they would be willing to engage in with the former mental patient, such as showing the person the university library and taking the person to a party. For students who read about a person who fit their personal stereotype, Ramsey and her colleagues found a correlation of $r = .43$ between attitudes toward former mental patients and the number of activities in which they were willing to engage. For students who read about a person who did not fit their personal stereotype, the correlation was only $r = -.07$.

Attitude-behavior correspondence   The term *attitude-behavior correspondence* refers to how well an attitude matches, as it were, the behavior it is supposed to be associated with. A higher degree of correspondence results in a higher attitude-behavior correlation. One type of correspondence that is important to the prejudice-discrimination relationship is the degree to which people can control their responses on the attitude measure and the degree to which they can control the behavior being measured. Dovidio and his colleagues (1996) noted that explicit paper-and-pencil measures of prejudice assess controllable responses: People can think about how they want to respond and carefully choose their responses, so social desirability response bias can affect their answers; however, implicit attitude measures assess relatively uncontrollable attitudes, so there is less opportunity for social desirability response bias to affect responses (see Chapter 2). Similarly, some behaviors, such as the content of what a person says, are controllable and so can be affected by a social desirability response bias, whereas other behaviors, such as many nonverbal behaviors, are more automatic and difficult to control and so are less likely to be influenced by a social desirability response bias. Drawing on the correspondence principle, Dovidio and his colleagues proposed that scores on controllable measures of prejudice should be correlated with controllable behaviors but not with automatic behaviors and that scores on implicit measures of prejudice should be correlated with automatic behaviors but not with controllable behaviors.

John Dovidio, Kerry Kawakami, and Samuel Gaertner (2002) tested this hypothesis in a study in which White college students completed explicit and implicit measures of prejudice. The participants then discussed several race-neutral topics, such as what personal belongings were most useful to bring to college, with a Black student confederate who played the role of another research participant. The interactions were videotaped, and raters later coded the White students' behaviors for the friendliness of their (automatic) nonverbal behaviors and for the friendliness of what they said (controllable behavior). The researchers found that, as they had expected, implicit prejudice correlated with nonverbal friendliness but not with verbal friendliness and explicit prejudice correlated with verbal friendliness but not with nonverbal friendliness. Similarly, Denise Sekaquaptewa and her colleagues (Sekaquaptewa, Espinoza, Thompson, Vargas, & von Hippel, 2003) found that an implicit measure of prejudice was related to White students' tendency to choose to ask a Black student stereotypic rather than nonstereotypic questions from a list provided by the researchers.

Perceived social support   The term *perceived social support* refers to the extent to which people believe that others share their attitudes and opinions. Generally, attitudes for which people perceive more social support are more closely related to their behavior than attitudes for which they perceive less social support. For example, Gretchen Sechrist and Charles Stangor (2001) conducted a study in which White college students were pretested for level of racial prejudice and selected for participation in a study conducted several weeks later based on their having high or low scores. As part of the study, participants were told that either 81 percent of the students at their university agreed with his or her racial attitudes (high social support condition) or that 19 percent agreed with them (low social support condition). The researchers then used what is known as the waiting room ploy to assess discrimination: The research apparatus "malfunctioned" and the experimenter asked the participant to wait in the hallway, where seven chairs were lined up in a row, with a female African American student seated in the chair next to the door to the laboratory. Discrimination was assessed by how many chairs away from the Black student the participant sat. Not surprisingly, the students who had scored low on prejudice sat closer to the Black student than those who had scored high, an average of 2 seats versus 3.9 seats away. In addition, perceived social support affected the behavior of prejudiced participants, with those who thought that most of their fellow students also were prejudiced sitting farther from the Black woman than those who thought that most of their peers were unprejudiced, an average of 4.3 seats versus 3.4 seats. Perceived social support had no effect on seating distance of the students low on prejudice. Sechrist and Stangor also found a much higher prejudice-discrimination correlation for the students high in prejudice, $r = .76$, than for the students low in prejudice, $r = .33$.

Motivation to Control Prejudice

The theories of contemporary prejudice discussed in Chapter 5 postulate that all people are prejudiced to some degree, even if they are not consciously aware of it. A corollary to these theories is that, because of the prejudice that affects them, people sometimes feel an impulse to behave in a prejudiced or discriminatory manner but restrain that behavior because the egalitarian aspect of their value systems motivates them to act in an unprejudiced manner (Crandall & Eshleman, 2003). For example, a White person might find himself about to say something along the lines of, "Well, that's a typical X for you," with X being a derogatory term for an ethnic group. However, realizing what he was about to say, he restrains himself and says nothing. This section considers some factors that motivate that kind of control of prejudiced reactions. Two pairs of researchers, Bridget Dunton and Russell Fazio (1997) and Ashby Plant and Patricia Devine (1998), have studied the factors that motivate suppression of prejudiced behavior. Because these pairs of researchers worked on the issue separately, they developed somewhat different, yet compatible, approaches to the problem.

Motivation to control prejudiced reactions   Dunton and Fazio (1997) proposed that people experience a **motivation to control prejudiced reactions.** In

Dunton and Fazio's view, this motivation has two aspects, *concern with acting prejudiced* and *restraint to avoid dispute.* The first aspect involves concern that others might think that one is prejudiced, being personally bothered by having prejudiced thoughts or feelings, and having a personal commitment to avoid acting in a prejudiced manner. This concern is reflected in statements such as those shown in the first section of Table 10.2. Restraint to avoid dispute involves the awareness that saying and doing some kinds of things (such as telling racial jokes) would cause trouble, combined with a willingness to not say or do those things as a way of avoiding arguments. This characteristic is reflected in statements such as those shown in the second section of Table 10.2. Thus, people avoid doing some things so they will not appear to be prejudiced to themselves and other people, to avoid arguments, or both.

The usefulness of Dunton and Fazio's (1997) approach is shown by research they conducted using implicit and explicit measures of prejudice. As would be expected, people with positive implicit attitudes toward African Americans exhibited positive explicit attitudes. Because they have unprejudiced implicit attitudes, these people are unlikely to experience impulses toward prejudiced behavior, so they have no reason to control their explicit responses. Similarly, people with negative implicit attitudes but low motivation to control prejudiced responses exhibited negative explicit attitudes. Because they are not motivated to suppress their

---

TABLE 10.2 STATEMENTS ILLUSTRATING DIFFERENT TYPES OF MOTIVATION TO SUPPRESS PREJUDICED RESPONSES

Concern with Acting Prejudiced (Dunton & Fazio, 1997, p. 319)

"It's important to me that other people not think I'm prejudiced."

"I get angry with myself when I have a thought or feeling that might be considered prejudiced."

"It bothers me a great deal when I think I've offended someone, so I'm always careful to consider other people's feelings."

Restraint to Avoid Dispute (Dunton & Fazio, 1997, p. 319)

(Agreement with these items indicates low restraint)

"I always express my thoughts and feelings, regardless of how controversial they might be."

"I think that it is important to speak one's mind rather than to worry about offending someone."

Internal Motivation (Plant & Devine, 1998, p. 630)

"Because of my personal values, I believe that using stereotypes about Black people is wrong."

"Being nonprejudiced toward Black people is important to my self-concept."

External Motivation (Plant & Devine, 1998, p. 630)

"I attempt to appear nonprejudiced toward Black people in order to avoid disapproval from others."

"If I acted prejudiced toward Black people, I would be concerned that others would be angry with me."

---

prejudiced behavior, they express prejudice freely. However, people with negative implicit attitudes and high motivation to control prejudiced responses exhibit overly positive behaviors. That is, like people experiencing ambivalent prejudice, they overcompensate for their negative implicit attitudes with overly positive behavior.

These factors also are related to intergroup interaction. Tamara Towles-Schwen and Russell Fazio (2003) found that people who are low on restraint to avoid dispute express a willingness to interact with African Americans regardless of their implicit attitudes. People who are low on restraint also have more experience interacting with African Americans, so presumably they have learned how to carry on interracial interactions without letting any negative attitudes they may hold get in the way. However, people with negative implicit attitudes who are low on concern with appearing prejudiced but high on restraint prefer to avoid interracial interactions, perhaps as a way of avoiding the trouble that expressing their negative attitudes might cause.

Motivation to respond without prejudice   Plant and Devine (1998) proposed that people experience what they refer to as **motivation to respond without prejudice.** Working from the perspective that a norm exists in the United States that discourages expressions of prejudice, Plant and Devine postulated that motivation to comply with that norm can come from two sources. The first source is internal, stemming from a personal belief system that holds that prejudice is wrong; this type of motivation is reflected in statements such as those shown in the third section of Table 10.2. The other source of motivation to comply with the nonprejudiced norm is external, a result of social pressure. This type of motivation is reflected in statements such as those shown in the last section of Table 10.2. In essence, internally motivated people act in a nonprejudiced way because it is personally important to them to do so; externally motivated people act in a nonprejudiced way to avoid negative reactions from other people.

In contrast to Dunton and Fazio (1997), who combined internal and external motivation into a single concern with acting prejudiced dimension, Plant and Devine (1998) conceptualize internal and external motivation as separate dimensions, so that a person can experience one type of motivation but not the other, experience both types of motivation simultaneously, or experience neither type of motivation. As a result, Plant and Devine's approach allows researchers to determine the factors that are specifically associated with each source of motivation. For example, people high in internal motivation judge their intergroup behavior by their personal standards; if they act in a prejudiced way, they feel guilty and criticize themselves because they have violated personal values that are important to them. In contrast, people high in external motivation who act in a prejudiced manner feel threatened because they anticipate a negative response from other people.

As might be expected, people who are high in internal motivation to control prejudice exhibit less explicit prejudice than people low in internal motivation. In addition, people high in internal motivation who are also low in external motivation (remember, it is possible to be high on both) score lower on physiological and implicit cognition measures of prejudice (Amodio, Harmon-Jones, & Devine,

2003; Devine, Plant, Amodio, Harmon-Jones, & Vance, 2002). Devine and her colleagues interpret these results to mean that people high in internal motivation to control prejudice, especially those who are also low on external motivation, have so thoroughly integrated their nonprejudiced standards into their personal belief systems that they automatically control even implicit and physiological indicators of prejudice. Furthermore, people who are both high in internal motivation and low in external motivation show low levels of implicit prejudice when distracted, suggesting that they control their negative attitudes automatically, without conscious effort (Devine et al., 2002).

An interesting finding that has emerged from the research of Plant and her colleagues is that although high internal motivation to control prejudice is associated with *low* scores on measures of explicit prejudice (average $r = -.65$), external motivation is associated with *high* scores on those measures (average $r = .28$) (Amodio et al., 2003; Devine et al., 2002; Plant & Devine, 1998; Plant, Devine, & Brazy, 2003). Why would external motivation to *control* prejudice be associated with *more* prejudice? Plant and Devine (1998) hypothesize that people high in external motivation, especially those who are also low in internal motivation, probably try to avoid situations where they have to interact with members of minority groups so as to avoid pressure from others to control their prejudices in that situation. When put in settings where they cannot avoid intergroup contact and must control public expression of prejudice (such as classrooms and the workplace), they try to do so (Plant & Devine, 1998; Plant et al., 2003) and are generally able to do so (Monteith, Spicer, & Tooman, 1998), but feel frustrated by the process. They also report generally feeling more pressure to act in a "politically correct" manner than do other people (Plant & Devine, 2001).

Plant and Devine (2001) believe that these negative feelings cause an anti-minority backlash in people high in external motivation to control prejudice. This backlash against pressure from others is reflected in higher levels of explicit prejudice. In addition, when put under pressure to favor a Black person over a White person or to support a policy that benefits Blacks over Whites, people high in external motivation to control prejudice will do so. However, those who are also low in internal motivation to control prejudice feel more angry and resentful about the pressure than other people and are less favorable toward African Americans and pro-Black policies after the pressure has been released (Plant & Devine, 2001). Consequently, putting pressure on other people to change negative intergroup attitudes they hold could backfire, reinforcing rather than reducing their prejudice.

Social norms   An important aspect of external motivation to control prejudice that deserves a little more discussion is motivation to comply with social norms. **Social norms** are informal rules that groups develop that describe how to be a good group member (Forsyth, 2006). These rules govern both behavior—how a group member is supposed to act—and attitudes—the types of beliefs a group member is supposed to hold. For example, members of the Democratic Party expect one another to vote for Democratic candidates and to hold relatively liberal political attitudes whereas members of the Republican Party expect one another to vote for Republican candidates and to hold relatively conservative political attitudes.

Attitude norms sometimes include prejudices; group norms promote some prejudices, such as "Students at our college are better than students at the college that is our biggest rival," and forbid others, such as racial prejudice. Because being a good group member means adhering to group norms, "to be a good group member, one must adopt the prejudices that the group holds and abstain from those prejudices that the group frowns upon" (Crandall et al., 2002, p. 360). The normativeness of discrimination against a group is a function of the normativeness of prejudice against that group. In a study of these hypotheses, Crandall and his colleagues (2002) had college students rate the acceptability of prejudice and discrimination against a number of social groups. They found an average correlation of $r = .82$ between the acceptability of prejudice against a group and the acceptability of discrimination against the group. Thus, people feel comfortable expressing normative prejudices and discriminating against targets of those prejudices because they believe that other people will approve; similarly, they are reluctant to express nonnormative prejudices and to discriminate against members of normatively protected groups because they believe that others will disapprove (see also Franco & Maass, 1999).

Researchers have typically investigated the effects of people's perceptions of social norms on discriminatory behavior by providing research participants made-up information about a group norm and then assessing the attitudes they express. For example, Fletcher Blanchard, Terri Lilly, and Leigh Ann Vaughn (1991) conducted an on-campus survey of responses to racist behavior. When the person conducting the survey approached a student to participate, one or two student confederates of the researchers joined the participant and interviewer. The interviewer told the students that all of them could answer the questions. The confederates always answered first, responding with either the most pro-racist answer to each question, the most anti-racist answer to each question, or with a neutral (middle of the response scale) answer. These different responses created the three conditions of the experiment. Blanchard and his colleagues found that students provided with a racist norm responded in a more racist manner than those provided with a neutral norm and those provided with an anti-racist norm responded in a more anti-racist manner. Other researchers have obtained similar results (for example, Blanchard, Crandall, Brigham, & Vaughn, 1994; Crandall et al., 2002; Monteith, Deneen, & Tooman, 1996), although the effect is more consistent for anti-racist norms than for pro-racist norms.

Social norms will have greater influence on some people than on others. For example, David Trafimow and Krystina Finlay (1999) compared the extent to which personal attitudes versus social norms influenced people's performance of 30 behaviors. They found that normative influence was more important than personal attitudes for 21 percent of the participants in their research. In addition, social identity theory (see Chapter 8) predicts that group norm effects will be stronger for people who identify more strongly with the group (Hogg & Mullin, 1999). This prediction was borne out in a study conducted by Charles Stangor, Gretchen Sechrist, and John Jost (2001), who provided college students with information that indicated that their racial stereotypes were less positive than those of students at either their own college (their ingroup) or another college (an outgroup). A week later, in what was supposedly a different experiment, Stangor and his colleagues found that students who were given information about their ingroup norm expressed more positive racial attitudes than those given information about the outgroup norm.

The development of motivation to control prejudice

Where does motivation to control prejudice come from? Two sets of researchers have taken somewhat different, but nonetheless compatible, approaches to answering this question. Working with the concepts used in Dunton and Fazio's (1997) model, Towles-Schwen and Fazio (2001) looked for the childhood correlates of concern with appearing prejudiced and restraint to avoid dispute by asking college students about their childhood experiences. They found that high concern with appearing prejudiced was associated with parental emphasis on egalitarian values and positive contact with Black people during childhood (although the absolute number of contacts was not important). "These children learned that they should not act prejudiced from their parents while still very young and these values were reinforced by positive interactions early in childhood" (Towles-Schwen & Fazio, 2001, p. 173). People high in restraint to avoid dispute reported having grown up with prejudiced parents, having had little contact with Black people during childhood, and that their primary exposure to Black people was through media portrayals. In addition, they remembered the few contacts they did have with Black people as being negative. Towles-Schwen and Fazio (2001) concluded that "restraint promotes control because the individuals' backgrounds are such that their inexperience with Blacks and/or their prejudiced home environment provide cause for their believing that their actions might provoke dispute" (pp. 173–174).

Crandall and his colleagues (2002) view the development of internal and external motivation to control prejudice as a matter of accommodation to group norms, a perspective similar to that of Plant and Devine (see, for example, Devine et al., 2002). As shown in Figure 10.1, this model begins with people's being embedded a normative context, such as that of their childhood, for which they have learned the governing norms without being aware of having done so. These norms, including those dealing with the expression and control of prejudice, comprise the "natural" rules of behavior for people raised as part of that social group. These individuals have no need for specific sources of motivation to control prejudice; they know what behaviors the group will and will not accept and "naturally" comply with the group's norms. When people move to a new normative environment, such as by leaving home to go to college, some of the expressions of prejudice that were permissible in their previous environment may no longer be acceptable. People in the new environment provide external motivation to control prejudice by putting pressure on the new arrivals to comply with the new group's norms concerning prejudice, although at this point the new arrivals may have little internal motivation to do so. One possible response to this pressure would be to leave the new group to escape the pressure.

However, if the people are attracted to the new group, they will try to fit in by complying with the group's norms. To the extent that people begin to identify with the new group, that is, as membership in the group becomes important to their self-concepts, they develop an internal motivation to control prejudice based on

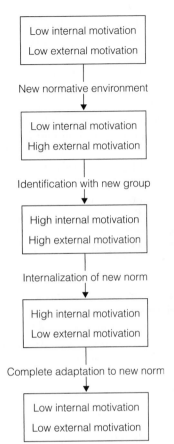

FIGURE **10.1**

THE NORMATIVE CONTEXT AND MOTIVATION TO CONTROL PREJUDICE

When people are fully embedded in a normative context they experience no motivation to control prejudice because they automatically comply with the relevant norms. When they move to a new normative environment, they first experience external motivation as people in the new environment external pressure to comply with their norms. As the new arrivals come to identify with the new group, they develop an internal motivation to control prejudice. As the new norm becomes part of their value system, external motivation declines. Finally, when compliance with the new norm becomes fully automatic, internal motivation is no longer needed.

Based on Crandall, Eshleman, & O'Brien (2002).

their desire to fit in with the group. At this point they experience external motivation as well as internal because they still depend on the group for information about what the norm entails. As people internalize the new norm and make it part of their value system, internal motivation remains, but external motivation declines. When people become fully adapted to the group norm, internal motivation declines because they no longer need to monitor their behavior; behaving in accord with the norm has become automatic.

Regressive Prejudice

Earlier, we gave the hypothetical example of a White person who was about to make a derogatory comment about a minority group but kept himself from doing so. Crandall and Eshleman (2003) have noted that exerting that kind of control over prejudiced responses requires a great deal of mental work: One must recognize that prejudice might be affecting one's behavior and then consciously change that behavior to produce a nonprejudiced response. Although, as postulated by Plant and Devine (1998; Devine et al., 2002), this process might become automatic for some people, others have to work at it. The laborious nature of this process is demonstrated by research showing that people experience a sense of relief when they are allowed to express prejudices they have been controlling (Crandall & Eshleman, 2003). Thus, it is not surprising that even people who score low on measures of prejudice report sometimes making prejudiced responses toward members of other groups (Monteith & Voils, 1998; Voils, Ashburn-Nardo, & Monteith, 2002). That is, even people who see themselves as unprejudiced and who score low on measures of prejudice sometimes find themselves acting in prejudiced ways. Box 10.2 provides an example of how an everyday event can trigger prejudiced reactions even in unprejudiced people. Ronald Rogers and Steven Prentice-Dunn (1981) labeled such expressions of prejudice by people who are otherwise low in prejudice **regressive racism (prejudice).** Rogers and Prentice-Dunn proposed that regressive prejudice occurs because controlling prejudiced responses requires attention and mental resources; when those resources are not available or when the control process is short-circuited people regress from controlling prejudice to expressing it. This section examines some of the factors that can produce regressive prejudice.

Control over behavior   To avoid responding in a certain way, people must be able to control the behavior. As we noted earlier, some behaviors, such as nonverbal responses, are less under voluntary control than others, such as the content of what one says. Consequently, people may give off nonverbal cues that imply dislike of or discomfort with a member of a stereotyped group even while trying to behave in a positive manner (see, for example, Dovidio et al., 2002; Dovidio, Kawakami, Johnson, Johnson, & Howard, 1997; Fazio, Jackson, Dunton, & Williams, 1995). In one study of this process, Dovidio and his colleagues (2002) tested White research participants for implicit prejudice against African Americans. Each participant then held a 3-minute conversation with a Black student who was working for the researchers; because the conversation was about a race-neutral topic, the White participants were presumably motivated to act in a nonprejudiced manner. However, compared to the nonverbal behavior of participants with lower prejudice scores, the behavior of those with higher scores was rated as less friendly by both the participants' Black conversational partners and White raters who saw videos of the participants' side of the conversation. Thus, when people hold stereotyped views of other groups, those views may "leak out" through their nonverbal behavior even while they are trying to control the effects of those stereotypes on other behaviors (see also Sekaquaptewa et al., 2003).

Cognitive demands   As we saw in Chapter 4, cognitive demands, such as trying to remember an 8-digit number or working under time pressure, make it difficult for people to control the effects of stereotypes and prevent stereotypes from affecting their judgments. The same processes affect the expression of prejudice: Even for people who are motivated to control their prejudices, cognitive demands can reduce their mental resources and so reduce control. To demonstrate this effect, Daniel Wegner and his colleagues (reported in Wegner, 1994) had research participants complete sentences about women such as "Women who go with a lot of men are . . ." (Wegner, 1994, p. 47). Half the participants were instructed not to be sexist in their responses and half received no special instructions; in addition,

10.2   *Stereotype Arousal in Everyday Life*

Most research on stereotype arousal uses laboratory methods, so you might wonder how well those procedures generalize to everyday life. Consider the following commercial that was televised in 1995.

The commercial opens with a picture of a poker-faced, vaguely threatening and ominous Black man with his head shaved that takes up the left two-thirds of the screen. After a moment, the following lines appear one at a time down the right side of the screen, with a pause between each:

Michael Conrad.
Male. Age 28.
Trafficking.
Armed Robbery.
Assault and Battery.
Extortion.

Rape.
Murder.
Apprehended
January 1994 by
Joseph Cruthers,
Shown here. (Urban Alliance on Race
Relations, 1995)

By the time "Apprehended" appears, most people assume the picture is that of the criminal, Michael Conrad. When they learn that the picture is that of a policeman, they feel both surprised and upset that they have operated on the social stereotype that Black men are dangerous and made the racist assumption that the pictured Black man must be a criminal (Fazio & Hilden, 2001).

half the participants in each of these groups were put under time pressure to respond and half were not. Wegner and his colleagues found that participants who had been instructed to avoid sexist responses (and therefore were motivated to do so) and were not under time pressure to respond provided fewer sexist responses (such as "sluts" to the sentence stem just given) than participants who received no such instructions. However, time pressure undermined the ability to control prejudice of the participants who were motivated to be nonsexist: They made sexist responses at the same rate as the participants who were not motivated to control their sexism.

Disinhibitors   Because motivation to control prejudice derives from social norms to avoid being prejudiced, factors that reduce people's motivation to comply with social norms can also reduce motivation to control prejudice and disinhibit its expression. Two factors that motivate norm compliance are the desire to avoid the social punishments that other people would mete out for violating norms and the desire to receive the rewards that others provide for norm compliance. As a result, when people are anonymous and cannot be identified, they are less motivated to comply with norms than when they are identifiable (see, for example, Myers, 2002). Edward and Marcia Donnerstein (1976) tested the effects of anonymity on the release of prejudice in a study in which White research participants gave what they thought were electric shocks to a Black or White confederate for making errors on a learning task. Donnerstein and Donnerstein assessed aggressive discrimination in two ways. Because participants used a dial to set a shock level, they used shock intensity as an indicator of overt, direct aggression; however, because the length of time the participants pressed the button that administered the shock was a less clear-cut behavior than setting the shock level, they used shock duration as an indicator of covert, indirect aggression. Half the participants thought that their behavior was being monitored and half thought they were anonymous. Donnerstein and Donnerstein found that anonymous participants showed more direct aggression toward the Black than the White person, indicating that anonymity facilitated discriminatory behavior.

Two other of Donnerstein and Donnerstein's findings also are interesting. In contrast to their anonymous peers, participants who were identifiable favored the Black person by showing less direct aggression toward him than toward the White person, perhaps reflecting a motivation not to appear prejudiced similar to that felt by people experiencing ambivalent prejudice. In addition, nonanonymous participants showed a higher level of indirect aggression toward the Black person than the White person, perhaps reflecting the tendency of people experiencing aversive prejudice to let their attitudes show in covert ways. (See Chapter 5 for a discussion of ambivalent and aversive prejudice.)

Strong emotions also can lead people to ignore social norms. In another study of interracial aggression, Rogers and Prentice-Dunn (1981) gave angered and calm White research participants the opportunity to administer electric shocks to a Black or White person. Their results paralleled those Donnerstein and Donnerstein (1976) found for anonymity: Angry participants gave stronger shocks to the Black person than to the White person, whereas calm participants gave stronger shocks to the White person. Alcohol consumption is another notorious disinhibitor of compliance with social norms. Not surprisingly, then, Laurie O'Brien and her colleagues (as reported in Crandall & Eshleman, 2003) found a correlation of .31 between alcohol intoxication (as measured by Breathalyzer tests of people leaving bars) and willingness to express prejudice against racial and religious groups.

The expression of prejudice is a forbidden act, but the implied approval of an authority figure can release normative restraints. For example, Donnerstein and Donnerstein (1976) reported a study in which White participants observed a peer delivering an intense electric shock to a Black person. Some of the participants then saw the experimenter overseeing the study severely reprimand the person for delivering such a strong shock; other participants saw the experimenter ignore the shock level, thus implicitly giving approval to it. Participants in a control condition saw a shock being administered but did not know its intensity. All the participants then took part in the experiment. Compared to the control participants, those who saw a peer reprimanded for administering a strong shock gave weaker shocks, but those who saw no reprimand gave much more severe shocks.

Finally, other people's behavior can disinhibit prejudice. Linda Simon and Jeff Greenberg (1996) created a situation in which four White research participants and a Black confederate worked in separate cubicles on a creativity task. The

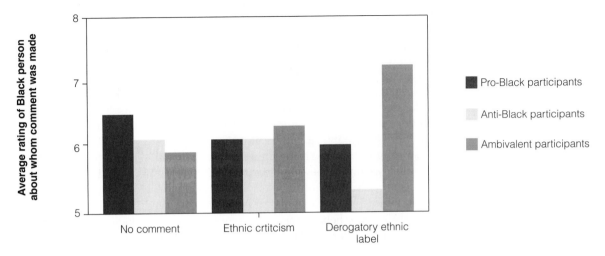

Type of comment overheard

FIGURE **10.2**

PRIMING AS A RELEASER OF REGRESSIVE PREJUDICE

White research participants overheard either no comment about a Black confederate, a critical comment that included a reference to race ("Black person"), or a critical comment that included a derogatory ethnic label ("nigger"). Ratings of the Black person made by participants who had positive attitudes toward Blacks were not affected by the type of comment overheard. However, participants with negative attitudes toward Blacks made more negative ratings when they overheard the derogatory ethnic label. In contrast, the ratings made by participants characterized by ambivalent prejudice were higher when they overheard the derogatory ethnic label.

Data from Simon and Greenberg (1996), Table 1, p. 1199.

participants had been earlier determined to have positive, negative, or ambivalent attitudes toward African Americans. The participants labeled their answers with a code letter they wrote on a yellow sticky note attached to the answer sheet. They then evaluated what they thought were the other participants' responses (actually standard responses created by the researchers) that the experimenter passed around one at a time. Some participants received a list with no comment added to the sticky note, others received a list with a handwritten addition to the sticky note that read "I can't believe they stuck us with this Black person! (please erase this)" (the ethnic criticism condition), and a third group of participants received a list with a note that read "I can't believe they stuck us with this nigger! (please erase this)" (the derogatory ethnic label condition). As shown in Figure 10.2, participants with positive attitudes toward African Americans were unaffected by the comment manipulation, giving the Black participant's contribution a rating of about 6 in all conditions. Consistent with the theory of ambivalent prejudice, racially ambivalent participants inflated their ratings in the derogatory label condition, presumably to emphasize that they were not prejudiced. However, anti-Black participants who had been primed by the derogatory label felt free to express their prejudice, resulting in lower ratings than in the other two conditions.

Moral credentials   When we, the authors, were growing up, it was not unusual for a White person who was accused of anti-Black prejudice to defend himself by saying something along the lines of, "How can you call me prejudiced? Why, some of my best friends are Black!" The claim of friendship was used as a kind of credential to establish the person's lack of prejudice. More recently, Benoît Monin and Dale Miller (2001) have suggested that complying with the norm to avoid prejudiced behavior can have an ironic effect: It can increase the likelihood of behaving in a prejudiced way in the future by reducing the motivation to appear unprejudiced. They believe that acting in a nonprejudiced way establishes what they call *moral credentials* by allowing people to show others that they are not prejudiced and by reinforcing their own beliefs that they are not prejudiced. Having established to themselves and to others that they are not prejudiced then allows them to act in a prejudiced manner if they are disposed to do so; if challenged, they can point to their earlier behavior as evidence of their lack of prejudice.

Monin and Miller (2001) tested their theory in a set of studies in which some research participants had an opportunity to establish their unprejudiced credentials by either rejecting a set of stereotypical statements about women or by selecting a well-qualified woman or African American for a job. Other participants had no opportunity to act in a nonprejudiced manner. All participants then rated the extent to which they thought a given job (such as construction foreman or police officer) was better suited for a man or woman, or a Black person or a White person. In all three experiments, participants who had had the opportunity in the first part of the study to establish that they were nonprejudiced rated the job in the second part of the study as better filled by a man or White person. Monin and Miller (2001) concluded that "the more confident people are that their past behavior reveals a lack of prejudice, the less they will worry that their future behavior is, or can be construed as, prejudiced. . . . By fostering self-image security . . . the establishment of moral credentials emboldens the [person] to respond honestly in circumstances in which political correctness pressure militates against honest expression" (p. 40).

Reactions to Having Acted in a Prejudiced Manner

Given that situations can arise that can lead people to make prejudiced responses, how do they then react to having acted in a prejudiced manner? The initial research on this topic focused on differences between people high and low in explicit prejudice. Patricia Devine and her colleagues (Devine, Monteith, Zuwerink, & Elliot, 1991; Monteith, Devine, & Zuwerink, 1993; Zuwerink, Devine, Monteith, & Cook, 1996) hypothesized that people with nonprejudiced self-images who act or think in a prejudiced manner experience a discrepancy between how they think they *should* respond (that is, in a nonprejudiced manner) and how they *do* respond (that is, in a prejudiced manner). This discrepancy then leads to feelings of discomfort and guilt. To test this hypothesis, they examined differences in how people believed they should respond in interactions with an African American or a gay man and how they thought they would actually respond. Not surprisingly, Devine and her colleagues found that people low in prejudice had more stringent personal standards for nonprejudiced behavior than did people high in prejudice. Nonetheless, people both high and low in prejudice felt discomfort over discrepancies between how they thought they should act and how they thought they would act. However, whereas people low in prejudice felt guilty about their discrepancies, people high in prejudice did not. Rather than feeling negative toward themselves over their discrepancies, people high in prejudice experienced negative emotions about other people, such as feeling angry and irritated at them, perhaps because they believed that other people expected them to be unprejudiced and would pressure them to behave in unprejudiced ways.

Recent research has focused on how people with specific motivations to control prejudice respond to having acted in a prejudiced manner. As might be expected, college students with high internal motivation to respond without prejudice experience strong negative emotions, particularly guilt and self-criticism, when they violate their personal standards for behavior (the sources of their internal motivation). Conversely, students with high external motivation to respond without prejudice experience strong negative emotions, particularly feelings of threat, when their actions violate what they see as campus (that is, externally imposed) standards for behavior (the source of their external motivation; Plant & Devine, 1998). In addition, people who are high on restraint to avoid dispute feel uneasy and distressed after having been induced to respond in terms of racial stereotypes, perhaps because they see such responses as being likely to provoke conflict with others (Fazio & Hilden, 2001).

In addition to discovering their own prejudiced behavior, people may be confronted by others who point out behaviors that could indicate prejudice. How do people respond then? Alexander Czopp and Margo Monteith (2003) found that the response depended on two factors. The first was the type of prejudice involved. People felt more concerned and guilty over racial prejudice than over sexism. In fact, "the predominant evaluative sentiment resulting from confrontations about gender-biased behavior was amusement" (Czopp & Monteith, 2003, p. 541), suggesting that many people do not take gender-based prejudice very seriously. The second factor was the person who did the confronting. People were more likely to dismiss an accusation of prejudice when it came from a member of the group toward which their prejudiced behavior was directed than when it came from a member of their own group. Czopp and Monteith suggested that this reaction occurred because people felt less threatened when confronted by a member of their own group, perhaps reflecting Dunton and Fazio's (1997) concept of restraint to avoid dispute. Thus, it appears that the greatest guilt and discomfort over acting in a prejudiced manner is elicited when people have a high internal motivation to control prejudice and when they become aware of their prejudiced responses themselves or have those responses pointed out by a member of their own group.

Researchers have found that guilt over having acted in ways that are discrepant from one's self-image leads to action that reaffirms that image (Steele, 1988). Interestingly, there seems to be no recent research on whether feelings of guilt about having acted in a prejudiced manner affects future behavior, but several older studies have done so. For example, Steven Sherman and Larry Gorkin (1980) induced some research participants to make a sexist decision by leading them to assume that a surgeon depicted in a story was male rather than female; participants in a control condition made no such decision. Later, all participants took part in a seemingly unrelated study in which they acted as mock jurors in a sex discrimination case involving a woman who alleged that she had been refused a job because of her sex, with a man being hired instead. Sherman and Gorkin found that compared to participants in the control condition, those who had been induced to make the sexist decision in the first part of the experiment were more likely to see the hiring of the man as unjustified and were more likely to decide the case in favor of the woman.

Perhaps more telling are the results of an experiment conducted by Donald Dutton and Robert Lake (1973). Based on a pretest, they selected 80 students who were low on prejudice and who had also rated equality as a value that was important to them. The participants thought they were taking part in a study of physiological responsiveness to various stimuli and that high physiological arousal indicated the presence of unconscious negative attitudes toward a stimulus. While their physiological responses were recorded participants watched a series of slides that included pictures of Black people. Half the participants received feedback that indicated unusually high responsiveness to the picture of Black people relative to neutral stimuli (thus threatening their nonprejudiced self-images) whereas the other participants received feedback that indicated similar responses to the two types of stimuli (thus leaving their nonprejudiced self-images unthreatened). All participants were paid $2.00 in quarters (to ensure that they had change for what happened next) for their participation. On leaving the building, participants were approached by either a Black or a White panhandler who asked "Can you spare some change for some food?" Eighty-five percent of the participants in the self-image threat condition gave money to the Black panhandler compared to 45 percent of those in the nonthreat condition. In addition, the participants in the threat condition gave more money (an average of 47 cents) than the participants in the nonthreat condition (an average of 17 cents). Threat condition did not affect donations to the White panhandler. By the way, if 47 cents does not seem like much money, it is equivalent to about $1.95 today when corrected for inflation.

Thus, when people who have nonprejudiced self-images have that image called into question, they feel guilty and that guilt motivates them to reaffirm their self-images of low prejudice by acting in an especially nonprejudiced manner. One question that has not been addressed, though, is the role of motivation to reduce prejudice. Both Sherman and Gorkin (1980) and Dutton and Lake (1973) assumed that, in Plant and Devine's (1998) terms, their participants were internally motivated. It would be interesting to see how externally motivated people would react, especially in light of the research that indicates that they show an anti-minority backlash when pressured to act in an unprejudiced manner (Plant & Devine, 2001).

DISCRIMINATION IN ORGANIZATIONS

As we noted earlier, organizational discrimination occurs when "the practices, rules, and policies of formal organizations, such as corporations or government agencies" result in different outcomes for members of different groups (Benokraitis & Feagin, 1995, p. 44). Although more than 40 years have passed

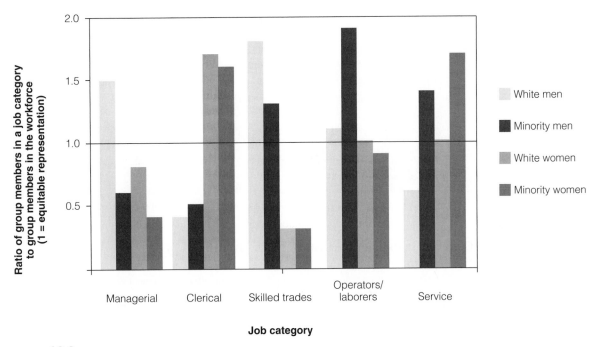

Job category

FIGURE **10.3**

REPRESENTATION OF MEMBERS OF RACIAL/ETHNIC AND GENDER GROUPS IN SELECTED OCCUPATIONAL CATEGORIES IN 2002

This figure shows the ratio of the number of members of each social group employed in a job category to their number in the U.S. workforce. If members of a group were equitably represented in a category, the ratio for that category would be 1.0. Thus, White men are overrepresented in the managerial category, women are overrepresented in clerical jobs and underrepresented in the skilled trades (such as carpenters, electricians, and so forth), minority men are overrepresented in the operators/laborers category (such as drivers, warehouse workers, and so forth), and both minority men and women are overrepresented in service jobs.

Source: U.S. Equal Opportunity Employment Commission, 2004.

since enactment of the landmark Civil Rights Act of 1964, racial/ethnic and gender discrimination still exist in the workplace. For example, Figure 10.3 shows the ratio of White and minority men and women employed in selected job categories to their representation in the workforce in 2002 (U.S. Equal Employment Opportunity Commission [EEOC], 2004). If members of various groups were equitably represented in different job categories, the ratio would be 1.0; ratios greater than 1.0 indicate overrepresentation—more members of the group hold that type of job than would be expected based on their numbers in the workforce—and ratios less than 1.0 indicate underrepresentation. For example, White men make up 37 percent of the workforce but hold 56 percent of managerial jobs, resulting in a ratio of 1.5; that is, White men are 50 percent more likely to be managers than one would expect from their number in the workforce. In contrast, Black women make up 15 percent of the workforce but hold only 6 percent of managerial jobs, resulting in a ratio of 0.4; that is, Black women are

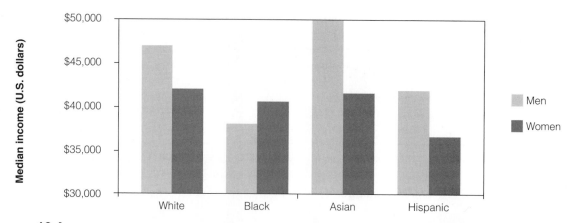

FIGURE **10.4**

MEDIAN INCOME FOR COLLEGE GRADUATE FULL-TIME WORKERS AGE 25 TO 34 IN 2002 BY RACE/ETHNICITY AND GENDER

Except for African Americans, men earned more than women and with the exception of Asian men, Whites earned more than minority group members despite all having a college degree.

Source: U.S. Bureau of the Census, 2003.

60 percent less likely to be managers than one would expect from their number in the workforce. The EEOC data shown in Figure 10.3 indicate that White men are overrepresented as managers whereas White women and members of minority groups are underrepresented; women are overrepresented in clerical jobs whereas men are underrepresented, but the reverse is true for skilled trades (jobs such as carpenter and electrician); Black men are overrepresented as operators and laborers (jobs such as truck driver and assembly worker); and members of minority groups are overrepresented in service occupations whereas White men are underrepresented. In sum, White men still tend to be overrepresented in the more prestigious, higher paying occupations.

One might argue that the employment data are misleading because they include older female and minority workers who were never given the opportunity to get the kind of education and develop the skills that are required for higher paying jobs. However, consider Figure 10.4, which shows median salaries for college graduates of various racial/ethnic and gender groups aged 25 to 34 years and employed full time during 2002 (U. S. Bureau of the Census, 2003). Members of this cohort all have the same level of education, are all at equivalent stages of their careers, and all entered the workforce well after equal employment opportunity legislation took effect. As you can see, except for African Americans, men were paid more than women and White men were paid better than any group except Asian men. The disparity is even greater for people with a high school education but no college: Men of all racial/ethnic groups were paid more than women of any group and White men were the highest paid.

We have divided our discussion of organizational discrimination into two parts. The first part examines employment discrimination at the organizational level. The second part examines some of the psychological variables that influence the discriminatory behavior of people who make decisions in organizations. As you read this section bear in mind that although the effects of gender and racial bias tend to be small (see, for example, Barrett & Morris, 1993), small effects can cumulate over time to have a large impact on career outcomes. For example, Richard Martell, David Lane, and Cynthia Emrich (1996) conducted a computer simulation that modeled the potential effects of gender discrimination in an organization that had eight levels of promotion. The simulation started with an equal number of male and female new employees. Although job qualifications varied among both male and female employees, they were, on the average, the same for both groups; however, there was a very small pro-male bias for promotions at each level. After the simulation had run through all eight levels of promotion, 65 percent of the top-level jobs were filled by men. Therefore, even when discrimination has a small effect on any one decision, it can have larger effects in the long run.

Organizational Research

Organizational researchers have conducted an enormous amount of research to determine the forms discrimination takes in organizations and the ways in which discrimination is related to characteristics of organizations. As we will see, racial discrimination has been found at many points in the employment process, including hiring, job performance evaluations, and promotions. There appears to be less gender discrimination in hiring and performance evaluation, but evidence still supports gender discrimination in promotion. Let us look at the results of some of that research.

Hiring   The first step in the employment process is hiring, so quite a bit of research has been conducted on the hiring process, most of it focusing on racial discrimination. One technique that has been used to study discrimination in hiring is the *employment audit*. In an employment audit, members of two groups are matched on appearance, education, and relevant experience, and then sent to apply for the same job. Thus, one White person and one Black person, both with the same qualifications, dressed similarly, and trained to act similarly, would apply for the same job. The dependent variable in such studies is who is more likely to be hired, the Black applicant or the White applicant? A review of several such studies by James Heckman (1998) found that for the most part, Black and White applicants experience the same outcome: in 68 percent of the cases neither was offered a job and in 15 percent of the cases both were offered a job. However, when discrimination did occur, it favored the White applicant: overall, 27 percent of White applicant were offered jobs compared to 21 percent of Black applicants. That is, a White applicant was 1.3 times more likely to get a job than was a Black applicant.

The results of an employment audit study conducted by Marc Bendick, Charles Jackson, and Victor Reinoso (1994) illustrate some of the specific forms of discrimination that can occur. For example, they found that although employers accepted applications from Black and White job seekers at about the same rate—95 percent for Whites and 92 percent for Blacks—48 percent of the White applicants were offered interviews compared to 40 percent of the Black applicants. When more than one opening was available and the job was offered to both applicants, Black applicants were offered lower starting salaries. In addition, Black applicants were more likely to be steered toward a job at a lower level in the organization than the one they had applied for. Bendick and his colleagues also found that discrimination was more likely to occur when applications were made through employment agencies rather than directly to the company. One reason for this finding might be that the companies using employment agencies cued the agencies that they only wanted to see White applicants. For example, evidence was presented in one employment discrimination lawsuit that employers would use terms such as "all-American," "front-office appearance," and "corporate image" in the job descriptions they sent to employment agencies to indicate that they wanted to see only White job candidates (Wolff, 1989).

One shortcoming of employment audits is that it is impossible to perfectly match a Black and a White applicant in every regard: They are different people with different personalities, so it is always possible that any differences in the responses they received are a result of their individual characteristics rather than of their racial group membership. Therefore, researchers have begun to conduct studies using matched mailed-in résumés to see who is more likely to be called for an interview, a Black applicant or a White applicant. Marianne Bertrand and Sendhil Mullainathan (2003) conducted a large-scale study of this kind, sending out almost 5,000 résumés in response to 1,300 jobs advertised in newspapers in Chicago and Boston. They manipulated three independent variables using information in the résumés: race of the applicant, gender of the applicant, and how well qualified the applicant was for the job. They manipulated race and gender by varying the applicant's first name: "White" names included Kristin, Carrie, Brad, and Jay; "Black" names included Ebony, Latonya, Jermaine, and Leroy. The researchers chose the names based on the frequency of their appearance in birth records and checked the racial associations the names elicited by conducting a survey asking respondents to rate how "Black" and "White" each name sounded.

Bertrand and Mullainathan (2003) found that overall, only 17 percent of the applicants were called for an interview; however, 10.1 percent of the White applicants were called compared to 6.7 percent of the Black applicants. In other words, White applicants received an interview offer for every 10 résumés submitted, whereas Black applicants had to submit 15 résumés to get an interview. In addition, although White applicants with high quality résumés were more likely to be called than White applicants with low quality résumés, 11.3 percent compared to 8.8 percent, résumé quality had virtually no effect on the response rate for Black applicants: 7.0 percent for high quality résumés and 6.4 percent for low quality résumés. Note that a White applicant with a low quality résumé was 26 percent more likely to be called for an interview (8.8 percent) than a Black applicant with a high quality résumé (7.0 percent). The researchers obtained the same results in both Boston and Chicago, and for six types of jobs ranging from clerical worker to manager across six industries. Bertrand and Mullainathan put their results in this context: "in our sample, [having] a White name is equivalent to about 8 additional years of [job-related] experience" in being called for an interview (p. 10).

10.3 *Invisible Man*

Lawrence Graham (1995), a highly successful Harvard educated lawyer, set out to uncover what life was like as an employee at one of the all-White country clubs in Greenwich, Connecticut. In his essay on his experiences, he first describes applying for work. His goal was to be a waiter and he applied for this job at five country clubs. As he writes, "During each of my phone conversations, I made sure that I spoke to the person who would make the hiring decision. I also confirmed exactly how many waiter positions were available, and I arranged a personal interview within forty minutes to an hour of the conversation, just to be sure that they could not tell me that no such job was available" (p. 4). Upon arrival at each of the five clubs, he was told either that there were no openings or that he was not qualified. One receptionist threatened to call security. Another employer firmly insisted he could not have been the person she

talked to on the phone. No one would even accept his application for a waiter position.

Graham did secure a job as a busboy at one of the clubs. In that role, people made negative comments about "Negroes" and other minority groups right in front of him. Example comments included "My goodness. . . . That busboy had diction like an educated White person" (p. 12). He learned that the staff quarters were unselfconsciously called the "Monkey House" because at one time all the workers had been Black. At one point, he was instructed to find the "Chinaman," a supply clerk, and was told it was easy to remember his location because it was right next to the laundry. These and many similar experiences took place in less than a one-month period. They also took place in the 1980s, not, as you might expect by reading them, during the pre-civil-rights era of the 1960s.

An important part of the hiring process is the job interview. Based on a review of 31 studies of racial group differences in employment interview outcomes, Allen Huffcutt and Philip Roth (1998) found that, on the average, Whites received higher ratings than either Blacks or Hispanics. Such racial differences in evaluations were greater for low level jobs than for higher level jobs and discrimination increased as the proportion of Black applicants increased. Thus, White job applicants are more likely to get interviews than are their equally qualified Black peers and, once interviewed, are more likely to get high ratings on suitability for the job. Box 10.3 relates one Black man's experience in applying for a low-level job and a few of his experiences on that job.

There is less research on gender differences in hiring than on racial differences. However, Bertrand and Mullainathan (2003) found that male and female applicants were called for interviews at about the same rate, 17.2 percent for women and 15.3 percent for men. Also, Heather Davison and Michael Burke (2000) reviewed 49 studies in which participants evaluated the suitability of equally qualified male or female applicants for a job. Overall, they found virtually no discrimination, although men tended to receive slightly higher suitability ratings for male-stereotyped jobs and women tended to receive slightly higher suitability ratings for female-stereotyped jobs. Thus, the research appears to indicate that currently there is little gender discrimination in the hiring process. However, Davison and Burke noted that reviews of research published in 1979 and 1988 did find evidence of discrimination, suggesting that gender discrimination has decreased over time. For example, the 1988 study (Olian, Schwab, & Haberfeld, 1988) found that gender accounted for 4 percent of the variance in hiring evaluations whereas Davison and Burke found that it accounted for less than 1 percent.

Performance evaluation   Once a person is on the job, performance evaluations are important determinants of the person's career: Positive evaluations can lead to valuable training opportunities, promotions, and pay raises, whereas poor evaluations can lead to losing one's job. Chieh-Chen Bowen, Janet Swim, and Rick Jacobs (2000) reviewed 27 studies of gender differences in job performance ratings in organizations. They found that, overall, men and women received equal job performance ratings, although male evaluators tended to give somewhat higher ratings to men than to women. Unlike Davison and Burke, who found that both men and women received slightly higher suitability ratings for sex-stereotyped jobs, Bowen and her colleagues found that the sex typing of the job was not related to performance ratings. However, the sex stereotyping of the items on performance evaluation measures was: Men received higher ratings on measures that included mostly masculine-stereotyped items, women received higher ratings on measures that included mostly feminine-stereotyped items, and men and women received equal ratings on measures that contained mostly gender-neutral items. Bowen and colleagues also found that supervisors who had more opportunity to directly observe employees' job performance gave somewhat higher performance ratings to women. They concluded that "any overall gender discrimination that one might observe in the work force is . . . not directly attributable to biases in performance appraisal" (Bowen et al., 2000, p. 2206). However, their results do indicate that to the extent that performance evaluations are made by men, especially men who do not directly observe their employees' performance, and to the extent that the performance evaluations measures used by an organization include masculine-stereotyped items, men will receive higher evaluations than women.

Unlike the situation for gender, race/ethnicity does appear to affect job performance evaluations. Based on a review of 48 studies, Philip Roth, Allen Huffcutt, and Philip Bobko (2003) found that White employees received higher evaluations than Black employees, although there was no differences in evaluations of Hispanic and White employees. In contrast to Huffcutt and Roth's (1998) findings, which showed that racial bias in employment interview outcomes decreased as job complexity increased, Roth and his colleagues found that racial biases in performance evaluations were similar across levels of job complexity. Thus, although there is little racial bias in hiring for higher-level jobs, evaluation of performance in those jobs is biased in favor of Whites, especially when the raters are White (Roberson & Block, 2001). Even when numerical ratings of job performance are the same for Black and White workers, the narrative comments that supervisors make about employee performance might be biased. For example, Patricia Thomas and her colleagues (Thomas, Edwards, Perry, & David, 1998) compared the performance evaluation comments made by the supervisors of 582 male U.S. Navy officers who had received the highest numerical performance rating. They found that White officers were more likely to be described as outstanding leaders and were more likely to be recommended for positions of command than were Black officers. In addition, White officers were more likely to be recommended for early promotion and to be described as having characteristics that other research shows lead to early promotion (Johnson, 2001). That is, promotion boards seem to use certain characteristics as cues when selecting officers for early promotion and evaluators were more likely to attribute those characteristics to White officers than to Black officers.

Although racial group differences in job performance evaluations might reflect racial prejudice, they might also be accurate, reflecting actual racial group differences in average job performance. For example, Roth and his colleagues (2003) found that, compared to White workers, Black workers had lower average scores on objective measures of work performance, and that these differences were about twice as large as the differences in supervisor ratings. However, Jeffrey Greenhaus, Saroj Parasuramen, and Wayne Wormley (1990) have suggested that although minority group employees may actually perform at a somewhat lower level than White employees, that lower level of performance might itself be a result of prejudice and discrimination in the workplace. They proposed that differences in race may lead to differences in experiences in the organization, and that these differences in experiences might affect job performance, which is then reflected in performance evaluations. Organizational researchers have not paid much attention to issues such as these (Brief, 1998); however, organizational theorists have proposed a number of workplace characteristics could adversely affect minority group members' job performance (Roberson & Block, 2001).

One such characteristic is what Daniel Ilgen and Margaret Youtz (1986) called the *lost opportunities effect:* "Differential treatment of minority and majority group members may result in different on-the-job opportunities for these two groups. To the extent that minority group members have fewer and less favorable opportunities, lower performance for minorities may result" (p. 317). For example, minority group managers report that compared to their White peers, their supervisors appear to view them as less competent (such as by reviewing their work more frequently and more closely) and give them less support and encouragement (Blank & Slipp, 1994; Greenhaus et al., 1990; James, 2000). Prejudiced Whites also can create a chilly climate for their Black coworkers. For example, Black managers reported feeling less accepted than White coworkers by their White peers (Greenhaus et al., 1990; Blank & Slipp, 1994). In addition, Anne Tsui, Terri Egan, and Charles O'Reilly (1992) found that lower-level White workers showed more work avoidance, such as absences, as the proportion of minority workers in their work units increased and expressed stronger intentions to quit their jobs if another employment opportunity arose. Such coworker prejudice can have a direct effect on Black workers' job performance. For example, John Dovidio (2001) had Black research participants work on a task with either a prejudiced or unprejudiced White participant. He found that the work teams with a prejudiced White participant were 30 percent less productive than those with an unprejudiced White participant.

Ilgen and Youtz (1986) also proposed that workplace prejudice and discrimination could have an adverse affect on minority employees' morale, which, in turn, could affect job performance. For example, Elizabeth Deitch and her colleagues (2003) analyzed survey data on Black and White workers' experience of workplace mistreatment, such as being set up for failure, being treated as if they didn't exist, and being the target of insulting jokes or comments. They found that Black workers were more likely to report experiencing such mistreatment than White workers and that the experience of such mistreatment was related to lower morale in the form of reduced job satisfaction. Other research shows that lower job satisfaction is related to lower job performance (Judge, Thoresen, Bono, & Patton, 2001). For examples of some of the hassles that Black workers face, see Box 10.4.

Promotion   Promotion within an organization is based largely on job performance evaluations. However, as Bowen and colleagues (2000) have noted, even when women and members of minority groups receive the same performance evaluations as men and majority group members, decisions based on those evaluations can still be biased. And so it seems to be with promotions. Looking first at gender differences, researchers have found that although women and men receive, on average, equal job performance ratings, their supervisors often see them as having less promotion potential than men (Landau, 1995; Shore, 1992), they must wait longer for promotion (Cannings & Montmarquette, 1991; Maume, 1999), and receive fewer promotions the higher they move in the organizational structure (Lyness & Judiesch, 1999).

Even in situations in which women receive higher job performance ratings than men, they may be promoted no faster (Cannings & Montmarquette, 1991; Shore, 1992). For example, Ted Shore (1992) studied the results of assessment center ratings of male and female managers. Managers attending an assessment center undergo a set of written and performance tests designed to assess their potential for promotion. Shore found that, on the average, women and men received the same scores on measures of mental ability and similar ratings on interpersonal skill. In addition, women scored higher on measures of managerial job performance. Nonetheless, women received the same overall managerial potential ratings as men and were promoted at the same rate.

Ironically, the male advantage in promotion may be greater in female-dominated occupations, such as clerical and sales, than in male-dominated occupations, such as manufacturing (Maume, 1999). For example, David Maume (1999) found that men were 17 percent more likely than women to be promoted in female-dominated occupations. Being in a female-dominated job not only increased men's odds of promotion, it decreased women's.

In regard to race, Black workers are less likely to be promoted than their White counterparts (Roth et al., 2003) and must wait longer for promotion (Maume, 1999). As with women and men, when Black workers receive the same job performance ratings as their White peers, they are likely to receive lower ratings on promotion

10.4   *Everyday Racial Hassles at Work*

The editors of *Harvard Business Review* asked organizational consultants Keith Caver and Ancella Livers (2002) to write a fictional letter from a Black manager to a White boss describing some of the everyday, almost certainly unintentional, incidents that make Black managers feel like outsiders. The events they noted included:

- Being cast as a *de facto* diversity expert even though the managers' training gave them no special expertise in that field: "Despite my 15 years of experience, despite my solid track record, my new colleagues appeared to have little interest in my business expertise. Instead, they seemed to have assigned me some special role: official interpreter of minority concerns for the organization" (p. 78).
- Having one's presence questioned when others go unchallenged: "One weekend I went to the office in my normal, casual weekend attire. . . . Before getting into the elevator I was stopped by an informally dressed young white man who in a stern voice asked to see my identification. . . . I had worked here for two years, but because I was out of context, he assumed I was a thug. You might chalk it up to an honest mistake, but I can assure you he hadn't challenged any of the white people entering the building" (p. 79).
- Resentment over increased workplace diversity: Robert, a Black manager, hired a Black woman and promoted a Black man.

Afterwards, "Robert began to hear whispers in the halls—suggestions that he was building his own little 'ghetto fiefdom' and having a White colleague 'jokingly' say to him, 'So white people aren't good enough for you?'" (p.79)
- Not being trusted to do one's job properly: In addition to the comments of his peers, Robert's boss "suddenly seemed to take a greater interest in the details of his group's work—asking for reports and updates he'd never needed when Robert's team was primarily white. Subtly, his boss was letting him know that at some level he expected the team's performance to drop" (p. 79)
- Having others assume that because you are not White, you are a low-level employee: A Black woman "was recently hired as a senior vice president for a major financial institution. With the exception of a few initial interviews and meetings, she did not set foot in the organization until her first day at the office. As she emerged from the elevator, she was abruptly greeted by a white male who directed her to a small cubicle and asked her to quickly put her things away as they were expecting a new senior officer to arrive shortly" (p. 80).

The effect of experiences such as these is that for minority workers, "race is always with us. As a friend of mine said recently, 'I don't think a day goes by that I'm not reminded I'm black'" (p. 81).

potential (James, 2000; Landau, 1995; Thomas et al., 1998). In addition, White employees are paid more than Black employees in jobs with equivalent levels of authority (Dreher & Cox, 1996; Smith, 1997). Ryan Smith (1997) also found that although Black employees' absolute salary levels increased with promotion, the difference in Black and White workers' salaries increased with higher levels of authority: Black workers with no authority were paid 86 percent of what their White peers received, 81 percent at low levels of authority, and 77 percent at middle levels of authority (there were too few Black managers at high level of authority for Smith to make meaningful comparisons).

The problem begins at the lowest level of promotion. Using the results of separate surveys, David Maume (1999) and Ryan Smith and James Elliott (2002) both found that African Americans in nonmanagerial jobs were 50 percent less likely to be promoted to managerial jobs than were their White peers. Smith and Elliott further noted that when African Americans did hold first-level managerial positions, they were more likely to supervise Black workers than White workers. Because most Black workers are in low-level jobs, this ethnic matching of supervisors and employees means that most Black managers are found in low-level positions of authority. Smith and Elliott (2002) refer to this ethnic matching phenomenon as the "sticky floor" effect: "The relative position of one's ethnic group within an organization constitutes the 'sticky floor'—one to which individual opportunity for authority 'adheres.' If one's ethnic group dominates only entry-level jobs within an organization, then one's authority chances will be restricted largely to supervising entry-level workers. If one's ethnic group dominates higher-level positions, then one's authority chances will increase accordingly" (p. 274; see also James, 2000).

At least two other organizational factors are related to Black managers' slower promotion rates relative to their White peers. First, as we noted earlier, Black managers tend to be "tracked" into certain job categories, such as affirmative action officer (Collins, 1997). Jobs in these categories have slower promotion rates and "top out" at lower levels of authority than other jobs in other categories, such as sales and operations management, regardless of the race of the people holding the jobs (James, 2000). Second, one's mentor in an organization can have important effects on career progression because of the formal and informal training and social support mentors provide, and because of the connections they have with upper-level management (Roberson & Block, 2001). Because White men predominate in upper-level management positions, they can be especially helpful as mentors. For example, George Dreher and Taylor Cox (1996) found that having had a White male mentor added more than $22,000 per year to manager's salaries after 10 years of experience compared to managers who had had female or non-White mentors. They also found that women, African American men, and Hispanic men were less likely than White managers to have had a White male mentor.

Although it is tempting to attribute the differential treatment of female and Black workers that results in differential outcomes to intentional discrimination, Smith and Elliott (2000) see the situation differently: "We believe that something more subtle and profound occurs in the process of doing 'business as usual'— mere maintenance of the status quo is more than enough to perpetuate racial stratification" (p. 274); the same principle applies to gender stratification.

Individuals in Organizations

Although people very often talk about organizational discrimination and institutional discrimination, if you think about it, organizations and institutions do not discriminate: Individuals in organizations and institutions discriminate. That is, discriminatory policies are set and enforced by individuals, discriminatory decisions about hiring and promotions are made by individuals, and discriminatory performance evaluations are made by individuals. Even when decision are made by committees, individuals have input into those joint decisions. Given this situation, surprisingly little research has been conducted on how individual-level psychological processes influence discriminatory outcomes in organizations (Brief, 1998; Roberson & Block, 2001). This section discusses some of those processes: stereotype fit, intergroup respect, shifting standards, contemporary prejudice, and conformity to perceived organizational norms.

Stereotype fit   Madeline Heileman (1983, 2001) developed the **stereotype fit hypothesis** as an explanation for why women hold few managerial or executive positions in organizations relative to men. The hypothesis postulates that the characteristics associated with effective managers are very similar to the cultural stereotypes of men and very different from the cultural stereotypes of women. Therefore, men are perceived as fitting into the managerial role but women are not; as a result, women are less likely to be hired for managerial positions and, once hired, less likely to be promoted into higher positions (see also Eagly & Karau, 2002). More generally, people see men as better suited for "masculine" jobs such as business manager and construction worker and women as better suited for "feminine" jobs such as nurse and secretary (Biernat & Kobrynowicz, 1997; Cejka & Eagly, 1999).

Evidence for the manager-as-male stereotype has come from studies in which experienced male corporate managers rated the target groups *male manager* and *female manager* on traits that characterize effective managers (Dodge, Gilroy, & Fenzel, 1995; Heilman, Block, & Martell, 1995; Martell, Parker, Emrich, & Crawford, 1998). These studies have found that male managers as a group received higher ratings on the traits than did female managers as a group. However, the results of the studies were less consistent when the research participants rated *successful male managers* and *successful female managers*: two studies found a pro-male bias (Dodge et al., 1995; Heilman et al., 1995) but one found no difference in the ratings of successful male and female managers (Martell et al., 1998). Interestingly, the one study that included female managers as participants (Dodge et al., 1995) found that they expressed a pro-female bias when rating male and female managers in general, although not when rating successful male and female managers. These results suggest that an egocentric bias might be at work when rating managers in general: Because managers are making the ratings, they see managers as having characteristics similar to their own—male-stereotypical when men are making the ratings and female-stereotypical when women are making the ratings. However, given that men predominate in positions of power in organizations, their belief systems are more likely to influence organizational decisions than are women's.

An example of stereotype fit in operation comes from a study conducted by Annelies Van Vianen and Tineke Willemsen (1992). They studied the evaluations and decisions that employment interviewers made about male and female applicants for managerial jobs. Consistent with the stereotype fit hypothesis, they found that the interviewers believed that the ideal applicant for the job would have more masculine traits than feminine traits. They also found that although interviewers regarded the male and female applicants as being equally qualified for the jobs in terms of education and experience, they were more likely to recommend that male applicants be hired. Finally, Van Vianen and Willemsen found that the interviewers attributed more masculine traits to successful applicants than to unsuccessful applicants, indicating that masculinity played an important role in their decisions. Therefore, because the interviewers saw female applicants as less masculine than male applicants and viewed the jobs as requiring masculine traits, they were less likely to recommend that female applicants be hired even though they had the same objective qualifications as the male applicants.

Stereotype fit (or lack of fit) can also influence performance evaluations. Jennifer Boldry, Wendy Wood, and Deborah Kashy (2001) examined this influence in a study of ratings male and female ROTC cadets made of one another. They found that although male and female cadets scored equally well on objective measures of military performance, female cadets received lower ratings on motivation and leadership from their fellow cadets. Thus, equal performance, when filtered through gender stereotypes, can lead to different evaluations. Also recall the research discussed earlier that found that women are less likely to be promoted despite equal job performance evaluations (Landau, 1995; Lyness & Judiesch, 1999; Maume, 1999); similar processes might be operating in those situations.

Although Heilman (1983, 2001) developed the stereotype fit hypothesis to explain gender differences in organizational outcomes, it can also explain racial and ethnic group differences in outcomes; however, less research has been conducted in that context. One study that has addressed this question examined experienced White managers' ratings of *managers, African Americans,* and *Whites* on a set of traits characteristic of good managers (Tomkiewicz, Brenner, & Adeyemi-Bello, 1998). They found a correlation of $r = .54$ between the ratings of *managers* and *Whites* but a correlation of only $r = .17$ between the ratings of *managers* and *African Americans,* indicating that Whites were seen as fitting the managerial role better than were African Americans.

Similar processes operate for lower level jobs as well. For example, Joleen Kirschenman and Kathryn Neckerman (1990) interviewed 185 Chicago-area employers about their impressions of members of various racial and ethnic groups as workers in low-level jobs such as sales clerk, typist, restaurant worker, and assembly worker. They found that employers generally perceived Blacks and Hispanics as having none of the characteristics of good workers, seeing them as unskilled, illiterate, dishonest, unmotivated, involved with drugs and gangs, lacking a work ethic, and having few interpersonal skills. The employers contrasted Blacks and Hispanics with recent immigrants from central Europe, whom they saw as having all the characteristics of desirable workers. These stereotypes were reflected in employee recruitment strategies. For example, Kirschenman and

Neckerman (1990) noted that "one company advertised for skilled workers in Polish- and German-language newspapers, but hired all its unskilled workers, 97 percent of whom were Hispanic," through employee referrals (p. 210).

Employers did have subcategories within their stereotypes, however. For example, they differentiated between "desirable" Black workers—those who had middle- or working-class backgrounds—from "undesirable" Black workers—those who resided in urban ghettos. However, employers tended to use race as a marker for ghetto resident, assuming that Black job applicants were ghetto residents (and therefore would not be good workers) unless the applicants provided evidence of being "desirable." Such evidence included speaking standard English, dressing appropriately for the job interview, being able to demonstrate job-related skills, having a history of steady employment, and providing a non-ghetto address. In sum, Kirschenman and Neckerman (1990) found that employers assumed that Blacks and Hispanics were unqualified for even low level jobs unless the applicant proved otherwise, but applied less stringent criteria to members of other groups.

Finally, although stereotype fit can result in a disadvantage for some groups, it can confer an advantage on other groups. For example, the Asian stereotype includes being talented at math and computers whereas the female stereotype includes having little talent in those domains. Jennifer Steele and Nalini Ambady (2004) hypothesized that an Asian American woman's perceived qualification for a computer technician job would depend on whether her Asian identity or her female identity was salient to the decision maker. College student participants read the description of a student computer technician job, reviewed a completed application for the job, and then interviewed the applicant, an Asian American woman. The application form was designed to emphasize either the Asian or female aspect of the applicant's identity. Compared to participants in the condition in which the applicant's female identity was salient, those in the condition in which her Asian identity was salient gave her a stronger hiring recommendation and recommended a 12 percent higher starting salary.

Intergroup respect   One explanation for organizational discrimination, then, is stereotype fit: Because the stereotype of White men provides a better fit to the managerial stereotype than do the stereotypes of minority group members or women, White men are selected over equally, or even better, qualified members of other groups. Lynne Jackson, Victoria Esses, and Christopher Burris (2001) have proposed a different explanation. They have hypothesized that it is not a decision maker's stereotypes about a group that are the primary factors affecting discriminatory decisions, but rather it is the amount of respect the decision maker has for the group that affects decisions. They define respect as "feelings of esteem for another that manifest in both valuing the person's feelings, thoughts, and behaviors as well as willingness to be influenced by that person" (pp. 48–49). Jackson and her colleagues propose that people learn to hold different degrees of respect for various groups based on the amount of power the groups have in society. For example, "differential respect for men and women may have its origins in the social structure. In most contemporary cultures, men continue to hold higher social status than women. . . . Relatedly, men generally still have more power than women in society (e.g., in politics and economics), in the workplace, and in interpersonal relationships . . . Because many positions occupied by men are high in status, people are likely to more frequently act deferentially to men than to women" (Jackson et al., 2001, p. 49). Living in such a social context, they argue, leads people to develop more respect for men as a group than for women as a group (although, of course, individual women can be respected more than individual men).

Jackson and her colleagues (2001) conducted three studies to test the hypothesis that respect outweighs stereotypes in affecting hiring decisions. In the first two studies, research participants read a description of a gender-neutral job and an application for the job from a man or a woman. Participants rated the applicant on the degree of respect they felt for him or her, the extent to which sets of male and female stereotypes described the applicant, and how suitable the applicant was for the job. The researchers found that although both respect and stereotypes had positive correlations with job suitability ratings, respect had a much stronger relationship. The third study was an experiment in which the researchers manipulated how respected the applicant was by a previous employer and the applicant's male and female stereotypic characteristics using a letter of recommendation in the applicant's file. They also manipulated whether the applicant was applying for a high or low status job. They found that greater respect led to stronger hiring recommendations, especially for the high status job, and that having more masculine stereotypic traits led to stronger hiring recommendations for both types of job; feminine stereotypic traits were not related to hiring recommendations. As in the first two studies, respect had a stronger effect than stereotypes. Jackson and her colleagues' findings indicated that the effect group membership has on hiring goes beyond how decision makers think about groups (stereotypes) to include how they feel about groups (respect). This distinction is important because, as Jackson and her colleagues note, eliminating reliance on stereotypes in decision making may not eliminate discrimination that is rooted in differences in respect for different social groups.

Shifting standards   Think back to two of the sets of research results on gender discrimination in organizations that we presented earlier. First, on the average, women and men receive equal job performance evaluations. Second, on the average, women are less likely to get promoted than men. Given that rewards such as promotions are supposed to be based on performance, these two sets of findings appear to contradict one another: given equal performance, women and men should be promoted at equal rates. One explanation for this apparent contradiction lies in Monica Biernat's (2003) **shifting standards model** of evaluation that we introduced in Chapters 3 and 4. Recall that the model proposes that negative stereotypes lead people to hold lower performance expectations for women and members of minority groups. When evaluators use subjective criteria to rate performance, a person is rated relative to the expectations the evaluator has for the person's group. Because most workplace performance evaluation measures use subjective rating scales (see, for example, Murphy & Cleveland, 1995), job performance ratings are vulnerable to this bias. For example, a woman manager's performance would be rated relative to the evaluator's expectations for woman managers as a group. The top section of Figure 10.5 illustrates this process. Janet

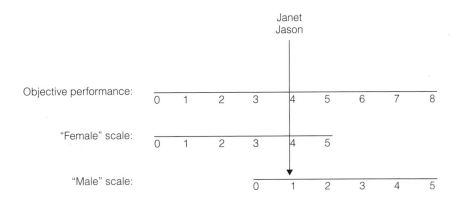

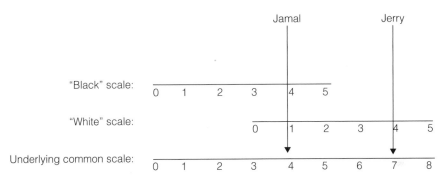

FIGURE 10.5

SHIFTING STANDARDS OF EVALUATION

Top Section: Janet and Jerry perform at the same objective level, but because the evaluator's expectations for female performance are lower than his expectations for male performance, Janet gets a higher performance rating. *Bottom Section:* Jamal gets a high rating of 4, but it is relative to the low expectations the rater has of Black employees. Jerry gets a high rating of 4, but it is relative to the higher expectations that the rater has for White employees. As a result, when the two ratings are transformed to a common scale, such as if the rater had to rank employees, Jerry comes out ahead of Jamal.

Adapted from Biernat (2003, Figure 1, p. 1021).

and Jason work for the same manager and perform at the same level. However, because their manager has lower expectations for female employees (that is, the female standards are shifted to the left of the male standards in this example), the same level of performance results in a higher rating for Janet than for Jason.

The bottom section of Figure 10.5 provides a hypothetical example of how shifting standards can also influence the interpretation of performance ratings. In this example, Jamal, who is Black, and Jerry, who is White, work for the same manager, who gives them both a (very good) rating of 4 on a 5-point scale. But their manager has, probably unconsciously, rated Jamal and Jerry relative to the expectations he has for the performance of Black and White employees. That is, he saw Jamal's performance as "very good for a Black employee" and Jerry's as "very good for a White employee." However, because of the different standards used for rating Black and White performance, Jamal actually scores lower on an objective common scale that takes both race-based scales into account. Biernat (2003) notes that it is the objective common scale, not the race-based subjective scales, that is used to determine the distribution of organizational rewards such as promotions and pay raises. Thus, although both Jamal and Jerry received ratings of 4 on their annual performance evaluations, Jerry is more likely to get a promotion or pay raise because his 4 translates to a 7 (very good) on the objective scale whereas Jamal's 4 translates to a 4 (average).

Recall, for example, the study conducted by Monica Biernat and Theresa Vescio (2002) that we described in Chapter 4, in which participants took the role of the manager of a coed softball team. Even when male and female players were evaluated as equal in athletic ability, men were more likely to be chosen as starting players and to be placed in the top of the batting order. Thus, men received more rewards than women, presumably because shifting standards put them higher on the objective scale the participants used to make their choices. These kinds of differential decisions are made not only by evaluators but also by other people who use the evaluations to make decisions. For example, Biernat (2003) reported the results of a study in which participants read a letter of recommendation; half the participants thought it was written on behalf of a Black job applicant and half that it was written on behalf of a White job applicant. The participants interpreted the letter to mean that, in objective terms, the Black applicant had performed less well on the job described in the letter than had the White applicant. Participants apparently assumed that the letter writer had used lower standards to evaluate the Black applicant's performance.

Contemporary prejudice   In Chapter 5 we noted that because of contemporary social norms that condemn prejudice, prejudice and discrimination tend to manifest themselves in subtle ways and in situations in which prejudiced behavior can be attributed to causes other than prejudice. Thus, for example, a prejudiced person could claim that she voted against a Black political candidate not because he was Black, but because his platform was too liberal. In the employment context, a prejudiced employer may use applicant characteristics as a reason to reject a Black job applicant even while hiring a White applicant with the same characteristic. For example, Gordon Hodson, John Dovidio, and Samuel Gaertner (2002) asked White college student participants who had been classified as being high or low on racial prejudice to make college admission decisions about Black and White applicants. For this study the researchers created two mixed qualification applicant conditions, a clearly high qualification applicant condition, and a clearly low qualification applicant condition. In one mixed qualification condition the applicant had high Scholastic Assessment Test (SAT) scores but a low high school grade point average (GPA); in the other mixed qualification condition, the applicant had a high GPA but low SAT scores. The high qualification applicant had both high SAT scores and a high GPA; the low qualification applicant had both low SAT scores and a low GPA.

Both high and low prejudice participants accepted the highly qualified Black and White applicants at the same rate (100 percent) and rejected the poorly qualified Black and White applicants at the same rate (69 percent). However, high prejudice participants were more likely to accept the mixed qualification White applicant (74 percent) than the mixed qualification Black applicant (44 percent); the reverse was true for low prejudice participants although the difference was not as large: 86 percent accepted the Black applicant and 64 percent accepted the White applicant. Hodson and his colleagues also asked their participants to rate how much influence the applicant's SAT scores and GPA had on their decisions. The high prejudice participants who had evaluated the mixed qualification Black applicant rated whichever piece of negative information they had seen—SAT scores in the one condition and GPA in the other condition—as most important to their decisions. Low prejudice participants showed the opposite pattern, focusing on whichever piece of information was more positive. Thus, both high and low prejudice participants seized on the information that was consistent with their racial attitudes—positive for those low in prejudice and negative for those high in prejudice—and used that information to justify their decisions.

Employers may also use business-related factors to justify discrimination, the most common being maintaining workplace harmony and placating customers (Brief, 1998; Kirschenman & Neckerman, 1990). Kirschenman and Neckerman (1990) found that many of the employers they interviewed were reluctant to hire minority workers because they thought doing so would upset their White workers, leading to morale and productivity problems. This reluctance was reflected in hiring practices: Employers who said they valued teamwork highly were twice as likely to have racially homogeneous workforces than those who thought that teamwork was less important. Unfortunately, these employers' concerns may have a basis in reality: Recall that Tsui and her colleagues (1992) found that lower-level White workers showed more work avoidance as the proportion of minority workers in their work units increased. Kirschenman and Neckerman (1990) also noted that some employers believed that they would lose customers if they hired minority workers. They quoted one restaurant owner as saying, "I have all white waitresses for a very basic reason. My clientele is 95 percent white. I simply wouldn't last very long if I had some black waitresses out there" (p. 220). This concern may also be based in reality: A White suburban restaurant owner who had hired Black wait staff because he could not find enough White workers received comments from his White customers such as "Why do you have *those* people out here?" (p. 220, emphasis in original). Customer demand can also work in the other direction: Harry Holzer (1996) found that employers with a predominantly Black customer base were more likely to hire Black workers than White workers.

Conformity to perceived norms   Finally, individuals might make discriminatory decisions because they believe those decisions are consistent with company norms. For example, Arthur Brief and his colleagues (Brief, Dietz, Cohen, Pugh, & Vaslow, 2000) conducted a study in which White participants were classified as high or low on racial prejudice. The participants' took the role of a company personnel officer and reviewed the files of 10 applicants for a sales position.

Their task was to select three applicants for job interviews. The files presented information on three well-qualified Black applicants, two well-qualified White applicants, and five poorly qualified White applicants. Before reviewing the files, participants read one of two versions of a memo from the company president. In one version, the president discouraged hiring minority applicants because the person hired would be working with an all White customer base and many of the customers would not like dealing with a member of a minority group. In the other version of the memo, the company president encouraged the personnel officer to select the best possible applicants and made no reference to race.

Low prejudice participants who read the "best applicants" memo selected an average of 60 percent of Black applicants for interviews, a proportion equal to their representation in the group of qualified applicants. As predicted by theories of contemporary prejudice, prejudiced participants who did not have a justification for discrimination also acted in a nondiscriminatory manner, selecting an average of 62 percent of Black applicants. In contrast, high prejudice participants who did have a justification for discrimination—the company president's preference for hiring a White person—chose an average of only 17 percent of the Black applicants for interviews. Interestingly, even low prejudice participants discriminated against the Black applicants when that reflected the company president's wishes. They chose an average of 37 percent Black applicants, more than the high prejudice participants who had read the "no minorities" memo but fewer than those who had read the "best applicants" memo. Therefore, even low prejudice people may make discriminatory decisions when they believe that doing so will please their boss. By the way, if pressure from a company president to discriminate seems far-fetched, see Box 10.5, which describes the event that led to Brief and colleagues' research.

HATE CRIMES

Hate crimes (also called bias crimes) are, perhaps, the most severe form of discrimination. **Hate crimes** are criminal offenses in which there is evidence that the victims were chosen because of their race, ethnicity, national origin, religion, disability, or sexual orientation (U.S. Federal Bureau of Investigation [FBI], 1999). Although whether a crime is caused by bias rather than some other motive (such as personal animosity rather than prejudice) is sometimes a matter of judgment, in many cases the evidence is fairly obvious. For example, a survey of gay, lesbian, and bisexual hate crime victims found that in 53 percent of the cases the offender made an explicit statement about the victim's sexual orientation (Herek, Cogan, & Gillis, 2002). In addition, hate crimes usually have no motivation other than attacking a member of a particular group. "There appear to be no gains for the assailant: There is no attempt to take money or personal items and there is no prior relationship between the victim and offender" that could provide a personal motive, such as revenge (McDevitt, Levin, & Bennett, 2002, p. 304).

10.5 *"Lightening Up" Shoney's*

In 1992, the restaurant chain Shoney's Incorporated paid $132.5 million to settle an employment discrimination lawsuit. The evidence in the case revealed a long-standing policy of minimizing the number of Black employees in the company, especially in customer-contact jobs. For example, 75 percent of Shoney's Black restaurant workers held minimum-wage jobs such as dishwasher, cook, and breakfast-bar attendant (Watkins, 1993). These employment policies were a direct reflection of Chief executive Officer Ray Danner's views. For example, one former Shoney's vice president described what he called Danner's Laws: "Blacks were not qualified to run a store. Blacks were not qualified to run a kitchen of a store. Blacks should not be employed in any position where they would be seen by customers" (Watkins, 1993, p. 427).

Danner's justification for his policies was that White customers did not want to see Black employees and would not patronize restaurants that employed Black customer service staff. In pretrial testimony Danner said, "In looking for anything to identify why [a restaurant] is underperforming in some cases, I would probably have said that this is a neighborhood of predominantly white neighbors, and we have a considerable amount of black employees and this might be a problem" (Watkins, 1993, p. 427). Steve Watkins (1993) reported that "the smoking gun in the case came in the form of a letter Danner wrote complaining about the performance of [one restaurant] and comparing the racial makeup of the store, which had several black employees—some of whom were later fired—to the all-white, or nearly all-white, composition of other fast-food restaurants Danner visited in the area" (p. 427).

When executives from company headquarters visited restaurants, they would tell managers whom they thought had hired too many Black workers "to 'lighten up' their store—a company euphemism for reducing the number of black workers—and hire 'attractive white girls' instead" (Watkins, 1993, p. 424). In another instance, "two black Shoney's employees said they were ordered by their manager to hide in a restroom because some company executives had shown up for a surprise visit and there were 'too many' blacks at work that day" (Watkins, 1993, p. 426). These anti-Black policies did not affect only Black employees: Watkins reported that White restaurant managers who disobeyed orders to "lighten up" their staff were fired.

Table 10.3 presents some of the characteristics of the hate crimes reported to the FBI from 1997 to 1999 (Strom, 2001). The FBI received 2,976 reports of hate crimes during that period, which is probably fewer than the true number given that most crimes of all kinds go unreported (Strom, 2001). As Table 10.3 shows, a little more than half the victims of hate crimes are members of racial or ethnic minority groups; however, one does not have to be a member of a minority group to be a victim of a hate crime: 19 percent of the victims during the 1997 to 1999

TABLE 10.3	CHARACTERISTICS OF HATE CRIMES REPORTED 1997–1999
Victim Group	
Racial/ethnic minority	53%
White	19%
Religion	14%
Sexual orientation	13%
Disability	1%
Victim Gender	
Male	62%
Female	38%
Victim Age	
Under 18 years	23%
18 to 24 years	21%
25 to 34 years	21%
35 to 44 years	19%
45 years or older	16%
Type of Offense	
Violent	
Aggravated assault	13%
Simple assault	22%
Intimidation	23%
Other violent crime	2%
Property	
Vandalism	28%
Burglary or theft	8%
Other property crime	2%
Other	2%
Weapon Used in Violent Offenses	
Deadly weapon	18%
Hands, feet, or fist	35%
None	47%

Source: Strom, 2001.

period were White. Most victims were male (62 percent) and young (65 percent were under 35 years of age), most of the crimes were violent (60 percent), and 18 percent involved the use of a deadly weapon. Jack Levin and Jack McDevitt (2002) have further noted that hate crimes are excessively brutal compared to crime in general: 58 percent of hate crimes involve assaults compared to 7 percent of all crimes and 30 percent of hate crime assault victims receive physical injuries compared to 7 percent of victims for assaults in general.

In this section, we discuss three aspects of hate crimes. First, we look at some of the characteristics of hate crime offenders. We then examine the motivations that offenders have for taking part in hate crimes. We conclude with a brief discussion of the effects of hate crimes on the victims.

Hate Crime Offenders

Who commits hate crimes? There are two ways of looking for answers to this question. One approach is to examine victim descriptions of offenders, such as those contained in the reports of hate crimes collected by the FBI. Strom's (2001) analysis of these data showed that, like most offenders, hate crime perpetrators are disproportionately male (84 percent) and young: 62 percent are under 24 years of age and 79 percent are under 35 years of age. Another approach to determining offender characteristics is to conduct surveys and examine the characteristics of people who admit to having participated in hate crimes. Karen Franklin (2000) investigated anti-gay behavior and found that 10 percent of her sample of 489 community college students admitted having assaulted a lesbian or gay man (or someone the respondent thought was lesbian or gay) and that an additional 24 percent admitted engaging in verbal abuse. Like Strom, Franklin found that offenders were disproportionately male. (She did not report results by age of respondent.) Franklin also found that men were increasingly likely to be offenders as the violence of the behavior increased: Men were the perpetrators in 64 percent of name-calling incidents, 79 percent of intimidation incidents, and 92 percent of physical attacks. In addition, Franklin found that, relative to their representation in her sample, African Americans were more likely than members of other racial groups to admit to having engaged in anti-gay behaviors: African Americans constituted 19 percent of offenders versus 12 percent of the sample. African Americans were also more likely to admit to physical violence than members of other groups: 29 percent versus 4 percent to 11 percent for other groups.

Although one might think that hate crime offenders hold extremely negative intergroup attitudes or are unusually aggressive people, that is not always the case, as we will see shortly. Also, as we saw in Chapter 8, very few hate group members commit hate crimes. What factors, then, motivate people to commit hate crimes? The next section addresses that question.

Motivations for Hate Crimes

Why do people commit hate crimes? Based on an analysis of 169 hate crimes reported to the Boston police in 1991 and 1992, Jack Levin and Jack McDevitt (2002) proposed four motivations for engaging in hate crimes: thrill seeking, defending one's "territory" from outsiders, retaliation for a perceived offense committed by an outgroup member, and a commitment to a racist, anti-gay, or other bigoted ideology. Franklin (2000) has identified a fifth motivation, peer group dynamics, that Levin and McDevitt had included as part of thrill seeking (McDevitt, Levin, & Bennett, 2002) and Bryan Byers and Benjamin Crider (2002) have suggested that seeing hate crime as a normal behavior may facilitate, if not motivate, such behavior. Franklin (2000) also examined people's reasons for not carrying out anti-gay behaviors. Let us look at these motives.

Thrill seeking   Thrill seeking as a motivation for a hate crime entails committing the crime out of a desire for excitement, as an antidote for boredom. For example, McDevitt and his colleagues (2002) noted that young people who had been arrested for hate crimes "often told police that they were just bored and looking for some fun. . . . The attack in these thrill-motivated cases was triggered by an immature desire to display power and to experience a rush at the expense of someone else. . . . Several of these young offenders revealed that their only benefit from the attack was some vague senses of their own importance: a sadistic high as well as bragging rights with their friends" (pp. 307–308). Thrill-motivated hate crimes were the ones most commonly found in Levin and McDevitt's (2002) Boston sample, constituting 66 percent of the cases.

Thrill seekers generally have little commitment to bias and often express little animosity toward the group whose members they have attacked (Byers, Crider, & Biggers, 1999; Franklin, 2000; McDevitt et al., 2002). Rather, they are bored and see violence as a way of alleviating their boredom. For example, Byers and Crider (2002; Byers et al., 1999) interviewed young men who, as teenagers, had participated in criminal and harassing behavior against the Amish residents of the rural county in which they and their Amish victims lived. These offenses are so common, and so commonly accepted by the non-Amish, that there is a local word for them, *claping*. The role played by boredom in hate crimes is illustrated by the comments of one of Byers and colleagues' (1999) respondents, who offered this explanation for his behavior: "It was what our friends were doing at the time to pass the summer months away or whatever. That was what we were doing on Friday nights" (p. 85). The results of Byers and colleagues' (1999; Byers & Crider 2002) interviews suggest that a lack of respect rather than animosity might be the emotional facilitator of thrill seekers' behavior. One of their respondents told them, "I just had the mentality that they are just Amish. . . . It is like, we can pick on them because they are so different" (Byers et al., 1999, p. 87) and another said, "It is because I still have some feeling that they almost 'deserved it' for some unknown reason because they are different" (p. 88).

Thrill seekers tend to choose as targets people they see as providing easy and safe opportunities for violence. For example, an offender who, along with a friend, targeted gay men as robbery victims said, "It wasn't because we had something against gays, but because we could get some money and have some fun. It was a *rush*. A serious rush. Massive rush. . . . It was nothing at all against gays. They're just an easy target. Gays have a reputation that they can't fight [back]" (Franklin, 1998, p. 14, emphasis in original). Similarly, one of Byers and Crider's (2002) respondents said of the Amish, "They are an easy target. They offer an easy target because they 'turn the other cheek' and don't fight back" (p. 131). Another characteristic that makes a group an easy target for thrill seekers is an unwillingness or inability to report the crime. For example, one of Byers and Crider's (2002) interviewees noted that the Amish "can't call the cops [because of their rejection of modern technology, such as telephones] and don't believe in suing" (p. 135). Similarly, lesbians, gay men, and bisexuals may be seen as easy targets because they are reluctant to report hate crimes due to concern over police harassment or public disclosure of their sexual orientation (Herek et al., 2002).

Thrill seekers often justify their actions by minimizing the crime's impact on the victims and by portraying their actions as harmless fun (Byers et al., 1999; Franklin, 1998). One of Byers and colleagues' (1999) respondents said, "It was all, I always thought clean fun. . . . We always looked at it as there are a lot worse things that we could be doing" (p. 85). Byers and his colleagues found that denying that they had hurt anyone was a common justification offenders gave for their behavior. One of their respondents said about destroying an outhouse, "No one ever really got hurt, and it wasn't really that much property damage. It was pretty much just a mess to clean up" (p. 85). Besides, one respondent explained, claping causes no real injury because the Amish should expect to be harassed: "Stuff like that happens to them. It happens to them all the time. They are used to it I think" (Byers et al., 1999, p. 86).

Territorial defense   In defensive hate crimes, the perpetrators see themselves as protecting their own territory from invasion by outsiders. The purpose of this type of hate crime is to coerce the outsiders to go away and to send a more general message that members of the victim's group are not wanted in the offenders' neighborhood. For example, Donald Green, Dara Strolovitch, and Janelle Wong (1998) found that the incidence of hate crimes was higher in all-White neighborhoods into which minority group members were moving compared to similar neighborhoods which remained all White. Defensive hate crimes constituted 25 percent of Levin and McDevitt's (2002) sample of cases.

Retaliation   In retaliatory hate crimes, the offenders are seeking revenge for a real or rumored attack on a member of their ingroup. McDevitt and his colleagues (2002) note that "whether the [attack] actually occurred is often irrelevant. Sometimes a rumor of an incident may cause a group of offenders to take vengeance, only to learn later that their original information was merely unfounded hearsay" (p. 309). Although the reason retaliatory attackers give for their actions is revenge, they usually do not seek out the person they believe committed the offense against their group, but target any available member of the group. This kind of generalized retaliation may be especially likely to occur when the real target of the offenders' anger is out of their reach. As Levin and McDevitt (2002) noted, "After [the September 11, 2001, terrorist attacks], what made it especially tempting to target college students who spoke with an accent and had a dark complexion was the ambiguity in identifying the real enemy. President Bush blamed Osama bin Laden, a shadowy figure who resided in a far-off land and had been seen only a few times on videotape. For most Americans, bin Laden . . . was an abstraction, little more than a caricature. It was therefore far more satisfying psychologically to target flesh-and-blood human beings [who were close at hand]—international students" (p. 5). Retaliatory hate crimes constituted 8 percent of Levin and McDevitt's (2002) sample of cases.

Mission   Mission-motivated hate crimes are carried out because of a commitment to a bigoted ideology. In these kinds of crimes, "the perpetrator seeks to rid the world of evil" (McDevitt et al., 2002, p. 309). Some mission-oriented offenders are members of hate groups, although they may be acting without the knowledge or support of the group's leadership. As we saw in Chapter 8, the leadership of many hate groups publicly oppose violence, seeing it as a threat to their recruitment efforts. Other mission-oriented offenders act on their own, seeing themselves as victims of conspiracies by groups against whom they seek revenge (Levin & McDevitt, 2002). Mission hate crimes are extremely rare; they constituted less than 1 percent of Levin and McDevitt's (2002) sample of cases.

Peer group dynamics   Many hate crimes, especially thrill- and defense-motivated crimes, are committed by groups of offenders, almost always young men who know one another (Levin & McDevitt, 2002), so peer group dynamics can play an important part in motivating participation in these crimes (Byers et al., 1999; Franklin, 1998, 2000; McDevitt et al., 2002). Offenders motivated by peer group concerns act out of "the desire to feel closer to friends, to live up to friends' expectations, and to prove toughness and [in the case of anti-gay crimes] heterosexuality to friends" (Franklin, 2000, p. 347). As this emphasis on toughness and heterosexual masculinity suggests, Franklin (1998) noted that men are more strongly motivated by this factor than are women, at least in the anti-gay context (see also Chapter 9). The group-centered nature of some hate crimes is illustrated in the interviews Byers and his colleagues (1999) conducted with perpetrators of hate crimes against the Amish: "When asked if a person were to clape alone, subjects responded that the person would have to be 'sick' to do such a thing" (p. 84). Another said, "It was a kind of male bonding. . . . It kind of drew us all closer because we went out and did something" (p. 89).

Like thrill seekers, peer-motivated hate crime offenders exhibit little animosity toward their victims' groups, but also exhibit little respect for them (Byers et al., 1999; Franklin, 1998). However, unlike thrill seekers, they sometimes do acknowledge that the victim was harmed, but tend to minimize their personal responsibility. Instead, they portray themselves as having had little choice in the matter (Byers et al., 1999; Franklin, 1998). For example, some of Byers and colleagues' (1999) respondents blamed their behavior on peer pressure or local norms, giving explanations such as "The harassment was almost common nature" and "[It] is because of the way I was raised" (p. 92).

McDevitt and his colleagues (2002) note that many offenders who act on the basis of peer group concerns may be unwilling participants in the crime: They do not approve of violence (or, perhaps, even prejudice), but go along with the group because they feel that if they do not they will lose the approval of their friends. In many instances, unwilling participants do not actively take part in the crime, but also do nothing to prevent it or stop it once it has begun and are unwilling to provide information to authorities afterwards (see also Byers et al., 1999).

Normalization   Based on their interviews with participants in anti-Amish hate crimes, Byers and Crider (2002) have suggested that one factor that facilitates, if not motivates, such crimes is community acceptance of such behavior. That is, the community in which the offenders live views such actions as normal behavior and so do not strongly condemn it, try to prevent it, or punish it. Byers and Crider (2002) noted that "victimization of the Amish was sometimes considered a rite of passage [in the local non-Amish community]. . . . If people believe that claping is harmless, there is a lower likelihood of intervention from parents, teachers, or criminal justice officials" (pp. 133–134). This attitude was reflected in comments made by Byers and Crider's (2002) interviewees. For example,

> [Claping] is socially acceptable here. . . . [Interviewer: In this community?] Extremely, in this community. They just pretty much shrug and it is "boys growing up." If I lived here and I had kids and they were 16 or 17, then it would not surprise me if I just said it is just "kids growing up." . . . I think that most people would see it as something as I will turn my back to it and pretend that it is not there. Like when people are watching t.v. and you see the starving kids, everyone just turns the channel. It is the same thing. . . . If something bad really did happen like say somebody got killed or whatever I would say that the community would be, "That is a shame and all that," but then the entire town would be like "Oh well." I really think it would be that way. (pp. 136–137)

Claping is so acceptable in the community where Byers and Crider conducted their interviews that one of the researchers was invited out on a claping expedition (he declined the invitation).

Inhibiting factors   It is often as informative to understand why people do *not* engage in a behavior as why they do engage in it. A unique aspect of Franklin's (2000) study is that she asked the nonoffenders in her sample why they "have never harassed or beaten up a homosexual" (p. 353). She identified a number of reasons, although she did not report the number of people giving each type of reason. Some people's responses implied that they refrained from anti-gay behavior because of a lack of opportunity, saying they avoid homosexuals or never see homosexuals. Others reported a fear of negative consequences, such as getting into trouble with authorities or peer disapproval. Some respondents cited a belief in nonviolence or other religious or moral beliefs. A final reason was knowing someone who was homosexual. Franklin also noted that these restraining beliefs may be fairly weak and so may easily break down under pressure. For example, 38 percent of her respondents who had never engaged in anti-gay behavior "reported some likelihood to verbally or physically assault a homosexual who flirted with or propositioned them" (Franklin, 2000, p. 353).

Effects on Victims

Surveys conducted in different parts of the United States over a period of 10 years have provided an unusually consistent set of results regarding the effects hate crimes have on their victims: Hate crime victims suffer more severe psychological consequences from their victimization and these negative effects last longer compared to

---

TABLE 10.4   EFFECTS OF HATE CRIMES ON VICTIMS

Compared to victims of similar crimes that were not motivated by bias, hate crime victims experience more:

- Nervousness, anxiety, depression, and stress
- Intrusive thoughts about the crime
- Trouble concentrating or working
- Anger and a desire to retaliate
- Feelings of being exhausted and weak for no reason
- Fear of future trouble in life
- Distrust of people
- Fear of crime and feelings of personal vulnerability
- Difficulty coping with the effects of victimization
- Difficulty in relationship with spouse or significant other

Sources: Ehrlich, Larcom, and Purvis (1995); Herek, Gillis, and Cogan (1999); McDevitt, Balboni, Garcia, and Gu (2001).

---

victims of similar crimes that were not motivated by bias (Ehrlich, Larcom, & Purvis, 1995; Herek, Gillis, & Cogan, 1999; McDevitt, Balboni, Garcia, & Gu, 2001). Table 10.4 lists some of the outcomes that hate crime victims experience to a greater extent than victims of other crimes. In addition, compared to victims of non-bias crimes, hate crime victims report feeling less control over their lives. One factor that helps crime victims deal psychologically with their victimization is the feeling that they can control what happens to them and, as a result, do things that will prevent them from being victimized again (Davis, Taylor, & Titus, 1997). However, hate crime victims tend to be chosen at random and so believe that there is nothing they can do to avoid becoming a victim again: "Victims are aware that their overt actions did nothing to precipitate their victimization; being the 'wrong person,' at the wrong time and place, qualifies the bias victim [to become a victim]. Therefore, if the impetus for victimization is something that is outside the bias victim's control before the incident, it is reasonable that there would be little the victim would do differently subsequent to the incident" (McDevitt et al., 2001, p. 711). These feelings of lack of control exacerbate the negative psychological consequences of having been a crime victim.

A special characteristic of hate crimes is what McDevitt and his colleagues (2001; see also Ehrlich, 1999) call **secondary victimization:** A hate crime has psychological effects not only on the victim but also on members of the victim's group. These secondary victims experience, at least temporarily, heightened anxiety over the possibility of becoming victims themselves. Secondary victimization is a major goal of defense-motivated hate crimes and is often a secondary goal of others (McDevitt et al., 2001). As McDevitt and his colleagues (2001) note, "a cross burning not only affects the immediate family [that was victimized], but any African American who becomes aware of the incident" (p. 698). There are few data on the extent of secondary victimization in hate crimes, but Howard Ehrlich (1999) reported that surveys of college students following on-campus hate crimes have found that about two-thirds of other members of the victim's group experience fear of becoming victims themselves. Thus, hate crimes victimize not just individuals, but entire social groups.

Chapter Summary

Discrimination consists of treating people differently, and usually unfairly, based solely or primarily on their membership in a social group. Discrimination is therefore a matter of behavior (including verbal behavior), whereas prejudice is an attitude that can motivate discriminatory behavior. Discrimination can take any of three forms. Blatant discrimination is intentional and obvious. Subtle discrimination is less visible and obvious than blatant discrimination, is often unintentional, and derives from people having internalized discriminatory customs and social norms. Covert discrimination is hidden but intentional, and often motivated by malice. Each form of discrimination can occur at any of four levels of society. Interpersonal discrimination consists of behaviors that individuals direct at other individuals. Organizational discrimination occurs when the policies and practices of an organization put members of some groups at a disadvantage relative to members of other groups. Institutional discrimination occurs across organizations that are part of a particular social institution. Cultural discrimination consists of discriminatory assumptions and practices that are so deeply embedded in a culture that members of the culture take them for granted and see them as normal.

Although prejudice can motivate discrimination, not all prejudiced people discriminate when they have the opportunity and nonprejudiced people can discriminate without intending to. A number of factors influence the relationship between prejudice and discrimination. Prejudice is more likely to manifest itself in discrimination when the target of the discrimination matches the prejudiced individual's personal stereotype of the outgroup. Implicit prejudice is most likely to result in automatic, uncontrollable behaviors, whereas explicit prejudice is most likely to affect controllable behaviors. Finally, people are more likely to act on their prejudices when they believe that other people agree with them.

Because of the egalitarian norm that exists in modern society, most people are motivated to control any prejudice they feel and to avoid discriminatory behavior. There are two theories of motivation to control prejudice. Dunton and Fazio (1997) postulate that motivation to control prejudiced reactions has two components. Concern with acting prejudiced involves concern that others might think that one is prejudiced and a personal desire to avoid being prejudiced. Restraint to avoid dispute involves the awareness that acting in a prejudiced manner would cause trouble coupled with a willingness not to act prejudiced as a way of avoiding arguments. Plant and Devine (1998) postulate that what they call motivation to respond without prejudice consists of two types of motivation. Internal motivation stems from a personal belief that prejudice is wrong and external motivation stems from a desire to avoid the negative reactions from other people that would be elicited by a display of prejudice. Social norms—informal rules that define how a good group member thinks and behaves—are an important part of both theories. Group norms define what prejudices and forms of discrimination are acceptable and unacceptable and people are motivated to behave in ways that are consistent with what they believe the norm to be.

The two theories take somewhat different, but not necessarily contradictory, approaches to the development of motivation to control prejudice. Research on Dunton and Fazio's (1997) theory has focused on childhood correlates of the theory's two components. Concern with appearing prejudiced is associated with parental emphasis on egalitarian values and positive contact with Black people. Restraint to avoid dispute is correlated with having prejudiced parents, having little childhood contact with Black people, and experiencing the contacts that did occur as negative. Plant and Devine's (1998) theory views the development of internal and external motivation to control prejudice as a matter of accommodation to group norms. People start out in a given normative context and, if they move to a new context, experience external motivation to control prejudices that were acceptable in the old context but are not acceptable in the new context. To the extent that people try to abide by the new norms, they develop an internal motivation while external motivation fades.

Regressive prejudice occurs when people lose control over their prejudiced responses and act in a discriminatory manner. Thus, people can exhibit nonverbal indicators of prejudice, which are usually not under voluntary control, while trying to appear unprejudiced through their controllable behaviors. Just as high cognitive demands can lead people to apply stereotypes, such demands can let prejudiced behaviors "leak out" by undermining control. Alcohol consumption and strong emotions, such as anger, can also reduce control over behavior. Because people are less motivated to comply with social norms when other people cannot identify them, anonymity facilitates discriminatory behavior, as does the actual or implied approval of authority figures. Seeing other people act in a prejudiced manner can also disinhibit prejudice. Finally, if individuals believe that they have established their credentials as unprejudiced people, they may let their control lapse and act in a discriminatory manner.

People who see themselves as unprejudiced but realize that they have acted in a prejudiced manner often feel guilty about the behavior, but prejudiced people do not. People with a strong internal motivation to avoid prejudice also feel guilty over violating their principles, but externally motivated people and people high on restraint to avoid dispute feel threatened by what others might think of their behavior. When confronted for having acted in a prejudiced manner, people are more likely to accept the feedback from a member of their own group than from a member of the group against which their prejudice was directed, perhaps because they feel less defensive and threatened when confronted by a member of their ingroup. Finally, when people feel guilty over having acted prejudiced, they try to make up for it by doing things to show how unprejudiced they really are.

Data on the nature of the American workforce indicate that White men still disproportionately hold the most powerful and prestigious jobs. Research indicates that Black job applicants who submit résumés are less likely to be called for interviews than equally qualified White applicants and receive lower ratings on interview performance. As a result, they are less likely to be hired. In contrast, there currently seems to be little gender discrimination in hiring. Once on the job, although there seems to be little gender bias in performance evaluations, Black workers receive lower performance evaluations than White workers. Even when numerical ratings for Black and White employees are identical, White employees tend to get more positive narrative comments. Black employees perform less well on objective measures of job performance, so evaluations might simply be reflecting that difference. However, the lower objective performance might itself be a result of prejudice, reflecting lost opportunities, such as for additional training, and lower morale caused by prejudice and discrimination.

Even when women and members of minority groups receive the same performance evaluations as men and Whites, they are less likely to be promoted, are promoted more slowly, and are more likely to end their careers at a lower organizational level. In addition, the pay differential between Black and White workers increases as level of authority increases. Black workers may experience slower promotions because of the sticky floor effect—Black managers tend to supervise Black workers who are disproportionately found at lower organizational levels, are tracked into jobs with little promotion potential, and have fewer influential mentors to help them in their careers.

A number of individual-level processes contribute to discrimination in organizations. The stereotype fit hypothesis holds that women and members of minority groups are underrepresented in managerial positions relative to White men because the White male stereotype matches the stereotype of the effective manager whereas the female and minority stereotypes do not. As a result, women and minority group members are perceived as less qualified despite their objective qualifications. Similar processes also can operate for lower level jobs: The generally negative stereotypes of minority groups contradict the "good worker" stereotype. Women and members of minority groups also may be excluded from prestigious jobs because, as groups, they garner less respect than White men. The finding that women and members of minority groups are less likely to be promoted even when they receive the same performance evaluations as men and Whites may be a result of the shifting standards effect: Because evaluators have lower expectations for women's and minority groups' performance relative to men's and Whites', the same subjective rating translates into a lower rating on an objective common scale that takes the race-based evaluations into account. Rewards such as promotions are based on the common scale.

Contemporary prejudice can lead prejudiced decision makers to put more weight on the negative aspects of a minority group member's qualifications when both positive and negative information is available, leading to an adverse decision that can be justified by the negative information. Employers also may use business-related justifications, such as maintaining work group harmony and customers' prejudices, as justifications for not hiring minority workers. Finally, people tend to comply with what they perceive to be the requirements of organizational norms and authority figures. Thus, if they perceive the organizational norm as calling for discrimination or perceive that authority figures prefer to have as few minority workers as possible, even low prejudiced people may discriminate to comply with those demands.

Hate crimes are criminal offenses in which evidence shows the victims were chosen because of their group membership. Hate crime offenders are primarily young men. Several motives exist for hate crime. The most common seems to be thrill seeking: People are bored and see picking on or assaulting a member of an outgroup as a way of getting some excitement. They often have no strong animosity toward their victims' groups; they choose as targets members of groups they believe are unlikely to fight back or to report the crime. They often justify their actions by minimizing their impact or the victim or portraying their actions as harmless fun. Defensive hate crimes are designed to drive outgroup members from ingroup "territory" and to send a general message to other members of the victim's group to stay away. Retaliation crimes are carried out in response to an actual or rumored hate crime against a member of the offender's group. Mission hate crimes occur because of a commitment to a bigoted ideology and to rid the world of a perceived evil. Peer group dynamics contribute to hate crimes because offenders are often trying to impress members of the peer group, are going along with what they see as the group norm, or have succumbed to group pressure to participate. Community norms also can facilitate hate crimes by viewing them as normal behavior and refraining from disapproving of or punishing them. Factors that can inhibit people from committing hate crimes include lack of opportunity, fear of negative consequences, religious or moral beliefs, or knowing a member of the targeted group.

Hate crimes generally have more severe psychological consequences for their victims than do non-bias-motivated crimes, and those effects last longer. The effects may be more severe and longer lasting because hate crime victims feel that they cannot do anything to avoid being victimized in the future. Hate crimes also result in secondary victimization: A hate crime has negative psychology effects not only on the victim, but also on other members of the victim's group, who experience heightened anxiety over the possibility of becoming victims themselves.

SUGGESTED READINGS

The Relation of Prejudice to Discrimination

Crandall, C. S., Eshleman, A., & O'Brien, L. (2002). Social norms and the expression and suppression of prejudice: The struggle for internalization. *Journal of Personality and Social Psychology, 82*, 359–378.
  Crandall and his colleagues present a set of studies on the role of social norms in prejudice and discrimination.

Motivation to Control Prejudice

Dunton, B. C., & Fazio, R. H. (1997). An individual difference measure of motivation to control prejudiced reactions. *Personality and Social Psychology Bulletin, 23,* 316–326.

Plant, E. A., & Devine, P. G. (1998). Internal and external motivation to respond without prejudice. *Journal of Personality and Social Psychology, 75,* 811–832.

These articles present the two major models of motivation to control prejudice. Plant and Devine comment on the similarities and differences of the models.

Regressive Prejudice

Crandall, C. S., & Eshleman, A. (2003). A justification-suppression model of the expression and experience of prejudice. *Psychological Bulletin, 129,* 414–446.

This article includes a comprehensive review of factors that act as releasers of regressive prejudice, which Crandall and Eshleman refer to as justifications.

Reactions to Having Acted Prejudiced

Czopp, A. M., & Monteith, M. J. (2003). Confronting prejudice (literally): Reactions to confrontations of racial or gender bias. *Personality and Social Psychology Bulletin, 29,* 532–544.

Devine, P. G., Monteith, M. J., Zuwerink, J. R., & Elliot, A. J. (1991). Prejudice with and without compunction. *Journal of Personality and Social Psychology, 60,* 817–830.

Fazio, R. H., & Hilden, L. E. (2001). Emotional reactions to a seemingly prejudiced response: The role of automatically activated racial attitudes and motivation to control prejudice. *Personality and Social Psychology Bulletin, 27,* 538–549.

Plant, E. A., & Devine, P. G. (1998). Internal and external motivation to respond without prejudice. *Journal of Personality and Social Psychology, 75,* 811–832.

Devine and colleagues' article describes some of the initial theory and research on how people with unprejudiced self-concepts react to having acted in a prejudiced manner. Plant and Devine and Fazio and Hilden examine the issue in the context of their models of motivation to control prejudice. Czopp and Monteith examine the issue in the context of responses to having acted in a prejudiced manner toward different groups.

Organizational Discrimination

Roberson, L., & Block, C. J. (2001). Racioethnicity and job performance: A review and critique of theoretical perspectives on the causes of group differences. *Research in Organizational Behavior, 23,* 247–325.

Roberson and Block discuss four models of factors that affect minority group members' work performance. Although the discussion focuses on work performance, the principles they discuss generalize to other processes, such as hiring and promotion.

Hate Crimes

Ehrlich, H. J. (1999). Campus ethnoviolence. In F. L. Pincus & H. J. Ehrlich (Eds.), *Race and ethnic conflict: Contending views on prejudice, discrimination, and ethnoviolence* (2nd ed., pp. 277–290). Boulder, CO: Westview.

Levin, J., & McDevitt, J. (2002). *Hate crimes revisited: America's war on those who are different.* Boulder, CO: Westview.

McDevitt, J., Balboni, J., Garcia, L., & Gu, J. (2001). Consequences for victims: A comparison of bias- and non-bias-motivated assaults. *American Behavioral Scientist, 45,* 697–713.

McDevitt, J., Levin, J., & Bennett, S. (2002). Hate crime offenders: An expanded typology. *Journal of Social Issues, 58,* 303–317.

The article by McDevitt and his colleagues (2002) presents an overview of Levin and McDevitt's (2002) typology of hate crime offenders. Levin and McDevitt's (2002) book discusses the typology in more detail and provides a number of case descriptions for each type. They also discuss issues involved in policing, public policy, and prevention, among others. Ehrlich (1999) discusses the problem of hate crime on college campuses, usually considered to be bastions of tolerance (see also Levin and McDevitt's Chapter 9).

KEY TERMS

blatant discrimination	motivation to respond without prejudice
covert discrimination	organizational discrimination
cultural discrimination	regressive racism (prejudice)
discrimination	secondary victimization
hate crimes	shifting standards model
institutional discrimination	social norms
interpersonal discrimination	stereotype fit hypothesis
motivation to control prejudiced reactions	subtle discrimination

QUESTIONS FOR REVIEW AND DISCUSSION

1. Define *discrimination.* How does discrimination differ from prejudice? How are the two concepts similar?
2. Define the three forms discrimination can take and give an example of each. Explain the four societal levels at which discrimination can occur and give an example of discrimination at each level.
3. Review the types of contemporary prejudice we discussed in Chapter 5. What forms of discrimination do you think those types of prejudice likely result in?
4. Describe the factors that influence the relationship between prejudice and discrimination. That is, under what conditions is prejudice most likely to result in discrimination?
5. Describe the sources of motivation to control prejudice proposed by Dunton and Fazio (1997) and Plant and Devine (1998). In what ways are these models similar and in what ways do they differ? Which model do you think is more accurate? Explain your reasons for your choice.

6. Plant and her colleagues have found that people with high scores on external motivation to control prejudice express more prejudice than people with low scores. How do they explain this apparent contradiction?

7. What are social norms? How are they related to prejudice and discrimination? What experiences have you had with social norms and prejudice and discrimination?

8. Describe the two models of the development of motivation to control prejudice.

9. What is regressive prejudice? Describe the factors that can precipitate it. Have you observed any instances of regressive prejudice? If so, describe them and explain what factors led to the release of discriminatory behavior in those cases.

10. How do people who see themselves as unprejudiced react to having acted in a prejudiced manner? How are the reactions of people with internal and external motivation to control prejudice similar and how do they differ?

11. What is an *employment audit*? Do you think that employment audits are effective tools for studying discrimination in hiring? Why or why not?

12. What has research discovered about race and gender discrimination in hiring? What has research discovered about race and gender discrimination in performance evaluation?

13. Researchers have found that Black workers usually get lower scores on objective measures of job performance than do White workers. What is the relevance of this finding for interpreting race differences in supervisor evaluations, which generally have a strong subjective element?

14. What has research discovered about race and gender discrimination in promotions? What organizational factors might contribute to these differences?

15. What is the stereotype fit hypothesis? How does it explain race and gender differences in hiring, performance evaluation, and promotion?

16. Describe how differences in the amount of respect that different social groups receive are related to organizational discrimination.

17. What is the shifting standards effect? How does it explain race and gender differences in hiring, performance evaluation, and promotion?

18. Explain the role contemporary prejudice plays in organizational discrimination.

19. Explain the role conformity to perceived norms plays in organizational discrimination.

20. Rather than attributing the differential outcomes minority and female workers experience in organizations to intentional discrimination, Smith and Elliott (2002) wrote that "We believe that something more subtle and profound occurs in the process of doing 'business as usual'—mere maintenance of the status quo is more than enough to perpetuate . . . stratification" (p. 274). Do you agree or disagree? Explain the reasons for your position.

21. What are hate crimes?

22. Describe the characteristics of hate crime offenders.

23. Explain how thrill seeking can motivate hate crimes. Who do thrill seekers choose as victims? How do they justify their behavior?

24. Some researchers believe that thrill-seeking hate crime offenders feel little animosity toward their victims or their groups. Do you agree or disagree? Explain the reasons for your position.
25. Explain territorial defense as a motivation for hate crimes.
26. Explain retaliation as a motivation for hate crimes.
27. What are mission-motivated hate crimes? Why do you think they are so rare?
28. Explain the role that peer group dynamics play in hate crimes.
29. Explain how community attitudes can affect the occurrence of hate crimes.
30. In what ways do the psychological consequences differ for the victims of hate crimes and those of crimes not motivated by bias? Why causes these differences?
31. Explain the concept of *secondary victimization.*

THE EXPERIENCE OF DISCRIMINATION

Oh, is there still racism?

—Anonymous student, on hearing that a course on racism was being offered on her campus, quoted in Tatum, 1997 (p. 3)

I don't think White people, generally, understand the full meaning of racist discriminatory behaviors directed toward Americans of African descent. They seem to see each act of discrimination or any act of violence as an "isolated" event. As a result, most White Americans cannot understand the strong reaction manifested by Blacks when such events occur. They feel that Blacks tend to "overreact." They forget that in most cases, we live lives of quiet desperation generated by a litany of *daily* large and small events that, whether or not by design, remind us of our "place" in American society.

—Anonymous Black professor, quoted in Feagin and Sikes, 1994 (pp. 23–24, emphasis in original)

As we saw in Chapter 5, many White Americans think prejudice is more or less a thing of the past. It is certainly true that more blatant forms of prejudice have declined in the United States, because of both legislative and social changes. It is also true, however, that the existence of prejudice and discrimination can simply be invisible to many members of the majority group. It is sometimes difficult for the majority group to accept that, for many people, prejudice and discrimination are a "lived experience" (Feagin & Sikes, 1994, p. 15) and are not inconsequential beliefs and actions that can simply be overlooked while "getting on with one's life." Instead, for members of stereotyped groups, these experiences are woven into the fabric of their lives. Much of this book has focused on theories about and research on prejudiced people. In this chapter, we tell the story of prejudice and discrimination from the point of view of those lived experiences, focusing on the social psychological research that describes and explains them.

As we have seen in earlier chapters, prejudice and discrimination can take many forms, depending on the actor, the situation, and the historical time period in which a person lives. These factors similarly affect those who experience prejudice, creating a dynamic interchange between those who treat others unfairly and those who are the recipients of this injustice (Dovidio, Major, & Crocker, 2000). This chapter focuses on the consequences of this exchange as they affect every aspect of the stigmatized person's life, including their academic and economic achievement and their physical and mental well-being.

Social Stigma

To fully understand what it is like to experience discrimination, it is important to know what factors set others apart from the dominant group, increasing the likelihood that they will be discriminated against. Recall from Chapter 1 our discussion of *group privilege*. This privilege is defined as membership in the dominant group, a status that is seen as normal and natural and is usually taken for granted (Johnson, 2006). Dominant group membership is sometimes referred to as majority group membership, but this is somewhat of a misnomer. Privileged status often comes from being in the majority; however, it is not defined simply by a group's numerical advantage. For example, the British rule of India lasted more than 300 years; during that time, Indians faced severe racial discrimination from the British even though the Indians clearly outnumbered the British (Dirks, 2001). Similarly, although Blacks in South Africa outnumber Whites four to one, until 1994 Blacks were subjected to apartheid laws that enforced their segregation from Whites, governed their social life, and limited their employment options (Beck, 2000). Privileged status, then, is defined less by a group's numbers and more by its power and influence. We begin our discussion by outlining the factors that delineate a group's privileged or disadvantaged status.

What Defines a Stigmatized Group?

Whether they are consciously aware of it or not, individuals with privileged status define which groups do or do not share this status. In social psychological terms, those groups that do not share this status are **stigmatized** or deviant. Stigmatized groups differ from the privileged or dominant groups in terms of appearance or behavior. Members of stigmatized groups violate the norms established by the dominant group on these dimensions and, as such, are marked by the resulting social stigma (Jones et al., 1984). Because of this, members of stigmatized groups are sometimes referred to as *the marked* and those who are the actors, or the ones who stigmatize, are sometimes referred to as *the markers*. Marked individuals are "devalued, spoiled, or flawed in the eyes of others" (Crocker, Major, & Steele, 1998, p. 504). The consequences of this devaluation are far reaching and can include dehumanization, threat, aversion, and other negative treatment, including subtle forms of discrimination (Dovidio et al., 2000).

Which groups are stigmatized by the privileged or dominant group? The answer depends on the culture and on the historical events that led to the current cultural context. As we saw in Chapter 1, for example, the Irish and Italians were once considered non-White and were targets of discrimination in the United States; today, they are accepted as part of the White majority (Rubin, 1998). Returning to our earlier examples, India is now governed by its own people and is not subject to British dominance and Blacks in South Africa have made significant strides toward undoing the effects of apartheid. Hence, historical events and changes in laws and social norms affect cultural beliefs about who can or should be stigmatized, even if it sometimes takes many years to see their effects. More generally, dominant group members determine which individuals are stigmatized, based on any number of characteristics, including membership in an underrepresented basic social category, such as ethnicity, age, or gender, or in a socially deviant category defined by physical or mental disability, weight, socioeconomic status, or sexual orientation. People also can be stigmatized because of their acne, their mother's alcoholism, a speech impediment, or illness, among many other things (Jones et al., 1984). To be stigmatized, then, individuals must have a characteristic that is devalued by the dominant group and that sets them apart from that group. Regardless of the source of the stigma, in all cases, there is shame associated with being marked (Goffman, 1963).

As you read this list of stigmatized groups, you might have concluded that almost everyone has had the experience of being different from the majority and has suffered because of it. It is true that being different from the group is often part of normal human life. If you have had such experiences, it may give you some insight into what it is like to be a member of a stigmatized group. But for majority group members, many times these experiences are short-lived or otherwise *benign*. Benign stigmas, such as acne, a correctable speech impediment, or a short-term illness, differ in important ways from the more harmful stigmas social scientists most often study, such as those based on ethnicity, severe mental illness, or sexual orientation. Because these latter stigmas typically have more negative consequences, ranging from depression to extreme violence against the stigmatized group, they are the focus of this chapter. Edward Jones and his colleagues (1984) have identified five dimensions that are particularly helpful in differentiating between harmful and benign stigmas: course, concealability, aesthetic qualities, origin, and peril.

1. *Course*   Benign stigmas are often temporary; acne is usually outgrown or can be cured by a dermatologist. That is, the *course* of the stigma is short. In contrast, the course of many negative stigmas generally cannot be changed. An individual's ethnicity is typically part of his or her lifelong identity, for example. This factor is sometimes referred to as *stability;* some stigmas are stable, or irreversible, whereas others are unstable and can change over time. In general, people believe that physically based stigmas, such as blindness or cancer, are stable and that mental-behavioral stigmas, such as drug abuse or obesity, are unstable (Weiner, Perry, & Magnusson, 1988). In general, stable stigmas have more negative consequences for the stigmatized person.

2. *Concealability*   Some stigmas are concealable, which means they can be hidden or controlled by the stigmatized person. Such stigmas can be avoided simply by keeping the stigma private, such as by not talking about one's alcoholic mother, or can be hidden, such as by wearing makeup to cover a scar or birthmark. Moreover, some individuals can and do choose to "pass" for a member of a different ethnic group, thus concealing their group membership. However, as Jones and his colleagues (1984) explain, concealing a stigma does not reduce the guilt and shame associated with that stigma. Moreover, concealment of a stigma may also mean hiding an important part of one's identity. Many gay men and lesbians are not open about their relationships out of fear of social rejection, loss of employment, or the threat of physical violence; as a result they often find themselves lying about or hiding an important part of their life and they feel guilt and shame because they must do so (Meyer, 2003). Similarly, people often fail to seek treatment for mental illness because of the stigma associated with revealing their problem (Corrigan, 2004). People who have stigmas that cannot be concealed have a different set of problems; they realize their membership in a stigmatized group is apparent and this, in turn, affects their thoughts, feelings, and behavior. They must always directly cope with the prejudice and discrimination associated with their group membership (Crocker et al., 1998).

3. *Aesthetic qualities*   Aesthetics refers to what is beautiful or appealing. As we discussed in Chapter 3, many stereotypes are triggered by physical appearance cues (Fiske & Taylor, 1991) and many stigmas are based on this dimension as well. In general, less physically attractive people are more likely to be stigmatized (Eagly, Ashmore, Makhijani, & Longo, 1991). One reliable indicator of physical attractiveness is facial symmetry, or the degree to which the left and right sides of the face are mirror images of each other (Langlois & Roggman, 1990). Individuals with facial disfigurement typically do not meet this standard and are likely to be stigmatized. In North American culture, slimness is emphasized and overweight people become the targets of discrimination (Crandall et al., 2001). Similarly, a central component of the old-age stereotype is a decline in physical attractiveness and mobility (Slotterback & Saarnio, 1996).

4. *Origin*   This term refers to how the stigma came to be and whether its onset was under the control of the stigmatized individual. Stigmas perceived to be controllable include drug addiction, acquisition of HIV, and obesity; those perceived to be uncontrollable include cancer and heart disease (Weiner et al., 1988). Physical characteristics that one is born with, such as race or many disabilities, also are perceived to be uncontrollable (Jones et al., 1984). People's beliefs about the controllability of a stigma have important implications for acceptance of the stigmatized other. When people believe that a stigma is uncontrollable, they feel more pity and less anger toward the stigmatized individual compared with when the stigma is perceived as controllable (Dijker & Koomen, 2003; Weiner et al., 1988). This viewpoint is evident in this excerpt from a letter to the editor that appeared in *The Chronicle Review:* "Race is something that a person has no control over; hence racism is wrong. Homosexuality is a choice a person makes, and therefore it is not wrong to disagree with it" (Colvin, 2003, p. B4). Research suggests that others share Colvin's viewpoint. For example, Bernard Whitley (1990) found that people who believed that sexual orientation was controllable had more negative attitudes toward lesbians and gay men than did people who believed sexual orientation was not controllable.

5. *Peril*   Members of some stigmatized groups are, correctly or incorrectly, perceived to be dangerous. Persons with a mental illness, for example, are stereotypically perceived to be dangerous, even though statistically they are no more likely to commit a violent crime than someone not so diagnosed (Corrigan & Penn, 1999). As we saw in Chapter 3, people stereotypically assume that Blacks are more dangerous than Whites (Duncan, 1976). Especially in the early years of the AIDS epidemic, the stigma associated with AIDS was found to be related to the belief that persons with AIDS were highly contagious and therefore dangerous (Triplet & Sugarman, 1987). In general, groups assumed to be more dangerous are more stigmatized than groups perceived as less dangerous (Jones et al., 1984).

Stigma by Association

So far, we have discussed what sets individuals apart from the dominant group. One underlying assumption is that the dominant group generally rejects members of stigmatized groups. But what happens when a member of the majority group does associate with a stigmatized person? Erving Goffman (1963) proposed that such an association would result in a "courtesy stigma" whereby the majority group member would also then be stigmatized. Until recently, mainly anecdotal data supported this possibility. However, two experiments by Steven Neuberg and his colleagues (Neuberg, Smith, Hoffman, & Russell, 1994) suggest that Goffman's hypothesis was correct. In the first study, male participants watched a social interaction that they believed was between either two friends or two strangers. In the course of the conversation, one of the men (Person A) discussed his relationship as being with either a woman or a man, which also revealed that he was either heterosexual or gay. Results showed that when the other man, Person B, was presented as a heterosexual, his being friends with the gay man produced a "courtesy stigma" or a stigma by association. Male research participants were less comfortable with Person B when they believed he was a friend to, rather than a stranger to, the gay Person A. A second study manipulated the social status of the heterosexual man as being high or low, based on the assumption that people like to associate with high status others. This status provided no buffer against the courtesy stigma, however. Instead, results showed that stigmatization of the heterosexual man was stronger when he was of higher status and associated with a gay man, perhaps because the association violates expectations about appropriate heterosexual behavior, particularly that of high status heterosexuals. Janet Swim and her colleagues (Swim, Ferguson, & Hyers, 1999) also found that people fear stigma by association with gay people. In their study, heterosexual women behaved in ways that socially distanced themselves from a lesbian, even when doing so required agreeing with socially unpopular positions or making sexist responses.

Additional research suggests that individuals who are dating a person with a disability are subject to stigma by association, including the perception that they are less intelligent and sociable than those dating a nondisabled person (Goldstein & Johnson, 1997). Yet some aspects of this stigma by association were positive, including the perception that those dating the disabled were more nurturant and trustworthy than those not doing so. Even so, these positive associations are consistent with the idea that stigmas label a person as different. As the authors note, respondents' positive comments focused on this difference, pointing out, for example, how much a person had to give up to date someone with a disability. In many cases, the comments indicated sympathy for the nondisabled person. Taken together, these studies suggest that Goffman's idea has merit; there are social consequences for associating with a deviant.

Tokenism

We noted above that being a numerical minority is not, in and of itself, sufficient to produce stigmatized status. That is, power and status are important components of defining privilege and nonprivilege. This does not mean, however, that being in the minority produces no negative effects, particularly in certain situations or settings. That is, one can be in the majority or near majority in a larger population, but still have stigmatizing experiences from being a minority within a particular context. Women, for example, are now represented in the labor force at numbers nearly equal to men. Many, however, still have negative experiences that result from being in the minority in some environments, such as being the only woman in a particular work group (Yoder, 2002). When individuals are a statistical minority within a particular setting, they can be treated as *tokens* and can be stigmatized because of it. In general, token status occurs when there is a preponderance of one group over another, such as when one gender or ethnicity is in the majority and only a few individuals from another gender or ethnicity are represented (Kanter, 1977).

Rosabeth Moss Kanter (1977) pioneered the research on tokenism in her case study of a multinational Fortune 500 corporation. Kanter highlighted three perceptual tendencies that affected the daily lives of tokens: visibility, contrast, and assimilation. *Visibility* refers to the tendency for tokens to get attention or, as she put it, "capture a larger awareness share" (p. 210). Consider, for example, this visual field containing a series of 10 Xs and only 1 O:

X X X X X X X O X X

Notice that your eyes tend to be drawn toward the O and not to any individual X. As we saw in Chapter 3, the perceptual process is similar in social situations; people's attention also tends to be drawn to the novel or unique person rather than to members of the majority group (Fiske & Taylor, 1991). Members of the minority, or token group, are simply noticed more than are other group members. *Contrast* refers to the polarization or exaggeration of differences between the token and the dominant group. A White person in a group comprised only of Whites, for example, might not think much about her or his racial identity. The presence of a Black person, however, brings race to the forefront, raising awareness of race for members of the dominant group. Similarly, adding a woman to an all-male work group can raise awareness of gender issues. Often, dominant group members are uncomfortable when this happens. *Assimilation* occurs when the token is stereotyped; in particular, the token's characteristics are distorted so that she or he fits the expected stereotype. A group of men, then, notice when a token woman behaves in a way that confirms their stereotypes about women and often generalize from that confirmation. However, the same men tend not to notice when the woman's behavior does not conform to their gender stereotypes.

These perceptual tendencies have important consequences for the token, which Kanter (1977) illustrated in her case study. She found, for example, that whenever the token women did something unusual, it stood out. As she describes it "[t]hey were the subject of conversation, questioning, gossip, and careful scrutiny . . . Their names came up at meetings, and they would easily be used as examples . . . [S]ome women were even told by their managers that they were watched more closely than the men" (p. 212). This was a double-edged sword; their achievements were noticed, but so were their mistakes. And, their actions were seen as representative of all women, not just of them as individuals. Because of this, even small decisions, such as what to wear to a business meeting, became important. Most people find such situations difficult to navigate, as the additional examples provided in Box 11.1 illustrate. Tokens often feel isolated but, at the same time, must go on as if the differences do not exist and do not affect their work. Solos, or people who are the only minority member in a majority group, often feel alone and without support (Benokraitis & Feagin, 1995). As one Black woman wrote, "the responsibility associated with being the only Black female in my college and only one of a handful in the university, was overwhelming. I have suffered several instances of burn-out and exhaustion. As a consequence I have learned to maintain a less visible profile as a coping and survival strategy" (Moses, 1989, p. 15). All told, the negative effects of being in the minority can create what has been called the "chilly climate" (Sandler & Hall, 1986). Tokens do not feel welcome or supported in their environment and often their work and personal lives suffer because of it.

11.1 *The Chilly Climate: Personal Experiences*

What does happen to the deviate? The deviate can convert, but short of a sex change operation, a time machine to age me, and a personality overhaul, conversion seems out of the question for me. Be isolated? That originally was all right with me, but that surely does not make me a team member. What can I do? Yet, the failure is placed squarely on my shoulders. "What is wrong with you?" "Why can't you get along?" These questions haunt me, undermining my self-image.

—Jan Yoder, 1985 (p. 67)

It is difficult to document exactly what form a token's negative experiences might take. That is, the actual events that comprise those experience are very personalized. Moreover, many of the individual instances that lead to the isolation and loneliness experienced by tokens seem harmless on the surface, especially to those who are not directly living with them. As you read the personal accounts described in this chapter they, too, may seem harmless. Keep in mind, however, that the research evidence suggests that, over time, such experiences affect those in token roles by isolating them from the dominant group, lowering their self-esteem, and creating loneliness. As a respondent in Paula Caplan's (1994) survey of women in academe

described, their cumulative impact is similar to "lifting a ton of feathers" (p. 9). Over time, their weight is unbearable.

This weight is illustrated by the opening quote in this box, which came from Jan Yoder's (1985) first person account of being the first female civilian faculty member at a United States military academy. Her writings captured her dilemma about how to respond to her interactions with the military officers who comprised 97 percent of the faculty. As she notes in her account, no one event seemed overly traumatic. Yet, because of their cumulative impact, she stayed only 6 months. Here are a few of her experiences: (1) Because she openly questioned the sexism of some exam questions, she was given a suggestion book so she could quietly record her objections without disrupting faculty meetings. (2) Her department chose to use "Macho Man" as its theme song, a song few women would choose to represent themselves. (3) Gossip about her ranged from "she's a lesbian" to "she is heterosexual, but promiscuous." (4) Despite her efforts to clarify her position in the academy, at social gatherings it was widely assumed that she was the wife of one of the officers.

Jan Yoder is now a highly successful faculty member at the University of Akron.

Although Kanter (1977) defined token status as simply being in the numerical minority, more recent work suggests numbers alone do not define token status. For example, women who pursue nontraditional occupations are more likely to experience the effects of tokenism than are women in traditional occupations (Yoder, 1991, 2002). A survey of undergraduates, for example, found that men's perceptions of current sex discrimination were not affected by their area of study; however, women in male-dominated academic areas, such as math, science, and engineering, reported higher levels of current sex discrimination than did women

Her study of Black women firefighters (Yoder, 1997) shows how the experience of being a token can threaten the safety of both the firefighters and those they are protecting. One Black woman in her study reported that, in response to a request for help, she received no constructive instruction, but instead was written up for presumed negligence. A coworker directly told another Black woman that when there was a fire, she was not to touch anything, but rather to stay out of the way. Many of the women reported receiving the "silent treatment," with the men literally walking out of the room when they entered. One reported that, during her formal testing, she was required to hoist a hose onto a shelf that suddenly had been raised 5 inches above where it was during training.

One of the ways tokens can be made to feel alienated is through the conversations Whites initiate with them. Black managers, for example, express frustrations with queries that seem to hold them accountable for other Blacks' behaviors, such as "Why do all the Blacks sit together?" and the relative lack of discussion about business-related topics, such as how to make the company succeed (Caver & Livers, 2002). Blacks often feel invisible as well.

Anderson Franklin (2004) describes the experience of a successful Black manager who took a White business client out for dinner in New York City. The maître d' ignored the Black manager, instead asking the White client if he had reservations. And, after dinner, the waiter returned the Black manager's credit card to the White client. After dinner, the White client easily found a cab, but the Black manager was not so successful and was ignored by cab drivers for over 15 minutes, even as other Whites successfully hailed a cab. Echoing the sentiments expressed by others in this chapter, at the individual level, such actions may seem harmless to Whites, but to tokens "[i]t's the cumulative effect that wears us down" (Caver & Livers, 2002, p. 78).

Many others have written about these individualized experiences. Researchers look across such events and, based on patterns, draw conclusions about the short- and long-term effects of being a token. On a positive note, research suggests that when the group composition changes, so that, for example, several women become part of an otherwise male-dominated group, these negative experiences dissipate and job satisfaction improves (Nieman & Dovidio, 1998).

in female-dominated academic areas, such as the arts, education, and social science (see Figure 11.1; J. Steele, James, & Barnett, 2002). This pattern also emerged in a measure of whether sex discrimination was expected in the future; women in male-dominated professions were most likely to hold this expectation and were most likely to consider changing their major. Research shows that men, such as male nurses, who are a statistical minority in their occupation or group, rarely have the same negative experiences as token women and may even be on the fast track to promotion (Benokraitis & Feagin, 1995; Maume, 1999; Yoder,

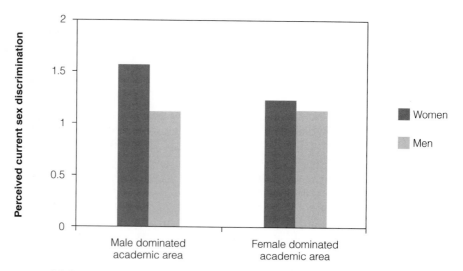

FIGURE **11.1**

PERCEIVED CURRENT SEX DISCRIMINATION BY GENDER OF RESPONDENT AND ACADEMIC AREA

Female undergraduates in a male-dominated academic area reported higher levels of sex discrimination than did female undergraduates in a female-dominated academic area or male undergraduates in either academic area.

Adapted from Steele, J., James, J. B., & Barnett, R. C. (2002). Learning in a man's world: Examining the perceptions of undergraduate women in male-dominated academic areas. *Psychology of Women Quarterly, 26*, 46–50.

1991), although there may be exceptions in some settings. Susan Murray (1997) found that male child-care workers were pushed away from tasks requiring nurturing and received the clear message that child care was women's work. These men reported feeling under suspicion, especially about their sexual motives for choosing a career in child care. Token status, then, is not all in the numbers.

The majority of the research on tokenism has focused on women who occupy nontraditional roles and remain the minority in those roles. Only a few studies have examined the experiences of people of color (see Moses, 1989, for one example). Jan Yoder (1997) studied the experience of Black women who were training to be firefighters; these women were a double minority in that setting. She found that their efforts were directly sabotaged by their superiors and coworkers (see Box 11.1). Additional factors, such as one's status in an organization, also may affect one's experience as a minority. Mary Kite and Deborah Balogh (1997) found that untenured women faculty were more likely than untenured men to report the kinds of negative interactions that are typically associated with the chilly climate, such as being excluded from social events or having their comments ignored at meetings. Tenured women and men did not differ in their reports about negative interactions, even though, at that time, both tenured and untenured women were a statistical minority at their university. This may be because their secure status or their experience in the environment provided a buffer from the effects of tokenism. Additional research is needed to explore how such factors affect the experience of being a solo.

RESPONSES TO PREJUDICE AND DISCRIMINATION

The personal experiences and experimental research we described in Chapter 10 provide a snapshot of the many and varied forms prejudice and discrimination can take. We focus here on how these behaviors affect stigmatized group members. The effects can be viewed on a continuum; at one end of the continuum are discriminatory behaviors that can make stigmatized group members uncomfortable. At the other end of the continuum are behaviors that cause members of stigmatized groups to lose job opportunities and can affect their health and well-being. Social psychologists have documented how stigmatizing experiences can create uncertainty for members of stigmatized groups, especially in how to interpret social and job-related interactions with the dominant group. We turn to this research next.

Attributional Ambiguity

Most people find it difficult to talk directly about stereotyping and prejudice. When members of dominant and stigmatized groups interact, the topic of prejudice can become the proverbial "elephant in the room." Recall from our discussion above, for example, that when tokens are present, it increases the likelihood the majority group members will think about their own group membership, even if they do not discuss this awareness. One cause of this discomfort is the generally ambivalent attitudes that dominant group members hold toward stigmatized groups. Research shows that dominant group members typically have mixed reactions to members of stereotyped groups (see Chapter 5). People who are not disabled, for example, often report feelings of both sympathy and anger toward those who are (Dijker & Koormen, 2003, Fichten & Amsel, 1986). Similarly, Whites often hold ambivalent attitudes about Blacks. Most Whites, for example, generally report having positive attitudes toward Blacks, but they also are less willing to interact with Blacks in more intimate settings (Muir, 1991). Moreover, as we discussed in Chapter 5, what people are willing to say about stigmatized groups has changed; in the United States, people today are much more accepting of the principle of equality for all people and most people want to avoid the appearance of being prejudiced.

Members of stigmatized groups are well aware of these mixed reactions. This awareness leads to a situation that Jennifer Crocker, Brenda Major, and their colleagues (Crocker, Voelkl, Testa, & Major, 1991) refer to as **attributional ambiguity**. That is, members of stigmatized groups often find it difficult to interpret feedback from dominant group members. Although such feedback may be based on the stigmatized group member's actual ability or achievement, it also may be based on feelings of sympathy or pity or on the desire on the part of the dominant group member to appear unbiased. Research shows, for example, that Whites sometimes give more positive feedback to Blacks than to Whites for the same poor performance, perhaps to avoid the appearance of being prejudiced (Harber, 1998; see also Chapter 5). Questions arise, then; for example, a Black person might wonder whether his supervisor's evaluation reflects his competence or stems from the supervisor's biases and prejudices. The answer to this question is unclear, leaving the stigmatized person unsure about how to interpret the feedback.

Crocker and her colleagues (1991) demonstrated the effects of attributional ambiguity in a study that was supposedly on friendship development. In this study, all participants were paired with a White student in an adjoining room; this student was actually a confederate of the experimenter. To manipulate whether the confederate knew the participant's race, either the blinds were drawn between the two rooms (so the participant could not be seen) or they were not. The participants described their likes and dislikes on a form that was allegedly shown to the confederate. Next, participants received bogus feedback indicating that the partner had either a positive or negative reaction to the information. Results showed that when the partner could not see them, Blacks were more likely to attribute negative than positive feedback to prejudice. Moreover, when Blacks knew their partner could see them, they attributed both the positive and negative feedback to prejudice. White participants' attributions to prejudice were unaffected by the valence of the feedback or by whether their partner knew their race. These results suggest that stigmatized group members sometimes *discount* feedback from the majority group because they believe it is based on factors other than their ability or performance (see also Major, Carrington, & Carnevale, 1984).

Members of stigmatized groups do not always discount positive feedback, however, and instead may *augment* it, or conclude that the positive evaluation was due to their own deservingness. In one study, for example, unattractive people found positive feedback to be more believable than did attractive people in a similar situation, perhaps because the unattractive participants did not think their partner had ulterior motives—in this case, an other-sex attraction toward them. Attractive people, in contrast, may have assumed attraction played a role and, as such, discounted the feedback (Major, Carrington, & Carnevale, 1984). When ulterior motives are not suspected, then, people are more likely to conclude that the feedback is due to their abilities or characteristics, but when such motives are suspected, members of stigmatized groups do not believe the positive feedback and conclude that it was due to factors such as the evaluators' desire to appear unbiased or their sympathy or pity.

What are the psychological consequences of receiving unclear feedback? Research shows that such consequences depend on whether stigmatized group members augment or discount the feedback and on the valence of the feedback. Discounting negative feedback, for example, has self-protective consequences. In the Crocker and colleagues (1991) study described above, Blacks who could attribute negative feedback to prejudice were less depressed than those who could not. In contrast, discounting positive feedback tended to produce lower self-esteem, even when compared to those individuals who received negative feedback (but see Branscombe & Ellemers, 1998, for a discussion of the limitations of these findings). Interestingly, these effects emerged even in a role-playing study in which undergraduates were asked to put themselves in the shoes of Blacks or women and imagine how they would feel if they were offered a job for one of two reasons (Blaine, Crocker, & Major, 1995). Participants who imagined the job offer came out of sympathy for past discrimination against their group reported that they would have lower self-esteem, higher depression, more hostility, and lower motivation than those who imagined the job offer was based on their qualifications. Follow-up studies showed that these effects were quite general. For example, similar patterns emerged regardless of whether the employer felt sympathy because of employment discrimination specifically or felt sympathy for the stigmatized group in general, in this case people with disabilities (Blaine et al., 1995).

Interestingly, self-esteem can be affected even if the stigmatized group member does not blame the evaluator for the negative feedback (Crocker, Cornwell, & Major, 1993). Overweight women who received negative social feedback from a male evaluator were more likely to attribute the negative feedback to their weight than were normal weight women, but did not dislike the evaluator for providing this feedback. That is, they did not attribute his feedback to prejudice. Even so, the overweight women who received negative feedback reported being in a more negative mood, and reported higher levels of depression and anxiety than did normal weight women who received negative feedback or women of any weight who received positive feedback. Overweight women are not getting a boost to their self-esteem, but instead may shoulder the blame for their weight. This may have harmful consequences. For example, the overweight may conclude that they will fail at dieting or following an exercise program and therefore not try or give up too easily. If, instead, the overweight had benefited from this buffer, they might be more willing to try and succeed in these endeavors.

In summary, research on attributional ambiguity shows that stigmatized people consider the source when receiving feedback and, if they believe the source is prejudiced against them, weigh that feedback differently. When the feedback is negative and can be attributed to prejudice they discount it. They also sometimes discount positive feedback because they doubt its validity, believing instead it stemmed from the evaluator's ulterior motives. Other times, for example when ulterior motives are not suspected, stigmatized individuals augment the positive feedback, deciding it must be due to their ability or characteristics. For minorities, discounting negative feedback has beneficial effects on self-esteem, but discounting positive feedback does not. Results of research on overweight women, however, suggests they do not to gain a psychological benefit from attributing negative feedback to prejudice.

Personal/Group Discrimination Discrepancy

In your study of social science, you have no doubt heard about serendipitous findings that are at first puzzling but later lead to important new theories and research. Faye Crosby (1984) stumbled across just such a finding when she surveyed working women who lived in a Boston suburb. Objective indicators showed that these women were being discriminated against; for example, the women earned between $5,000 and $8,000 less than men for equivalent jobs. Yet Crosby also found that the women were just as satisfied with their job as the men were. Perhaps even more puzzling was that the women were well aware that sex discrimination existed in the United States and, moreover, they were aggrieved by this state of affairs. They just did not believe this discrimination was happening in their own lives.

Crosby's (1984) surprising finding has led to a great deal of research on what is now known as the **personal/group discrimination discrepancy (PGDD);** that is, people believe their group, as a whole, is more likely to be discriminated against than they, themselves, are as individuals (Taylor, Wright, Moghaddam, & Lalonde, 1990). A number of studies, examining a number of disadvantaged groups, have reported findings consistent with this hypothesis, including Black college activists, French Canadians in Quebec, Canada (who live in a largely English-speaking country), English-speaking residents of Quebec (where French is the dominant language), unemployed workers in Australia, and lesbians (see Crosby, Pufall, Snyder, O'Connell, & Whalen, 1989; Taylor, Wright, & Porter, 1994, for reviews). Figure 11.2 illustrates the pattern the PGDD generally follows; lesbians perceived higher levels of discrimination for their group at a national and a local level than for themselves. They also believed lesbians at the local level and the national level had a greater need to hide their sexual orientation at work by appearing heterosexual than they themselves did (Crosby et al., 1989).

Cognitive explanations   There are two main categories of explanations for the PGDD: cognitive and motivational. Proponents of cognitive explanations suggest the personal/group discrimination discrepancy is simply a function of the way people process information. For example, Faye Crosby and her colleagues (1986) found that when participants evaluated information about discrimination in the aggregate form (that is, they read about patterns of discrimination compiled over several individuals), they believed that discrimination occurred. But when the same information was presented on a case by case basis, they failed to perceive discrimination. Hence, how the information was presented and processed either produced or inhibited the perception of discrimination. Research also has demonstrated that the PGDD is quite general, applying to domains unrelated to discrimination, such as the economy and the threat of AIDS (Moghaddam, Stolkin, & Hutcheson, 1997). People believe, for example, that a good economy is more likely to benefit their group as a whole than them as individuals. Such findings suggests a general process is operating that extends beyond perceptions of discrimination. It may be that the PGDD emerges because group examples more readily come to mind than do individual examples or because group information is more easily processed than is information about the self. Supporting this possibility, research shows that the PGDD is found for perceptions of positive events as well as negative events; people believe, for example, that the group, overall, is more likely than they, as individuals, to have warm and supportive friends and to benefit from the improved efficiency of computers (Moghaddam et al., 1997).

Another cognitive-based explanation is that people are using different comparison standards when judging their own versus the group's level of discrimination.

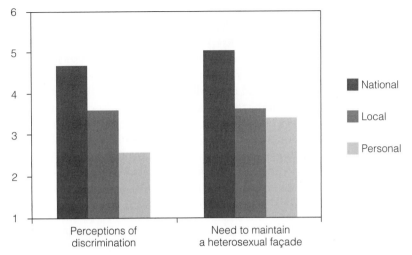

FIGURE 11.2

LESBIANS' RATINGS OF PERCEIVED DISCRIMINATION AT THE PERSONAL, LOCAL, AND NATIONAL LEVEL

Lesbian respondents saw more evidence of discrimination at the local level than at the personal level and the highest level of discrimination at the national level. They also believed lesbians at the local level and the national level had a greater need to hide their sexual orientation at work by appearing heterosexual than they themselves did.

Adapted from Crosby, F. J., Pufall, A., Snyder, R. C., O'Connell, M., & Whalen, P. (1989). The denial of personal disadvantage among you, me, and all the other ostriches. In M. Crawford & M. Gentry (Eds.), *Gender and thought: Psychological perspectives* (pp. 79–99). New York: Springer-Verlag.

That is, when deciding about their personal experience with discrimination, people consider their experiences in comparison with their own group members, but when deciding about the groups' discriminatory experiences, they compare themselves to other groups (Taylor et al., 1994). Women, then, may believe that they, personally, are better off than most women, but that their group is doing worse, on the whole, than men are. If this is the case, making the referent group explicit should reduce the PGDD. Research supports this possibility (Quinn, Roese, Pennington, & Olson, 1999). Ratings made in the absence of a referent led people to use ingroup comparisons for judgments of personal discrimination and outgroup comparisons for judgments of group discrimination. Moreover, providing a specific referent to an ingroup, in this case by asking women to compare their personal level of discrimination to other women's, reduced the PGDD. Perceptions of the frequency of discriminatory acts also affects the PGDD. Kathleen Fuegen and Monica Biernat (2000) asked women to read vignettes describing either a high- or low-severity act of discrimination that was either high or low in frequency. These women's ratings of their own and their group's experience with discrimination in general were affected by the vignette they read, with ratings of both personal and group discrimination being highest when the described discriminatory act was highly severe and frequent. This finding suggests that people associate discrimination with acts that are relatively rare and severe. Moreover, these beliefs affect the PGDD; this discrepancy was lower for those who read vignettes describing discriminatory events that occur frequently in society.

Taken as a whole, these studies show that how people process information in general, and about discrimination specifically, affects their views about their own and their group's experience with discrimination. It should be noted, however, that neither making the referent group explicit nor including information about frequency or severity of discrimination completely eliminates the PGDD. For example, making the referent explicit by asking women to compare their level of discrimination specifically to men's did not reduce the PGDD (Quinn et al., 1999). Cognitive explanations tell us something, but not everything, about why the PGDD occurs (Taylor et al., 1994).

Motivational explanations   Motivational explanations assume that people have reasons for believing that they are not personally discriminated against, even while recognizing that their group is. The motivational explanation that has received the most support is Crosby and colleagues' (1986) hypothesis that people want to deny or minimize their own experiences with discrimination. Recall from our earlier discussion that, in Crosby's studies (Crosby, 1984; Crosby et al., 1986), people did report little personal experience with discrimination, even though by objective indicators discrimination existed. There are several reasons why individuals might deny their personal experiences with discrimination (see Taylor et al., 1994, for a review). In some instances, individuals might take personal responsibility for their situation, and thus not acknowledge that the poor treatment they received could be due to discrimination. In other instances, people deny discrimination to justify their failure to accuse a specific discriminator or, relatedly, to justify not taking action about the discriminatory act. Finally, people may view their own situation as relatively harmless compared to more dramatic examples of discrimination, particularly those highlighted in the mass media.

Another reason people might deny personal discrimination is that they recognize that there are social costs to claiming discrimination and want to avoid these costs by distancing themselves from claims of unfairness (Kaiser & Miller, 2001a). These social costs include outcomes that create tension between themselves and the dominant group, such as being labeled a whiner or someone who takes advantage of possible discrimination for personal gain (Feagin & Sikes, 1994). To test this possibility Cheryl Kaiser and Carol Miller (2001a) asked introductory psychology students to read a description of a Black student who failed a test that had been evaluated by one of eight White judges. The potential bias he faced was manipulated: either none, four, or all of these White judges reportedly had a history of discriminating against Blacks. The research participants learned of this possible discrimination and that the student had failed the test. They also learned that the Black student attributed his failure to either the quality of his answers or to discrimination. Regardless of how much possible prejudice he had faced, participants were more likely to label the student as a complainer and to evaluate him less favorably when he made attributions to discrimination rather than ability.

Interestingly, however, the student who attributed his failure to discrimination also was seen as truer to himself than the student who attributed his failure to ability.

Additional research suggests that members of stigmatized groups are aware of such perceptions and this awareness affects their decision to report or confront discrimination. Women and Blacks who received a failing grade on a creativity test, for example, were more likely to attribute the failure to discrimination when reporting their attributions anonymously or when their explanation would be seen only by a stigmatized group member, compared to when the explanation would be seen by a dominant group member (Stangor, Swim, Van Allen, & Sechrist, 2002). For members of non-stigmatized groups, attributions were unaffected by who would see the results. The stakes of the encounter matter, too. Nicole Shelton and Rebecca Stewart (2004), for example, found that women who were being interviewed for a competitive, high paying job were less likely to confront a male interviewer who asked sexist questions than were women who were being interviewed for a low paying, less competitive job. This awareness also may play a role in the PGDD; supporting the idea that members of stigmatized groups want to distance themselves from negative attributes associated with their group, Gordon Hodson and Victoria Esses (2002) found that women were more likely to think that negative attributes (including discrimination) applied to the ingroup than to themselves, suggesting that they wanted to distinguish themselves from the group on these attributes. However, this distancing was not found for positive attributes; instead, they were more likely to report that positive attributes applied to themselves than to the ingroup. These effects were more pronounced for women who strongly identified with their group and, therefore, were more invested in how they and their group were perceived.

Perceiving discrimination   It would be incorrect to conclude, however, that people never recognize that they are personally being discriminated against. Donald Taylor and his colleagues (1990) found that both Haitian and Indian Canadian immigrants reported significant personal experience with discrimination, even though they reported that their group experienced more discrimination, as a whole, than they did as individuals. Similarly, single mothers receiving government assistance reported feeling that their life was somewhat unfair and evidenced resentment toward their situation, but still believed themselves to be better off than other mothers in their situation (Olson, Roese, Meen, & Robertson, 1995). There also may be individual differences in the tendency to minimize one's own experience with discrimination; the more typical of their group that Iranians perceived themselves to be, the less likely they were to exhibit the personal/group discrimination discrepancy (Verkuyten & Nekuee, 2001). Similarly, Don Operario and Susan Fiske (2001, Study One) found that non-Whites who were low and high identifiers with their group reported equal amounts of discrimination directed at their group, but differed in their perceptions of personal discrimination: high identifiers were more likely to report discrimination directed at themselves than were low identifiers. Results of a second study (Operario & Fiske, 2001, Study Two), suggest that this pattern emerged because high identified minorities are more sensitive to possible discrimination and, therefore, react to both subtle and obvious indicators of prejudice, whereas those less highly identified reacted only to obviously prejudiced actions. That is, those who identify strongly with their group may simply be more likely to notice and react to subtle forms of prejudice.

Interestingly, research suggests that this heightened sensitivity might be counterproductive. Elizabeth Pinel (2002) found that women who were high in *stigma consciousness*—that is, who believe that they live in a stereotyped world and that this affects their interactions with outgroups—were more critical of men who they believed to be sexist. This criticism, in turn, elicited more negative criticism from those men. The end result was that the women concluded that they were incompatible with the sexist men. No such effects emerge for women low in stigma consciousness or for women who believed they were interacting with nonsexist men. It is important to note that these results emerged independent of the men's actual sexist beliefs; the experimenter controlled who was described as sexist. Therefore, the differences in ratings were due to the women's expectations and how the interaction was affected by them, and not to sexist behavior on the men's part.

It may seem that there is a contradiction between the studies on attributional ambiguity, described above, which suggests that members of stigmatized groups are well aware that they personally might be discriminated against because of their stigmatized status and the PGDD, which suggests that people deny personal discrimination. As often happens in social science, bodies of literature address questions in different ways, resulting in seemingly subtle differences that account for such contradictions. In this case, studies of attributional ambiguity focus on a single, specific, instance of discrimination, whereas the personal/group discrepancy focuses on broad patterns of perceived discrimination. For example, studies of attributional ambiguity that focus on one interaction show that attributions to prejudice can protect self-esteem. This protection is not evident when individuals make attributions to broader, more stable patterns of discrimination; that is, when they consider, overall, how prejudice affects them as an individual, people report that their psychological well-being is adversely affected (Branscombe, Schmitt, & Harvey, 1999). But, as we saw with the personal/group discrimination discrepancy, they still may believe these effects are worse for their group than for themselves. We have more to say about the effects of experiencing discrimination on mental health later in this chapter.

CONSEQUENCES OF PREJUDICE TO THE TARGET

During the 1990s, there were impressive increases in minority group members' and women's participation in undergraduate and graduate education. Women, for example, are now more likely to enroll in college than are men and Blacks and Hispanics are enrolling in record numbers. These gains, however, do not necessarily translate into greater academic achievement for these groups. Minority student attrition rates are higher than Whites' at both the graduate and undergraduate level, and both women and minorities continue to be underrepresented in science and engineering (National Science Foundation, 2002). Moreover, college entrance exam scores continue to differ by sex and ethnicity. Boys, for example, score higher than girls on the math section of the SAT and Whites score higher on both the math and verbal sections than do Blacks and Latinos (College Board, 2003).

One explanation that has been offered for these differences is that women and minorities are not as able or as well prepared as their White male counterparts (Benbow & Stanley, 1980; Herrnstein & Murray, 1994). Yet, abundant evidence refutes this claim. For example, when women and minorities participate in programs designed specifically for underrepresented groups, they can and do succeed (Fullilove & Treisman, 1990; Grimmett, Bliss, & Davis, 1998). Moreover, despite their lower standardized test performance, girls receive higher grades in math courses than do boys, perhaps because girls perform better when the exam covers materials they have just studied (as a classroom test would) whereas boys perform better when the exam covers with new material (as a standardized test would; Kimball, 1995). Situational factors, then, have an important influence on the success of individuals who are underrepresented in a specific discipline (such as women in math and science) or in an academic setting more generally (such as Blacks at most colleges and universities; see C. Steele, 1997, for a review). In this section, we review research and theory on those situational factors and how they affect academic performance. We then describe the psychological outcomes that are related to being in these situations, specifically, or to prejudice and discrimination generally.

Stereotype Threat

If situational factors can raise the achievement of women and minorities, can they also hinder their performance? Research evidence suggests that they can. Consider, for example, that Blacks are well aware that a negative stereotype exists about their academic abilities. According to Claude Steele (1997), this knowledge produces a "threat in the air" (p. 617). Blacks realize that they can be judged or treated in terms of this negative stereotype and are fearful of confirming that judgment. If this fear is strong enough and also is personally relevant to the stereotyped group member, it can create a **stereotype threat** that interferes with academic achievement (Aronson, Quinn, & Spencer, 1998). As we will see, this affects the behavior of the person so threatened *even though* no discriminatory actions actually were directed toward her or him.

In one of the first demonstrations that stereotype threat affects Blacks' achievement, Claude Steele and Joshua Aronson (1995) asked Black and White undergraduates to take a test composed of the most difficult verbal questions from the Graduate Record Exam (GRE). Half of the participants were told the test was diagnostic of intellectual ability (the diagnostic condition); the other half were told the test was simply a laboratory problem-solving task (the nondiagnostic condition). Steele and Aronson proposed that the diagnostic condition induced stereotype threat for Blacks because their exam performance could support or refute the stereotype that Blacks have low verbal ability. Supporting this hypothesis, in two

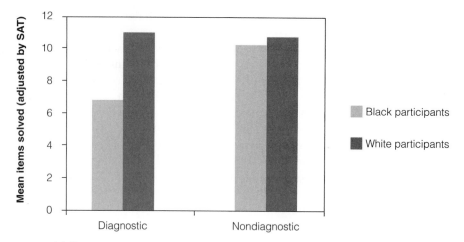

FIGURE **11.3**

MEAN ITEMS SOLVED BY PARTICIPANT RACE AND TEST DIAGNOSTICITY

Blacks' performance on a test of verbal ability were affected by whether the test was
described as diagnostic, and thus produced stereotype threat, or nondiagnostic
(nonthreatening). White's performance was unaffected by how the test was described.
These scores are adjusted for overall verbal ability, as measured by the SAT.

Adapted from Steele, C., & Aronson, J. (1995). Stereotype threat and the intellectual test performance of African Americans.
Journal of Personality and Social Psychology, 69, 797–811, Studies 1 and 2.

separate studies, Black participants in the diagnostic condition scored lower than
Blacks in the nondiagnostic condition or Whites in either condition. Figure 11.3
presents these results for the number of items solved correctly, collapsed across
Studies One and Two. Results of a third study showed that Blacks who were told
the test was diagnostic also were more likely to complete word fragments in Black
stereotypic ways (that is, completed _ _ Z Y as LAZY) than were Blacks who participated in the nondiagnostic condition, or Whites in either condition. Similarly,
compared with those in other conditions, Blacks in the diagnostic condition were
more likely to complete word fragments in a way that indicated self-doubt (that is,
completed L O _ _ _ as LOSER) and were more likely to distance themselves
from stereotypically Black activities, such as liking jazz or basketball. Because
these tasks were completed before the actual diagnostic test was taken, these findings suggest that the mere expectation of taking a potentially stereotype-confirming
test brought up stereotypic thoughts, self-doubt, and a desire to be seen as different from the Black stereotype.

General features of stereotype threat   There are several keys to understanding how stereotype threat operates (Aronson et al., 1998; C. Steele, Spencer, &
Aronson, 2003). One is that stereotype threat stems from situational pressures
that bring the stereotype to mind, not merely from internalization of the negative
stereotype. In fact, people need not *believe* the stereotype about their group, or

even be worried that it applies to them personally, for it to influence behavior. Claude Steele (1997) cites the example of a Black man waiting at an ATM machine for a woman to complete her transaction. This man is likely aware of the stereotypic belief that Black men are violent and, even though he himself has no violent intentions, he might be still concerned that the woman will fear him. The situations that produce stereotype threat vary widely and range from the diagnosticity of the test, as we saw in the Steele and Aronson (1995) experiment, to whether a person is a minority in a situation. Michael Inzlicht and Talia Ben-Zeev (2003), for example, showed that women who took a math test in a group of other women, and were therefore in the majority, scored higher than women who took the same test in a group of other men and were therefore in the minority. The effects of stereotype threat have been demonstrated both in the lab and in naturally occurring environments.

A second key feature of stereotype threat is that it is a quite general process that can affect any group for which a negative stereotype exists. Jean-Claude Croizet and Theresa Claire (1998), for example, investigated whether stereotype threat could result from the stereotypic belief that individuals from a lower socioeconomic status (SES) are less intelligent than those from a higher SES background. Participants were French undergraduates from both high and lower SES who completed the verbal portion of the GRE under one of two instruction sets: the test was described either as an assessment of intellectual ability for solving verbal problems (the diagnostic condition) or as an assessment of lexical memory (the nondiagnostic condition). Results supported the stereotype threat hypothesis. Lower SES participants in the diagnostic condition tried fewer items and answered fewer questions correctly than did lower SES participants in the nondiagnostic condition. Scores for the higher SES participants were not influenced by instruction set.

Stereotype threat also has been demonstrated for women and Latinos and has been shown to operate in a variety of academic settings ranging from middle schools to private and public colleges and universities (see C. Steele et al., 2003, for a review). Evidence for stereotype threat also has been found in a number of performance domains, such as athletics (Stone, Lynch, Sjomeling, & Darley, 1999) and the workplace (Roberson, Deitch, Brief, & Block, 2003). Despite this generality, certain conditions are more likely to produce stereotype threat; for example, more negative stereotypes generally produce stronger stereotype threat (C. Steele et al., 2003). Moreover, stereotype threat has its strongest effects on those individuals whose self-esteem is tied to their performance in a domain or who have the greatest chance for success in that area of achievement. As Joshua Aronson and his colleagues (1998) put it, "all other things being equal, the more a person cares about being good at something, the greater will be his or her distress about stereotypes alleging a lack of ability" (p. 87). Whites who believe their athleticism is important to their identity are more threatened by the stereotype that "Blacks are more athletic that Whites" than are Whites for whom athleticism is unimportant (Stone et al., 1999). Similarly, women who strongly identify with being a woman are more likely to experience stereotype threat on a test of their math ability than those who do not have a strong gender identification (Schmader, 2002).

A third key feature of stereotype threat is that the nature of the threat varies by the specific context of the negative stereotype. The type of threat that would affect women, for example, could be very different from the type of threat that would affect older adults or athletes. Women, for example, are likely threatened in the arena of mathematical ability, older adults in the area of memory, or athletes on the football field. Moreover, stereotype threat does not generalize to other situations. Women's performance on an English exam, for example, would not be hindered by a threat about their mathematical ability because that domain does not apply there. Stereotype threat also can be produced in groups whose members are not normally threatened by a belief. White men generally do not worry about their math ability, for example, and are not stereotypically believed to do poorly in math. Yet White men experienced significant performance drops when they believed the test was designed to determine why Asian males outperformed White males in math (C. Steele et al., 2003).

Evidence suggests that stereotype threat operates by changing the way information is processed, specifically by reducing people's working memory capacity (Schmader & Johns, 2003). That is, stereotype threat is not just an emotional reaction to the possibility of confirming a stereotype about one's group but also a cognitive reaction. In one relevant experiment, working memory was assessed by the operation span test, during which participants evaluated mathematical equations while memorizing words for later recall. Male and female undergraduates were told that this was a test of the ability to either remember two different pieces of information simultaneously (nonthreatening condition) or to solve complex mathematical equalities (condition threatening to women). Those in the threatening condition also were told that gender differences in this ability might explain gender differences in math performance. Results showed that men's operation span test scores did not differ based on how the test was described. Women, however, scored lower under stereotype threat conditions than under nonstereotype threat conditions (Schmader & Johns, 2003). Apparently, the added threat taxes cognitive resources, resulting in lowered attention for those under this threat. Interestingly, holding stereotypic beliefs also can impair the cognitive performance of nonthreatened group members; research demonstrating such effects is presented in Box 11.2

Reducing stereotype threat   While reading about research confirming that stereotype threat can affect achievement, you may have noticed an important point. That is, when participants believed the test did *not* provide information about their ability, those who would otherwise be threatened by group stereotypes performed well. Women, then, who believed a math test does not show gender differences performed as well as men did on that test (Spencer, Steele, & Quinn, 2001). This suggests that the way in which achievement tests are described to their takers may affect their scores. It is possible, for example, that the combination of describing IQ tests as diagnostic and the awareness of a test-related stereotype (for example, that those from a lower SES will achieve lower scores) actually produces those lower scores. If so, SES differences might disappear if the IQ tests generally were presented as nondiagnostic (Croizet & Claire, 1998).

11.2 *Holding Racial Stereotypes Can Be Hazardous to Your Performance*

In this chapter, we describe the many negative consequences of stereotyping and prejudice to those who are targets of these beliefs and actions. An implication one might draw from this discussion is that there are no negative consequences for those who hold stereotypic beliefs or discriminate against members of stigmatized groups. Research suggests, however, that this is not the case and that, instead, holding negative stereotypes or discriminating against others can impair people's cognitive performance. In one relevant study, Jennifer Richeson and Nicole Shelton (2003) examined the effects of interacting with a Black person on Whites' executive function. Executive function refers to the ability to plan, organize, and strategize; when this function is impaired, for example when resources are overextended, cognitive performance suffers. Participants in this study completed the Implicit Association Test (Greenwald, McGhee, & Schwartz, 1998), which, as you learned in Chapter 2, is an indirect measure of racial prejudice. Then, at the request of either a Black or White experimenter, they were videotaped while commenting on two controversial issues—one of which was racial profiling in post–September 11 America. Finally, they completed the Stroop test, which requires good executive function. Results showed that the more negative the participants' implicit attitudes were, the more likely it was that interacting with a Black person reduced their executive function. In contrast, interacting with a White person did not affect executive function, regardless of the participants' implicit racial attitudes. A subsequent study (Richeson et al., 2003) used a similar

procedure, but also assessed neural activity in the brain regions that control executive function. This activity was assessed as participants responded to familiar and unfamiliar photographs of Black faces. Changes in brain activity were significantly correlated with racial attitude, and these changes also predicted performance on the Stroop test. No such relationships were found when participants responded to White faces. These results further support the hypothesis that, for those who are racially biased, interracial contact impairs executive function.

Although Richeson and her colleagues (Richeson et al., 2003; Richeson & Shelton, 2003) found stronger effects for individuals with negative racial attitudes, evidence for more general effects also exists. Specifically, priming non-Blacks with the Black stereotype can lower performance on standardized tests (Wheeler, Jarvis, & Petty, 2001). Participants who wrote an essay about a day in the life of a Black college student, and thus had their stereotypes about Blacks primed, subsequently scored lower on the math section of the GRE than did students who wrote about a White student, and thus did not have their Black stereotypes primed. These effects emerged regardless of their scores on the Modern Racism Scale (McConahay, Hardee, & Batts, 1981). Results of a second study showed that these effects were stronger for those who included stereotypic content in their essays, supporting the argument that stereotypic beliefs played a role in producing them.

In this chapter, and throughout the book, we have provided many reasons why stereotyping

Holding Racial Stereotypes Can Be Hazardous to Your Performance (continued)

and prejudice are harmful. As social psychologists know well, personal involvement increases people's attention to persuasive messages, making it more likely that high quality arguments will be accepted (Petty & Cacioppo, 1979).

Perhaps raising awareness of findings such as these can produce such increased involvement, helping to convince reluctant individuals to recognize the harmful effects of prejudice.

Yet, as Steele and his colleagues (2003) note, the diagnostic purposes of standardized tests are well-known and it seems unlikely that simple instructions would override this effect outside the laboratory. Certainly, however, taking care that instructions are as neutral as possible is important, especially for tests that are not already labeled as diagnostic.

Research also has demonstrated that the effects of stereotype threat are most likely seen when the task at hand is difficult or frustrating, and least likely to emerge when the task is easier (Spencer et al., 2001). This may explain why women do better than men in math courses but not on standardized tests; as we noted earlier, course grades are based on material they have previously studied and so tests of those skills may be less threatening. Interventions that reduce the stress associated with a test, then, may reduce stereotype threat. Other promising interventions include encouraging students by letting them know that intelligence and achievement are improvable or by having them participate in well-designed programs for high-achieving (not remedial) students (Aronson, Fried, & Good, 2001). It is important to note that such strategies have produced long-term improvements in achievement (see Aronson, et al., 1998).

Providing role models also reduces stereotype threat. College women, for example, performed better on a difficult math test after reading about successful women, compared to women who read about successful corporations (McIntyre, Paulson, & Lord, 2003). Stereotype threat also can be reduced by changing how feedback is given. As we saw in our discussion of attributional ambiguity, Blacks have reasons to distrust feedback. But research shows that individuals who are told both that standards are high *and* that they can achieve those standards accept the feedback and are motivated to respond to it (Cohen, Steele, & Ross, 1999). As Steele and his colleagues (2002) point out, such statements de-emphasize negative stereotypes and affirm ability, thereby reducing stereotype threat. As Joshua Aronson and his colleagues (1998) put it "there is nothing special about the personalities, the belief systems, or the values of women and minorities that undermines their performance. Rather, we argue, they fall victim to a situation that undermines their performance. This situation, which we have labeled stereotype threat, arises when negative stereotypes are available as a possible explanation for performance. What is hopeful about this analysis is that situations can be changed" (p. 99). As researchers continue to discover ways to change these situations, and the threat that accompanies them, the negative consequences of that threat can be eradicated.

Stereotype lift   As we noted earlier, people are well aware of the diagnostic purposes of intelligence and achievement tests; cultural expectations about which groups tend to perform better on such tests also are well known (C. Steele, 1997). Research on stereotype threat documents how this knowledge can hinder achievement for members of those groups for whom expectations are low. But research also suggests that this same information can provide a performance boost, or *stereotype lift*, for members of nonstereotyped groups (Walton & Cohen, 2003). This lift can occur if members of nonstereotyped groups engage in downward social comparisons; that is, if they are evaluating their abilities by comparing themselves to others who are doing worse than they are (Fein & Spencer, 1997). The boost that accompanies this comparison theoretically occurs because these downward comparisons alleviate the doubt or anxiety associated with possible failure in achievement-related domains.

This idea was tested by Greg Walton and Geoffrey Cohen (2003) who reviewed 43 studies that assessed the test performance of members of stereotyped and nonstereotyped groups. Results showed that, overall, members of nonstereotyped groups performed better when the test situation produced stereotype threat for the members of the stereotyped groups. That is, what was a drain on performance for the threatened group became a boost in performance for the nonthreatened group. Moreover, the effects of stereotype lift emerged even when threat was introduced through situational cues, and thus was not made explicit in the study. Such outcomes suggests that members of nonstereotype groups automatically link negative stereotypes and intellectual tests and, therefore, receive the resulting performance lift.

The real world implications of this are significant. Walton and Cohen, for example, note that stereotype lift results in a 50-point advantage on the SAT for White men compared to stereotype-threatened groups, a difference large enough to make the difference in college admission decisions or awarding of scholarships. Awareness of, and advocacy against, such inequities can result in positive changes. The outcome of a legal challenge illustrates how this can happen. Fair Test recently reached a settlement in their complaint against the Educational Testing Service and the College Entrance Examination Board (*Test makers to revise national merit exam to address gender bias,* 1996); this group charged that the Preliminary SAT (PSAT) was gender biased, resulting in girls being underrepresented in the group of National Merit Scholarships. This bias resulted in boys receiving millions of dollars more in scholarships than girls. As part of the settlement, the PSAT was revised; the new test has significantly increased the number of female National Merit Semi-Finalists. Consistent with research on reducing stereotype threat, these gains were achieved by adding a writing component, an area of the test that is not threatening to girls. Doing so should also theoretically reduce stereotype lift to boys on the PSAT.

Vulnerability to Stress

Research on stereotype threat and stereotype lift addresses how prejudice and discrimination can affect the economic and academic success of stigmatized group members. Experiencing discrimination also can have a profound influence on an individual's physical and mental health. Such effects are linked to the stress associated with chronic exposure to discriminatory actions and can have both short- and long-term effects.

How prejudice and discrimination can produce stress   It is well-established that stress can produce psychological and biological changes that result in disease (Lazarus, 1993). Kevin Allison (1998) has argued that either the chronic experience of prejudice, such as repeatedly being stared at in social situations, or the experience of a major individual incidence of prejudice, such as the experience or threat of physical violence, can produce the chronic stress commonly associated with disease. The impact of subtle prejudice is less intense than the impact of major incidents, but both can have mental and physical health consequences.

Experimental evidence supports Allison's (1998) assertion. For example, Blacks who completed an achievement test under stereotype threat conditions had elevated blood pressure levels, compared to Blacks who took the test under nonthreatening conditions or Whites under either condition (Blascovich, Spencer, Quinn, & C. Steele, 2001). This finding suggests that Blacks' higher incidence of hypertension compared with Whites may stem, at least in part, from their real-life experience in threat-producing situations. Evidence further suggests that the effects are not limited to situations that meet the conditions for stereotype threat. A study of nearly 2,000 Black Americans found a positive relationship between experience with racial discrimination and high blood pressure (Krieger & Sidney, 1996). Similarly, research shows that gay men who reported experiencing anti-gay violence or discrimination during the previous year showed higher levels of psychological distress than gay men who did not report such experiences (Meyer, 2003).

A second way in which experiencing prejudice and discrimination can produce stress is through events that are normative and nonnormative for certain stigmatized groups (Allison, 1998). Examples of normative events include identity development and school socialization; these experiences are part of the developmental process but differ across stigmatized groups. For example, it is typical for adolescents to struggle with their sexual identity development. Yet, for gay and lesbian adolescents, this normative experience has the added stress that stems from knowing prejudice toward their group is widespread. Heterosexuals, for example, do not worry about "coming out" to parents or friends about their attraction to members of the other sex; gay men and lesbians know that telling others of their attraction to same-sex others can result in personal rejection or physical and verbal abuse (Pilkington & D'Augelli, 1995). Correlational data reveal that lesbian, gay, and bisexual (LGB) youth who have disclosed their sexual orientation to family and friends are at a greater risk for suicide attempt than LGBs who have not made such a disclosure (Rotheram-Borus & Fernandez, 1995). Nonnormative life stresses are those experienced only by members of stigmatized groups. Minority immigrants, for example, often experience prejudice and discrimination during the acculturation process either because of language difficulties or because they violate cultural norms, increasing their stress levels as they try to adapt to their new environment (Allison, 1998).

Prejudice and discrimination also can produce stress through indirect means. That is, some life events are more likely to happen to individuals from stigmatized groups—not because of their group membership, per se, but because of situational factors related to their group membership. Children from a low SES background, for example, are more likely to attend poorly funded schools, live in lower quality housing, and have poorer nutrition than students from higher SES backgrounds, all of which affect their physical and mental health and their success in school. These effects are indirectly related to ethnicity (Arnold & Doctoroff, 2002). That is, race in and of itself does not predict academic achievement; given similar opportunities, both Blacks and Whites are successful in school, for example. However, because ethnic minority children are overrepresented in lower SES groups, they are more likely than White children to experience academic failure that results from poverty. African Americans are more likely than their White counterparts to experience a variety of stressful events, including the divorce or separation of their parents, death of a friend, birth of a sibling, or residence in a violent neighborhood (Garrison, Schoenbach, Schluchter, & Kaplan, 1987). These stressors create a cycle of stress; research has demonstrated, for example, that experiencing a high level of stress makes individuals more vulnerable to the effects of subsequent stressors (see Allison, 1998 for a review). Evidence also suggests possible indirect effects of *higher* SES for Blacks. Specifically, mortality rates are higher for Blacks with more advantaged socioeconomic status, perhaps because these individuals have more day-to-day contact with Whites in traditionally all-White workplaces (Feagin & McKinney, 2003). As we saw in our discussion of tokenism, when a person of different ethnicity joins a formerly all-majority group, the majority is more likely to think about ethnicity, and perhaps to be uncomfortable with having to do so. This discomfort can affect interactions between minority and majority members which, in turn, can result in stress for the minority group member that may affect both mental and physical health. Famous minorities are not immune from this stress, as the examples in Box 11.3 illustrate.

Stress-related responses to prejudice and discrimination

As we noted above, stress produces physiological changes that can affect both mental and physical health. What effects do those stressors have on the people who experience them? To find out, Joe Feagin and Karyn McKinney (2003) conducted focus groups with economically successful African Americans to explore their perceptions of the effects of racism on their physical and mental health. Respondents often noted that racially related stress affected their immune systems, making them more susceptible to colds and other diseases. Reports of elevated blood

11.3   *Can Discrimination Affect the Rich and Famous?*

People of color remain a minority in many arenas, including certain sports and in the television and movie industry. Are the effects of this minority status outweighed by success? Consider this: Arthur Ashe, the nation's first Black male tennis star, suffered much adversity in his life, including losing his mother at a young age and acquiring AIDS from a blood transfusion, which led to his death. Yet when asked to describe his most difficult challenge, he replied, "Being Black is. No question about it. Even now it continues to feel like an extra weight tied around me" (quoted in Schuster, 1993, p. 1C).

Another example of how minority status can affect even the most successful comes from the media's response to the question of whether the prestigious Master's golf tournament should open its doors to women (Vitello, 2004). The club that hosts this tournament only allows male members, a tradition that was challenged publicly by Martha Burk, head of the National Council of Women's Organization. Yet who was put on the spot to respond to this challenge? Which of the following do you think is the likely candidate? Paul Vitello (2004) asked his readers to consider these possibilities: (a) the club members themselves; (b) the Professional Golfer's Association; (c) any number of White male golfers who have played in or won the tournaments and/or the women they love; and (d) CBS, the network that broadcasts the Masters. The answer is none of the above; Tiger Woods, the golf phenomenon of Black and Thai ethnicity, was the person singled out and asked to boycott the tournament. As Vitello (2004) writes, "somehow, because the subject was discrimination, the attention turned to the man of color—the guy whose ancestors were hurt most by the ugly history of white-men-only discrimination in America" (p. 253). Never mind that the issue concerned *sex* discrimination and that, by boycotting the tournament, Woods would be giving up the chance to win the Masters three years in a row, a feat no one has accomplished. As is often the case for tokens, Woods was put in the position of responding, not only to actions against his race but for all discriminatory actions.

One of the stressors these athletes were responding to concerned being asked to serve as a spokesperson for their race. Ashe, for example, was referring both to his experiences with discrimination and to his position as the first Black tennis star, noting that this role often put him in the position of being spokesperson for his race, a common experience for members of underrepresented groups (Sandler & Hall, 1986). He could never be quite confident that the attention he received was due to his success and not his race. Woods was asked to be a spokesperson for all underrepresented groups.

On the surface, asking individuals to speak for their group or to stand up for discrimination seems like a supportive gesture on the part of the majority. After all, it does recognize that differences in perspectives can exist. A closer examination, however, shows the problem with the approach. First, it is possible that the majority and minority groups *agree* on an issue. Second, as we saw in Chapter 3, it reflects a belief in outgroup homogeneity—that outgroup members are all alike and one person can speak for the entire group. Third, it puts the minority group member in the spotlight, which results in her or his actions being highly scrutinized (Fiske & Taylor, 1991). Not surprisingly, most minority group members find this extra attention uncomfortable and would prefer that all perspectives representing their group's viewpoints were heard (Sandler & Hall, 1986).

pressure, headaches, insomnia, and stomach problems also were common. Some respondents referred to "nine-to-five" headaches that would be present while they were at the workplace, but would lift on leaving. As one respondent put it, "I would have this headache. And it would be for eight hours until I walked out the door and then it was like a weight was lifted off" (p. 73). Feagin and McKinney also found that one way many Blacks cope with these stressors is through more or less socially accepted but unhealthy behaviors such as alcohol and tobacco use or excessive eating. Such coping mechanisms helped reduce stress in the short-run, but obviously have long-term health consequences for the users. This method of coping may also affect their children's well-being. Fredrick Gibbons and his colleagues (Gibbons, Gerrard, Cleveland, Wills, & Brody, 2004) found that parents' experience of racial discrimination led to increased parental distress, which indirectly increased parental substance use at the time and 2 years later. Moreover, their children were aware of their parent's distress and this awareness was related to the children's future substance use. Results also showed, however, that effective parenting reduced the chances that the child would smoke or drink alcohol in the future.

A common, but far from universal, response to racism is frustration, anger, and even rage (Feagin & McKinney, 2003; Swim, Aikin, Hall, & Hunter, 1995). Although members of minority groups may be reluctant to express these feelings, failing to do so can produce higher blood pressure and greater sleep disturbance (E. Johnson & Greene, 1991). What is the best way to cope? Feagin and McKinney (2003) offer several effective strategies including internally-focused or cognitive-based coping, such as adjusting one's own attitudes, being more accepting of what appears to be unintentional discrimination, becoming desensitized to discriminatory acts, or framing the acts as due to White ignorance. Also effective are behavioral strategies, such as verbally confronting discrimination or protesting through formal channels. Box 11.4 describes how such verbal confrontations are received by those being confronted.

Also central to effective coping is knowing when one has or lacks control in either the situation or the response to it. As one respondent from Feagin and McKinney's (2003) sample put it, "When I feel that I'm in control, I never get angry. . . . And I am in control of every racial situation. I am not the sick one. . . . I'm in control, I don't get mad anymore" (p. 140). By recognizing what can and cannot be controlled, members of stigmatized groups can minimize the psychological costs they incur by reacting—that is, how their own anger can affect their lives—and also can reduce the likelihood that they will internalize the incident, realizing it is not them but the other person or the situation that is to blame. If parental socialization includes a discussion about racism, this strategy also appears to provide a buffer against the negative mental health consequences of experiencing discrimination (Fischer & Shaw, 1999). These strategies focus on how members of stigmatized groups can address prejudice and discrimination. Of course, the burden of addressing these beliefs and behaviors does not rest solely with them. In Chapter 12, we discuss in detail strategies privileged group members can use to reduce prejudice and discrimination.

11.4   *Reactions to Being Confronted about Discrimination*

How is confrontation accepted by those being confronted? Alexander Czopp and Margo Monteith (2003) asked participants to imagine their reaction to verbal confrontations about discrimination in three different scenarios. Results showed that people would feel more guilt and discomfort when confronted about racial bias than about gender bias. Moreover, respondents low in prejudice were more likely to express guilt in response to racial bias than were those high in prejudice. Interestingly, results of a second study showed that people felt more guilty about both gender and racial bias when the confrontation was initiated by a man or White person, respectively, than by woman or Black person; conversely, a confrontation by a woman or Black person made them more uncomfortable than the same confrontation by a man or White person. Taken together, these results suggest that confrontation does make biased people reconsider their actions, especially if they are low in prejudice.

Threats to Self-Esteem

Fifty years ago, most social scientists would have believed that minority group members have low self-esteem. Theoretically, this result was expected because it was assumed that these individuals would have accepted and internalized the dominant group's stigmatizing beliefs about them. This viewpoint was consistent with important theories of the time, such as the concept of the "looking glass self" proposed by Charles Horton Cooley (1902). According to this and similar theories, our self-images are, in part, formed by imagining how we look to others and how others judge us. When those imaginings are negative, self-worth suffers. As we have seen throughout this book, stigmatized group members have a multitude of experiences, both historical and personal, that suggest such negative evaluations exist. But do these experiences affect their self-esteem?

It turns out that this question cannot be answered with a simple "yes" or "no." Recent research suggests that the answer is considerably more complex. We focus here on the results of a major review of this literature, conducted by Jean Twenge and Jennifer Crocker (2002), who examined data from 712 studies that encompassed over 375,000 participants. Results showed that important differences in self-esteem emerged across ethnic groups. One major finding is that Blacks have higher self-esteem than any other ethnic group studied, including Whites. This pattern of results is particularly interesting because studies of Americans' general attitudes toward social groups find Blacks to be more devalued than Whites, Asians, or Hispanics (Wilson, 1996a). Clearly, Black's self-concepts are not simply reflecting societal attitudes toward their group. Interestingly, the evidence also suggests that Blacks' higher self-esteem is linked to their racial identity. For example, by looking at studies across time, Twenge and Crocker showed that there were larger differences between Blacks' and Whites' self-esteem around and after the time of the civil rights and Black power movements in the United States (see also Gray-Little & Hafdahl, 2000), presumably because such actions raised awareness of and confidence in their group identity. Moreover, self-esteem was higher among college-age Blacks, who may be learning more about their culture and heritage (Twenge & Crocker, 2002).

However, the different patterns observed across ethnic groups suggest that a single theory is unlikely to account for the data. In contrast to Blacks, Asians and Hispanics had lower self-esteem than Whites, so not all ethnic groups form a positive social identity relative to the dominant group. In addition, Twenge and Crocker (2002) found little evidence that racial identity improved self-esteem for Asians and Hispanics. Instead, the data for these groups appear to be most consistent with the idea that there are cultural differences in how people evaluate themselves. For example, cultures differ in their endorsement of individualism or collectivism. *Individualism* refers to the idea that people are independent of one another and that individuals should focus on their personal goals, personal uniqueness, and personal controls. *Collectivism* refers to the idea that group members are bound together and are obligated to one another (Oyserman, Coon, & Kemmelmeier, 2002). People with an individualist perspective tend to see the self as stable and transcending relationships and situations. That is, they emphasize the individual over the group. In contrast, people with a collectivist perspective tend to believe the self is flexible and varies with the situational context and, accordingly, de-emphasize the importance of the self relative to the group. Maintaining and enhancing self-esteem is associated with individualism; it is acceptable in an individualist culture to stand out from and be superior to others. Collectivist cultures, in contrast, emphasize self-criticism both because it is believed this leads to self-improvement and because it promotes harmony with others. Because the commonly used self-esteem measures contain items consistent with the individualist perspective, self-esteem should be higher in groups that come from those cultures rather than from collectivist cultures.

Twenge and Crocker's (2002) results are consistent with this perspective. The self-esteem of individuals from collectivist cultures, such as Asian Americans, Hispanics, and Native Americans was lower than the self-esteem of individuals from individualist cultures, such as Whites and Blacks in the United States. It might surprise you to learn that Asian Americans experience lower self-esteem than do Blacks or Whites. Many people view this group as a so-called model minority and, as such, expect them to be unaffected by prejudice and discrimination. See Box 11.5 for more about this stereotypic perception.

The question of whether and why stereotyping and prejudice affect self-esteem is far from settled. We saw in our discussion of attributional ambiguity that attributing discrimination to prejudice can actually buffer self-esteem. However, this buffering effect is far from universal, particularly when viewed outside of the context of a particular instance of discrimination. Women who perceive high levels of discrimination, for example, also report higher levels of

11.5   *Are Asians Americans a "Model Minority?"*

Statistically, Asian Americans are an underrepresented group in the United States. Yet when people think about minorities, particularly those who are stigmatized, this group does not readily come to mind. You may have noticed, for example, that Asian Americans are rarely a subject of social psychological research on prejudice and discrimination, especially when compared to Blacks and women. One reason Asian Americans are often overlooked may stem from the perception that they are the "model minority." That is, as a group, they are well-integrated into the culture of the United States and the characteristics associated with them—high achievement and economic success—are the same characteristics associated with Americans in general (Lee, 1996). As Daphna Oyserman and Izumi Sakamoto (1997) point out, however, the blurred boundaries between "Asian" and "American" is a mixed bag. It is a good thing to be seen as a model, but viewing Asian Americans in this light is also a way to marginalize the group.

Oyserman and Sakamoto (1997) studied Asian Americans' perceptions of the stereotypes held about their group and their reaction to those stereotypes. Results showed that some respondents believed that non-Asians perceive them as high achieving and highly motivated—in short, a model minority. Those who made this observation also believed this to be a positive perception that held a kernel of truth. Other respondents, however, viewed the "model minority" label negatively and believed it overlooked their personal role in their success. That is, they thought their success was being attributed to their group membership, rather than their own abilities and efforts. They also believed that the label kept them out of the societal mainstream.

Research suggests this perception has validity. Monica Lin and her colleagues (Lin, Kwan, Cheung, & Fiske, 2005) showed that Whites believe Asian Americans have poor social skills. Indeed, a variety of negative stereotypes about Asians exist in concert with the "model minority" label. Oyserman and Sakamoto (1997) found that Asian Americans believe non-Asians hold negative stereotypes about their physical appearance and mannerisms, stereotyping them as short, glasses wearers, and having poor English-speaking ability. Asian Americans also believed others perceived them as exclusionist, keeping with their own race and holding condescending

depression than women who perceive less discrimination (Kobrynowicz & Branscombe, 1997). And, asking women to think specifically about the ways they have been discriminated against leads to reductions in self-esteem (Branscombe, 1998). It seems clear that there is no one answer to the question of whether one's group membership, or experiencing prejudice and discrimination related to that membership, affects self-esteem. The outcomes depend on when and how the question is asked, the cultural context within which a stigmatized group lives, and whether the individuals themselves readily perceive discrimination in their lives. Research questions related to this issue will no doubt continue to attract the attention of social science researchers.

views about other races. These perceptions also are not unfounded; research shows that Whites do view Asians more negatively than Americans in general or Whites specifically (Stangor, Sullivan, & Ford, 1991).

The belief that Asian Americans are highly competent workers appears to coexist with the belief that they are unsociable. Research suggests this latter belief is used to justify discrimination against Asian Americans (Lin et al., 2005). That is, Asian Americans are characterized as working too hard and unfairly succeeding at the cost of positive social relations. The "model minority," then, pays a price for being perceived as competent. This price is evident in Asian American's reports about their experiences. Oyserman and Sakamoto (1997), for example, found that about half of their Asian American sample reported having a set of coping strategies to deal with these negative perceptions. Many of these experiences are similar to those of other stigmatized group members, including the experience of being singled out, being stared at, not having their groups' voice represented in the media, or, relatedly, having people make assumptions about their perspective based solely on their group membership.

Moreover, model minority status does not appear to ameliorate workplace discrimination; Asian Americans report levels of workplace discrimination that are similar to Hispanics, and significantly less than Whites (although Blacks report higher levels of such discrimination; Bell, Harrison, & McLaughlin, 1997). Another downside to model minority status is that needed help is sometimes not offered. Asian Americans who are poor at math (and so violate the stereotype that all Asian Americans are mathematically talented), for example, might not receive mentoring or other help (Goto, 1999). Research shows that successful Asians Americans are less likely to have a mentor than are successful managers from other minority groups and they report being less satisfied with the mentoring experiences they do have (Thomas, 1991). It may be that the "model minority" stereotype is preventing Asian Americans from getting effective mentoring, perhaps because of the very success that led to this label (Goto, 1999). Some Asian Americans have succeeded in spite of this, but that does not mean it has not hindered others' progress.

COPING WITH DISCRIMINATION

As we have seen throughout this chapter, living with prejudice and discrimination creates a threatening situation that can be difficult to deal with and individuals who are in this situation use a variety of coping strategies to do so. Some of these strategies were discussed in the section on stress-related responses to prejudice and discrimination. We next consider two additional coping strategies that have been studied by social justice researchers: psychological disengagement and behavioral compensation.

Psychological Disengagement and Disidentification

One coping strategy employed by stigmatized group members is **psychological disengagement,** "a defensive detachment of self-esteem from outcomes in a particular domain, such that feelings of self-worth are not dependent on successes or failures in that domain" (Major, Spencer, Schmader, Wolfe, & Crocker, 1998, p. 35). That is, when individuals disengage, they produce a psychological separation from themselves and the arena in which they might fail, thereby protecting their self-esteem. A person who fears poor performance in an achievement-related area, for example, might psychologically prepare for failure by de-emphasizing the importance of success in that area. One way to manage this is by **disidentification** or devaluing the domain (Schmader, Major, & Gramzow, 2001; C. Steele, 1997). When people disidentify with a domain, they define or redefine their self-concept so that the domain is no longer an area of self-identification. Women who believe they might be unsuccessful at math, then, might disidentify with a career in mathematics, and instead associate their self-worth with literature. For these women, then, failure at math would not affect their self-esteem. A second way to separate stereotypic expectations of failure from individual self-esteem is by *discounting* the feedback as inaccurate or invalid, particularly because its source was a prejudiced other (Crocker et al., 1991). We discussed this process under the section of this chapter on attributional ambiguity.

It is important to note that psychological disengagement refers to the distancing of the self from areas in which one's group is negatively stereotyped and, therefore, expected to fail. In our example, a woman's belief that she might fail at math is tied to the cultural stereotype that women, in general, are not mathematically inclined. This process also can operate on an individual level—that is, for reasons not linked to group stereotypes. Sabotaging one's performance out of fear of failure, called self-handicapping, can have similar self-protective outcomes (Berglas & Jones, 1978). Our focus, here, however, is on disengagement that is related to group membership. Theoretically, the disengagement emerges in response to *systemic injustice,* or the belief that discrimination has produced differences between social groups that cannot be overcome at a personal level, no matter how motivated or competent an individual member of that group is (Schmader et al., 2001).

Research suggests that Black students are particularly likely to disengage their self-esteem from their performance in intellectual or academic domains, especially when compared to Whites. A study of a large, nationally representative sample of middle and high school–aged children found that Blacks' achievement was lower than Whites' in three of the four content areas studied (Osborne, 1995). Despite this, Blacks reported higher self-esteem than did Whites. Moreover, the relationship between grade point average and self-esteem weakened for Blacks as the children reached more advanced grade levels, suggesting that more disengagement occurs with more academic feedback and experience. A similar pattern emerged for Black males, but not Black females, when the relationship between academic achievement and self-esteem was examined. No such weakening occurred for White students. Moreover, based on both empirical data and a recent review of this literature, Toni Schmader and her colleagues (Schmader et al.,

2001) concluded that this disengagement of the self from academic domains occurs not because ethnic minorities devalue education but rather because they discount the academic feedback they receive from White evaluators.

Much of the evidence on ethnic differences in engagement is based on correlational data that cannot definitely confirm the cause. To test the role of engagement experimentally, in their first study Brenda Major and her colleagues (1998) had Blacks and Whites take either an easy or difficult test, so that participants experienced success or failure in an academic domain. If Blacks are disengaging from academic performance in general, their self-esteem should be less affected by negative feedback in such situations than should the self-esteem of Whites. Results supported this prediction; White's performance-related self-esteem was lower when they took the difficult test and experienced failure than when they took the easy test and succeeded. In contrast, Blacks' performance-related self-esteem was unaffected by which test they took.

Major and her colleagues (1998) conducted a follow-up study that examined whether test failure would be more likely to affect individuals who were chronically disengaged intellectually, compared with those who chronically engaged on this factor. Level of intellectual engagement was assessed in advance on a measure designed for that purpose. Procedures were otherwise similar to Study One, except that all participants in Study Two believed they performed poorly on the test. Results showed that Blacks who were chronically disengaged with intellectual tests tended to have higher self-esteem following failure than Blacks who were not so disengaged. Whites' self-esteem was unrelated to their level of intellectual engagement. Taken together, research on psychological disengagement suggests that Blacks can protect their self-esteem by disengaging themselves from academic or achievement-related domains. Yet, doing so has costs; disconnecting from academic achievement may result in poor performance in school, which is linked to higher dropout rates, lower college acceptance rates, and the receipt of fewer scholarships to support higher education. It is also linked to fewer opportunities for job success (C. Steele, 1997).

Behavioral Compensation

As we have seen throughout this chapter, for members of stigmatized groups the experience of prejudice and discrimination is not a one-time or unusual event. Because of this, individuals develop strategies that help them cope with the experience. A strategy that has recently received attention concerns how people behave when they expect to be discriminated against. Carol Miller and her colleagues (Kaiser & Miller, 2001b; Miller & Myers, 1998) have proposed that, in such situations, people sometimes **compensate** for potential discrimination by changing their behavior in ways that disconfirm the stereotype.

According to this perspective, individuals develop a set of skills to help them achieve desired outcomes. In the case of potential discrimination, these skills are above and beyond what is needed to succeed in a typical social interaction. This is because when prejudice is a possibility, the individual must overcome an added burden to be successful in an interaction. Heavyweight people, for example, know that they may face discrimination because of their weight; this discrimination can take the form of overhearing unflattering comments about their size, being avoided or excluded, job discrimination, and even physical violence (see Miller & Myers, 1998, for a review). To compensate for possible discrimination, a heavy-weight individual might use humor in a social interaction to increase the chances that they will be liked. According to Miller and Myers (1998), as levels of prejudice increase higher and higher levels of compensation are required to overcome it. Increased prejudice also reduces the chances that the compensation will be successful.

Experimental evidence suggests stigmatized people do compensate for potential discrimination. In one relevant experiment, Cheryl Kaiser and Carol Miller (2001b) asked women to complete a test of their future career success. This test required them to write an essay about what their lives would be like in 10 years. The women also were told, either before or after completing the essay, that the panel of men who would be evaluating their results was composed entirely of prejudiced men or that either 50 percent or none of the panelists were prejudiced men. Independent evaluators rated the essays on the extent to which they conformed to gender stereotypes and gave their overall impression of the essays. Results showed the content of the essays did vary depending on who the participants thought would evaluate them: The essays of those forewarned about prejudice included fewer references to stereotypically feminine topics, such as the importance of family and niceness, compared to essays written by those who believed none of the panelists were prejudiced or who were informed of possible discrimination after the fact. The authors believe that these differences were due to the women's desire to distance themselves from femininity as a way to compensate in advance for the judges' possible sexism. An interesting additional finding was that those who wrote the essays that distanced themselves from femininity created a more negative impression overall; Kaiser and Miller speculate that this outcome was due to overcompensation—perhaps creating an impression of being *too* unfeminine and appearing strident.

To test the possibility that behavioral compensation varies by the demands of the situation, Miller and her colleagues (Miller, Rothblum, Felicio, & Brand, 1995) studied the impressions overweight and normal weight women made in a telephone conversation. In some cases, their conversational partner could see them, in others the partners could not be seen. This manipulation was designed to increase the demands of the situation for those who could be seen; presumably, the overweight women felt an extra burden because they expected discrimination based on their weight. The authors also varied whether the overweight women believed or did not believe their partner could see them. In all cases, the interaction was videotaped, so a visual record was created. Of interest were the partners' ratings of the overweight women's social skills after the conversation. Results showed that overweight women received more negative evaluations than normal weight women when their partner could see them *and* they were not aware that they could be seen. When they *were* aware that they could be seen, overweight women were rated similarly to normal weight women. That is, they were able to successfully compensate for potential prejudice by using their social skills more effectively.

People's ability to compensate for prejudice depends on a number of factors. First, the demands of the prejudice-related situation must not be so high that the person cannot overcome them. Second, the person must acquire the skills needed for compensation; individual differences in the ability to gain and effectively use these skills probably exist (see Miller & Myers, 1998). Finally, there may be unintended consequences to behavioral compensation. People who expect to compensate for the effects of prejudice may "slack off" in situations where prejudice is not a factor and, in doing so, fail to use the appropriate level of effort required in that social setting. They also may overcompensate, as we saw in the Kaiser and Miller (2001b) study, by trying too hard, talking too much, or coming on too strong. In short, stigmatized individuals may misjudge the requirements of the social interaction and either do too much or too little. Certainly, this is a burden not faced by members of nonstigmatized groups.

Chapter Summary

This chapter reviews the research on stereotyping and prejudice from the perspective of those individuals who are members of a stigmatized group. Five factors distinguish whether a stigma is benign or harmful: course, concealability, aesthetic qualities, origin, and peril. Erving Goffman (1963) proposed that there is also a possibility for stigma by association; research testing this hypothesis has shown that people do associate negative characteristics with dominant group members who socialize with or support stigmatized others. Tokens are individuals who are a minority in a majority group; these individuals stand out from the group and often have negative experiences because of it. Rosabeth Kanter (1977) emphasized the perceptual tendencies of visibility, contrast, and assimilation that produce these negative experiences. More recent work describes the chilly climate that can accompany tokenism and its effect on the individuals who experience it.

Social psychologists have proposed several theories about how people respond to prejudice and discrimination. Work on attributional ambiguity shows that members of stigmatized groups know that dominant group members have both positive and negative reactions to them and that these reactions can lead to both favorable and unfavorable evaluations. What is important is that, in both cases, the stigmatized person believes these evaluations may be due to their group membership, not their ability. Ironically, this makes it difficult for members of stigmatized groups to know which actions and behaviors are sincere and which stem from prejudice or from a desire to appear unbiased. Attributing negative feedback to prejudice can provide a buffer to self-esteem, but this buffer may come at a cost. One potential cost can be seen in research on the personal/group discrimination discrepancy (PGDD)—the tendency to believe that one's group is more likely to experience discrimination than one is as an individual group member. The PGDD has been demonstrated in a number of contexts and may be explained by cognitive factors, such as differences in how information about individuals and groups is processed, or by motivational factors, such as the desire to deny personal discrimination as a justification for not taking action against it.

Experiencing discrimination has a number of personal consequences to the target. For example, research on stereotype threat suggests that stigmatized group members are aware that they are stereotyped and that, especially in achievement settings, they fear confirming those stereotypes. The threat itself actually harms academic achievement. The general features of stereotype threat include the importance of situational factors in producing the threat and the generality of its effects. Stereotype threat also can change the way information is processed. However, researchers have shown that under certain conditions, stereotype threat can be reduced. Finally, nonstereotyped group members sometimes experience stereotype lift, a gain that emerges from the same situations that produce stereotype threat for the stereotyped group.

Throughout this chapter, the stressful by-products that result from experiencing prejudice were emphasized. These by-products affect physical health, producing hypertension, headaches, and other ailments, and mental health, such as depression and coping. Although strategies are available that reduce these effects, some are unhealthy and many put the burden on the stigmatized group member rather than the actor. One negative outcome of discrimination is low self-esteem, which appears to affect Asians and Hispanics more than Blacks and Whites. Differences between individualist and collectivist cultures may explain these effects, particularly because the former emphasizes the self and the latter emphasizes the group.

Individuals can cope with discrimination by psychologically disengaging or putting a psychological separation between themselves and the arena in which they might fail. This can be accomplished by disidentification, or devaluing the domain, or by discounting the feedback. Doing so often has the unfortunate effect of lowering academic achievement. Individuals may also use behavior compensation as a way to cope with prejudice and discrimination. That is, they develop a set of skills that allow them to compensate for potential discrimination by changing their behavior in ways that disconfirm the stereotype. Doing so has both an upside and a downside.

This chapter includes a number of personal stories of the effects of experiencing prejudice and discrimination. It is important that dominant group members listen to those stories and understand the cumulative effect of even seemingly small incidents of discrimination. It is this cumulative impact that is often most detrimental to those who experience discrimination because of their group membership.

SUGGESTED READINGS

The Target's Perspective

Oyserman, D. & Swim, J. K. (Ed.) (2001). Stigma: An insider's perspective [Special Issue]. *Journal of Social Issues, 57.*

Swim, J. K. & Stangor, C. (Eds.) (1998). *Prejudice: The target's perspective.* San Diego: Academic Press.

Both resources have a number of articles that are relevant to the issues in this chapter. Both include general discussions of theories and data as well as articles devoted to specific stigmatized groups, such as the overweight, women, or specific racial groups.

Social Stigma

Corrigan, P. W., & Penn, D. L. (1999). Lessons from social psychology on discrediting psychiatric stigma. *American Psychologist, 54,* 765–776.
  Discusses social psychological processes as they relate to the stigma associated with severe mental illness. The article includes sections on public education and the effects of contact on diminishing this stigma.

Jones, E. E., Farina, A., Hastorf, A. H., Markus, H., Miller, T., & Scott, R. (1984). *Social stigma: The psychology of marked relationships.* New York: W. H. Freeman.
  Although a great deal of research has addressed stigma since the publication of this book, it remains one of the best resources on this topic because of its clear explanations.

Weiner, B., Perry, R. P., & Magnusson, J. (1988). An attributional analysis of reactions to stigmas. *Journal of Personality and Social Psychology, 55,* 738–748.
  An accessible research article that examines people's perceptions of and reactions to stigmatized individuals.

Personal Experiences as Tokens or Members of Stigmatized Groups

Dews, C. L. B. (Ed.) (1995). *This fine place so far from home.* Philadelphia: Temple University Press.

Tokarczyk, M. M. & Fay, E. A. (Eds.) (1993). *Working-class women in the academy: Laborers in the knowledge factory.* Amherst, MA: The University of Massachusetts Press.
  Both books contain collections of essays from women and men from lower class and/or ethnic minority backgrounds who are currently working in academia. Many essays explore their experiences, including their feelings of isolation and the ways in which the subtle message that they are "different" is conveyed. Many students, especially students of color and first generation college students, will resonate with their experiences.

Graham, L. O. (1995). *Member of the club: Reflections on life in a racially polarized world.* New York: HarperCollins.
  This highly readable book contains a series of essays that address racism in the United States. Graham is a highly successful Harvard trained lawyer who writes about his difficulty in finding acceptance in either the White professional or the Black community. One essay, for example, describes his undercover job as a busboy in an all-White Connecticut country club. Others address topics from interracial marriage to Black men's dining experiences in top New York restaurants.

Herek, G. M. & Berrill, K. T. (Eds.) (1992). *Hate crimes: Confronting violence against lesbians and gay men.* Newbury Park, CA: Sage.
  This excellent volume contains a number of powerful "Survivor Stories" of victims of anti-gay and lesbian violence. Many were based on testimony at the 1996 anti-gay violence hearing before the Subcommittee on Criminal Justice of the Committee on the Judiciary, House of Representatives. The stories are brief and memorable and put a human face on the problem of violence against gays and lesbians.

Responses to Negative Behaviors

Crocker, J., Voelkl, K., Testa, M., & Major, B. (1991). Social stigma: The affective consequences of attributional ambiguity. *Journal of Personality and Social Psychology, 60*,
218–228.
> This paper provides an overview of the theoretical basis for attributional ambiguity and
> describes two studies that test hypotheses derived from this theory.

Crosby, F. J. (1984). The denial of personal discrimination. *American Behavioral Scientist,
27*, 371–386.

Taylor, D. M., Wright, S. C., & Porter, L. E. (1994). Dimensions of perceived discrimina-
tion: The personal/group discrimination discrepancy. In M. P. Zanna & J. M. Olson
(Eds.), *The psychology of prejudice: The Ontario symposium* (Vol. 7, pp. 233–255).
Hillsdale, NJ: Lawrence Erlbaum.
> Crosby's paper provides a highly readable discussion of the personal group discrimina-
> tion discrepancy. Taylor's review is more up to date and discusses newer theories about
> the causes of the PGDD.

Stereotype Threat

Steele, C. (1997). A threat in the air: How stereotypes shape intellectual identity and
performance. *American Psychologist, 52*, 613–629.

Steele, C., & Aronson, J. (1995). Stereotype threat and the intellectual test performance of
African Americans. *Journal of Personality and Social Psychology, 69*, 797–811.
> These widely cited articles provide both a theoretical overview of stereotype threat and
> a description of research demonstrating the basic effects. The authors also discuss the
> applied implications of their findings and offer suggestions for overcoming stereotype
> threat. Although many more recent articles exist, including more current review arti-
> cles, these remain the standards for those new to the literature.

Coping with Discrimination

Feagin, J. R., & McKinney, K. D. (2003). *The many costs of racism.* Lanham, MD:
Rowman & Littlefield.
> Reviews the cost of White racism from the perspective of African Americans, covering
> physical and mental health costs and family and community costs. The book has many
> engaging examples and also focuses on strategies for overcoming racism.

Kaiser, C. R., & Miller, C. T. (2001). Reacting to impending discrimination: Compensation
for prejudice and attributions to discrimination. *Personality and Social Psychology
Bulletin, 27*, 1357–1367.
> Relatively little research has addressed how people's behavior changes when they
> expect to be discriminated against. This clever study gets at both the behavior of the
> person expecting discrimination and independent assessments about how those
> behavioral changes might affect the interaction.

Major, B., Spencer, S. J., Schmader, T., Wolfe, C., & Crocker, J. (1998). Coping with
negative stereotypes about intellectual performance: The role of psychological disengagement. *Personality and Social Psychology Bulletin, 24*, 34–50.
> This groundbreaking paper provides experimental evidence for psychological
> disengagement.

KEY TERMS

attributional ambiguity
compensate
disidentification
personal/group discrimination
   discrepancy (PGDD)

psychological disengagement
stereotype threat
stigmatized

QUESTIONS FOR REVIEW AND DISCUSSION

1. Explain the concept of *stigma* and describe the five factors that distinguish between harmful and benign stigmas.
2. Do you think the basis of their stigma matters from the point of view of marked, or stigmatized, individuals?
3. Give examples of groups in the modern world who are numerically a majority but are nonetheless stigmatized.
4. Explain why researchers often consider women to be a stigmatized group.
5. Define *stigma by association*. How are your own interactions affected by the possibility of this stigma?
6. Give examples of token groups outside the corporate setting studied by Kanter (1977). Explain how the concepts of visibility, assimilation, and contrast relate to these groups.
7. If you were doing research on the effects of tokenism, how would you determine whether a particular person's experiences were unique to them or part of an overall pattern?
8. Explain the concept of *attributional ambiguity*. Why would a stigmatized group member experience attributional ambiguity?
9. What are the possible reactions to positive feedback given by a majority group member to a stigmatized group member? Think of situations where each reaction might be more likely.
10. What is the *personal/group discrimination discrepancy*? Outline the available support for cognitive and motivational explanations for the personal/group discrimination discrepancy. Which explanation do you think is more accurate and why?
11. Explain the concept of *stereotype threat*. Outline the keys to understanding how stereotype threat operates.
12. If you were an elementary school teacher, how would you prepare your students for standardized tests so that the effects of stereotype threat would be minimized?
13. What is *stereotype lift* and is it detrimental? Why or why not?
14. Describe the stressors that result from experiencing discrimination. How could these stressors be minimized? Is the stress associated with experiencing

discrimination the same or different from other types of stressors? Explain your reasoning.

15. Who is most responsible for reducing the mental health consequences of experiencing discrimination, the stigmatized or the majority group member? Explain your reasoning.

16. Consider the current literature addressing how experiencing discrimination affects self-esteem. What are the most important questions that remain unanswered? If you were planning to conduct research on this issue, what would be your focus? Why?

17. Explain the concept of *psychological disengagement*.

18. Distinguish between disidentification and discounting.

19. How might psychological disengagement affect the school performance of Hispanics in the United States?

20. Explain the concept of *behavioral compensation*. Explain how members of stigmatized groups use behavioral compensation in situations where they might be discriminated against. Does behavioral compensation do more harm than good? Explain your reasoning.

21. The work cited in this chapter examines social psychological theory, but also emphasizes individual experience. How should researchers balance these two perspectives?

22. Consider the opening quotes of this chapter. Do you believe dominant group members can ever understand racist or other discriminatory behaviors? Why are why not? Are there factors that will make this understanding more likely?

REDUCING PREJUDICE AND DISCRIMINATION

The question may be posed whether a world in which prejudice has been eliminated is at all possible. . . . Contrary to the currently fashionable conclusion that stereotyping and even prejudice may be inevitable and universal outcomes of basic and unchangeable human cognitive processes, . . . it is only the potential for prejudice that is inherently human, and this potential is realized only under particular social circumstances. No matter how depressingly common these circumstances may be today, it does create the possibility of structuring societies and circumstances in order to make tolerance rather than prejudice the norm.

—John Duckitt, 1994 (p. 262)

As John Duckitt (1994) implied in the quotation that opened this chapter, much of the research on prejudice and discrimination paints a pessimistic picture of the situation: Because prejudice and discrimination are, in large measure, rooted in normal human psychological processes, they seem to be unavoidable. However, like Duckitt, we are optimists. We also believe that human nature only provides the potential for prejudice—it does not make prejudice unavoidable or render prejudices that already exist unchangeable. In this chapter we discuss theory and research that addresses the question of how prejudice can be reduced. We begin with processes that operate within individuals: people's attempts to suppress stereotypes when they are activated; the self-regulation or self-control of prejudiced thoughts, feelings, and behaviors; and people's responses to the discovery of contradictions between their prejudiced behavior and their personal values and self-images as nonprejudiced people. The second part of the chapter discusses the role of intergroup contact in prejudice reduction: the conditions under which interacting with members of other groups can lead to reduced prejudice and the psychological processes triggered by contact that bring the changes about. We then look at educational and workplace interventions designed to reduce prejudice in those settings, followed by a brief discussion of the kind of attitude that should replace prejudice. We close by presenting a list of things that you can personally do to help reduce prejudice.

An important point to bear in mind while reading this chapter is that despite the fact that a number of processes can be called on to reduce prejudice, prejudice reduction is not an easy task. Attitudes in general tend to be very resistant to change; once an attitude is formed a number of psychological factors operate to keep it in place (see, for example, Wegener, Petty, Smoak, & Fabrigar, 2004). Intergroup attitudes and prejudices may be especially resistant to change because they are often rooted in values and beliefs that are important to the person, involve the person's social and personal identities, and are reinforced and supported by the person's social network of family and friends (Goodman, 2001). Because changing prejudiced attitudes means making changes in these psychologically important systems, challenges to prejudice often arouse feelings of threat, psychological tension, and anxiety. For example, because our society defines prejudice as bad, people are likely to think that having prejudices makes them bad people, a thought that engenders a threat to the person's positive self-image. In addition, because most people do not want to be prejudiced, acknowledging one's prejudices arouses psychological discomfort and anxiety. To avoid this discomfort, people may find it easier to avoid thinking about their behavior and so forestall any change. As we will see, individual-level models of prejudice reduction are based on people's acknowledgment of their behavior as at least sometimes being based on stereotyping or prejudice. Without this acknowledgment, attitude change cannot occur. Therefore, changing prejudiced attitudes is not an easy task: it takes time and persistence whether one is trying to change one's own attitudes or those of another person. However, persistence can lead to success, at which point the factors that supported the old, prejudiced attitudes come into play to support and maintain the new, unprejudiced attitudes.

INDIVIDUAL LEVEL PROCESSES

Theories of prejudice reduction at the individual level focus on cognitive and emotional processes that result in changes in intergroup attitudes. In this section, we examine three of those processes: stereotype suppression, self-regulation, and value confrontation.

Stereotype Suppression

As we saw in Chapter 10, even unprejudiced people sometimes have prejudiced thoughts and feelings, such as thinking about people in terms of group stereotypes. One way in which people try to deal with unwanted thoughts is with suppression—trying to push the unwanted thoughts out of mind and replace them with other, more acceptable thoughts (see, for example, Macrae, Bodenhausen, & Milne, 1998; Wyer, Sherman, & Stroesser, 1998). For example, someone who found himself thinking about another person in terms of stereotypes might try to ignore the stereotype and focus on characteristics of the person that run counter to the stereotype.

However, thought suppression can be a two-edged sword: Although it is effective while a person is focusing on suppressing an unwanted thought, the thought can return in greater strength after the person stops trying to suppress it (Wegner, 1994). For example, Daniel Wegner and his colleagues (Wegner, Schneider, Carter, & White, 1987) instructed research participants not to think about a white bear for a period of 5 minutes, but to ring a bell every time they did think of one. They were then given a 5-minute period during which they were allowed to think about white bears. Compared to participants in a control group who were allowed to think of white bears for the entire 10 minutes, participants in the suppression group rang their bells less often during the suppression period, showing that thought suppression is effective, but more often during the free-thought period, showing that suppression leads to increased thoughts about the previously suppressed topic. In what is perhaps a more realistic example, Daniel Wegner and David Gold (1995) found that people who were instructed not to think about a former love interest showed an increased number of thoughts about the person after the end of the suppression period. This enhanced return of suppressed thoughts is called the **rebound effect.**

Stereotype rebound   Neil Macrae and his colleagues (Macrae, Bodenhausen, Milne, & Jetten, 1994) conducted a series of experiments to see if the rebound effect occurred when people tried to suppress stereotypic thoughts. In the first experiment, participants viewed a picture of a male skinhead and wrote a brief essay about a typical day in the man's life. Before the participants began to write, the researchers told those in the stereotype suppression condition that group stereotypes could bias their essays, so they were to try as hard as they could not to think of the person they were writing about in stereotypic terms. Participants in the control condition received no instructions concerning stereotypes. When they had finished their essays, participants in both conditions viewed a picture of another male skinhead and wrote about a typical day in his life. This time, no instructions about stereotypes were given to either group of participants. Judges rated the extent to which participants used skinhead stereotypes in their essays. Analysis of the first essays showed that participants who had been instructed to suppress their stereotypes did so: The judges rated their essay as lower in stereotype use than the essays written by the control group participants. However, in the second essay, the participants who had originally been told to suppress their stereotypes showed a rebound effect: They used stereotypes to a greater extent than did the control group participants.

In their second experiment, Macrae and his colleagues (1994) used the same stereotype suppression manipulation they used in the first experiment. However, in the second part of this experiment, participants thought they were going to sit in a waiting room with a male skinhead. The researchers found that participants in the suppression condition sat farther away from the chair they expected the skinhead to use than did participants in the control condition. Thus, stereotype rebound can have behavioral effects as well as cognitive effects. In their third experiment, Macrae and his colleagues found that stereotypes are more accessible—that is, they come to mind more easily—after suppression, another indicator of rebound (see also Gordijn, Hindriks, Koomen, Dijksterhuis, & Van Knippenberg, 2004).

The stereotype rebound effect also manifests itself in other ways. For example, people who have suppressed stereotypes later show better memory for traits that are stereotypic of the target group than for nonstereotypic traits. People also show decreased memory for individuating information about a person that contradicts stereotypes of the person's group (Macrae, Bodenhausen, Milne, & Wheeler, 1996; Sherman, Stroesser, Loftus, & Deguzman, 1997). Lack of memory for individuating information is especially important because, as you will recall from Chapters 3 and 4, attention to individuating information helps people avoid applying stereotypes to others. Stereotype suppression also leads people to make greater use of stereotypes in general, including stereotypes of groups other than the one whose stereotypes they had suppressed. For instance, Ernestine Gordijn and her colleagues (2004, Study 4) had participants write about a day in the life of a male skinhead. Half the participants were in a stereotype suppression condition and half were in a control condition. In the second part of the experiment, all the participants wrote about a day in the life of an older woman. The researchers found that participants who had earlier suppressed the skinhead stereotype made greater use of the older adult stereotype when writing their second essay.

What the research on stereotype suppression shows, then, is that people can effectively suppress stereotypes while they are focusing on doing so; however, the stereotypes come back with greater force once people stop trying to suppress them. This rebound effect increases the accessibility of stereotypes, improves memory for stereotypic information, decreases attention to individuating information, increases stereotype use, and affects behavior toward stereotyped groups. In addition, suppressing stereotypes of one group can activate stereotypes of other groups.

Why do stereotypes rebound?   Stereotypes rebound, but why? Theorists have proposed several processes to explain the rebound effect. Wegner (1994) proposed that the suppression process itself primes suppressed thoughts such as stereotypes, making them more readily available for use when suppression is lifted. Wegner's explanation is based on his conception of how thought suppression operates, which includes two components. First, suppression involves an active, conscious attempt to find something to think about other than the suppressed thought. Second, there is a unconscious monitoring process that maintains a lookout for indications that the unwanted thought is breaking through the suppression barrier. However, Wegner proposed, to be able to keep unwanted thoughts suppressed, the unconscious process must be aware of what those thoughts are. This continual monitoring primes, or makes salient, those very thoughts. Consider Wegner and colleagues' (1987) white bear experiment. While people are consciously thinking about pink elephants, for example, to avoid thinking about white bears, the unconscious process continually focuses on white bears so that it can keep thoughts about them from reaching the conscious level. In a sense, while not thinking about white bears at the conscious level, people are continually thinking about them at the unconscious level. When the conscious suppression is released, the formerly suppressed thoughts come back with increased strength because they have been primed: What was previously unconsciously salient becomes consciously salient. Evidence for this unconscious priming comes from research showing that stereotypes come to mind more easily after suppression than if they are not suppressed (Gordijn et al., 2004; Macrae et al., 1994). Such enhanced accessibility is one effect of priming.

A second explanation for stereotype rebound focuses on the fact that suppression requires cognitive effort: People have to work to keep their suppressed thoughts under control (Gordijn et al., 2004; Macrae et al., 1994). Researchers who study self-control have found that repeated efforts at mental control use up one's ability to exert control; eventually, all of one's control resources are depleted and control fails (see, for example, Muraven & Baumeister, 2000). Mark Muraven and Roy Baumeister (2000) use the analogy of muscles: Repeated use of a muscle tires it to the point at which it can no longer function properly. In the context of stereotype suppression, when people suppress stereotypes they draw on their self-control resources; when those resources are depleted, control fails and the stereotype breaks through (Gordijn et al., 2004). However, as with a muscle, self-control resources can recuperate and regain their strength with rest (Muraven & Baumeister, 2000), permitting stereotypes to be suppressed again in the future.

Finally, Nira Liberman and Jens Förster (2000) have proposed a motivational explanation for stereotype rebound. They suggest that suppression of a stereotype creates a need to use it and this need is manifested in the rebound effect. Liberman and Förster (2000) hypothesized that if people are given a chance to express a stereotype after a period of suppression, that expression would reduce the motivational pressure and prevent the rebound effect. They conducted several studies that supported their hypothesis (see also Hodson & Dovidio, 2001). Note that none of the proposed explanations contradicts any of the others, so they all could be correct. That is, priming, control depletion, and use motivation could all operate simultaneously, or different processes could operate in different situations or affect different people.

Are rebound effects inevitable?   Although there is considerable evidence that stereotype suppression leads to rebound effects, Margo Monteith, Jeffrey Sherman, and Patricia Devine (1998) proposed some circumstances in which stereotype rebound might not occur. One such circumstance is when the suppressor is low in prejudice. They suggested three reasons why people who are low in prejudice might not experience stereotype rebound. First, as we noted in Chapter 4, low prejudice people are less likely to experience stereotype activation than are high prejudice people. Without stereotype activation, there are no stereotypes to suppress, so the stereotype suppression-rebound process might be initiated less often in low prejudice people. Second, when people low in prejudice experience stereotypical thoughts, they are highly motivated to suppress them. This strong motivation may keep stereotypes suppressed in the face of factors that usually cause rebound. Finally, low prejudice people might be able to avoid stereotype rebound because their egalitarian beliefs provide easily accessible replacements for stereotypic thoughts, such as positive beliefs about the stereotyped group. Recall that under Wegner's (1994) thought suppression model focusing on alternative thoughts facilitates suppression.

Monteith, Sherman, and Devine (1998) also suggested that social norms that proscribe certain prejudices could reduce some types of rebound effects for stereotypes associated with these prejudices (see Chapter 6 for a discussion of proscribed prejudices). For example, noting that stereotype activation does not necessarily lead to stereotype use (see Chapter 4), Monteith and her colleagues proposed that when proscribed prejudices are involved, high prejudice people might experience stereotype rebound in terms of stereotype activation and accessibility but not in terms of application. That is, the social norm against acting in a prejudiced manner is so strong that even high prejudice people will exert extra effort to avoid applying proscribed stereotypes.

The results of research have supported Monteith, Sherman, and Devine's (1998) suggestions. For example, high prejudice people, but not low prejudice people, exhibit stereotype activation after suppression (Hodson & Dovidio, 2001; Monteith, Spicer, & Tooman, 1998), supporting the proposition that low prejudice prevents stereotype rebound by inhibiting stereotype activation. In addition, Gordijn and colleagues (2004) and Macrae and colleagues (1998) showed that internal motivation to suppress stereotypes, a characteristic of low prejudice people, can inhibit stereotype rebound. Margo Monteith, Clarence Spicer, and Gregory Tooman (1998) also showed that although high prejudice people experience enhanced stereotype activation for a target of proscribed prejudice after suppression, they are no more likely than low prejudice people to apply the stereotype. Finally, Natalie Wyer, Jeffrey Sherman, and Steven Stroesser (2000) showed that external motivation to avoid a proscribed prejudice can also inhibit rebound effects, supporting the proposition that it is the normative proscription of prejudice that inhibits stereotype application in high prejudice people.

Wyer and her colleagues (2000) also demonstrated an important limitation of external motivation: It only inhibits rebound effects when people have cognitive resources available to prevent rebound. For example, in Wyer and colleagues' Experiment 2, participants who had the motivation to avoid rebound effects were unable to do so when they had to divert cognitive resources to remembering an 8-digit number. Thus, to avoid rebound effects, a person must have the cognitive capacity to carry out suppression tasks, such as searching for and focusing on distracting thoughts, as well as the motivation to avoid stereotype use.

Self-Regulation

The research on stereotype suppression shows that people who are motivated to act in an unprejudiced manner can do so. Based in part on the results of this research, Margo Monteith (1993; Monteith, Ashburn-Nardo, Voils, & Czopp, 2002) proposed a **self-regulation model** for the control of prejudice. This model, shown in Figure 12.1, proposes that, based on their experience of acting in a prejudiced manner, people who see themselves as unprejudiced become sensitized to environmental cues that warn them when they might respond in a prejudiced manner to a member of a stereotyped group. Forewarned by these cues, these people then suppress their prejudiced responses and replace them with appropriate nonprejudiced responses.

Developing cues for the control of prejudice   The left side of Figure 12.1 shows the process of developing cues for the control of prejudice. When a person encounters a member of a stereotyped group, characteristics of the group member, such as skin color or facial features, can trigger the activation of the group stereotype in the person's mind. If the stereotype is activated (recall from Chapter 4 that stereotype activation is not inevitable) and the person has not developed cues that would warn her that she might respond to the outgroup member in a prejudiced manner, she makes a prejudiced response, such as applying the group stereotype to the group member. Monteith and her colleagues illustrate this process using a hypothetical man named Pat who is grocery shopping. While trying to find a particular item, he sees a Black woman standing by a shelf and assumes the woman is an employee of the store. (As Feagin, 1991, has pointed out, Black people are often stereotypically assumed to be "the help.") When Pat asks the Black woman for assistance in finding the item he is looking for, she explains that she is a shopper, not a store employee. Seeing the Black woman standing by a shelf in the store thus activated Pat's stereotype that Black people must be low-level employees.

Acting in a prejudiced manner contradicts the self-image of people who see themselves as unprejudiced. If those people become aware of the contradiction between their self-images and their behavior, they feel guilty. Awareness of the contradiction is important because people do not always consciously realize that their behavior contradicts their beliefs; people are very adept at repressing such contradictions (Wilson, Lindsey, & Schooler, 2000). Awareness of the contradiction also leads people to reflect on their behavior, asking themselves what caused them to act in the way they did and how they can behave differently (that is, in an unprejudiced manner) in the future. They then use the results of this reflective process to develop cues that can warn them that they might be about to act in a prejudiced manner.

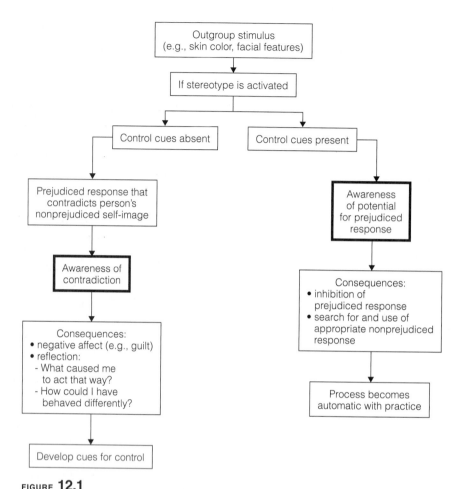

FIGURE **12.1**

THE SELF-REGULATION MODEL OF PREJUDICE REDUCTION

The presence of a stimulus associated with an outgroup can activate the stereotypes of the outgroup. In people who have not developed cues for the control of prejudice, the stimulus produces a prejudiced response that contradicts their self-images as nonprejudiced people. If they become aware of the contradiction, they experience negative emotions, such as guilt. The negative emotions motivate them to think about why they responded the way they did and about how they could have responded differently. These reflections lead to the development of cues for controlling prejudice, which are activated when a similar situation arises in the future. People who have developed cues for the control of prejudice become aware of the potential for making a prejudiced response. They inhibit the prejudiced response and replace it with a nonprejudiced response. With practice, the search for and use of replacement responses becomes automatic and conscious awareness is no longer needed.

Adapted from Monteith, Ashburn-Nardo, Voils, and Czopp (2002).

Continuing Monteith and colleagues' (2002) example, the Black woman's response makes Pat aware of the mistaken assumption that led him to apply a stereotype to her. He feels guilty about having made and acted on a prejudiced assumption, and thinks about ways he can avoid doing so in the future. One cue that Pat might develop would be to decide to always check to see if a Black person is wearing a store name tag or some other indicator of being an employee before asking for help. Seeing a Black person in store would then act as a cue to stop and check the situation before assuming that the person is an employee.

Using cues to control prejudice   The right side of Figure 12.1 illustrates what happens after people have developed cues for controlling prejudice. In this case, the cues people have developed warn them that they might respond to the situation in a prejudiced manner. They then suppress any prejudiced responses that they become aware of and search for appropriate nonprejudiced responses to use in their place. For example, the next time Pat is looking for something in a store and sees a Black person, that acts as a cue that he might make a prejudiced response. Pat then suppresses his impulse to ask the person for help and carries out his substitute behavior, checking for indicators that the person is, in fact, an employee. If such indicators are present, he asks the person for help; if they are not present, he looks for a store employee.

Monteith and her colleagues (2002) conducted a number of laboratory studies that supported the self-regulation model. One limitation of the model that they acknowledge is that it probably works best for people who are already low in prejudice. Those are the people who are most likely to feel guilty over having acted in a prejudiced manner and are most likely to be internally motivated to change their behavior. However, Margo Monteith and Gina Walters (1998) have found that some relatively prejudiced people, especially those who place high value on equal opportunity, are motivated to try to act in an unprejudiced manner. Monteith and her colleagues (2002) also investigated the "real world" applicability of the self-regulation model by conducting interviews in which they asked people about they experiences of having acted in a prejudiced manner. Two of the examples they found are shown in Box 12.1.

Automatic control of prejudice   Monteith and her colleagues (Devine & Monteith, 1999; Monteith et al., 2002) also suggested that the self-regulation of prejudice becomes automatic over time. That is, once people have developed cues for controlling prejudice and have practiced them sufficiently, they no longer have to stop and think about putting replacement behaviors into action; the use of those behaviors becomes unconscious and automatic. For example, Kerry Kawakami and her colleagues (Kawakami, Dovidio, Moll, Hermsen, & Russin, 2000) gave people practice in negating stereotypes by having them respond "No" each time a stereotypic trait was presented on a computer screen along with a picture of a member of the stereotyped group. They found that negating stereotypes became easier with practice and that the procedure reduced stereotype activation. However, they also found that practice affected only the stereotype of the group that the participants practiced with. For example, negation practice on racial stereotypes reduced the

12.1   *Self-Regulation in Action*

To investigate the "real world" applicability of the self-regulation model of prejudice reduction, Margo Monteith and her colleagues (2002) conducted interviews with students. Their first question was whether the students had "had a racial experience in which they did something related to Blacks that they then thought they should not have done, either because of their own reactions or because of others' reactions" (p. 1046). In response, an interviewee who had scored low on a measure of racial prejudice related this experience:

> Me and my roommate got approached several times last year in the parking lot by some homeless people and they were Black. After the first 2 or 3 times they asked for money, whenever we would see a group of Black people near there we would automatically assume that we better go the other way because they were going to ask for money. It made me feel bad because I didn't even give them a chance. Maybe they wanted directions to go somewhere, or wanted to know where to get some

coffee or something. We just automatically assumed that they wanted money. That was being judgmental, and I really didn't feel too good about that. (p. 1046)

Note the aspects of development of cues for control that appear in this student's story: The student was aware of having done something—avoiding the homeless people—that contradicted his value system and the student experienced negative emotions as a result of the behavior.

Monteith and her colleagues next asked their interviewees if they had ever thought about the experience again. The interviewee quoted above related this incident:

> This summer my girlfriend and I were looking at the horses downtown, and we were looking at one and this Black guy started walking toward us. Of course I figured that he was probably a homeless guy, and I immediately thought, here comes some homeless guy—he's going to ask us for money. But from my past experience I had in the parking lot with my roommate, I had to stop and think to myself, "Maybe he's not homeless,

activation of those stereotypes but other stereotypes, such as those associated with older people, were activated just as easily as they had been before the practice sessions that used racial stereotypes.

Self-regulation in action   How successful are people's attempts to be unprejudiced? Interestingly, few researchers have examined this question. One exception is Nicole Shelton (2003), who studied the interactions of White and Black college students. She found that White students who were motivated to avoid acting in a prejudiced manner were better liked by their Black interaction partners than were White students who were not so motivated, suggesting the efforts not to appear prejudiced were successful. However, she also found that the motivated White students enjoyed the interaction less and felt more anxious maybe he's not going to ask me for money. He might not say anything to me." I stopped and I thought about the past experience and it made me change my decision to something I probably wouldn't have made. (pp. 1046–1047)

Note how the student's previous experience led him to develop a cue for controlling his behavior, in this case being approached by a homeless person. This cue led him to think about how he wanted to respond and to respond in a nonprejudiced manner by not avoiding the man.

Through their interviews, Monteith and her colleagues also found that even prejudiced people sometimes engage in self-regulation, although apparently from external rather than internal motives. They gave this example from a student who scored relatively high on their measure of prejudice:

My roommate's Black and sometimes when we're watching shows [on television] they kinda like make the Blacks look trashy, you know like

on Jerry Springer. . . . I was laughing at it and he wasn't really and it kind of automatically made me feel like I had done something wrong so I felt bad. . . . I didn't want him to think, "Well, he looks like some kind of racist." . . . [Now,] if something on the TV comes up that's like shady you know it's like I think about it . . . you know I think about it to make sure that it doesn't happen again in case he actually was mad about it. I wouldn't laugh out loud if I thought maybe it would be offensive to someone else. I'm just a little more careful now. (p. 1047)

Note that in this case the student does not feel upset about his behavior because it contradicts his values, but because it might upset his roommate. Nonetheless, he developed and uses a cue for controlling his behavior.

than their unmotivated counterparts, perhaps because their efforts required a lot of work and they were concerned about the success of those efforts.

However, people need to be careful of the behaviors they use to communicate their desire not to be prejudiced. For example, Teri Conley and her colleagues (Conley, Calhoun, Evett, & Devine, 2001) asked lesbian, gay, and bisexual (LGB) people to list the mistakes heterosexual people make when trying to appear nonprejudiced and to rate how annoying they found those mistakes to be. The four most annoying mistakes were not admitting to any discomfort they might feel when interacting with an LGB person; using subtly prejudiced language, such as talking about heterosexuality as "normal;" making stereotypic assumptions about LGB people; and ignoring gay issues, such as by acting as if sexual orientation had no effect on people's lives. Other annoying behaviors included heterosexuals' stating that they knew another gay person, as though that were a credential of their lack of prejudice; asking inappropriate questions, such as questions about sexual behavior; and pointing out how unprejudiced they are. Conley and her colleagues did not question the good intentions underlying these behaviors, but saw them as a form of overcompensation by people who felt uncomfortable in the presence of LGB people, felt guilty over their discomfort, and so tried too hard in their efforts to overcome their discomfort.

Value Confrontation

Self-regulation processes occur when people become aware of a contradiction between their egalitarian belief systems and instances of nonegalitarian behaviors they have carried out. Can these kinds of processes be initiated externally? That is, can one design an intervention to change people's intergroup attitudes and behavior by making them aware of contradictions among their beliefs or between their beliefs and behavior?

The first attempt to do so was made by Milton Rokeach (1973). As part of his research on personal value systems, Rokeach had students rank order the personal importance of 18 values, including freedom and equality. He found that the students (and, in other studies, other adults as well) typically ranked freedom higher than equality. He also found that people who ranked freedom and equality close together had more positive attitudes toward the civil rights movement then under way than did other people. Rokeach therefore developed the **value confrontation technique** as an intervention that might be used to make positive changes in people's racial attitudes. The technique calls people's attention to the contradictions implied by placing a high value on freedom while placing a low value on equality. For example, in a series of studies conducted at Michigan State University, student research participants were shown data on value rankings. Afterwards, Rokeach (1973) told them, "Apparently, Michigan State students value *Freedom* more highly than they value *Equality*. This suggests that MSU students in general are much more interested in their own freedom than they are in freedom for other people" (p. 237; italics in original). He then asked the participants to think about their own rankings. He next informed the students about his findings concerning the relationship between value rankings and racial attitudes, and said, "This raises the question of whether those who are *against* civil rights are really saying that they care a great deal about *their own* freedom but are indifferent to other people's freedom. Those who are *for* civil rights are perhaps really saying they not only want freedom for themselves, but for other people, too" (p. 238; italics in original). He concluded by asking the students to think about the implications of this information for their own lives.

Rokeach (1973) hypothesized that being confronted with having a personal value system that contradicted the basic American value system that they presumably espoused—in this case ranking freedom high and equality low, thereby implying that they opposed civil rights for minority groups—would make people feel uneasy. This unease would lead them to revise their value systems to place an equally high value on freedom and equality, which, in turn, would lead to more favorable racial attitudes. How well did the procedure work? In three studies that compared students who underwent the value confrontation with students who did not, Rokeach (1973) believed he had found evidence supporting the value confrontation procedure. However, based on a review of Rokeach's studies and later research, Thomas Cook and Brian Flay (1978) concluded that the value confrontation procedure was not, in fact, very effective. They pointed to statistical flaws in Rokeach's data analysis that undermined his case for concluding that the intervention was effective and noted that the later studies produced inconsistent results, with some finding support for the procedure and others not. More recently, Bob Altemeyer (1994) conducted two value confrontation studies whose results were also inconsistent, with one finding value confrontation to be effective and the other not. Based on this evidence, it might appear that value confrontation is not a consistently effective means of changing intergroup attitudes.

However, the results of recent research by Leanne Son Hing, Winnie Li, and Mark Zanna (2002) suggest that value confrontation can be effective under certain conditions: It must be used with the right people and it must draw on value-behavior contradictions that are specific to the person. Son Hing and her colleagues proposed that value confrontation would be most effective with people who exhibit aversive prejudice (see Chapter 5). Such people endorse egalitarian values, yet still unconsciously harbor prejudices that lead them to behave in prejudiced ways. One reason, then, why previous value confrontation studies might not have found support for the technique is because those studies included two types of people who may not have been amenable to the technique: nonprejudiced people, whose non-prejudiced behavior does not conflict with their nonprejudiced values, and extremely prejudiced people, whose prejudiced behavior does not conflict their prejudiced values. Son Hing and her colleagues further proposed that for value confrontation to be effective, the procedure must expose people to specific instances of their own behavior that contradicts their values. Making the contradiction concrete and personally relevant by using behaviors the person has performed is more likely to have an impact than is Rokeach's (1973) procedure in which people are confronted with contradictions between abstract value positions (Aronson, 1999).

To test their hypothesis, Son Hing and her colleagues (2002) conducted an experiment in which they first screened college student research participants to identify two types of people: Those who scored low on an explicit measure of prejudice toward Asians but high on an implicit measure were classified as experiencing aversive prejudice toward Asians; those who scored low on both measures were classified as unprejudiced. To make participants' egalitarian values salient to them, they wrote an essay on the importance of treating minority students on campus fairly. To motivate the participants, the researchers told them that their essays might be used as part of a universitywide program promoting racial equality. To make participants aware of contradictions between their values and their behavior, those in the value confrontation condition then wrote about two situations in which they had reacted more negatively to an Asian person than they thought they should have or had treated an Asian person in a prejudiced manner. Participants in the

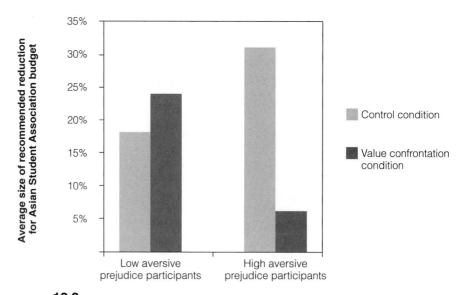

FIGURE **12.2**

**INFLUENCE OF VALUE CONFRONTATION ON PEOPLE LOW AND HIGH
IN AVERSIVE PREJUDICE**

White research participants who were low in aversive prejudice recommended equitable
cuts to the Asian Student Association (ASA) budget regardless of whether they had been
confronted with a contradiction between their egalitarian values and their previous behavior
toward Asians. In contrast, participants high in aversive prejudice recommended larger
cuts than low prejudice participants, whereas those in the value confrontation condition
recommended much smaller cuts than any of the other participants.

Adapted from Son Hing, Li, and Zanna (2002), *Journal of Experimental Social Psychology* 38(1): 71–78, 2002, Figure 1,
p. 76. Used by permission of Elsevier.

control condition did not write a second essay. To assess participants' attitudes
toward Asians, the researchers asked them to help the university's student government cut their budget by 20 percent. They were given a list of student organizations that included the Asian Student Association (ASA) and their current budgets
and asked to recommend how much each organization's budget was to be cut. The
task was designed so that cutting one organization's budget less than the overall
20 percent required cutting other organizations' budgets by more than 20 percent.
Thus, the fairest decision would have been to cut all organizations' budgets by
20 percent.

   As shown in Figure 12.2, Son Hing and her colleagues (2002) found that, in
both the value confrontation and control conditions, low prejudice participants recommended similar budget cuts for the ASA—18 percent in the control condition
and 24 percent in the value confrontation condition—both of which are close to the
20 percent cut that would indicate equal treatment of all organizations. Aversive
prejudice participants in the control condition recommended an average 31 percent
cut in the ASA's budget compared to the 18 percent recommended by the low prejudice participants. In contrast, aversive prejudice participants in the value

confrontation condition recommended an average budget cut of only 6 percent for the ASA, far less than that recommended by the other participants. The researchers also found that after describing ways in which they had discriminated against Asians, the aversive prejudice participants in the value confrontation condition reported feeling more negative emotions than those in the control condition. Son Hing and her colleagues interpreted these results as indicating that, for people experiencing aversive prejudice, becoming aware of a contradiction between their values and their behavior induced negative emotions, and that they tried to improve their emotional state by acting in a positive manner toward the group they had discriminated against in the past.

The results of Son Hing and her colleagues' (2002) research therefore indicates that under certain circumstances, value confrontation might be effective in changing intergroup attitudes. However, more research is needed to see whether Son Hing and colleagues' results can be replicated for other targets of discrimination. Research is also needed to see whether the intervention produces long-term effects or if people's attitudes revert to their old positions after they leave the laboratory.

INTERGROUP CONTACT

For most of World War II (as it had been for most of its history), the United States military was strictly segregated by race. In the Army, with the exception of a few all-Black units, combat formations were all White. Most Black soldiers were assigned to supply units and held jobs such as stevedore, warehouse worker, and truck driver. However, by late 1944, the Army in Europe was severely short of combat troops. This shortage led General Dwight Eisenhower, commander of Allied Forces in Europe, to approve what many senior officers saw as a radical solution to the problem: Black soldiers assigned to supply units in Europe would be allowed to volunteer for combat duty, formed into platoons led by White officers, given an accelerated combat training course, and, once trained, assigned to infantry companies that would consist of a Black platoon and three all-White platoons (Ambrose, 1997). One of the major concerns that Army authorities had was how serving with Black soldiers would affect the morale of the White soldiers, so the Army commissioned a survey to find out. White soldiers' reactions depended on who was asked. For example, when asked how they would feel about serving in a semi-integrated unit such as the ones described, 62 percent of White soldiers in segregated units said they would dislike it very much, compared to only 7 percent of the White soldiers actually serving in semi-integrated units (Stouffer, Suchman, DeVinney, Star, & Williams, 1949).

Results of this study and other research conducted in the middle of the 20th century led to the development of what is known as the **contact hypothesis** or **intergroup contact theory:** "Interaction between people changes their beliefs and feelings toward each other. . . . Thus, if only one had the opportunity to communicate with others and appreciate their way of life, understanding and reduction of prejudice would follow" (Amir, 1976, p. 245). Stated that way, the contact hypothesis is clearly simplistic and overly optimistic, a point Amir went on to make. As we saw in the Robbers Cave studies described in Chapter 8, simply bringing two competing groups together is more likely to result in hostility than in friendship. Indeed, increased contact of and by itself can lead to increased negative attitudes rather than positive attitudes, and negative contact leads to negative attitudes (see, for example, Eller & Abrams, 2004; Islam & Hewstone, 1993; Plant & Devine, 2003). Nonetheless, as we will see, some 60 years of research has found that under the proper conditions increased intergroup contact can lead to improved intergroup attitudes. In this section, we discuss three aspects of intergroup contact as a prejudice-reduction tool: the conditions necessary for successful intergroup contact, the effectiveness of intergroup contact, and recent theories concerning how contact brings about attitude change.

Conditions for Success

Allport (1954) noted that although bringing members of different groups into contact did not always improve intergroup attitudes, many times it did. Based on a review of the research conducted up to that time, Allport proposed four conditions that had to be met if intergroup contact were to lead to improved intergroup attitudes (see also Brewer & Brown, 1998):

- Members of each group must have equal status in the situation.
- The groups must work cooperatively to achieve common goals.
- The situation must allow participants to get to know each other as individuals (referred to as *acquaintance potential*).
- The intergroup effort must have the support of authorities, law, or custom (referred to as *institutional support*).

In addition to these necessary conditions, researchers have also identified what Thomas Pettigrew (1998a) has referred to as facilitating conditions: factors that are not necessary for success but which, when present in addition to the necessary conditions, increase the likelihood of success. Some of these factors are listed in Table 12.1. However, for the sake of simplicity, we focus our discussion on the necessary conditions.

Equal status   One factor that is essential to the success of intergroup contact as a prejudice reduction technique is that the groups have equal status within the contact situation (Amir, 1976). Because minority groups usually have lower status in society than do majority groups, replicating those status differences in interacting groups is likely to reinforce stereotypical beliefs and prejudicial attitudes (Cohen, 1984). In contrast, establishing group equality within the contact situation works against the reinforcement of social stereotypes and can promote positive views of outgroup members.

Fletcher Blanchard, Russell Weigel, and Stuart Cook (1975) conducted a classic study of the role of equal status with U.S. Air Force enlisted men as the participants. White airmen worked cooperatively on a task with either a Black or a White confederate of the researchers. The independent variable of partner

TABLE **12.1**	**FACTORS FACILITATING THE SUCCESS OF INTERGROUP CONTACT**

In addition to the four conditions that are necessary for intergroup contact to bring about improved intergroup attitudes, there are a number of factors that, if added to the necessary conditions, increase the likelihood of success. Among these factors are (Stephan, 1985):

- Members of the interacting groups should be of equal status outside the contact situation as well as in the situation.

- Members of the interacting groups should hold similar attitudes, values, and beliefs on issues not related to relations between the groups.

- Members of the interacting groups should have equal ability on the task the groups will be working on together.

- The group interaction should result in successful completion of the task.

- There should be opportunities for group members to interact outside the immediate situation.

- Efforts should be made to ensure that group members are viewed as individuals.

- The contact should be voluntary.

- Longer-term contact is more likely to bring positive results than shorter-term contact.

- There should be opportunities for contact in a variety of situations and with a variety of both ingroup and outgroup members.

- There should be an equal number of members from each group.

status was operationally defined in terms of competence on the task: a participant's partner was portrayed as being less competent than the participant, equally competent, or more competent. (Task competence is related to individual status in a variety of situations; see, for example, Cohen, 1984.) A second independent variable was success on the task; the researchers manipulated the situation so that a pair either succeeded or failed. After completing the task, the participants rated how much they liked their partner. When the pair succeeded, White and Black confederates received equal liking ratings in all three status conditions. However, the failure condition was really the crucial one: Recall from Chapter 5 that modern forms of prejudice are most likely to be expressed when a person has an excuse to derogate a member of a minority group; task failure would provide such an excuse, allowing the participant to blame his partner for the failure. This is what happened when participants whose team had failed at the task had a lower-status partner: the Black confederate was rated lower than the White confederate. However, Black partners whose status was equal to or greater than the participants' received ratings equal to those given the White confederates in the failure conditions. Thus, having interacted with an equal or higher status Black peer counteracted the effects of the prejudice that was shown in the derogation of the lower status Black partner.

Cooperation   A second condition for successful intergroup contact is that the groups work cooperatively in pursuit of common goals. As Sherif's (1966) Robbers Cave study showed, cooperating to achieve common goals helps unite interacting groups by giving them a purpose to strive toward that extends beyond the boundaries of each group and encompasses both groups: It helps turn two groups into one group with a common aim. For example, Donna Desforges and her colleagues (1991) had college student research participants work with another person on a learning task that involved either individual study or working together to learn the material. The other person was a confederate who portrayed a former mental patient whom the participants initially expected to act in a stereotypic manner, although he did not, in fact, do so. After working with the person, participants in the cooperative learning condition expressed more positive attitudes toward former mental patients in general than did participants in the individual study condition.

Athletic teams provide a more everyday example of cooperation in pursuit of common goals: Team members must work together to win. To see whether athletic participation affected intergroup attitudes Kendrick Brown and his colleagues (Brown, Brown, Jackson, Sellers, & Manuel, 2003) studied college athletes at 24 predominantly White colleges and universities in the United States. The researchers expected that the White athletes' racial attitudes would be affected by two factors, the amount of contact they had with minority teammates (defined in terms of the percentage of minority players on their teams) and whether the athletes played an individual or team sport. Team sports, such as basketball and soccer, require players to work together to win; in contrast, in individual sports, such as swimming and track, winning in most events is a result of individual effort. As shown in Figure 12.3, the White athletes' racial attitudes were affected by a combination of contact and pursuit of common goals: The attitudes of athletes who competed in individual sports were unrelated to the amount of intergroup contact they experienced whereas the attitudes of athletes who competed in team sports became more positive as contact increased. Thus, contact itself had no affect on attitudes in the absence of cooperation. Brown and his colleagues pointed out that sports also tend to emphasize equal status among racial groups: Higher status within a team, such as becoming a starting player, depends on athletic performance rather than race.

Acquaintance potential   Acquaintance potential is the opportunity for the members of the interacting groups to get to know one another as individuals. This process leads to individuation of outgroup members which, as we saw in Chapters 3 and 4, undermines stereotypes. Getting to know one another also gives people the opportunity to see that, despite some differences, they share many of their attitudes and values with members of the outgroup, which may help reduce intergroup anxiety and increase empathy for members of the other group (Miller, 2002). Perceptions of similarity also are an important factor in interpersonal liking and can lead to friendship formation (Berscheid & Reis, 1998). Intergroup friendships have been found to be related to lower prejudice in a number of situations, including Europeans' attitudes toward immigrant groups (van Dick et al., 2004), Catholic and Protestant Northern Irelanders' attitudes toward one another (Paolini, Hewstone, Cairns, & Voci, 2004), U.S. college students' attitudes toward members of other ethnic groups (Levin, van Laar, & Sidanius, 2003), Black and White American adults' attitudes toward one another (Ellison & Powers, 1994; Jackman &

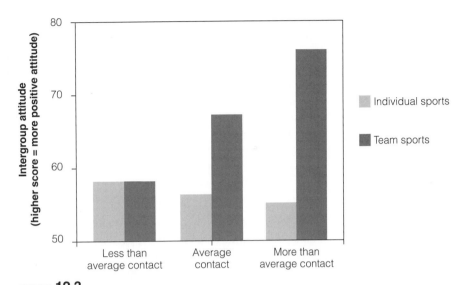

FIGURE **12.3**

TEAM SPORT PARTICIPATION AND PREJUDICE

Compared to individual sports such as track or golf, team sports such as basketball and soccer tend to more fully meet the conditions that facilitate the reduction of prejudice through intergroup contact. Thus, as shown above, Brown and colleagues found that amount of intergroup contact was not related to intergroup attitudes among participants in individual sports, but that for members of team sports, attitudes become more positive as contact increased.

Adapted from Brown et al. (2003), Figure 1, p. 1390.

Crane, 1986), and heterosexuals' attitudes toward lesbians and gay men (Herek & Capitanio, 1996). Pettigrew (1997) also found that friendships were more strongly related to low prejudice measured in a variety of ways than were other kinds of interpersonal relationships, such as having outgroup members as coworkers or neighbors. These latter relationships are not unimportant, however; not surprisingly, Pettigrew found that having more outgroup members as neighbors was associated with having more intergroup friendships (see also Ellison & Powers, 1994).

Indirect friendships may also ameliorate prejudice. That is, having a friend who has a friendship with an outgroup member is related to lower prejudice toward that group. For example, Stephen Wright and his colleagues (Wright, Aron, McLaughlin-Volpe, & Ropp, 1997) found that having an indirect friendship was related to lower prejudice for both White and minority college students. They also conducted two experiments that showed that learning that a friend has a friendship with an outgroup member leads to reduced prejudice. Indirect friendships can affect prejudice even in situations of extreme intergroup hostility: Stefania Paolini and her colleagues (2004) found that intergroup prejudice was lower for Catholics and Protestants in Northern Ireland who had indirect cross-group friendships. Wright and his colleagues (1997) proposed three reasons why indirect friendships are related to lower prejudice. First, having a friend who has an outgroup friendship provides a role model for positive intergroup behavior. Second, the friendship implies that outgroup members have positive characteristics, otherwise one's own friend would not like the outgroup member. Finally, disliking someone liked by a friend creates a cognitive conflict and people prefer their likes and dislikes to be mutually consistent. One way to resolve the conflict created by having a friend who likes a member of a group that one dislikes is to change one's attitude toward the group. In addition, Norman Miller (2002) points out that the friend can provide information about the outgroup that can undermine negative stereotypes, leading to a more positive attitude toward the group. This information can be especially powerful because it is provided by a trustworthy source: one's own friend.

Institutional support   The fourth condition for successful intergroup contact is institutional support: Authorities, law, or social norms must establish a clear expectation for attitude change in the direction of lower prejudice and behavior change in the direction of less discrimination. Authority figures in organizations and institutions can support effective intergroup contact in a number of ways (Cox, 2001; Schofield, 2001a). For example, people behave in ways for which they are rewarded and authorities can provide reward structures that reinforce nondiscriminatory behavior. Authorities also can work to establish a climate that communicates nonprejudiced norms by clearly stating their expectations, establishing and enforcing appropriate policies, setting a good example, and providing resources to help people deal with the stresses that change always brings. See Box 12.2 for one example of leadership effectively applied to producing successful intergroup contact.

Unfortunately, not much research has been conducted on the effects of institutional support, probably because of the difficulty of disentangling its effects from the effects of other factors (Schneider, 2004). However, Marylee Taylor (1995) conducted a study in which she compared the racial attitudes of White employees in companies that did and did not practice affirmative action. She took the presence of an affirmative action program as evidence of institutional support for interracial equality. Taylor found that even after controlling for interracial contact at work, White employees of affirmative action companies held more positive racial attitudes than employees of companies without affirmative action programs.

Effectiveness of Intergroup Contact

How effective is intergroup contact as a means of reducing prejudice? Since Allport's (1954) statement of the contact hypothesis, more than 200 studies have been conducted to try to answer that question. Based on a review of those studies, Thomas Pettigrew and Linda Tropp (2000) concluded that when the four necessary conditions for success are met, intergroup contact has a moderate effect on prejudice reduction, equivalent to a correlation of $r = .27$. Although this effect may not seem to be very large, it is about the same magnitude of the effect that psychotherapy has on the alleviation of mental disorder (see, for example, Lambert & Bergin, 1994).

12.2   *The Importance of Institutional Support*

Social psychologist David Schneider worked as a consultant for high schools implementing desegregation plans during the 1960s and 1970s. He related this case of the effect of institutional support on the outcome of intergroup contact:

> My observation was that desegregation did "work" in some schools. . . . And in each school where it did work, it was because the school board and especially the principal moved the faculty and students beyond the "this is being shoved down our throats" mentality. I spent time in one school that seemed to be well integrated behaviorally (in terms of clearly friendly relationships among at least some black and white students, and no overt hostility). I questioned some teachers about this, since the atmosphere contrasted so vividly with other schools I had visited. They all pointed to the principal, who had made it clear that desegregation was an opportunity rather than a constraint, and that they were going to make it work. He also had moved quickly to set up in-house teacher workshops to prepare the teachers for the increased demands he was placing on them. (Schneider, 2004, p. 432)

Pettigrew and Tropp also found that the intergroup contact effect applies to many outgroups, including those based on sexual orientation, race and ethnicity, physical disability, mental illness, nationality, and age. However, contact has a larger effect on prejudice against some groups than others. For example, Pettigrew and Tropp found that the effect for sexual orientation was equivalent to a correlation of $r = .27$; for race and ethnicity, equivalent to $r = .20$; and for age, equivalent to $r = .05$. It is not clear why these group differences exist, but it may be that contact has a greater effect on attitudes toward more stigmatized groups; surveys generally find that attitudes toward lesbians and gay men are more negative than attitudes toward African Americans (Sherrill, 1996).

Pettigrew and Tropp (2000) also found that contact had more effect on prejudice in some settings than in others. For example, the effect in work settings was equivalent to a correlation of $r = .33$ but equivalent to a correlation of only $r = .18$ in school settings. Again the reasons for this difference are not clear, but work settings may require a higher level of cooperation in pursuit of common goals than do school settings. Finally, intergroup contact early in life is important. For example, Peter Wood and Nancy Sonleitner (1996) found that adults who had more childhood contacts with African Americans had more positive racial attitudes. Similarly, Tamara Towles-Schwen and Russell Fazio (2001) found that college students who had had more contact with African Americans in school had a higher motivation to control prejudiced responses. As we noted earlier, that kind of motivation can lead to self-generated prejudice reduction.

Types of changes produced   Intergroup contact appears to have its effect on prejudice by producing cognitive and emotional changes. In terms of cognitive change, intergroup contact tends to increase knowledge about the outgroup (for example, Eller & Abrams, 2003), reduce stereotyping (for example, Aberson, Haag, Shoemaker, & Tomolillo, 2004), reduce expectations that intergroup interactions will have negative outcomes (for example, Plant & Devine, 2003), reduce ingroup favoritism (for example, Bettencourt, Brewer, Croak, & Miller, 1992), and lead to perceptions of unity between the ingroup and outgroup (for example, Eller & Abrams, 2003, 2004). Intergroup contact also has effects on intergroup emotions. Contact, including indirect contact, reduces intergroup anxiety (for example, Eller & Abrams, 2003, 2004; Levin et al., 2003; Paolini et al., 2004). Contact also leads to increases in empathy for the other group (for example, Aberson et al., 2004; Stephan & Finlay, 1999); as we saw in Chapter 6, greater empathy tends to be associated with less prejudice.

Intergroup contact also can lead people to engage in new behaviors, which can then lead to attitude change. Interacting with members of an outgroup may be a novel behavior for participants in intergroup contact situations who hold negative attitudes toward the outgroup. When people act in ways that are inconsistent with their attitudes, such as by holding a friendly conversation with members of a group they dislike, the contradiction leads to unpleasant feelings collectively referred to as *cognitive dissonance.* Because cognitive dissonance is unpleasant, people are motivated to reduce it. One way of reducing dissonance is to change one's attitude to be consistent with one's behavior. Thus, Michael Leippe and Donna Eisenstadt (1999) have found that inducing prejudiced people to behave in nonprejudiced ways, such as by having White college students write essays in favor of increasing scholarship money for Black students, leads to reductions in prejudice.

Limiting factors   As we saw, Pettigrew and Tropp (2000) found that although intergroup contact does reduce prejudice, its effect is only moderate in size. Another way of looking at this finding is that intergroup contact reduces prejudice in some people but not others. For example, in a study that was carefully designed to meet all the necessary conditions for successful intergroup contact, Stuart Cook (1984) found that only 40 percent of the participants showed a meaningful reduction in prejudice. Although this number was greater than the 12 percent of participants in a no-contact control group whose attitudes changed meaningfully over the same period of time, the results still suggest that about 60 percent of people who experience intergroup contact will not show meaningful attitude change. Several factors may inhibit attitude change in even the best-designed intergroup contact situations.

One such factor is the participants' preexisting intergroup attitudes. On the one hand, intergroup contact will probably result in very little attitude change for people who are already low in prejudice because their intergroup attitudes are already positive. On the other hand, the more prejudiced people are, the more likely they are to avoid intergroup contact. For example, Lilach Sagiv and Shalom Schwartz (1995) found that holding values related to lower prejudice, such as universalism, was positively correlated with readiness for intergroup contact among Israeli Christians, Jews, and Muslims, whereas holding value positions related to higher prejudice, such as security and conformity, was negatively correlated with readiness for intergroup contact. In addition, Oscar Ybarra and his colleagues (Ybarra, Stephan, Schaberg, & Lawrence, 2003) found that more prejudiced people required a greater amount of disconfirming evidence than less prejudiced people before they would give up an outgroup stereotype. Thus, more prejudiced people might be less likely to individuate outgroup members based on intergroup contact, reducing the impact that contact can have on their attitudes.

Another factor, related to prejudice, is intergroup anxiety. People higher in intergroup anxiety are more likely to avoid contact with members of outgroups that are the focus of their anxiety (Britt, Boniecki, Vescio, Biernat, & Brown, 1996; Plant & Devine, 2003). In contrast, White people who associate positive emotions with minority groups are more willing to engage in intergroup contact (Esses & Dovidio, 2002). Intergroup anxiety may be enhanced if anxious people are required to have contact with outgroup members and that enhanced anxiety may offset any benefits the contact might otherwise have (Hewstone, 1996). The quality of a person's prior experience with the outgroup also may be a factor. White people who have had negative experience with Black people tend to be higher on intergroup anxiety and to be more likely to expect the outcomes of intergroup contact to be negative, and so are more likely to avoid intergroup contact (Plant & Devine, 2003). Similarly, Linda Tropp (2003) found that members of minority groups who reported more personal experiences of discrimination had more pessimistic expectations for intergroup contact than did members of minority groups who reported fewer experiences of discrimination.

Finally, Walter and Cookie Stephan (1984) note that the normative climate outside the contact situation can have an effect on intergroup contact. They found that Anglo children whose friends had more positive attitudes toward Hispanics were more likely to have contact with Hispanic children than were Anglo children whose friends had more negative attitudes. They also found that peers' attitudes toward Hispanics had more effect on the Anglo children's intergroup contact than did their parents' attitudes. Thus, a number of factors exist that can attenuate the beneficial effects of intergroup contact, so perhaps it is not surprising that it does not have a larger impact on intergroup attitudes.

Models of the Contact Process

In his review of research on the contact hypothesis, Pettigrew (1998a) noted that after a great deal of activity during the 1950s and 1960s, research on the topic waned during the late 1970s. He attributed the decline in research to a lack of theories to explain how intergroup contact caused reductions in prejudice. That is, researchers had established that intergroup contact did, in fact, reduce prejudice and had established the conditions necessary for it to be effective, but no one had proposed any ideas about *how* it reduced prejudice. As a result, researchers felt that they had found out just about everything that they could about intergroup contact. That situation changed with the development of three models of processes by which contact reduces prejudice: Marilynn Brewer and Norman Miller's (1984) personalization model (see also Miller, 2002), Miles Hewstone and Rupert Brown's (1986; Hewstone, 1996) salient categorization model, and Samuel Gaertner and colleagues (Gaertner, Dovidio, Anastasio, Bachman, & Rust, 1993) common ingroup identity model (see also Gaertner & Dovidio, 2000).

All three models draw on social identity theory to explain how intergroup contact reduces prejudice. Recall from Chapter 8 that one aspect of social identity theory is that prejudice develops because people categorize others into ingroups and outgroups. Because people identify with their ingroups, they like members of those groups better than members of outgroups. Each of the models holds that intergroup contact that meets the conditions for success affects prejudice by changing how people conceptualize ingroups and outgroups. However, each model proposes that a different type of categorization process results in reduced prejudice.

Personalization   The **personalization model** (also called the **decategorization model**) proposes that intergroup contact reduces prejudice by leading people to see members of the outgroup as individuals rather than as members of social categories: Viewing people in personal terms rather than as members of groups then leads to liking for them and so to less prejudice toward them (Brewer & Miller, 1984; Miller, 2002). The process operates in this way: When equal status groups work cooperatively toward a common goal, the members of each group come to see the other group in complex terms rather than as a simple, stereotypic social category (hence, the term *decategorization*). For example, rather than thinking of outgroup members as stereotypically identical, participants in intergroup contact begin to identify subgroups within the overall group and become aware of the unique characteristics of individual group members. They also come to see that members of the other group have multiple social identities. For example, a White participant may come to realize that a Hispanic woman's social identity consists of more than just her ethnic identity; in addition, she is a woman, she is a member of an occupational group, she has particular hobbies and interests, she may be a mother, and so forth. Intergroup contact also may lead the White participant to think of herself in more complex terms (Roccas & Brewer, 2002) and to see similarities between aspects of her social identity (such as woman, mother, worker) and those of the Hispanic woman.

The awareness that members of both ingroup and outgroup members have complex social identities lessens the importance of group boundaries, which come to be seen as "fuzzy" and permeable rather than distinct and impenetrable. It also makes group categories less useful as a source of information about individual group members; recall from Chapter 3 that one reason stereotypes form is that they presumably provide useful information about other people. However, as one gets to know a member of an outgroup and see all the ways that person is similar to and different than the stereotypical member of that group, the group stereotype loses its usefulness as a source of information about the person.

An experiment conducted by Benjamin Crisp, Miles Hewstone, and Mark Rubin (2001, Experiment 2) illustrates the decategorization process. They operationally defined ingroup and outgroup in terms of competing universities in the United Kingdom. Participants in the experimental group were induced to think of outgroup members in terms of multiple social identities: not only their university affiliation, but also their gender, age, academic major, whether they lived in university housing or off-campus, and national origin (British or international student). Participants in the control group were induced to think of outgroup members solely in terms of their university affiliation. The researchers found that, compared to participants in the control group, those in the experimental group viewed the outgroup members more in terms of individual characteristics and less in terms of being members of a competing group; that is, they decategorized the outgroup. Participants in the experimental group also made more positive evaluations of the outgroup members.

Although Crisp and his colleagues (2001) found that decategorization reduced intergroup bias, they also found that it did not completely eliminate the bias. To fully reduce prejudice, outgroup members must be personalized; relations with outgroup members must take a person-to-person rather than a group-to-group form. That is, one must think of individual group members in terms of the ways in which they are similar to and different from oneself personally rather than oneself as a member of one's ingroup. This change in viewpoint is facilitated by the extent to which the intergroup contact situation has acquaintance potential and provides the opportunity for the formation of intergroup friendships. As we saw earlier, such friendships increase empathy for members of the other group and reduce intergroup anxiety and prejudice. Friendships are promoted through self-disclosure, providing the other person with information about oneself and one's attitudes, values, beliefs, and so forth. Although the discovery that one shares attitudes and values with another person does promote liking and friendship, self-disclosure can be a two-edged sword: If dissimilarities are discovered, liking may not increase, and, in cases of extreme disagreement, can actually decrease (Berscheid & Reis, 1998). Intergroup contact should therefore be structured in ways that emphasize similarities between members of different groups.

One shortcoming of the personalization process is that increased liking for some outgroup members does not always generalize to liking for the outgroup in general. That is, people may come to like the specific outgroup members they have contact with, but their attitudes toward the outgroup as a whole may not change. For example, Nikki Scarberry and her colleagues (Scarberry, Ratcliff, Lord, Lanicek, & Desforges, 1997) had college students work on a cooperative task with a confederate they thought was a gay man. Before they started the task, participants reported how much they thought they would like the gay man they would work with. Then during the task, the confederate made analogies linking information that was used in the task to other events. In one condition of the experiment, the analogies involved self-disclosure, such as "Like when I got this bruise and it swelled;" in the other condition, the analogies were impersonal, such as "Like when a person bruises" (Scarberry et al., 1997, p. 1297). After the task was completed, the participants reported how much they liked the other person. The researchers found that personalization made no difference: In both conditions the participants reported that they liked the confederate better than they had expected and the amount of change was the same in both conditions. However, the researchers also found that attitudes toward gay men in general improved in the impersonal analogies condition but not in the self-disclosure condition. That is, cooperative contact improved liking for an individual gay man with and without self-disclosure on his part, but the interaction led to more liking for gay men in general only when there was no self-disclosure.

Scarberry and her colleagues (1997) suggested that the self-disclosures may have led the participants to see the confederate as not being a typical member of his group—he was "an exception to the rule" (see Chapter 3)—so the participants' liking for him did not apply to the group as a whole. Supporting this interpretation, Nurcan Ensari and Norman Miller (2002) found that self-disclosure by outgroup members improved attitudes toward the outgroup as a whole when the disclosers were seen as a typical member of the outgroup but not when they were seen as atypical.

Salient categorization   The **salient categorization model** (also called the **mutual intergroup differentiation model;** Hewstone & Brown, 1986; Hewstone, 1996) proposes that generalization occurs only if group members are seen as typical of their group. Like the personalization model, the salient categorization model holds that it is essential that outgroups be differentiated—that is, the outgroup must come to be seen in nonstereotypic terms—and that intergroup cooperation under conditions of equality promotes this process. However, for group members to be seen as typical so that generalization can occur, group membership must remain salient during intergroup contact. Thus, whereas the personalization model holds that group categories must be made less salient for intergroup attitudes to improve, the salient categorization model holds that group categories must remain salient for generalization to occur.

Jan van Oudenhoven, Jan Groenewoud, and Miles Hewstone (1996) showed the importance of maintaining group salience in a study conducted in the Netherlands. Dutch high school students worked on two cooperative problem-solving tasks with a same-age confederate of Turkish descent (Turks are a negatively stereotyped group in the Netherlands). In the experimental condition, the confederate's Turkish group identity was made salient by the experimenter before the students started the first task and during a break between tasks; in the control condition, the confederate's nationality was not made salient. The researchers found that high group salience for the confederate led to more positive ratings of Turks in general than did low group salience. High group salience has also been found to boost the positive effects of intergroup contact for adults in natural contact settings. For example, compared to low group salience, under conditions of high salience, contact results in lower intergroup anxiety and more positive attitudes toward the outgroup as a whole (Greenland & Brown, 1999; Voci & Hewstone, 2003).

The importance of the outgroup members' being seen as typical of their group while still disconfirming aspects of the group stereotype was shown in a classic study conducted by David Wilder (1984). College students interacted with a confederate who portrayed a student from a rival college who appeared to be either typical or atypical of students of that college on a number of characteristics. The confederate also either confirmed an additional aspect of the outgroup stereotype by acting in an unfriendly manner or disconfirmed it by acting in a friendly manner. Wilder found that friendliness resulted in more positive ratings of students at the other college only when the confederate was otherwise seen as typical of its students. Other researchers have confirmed that for positive attitudes to generalize from the group member to the group as a whole, a stereotype-disconfirming member must be seen as otherwise typical. These results have been replicated for artificial groups set up for laboratory research (Wilder, Simon, & Faith, 1996), political groups (Ensari & Miller, 2002; Wilder et al., 1996), religious groups (Ensari & Miller, 2002), and nationality groups (Brown, Vivian, & Hewstone, 1999). However, perceptions of why a typical outgroup member acts in a nonstereotypic way can limit attitude change. Attitudes improve only if the behavior is seen as representing a true characteristic of the person that is part of the person's normal behavior pattern. If the behavior is seen as a result of the person making a special effort to behave in a nonstereotypic manner or if the behavior is seen as caused by situational factors (such as adherence to situation-specific norms), then there will be no change in intergroup attitudes (Wilder et al., 1996).

Hewstone and Brown (1986; Hewstone, 1996) acknowledge that their model requires intergroup contact to balance two competing processes: Although stereotypes initially define what the typical outgroup member is like, group members must come to be seen in nonstereotypical terms; at the same time, they must be perceived as typical of their group. Hewstone and Brown suggest that this balance can be achieved by structuring intergroup contact in two ways. First, the contact situation should emphasize the unique strengths that each group has to contribute. This procedure allows each group to maintain a positive view of its own contributions to the intergroup effort and to see the positive contributions made by the other group. At the same time, group categories can remain salient because each group makes a unique contribution to goal attainment. Second, although group members should act in ways that disconfirm the stereotype the other group holds of them, and thus promote decategorization, these behaviors should involve aspects of the stereotype that do not have negative implications for the other group. Such negative implications can arouse ingroup identification; increased ingroup identification leads to seeing outgroups in stereotypic terms (see Chapter 8), which impedes decategorization. For example, the stereotype of "they think they're better than us" is relevant to the ingroup and so bringing it to mind can have negative effects; in contrast, the stereotype of "they're lazy" has no implications for the ingroup.

Common ingroup identity   Whereas the personalization model focuses on decategorizing outgroup members and the mutual intergroup differentiation model focuses on salient categorization of outgroup members, the **common ingroup identity model** (Gaertner et al., 1993; Gaertner & Dovidio, 2000) focuses on inducing ingroup and outgroup members to recategorize themselves into a single group for which they share a common identity. The model proposes that the presence or absence of the four conditions necessary for successful intergroup contact affect how people view the intergroup situation (what the model calls their *group representation*): The members of two groups can

- recategorize themselves as belonging to one group with a common ingroup identity (the *one group representation*);
- recategorize themselves as belonging to one group with two subgroups in which the two subgroups retain their original identities while adding a common ingroup identity (the *dual identity representation*);
- retain the view that they constitute two separate groups with no common identity (the *separate groups representation*); or
- personalize the members of the other group and see them in individual rather than group terms (the *individuals representation*).

People's group representation influences their attitudes and behaviors toward members of the other group:

- a separate groups representation results in no change in attitudes and holds the potential for intergroup conflict;
- an individuals representation (personalization) leads to more positive attitudes toward the individual members of the outgroup who take part in the intergroup contact, but there is little or no generalization to the outgroup as a whole; and
- a one group or dual identity representation (development of a common ingroup viewpoint) leads to positive attitudes toward all members of the former outgroup.

Inducing members of two groups to develop a common identity as a means of reducing prejudice makes use of some of the social identity processes we discussed in Chapter 8. For example, identification with a group leads to ingroup favoritism, so recategorizing oneself and the members of another group as belonging to a single group should result in viewing them in favorable terms. In addition, people see ingroup members as sharing their attitudes, values, beliefs, and so forth, and such perceptions of similarity can lead to liking and friendship. That is, thinking of oneself and others as "we" rather than as "us and them" fosters a positive view of the others and so results in the elimination of, or at least a great reduction in, prejudice. After all, it is difficult to be prejudiced against people with whom one identifies.

Samuel Gaertner, John Dovidio, and their colleagues have conducted a great deal of laboratory research on the validity of their model. The general pattern of the research has been to form two groups, using either natural groups such as political parties (Gaertner et al., 1999) or randomly assigning participants to artificial groups, such as by telling them they share a common personality trait (Dovidio, Gaertner, & Validzic, 1998) or having them wear color-coded badges (Gaertner, Mann, Murrell, & Dovidio, 1989). (Recall from Chapters 3 and 8 how easy it is to create ingroups and outgroups.) The researchers then bring the members of the two groups together to work on a cooperative task and induce them to form either a one group or separate groups representation of the intergroup situation. Group representations are manipulated by having members of the two groups sit across a table from each other versus sitting alternately around the table (Gaertner et al., 1999), dress in common clothing (such as lab coats) versus individual clothing (Dovidio, Gaertner, Isen, & Lowrance, 1995), or share a prize for successful task completion versus separate prizes for each group (Gaertner et al., 1999). After they complete the task, participants make two sets of ratings: the extent to which they thought of themselves and the other participants as members of one group, as members of two groups, or as individuals, and the extent to which they liked the members of the two groups and thought they had positive traits such as being honest, cooperative, friendly, and so forth. These studies found that compared to a separate groups representation, perceptions of a common identity led to less bias, as did perception of the other participants as individuals (as the personalization model would predict). In addition, one group and individuals representations led to an increase in positive behaviors such as self-disclosure and helping (Dovidio et al., 1997).

Support for the common ingroup identity model has also come from field research. In these studies, in addition to assessing participants' group representations and attitudes toward the outgroup, this research has also assessed the extent to which the conditions necessary for successful intergroup contact were present in the research setting. This research has involved managerial employees at two banks being merged (Gaertner, Dovidio, & Bachman, 1996), nationality groups (Eller & Abrams, 2003, 2004), and children in stepfamilies (with the dependent variable in this case being stepfamily harmony; Banker & Gaertner, 1998). These studies have found that positive contact was related to a stronger one group representation and a weaker separate groups representation, and that a one group representation was in turn related to more positive perceptions of the outgroup members in the contact situation, less intergroup anxiety, and less prejudice toward the outgroup in general.

One situation in which group representations have not been found to be related to bias is intergroup contact in schools (Gaertner, Rust, Dovidio, Bachman, & Anastasio, 1996; Wittig & Molina, 2000). These studies have found that although the conditions of intergroup contact are related to group representations in the manner the common ingroup identity model predicts, there is little or no relationship between group representations and bias. Instead, Michele Wittig and Ludwin Molina (2000) found that the extent to which students were interested in interacting with members of other groups had the strongest relationship to bias. It is not clear why the common ingroup identity model does not fit the school situation as well as it does other situations. One possible explanation is that attending the same school does not provide a strong enough common identity to produce reductions in bias.

Although there is good support for the common ingroup identity model, researchers have identified two potential drawbacks to the creation of a common ingroup identity. The first is that if ingroup members define the common ingroup in terms of themselves (that is, if they assume that the outgroup will take on the ingroup identity), then intergroup bias can increase (Mummendey & Wenzel, 1999). For example, Sven Waldzus and Amélie Mummendey (2004) conducted an experiment in which Germans were induced to think of themselves in terms of one of two higher-level groups: Europeans, a category that included Poles, or Western Europeans, a category that excluded Poles. In each case, the researchers found that the participants thought of the higher-order category in terms of their German nationality. The researchers also found that the participants expressed more bias against Poles in the European condition than in the Western European condition. Waldzus and Mummendey explained the outcome by suggesting that sharing a common ingroup identity with what, from many Germans' point of view, is a lower status subgroup (Poles) made the German-Polish ingroup-outgroup contrast more salient. This salient contrast increased the participants' German social identity, which increased their bias (see Chapter 8).

The second problem is that creation of a common ingroup identity may lead to increased bias against common outgroups, groups that the former ingroup and outgroup both view as outgroups. For example, Thomas Kessler and Amélie Mummendey (2001) conducted a survey of people living in former East and West Germany. Prior to German reunification, residents of the two regions had looked on each other as outgroups; afterwards, some developed a strong common identity as Germans while others placed more importance on their regional identities and developed a weaker common identity. The researchers found that respondents who had developed a stronger common identity expressed less bias against members of the former outgroup, as common ingroup identity theory would predict. However, they also found that a stronger identity as German was associated with greater bias against non-Germans. Kessler and Mummendey explained their finding by suggesting that although the development of a common ingroup identity reduces the salience of former ingroup-outgroup distinctions, it increases the salience of common outgroups, leading to increased bias against them. Thus, development of a common ingroup identity can be a two-edged sword, decreasing bias against some targets while having the potential to increase bias against others.

Pettigrew's combined model   It seems at first glance that the three models of how intergroup contact reduces prejudice contradict one other: The personalization model holds that prejudice reduction derives from decategorization, the salient categorization model holds that it derives from maintaining group categories, and the common ingroup identity model holds that it derives from recategorizing the ingroup and outgroup into one common group. All have research to support them, so which is correct? Pettigrew's (1998a) answer to this question is that all are correct, but that each represents a different stage of the prejudice reduction process.

Figure 12.4 shows Pettigrew's (1998a) combined intergroup contact model. As do all three individual models, the combined model begins by saying that for intergroup contact to reduce prejudice, it must involve groups of equal status who cooperate to attain common goals. The situation must also provide acquaintance potential and the prejudice reduction effort must have institutional support. In addition, as noted earlier, there are conditions that although not necessary for successful intergroup contact, make success more likely (see Table 12.1). Pettigrew's

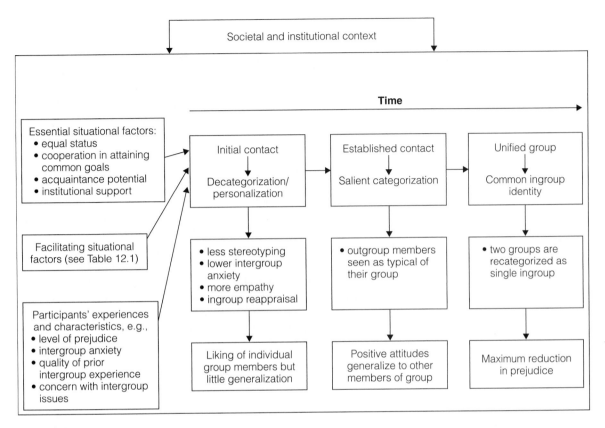

FIGURE **12.4**

PETTIGREW'S COMBINED INTERGROUP CONTACT MODEL

Situational and individual factors facilitate or hinder the effectiveness of intergroup contact. Under the proper conditions, contact leads to decategorization: less stereotyping, lower intergroup anxiety, increased empathy, reappraisal of the ingroup, and behavior change. As a result, participants like the members of the outgroup they are interacting with, but this liking does not generalize to other members of the outgroup. Over time, outgroup members may come to be seen as typical of their group through salient categorization, so that their positive characteristics are attributed to their group as a whole and positive attitudes generalize to the group as a whole. Finally, the members of the old ingroup and outgroup may come to develop a common ingroup identity and see themselves as members of a single ingroup, resulting in maximum reduction of prejudice.

Adapted from Pettigrew (1998a), Figure 2, p. 77. Used with permission from *Annual Review of Psychology.* Vol. 49. Copyright © 1998 by Annual Reviews. www.annualreviews.org.

model also acknowledges that people bring their unique personalities and sets of experiences with them into the contact situation and that these factors, such as level of prejudice and ingroup anxiety, can influence their individual contact experiences. In addition, Pettigrew notes that every intergroup contact situation is nested within broader societal and institutional contexts that can affect both the outcome of the process and the extent to which attitudes that are formed by contact generalize outside the contact setting.

Pettigrew (1998a) proposes that, within those constraints, personalization is the most likely first outcome of intergroup contact. Personalization of outgroup members reduces stereotyping and intergroup anxiety, increases empathy for outgroup members, and leads people to rethink their concepts of the ingroup. These changes lead to liking for the outgroup members with whom people have contact, but that liking does not necessarily generalize to the outgroup as a whole. Over time, continued contact with the outgroup can lead to salient recategorization, in which the outgroup members with whom people have contact come to be seen as typical of their group as whole. This change in perception increases the likelihood that the attitudes developed in the contact situation will generalize to the outgroup as a whole. Finally, continued contact might lead to the development of a common ingroup identity in which subgroup identities are subsumed within an overreaching common identity (the dual identity representation) or in which subgroup identities are abandoned in favor of a common identity (the one group representation). Reaching this stage results in the maximum reduction of prejudice.

Pettigrew (1998a) also notes that while it is conceptually useful to present the contact process as a series of discrete steps, the stages are not always distinct from one another and the processes they represent can overlap. For example, in regard to personalization and salient categorization, Hewstone (1996) and Miller (2002) have pointed out that cues that keep group membership salient often persist even as personalization takes place. As Miller (2002) noted,

> Skin color, hair texture and pigmentation, and facial features make the racial/ethnic identity of Black and Anglo Americans clear to members of both categories when they interact. Linguistic cues identify northerners and southerners to each other. Secondary sex traits, such as facial hair and pitch of voice, make sexual identity manifest when males and females interact. With less consistency, habitually worn religious emblems (a cross versus a Star of David and a skull cap) identify Palestinian Christians and Jews, and modes of dress identify blue- and white-collar workers in the United States. For most groups between whom there is strife, any contact at the interpersonal level occurs in the presence of category-identifying information. (pp. 399–400)

Marilynn Brewer and Samuel Gaertner (2001) have further suggested that the order in which the processes described in the combined model take place depends on the nature of the contact situation. For example, contact that emphasizes group-to-group interactions, such as the Robbers Cave study described in Chapter 8, may initially elicit salient categorization or development of a common ingroup identity prior to personalization. In contrast, contact that emphasizes person-to-person interactions, such as among neighbors or coworkers, may initially elicit personalization. Thus, Gaertner, Dovidio, Banker, and colleagues (2000) noted that in the Robbers Cave study, formation of a common group identity preceded personalization. In addition, they pointed out that intergroup contact moved back and forth among the stages of the combined model, with intergroup relations sometimes regressing to hostility, albeit at a lower level, following periods of successful cooperation. Thus, the improvement of intergroup relations through intergroup contact is complex and sometimes difficult process, but one that holds great potential for success.

EDUCATIONAL INTERVENTIONS

In Chapter 7, we saw that prejudice begins to develop in childhood. To counter this development, psychologists and educators have developed a number of school-based interventions aimed at reducing or preventing the development of prejudice in children. This section examines two commonly used interventions, cooperative learning and multicultural and anti-bias education. First, though, we look at school desegregation, a social policy that many hoped would improve intergroup relations among children by fostering intergroup contact.

School Desegregation

In deciding the landmark 1954 case *Brown v. Board of Education,* the United States Supreme Court ruled that segregated public education violated minority group children's right to equal protection of the law and ordered that public schools be desegregated. The Court's focus was on providing equality of education for all children, but a group of 32 social scientists had written an *amicus curiae* (friend of the court) brief expressing their opinion that desegregation would have a variety of positive educational, social, and psychological effects (Effects of segregation, 1953). One of the effects listed in what became known as the *Social Science Statement* was the potential for improved intergroup relations. According to the Social Science Statement, this potential was based on the belief that desegregated schools would provide the opportunity for positive intergroup contact. In effect, the drafters of the Social Science Statement saw school desegregation as an opportunity to implement the principles of the contact hypothesis on a national scale.

The eventual implementation of school desegregation led to a flurry of research on its effectiveness in improving the outcomes discussed in the Social Science Statement (see Schofield, 2001b, for a summary of the results of this research). In terms of intergroup relations, the research findings indicated that desegregation had inconsistent effects. Harold Fishbein (2002) examined the results of 26 studies of the effect of school desegregation on intergroup attitudes, 16 of which assessed Black students' attitudes and 22 of which assessed White students' attitudes. He found that the most common outcome was an increase, rather than a decrease in prejudice: 44 percent of the studies of Black students' attitudes and 45 percent of the studies of White students' attitudes found more prejudice among students in desegregated schools than among students in schools that were still racially segregated. Fishbein did note that 38 percent of the studies of Black students' attitudes found less prejudice among students attending desegregated schools, but only 23 percent of the studies of White students' attitudes did so. These findings led Schneider (2004) to conclude that "desegregation is no poster child for the contact hypothesis" (p. 391). However, two issues need to be considered in evaluating these findings: the distinction between desegregation and integration and the distinction between short-term effects and long-term effects.

Desegregation versus integration   In 1969, Thomas Pettigrew made a famous distinction between desegregation and integration. As he later phrased it, "Mere desegregation involves only a mixture of groups no longer formally separated. It does not refer to the quality of the intergroup interaction. Desegregated campus life can range from positive intergroup contact to a living hell of intergroup strife. . . . Genuine integration refers to positive intergroup contact that meets [the necessary] conditions for prejudice-reducing contact. . . . Integration goes beyond present-day U.S. society by providing the conditions for removing the racial and ethnic threats and stereotypes that divide Americans" (Pettigrew, 1998b, p. 272). Although the Social Science Statement (Effects of segregation, 1953) had said that, in Pettigrew's terms, integration, not mere desegregation, was necessary for intergroup contact to improve intergroup attitudes, researchers have noted from the outset that, in most cases, schools desegregated but did not integrate (see, for example, Cook, 1979; Schofield, 2001b). That is, most school desegregation programs did not implement the conditions necessary for successful intergroup contact.

Janet Schofield (2001a; Schofield & Eurich-Fulcer, 2001) has pointed out that many schools that are officially desegregated are actually segregated internally. One way in which this internal resegregation occurs is through the use of ability grouping or academic tracking, in which students who score high on standardized achievement tests are grouped together in accelerated classes while those with average or below average scores are grouped together in standard or remedial classes. For example, Schofield (1989) found that in one desegregated school more than 80 percent of the accelerated track students were White whereas more than 80 percent of the standard track students were Black (see also, Oakes, 1996). One ironic aspect of Schofield's finding was that the school she studied had been specifically established to be a model of integrated, not just desegregated, education. In addition to academic tracking, bilingual education programs, by their nature, segregate students less fluent in English from other students for most of the school day (Khmelkov & Hallinan, 1999; Schofield, 2001a). Vladimir Khmelkov and Maureen Hallinan (1999) further note that extracurricular activities are also frequently segregated: "White students . . . are more likely than Black students to participate in such activities as academic or art clubs, student government, or individual sports requiring special equipment. Black students, on the other hand, tend to participate more often than Whites in sports teams and band" (p. 638). Finally, as we noted in Chapter 7, students often voluntarily segregate themselves by race. For example, in a school with a student body that was almost exactly 50 percent Black and 50 percent White, Janet Schofield and Andrew Sagar (1977) found that on a typical day 95 percent of the students sat next to a student of the same race at lunch.

This internal resegregation has negative effects on two of the conditions necessary for intergroup contact to result in improved intergroup relations. First, it clearly undermines acquaintance potential (Khmelkov & Hallinan, 1999; Schofield, 2001a): Students who rarely meet one another cannot get to know each other. For example, Lincoln Quillian and Mary Campbell (2003) found that interracial friendships were more common at schools with more diverse student bodies than at schools where almost all the students were of the same race. Second, and perhaps less obviously, resegregation undermines the equal status of majority and minority students. For example, academic tracking produces a status hierarchy among students, with, as we noted earlier, the higher status accelerated track being populated primarily by White students and the lower status standard track being populated primarily by Black students. "This means that students are not only resegregated but resegregated in a way that can reinforce traditional stereotypes and engender hostility" (Schofield, 2001a, p. 638).

In addition to the effect academic tracking has on acquaintance potential and equal status, other school policies can also undermine the necessary conditions for successful intergroup contact. For example, administrative decisions, such as the choice of students to represent a school at public events, can influence students' perceptions of relative group status. Schofield (2001a) relates an incident in which a Black student refused to watch a televised quiz show in which a team from his school competed. "He explained that he did not want to see the program because the team from his school, which had a student body that was just over half Black, consisted entirely of White children. He said bitterly, 'They shouldn't call this school Wexler [a pseudonym]; they should call it White School'" (p. 639; brackets in original). In addition, school and teacher policies that emphasize competition rather than cooperation between students reduce the potential for creating situations in which members of different racial and ethnic groups cooperate to achieve common goals (Schofield, 2001a). Finally, as we noted in our discussion of the contact hypothesis, institutional support, especially in the form of the commitment of school principals to integration is essential for success. If that commitment is absent, nothing will change (Khmelkov & Hallinan, 1999; Schofield, 2001a).

Long-term versus short-term effects   Schofield (2001b) has noted that one of the shortcomings of most research on school desegregation is that it focused primarily on short-term effects, ignoring any long-term benefits desegregation may have (see also Stephan, 1986). That is, researchers generally assessed the effects of desegregation after only a brief period of implementation, usually a year or less, and paid little attention to later life outcomes (Schofield, 1991). However, Schofield (2001b) has pointed out that the research that has been conducted on the long-term effects of school desegregation has uncovered some positive effects. For example, as adults, Blacks who attended desegregated schools are more likely to live in integrated neighborhoods, are more likely to have White friends, and are more likely to work in desegregated settings (which often provide more in salary and benefits than predominantly Black work settings). Although there has been less research on long-term outcomes for Whites, as adults those who attended desegregated schools say they are more willing to live in integrated neighborhoods, are more likely to have Black friends, and are more likely to work in desegregated settings. Also, as we noted in our discussion of the contact hypothesis, White adults who attended desegregated schools exhibit less prejudice than those who attended segregated schools. Thus, despite the pessimistic results of research on the short-term effects of school segregation on intergroup relations, the research on its longer term effects provides a basis for optimism. In addition, as Janet Schofield and Rebecca Eurich-Fulcer (2001) note, the research provides guidance on how *not* to implement intergroup contact. Conversely, by highlighting the mistakes one must avoid, the results provide guidance on how to best structure intergroup contact to obtain its benefits.

Cooperative Learning

Although most school desegregation programs did not establish the conditions necessary for successful intergroup contact, what happens when those conditions are met? A number of educational techniques, collectively referred to as **cooperative learning,** have been devised to create group learning environments which implement the necessary contact conditions as part of the day-to-day educational process (see, for example, Slavin, 2001; Stephan & Stephan, 2001). One example of these techniques is the *jigsaw classroom* developed by Elliot Aronson and his colleagues (Aronson, Blaney, Stephan, Sikes, & Snapp, 1978; Aronson & Patnoe, 1997). In the jigsaw classroom:

- Students are divided into teams of six members, balanced in terms of gender, ethnicity, and academic ability.
- Each lesson is divided into six parts, with each team member responsible for becoming an "expert" on one part. For example, in a geography class focusing on a particular country, one team member becomes an expert on the country's history, another on its economics, another on its culture, and so forth.
- The students study their topics and then discuss them with the experts on their topics from the other teams.
- The students then meet as teams and each member teaches the others his or her area of expertise. This is where the term *jigsaw classroom* comes from: Each lesson is like a jigsaw puzzle, divided into pieces; the students then put their pieces together to form the "big picture" (Aronson et al., 1978).
- Finally, students take a quiz on the material with their individual scores being combined into a single team score.

As Iain Walker and Mary Crogan (1998) note, the cooperative learning process creates conditions necessary for successful intergroup contact: "Students have equal status contact (each has a unique and necessary piece of information), they work interdependently (each depends on the others to be able to achieve their desired goals), and they work in pursuit of a common goal (good grades, learning, teacher praise), all with the sanction of authorities (teachers)" (p. 382). In addition, interacting across teams with fellow experts and within teams with other team members provides acquaintance potential.

How effective is cooperative learning in reducing prejudice? David Johnson and Robert Johnson (2000) examined the results of 61 studies that compared the effects of cooperative learning versus individual study on intergroup relations. Sixty-one percent of the studies found that cooperative learning reduced prejudice and discrimination toward outgroup members who were teammates. However, Fishbein (2002) has noted that studies of cooperative learning have provided little evidence that its effects generalize to attitudes toward teammates' outgroups as a whole. More optimistically, Robert Slavin (2001) has noted that cooperative learning frequently results in the development of cross-ethnic group friendships. As we saw in our earlier discussion of the contact hypothesis, such friendships can play an important role in the generalization of prejudice reduction from individual outgroup members to the group as a whole.

Multicultural and Anti-Bias Education

Whereas cooperative learning reduces prejudice by providing experiences that allow students to get to know members of other groups and see them in a positive light, multicultural and anti-bias education take a more didactic approach using traditional teaching techniques (Stephan & Stephan, 2001). Although multicultural and anti-bias education overlap to some extent, they have somewhat different goals (Aboud & Levy, 2000), so we will discuss them separately.

Multicultural education   **Multicultural education** is an umbrella term that covers a variety of programs designed to teach students about the ethnic, racial, religious, and other groups in society. Multicultural education has five components (Banks, 2001):

- The integration of information on the history and culture of the groups and their contributions to society as a whole into the curriculum.
- Educating students on the ways in which cultural assumptions and perspectives influence the interpretation of events. For example, James Banks (2001) suggests that a history teacher could have students discuss how a Lakota Sioux historian might describe the westward expansion of the United States.
- Helping students develop positive attitudes toward social groups other than their own.
- Using teaching strategies that accommodate different learning styles.
- Creating a school culture that promotes equality.

The multicultural education approach is based on the belief that ignorance is a major cause of prejudice, with a lack of accurate information about other groups leading to intergroup anxiety and the use of stereotypes (Stephan & Stephan, 2001). Therefore, these programs try to "provide students with the knowledge and attitudes necessary to understand, respect, and interact harmoniously as equals with members of different ethnic groups" (Aboud & Levy, 2000, pp. 277–278).

There is disagreement about just how effective multicultural education is in reducing prejudice. Walter Stephan and Cookie Stephan (2001) take an optimistic view based on their review of the results of 41 studies of the effectiveness of multicultural education. They classified 88 percent of the studies as showing that the programs evaluated had some positive effects and no negative effects on prejudice, and classified only 5 percent of the studies as having found predominantly negative effects. Stephan and Stephan concluded that, despite some weaknesses, multicultural education is an effective tool for reducing prejudice. In contrast, Rebecca Bigler (1999) has taken a more pessimistic view, pointing out a number of weaknesses in the research (some of which Stephan and Stephan also noted). For example, Bigler called attention to the fact that although the results of published studies tend to support the effectiveness of multicultural education, many unpublished studies (such as doctoral dissertations) show no effect. Bigler also noted that within studies the effects of multicultural education are not consistent across dependent variables, with positive effects being found with some measures but not with others. There is also little evidence for long-term effects. Based on her review of the literature, Bigler concluded that multicultural education has been relatively ineffective in reducing prejudice in children. However, she also noted that such programs are potentially beneficial but need a stronger grounding in current understanding of the nature of children's racial attitudes and how education influences (and does not influence) those attitudes.

Anti-bias education   **Anti-bias education** "aims to provide students with a heightened awareness of institutional racism [and other forms of institutional bias] and with the skills to reduce it within their sphere of influence" (Aboud & Levy, 2000, p. 278). Anti-bias education programs instruct students about the nature of bias, its history, and its current forms and effects. The programs use lectures, media presentations, role-playing (such as the blue eyes/brown eyes exercise described in Chapter 7), and class discussion as teaching tools. Anti-bias education can either be part of a multicultural education program or can be a separate program.

Josette McGregor (1993) reviewed the results of 26 studies of the outcomes of anti-bias education programs and concluded that they were generally effective in reducing prejudice. She did note, however, that they tended to produce more change in younger students than in older students and that about 12 percent of the studies found more prejudice after the program than before. In addition, as with multicultural education, there is little research evaluating the long-term effects of anti-bias education. Overall, then, it would seem that multicultural education and anti-bias education are promising programs, but require more research on what makes them work so that they can be implemented more effectively (Bigler, 1999; McGregor, 1993).

WORKPLACE INTERVENTIONS

The increasing diversity of the North American workforce has led to an increased interest in the dynamics of diversity in organizations. One result of this interest has been the development of programs designed to increase the representation of women and minority group members in the workplace, to remove barriers to their career advancement, and to deal with the intergroup tensions that can accompany increased workforce diversity (see, for example, Cox, 1994, 2001; Thomas, 1991). Roosevelt Thomas (1991) identified three broad types of workplace diversity initiatives: affirmative action, valuing diversity (also called valuing differences), and managing diversity. We briefly discuss each type below. When thinking about these programs it is important to bear in mind that, unlike the educational programs we just discussed, workplace programs generally are not directly aimed at creating long-term, generalized attitude change. Rather, their goal is to create more diverse organizations and to help those organizations and their employees work more effectively and efficiently (Bendick, Eagan, & Lofhjelm, 2001); any effect on intergroup attitudes outside the workplace is seen as a side benefit.

Affirmative Action

Affirmative action programs consist of "voluntary and mandatory efforts undertaken [by organizations] to combat discrimination and to provide equal opportunity in . . . employment for all" (American Psychological Association, 1996, p. 2). Although the word "mandatory" is part of the definition of affirmative action, most programs are voluntary: In the United States, only federal government agencies, federal government contractors, and a few companies under court orders are required to have affirmative action programs. Thus, in the private sector in 1995, only about 3 percent of U.S. companies were required to have affirmative action plans (Reskin, 1998). However, voluntary affirmative action programs are fairly common. For example, Barbara Reskin (1998) found that 40 percent of a sample of large corporations in the New York City area had affirmative action plans for recruiting members of minority groups. Although affirmative action originated in the United States, affirmative action policies have been established in a number of other countries as well (Crosby, Ferdman, & Wingate, 2001). In thinking about affirmative action, it is important to bear in mind that, as noted in Box 12.3, the term *affirmative action* can mean different things to different people and that not all those meanings are correct.

Affirmative action programs are not intended to reduce prejudice or to improve intergroup relations. As Thomas (1991) noted, the goals of affirmative action are the "creation of [a] diverse work force [and] upward mobility for minorities and women" (p. 28). Affirmative action programs have generally met these goals, resulting in increased representation of and more promotions for women and minority group members in organizations with affirmative action policies (Crosby, Iyer, Clayton, & Downing, 2003). Affirmative action also can have economic benefits for companies. For example, researchers have found that, compared to companies with less diverse workforces, more diverse companies have higher stock prices, productivity, profitability, and market share, and their shareholders have a higher return on investment (see, for example, Johnson, 1998; Richard, 2000; Wright, Ferris, Hiller, & Kroll, 1995).

Although affirmative action programs are not designed to affect prejudice, the results of some research suggest that they can. For example, a fairly large number of laboratory studies have found that people hold more negative attitudes toward employees who may have benefited from affirmative action, seeing them as less competent and less qualified than other employees (see Crosby et al., 2003, for a summary of this research). In addition, Gregory Maio and Victoria Esses (1998) found that reading about affirmative action primed negative attitudes toward immigrants in a sample of Canadian college students. Their findings suggest that negative attitudes toward beneficiaries of affirmative action may generalize to entire outgroups. However, the results of field research paint a different

12.3   *What Does Affirmative Action Mean?*

Most people interpret affirmative action to mean a program that gives preference to or sets quotas for hiring and promoting women and members of minority groups regardless of their qualifications as a way to make up for past societal discrimination (Eberhardt & Fiske, 1994). However, preferential affirmative action programs are legal in the United States only if they are designed to remedy past discrimination carried out by the organization using the program; they cannot be used as a remedy for general societal discrimination and they cannot involve quota systems (see, for example, Stoker, 1998). A problem for research lies in the fact that most researchers simply ask people about affirmative action and allow them to apply their own, perhaps mistaken, meaning to the term. For example, Laura Stoker (1998) found that opposition to affirmative action among respondents to a national survey varied as a function of how the program was described: 76 percent opposed it when it was described in general terms, but opposition was reduced to 59 percent when it was described as a remedy for past discrimination by an organization.

Affirmative action programs can also take various forms (see, for example, Bobocel, Son Hing, Davey, Stanley, & Zanna, 1998): *Equal treatment* programs are designed to remove organizational barriers to members of target groups, such as women and minorities, but everyone in the organization can take advantage of these programs, even if they are not members of a targeted group. Mentoring and parental leave are examples of such programs. *Differential treatment* programs treat members of targeted and nontargeted groups differently, but only in limited circumstances that recognize individual merit. For example, membership in a targeted group might be used to break a tie between two equally qualified job applicants or candidates for promotion. *Preferential treatment* programs use group membership as a direct factor in a selection process. For example, selection for promotion might be based on points awarded for various factors such as education, work experience, and so forth. In a preferential treatment program, points toward promotion would be awarded for membership in some groups but not others. Ramona Bobocel and her colleagues (1998) found that college student participants in their research were opposed to preferential treatment programs, neutral toward differential treatment programs, and in favor of equal treatment programs.

picture. For example, Christopher Parker, Boris Baltes, and Neil Christiansen (1997) found that, overall, the White male employees of a U.S. government agency did not hold negative attitudes toward coworkers who had benefited from affirmative action. In addition, as noted earlier, Taylor (1995) found that employees of companies that had affirmative action programs held more positive intergroup attitudes than employees of companies without such programs. Thus, affirmative action does not, for the most part, seem to engender prejudice among people who work in organizations that practice it, and may help to reduce it.

Valuing Diversity

Although affirmative action does not seem to produce prejudice, increasing the representation of women and members of minority groups in organizations can cause tensions (see, for example, Williams & O'Reilly, 1998). As a result, about one-third to one-half of U.S. companies carry out programs designed to help employees work more effectively with colleagues of different backgrounds (Bendick et al., 2001). The goal of **valuing diversity** programs is the "establishment of quality interpersonal relationships [through] understanding, respecting, and valuing differences among various groups in the context of the business enterprise" (Thomas, 1991, p. 28). Like multicultural and anti-bias education, valuing diversity programs take the form of diversity training, using seminars, discussions, media presentations, and so forth to achieve its goals.

How effective are such programs at reducing prejudice and improving intergroup relations? It is hard to tell. Stephan and Stephan (2001) reviewed research on diversity training programs and found the results to be mixed: some programs were successful and others were not. They concluded that "[e]very year, thousands of diversity training programs are conducted in the United States and other countries, yet almost none of them are evaluated. The result is that we have no idea whether or not these programs are successful or are an enormous waste of time and effort" (p. 89). In addition, McGregor (1993) found that about 30 percent of the studies of adult-targeted anti-bias education programs actually resulted in increased prejudice.

A number of factors probably contribute to these mixed results. One is resistance on the part of trainees. Stephan and Stephan (2001) note that, in general, people feel anxious about change and diversity training involves learning how to change attitudes and behavior. In addition, some people may feel threatened by increased diversity in their organizations. For example, Erika James and her colleagues (James, Brief, Dietz, & Cohen, 2001) found that prejudiced employees saw increased diversity as reducing their chances of promotion whereas unprejudiced employees did not. In addition, resistance can arise because people do not see diversity training as relevant. As one manager told an interviewer, "I'm not in the business of dealing with social issues. The people in my division have jobs to do, and this touchy-feely diversity stuff doesn't help us do our jobs. I'm not wasting my people's time trying to change the way they 'feel' about people who are different from them. If there's a problem, just tell us what you want us to do. Don't waste our time with this diversity stuff" (Paskoff, 1996, p. 43).

Another factor contributing to the failure of diversity training is that the training is sometimes poorly conducted. Box 12.4 lists some of the problems one pair of experts noted in diversity training programs. As one example, in an analysis of a series of videos used in corporate diversity training, Jacqueline Layng (1998) noted that White male managers, presumably a major target audience for the videos, were portrayed as uniformly biased and incompetent in intergroup interactions. Such portrayals are likely to turn that audience off and induce resistance to the training program. Finally, the training that is given may be insufficient.

12.4   *Potential Pitfalls in Diversity Training*

Why do diversity training, multicultural education, and anti-bias education programs sometimes fail? Michael Mobley and Tamara Payne (1992) suggest some problems, whether real or thought to exist by the trainees, that commonly afflict the implementation programs and can cause a boomerang effect:

- Trainers who have political agendas or support some groups over others.
- The training is based on a philosophy of political correctness rather than on dealing with important issues in the organization.
- The training is presented as remedial, implying that the trainees are the cause of the problems that that training is designed to solve.
- The training pressures only one group to change.
- The relevance of the training is not made clear to the trainees, such as by explaining how prejudice and discrimination undermine affected employees' ability to work effectively and the effect these problems have on organizational performance.
- The content of the training appears to be irrelevant because it is not adapted to the trainees' needs, skills, and expertise.
- The training uses a limited definition of whose differences should be valued, such as by ignoring the contributions of White men.
- Resource materials, such as readings, videos, and so forth, are outdated.
- The discussion of certain issues, such as reverse discrimination or the problems that can accompany increased diversity, is forbidden either explicitly or implicitly.
- The trainers themselves are not adequately familiar with the issues the training addresses or have not been properly trained to conduct discussions of sensitive issues.

For example, in a survey of 108 diversity training providers, Marc Bendick, Mary Lou Eagan, and Suzanne Lofhjelm (2001) found that the average training program lasted only 10 hours and some lasted 4 hours or less. Brief programs such as these may not provide trainees with sufficient information or give them enough opportunity to practice new skills.

It is important to note that, although some diversity training programs fail, properly designed and implemented programs can succeed (Stephan & Stephan, 2001). In addition, valuing diversity does not have to take the form of formal training programs. As Nurcan Ensari (2001) notes, individual managers can underline the value of diversity in the context of day-to-day work. They can, for example, encourage members of different groups to get to know each other as individuals, note the contributions of individual workers (both White and minority, male and female) to work team success, and encourage the development of a common group identity. In short, they can put intergroup contact theory into practice.

Managing Diversity

Affirmative action focuses on achieving greater representation of minority group members and women in all types of jobs and at all levels of organizations. Valuing diversity focuses on teaching people how to deal with the issues raised by a more diverse workforce. **Managing diversity** focuses on changing organizational systems to "create an environment appropriate for utilization of a diverse workforce [with an] emphasis on [organizational] culture and systems [that] includes White males" (Thomas, 1991, p. 28). That is, while diversity training might change individuals' intergroup attitudes and behaviors, it can do nothing to change the organizational policies and procedures, such as those we discussed in Chapter 10, that impede women's and minority group members' feelings of acceptance by the organization and their advancement to higher levels in it. Recall, for example, the finding of Chieh-Chen Bowen, Janet Swim, and Rick Jacobs (2000) that many job performance evaluation instruments emphasize characteristics generally associated with men and that women receive lower performance ratings when such forms are used.

Diversity management programs have two main thrusts (see, for example, Cox, 1993, 2001). One focuses on making organizational systems more responsive to the needs of women and minority group members. This aspect of diversity management searches for and modifies policies and procedures that, intentionally or unintentionally, have adverse effects on members of those groups, such as gender-biased performance evaluation instruments. Other examples include (Cox, 1993):

- Using recruitment procedures that target women and minority group members, such as by placing job ads in publications designed for members of those groups.
- Ensuring that women and minority group members receive training in skills needed for effective job performance and promotion.
- Establishing new benefit programs, such as child care.
- Monitoring promotions to see if any groups are being underrepresented and, if so, determining and remedying the causes.

Many of these initiatives comprise good human resources management practice (see, for example, Cascio, 1998). Therefore, they do not have to be specifically targeted at women and members of minority groups; they can benefit White men as well. For example, an organizationwide program to develop skills needed for promotion would include White men as well as members of other groups and so also improve their chances of promotion. Similarly, a child-care program can benefit working fathers as well as working mothers.

The second thrust of diversity management programs is changing organizational culture to create a climate in which diversity is normative and valued, not merely tolerated. Procedures that help create and maintain a positive diversity climate include (Cox, 1993):

- Giving priority in hiring and promotion to individuals who value diversity.
- Making the organization's commitment to diversity and diversity skills training part of new employee orientation programs.

- Making diversity compliance and competence part of job performance evaluations.
- Rewarding diversity initiatives and suggestions made by employees.
- Making sure that policy-making committees have diverse representation.

Clearly, diversity management can take a long time and requires a substantial commitment of resources by the organization: Policies and procedures must be reviewed, new programs must be developed, and employees must be trained so they can work effectively under the new system. Unfortunately, there is not much published research evaluating efforts at changing organizational diversity climates, perhaps because diversity management programs are carried out by consultants who, as a group, do not have much interest in publishing research (Stephan & Stephan, 2001). The published evaluations of these programs that do exist tend to be found in books in which diversity management consults describe their own work (for example, Cox, 2001; Norton & Fox, 1997; Thomas, 1991). The available evidence does suggest, however, that efforts to improve the diversity climate of organizations can have positive results. For example, Taylor Cox (2001) reported that improvements in the diversity climates of two manufacturing plants of a large corporation led not only to improved intergroup relations but also to increases in work productivity and quality.

What Should Be Our Goal? Color-Blindness versus Multiculturalism

When we attempt to reduce prejudice, what attitude should replace it? One answer to this question is, of course, "nonprejudice"—we want people not to be prejudiced. But that answer raises another question: What does *nonprejudiced* mean in practice? In the United States today, there appear to be two viewpoints on the "best" way in which to be nonprejudiced: the color-blind perspective and the multicultural perspective.

The **color-blind perspective** holds that people should ignore racial and ethnic group membership in their dealings with other people, acting as though racial and ethnic groups do not exist. Proponents of the color-blind perspective believe that acknowledging racial or ethnic group membership inevitably leads either to discrimination against minority group members or reverse discrimination in their favor (Schofield, 1986). Although, as Schofield notes, the color-blind perspective is attractive because it appeals to traditional American values of individualism and equality, it is, in many ways, a game of "let's pretend": If we pretend that racial and ethnic group categories do not exist then, by definition, race and ethnicity pose no social or interpersonal problems. Therefore, this viewpoint "easily leads to a misrepresentation of reality in ways which allow and sometimes even encourage discrimination against minority group members" (Schofield, 1986, p. 233).

Schofield (1986) illustrates her point about the potential negative effects of the color-blind perspective with observations she made in a desegregated school in which the faculty had turned color-blindness into a rule for conducting intergroup relations. She noted that the faculty treated even mentioning the race of another person as a possible sign of prejudice. Consequently, race became a taboo topic at the school. The establishment of this taboo had at least three effects. One was that it led to behaviors, such as those described in Box 12.5, that might otherwise appear to be bizarre. A second effect was that pretending that race did not exist made it impossible for the students and faculty to deal with real racial issues. As a result the taboo "tended to inhibit the development of positive relations between black and white students. These students were vividly aware of differences and tensions between them that were related to their group membership. Yet such issues could not be dealt with in a straightforward manner in the colorblind climate. Thus, anger sometimes festered and stereotypes built when fuller discussion of the situation might have made it easier for individuals to see each other's perspectives" (Schofield, 1986, p. 246). Finally, pretending that racial and ethnic differences did not exist led to a lack of sensitivity to minority culture, which led to racially discriminatory behavior. Thus, the color-blind perspective led to "a predisposition to ignore or deny the possibility of cultural differences between white and black students which influenced the way they functioned in school. For example, . . . black boys saw certain types of ambiguously aggressive acts as less mean and threatening and more playful and friendly than their white peers. These behaviors were ones which sometimes began conflicts between students which resulted in suspensions. Awareness of the differential meaning of such behaviors to white and black students might have at least suggested ways of trying to reduce the disproportionate suspension of black students" (Schofield, 1986, p. 248).

The color-blind perspective on interpersonal relations is related to the **assimilationist perspective** on intergroup relations (Neville, Lilly, Duran, Lee, & Browne, 2000). This perspective holds that minority and immigrant groups should give up their own cultures and replace them with the language, values, behavior patterns, and other aspects of the majority culture (see, for example, Berry, 1984, 2001). Advocates of assimilation believe that if everyone shares the same culture, then intergroup differences are not possible because there is only one group (Frederickson, 1999). However, the assimilationist perspective effectively denies the value of any culture other than the majority group's. For example, drawing on Ray Rist's (1974) analysis of school desegregation as a tool of assimilation, Schofield (1986) pointed out that in the context of schooling, the color-blind perspective leads to the assumption that White middle-class culture is the norm and that it is up to Black students to learn and live within that culture. (Recall how Waldus and Mummendey, 2004, found that Germans tended to define "Europeanness" as "Germanness.") As Schofield (1986) noted, "this view does not grant any positive status to lower-class values or modes of behavior. Regardless of whether these values and behaviors reflect pathological reactions to a deprived childhood or creative adaptations to a lower-class environment, they are seen as a problem, standing in the way of the child's success at school and in the larger society" (p. 233).

In contrast to the color-blind perspective, the **multicultural perspective** emphasizes the importance of ethnic group membership. It views "ethnic identities [as] cognitively inescapable and fundamental to the self-concept; as a result,

12.5   *The Bizarre World of Racial/Ethnic Color-Blindness*

When color-blindness becomes a dominating ideology, as it did at the school to which Janet Schofield (1986) gave the pseudonym "Wexler," the result can be apparently bizarre behavior. One behavior she noticed was teachers' assertions that they were literally blind to the race of their students and did not know who was Black and who was White. For example, "When I was arranging . . . student interviews, I mentioned to Mr. Little [white] that I thought there was only one white girl in one of his classes. I asked if I was right about this and he said, 'Well, just a minute. Let me check.' After looking through the class roster in his roll book he said, 'You know, you're right. I never noticed that'" (p. 237).

The color-blind ideology also led to a reluctance to mention race even in race-neutral contexts:

Interviewer: The other day I was walking around the school and heard a sixth grade student describing a student from the seventh grade to a teacher who needed to find this student in order to return something she had lost. The sixth grader said the seventh grader was tall and thin. She described what the girl had been wearing and said her hair was dark, but she didn't say whether the girl was black or white. . . . Why do you think she didn't mention that?

Sylvia (black): The teacher might have got mad if she said whether she was white or black.

Interviewer: Do some of the teachers get mad about things like that?

Sylvia: Some do . . . they holler. . . .

Interviewer: Now when you talk to kids who are black, do you ever mention that someone is white or black?

Sylvia: No.

Interviewer: What about when you are talking to kids who are white?

Sylvia: Nope.

Interviewer: You never mention race? Why not?

Sylvia: They might think I'm prejudiced. (p. 240; ellipses in original)

Finally, the color-blind ideology undermined aspects of the students' education: "In a lesson on the social organization of ancient Rome, one social studies teacher discussed the various classes in Roman society, including the nobles and plebeians at length but avoided all references to slaves. Another teacher included George Washington Carver on a list of great Americans from which students could pick individuals to learn about but specifically decided not to mention he was black for fear of raising racial issues. . . . [In another instance a] white child was surprised to learn from a member of our research team that Martin Luther King was black, not white." As Schofield commented, "highlighting the accomplishments of black Americans and making sure that students do not assume famous figures are white is a reasonable practice" (p. 249).

individuals are motivated to retain their cultural heritages. Rather than trying to eclipse ethnic identities, multiculturalism aims to preserve their integrity while encouraging ethnic groups to interact and coexist harmoniously" (Hornsey & Hogg, 2000, p. 145). This viewpoint is the one that multicultural education attempts to instill. As we noted in our discussion of those programs, one premise of multicultural education is that an understanding and appreciation of other groups' cultures reduces intergroup anxiety and so reduces prejudice.

Multiculturalism has often been criticized as encouraging separation, division, and disharmony among racial and ethnic groups, in contrast to assimilation, which the critics see as a unifying process (Frederickson, 1999). However, from the perspective of psychology, multiculturalism embodies two aspects of intergroup contact theory. First, by emphasizing group membership, it encourages salient categorization, which, as we saw earlier, can promote the undermining of group stereotypes. Second, multiculturalism encourages people to view themselves simultaneously in terms of their ethnic identities and their national identities. In doing so, it embodies the dual identities variant of a common ingroup identity: People maintain their group identities along with a higher level, or superordinate, common identity (Dovidio, Kawakami, & Gaertner, 2000; Hornsey & Hogg, 2000). Thus, for example, many Americans feel proud of their various ethnic heritages while simultaneously holding a common American cultural identity (see, for example, Taylor & Lambert, 1996). In such a situation, identification with an ethnic group does not detract from national identity, nor does holding a common national identity detract from ethnic group identity: The two identities are overlapping, not competing (Hornsey & Hogg, 2000). For example, researchers have found that members of minority groups often see having a dual ethnic and national identity as the best way to thrive in the majority culture, a view that many majority group members share (Taylor & Lambert, 1996; van Oudenhoven, Prins, & Buunk, 1998). As we saw earlier, as with salient categorization, holding a common group identity promotes intergroup harmony.

To return to the question we asked at the beginning of this section, which perspective is more likely to result in low prejudice? Interestingly, although the concepts of assimilation and multiculturalism (or cultural pluralism) have been around for a long time (Frederickson, 1999), researchers have only just begun to investigate the relationship of the color-blind and multicultural perspectives to prejudice. The results of that research have favored multiculturalism. For example, Helen Neville and her colleagues (2000) found that people who scored higher on a measure of color-blind racial attitudes also scored higher on measures of racial prejudice. In addition, Jennifer Richeson and Richard Nussbaum (2004) found that priming a color-blind perspective versus a multicultural perspective in White college students led to greater pro-White bias relative to Blacks, Asians, and Hispanics (see also Wolsko, Park, Judd, & Wittenbrink, 2000). Richeson and Nussbaum found greater pro-White bias on implicit as well as explicit attitude measures.

There are probably several reasons for this relationship. On the one hand, as we noted earlier, multiculturalism incorporates aspects of intergroup contact theory that are associated with reduced prejudice. In addition, from a social identity theory point of view (see Chapter 8), the multicultural perspective emphasizes the value and contributions of both majority and minority groups to the common culture. This validation of their respective cultures allows people to feel more secure in their group identities and therefore feel less animosity toward other groups (Hornsey & Hogg, 2000). On the other hand, a number of writers have suggested that the color-blind perspective, despite its appearance of egalitarianism, is actually a form of contemporary prejudice (see for example, Bonilla-Silva, 2003; Carr, 1997; Schofield, 1986). Recall from Chapter 5 that people who experience aversive prejudice tend to see themselves as unprejudiced, but act in a prejudiced manner when their behavior can be attributed to causes other than prejudice. Schofield (1986) pointed out that the color-blind perspective, especially in situations in which it is a dominant ideology, encourages the expression of aversive prejudice. For example, she noted that in the school she studied, "to the extent that the taboo [about discussing race] . . . inhibited individuals from challenging each others' behavior as racist in outcome or intent, it removed a potential barrier to racist behavior because it minimized the probability that such behavior would pose a threat to [an unprejudiced] self-concept" (p. 247). Thus, both research and theory converge to indicate the goal in reducing prejudice should be to encourage people to adopt a multicultural, rather than a color-blind, perspective.

WHAT YOU CAN DO TO REDUCE PREJUDICE

To close this chapter and the book, let's move from the theoretical to the personal: What you can do to reduce prejudice. Listed below are a number of steps that individuals can take to reduce prejudice in themselves and to influence others' intergroup attitudes. These suggestions are derived from the theories we have discussed in this book and from practitioners who work to help others become less prejudiced (Anti-Defamation League, 2001; Blaine, 2000; Johnson, 2006; Sue, 2003).

Influencing Your Own Attitudes

As self-regulation theory, discussed earlier in this chapter, implies, we can each do a lot to change our own prejudices. However, such change is not an easy process. As we noted in the beginning of the chapter, attitudes are resistant to change and so the process can be a long and difficult one. Patricia Devine, Ashby Plant, and Brenda Buswell (2000) noted that, like a bad habit, our prejudices are well-learned and can rear their ugly heads when we least expect or want them to and, like a bad habit, they are difficult to change. But, given the desire to change and persistence in working on it, like a bad habit, prejudice *can* be changed. Some suggestions:

REFLECT ON YOUR THOUGHTS AND BEHAVIOR:

- Acknowledge that you have prejudices. Having prejudices does not make you a bad person. Almost everyone has prejudices; they are a by-product of growing up in a society in which prejudice is still common. The first step in breaking a habit is to acknowledge its existence so that one can think about ways of getting rid of it.

- Think about the nature of your prejudices: the beliefs and emotions that they are based on. Where did those beliefs and emotions come from? Do they have a real basis or are they just things that have been accepted because "everybody knows" they are true?
- For every negative belief you have about a group, search for examples that contradict that belief.
- Pay attention to your behavior. If you find yourself acting in a prejudiced manner, think about why you reacted that way and how you could behave differently in the future. Then carry out those new behaviors.
- If someone suggests that you've acted in a biased way, don't immediately deny it. Instead, ask the person why your behavior gave that impression. What you said or did may have one meaning for you but a different meaning for a member of another group. Rather than focusing on who is right and who is wrong, examine why people may differ in how they interpret an event. See Box 12.6 for an example.
- If you find yourself thinking that a member of a group is "acting just like a typical X," think about other factors that might be influencing the person's behavior. For example, is anxiety over being in a new situation leading the person to act in a cool and distant rather than a warm and friendly manner?
- Resist the tendency, present in all people, to judge an entire group by the actions of one or a few of its members.
- Think about intergroup issues in intergroup terms. That is, think of them as *our* issues, to which we all contribute problems and solutions, not as "their" issues that someone else is responsible for dealing with.

PUT INTERGROUP CONTACT THEORY INTO PRACTICE:

- Seek out contact with members of other groups.
- Bear in mind that, at least at first, intergroup contact may arouse some anxiety. Be ready for it and work your way through it. The anxiety will moderate as your experience with intergroup contact increases.
- When interacting with members of other groups, personalize them. For example, when interacting with a member of another race, look beyond the person's race to other characteristics, especially those that the two of you have in common. Some examples include gender, being a student or employee (or both), common interests, and so forth.
- Invite members of other groups to social events you host and accept invitations made by members of other groups.
- Be persistent; don't let one bad experience discourage you.

LEARN MORE ABOUT OTHER GROUPS:

- Be willing to discuss intergroup issues with members of other groups to get their perspectives. Compare those perspectives with your own and think about the reasons for any differences that exist. However, be careful not to treat the people with whom you talk as spokespersons for their groups; they will be giving you *their* opinions, *not* their group's opinions.
- Join and be active in organizations that work to improve intergroup relations.

12.6   *Prejudice and the Gold Dust Twins*

Several years ago, I (B.W.), who am White, was talking with a Black colleague when I made a reference to "the gold dust twins." She told me that she was surprised that I would use a racist term like that. I was puzzled because I did not know that the term had a racist meaning. I had learned it when I was a child. The adults in our all-White neighborhood had used the term to refer to two boys who were always in each other's company; you almost never saw the one without the other. Because of that experience, to me, "gold dust twins" meant inseparable friends, and that is the context in which I used it when speaking with my colleague. However, my colleague explained to me that the term originated with the Gold Dust Flour Mill (which had gone out of business before I was born). The logo on their packages included the picture of two stereotypically drawn Black children, whom the company's advertising called "the Gold Dust Twins." So, unknown to me, the term had originated as a reference to a racist depiction of African Americans, which rightly offended my Black colleague. I have not used the term, except to make points like this one, since my colleague explained its origins to me.

I think that there are at least two lessons to be learned from this incident. One lesson is that if someone makes a remark or does something that appears to disparage your social group, the insult may not be intentional. The person may have learned the term or behavior in an innocent context, but differences in social group history may give it a very different meaning for your group. When such a misunderstanding occurs, discuss the different perspectives with the other person so that he or she can learn and act differently in the future. The second lesson is that if someone informs you that something you said or did had a biased meaning, don't immediately reject the information. Ask the person why he or she saw it as biased and adjust your behavior accordingly.

- Read books and watch movies that realistically depict life as experienced by members of other groups. Derald Wing Sue (2003) presents a list of recommended books on pages 220 to 222 of his book and list of recommended movies on pages 226 to 228.
- Actively listen to what people from other groups have to say about their experiences and the effects those experiences have had on their lives. While doing so, be careful not to invalidate their experiences. That is, do not assume that because their viewpoint differs from yours that yours is correct and theirs is not. If something sounds too astonishing to be true, that may just mean that that the event is far outside your experience. Also, if you have a different interpretation of an event, share your view as an alternative, not as a challenge to the other person.
- Attend multicultural community events such as ethnic festivals and visit museums and attend concerts that feature the art and music of other cultures.

Influencing Other People's Attitudes

In addition to working to change your attitudes, you can also try to influence other people's attitudes. Doing this will not be easy: Not only are attitudes resistant to change, almost everyone is brought up to believe that it is not polite to question other people's beliefs and behavior. But, like ourselves, other people must become aware of any prejudiced beliefs they hold before they can change those beliefs. Some suggestions:

HELP PEOPLE BECOME AWARE OF THEIR ATTITUDES AND BEHAVIOR:

- Tactfully let other people know when their behavior appears to reflect bias and your reasons for believing that it does.
- If a person's behavior is blatantly racist or sexist, speak out against it. This can be especially difficult if you are dealing with friends or relatives, but you may also be especially influential with them.
- If someone provides you with negative information about a group, ask about the reliability of the source of the information: How likely is it that the information is correct? Provide counterexamples to help the person see the group in more accurate terms.
- Challenge the status quo by asking pertinent questions. For example, at a school board meeting you could ask (if this is the case) why almost all principals and administrators are White men while almost all the teachers they supervise are women and members of minority groups (Johnson, 2006).
- Write letters to companies whose advertising includes stereotypical or sexist portrayals and to the media organizations that publish or broadcast them.

ENCOURAGE INTERGROUP CONTACT:

- Encourage organizations you belong to (such as sororities, fraternities, clubs, and so forth) to recruit a more diverse membership and to become involved in community projects that bring them into contact with members of other groups.
- Encourage the leaders of your house of worship to invite clergy of other faiths to deliver sermons or to speak as part of religious education programs.

HELP OTHERS BECOME BETTER INFORMED:

- Investigate your cultural heritage and share it and your pride in it with others.
- Invite speakers on cultural or social issues to address your organizations.
- Invite friends of other faiths to visit a service at your place of worship.
- Encourage your local public library to periodically highlight the books, movies, and other materials it holds that provide information about the cultural groups in your community.
- Finally, and here is where you are likely to have the most influence, be a nonprejudiced role model for your children or younger siblings. Act in nonprejudiced ways so they can imitate your behavior and correct their inappropriate

behavior. With older children, discuss the stereotypical portrayals they see in the media or hear from others to help them avoid acquiring stereotypical beliefs.

Envoi

Change is difficult and the obstacles to change can appear to be insurmountable, especially at the outset. But always remember the Chinese proverb: "A journey of a thousand miles begins with a single step."

Chapter Summary

This chapter presented a number of approaches to reducing prejudice and discrimination. The first set of approaches discussed focused on changes within individuals. One of those approaches is trying to suppress stereotypes and other prejudiced thoughts while replacing them with nonprejudiced thoughts. Trying to suppress stereotypic thoughts will work, at least for a while. But when the suppression is released, the stereotypic thoughts return in greater force than before. This enhanced stereotyping may result from suppression's having primed the stereotype, depletion of cognitive control abilities, or suppression's causing a motivation to use the stereotype. However, rebound effects might not occur for people who are low in prejudice, and even people high in prejudice inhibit the application of socially proscribed stereotypes when they have the cognitive resources available to help them do so.

Another individual-level approach to the reduction of prejudice is self-regulation. In the self-regulation process, people learn to recognize situational cues that alert them to the possibility that they will act in a prejudiced manner in that situation. Having been alerted by these cues, people replace the prejudiced response with an appropriate nonprejudiced response. People learn the cues through experience: Having acted in a prejudiced manner, they regret doing so, think about their behavior and what caused it, and come up with ways of responding differently in the future. Over time, the process of substituting nonprejudiced responses for prejudiced responses can become automatic and the person does it without thinking about it. One problem that can arise with this process is that the behaviors that people think are unprejudiced might actually be viewed differently by members of the group to which they are directed.

A third individual-level approach to the reduction of prejudice is value confrontation. In this approach, people are made aware of contradictions between the egalitarian values they hold and their prejudiced thoughts or behaviors. The theory underlying the technique holds that people should feel uncomfortable over this contradiction and change their thoughts and behaviors to match their values. Early versions of this technique that made people aware of contradictions between abstract value positions were not very successful at reducing prejudice. However, a more recent version of the technique makes people aware of contradictions between their values and their actual behavior toward members of other groups, and is targeted at people who exhibit aversive prejudice and so may be especially sensitive to such contradictions. Initial research on this approach suggests that it might be more effective than the earlier one.

One of the longest standing approaches to prejudice reduction is embodied in the contact hypothesis, or intergroup contact theory. This approach holds that, given the proper circumstances, contact between members of different groups can lead to a reduction of prejudice on both sides. For intergroup contact to reduce prejudice, four conditions must be met: members of each group must have equal status in the situation, the groups must work cooperatively to achieve common goals, the situation must allow participants to get to know each other as individuals (acquaintance potential), and the intergroup effort must have the support of authorities, law, or custom (institutional support). When properly implemented, intergroup contact is reasonably successful at reducing prejudice, although it is more successful in some situations and for some groups than others. Intergroup contact appears to have its effect on prejudice by producing cognitive changes such as increased knowledge about the outgroup, reduced stereotyping, reduced expectations that intergroup interactions will have negative outcomes, reduced ingroup favoritism, and perceptions of unity between the ingroup and outgroup; emotional changes such as reduced intergroup anxiety and increased empathy for the other group; and behavioral changes that can lead to attitude change. The extent of these changes can be limited by such factors as preexisting intergroup attitudes (people very high and very low on prejudice are likely to show the least change); intergroup anxiety, which might be exacerbated by intergroup contact; and the normative climate, which can either encourage or inhibit attitude change.

Theorists have proposed three models of how intergroup contact affects prejudice, all based on the concepts of social categorization and social identity. The personalization model proposes that intergroup contact reduces prejudice by leading people to see members of the outgroup as individuals rather than as members of social categories: Viewing people in personal terms rather than as members of groups then leads to liking for them and so to less prejudice. One shortcoming of the personalization process is that although it increases liking for the outgroup members with whom people interact, that liking does not always generalize to liking for the outgroup in general. The salient categorization model addresses the issue of generalization by holding that generalization will occur only if group members are seen as typical of their group; for group members to be seen as typical so that generalization can occur, group membership must remain salient during intergroup contact. Thus, whereas the personalization model holds that group categories must be made less salient for intergroup attitudes to improve, the salient categorization model holds that group categories must remain salient for generalization to occur. The common ingroup identity model focuses on inducing ingroup and outgroup members to recategorize themselves into a single group for which they share a common identity; prejudice will be eliminated if people see themselves as members of a single unified group rather than as two competing groups.

These three models all have research to support them, yet they seem to contradict each other. However, Pettigrew (1998a) has reconciled them by suggesting that they represent three stages of intergroup contact that develop over time. Generally, personalization comes first, followed by salient categorization, with the process being completed with the development of a common ingroup identity. In practice, the stages of the contact process are not always distinct from one another and the processes they represent can overlap. Cues that keep group membership salient often persist even as personalization takes place. In addition, the order in which the processes described in the combined model take place depends on the nature of the contact situation. Contact that emphasizes group-to-group interactions may initially elicit salient categorization or development of a common ingroup identity whereas contact that emphasizes person-to-person interactions may initially elicit personalization.

Because prejudice begins to arise in childhood, psychologists and educators have developed a number of school-based interventions aimed at reducing or preventing the development of prejudice in children. Although school desegregation was not motivated by a desire to reduce prejudice, social scientists hoped that the resulting intergroup contact would do so. However, the results of research on the outcomes of school desegregation generally found that desegregation led to an increase rather than a decrease in prejudice. One reason for this outcome is that, for the most part, desegregation programs did not put into practice the condition necessary for successful intergroup contact. Nonetheless, the limited research that has been conducted on the long-term effects of desegregation show more positive results.

Cooperative learning interventions are designed to implement the conditions necessary for successful intergroup contact within the everyday classroom context: Students have equal status contact, they work cooperatively to achieve common goals, they interact closely and so get to know each other, and the process is supported by authority in the form of the teachers. Research on the effectiveness of cooperative learning has found that it reduces prejudice and discrimination toward outgroup members who are learning partners; however, there is little evidence that its effects generalize to attitudes toward teammates' outgroups as a whole.

Multicultural and anti-bias education programs attempt to provide students with knowledge about cultural groups, to instill respect for other groups, and to help children develop the attitudes and skills needed to interact effectively with members of other groups. Researchers disagree on how effective such programs are. On the optimistic side, most such programs have been found to have generally positive effects. On the pessimistic side, the research showing positive effects has often found them on some measures of change but not others and there has been little research on the long-term effects of these kinds of programs.

The increasing diversity of the workforce has led to the development of programs designed to increase the representation of women and minority group members in the workplace, to remove barriers to their career advancement, and to deal with the intergroup tensions that can accompany increased workforce diversity. Affirmative action programs are designed to increase the diversity of an organization's workforce and to ensure that members of all groups are treated fairly in terms of promotions and other personnel decisions. Affirmative action programs are not designed to affect prejudice. However, the results of laboratory research have suggested that people hold negative attitudes toward individuals they believe have benefited from affirmative action, and some research suggests that these attitudes generalize to groups as a whole. On a more optimistic note, field research involving employees of organizations with affirmative action programs have found little evidence that the programs generate prejudice and some evidence that they might reduce it.

Valuing diversity programs are the workplace equivalent of multicultural and anti-bias education. There is little research on the effectiveness of these programs, and what there is has produced mixed results, some finding that the programs evaluated had been successful, others finding no change or even a boomerang effect. A number of factors probably contribute to these mixed results including resistance on the part of trainees, a perception that diversity training is not relevant to organization goals, training that is poorly designed and poorly conducted, and training programs that are too short to accomplish their goals effectively.

Managing diversity focuses on changing organizational systems and the organizational culture to make the organization more welcoming to a diverse workforce and to help the organization effectively utilize the talents of a diverse workforce. These programs have two main thrusts. One focuses on making organizational systems more responsive to the needs of women and minority group members by searching for and modifying policies and procedures that have adverse effects on members of those groups. The second thrust of diversity management programs is changing organizational culture to create a climate in which diversity is normative and valued, not merely tolerated. There is very little published research on the effectiveness of diversity management programs, but what there is indicates that they can be successful even though it can take a long time and requires a substantial commitment of resources by the organization.

There is some controversy about what kind of attitude should replace prejudice. The color-blind perspective holds that people should ignore racial and ethnic group membership in their dealings with other people, acting as though racial and ethnic groups do not exist. Proponents of this perspective believe that acknowledging racial or ethnic group membership inevitably leads either to discrimination against minority group members or reverse discrimination in their favor. However, color-blindness ignores the real effects that race has on people's lives and can open the door to the expression of contemporary prejudices. The color-blind perspective on interpersonal relations is related to the assimilationist perspective on intergroup relations, which holds that minority and immigrant groups should give up their own cultures and replace them with the majority culture. Advocates of assimilation believe that if everyone shares the same culture, then intergroup differences are not possible because there is only one group. However, the assimilationist perspective effectively denies the value of any culture other than the majority group's and can in that way support prejudiced attitudes.

In contrast, the multicultural perspective emphasizes the importance of ethnic group membership. Rather than trying to do away with ethnic identities, multiculturalism aims to preserve them while encouraging ethnic groups to interact and coexist harmoniously. Multiculturalism has been criticized as encouraging separation, division, and disharmony among racial and ethnic groups, in contrast to assimilation, which the critics see as a unifying process. However, multiculturalism embodies two aspects of intergroup contact theory that promote positive intergroup relations. First, by emphasizing group membership, it encourages salient categorization, which can promote the undermining of group stereotypes. Second, multiculturalism encourages people to view themselves simultaneously in terms of their ethnic identities and their national identities. In doing so, it embodies the dual identities variant of a common ingroup identity, which also leads to reduced prejudice.

The results of research that has investigated the relationship of the color-blind and multicultural perspectives to prejudice have favored multiculturalism. There are several reasons for this finding. First, multiculturalism incorporates aspects of intergroup contact theory that are associated with reduced prejudice. In addition, from a social identity theory point of view, the multicultural perspective emphasizes the value and contributions of both majority and minority groups to the common culture. This validation of their respective cultures allows people to feel more secure in their group identities and therefore feel less animosity toward other groups. In contrast, a number of writers have suggested that the color-blind perspective, despite its appearance of egalitarianism, is actually a form of contemporary prejudice in which a veneer of egalitarianism hides unacknowledged negative intergroup attitudes. Thus, researchers have found that endorsement of the color-blind perspective is correlated with endorsement of beliefs that reflect contemporary prejudices.

The chapter closed with a list of things that you can do to help reduce prejudice. You can influence your own attitudes by reflecting on your thoughts and behaviors, putting intergroup contact theory into practice, and learning more about other groups. You can influence other people's attitudes by helping them become aware of their attitudes and behavior, encouraging intergroup contact, and helping them become better informed. These tasks are not easy, but they hold the promise of a better world.

SUGGESTED READINGS

Stereotype Suppression

Monteith, M. J., Sherman, J. W., & Devine, P. G. (1998). Suppression as a stereotype control strategy. *Personality and Social Psychology Review, 2,* 63–82.

Monteith and her colleagues summarize the research literature on stereotype suppression and rebound, and provide some hypotheses (most of which have subsequently been supported) about the conditions under which rebound effects occur.

Self-Regulation of Prejudiced Behavior

Monteith, M. J., Ashburn-Nardo, L., Voils, C. I., & Czopp, A. M. (2002). Putting the brakes on prejudice: On the development and operation of cues for control. *Journal of Personality and Social Psychology, 83,* 1029–1050.

This article presents a recent conceptualization on Monteith's model of the self-regulation of prejudiced behavior.

Value Confrontation

Rokeach, M. (1973). *The nature of human values.* New York: Free Press.

Son Hing, L. S., Li, W., & Zanna, M. P. (2002). Inducing hypocrisy to reduce prejudicial responses among aversive racists. *Journal of Experimental Social Psychology, 38,* 71–78. Rokeach describes his value confrontation technique in Chapter 9. Son Hing and her colleagues describe a newer version of the technique. The term they use, *hypocrisy induction,* comes from the theory on which they based their research.

Intergroup Contact

Amir, Y. (1976). The role of intergroup contact in the change of prejudice and ethnic relations. In P. A. Katz (Ed.), *Towards the elimination of racism* (pp. 245–308). New York: Pergamon.

Brewer, M. B., & Miller, N. (1984). Beyond the contact hypothesis: Theoretical perspectives on desegregation. In N. Miller & M. B. Brewer (Eds.), *Groups in contact: The psychology of desegregation* (pp. 281–302). Orlando, FL: Academic Press.

Gaertner, S. L., & Dovidio, J. F. (2000). *Reducing intergroup bias: The common ingroup identity model.* Philadelphia: Psychology Press.

Gaertner, S. L., Dovidio, J. F., Nier, J. A., Banker, B. S., Ward, C. M., Houlette, M., & Loux, S. (2000). The common ingroup identity mode for reducing intergroup bias: Progress and challenges. In D. Capozza & R. Brown (Eds.), *Social identity processes: Trends in theory and research* (pp. 134–148). Thousand Oaks, CA: Sage.

Hewstone, M. (1996). Contact and categorization: Social psychological interventions to change intergroup relations. In C. N. Macrae, C. Stangor, & M. Hewstone (Eds.), *Stereotypes and stereotyping* (pp. 323–368). New York: Guilford.

Pettigrew, T. F. (1998). Intergroup contact theory. *Annual Review of Psychology, 49,* 65–85. Amir's chapter is a classic summary of the early research on the contact hypothesis. The chapters by Brewer and Miller, Hewstone, and Gaertner and his colleagues present their respective models; the Gaertner and Dovidio book provides a more extensive discussion of their model. Pettigrew's chapter provides a recent summary along with his model integrating the process theories proposed by Brewer and Miller, Hewstone and Brown, and Gaertner and Dovidio.

Educational Interventions

Bigler, R. S. (1999). The use of multicultural curricula and materials to counter racism in children. *Journal of Social Issues, 55,* 687–705.

Schofield, J. W., & Eurich-Fulcer, R. (2001). When and how school desegregation improves intergroup relations. In R. Brown & S. L. Gaertner (Eds.), *Blackwell handbook of social psychology: Intergroup processes* (pp. 475–494). Malden, MA: Blackwell.

Stephan, W. G., & Stephan, C. W. (2001). *Improving intergroup relations.* Thousand Oaks, CA: Sage. Schofield and Eurich-Fulcer present a recent summary of the research on the effects of school desegregation on intergroup relations. Stephan and Stephan provide a concise description of cooperative learning interventions in their Chapter 7, and an optimistic review of multicultural education in their Chapter 3. Bigler presents a more pessimistic view of the effects of multicultural education.

Workplace Interventions

Crosby, F. J., Iyer, A., Clayton, S., & Downing, R. A. (2003). Affirmative action: Psychologi-cal data and the policy debates. *American Psychologist, 58*, 93–115.

Ensari, N. (2001). How can managers reduce intergroup conflict in the workplace? Social psychological approaches to addressing prejudice in organizations. *Psychologist-Manager Journal, 5*(2), 83–93.

Stephan, W. G., & Stephan, C. W. (2001). *Improving intergroup relations.* Thousand Oaks, CA: Sage.

Crosby and her colleagues summarize the psychological research on affirmative action. Stephan and Stephan discuss valuing diversity and managing diversity in their Chapter 4. Ensari presents some ways in which managers can carry out "on-the-job" diversity training.

Color-Blindness versus Multiculturalism

Frederickson, G. M. (1999). Models of American ethnic relations: A historical perspective. In D. A. Prentice & D. T. Miller (Eds.), *Cultural divides: Understanding and overcom-ing group conflict* (pp. 23–34). New York: Russell Sage Foundation.

Schofield, J. W. (1986). Causes and consequences of the colorblind perspective. In J. F. Dovidio & S. L. Gaertner (Eds.), *Prejudice, discrimination, and racism* (pp. 231–253). Orlando, FL: Academic Press.

Frederickson discusses the history of assimilationism and multiculturalism in the United States. Schofield discusses some of the shortcomings of the color-blind per-spective using examples from a desegregated public school.

What You Can Do

Anti-Defamation League. (2001). *101 ways to combat prejudice.* Retrieved August 11, 2004, from http://www.adl.org/prejudice/closethebook.pdf.

Sue, D. W. (2003). *Overcoming our racism: The journey to liberation.* San Francisco, CA: Jossey-Bass.

As its title indicates, the Anti-Defamation League pamphlet presents 101 things individ-uals can do to combat prejudice. Sue's book includes chapters addressed to both Whites and members of minority groups that discuss what individuals can do to overcome prejudice.

KEY TERMS

affirmative action
anti-bias education
assimilationist perspective
color-blind perspective
common ingroup identity model
contact hypothesis
cooperative learning
decategorization model
intergroup contact theory
managing diversity

multicultural education
multicultural perspective
mutual intergroup differentiation model
personalization model
rebound effect
salient categorization model
self-regulation model
value confrontation technique
valuing diversity

QUESTIONS FOR REVIEW AND DISCUSSION

1. What is stereotype suppression? What is the rebound effect? How does the rebound effect manifest itself?

2. Why does stereotype suppression result in rebound? Under what conditions might stereotype suppression *not* result in rebound? What role do cognitive resources play in the rebound effect?

3. Describe the self-regulation model of prejudice reduction. Include both the development and use of cues for control. What types of people are most likely to engage in the self-regulation of prejudice?

4. What kind of mistakes can people make when they try to act in an unprejudiced manner?

5. Think about the stereotype suppression and self-regulation of prejudice models. In what ways are they similar and in what ways are they different?

6. Have you had any experiences with suppressing stereotypes or trying to regulate prejudiced behavior? How well do your experiences match the propositions of the models? If your experiences have differed from what the models say happens, how would you change the models to account for your experiences?

7. Describe the value confrontation approach to reducing prejudice. How does the current approach developed by Son Hing and colleagues (2002) differ from Rokeach's (1973) original approach? How are these differences related to the effectiveness of the two approaches?

8. Explain the contact hypothesis. What four conditions are necessary for intergroup contact to result in reduced prejudice? Explain how each of these conditions contributes to the reduction of prejudice. Think about this question not only in terms of the contact hypothesis itself but also in terms of the three models of how intergroup contact reduces prejudice.

9. What does the research on the contact hypothesis have to say about its effectiveness in reducing prejudice? What types of changes does intergroup contact produce? What factors limit the effectiveness of intergroup contact in reducing prejudice?

10. Describe the personalization model of intergroup contact. How does personalization differ from decategorization? What are the shortcomings of the model?

11. Describe the salient categorization model of intergroup contact. How does it address the shortcomings of the personalization model? What issues of stereotyping does the model raise? How does it deal with those issues?

12. Describe the common ingroup identity model of intergroup contact. What types of group representations does the model say can result from intergroup contact? How are those representations related to prejudice? What drawbacks might emerge from a common ingroup identity?

13. Explain how Pettigrew's (1998a) combined intergroup contact model resolves the apparent contradictions among the personalization, salient categorization, and common ingroup identity models.

14. Think about the intergroup contact experiences that you have had. To what extent were the necessary and facilitating conditions for successful contact present? To what extent did the contact process follow the stages of Pettigrew's

combined model? How did these experiences affect your attitudes toward the other group?

15. Monteith and colleagues' (2002) self-regulation model of prejudice reduction focuses on individual cognitive and emotional processes whereas the contact model focuses on intergroup processes. In what ways might intergroup contact affect the self-regulation of prejudice, and in what ways might efforts at self-regulation affect what happens during intergroup contact?

16. What was the basis for expecting that school desegregation would reduce prejudice? Why did it, for the most part, fail to do so, at least in the short term? What long-term effects has it had?

17. Did you attend a desegregated elementary, middle, or high school? If so, how well did the school environment embody the conditions for effective intergroup contact? Think in terms of both the contact hypothesis itself and the three models of how contact affects intergroup attitudes. What effect did these factors have on intergroup relations in the school? What additional factors seemed to affect intergroup relations?

18. What is cooperative learning? Explain why cooperative learning programs should reduce prejudice. How well do they work? What limitations do they have?

19. Have you ever been involved in a cooperative learning situation? If so, how well did the situation embody the conditions for effective intergroup contact? Think in terms of both the contact hypothesis itself and the three models of how contact affects intergroup attitudes. What effect did these factors have on your attitudes? What is your personal evaluation of the experience?

20. What are multicultural and anti-bias education? What are their goals? How effective are they at reducing prejudice?

21. What are the goals of affirmative action programs? What effect do these programs appear to have on prejudice?

22. What are valuing diversity programs? What are their goals? How effective are they at reducing prejudice?

23. What are some of the reasons why diversity education programs fail?

24. Have you ever been in a multicultural education or anti-bias class, either in school or in the workplace? If so, what did it consist of? What effect did the experience have on your attitudes? What is your personal evaluation of that experience?

25. What are the goals of diversity management programs? What kinds of changes must organizations make to meet those goals?

26. Compare and contrast color-blindness and multiculturalism as replacements for prejudiced attitudes. Which do you think is better? What are your reasons for your opinion?

27. Describe the things you can do to reduce prejudice. What things can you think of that are not on the list we made?

Glossary

affirmative action   Programs within organizations designed to combat discrimination and to provide equal opportunity in employment for all members of the organization. Most affirmative action programs are voluntary. (Chapter 12).

ageism   Evaluative judgments about persons made simply due to their advanced age (Chapter 9).

ambivalent prejudice (or racism)   A form of prejudice in which people have a mixture of positive and negative beliefs about and feelings toward an outgroup, resulting in ambivalent attitudes toward members of that group (Chapter 5).

anti-bias education   A form of education that aims to give people a heightened awareness of institutional racism and bias and to provide them with the skills to reduce racism and bias within their spheres of influence (Chapter 12).

assimilationist perspective   The perspective that minority and immigrant groups should give up their own cultures and replace them with the language, values, behavior patterns, and other aspects of the majority culture (Chapter 12).

attention sequence   One of two overlapping waves in Aboud's cognitive developmental theory of racial attitudes; this concept involves the shift of attention from the self to groups or individuals (Chapter 7).

attributional ambiguity   The proposition that members of stigmatized groups often find it difficult to interpret feedback from dominant group members because they do not know whether the feedback reflects their ability or stems from the evaluator's biases and prejudices (Chapter 11).

attribution-value model   The hypothesis that prejudice results from the perception that members of minority groups have characteristics that are contrary to majority group values. Coupled to that perception is the belief that members of those groups are responsible for their undesirable characteristics. Because people who are seen as responsible for their negative characteristics arouse negative emotions in others, prejudice results when groups are perceived to be responsible for their negative stereotypic characteristics. (Chapter 6).

authoritarian personality   A personality type that is especially susceptible to unquestioning obedience to authority (Chapter 6).

aversive prejudice (or racism)   A form of prejudice in which people feel uncomfortable with interacting with members of minority groups and so try to ignore their existence and avoid contact with them, although they try to be polite and correct when they do have contact with members of minority groups (Chapter 5).

basic social category   Categories such as age, race, and gender, for which perceivers have a wealth of information available in memory (Chapter 3).

benevolent prejudice   A form of prejudice that is expressed in terms of apparently positive beliefs and emotional responses to targets of prejudice (Chapter 5).

blatant discrimination   Discrimination that consists of unequal and harmful treatment that is typically intentional, quite visible, and easily documented (Chapter 10).

bogus pipeline research   A research method used to convince participants that the true answers to their questions can be determined by a lie detector even though they actually can not be (Chapter 5).

categorization   The process of simplifying our environment by creating categories on the basis of characteristics (such as hair color or athletic ability) that a particular set of people appear to have in common (Chapters 3 & 4).

centration   The tendency to focus on a single piece of information when multiple pieces of information are relevant (Chapter 7).

chronic identities   Social identities that are always with group members, regardless of how much the situation changes (Chapter 8).

cognitive developmental theories   A set of theories that emphasize the ongoing interplay between children's mental development and their environments, accounting for social-cognitive processes such as prejudice in terms of both nature and nurture (Chapter 7).

color-blind perspective   The point of view that people should ignore racial and ethnic group membership in their dealings with other people, acting as though racial and ethnic groups do not exist (Chapter 12).

common ingroup identity model   A theory of prejudice reduction that holds that ingroup and outgroup members can be induced to recategorize themselves into a single group that shares a common identity (Chapter 12).

compensation   A method individuals use to prevent potential discrimination by changing their behavior in ways that disconfirm the stereotype (Chapter 11).

conditions   Sets of experiences that represent different aspects of the independent variable (Chapter 2).

contact hypothesis   A theory of prejudice reduction that holds that, under the proper conditions, interaction between ingroup and outgroup members changes their beliefs and feelings toward each other in a positive manner (Chapter 12).

content analysis   A research method by which researchers study documents, photographs, and works of art, to identify themes that help them understand the topic being studied (Chapter 2).

continuous measure   A measure of prejudice in which children are not forced to choose one of two options presented, therefore allowing researchers to measure complex attitudinal judgments and make fine-grained distinctions (Chapter 7).

convenience sampling   A method of recruiting people to participate in research that focuses on people from whom the researchers can easily collect data (Chapter 2).

convergent validity   The degree to which scores on a measure correlate with scores on measures of the same or related characteristics and with behaviors that are related to the characteristic being measured (Chapter 2).

cooperative learning   A type of group learning environment that implements the necessary contact conditions thought to reduce prejudice as part of the day-to-day educational process (Chapter 12).

correlation coefficient   A statistic that represents the relationship between two variables (Chapter 2).

correlational research strategy   A strategy used by researchers who measure two or more variables and look for relationships among them (Chapter 2).

covert discrimination   Unequal and harmful treatment that is hidden, purposeful, and, often, maliciously motivated and stems from conscious attempts to ensure failure (Chapter 10).

cultural discrimination   Occurs when one group within a culture retains the power to define cultural values as well as the form those values should take. This power results in discrimination and inequality built into literature, art, music, language, morals, customs, beliefs, and ideology to such a degree that they define a generally agreed-on way of life (Chapters 1 & 10).

cultural racism   See *everyday racism* (Chapter 8).

decategorization model   See *personalization model*.

dependent variable   In research, the proposed effect in a hypothesized cause-and-effect relationship between two variables (Chapter 2).

discriminant validity   Refers to the extent to which a measure does not assess characteristics that it is not supposed to assess (Chapter 2).

discrimination   Treating a person differently from others based solely or primarily on the person's membership in a social group (Chapters 1 & 10).

disidentification   Redefining one's self-concept so that a domain is no longer an area of self-identification (Chapter 11).

distributive justice   The perception that outcomes are being distributed on the expected basis that people who deserve more get more, rather than on some other, unfair, basis such as ingroup favoritism (Chapter 8).

doll technique   A measure of racial category awareness where the child is presented with two (or more) dolls and asked to identify the dolls' ethnicity (Chapter 7).

egalitarianism   A value system that reflects the belief that all people are equal and should be treated identically. People high on egalitarianism place a strong emphasis on the principles of equal opportunity, equal treatment for all people, and concern for others' well-being (Chapters 5 & 6).

egocentrism   A focus on oneself as the center of everything coupled with the inability to take the perspective of another person (Chapter 7).

egoistic relative deprivation   See *personal relative deprivation* (Chapter 8).

empathy   An other-oriented emotional response congruent with another's perceived welfare; empathic feelings include sympathy, compassion, and tenderness (Chapter 6).

ethnographic research   A set of qualitative data collection techniques, including participating in events, observing behavior, and conducting interviews, that researchers use to understand how people experience and interpret events in their daily lives (Chapter 2).

everyday racism   The assumption inherent in much of North American culture that the only correct social and cultural values are European Christian values (Chapter 8).

experimental research strategy   A research strategy whereby researchers take control of the research situation to ensure that the criteria for determining whether one variable causes another are met. It is the only research method that can be used for determining causality. (Chapter 2).

extraordinary racism   An organizational socialization process that occurs when the everyday racism of those who are recruited into hate groups is converted into extreme racism (Chapter 8).

extrinsic religious orientation   The use of religion as a way to achieve nonreligious goals and thus to provide security and solace, sociability and distraction, status and self-justification (Chapter 6).

false consciousness   The holding of false or inaccurate beliefs that are contrary to one's own social interest and that thereby contribute to maintaining the disadvantaged position of the group (Chapter 8).

field experiment   A research strategy wherein an independent variable is manipulated in a natural setting but as much control as possible is maintained over the research situation (Chapter 2).

forced choice method   A methodology in which the research participant must choose one of two options presented (Chapter 7).

gender constancy   The understanding that gender is permanent despite superficial changes in hairstyle, clothing, behavior, or age (Chapter 7).

gender polarization   The assumption that gender-associated characteristics are bipolar and that what is masculine is not feminine and what is feminine is not masculine (Chapter 9).

generalizability   The principle that the results of research on a hypothesis should be similar regardless of how a study is conducted. That is, the hypothesis should be supported generally, not just in one specific study. (Chapter 2).

group (or fraternal) relative deprivation   The degree to which a person feels that a group he or she identifies with has been deprived of some benefit (Chapter 8).

group privilege   An unearned favored state conferred simply because of one's race, gender, or sexual orientation (Chapter 1).

hate crimes   Criminal offenses in which there is evidence that the victims were chosen because of their race, ethnicity, national origin, religion, disability, or sexual orientation (Chapter 10).

hate group   An organization whose central principles include hostility toward racial, ethnic, and religious minority groups (Chapter 8).

homosociality   The tendency to interact socially only with members of one's own sex (Chapter 7).

hostile prejudice   A traditional form of prejudice that is expressed in terms of negative beliefs about and emotional responses to targets of prejudice (Chapter 5).

hypothesis   A proposed relationship between two variables that is tested in research (Chapter 2).

hypothetical construct   The technical term for an abstract concept that is used in theories and studied in research (Chapter 2).

ideology   A set of attitudes and beliefs that predisposes people to view the world in certain ways and to respond in ways consistent with those viewpoints (Chapter 6).

illusory correlations   Beliefs that incorrectly link two characteristics, such as race and a personality trait (Chapter 3).

Implicit Association Test (IAT)   A technique for measuring prejudice that uses the principle of response competition to pit two responses (an habitual response and an opposing response) against one another. In assessing prejudice, the technique assumes that negative responses are more closely associated with outgroups than are positive responses, so prejudiced people's negative responses to stimuli associated with an outgroup will be faster than positive responses to the outgroup. (Chapter 2).

implicit prejudices   Prejudices that people are not aware of having but that can be assessed through implicit cognition and some behavioral measures (Chapters 2 & 5).

independent variable   In research, the proposed cause in a hypothesized cause-and-effect relationship. In experimental research, it is also the term used for the variable the experimenter manipulates. (Chapter 2).

individualism   A value system based on a strong emphasis on self-reliance and independence from others (Chapter 6).

individuating information   In the context of making judgments of others, information that is specific to the person, regardless of whether it is stereotypic to the person's group (Chapter 4).

ingroup bias   People's bias in favor of members of their own group (Chapter 8).

inner state theories   Theories of individual differences, such as differences in personality (Chapter 7).

institutional discrimination   Discrimination that occurs when beliefs about group superiority are sanctioned by institutions or governing bodies. It is rooted in the norms, policies, and practices associated with a social institution such as the family, religious institutions, the educational system, and the criminal justice system. (Chapters 1 & 10).

intergroup anxiety   The feelings of discomfort many people experience when interacting with, or anticipating an interaction with, members of other groups (Chapter 6).

intergroup contact theory   See *contact hypothesis* (Chapter 12).

internal consistency   The extent to which people respond in the same way to all the items on a measure; high internal consistency is a desirable feature of measures (Chapter 2).

interpersonal discrimination   One individual's unfair treatment of another based on the other person's group membership (Chapters 1 & 10).

intrinsic religious orientation   People with an intrinsic religious orientation truly believe in their religions' teachings and try to live their lives according to those teachings. (Chapter 6).

Jim Crow racism   The form of overt prejudice by the White majority against members of other racial groups, often embodied in law, that was the social norm prior to World War II (Chapter 5).

laboratory experiment   Experimental research that is carried out in a highly controlled environment (Chapter 2).

legitimizing myths   Sets of attitudes and beliefs that people use to justify their social group's dominant position in society (Chapter 6).

linguistic intergroup bias   The hypothesis that positive descriptions of ingroups and negative descriptions of outgroups tend to be made in abstract terms and that negative ingroup and positive outgroup actions tend to be described in concrete terms (Chapter 3).

managing diversity   Programs aimed at analyzing and changing organizational systems to create an environment appropriate for utilization of a diverse workforce (Chapter 12).

minimal group paradigm   A standard set of research procedures that creates artificial ingroups and outgroups based on bogus information given to research participants about minimally important differences between groups (Chapters 3 & 8).

modern-symbolic prejudice (racism)   A form of prejudice that avoids blatant derogation of outgroups; it is rooted in abstractions, such as cultural stereotypes of outgroups and cultural values, rather than in people's direct experiences with members of those groups (Chapter 5).

motivation to control prejudiced reactions   A desire to appear unprejudiced that reflects both the concern that others might think that one is prejudiced (concern with acting prejudiced) and the awareness that saying and doing some kinds of things would cause trouble (constrain to avoid dispute) (Chapter 10).

motivation to respond without prejudice   A desire to appear unprejudiced that is rooted in either a sincere belief that prejudice is wrong (internal motivation), a concern with others' reactions if one were to act in a prejudiced manner (external motivation), or both (Chapter 10).

multicultural education   An umbrella term that covers a variety of programs designed to teach people about ethnic, racial, religious, and other groups in society (Chapter 12).

multicultural perspective   The viewpoint that ethnic identities are fundamental to the self-concept and that, as a result, individuals are motivated to retain their cultural heritages; holds that intergroup relations are optimized when people both retain their cultural identities and develop a higher-order identity (such as national identity) that is also held by other groups (Chapter 12).

mutual intergroup differentiation model   See *salient categorization model* (Chapter 12).

old-fashioned racism   Prejudice that is reflected in beliefs such as the biological superiority of Whites, support for racial segregation, and opposition to interracial marriage (Chapter 5).

operational definitions   Directly observable, concrete representations of hypothetical constructs (Chapter 2).

organizational discrimination   The manifestation of institutional discrimination in the context of a particular organization (Chapter 10).

outgroup homogeneity effect   The proposition that people tend to see members of their own group as very different from one another and, at the same time, tend to underestimate the differences between members of other groups (Chapters 3 & 8).

patronizing speech   A change in conversational strategies in ways that reflect age stereotypic beliefs (Chapter 9).

personal/group discrimination discrepancy (PGDD)   The proposition that people believe their group, as a whole, is more likely to be discriminated against than they, themselves, are as individuals (Chapter 11).

personal relative deprivation   The degree to which a person feels deprived of some benefit as an individual relative to other individuals (Chapter 8).

personalization model   The proposition that intergroup contact reduces prejudice by leading people to see members of the outgroup as individuals rather than as members of social categories (Chapter 12).

predictions   The restatement of hypotheses in terms of operational definitions (Chapter 2).

prejudice   An attitude directed toward people because they are members of a specific social group (Chapter 1).

priming   The exposure to an example of a member of a category, such as a picture of a Black person, that activates concepts associated with the category (Chapter 2).

probability sampling   A sample of research participants that is constructed to be an accurate representation of the population of interest (Chapter 2).

procedural justice   The fairness of the process by which rewards are distributed (Chapter 8).

process sequence   One of two overlapping waves in Aboud's cognitive developmental theory of racial attitudes; this sequence proceeds from being dominated by emotions, to relying on observable differences between the self and others, to categorizing people based on deeper conceptual differences (Chapter 7).

prototypicality   The extent to which a member of a social group or category fits the observer's concept of the essential features characteristic of that social group or category (Chapter 4).

psychological disengagement   A defensive detachment of self-esteem from outcomes in a particular domain, such that feelings of self-worth are not dependent on successes or failures in that domain (Chapter 11).

quest religious orientation   The view that religiosity is a search, or quest, for answers to questions about the meaning of life (Chapter 6).

rebound effect   The enhanced return of suppressed thoughts that follows an attempt to suppress those thoughts (Chapter 12).

regressive prejudice (racism)   Unintended expressions of prejudice by people who are otherwise low in prejudice (Chapter 10).

relative deprivation   The degree to which a person feels deprived as an individual (personal relative deprivation) or as a member of a group (group relative deprivation) (Chapter 8).

relative gratification   The perception that things are getting better (in contrast to relative deprivation, in which people perceive things to be getting worse) (Chapter 8).

reliability   The consistency with which a measure provides essentially the same result each time it is used with the same person (Chapter 2).

religious fundamentalism   The belief that there is one set of religious teachings that clearly contain the fundamental, basic, intrinsic, essential, inerrant truth about humanity and deity and that those who believe and follow these fundamental teachings have a special relationship with the deity (Chapter 6).

response amplification   A behavior toward a stigmatized person that is more extreme than behavior toward a nonstigmatized but similar person in the same type of situation (Chapter 5).

right-wing authoritarianism (RWA)   A set of attitudes—*authoritarian submission, authoritarian aggression* and *conventionalism*—that lead people to be prejudiced against groups that authority figures condemn and that are perceived to violate traditional values (Chapter 6).

salient categorization model   The proposition that the positive attitudes generated by contact with individual members of an outgroup will generalize to the group as a whole only if the individual outgroup members are seen as typical of their group (Chapter 12).

scapegoating   The process of blaming (and sometimes punishing) an innocent outgroup for the misfortunes of one's ingroup (Chapter 8).

scientific racism   The interpretation (and frequently misinterpretation) of research results to show minority groups in a negative light (Chapter 1).

secondary victimization   The psychological effects a hate crime has on members of the victim's group (Chapter 10).

self-enhancement   Looking down on others to make one feel better about oneself (Chapter 6).

self-fulfilling prophecy   Occurs when Person A's stereotype of Person B's group leads Person A to behave in ways that elicit stereotype-consistent behavior from Person B (Chapter 4).

self-protection   The tendency to look down on others when one's self-esteem is threatened in order to make one feel better about oneself, especially when doing so can directly counteract the threat (Chapter 6).

self-regulation model   The proposal that through the experience of acting in a prejudiced manner, people who see themselves as unprejudiced become sensitized to environmental cues that warn them when they might respond in a prejudiced manner so that they can act appropriately in the future (Chapter 12).

self-report   A research technique that relies on asking people to report their attitudes, opinions, and behaviors (Chapter 2).

self-stereotyping   The proposition that when group members view themselves in terms of the (usually positive) stereotypes they have of their group, the self becomes one with the group and the positive view of the group is reflected in a positive view of the self (Chapter 8).

sexual orientation hypothesis   The proposition that people are more likely to believe feminine men are gay than to believe that masculine women are lesbian (Chapter 9).

shifting standards model   The proposition that people are evaluated relative to the stereotypic expectations of their group, such that the same level of performance elicits higher evaluations for members of groups for which expectations are low than for members of groups for which expectations are high; conversely, a given evaluation is interpreted as reflecting lower levels of performance for members of low-expectation groups than for members of high-expectation groups (Chapters 3, 4, & 10).

social desirability response bias   People's tendency to act and to respond to researchers' questions in ways that make them look good (Chapter 2).

social dominance orientation (SDO)   An individual difference variable that reflects the extent to which one desires that one's ingroup dominate and be superior to outgroups (Chapter 6).

social identity   The part of a person's self-concept that derives from membership in groups that are important to the person (Chapter 8).

socialization   The process of learning one's culture in childhood by being directly taught what things are important and by observing and imitating adults' behaviors and attitudes (Chapter 5).

social learning theory   The proposition that we learn social behaviors and attitudes either directly (for example, by being rewarded or punished for our actions) or vicariously (for example, by observing the consequences of others' behavior) (Chapters 3 & 7).

social norms   Informal rules that groups develop that describe how to be a good group member (Chapter 10).

social role theory   The proposition that when we observe others, we pay attention to the social roles they occupy and, in doing so, come to associate the characteristics of the role with the individuals who occupy it (Chapter 3).

sociometric ratings   One of two types of sociometric procedures (the best friends procedure and the roster and rating procedure) that are used to measure peer status (Chapter 7).

stereotype activation   The extent to which a stereotype is accessible in one's mind (Chapter 4).

stereotype application   The extent to which one uses a stereotype to judge a member of the stereotyped group (Chapter 4).

stereotype endorsement   The extent to which a person agrees with the social stereotype of a group (Chapter 4).

stereotype fit hypothesis   The hypothesis that the characteristics associated with a social role (such as manager) are very similar to the cultural stereotypes of one group (such as men) and very different from the cultural stereotypes of another group (such as women). As a result, members of the first group are perceived as being more qualified for the role than members of the second group. (Chapter 10).

stereotypes   Beliefs and opinions about the characteristics, attributes, and behaviors of members of various groups (Chapter 1).

stereotype threat   The proposition that stigmatized group members are aware that they are stereotyped and that, especially in achievement settings, they fear confirming those stereotypes (Chapter 11).

stigmatized   Members of groups who violate the norms established by the dominant or privileged group and, as such, are marked as deviant (Chapter 11).

subtle discrimination   Unequal and harmful treatment of social group members that is typically less visible and obvious than blatant discrimination (Chapter 10).

subtle prejudice   A form of prejudice characterized by the presence of low positive affect but the absence of negative affect toward members of outgroups (Chapter 5).

subtypes   Categories that are subordinate to the more basic categories of sex, race, and age (Chapters 3 & 9).

symbolic beliefs   The perception that outgroups hold different values that are substantially different than those held by one's ingroup (Chapter 6).

symbolic prejudice (or racism)   See *modern-symbolic prejudice.*

symbolic threats   The perception that outgroup values threaten the values of one's ingroup; see also *symbolic beliefs.* (Chapter 6).

terror management theory   The proposition that people's desire to promote and defend their belief and value systems results in prejudice (Chapter 6).

test-retest reliability   A method of evaluating a measure's reliability by having a group of people complete the measure at two different times and correlating the scores (Chapter 2).

ultimate attribution error   The assumption that one's own group's negative behavior can be explained by situational processes, but similar negative actions by members of other groups are due to their internal stable characteristics (Chapter 3).

unobtrusive measures   Subtle measures of prejudice that appear to have nothing to do with prejudice or that appear to be unrelated to the research study taking place (Chapter 2).

validity   The accuracy of a measure, assessed in terms of how well scores on the measure correlate with scores on measures of related traits and behaviors and the extent to which scores on the measure are uncorrelated with scores on measures of unrelated traits and behaviors (Chapter 2).

value confrontation technique   An intervention used to make positive changes in people's intergroup attitudes by calling their attention to the contradictions implied by placing a high value on freedom while placing a low value on equality (Chapter 12).

value difference hypothesis   The proposition that prejudice is based, in part, on the perception that the outgroups' value systems differ from one's own (Chapter 6).

valuing diversity   Programs that establish quality interpersonal relationships through understanding, respecting, and valuing differences among various groups (Chapter 12).

variable   A characteristic on which people differ and so takes on more than one value when it is measured in a group of people (Chapter 2).

References

Aberson, C. L., Haag, S. C., Shoemaker, C., & Tomolillo, C. (2004, January). *Contact, anxiety, perspective taking, and stereotype endorsement as predictors of implicit and explicit biases.* Poster presented at the meeting of the Society for Personality and Social Psychology, Austin, TX.

Aberson, C. L., Healy, M., & Romero, V. (2000). Ingroup bias and self-esteem: A meta-analysis. *Personality and Social Psychology Review, 4,* 157–173.

Aboud, F. E. (1977). Interest in ethnic information: A cross-cultural developmental study. *Canadian Journal of Behavioural Science, 9,* 134–146.

Aboud, F. E. (1980). A test of ethnocentrism with young children. *Canadian Journal of Behavioural Science, 12,* 195–209.

Aboud, F. E. (1988). *Children and prejudice.* New York: Basil Blackwell.

Aboud, F. E. (2003). The formation of in-group favoritism and out-group prejudice in young children: Are they distinct attitudes? *Developmental Psychology, 39,* 48–60.

Aboud, F. E., & Amato, M. (2001). Developmental and socialization influences on intergroup bias. In R. Brown & S. L. Gaertner (Eds.), *Blackwell handbook of social psychology: Intergroup processes* (pp. 65–85). Malden, MA: Blackwell.

Aboud, F. E., & Doyle, A. B. (1995). The development of in-group pride in Black Canadians. *Journal of Cross-Cultural Psychology, 26,* 243–254.

Aboud, F. E., & Doyle, A. B. (1996a). Does talk of race foster prejudice or tolerance in children? *Canadian Journal of Behavioural Science, 28,* 161–170.

Aboud, F. E., & Doyle, A. B. (1996b). Parental and peer influences on children's racial attitudes. *International Journal of Intercultural Relations, 20,* 371–383.

Aboud, F. E., & Fenwick, V. (1999). Exploring and evaluating school-based interventions to reduce prejudice. *Journal of Social Issues, 55,* 767–768.

Aboud, F. E., & Levy, S. R. (2000). Interventions to reduce prejudice and discrimination in children and adolescents. In S. Oskamp (Ed.), *Reducing prejudice and discrimination* (pp. 269–293). Mahwah, NJ: Erlbaum.

Aboud, F. E., & Mitchell, F. G. (1977). Ethnic role-taking: The effects of preference and self-identification. *International Journal of Psychology, 12,* 1–17.

Ackman, D. (2004). *Morgan Stanley: Big bucks for bias.* Retrieved July 21, 2004, from www.forbes.com.

Adams, H. E., Wright, L. W., & Lohr, B. A. (1996). Is homophobia associated with homosexual arousal? *Journal of Abnormal Psychology, 105,* 440–445.

Adorno, T. W., Frenkel-Brunswik, E., Levinson, D. J., & Sanford, R. N. (1950). *The authoritarian personality.* New York: Harper and Row.

Agnew, C. R., Thompson, V. D., & Gaines, S. O., Jr. (2000). Incorporating proximal and distal influences on prejudice: Testing a general model across outgroups. *Personality and Social Psychology Bulletin, 26,* 403–418.

Agnew, C. R., Thompson, V. D., Smith, V. A., Gramzow, R. H., & Currey, D. P. (1993). Proximal and distal predictors of homophobia: Framing the multivariate roots of outgroup rejection. *Journal of Applied Social Psychology, 23,* 2013–2042.

Aho, J. A. (1988). Out of hate: A sociology of defection from neo-Nazism. *Current Research on Peace and Violence, 11,* 159–169.

Aho, J. A. (1990). *The politics of righteousness: Idaho Christian patriotism.* Seattle: University of Washington Press.

Allison, K. W. (1998). Stress and oppressed social category membership. In J. K. Swim & C. Stangor (Eds.), *Prejudice: The target's perspective* (pp. 145–170). San Diego: Academic Press.

Allon, N. (1982). The stigma of overweight in everyday life. In B. Wolman (Ed.), *Psychological aspects of obesity: A handbook* (pp. 130–174). New York: Van Nostrand Reinhold.

Allport, G. W. (1954). *The nature of prejudice.* New York: Perseus.

Allport, G. W., & Ross, J. M. (1967). Personal religious orientation and prejudice. *Journal of Personality and Social Psychology, 5,* 432–443.

Altemeyer, B. (1981). *Right-wing authoritarianism.* Winnipeg: University of Manitoba Press.

Altemeyer, B. (1988). *Enemies of freedom: Understanding right-wing authoritarianism.* San Francisco: Jossey-Bass.

Altemeyer, B. (1994). Reducing prejudice in right-wing authoritarians. In M. P. Zanna & J. M. Olson (Eds.), *The psychology of prejudice* (pp. 131–148). Mahwah, NJ: Erlbaum.

Altemeyer, B. (1996). *The authoritarian specter.* Cambridge, MA: Harvard University Press.

Altemeyer, B. (1998). The other "authoritarian personality." *Advances in Experimental Social Psychology, 30,* 47–92.

Altemeyer, B., & Hunsberger, B. (1992). Authoritarianism, religious fundamentalism, and prejudice. *International Journal for the Psychology of Religion, 2,* 113–133.

Ambrose, S. E. (1997). *Citizen soldiers: The U. S. Army from the Normandy Beaches to the Bulge to the surrender of Germany, June 7, 1944, to May 7, 1945.* New York: Simon & Schuster.

American Civil Liberties Union. (2003). ACLU of NJ wins $775,000 for victims of racial profiling by state troopers. Retrieved March 14, 2002, from www.aclu.org/RacialEquality.

American Psychological Association. (1996). *Affirmative action: Who benefits?* Washington, DC: Author.

American Psychological Association (2001). *Publication Manual of the American Psychological Association* (5th ed.). Washington, DC: American Psychological Association.

Amir, Y. (1976). The role of intergroup contact in the change of prejudice and ethnic relations. In P. A. Katz (Ed.), *Towards the elimination of racism* (pp. 245–308). New York: Pergamon.

Amodio, D. M., Harmon-Jones, E., & Devine, P. G. (2003). Individual differences in the activation and control of affective race bias as assessed by startle eye blink response and self-report. *Journal of Personality and Social Psychology, 84,* 738–753.

Anti-Defamation League. (2001). *101 ways to combat prejudice.* Retrieved August 11, 2004, from http://www.adl.org/prejudice/closethebook.pdf.

Archer, D., Iritani, B., Kimes, D. D., & Barrios, M. (1983). Face-ism: Five studies of sex differences in facial prominence. *Journal of Personality and Social Psychology, 45,* 725–735.

Armour, S. (2004, June 24). Wal-Mart is 'rife' with discrimination, lawsuit plaintiffs say. *USA Today,* B03.

Armstrong, K. (2000). *The battle for God: A history of fundamentalism.* New York: Ballantine.

Arnold, D. H., & Doctoroff, G. L. (2002). The early education of socioeconomically disadvantaged children. *Annual Review of Psychology, 54,* 517–545.

Aronson, E. (1999). Dissonance, hypocrisy, and the self-concept. In E. Harmon-Jones & J. Mills (Eds.), *Cognitive dissonance: Progress on a pivotal theory in social psychology* (pp. 103–206). Washington, DC: American Psychological Association.

Aronson, E., Blaney, N., Stephan, C., Sikes, J., & Snapp, M. (1978). *The jigsaw classroom.* Beverly Hills, CA: Sage.

Aronson, E., & Patnoe, S. (1997). *The jigsaw classroom: Building cooperation in the classroom* (2nd ed.). New York: Longman.

Aronson, J., Fried, C. B., & Good, C. (2001). Reducing the effects of stereotype threat on African American college students by shaping theories of intelligence. *Journal of Experimental Social Psychology, 38,* 113–125.

Aronson, J., Quinn, D. M., & Spencer, S. J. (1998). Stereotype threat and the academic underperformance of minorities and women. In J. K. Swim & C. Stangor (Eds.), *Prejudice: The target's perspective* (pp. 83–103). San Diego, CA: Academic Press.

Ashe, A., & Rampersad, A. (1993). *Days of grace: A memoir.* New York: Alfred A. Knopf.

Ashmore, R. D., & Del Boca, F. K. (1981). Conceptual approaches to stereotypes and stereotyping. In D. L. Hamilton (Ed.), *Cognitive process in stereotyping and intergroup behavior* (pp. 1–35). Hillsdale, NJ: Erlbaum.

Ashmore, R. D., & Longo, L. C. (1995). Accuracy of stereotypes: What research on physical attractiveness can teach us. In Y.-T. Lee, L. J. Jussim & C. R. McCauley (Eds.), *Stereotype accuracy: Toward appreciating group differences* (pp. 63–86). Washington, DC: American Psychological Association.

Atchley, R. (1997). *Social forces and aging.* Belmont, CA: Wadsworth.

Augoustinos, M., Innes, J. M., & Ahrens, C. (1994). Stereotypes and prejudice: The Australian experience. *British Journal of Social Psychology, 33,* 125–141.

Augoustinos, M., & Walker, I. (1995). *Social cognition: An integrated introduction.* Thousand Oaks, CA: Sage.

Averhart, C. J., & Bigler, R. S. (1997). Shades of meaning: Skin tone, racial attitudes, and constructive memory in African American children. *Journal of Experimental Child Psychology, 67,* 363–388.

Ayers, I., & Siegelman, P. (1995). Race and gender discrimination in bargaining for a new car. *American Economics Review, 85,* 304–321.

Babbie, E. (1990). *Survey research methods.* Belmont, CA: Wadsworth.

Babbie, E. (1999). *The basics of social research.* Belmont, CA: Wadsworth.

Bailey, W. T., Harrell, D. R., & Anderson, L. E. (1993). The image of middle-aged and older women in magazine advertisements. *Educational Gerontology, 19,* 97–103.

Baker, J. A., & Goggin, N. L. (1994). Portrayals of older adults in *Modern Maturity* advertisements. *Educational Gerontology, 20,* 139–145.

Baker, J. G., Fishbein, H. D. (1998). The development of prejudice towards gays and lesbians by adolescents. *Journal of Homosexuality, 36* (1), 89–100.

Bandura, A. (1977). *Social learning theory.* Upper Saddle River, NJ: Prentice Hall.

Bandura, A. (1986). *Social foundations of thought and action.* Upper Saddle River, NJ: Prentice Hall.

Banker, B. S., & Gaertner, S. L. (1998). Achieving stepfamily harmony: An intergroup-relations approach. *Journal of Family Psychology, 12,* 310–325.

Banks, J. A. (2001). Multicultural education: Characteristics and goals. In J. A. Banks & C. A. M. Banks (Eds.), *Multicultural education: Issues and perspectives* (4th ed., pp. 3–30). New York: Wiley.

Banks, R. R., & Eberhardt, J. L. (1998). Social psychological processes and the legal bases of racial categorization. In J. L. Eberhardt & S. T. Fiske (Eds.), *Confronting racism: The problem and the response* (pp. 54–75). Thousand Oaks, CA: Sage.

Bargh, J. A. (1999). The cognitive monster: The case against the controllability of automatic stereotype effects. In S. Chaiken & Y. Trope (Eds.), *Dual-process theories in social psychology* (pp. 361–382). New York: Guilford.

Bargh, J. A., Chen, M., & Burrows, L. (1996). Automaticity of social behavior: Direct effects of trait construct and stereotype activation on action. *Journal of Personality and Social Psychology, 71,* 230–244.

Barkun, M. (1997). *Religion and the racist right* (rev. ed.). Chapel Hill: University of North Carolina Press.

Barrett, G. V., & Morris, S. B. (1993). The American Psychological Association's amicus curiae brief in *Price Waterhouse v. Hopkins:* The values of science versus the values of the law. *Law and Human Behavior, 17,* 201–215.

Bar-Tal, D. (1996). Development of social categories and stereotypes in early childhood: The case of "the Arab" concept formation, stereotype and attitudes by Jewish children in Israel. *International Journal of Intercultural Relations, 20,* 341–370.

Bartholow, B. D., Decker, C. L., & Sestir, M. (2004, January). *Stereotype activation and control of prejudiced responses: Cognitive control of inhibition and its impairment by alcohol.* Paper presented at the meeting of the Society for Personality and Social Psychology, Austin, TX.

Bartlett, F. C. (1932). *Remembering.* Cambridge, UK: Cambridge University Press.

Basow, S. A. (1995). Student evaluations of college professors: Are female and male professors rated differently? *Journal of Educational Psychology, 87,* 656–665.

Basow, S. A., & Silberg, N. (1987). Student evaluations of college professors: Are female and male professors rated differently? *Journal of Educational Psychology, 79,* 308–314.

Batson, C. D. (1976). Religion as prosocial: Agent or double agent? *Journal for the Scientific Study of Religion, 15,* 29–45.

Batson, C. D., & Burris, C. T. (1994). Personal religion: Depressant or stimulant of prejudice and discrimination? In M. P. Zanna & J. M. Olson (Eds.), *The psychology of prejudice* (pp. 149–169). Hillsdale, NJ: Erlbaum.

Batson, C. D., Chang, J., Orr, R., & Rowland, J. (2002). Empathy, attitudes, and action: Can feeling for a member of a stigmatized group motivate one to help the group? *Personality and Social Psychology Bulletin, 28,* 1656–1666.

Batson, C. D., Eidelman, S. H., Higley, S. L., & Russell, S. A. (2001). "And who is my neighbor?" II: Quest religion as a source of universal compassion. *Journal for the Scientific Study of Religion, 40,* 39–50.

Batson, C. D., Flink, C. H., Schoenrade, P. A., Fultz, J., & Pych, V. (1986). Religious orientation and overt versus covert racial prejudice. *Journal of Personality and Social Psychology, 50,* 175–181.

Batson, C. D., Floyd, R. B., Meyer, J. M., & Winner, A. L. (1999). "And who is my neighbor?:" Intrinsic religion as a source of universal compassion. *Journal for the Scientific Study of Religion, 38,* 445–457.

Batson, C. D., Naifeh, S. J., & Pate, S. (1978). Social desirability, religious orientation, and racial prejudice. *Journal for the Scientific Study of Religion, 17,* 31–41.

Batson, C. D., Polycarpu, M. P., Harmon-Jones, E., Imhoff, H. I., Mitchener, E. C., Bednar, L. L., Klein, T. R., & Highberger, L. (1997). Empathy and attitudes: Can feelings for a member of a stigmatized group improve feelings toward the group? *Journal of Personality and Social Psychology, 72,* 105–118.

Batson, C. D., Schoenrade, P., & Ventis, W. L. (1993). *Religion and the individual: A social-psychological perspective.* New York: Oxford University Press.

Bayer, R. (1987). *Homosexuality and American psychiatry: The politics of diagnosis* (2nd ed.). Princeton, NJ: Princeton University Press.

Beck, R. B. (2000). *The history of South Africa.* Westport, CT: Greenwood.

Bell, D. W., & Esses, V. M. (1997). Ambivalence and response amplification toward Native peoples. *Journal of Applied Social Psychology, 27,* 1063–1084.

Bell, D. W., & Esses, V. M. (2002). Ambivalence and response amplification: A motivational perspective. *Personality and Social Psychology Bulletin, 28,* 1143–1152.

Bell, M. P., Harrison, D. A., & McLaughlin, M. E. (1997). Asian American attitudes toward affirmative action in employment: Implications for the model minority myth. *Journal of Applied Behavioral Science, 33,* 356–377.

Below, A., Molau, S., & Suchi, A. (1995). *The Homo Sapiens Americanus and the Homo Sapiens Germanus: Common stereotypes and our impressions.* Retrieved October 20, 2003, from www.iei.uiuc.edu/class.pages/daad95/stereotypes.html.

Bem, S. L. (1993). *The lenses of gender: Transforming the debate on sexual inequality.* New Haven, CT: Yale University Press.

Benbow, C. P., & Stanley, J. C. (1980). Sex differences in mathematical ability: Fact or artifact. *Science, 210,* 1262–1264.

Bendick, M., Jr., Brown, L. E., & Wall, K. (1999). No foot in the door: An experimental study of employment discrimination against older workers. *Journal of Aging and Social Policy, 10,* 5–23.

Bendick, M., Jr., Eagan, M. L., & Lofhjelm, S. M. (2001). Workforce diversity training: From anti-discrimination compliance to organizational development. *Human Resources Planning, 24*(2), 10–25.

Bendick, M., Jr., Jackson, C. W., & Reinoso, V. A. (1994). Measuring employment discrimination through controlled experiments. *Review of Black Political Economy, 23,* 23–48.

Benokraitis, N. V., & Feagin, J. R. (1995). *Modern sexism: Blatant, subtle, and covert discrimination* (2nd ed.). Englewood Cliffs, NJ: Prentice-Hall.

Berglas, S., & Jones, E. E. (1978). Drug choice as a self-handicapping strategy in response to noncontingent success. *Journal of Personality and Social Psychology, 36,* 405–417.

Berkowitz, L. (1993). *Aggression: Its causes, consequences, and control.* New York: McGraw-Hill.

Bernal, M. E., Knight, G. P., Ocampo, K. A., Garza, C. A., & Cota, M. K. (1993). Development of Mexican American identity. In M. E. Bernal and G. P. Knight (Eds.), *Ethnic identity: Formation and transmission among Hispanics and other minorities.* (pp. 31–46). Albany, NY: State University of New York Press.

Bernat, J. A., Calhoun, K. S., Adams, H. E., & Zeichner, A. (2001). Homophobia and physical aggression toward homosexual and heterosexual individuals. *Journal of Abnormal Psychology, 110,* 179–187.

Berndt, T. J., & Heller, K. A. (1986). Gender stereotypes and social inferences: A developmental study. *Journal of Personality and Social Psychology, 50,* 889–898.

Berry, J. W. (1984). Cultural relations in plural societies: Alternatives to segregation and their sociopsychological implications. In N. Miller & M. B. Brewer (Eds.), *Groups in contact: The psychology of desegregation* (pp. 11–27). Orlando, FL: Academic Press.

Berry, J. W. (2001). A psychology of immigration. *Journal of Social Issues, 57,* 615–631.

Berscheid, E., & Reis, H. T. (1998). Attraction and close relationships. In D. T. Gilbert, S. T. Fiske, & G. Lindzey (Eds.), *Handbook of social psychology* (4th ed., vol. 2, pp. 193–281). Boston: McGraw-Hill.

Bertrand, M., & Mullainathan, S. (2003). *Are Emily and Greg more employable than Lakisha and Jamal? A field experiment on labor market discrimination* (Working Paper 9873). Cambridge, MA: National Bureau of Economic Research. Retrieved September 23, 2003, from http://www.nber.org/papers/w9873.

Bettencourt, B. A., Brewer, M. B., Croak, M. R., & Miller, N. (1992). Cooperation and the reduction of intergroup bias: The role of reward structure and social orientation. *Journal of Experimental Social Psychology, 28,* 301–319.

Bieman-Copland, S., & Ryan, E. B. (1998). Aged-biased interpretation of memory successes and failures in adulthood. *Journal of Gerontology: Psychological Sciences, 53B,* P105–P111.

Biernat, M. (1994). Shifting standards and stereotype-based judgments. *Journal of Personality and Social Psychology, 66,* 5–20.

Biernat, M. (2003). Toward a broader view of social stereotyping. *American Psychologist, 58,* 1019–1027.

Biernat, M., & Crandall, C. S. (1999). Racial attitudes. In J. S. Robinson, P. R. Shaver, & L. S. Wrightsman (Eds.), *Measures of political attitudes* (pp. 297–411). San Diego, CA: Academic Press.

Biernat, M., & Kobrynowicz, D. (1997). Gender- and race-based standards of competence: Lower minimum standards but higher ability standards for devalued groups. *Journal of Personality and Social Psychology, 72,* 544–557.

Biernat, M., Manis, M., & Nelson, T. F. (1991). Comparison and expectancy processes in human judgment. *Journal of Personality and Social Psychology, 61,* 203–211.

Biernat, M., & Vescio, T. K. (2002). She swings, she hits, she's great, she's benched: Implications of gender-based shifting standards for judgment and behavior. *Personality and Social Psychology Bulletin, 28,* 66–77.

Biernat, M., Vescio, T. K., Theno, S. A., & Crandall, C. S. (1996). Values and prejudice: Understanding the impact of American values on outgroup attitudes. In C. Seligman, J. M. Olson, & M. P. Zanna (Eds.), *The psychology of values* (pp. 153–189). Mahwah, NJ: Erlbaum.

Biesanz, J. C., Neuberg, S. L., Smith, D. M., Asher, T., & Judice, T. N. (2001). When accuracy-motivated perceivers fail: Limited attentional resources and the reemerging self-fulfilling prophecy. *Personality and Social Psychology Bulletin, 27,* 621–629.

Bigler, R. S. (1999). The use of multicultural curricula and materials to counter racism in children. *Journal of Social Issues, 55,* 687–705.

Bigler, R. S., & Liben, L. S. (1993). A cognitive-developmental approach to racial stereotyping and reconstructive memory in Euro-American children. *Child Development, 64,* 1507–1518.

Bigler, R. S., Spears-Brown, C., & Markell, N. (2001). When groups are not created equal: Effects of group status on the formation of intergroup attitudes. *Child Development, 72,* 1151–1162.

Bizman, A., & Yinon, Y. (2001). Intergroup and interpersonal threats as determinants of prejudice: The moderating role of in-group identification. *Basic and Applied Social Psychology, 23,* 191–196.

Bjørgo, T. (1998). Entry, bridge-burning, and exit options: What happens to young people who join racist groups—and want to leave? In J. Kaplan & T. Bjørgo (Eds.), *Nation and race: The developing Euro-American racist subculture* (pp. 231–258). Boston: Northeastern University Press.

Blackwood, E., & Wieringa, S. E. (2003). Sapphic shadows: Challenging the silence in the study of sexuality. In L. D. Barnets & D. C. Kimmel (Eds.). *Psychological perspectives on lesbian, gay, and bisexual experiences* (pp. 410–434). New York: Columbia University Press.

Blaine, B., Crocker, J., & Major, B. (1995). The unintended negative consequences of sympathy for the stigmatized. *Journal of Applied Social Psychology, 25,* 889–905.

Blaine. B. E. (2000). *The psychology of diversity: Perceiving and experiencing social difference.* Mountain View, CA: Mayfield.

Blair, I. V. (2002). The malleability of automatic stereotypes and prejudice. *Personality and Social Psychology Review, 6,* 242–261.

Blair, I. V., Judd, C. M., Sadler, M. S., & Jenkins, C. (2002). The role of Afrocentric features in person perception: Judging by features and categories. *Journal of Personality and Social Psychology, 83,* 5–25.

Blair, I. V., Park, B., & Bachelor, J. (2003). Understanding intergroup anxiety: Are some people more anxious than others? *Group Processes & Intergroup Relations, 6,* 151–169.

Blakemore, J. E., LaRue, A. A., & Olejnik, A. B. (1979). Sex-appropriate toy preference and the ability to conceptualize toys as sex-role related. *Developmental Psychology, 15,* 339–340.

Blanchard, F. A., Crandall, C. S., Brigham, J. C., & Vaughn, L. A. (1994). Condemning and condoning racism: A social context approach to interracial settings. *Journal of Applied Psychology, 79,* 993–997.

Blanchard, F. A., Lilly, T., & Vaughn, L. A. (1991). Reducing the expression of prejudice. *Psychological Science, 2,* 101–105.

Blanchard, F. A., Weigel, R. H., & Cook, S. W. (1975). The effect of relative competence of group members upon interpersonal attraction in cooperating interracial groups. *Journal of Personality and Social Psychology, 32,* 519–530.

Blank, R., & Slipp, S. (1994). *Voices of diversity: Real people talk about problems and solutions in a workplace where everyone is not alike.* New York: American Management Association.

Blascovich, J. (2000). Using physiological indexes of psychological processes in social psychological research. In H. T. Reiss & C. M. Judd (Eds.), *Handbook of research methods in social and personality psychology* (pp. 117–137). New York: Cambridge University Press.

Blascovich, J., Spencer, S. J., Quinn, D. M., & Steele, C. (2001). African Americans and high blood pressure. *Psychological Science, 12,* 225–229.

Blascovich, J., Wyer, N. A., Swart, L. A., & Kibler, J. L. (1997). Racism and racial categorization. *Journal of Personality and Social Psychology, 72,* 1364–1372.

Blazak, R. (2001). White boys to terrorist men: Target recruitment of Nazi skinheads. *American Behavioral Scientist, 44,* 982–1000.

Blee, K. M. (2002). *Inside organized racism: Women in the hate movement.* Berkeley: University of California Press.

Bobo, L. (1988). Group conflict, prejudice, and the paradox of contemporary racial attitudes. In P. A. Katz & D. A Taylor (Eds.), *Eliminating racism: Profiles in controversy* (pp. 85–116). New York: Erlbaum.

Bobo, L., Kluegel, J. R., & Smith, R. A. (1997). Laissez-faire racism: The crystallization of a kinder, gentler antiblack ideology. In S. A. Tuch & J. K. Martin (Eds.), *Racial attitudes in the 1990s: Continuity and change* (pp. 15–42). Westport, CT: Praeger.

Bobocel, D. R., Son Hing, L. S., Davey, L. M., Stanley, D. J., & Zanna, M. P. (1998). Justice-based opposition to social policies: Is it genuine? *Journal of Personality and Social Psychology, 75,* 653–669.

Bodenhausen, G. V. (1990). Stereotypes as judgmental heuristics: Evidence of circadian variations in discrimination. *Psychological Science, 1,* 319–322.

Bodenhausen, G. V., Kramer, G. P., & Süsser, K. (1994). Happiness and stereotypical thinking in social judgment. *Journal of Personality and Social Psychology, 66,* 621–632.

Bodenhausen, G. V., & Lichtenstein, M. (1987). Social stereotypes and information-processing strategies: The impact of task complexity. *Journal of Personality and Social Psychology, 52,* 871–880.

Bodenhausen, G. V., & Macrae, C. N. (1998). Stereotype activation and inhibition. In R. S. Wyer, Jr. (Ed.), *Stereotype activation and inhibition* (pp. 1–52). Mahwah, NJ: Erlbaum.

Bodenhausen, G. V., Macrae, C. N., & Sherman, J. W. (1999). On the dialectics of discrimination: Dual processes in social stereotyping. In S. Chaiken & Y. Trope (Eds.), *Dual-process theories in social psychology* (pp. 271–290). New York: Guilford.

Bodenhausen, G. V., Mussweiler, T., Gabriel, S., & Moreno, K. N. (2002). Affective influences on stereotyping and intergroup relations. In J. P. Forgas (Ed.), *Handbook of affect and social cognition* (pp. 319–343). Mahwah, NJ: Erlbaum.

Bodenhausen, G. V., Sheppard, L. A., & Kramer, G. P. (1994). Negative affect and social judgments: The differential impact of anger and sadness. *European Journal of Social Psychology, 24,* 45–62.

Bodenhausen, G. V., & Wyer, R. S., Jr. (1985). Effects of stereotypes on decision making and information processing strategies. *Journal of Personality and Social Psychology, 48,* 267–282.

Bogardus, E. S. (1928). *Immigration and race attitudes.* Boston: Heath.

Bogdan, R., Biklen, D., Shapiro, A., & Spelkoman, D. (1990). The disabled: Media's monster. In M. Nagler (Ed.), *Perspectives on disability* (pp. 138–142). Palo Alto, CA: Health Markets Research.

Bohan, J. (1996). *Psychology and sexual orientation.* New York: Routledge.

Boldry, J., Wood, W., & Kashy, D. A. (2001). Gender stereotypes and the evaluation of men and women in military training. *Journal of Social Issues, 57,* 689–705.

Bolin, A. (1997). Transforming transvestism and transsexualism: Polarity, politics, and gender. In B. Bullough, V. L. Bullough, & J. Elias (Eds.). *Gender blending* (pp. 25–32). New York: Prometheus.

Bolinger, D. (1990). *The loaded weapon: The use and abuse of language today.* London: Longman.

Boniecki, K. A. (2004, January). *Prejudice, stereotypes, and perceived intergroup threat: A reanalysis of Stephan et al.* (2002). Poster presented at the meeting of the Society for Personality and Social Psychology, Austin, TX.

Bonilla-Silva, E. (2003). *Racism without racists: Color-blind racism and the persistence of racial inequality in the United States.* Lanham, MD: Rowman & Littlefield.

Bouchard, T. J., Jr., Segal, N. L., Tellegen, A., McGue, M., Keyes, M., & Krueger, R. (2003). Evidence for the construct validity and heritability of the Wilson-Patterson Conservatism Scale: A reared-apart twins study of social attitudes. *Personality and Individual Differences, 34,* 959–969.

Boulton, M. J., & Smith, P. K. (1996). Liking and peer perceptions among Asian and White British children. *Journal of Social and Personal Relationships, 13,* 163–177.

Bouman, W. P., & Arcelus, J. (2001). Are psychiatrists guilty of 'ageism' when it comes to taking a sexual history? *International Journal of Geriatric Psychiatry, 16,* 27–31.

Bowen, C.-C., Swim, J. K., & Jacobs, R. R. (2000). Evaluating gender biases on actual job performance of real people: A meta-analysis. *Journal of Applied Social Psychology, 30,* 2195–2215.

Boy Scouts of America and Monmouth Council v. James Dale, 530 U.S. 640 (2000).

Branscombe, N. R. (1998). Thinking about one's gender group's privileges or disadvantages: Consequences for well-being in women and men. *British Journal of Social Psychology, 37,* 167–184.

Branscombe, N. R., & Ellemers, N. (1998). Coping with group-based discrimination: Individualist versus group-level strategies. In J. K. Swim & C. Stangor (Eds.), *Prejudice: The target's perspective* (pp. 243–266). San Diego: Academic Press.

Branscombe, N. R., Schmitt, M. T., & Harvey, R. D. (1999). Perceiving pervasive discrimination among African Americans: Implications for group identification and well-being. *Journal of Personality and Social Psychology, 77,* 135–149.

Branscombe, N. R., & Wann, D. L. (1991). Physiological arousal and reactions to outgroup members during competitions that implicate an important social identity. *Aggressive Behavior, 18,* 85–93.

Brauer, M., Judd, C. M., & Jacquelin, V. (2001). The communication of social stereotypes: The effects of group discussion and information distribution on stereotypic appraisals. *Journal of Personality and Social Psychology, 81,* 463–475.

Brauer, M., Wasel, W., & Niedenthal, P. (2000). Implicit and explicit components of prejudice. *Review of General Psychology, 4,* 79–101.

Brenner, C. (1992). Eight bullets. In G. M. Herek & K. T. Berrill (Eds.), *Hate crimes: Confronting violence against lesbians and gay men* (pp. 11–15). Newbury Park, CA: Sage.

Breslau, K. (2001, October 15). Hate crime: He wasn't afraid. *Newsweek,* 8.

Brewer, M. B. (1979). In-group bias in the minimal intergroup situation: A cognitive motivational analysis. *Psychological Bulletin, 86,* 307–324.

Brewer, M. B. (1991). On being the same and different at the same time. *Personality and Social Psychology Bulletin, 17,* 475–482.

Brewer, M. B. (1999). The psychology of prejudice: Ingroup love or outgroup hate? *Journal of Social Issues, 55,* 429–444.

Brewer, M. B. (2003). *Intergroup relations* (2nd ed.). Philadelphia: Open University Press.

Brewer, M. B., & Brown, R. J. (1998). Intergroup relations. In D. T. Gilbert, S. T. Fiske, & G. Lindzey (Eds.), *Handbook of social psychology* (4th ed., vol. 2, pp. 554–594). Boston: McGraw-Hill.

Brewer, M. B., Dull, V., & Lui, L. (1981). Perceptions of the elderly: Stereotypes as prototypes. *Journal of Personality and Social Psychology, 41,* 656–670.

Brewer, M. B., & Feinstein, A. S. H. (1999). Dual processes in the cognitive representation of persons and social categories. In S. Chaiken & Y. Trope (Eds.), *Dual-process theories in social psychology* (pp. 255–270). New York: Guilford.

Brewer, M. B., & Gaertner, S. L. (2001). Toward the reduction of prejudice: Intergroup contact and social categorization. In R. Brown & S. L. Gaertner (Eds.), *Blackwell handbook of social psychology: Intergroup processes* (pp. 451–472). Malden, MA: Blackwell.

Brewer, M. B., & Miller, N. (1984). Beyond the contact hypothesis: Theoretical perspectives on desegregation. In N. Miller & M. B. Brewer (Eds.), *Groups in contact: The psychology of desegregation* (pp. 281–302). Orlando, FL: Academic Press.

Brewer, M. B., & Pickett, C. L. (1999). Distinctiveness motives as a source of the social self. In T. Tyler, R. Kramer, & O. John (Eds.), *The psychology of the social self* (pp. 71–87). Mahwah, NJ: Erlbaum.

Brewer, M. B., & Pierce, K. B. (2005). Social identity complexity and outgroup tolerance. *Personality and Social Psychology Bulletin, 31,* 428–437.

Brief, A. P. (1998). *Attitudes in and around organizations.* Thousand Oaks, CA: Sage.

Brief, A. P., Dietz, J., Cohen, R. R., Pugh, S. D., & Vaslow, J. B. (2000). Just doing business: Modern racism and obedience to authority as explanations for employment discrimination. *Organizational Behavior and Human Decision Processes, 81,* 72–97.

Brigham, J. C., & Malpass, R. S. (1985). The role of experience and contact in the recognition of faces. *Journal of Social Issues, 41*(3), 139–155.

Britt, T. W., Boniecki, K. A., Vescio, T. K., Biernat, M., & Brown, L. M. (1996). Intergroup anxiety: A person X situation approach. *Personality and Social Psychology Bulletin, 22,* 1177–1188.

Broughton, A. (2002). *The life of women and men in Europe: A statistical portrait of women and men in all stages of life.* Luxembourg: Statistical Office of the European Communities.

Broverman, I. K., Vogel, S. R., Broverman, D. M., Clarkson, F. E., & Rosenkrantz, P. S. (1972). Sex-role stereotypes: A current appraisal. *Journal of Social Issues, 28*(2), 59–78.

Brown v. Board of Education, 347 U.S. 483 (1954).

Brown, C. S., & Bigler, R. S. (2002). Effects of minority status in the classroom on children's intergroup attitudes. *Journal of Experimental Child Psychology, 83,* 77–110.

Brown, D. E. (1991). *Human universals.* New York: McGraw-Hill.

Brown, K. T., Brown, T. N., Jackson, J. S., Sellers, R. M., & Manuel, W. J. (2003). Teammates on and off the field? Contact with Black teammates and the racial attitudes of White student athletes. *Journal of Applied Social Psychology, 33,* 1379–1403.

Brown, R. (1995). *Prejudice: Its social psychology.* Cambridge, MA: Blackwell.

Brown, R., Croizet, J.-C., Bohner, G., Fournet, M., & Payne, A. (2003). Automatic category activation and social behavior: The moderating role of prejudiced beliefs. *Social Cognition, 21,* 167–193.

Brown, R., & Smith, A. (1989). Perceptions of and by minority groups: The case of women in academia. *European Journal of Social Psychology, 19,* 61–75.

Brown, R., Vivian, J., & Hewstone, M. (1999). Changing attitudes through intergroup contact: The effects of group membership salience. *European Journal of Social Psychology, 29,* 741–764.

Browning, C. R. (1992). *Ordinary men: Reserve Police Battalion 101 and the final solution in Poland.* New York: HarperCollins.

Bullock, H. E., & Fernald, J. L. (2003). "Feminism lite?" Feminist identification, speaker appearance, and perceptions of feminist and antifeminist messengers. *Psychology of Women Quarterly, 27,* 291–299.

Burnett, M. N., & Sisson, K. (1995). Doll studies revisited: A question of validity. *Journal of Black Psychology, 21,* 19–29.

Burnstein, E., & Vinokur, A. (1977). Persuasive argumentation and social comparison as determinants of attitude polarization. *Journal of Experimental Social Psychology, 13,* 315–332.

Buss, D. M., & Kenrick, D. T. (1998). Evolutionary social psychology. In D. T. Gilbert, S. T. Fiske, & G. Lindzey (Eds.), *The handbook of social psychology* (4th ed., vol. 2, pp. 982–1026). Boston: McGraw-Hill.

Bussey, K., & Bandura, A. (1992). Self-regulatory mechanisms governing gender development. *Child Development, 63,* 1236–1250.

Butler, R. N. (1969). Age-ism: Another form of bigotry. *Gerontologist, 9*(4, Pt. 1), 243–246.

Byers, B. D., & Crider, B. W. (2002). Hate crimes against the Amish: A qualitative analysis of bias motivation using routine activities theory. *Deviant Behavior, 23,* 115–148.

Byers, B. D., Crider, B. W., & Biggers, G. K. (1999). Bias crime motivation: A study of hate crime and offender neutralization techniques used against the Amish. *Journal of Contemporary Criminal Justice, 15,* 78–96.

Byrnes, D., & Kiger, G. (1988). Contemporary measures of attitudes toward Blacks. *Educational and Psychological Measurement, 48,* 107–119.

Cacioppo, J. T., Petty, R. E., Feinstein, J. A., & Jarvis, B. W. (1996). Dispositional differences in cognitive motivation: The life and times of individuals varying in need for cognition. *Psychological Bulletin, 119,* 197–253.

Cacioppo, J. T., Petty, R. E., Losch, M. E., & Kim, H. S. (1986). Electromyographic activity over facial muscle regions can differentiate the valence and intensity of affective reactions. *Journal of Personality and Social Psychology, 50,* 260–268.

Campbell, B., Schellenberg, E. G., & Senn, C. Y. (1997). Evaluating measures of contemporary sexism. *Psychology of Women Quarterly, 21,* 89–102.

Canetto, S. S., Kaminski, P. L., & Felicio, D. M. (1995). Typical and optimal aging in women and men: Is there a double standard? *International Journal of Aging and Human Development, 40*(3), 187–207.

Cannings, K., & Montmarquette, C. (1991). Managerial momentum: A simultaneous model of the career progress of male and female managers. *Industrial and Labor Relations Review, 44,* 212–228.

Caplan, P. J. (1994). *Lifting a ton of feathers.* Toronto: University of Toronto Press.

Caporael, L. R., & Culbertson, G. H. (1996). Verbal response modes of baby talk and other speech at institutions for the aged. *Language and Communication, 6,* 99–112.

Carlson, J. M., & Iovini, J. (1985). The transmission of racial attitudes from fathers to sons: A study of Blacks and Whites. *Adolescence, 20,* 233–237.

Carmines, E. G., & Layman, G. C. (1998). When prejudice matters: The impact of racial stereotypes on the racial policy preferences of Democrats and Republicans. In J. Hurwitz & M. Peffley (Eds.), *Perception and prejudice: Race and politics in the United States* (pp. 100–134). New Haven, CT: Yale University Press.

Carpenter, S., & Trentman, S. (1998). Subtypes of women and men: A new taxonomy and an exploratory analysis. *Journal of Social Behavior and Personality, 13,* 679–696.

Carr, L. G. (1997). *"Color-blind" racism.* Thousand Oaks, CA: Sage.

Carroll, R. (1988). *Cultural misunderstandings: The French-American experience* (C. Volk, Trans.). Chicago: University of Chicago Press.

Carver, C. S., & de la Garza, N. H. (1984). Schema-guided information search in stereotyping of the elderly. *Journal of Applied Social Psychology, 14,* 69–81.

Cascio, W. F. (1998). *Applied psychology in human resource management* (5th ed.). Upper Saddle River, NJ: Prentice Hall.

Castano, E., Yzerbyt, V., Bourguignon, D., & Seron, E. (2002). Who may enter? The impact of in-group identification on in-group/out-group categorization. *Journal of Experimental Social Psychology, 38,* 315–322.

Castano, E., Yzerbyt, V., Paladino, M.-P., & Sacchi, S. (2002). I belong, therefore I exist: ingroup identification, ingroup entitivity, and ingroup bias. *Personality and Social Psychology Bulletin, 28,* 135–143.

Caver, K. A., & Livers, A. B. (2002). Dear White boss. *Harvard Business Review, 80*(11), 77–81.

Cejka, M. A., & Eagly, A. H. (1999). Gender-stereotypic images of occupations correspond to the sex segregation of employment. *Personality and Social Psychology Bulletin, 25,* 413–423.

Chapman, L. J. (1967). Illusory correlation in observational report. *Journal of Verbal Learning and Verbal Behavior, 6,* 151–155.

Chen, M., & Bargh, J. A. (1997). Nonconscious behavioral confirmation processes: The self-fulfilling consequences of automatic stereotype activation. *Journal of Experimental Social Psychology, 33,* 541–560.

Chirumbolo, A. (2002). The relationship between need for cognitive closure and political orientation: The mediating role of authoritarianism. *Personality and Individual Differences, 32,* 603–610.

Christie, R. (1991). Authoritarianism and related constructs. In J. P. Robinson, P. R. Shaver, & L. S. Wrightsman (Eds.), *Measures of personality and social psychological attitudes* (pp. 501–571). San Diego, CA: Harcourt.

Chumbler, N. R. (1995). The development and reliability of a Stereotypes Toward Older People Scale. *College Student Journal, 28,* 220–229.

Cialdini, R. B., Borden, R., Thorne, A., Walker, M., Freeman, S., & Sloane, L. T. (1976). Basking in reflected glory: Three (football) field studies. *Journal of Personality and Social Psychology, 34,* 366–375.

Cialdini, R. B., & De Nicholas, M. E. (1989). Self-presentation by association. *Journal of Personality and Social Psychology, 57,* 626–631.

Cialdini, R. B., Kallgren, C. A., & Reno, R. R. (1991). A focus theory of normative conduct: A theoretical refinement and reevaluation of the role of norms in human conduct. *Advances in experimental social psychology, 24,* 201–234.

Clark, K. B., & Clark, M. P. (1947). Racial identification and preference in Negro children. In T. M. Newcomb & E.L. Hartley (Eds.), *Readings in social psychology* (pp. 169–178). New York: Holt.

Cloud, D. L. (1998). The rhetoric of <family values>: Scapegoating, utopia, and the privatization of social responsibility. *Western Journal of Communication, 62,* 387–419.

Cockburn, A., & St. Clair, J. (1998). *Driving while black.* Retrieved May 5, 2003, from www.counterpunch.org/drivingblack.html.

Cohen, C. E. (1981). Person categories and social perception: Testing some boundaries of the processing effects of prior knowledge. *Journal of Personality and Social Psychology, 40,* 441–452.

Cohen, E. G. (1984). The desegregated school: Problems in status power and interethnic climate. In N. Miller & M. B. Brewer (Eds.), *Groups in contact: The psychology of desegregation* (pp. 77–96). Orlando, FL: Academic Press.

Cohen, G. L., Steele, C.M., & Ross, L. D. (1999). The mentors' dilemma: Providing critical feedback across the racial divide. *Personality and Social Psychology Bulletin, 25,* 1302–1318.

Cohen, J. (1992). A power primer. *Psychological Bulletin, 112,* 155–159.

College bound seniors 2003: A profile of SAT program test takers. (2003). New York: The College Board.

Collins, S. M. (1997). Black mobility in White corporations: Up the corporate ladder but out on a limb. *Social Problems, 44,* 55–67.

Coltrane, S., & Messineo, M. (2000). The perpetuation of subtle prejudice: Race and gender imagery in 1990s television advertising. *Sex Roles, 42,* 363–389.

Colvin, E. (2003, December 5). Letter to the Editor. *The Chronicle Review,* B4.

Conley, T. D., Calhoun, C., Evett, S. R., & Devine, P. G. (2001). Mistakes that heterosexual people make when trying to appear non-prejudiced: The view from LGB people. *Journal of Homosexuality, 42*(2), 21–43.

Conway, M., Mount, L., & Pizzamiglio, M. T. (1996). Status, community, and agency: Implications for stereotypes of gender and other groups. *Journal of Personality and Social Psychology, 71,* 25–38.

Cook, S. W. (1979). Social science and school desegregation: Did we mislead the Supreme Court? *Personality and Social Psychology Bulletin, 5,* 420–437.

Cook, S. W. (1984). Cooperative interaction in multiethnic contexts. In N. Miller & M. B. Brewer (Eds.), *Groups in contact: The psychology of desegregation* (pp. 155–185). Orlando, FL: Academic Press.

Cook, T. D., & Flay, B. R. (1978). The persistence of experimentally induced attitude change. *Advances in Experimental Social Psychology, 11,* 1–57.

Cooley, C. H. (1902). *Human nature and the social order.* New York: Schocken.

Corenblum, B., & Annis, R. C. (1987). Racial identity and preference in Native and White Canadian children. *Canadian Journal of Behavioural Science, 19,* 254–265.

Corenblum, B., & Annis, R. C. (1994). Development of racial identity in minority and majority children: An affect discrepancy model. *Canadian Journal of Behavioural Science, 25,* 499–521.

Corenblum, B., & Stephan, W. G. (2001). White fears and Native apprehension: An integrated threat theory approach to intergroup attitudes. *Canadian Journal of Behavioural Science, 33,* 251–268.

Corley, T. J., & Pollack, R. H. (1996). Do changes in the stereotypic depiction of a lesbian couple affect heterosexuals' attitudes toward lesbianism? *Journal of Homosexuality, 32,* 1–17.

Correll, J., Park, B., Judd, C.M., & Wittenbrink, B. (2002). Targets of discrimination: Using ethnicity to disambiguate potentially threatening individuals. *Journal of Personality and Social Psychology, 83,* 1314–1329.

Corrigan, P. (2004). How stigma interferes with mental health care. *American Psychologist, 59,* 614-625.

Corrigan, P. W., & Penn, D. L. (1999). Lessons from social psychology on discrediting psychiatric stigma. *American Psychologist, 54,* 765–776.

Coupland, N., Coupland, J., Giles, H., Henwood, K., & Wiemann, J. (1988). Elderly self-disclosure: Interactional and intergroup issues. *Language and Communication, 8,* 109–133.

Cowan, G., Martinez, L., & Mendiola, S. (1997). Predictors of attitudes toward illegal Latino immigrants. *Hispanic Journal of Behavioral Sciences, 19,* 403–415.

Cox, O. C. (1948). *Caste, class, and race.* New York: Monthly Review Press.

Cox, T., Jr. (1993). *Cultural diversity in organizations: Theory, research, and practice.* San Francisco: Berrett-Koehler.

Cox, T., Jr. (2001). *Creating the multicultural organization.* San Francisco: Jossey-Bass.

Crandall, C. S. (1994). Prejudice against fat people: Ideology and self-interest. *Journal of Personality and Social Psychology, 66,* 882–894.

Crandall, C. S. (1995). Do parents discriminate against their heavyweight daughters? *Personality and Social Psychology Bulletin, 21,* 724–735.

Crandall, C. S., D'Anello, S., Sakalli, N., Lazarus, E., Wieczorkowska, G., & Feather, N. T. (2001). An attribution-value model of prejudice: Anti-fat attitudes in six nations. *Personality and Social Psychology Bulletin, 27,* 30–37.

Crandall, C. S., & Eshleman, A. (2003). A justification-suppression model of the expression and experience of prejudice. *Psychological Bulletin, 129,* 414–446.

Crandall, C. S., Eshleman, A., & O'Brien, L. (2002). Social norms and the expression and suppression of prejudice: The struggle for internalization. *Journal of Personality and Social Psychology, 82,* 359–378.

Crandall, C. S., & Martinez, R. (1996). Culture, ideology, and antifat attitudes. *Personality and Social Psychology Bulletin, 22,* 1165–1176.

Crawford, M., Stark, A., & Renner, C. H. (1998). The meaning of Ms.: Social assimilation of a gender concept. *Psychology of Women Quarterly, 22,* 197–208.

Crawford, M. T., & Skowronski, J. J. (1998). When motivated thought leads to heightened bias: High need for cognition can enhance the impact of stereotypes on memory. *Personality and Social Psychology Bulletin, 24,* 1075–1088.

Crisp, R. J., Hewstone, M., & Rubin, M. (2001). Does multiple categorization reduce intergroup bias? *Personality and Social Psychology Bulletin, 27,* 76–89.

Crocker, J., Blaine, B., & Luhtanen, R. (1993). Prejudice, intergroup behaviour and self-esteem: Enhancement and protection motives. In M. A. Hogg & D. Abrams (Eds.), *Group motivation: Social psychological perspectives* (pp. 52–67). New York: Harvester Wheatsheaf.

Crocker, J., Cornwell, B., & Major, B. (1993). The stigma of overweight: Affective consequences of attributional ambiguity. *Journal of Personality and Social Psychology, 64,* 60–70.

Crocker, J., Major, B., & Steele, C. (1998). Social stigma. In D. T. Gilbert, S. T. Fiske, & G. Lindzey (Eds.), *The handbook of social psychology* (4th ed., vol. 2, pp. 504–553). Boston: McGraw-Hill.

Crocker, J., Voelkl, K., Testa, M., & Major B. (1991). Social stigma: The affective consequences of attributional ambiguity. *Journal of Personality and Social Psychology, 60,* 218–228.

Croizet, J.-C., & Claire, T. (1998). Extending the concept of stereotype threat to social class: The intellectual underperformance of students from low socioeconomic backgrounds. *Personality and Social Psychology Bulletin, 24,* 588–594.

Crosby, F. J. (1976). A model of egoistical relative deprivation. *Psychological Review, 83,* 85–113.

Crosby, F. J. (1984). The denial of personal discrimination. *American Behavioral Scientist, 27,* 371–386.

Crosby, F. J., Clayton, S., Alksnis, O., & Hemker, K. (1986). Cognitive biases in the perception of discrimination. *Sex Roles, 14,* 637–646.

Crosby, F. J., Ferdman, B. M., & Wingate, B. R. (2001). Addressing and redressing discrimination: Affirmative action in social psychological perspective. In R. Brown & S. L. Gaertner (Eds.), *Blackwell handbook of social psychology: Intergroup processes* (pp. 495–513). Malden, MA: Blackwell.

Crosby, F. J., Iyer, A., Clayton, S., & Downing, R. A. (2003). Affirmative action: Psychological data and the policy debates. *American Psychologist, 58,* 93–115.

Crosby, F. J., Pufall, A., Snyder, R. C., O'Connell, M., & Whalen, P. (1989). The denial of personal disadvantage among you, me, and all the other ostriches. In M. Crawford & M. Gentry (Eds.), *Gender and thought: Psychological perspectives* (pp. 79–99). New York: Springer-Verlag.

Crosby, J. R., & Monin, B. (2004, January). *Failure to warn: Black students receive less realistic feedback about the consequences of difficult class loads.* Poster presented at the meeting of the Society for Personality and Social Psychology, Austin, TX.

Croteau, J. M. (1996). Research on the work experiences of lesbian, gay, and bisexual people: An integrative review of methodology and findings. *Journal of Vocational Behavior, 48,* 195–209.

Crowson, H. M., Thoma, S. J., & Hestevold, N. (2003, August). *On the development, uniqueness, and mediational role of RWA.* Paper presented at the meeting of the American Psychological Association, Toronto, Canada.

Cuddy, A. C., & Fiske, S. T. (2002). Doddering but dear: Process, content, and function in stereotyping of older persons. In T. D. Nelson (Ed.), *Ageism: Stereotyping and prejudice against older persons* (pp. 3–26). Cambridge, MA: MIT Press.

Cunningham, W. A., Nezlek, J. B., & Banaji, M. R. (2004). Implicit and explicit ethnocentrism: Revisiting the ideologies of prejudice. *Personality and Social Psychology Bulletin, 30,* 1332–1346.

Cummins, H. J. (2004, July 4). Wal-Mart case highlights covert bias. *Minneapolis Star Tribune.* Retrieved July 5, 2004, from www.startribune.com/stories.

Czopp, A. M., & Monteith, M. J. (2003). Confronting prejudice (literally): Reactions to confrontations of racial or gender bias. *Personality and Social Psychology Bulletin, 29,* 532–544.

Dail, P. W. (1988). Prime-time television portrayals of older adults in the context of family life. *The Gerontologist, 28,* 700–706.

Danso, H. A., & Esses, V. M. (2001). Black experimenters and the intellectual test performance of White participants: The tables are turned. *Journal of Experimental Social Psychology, 37,* 158–165.

Darley, J. M., & Gross, P. H. (1983). A hypothesis-confirming bias in labeling effects. *Journal of Personality and Social Psychology, 44,* 20–33.

Davey, A. G. (1983). *Learning to be prejudiced: Growing up in multi-ethnic Britain.* London: Edward Arnold.

Davies, J. C. (1969). The J-curve of rising and declining satisfactions as a cause of some great revolutions and a contained rebellion. In H. D. Graham & T. R. Gurr (Eds.), *The history of violence in America* (pp. 690–730). New York: Praeger.

Davies, M. (2004). Correlates of negative attitudes toward gay men: Sexism, male role norms, and male sexuality. *The Journal of Sex Research, 41,* 259–266.

Davis, J. A. (1959). A formal interpretation of the theory of relative deprivation. *Sociometry, 22,* 280–296.

Davis, M. H. (1994). *Empathy: A social psychological approach.* Madison, WI: Brown & Benchmark.

Davis, R. C., Taylor, B. G., & Titus, R. M. (1997). Victims as agents: Implications for victim services and crime prevention. In R. C. Davis, A. J. Lurigio, & W. G. Skogan (Eds.), *Victims of crime* (2nd ed., pp. 167–179). Thousand Oaks, CA: Sage.

Davison, H. K., & Burke, M. J. (2000). Sex discrimination in simulated employment contexts: A meta-analytic investigation. *Journal of Vocational Behavior, 56,* 225–248.

Deaux, K. (1996). Social identification. In E. T. Higgens, & A. W. Kruglanski (Eds.), *Social psychology: Handbook of basic principles* (pp. 777–798). New York: Guilford.

Deaux, K., & Kite, M. E. (1987). Thinking about gender. In B. B. Hess & M. M. Ferree (Eds.), *Analyzing gender: A handbook of social science research* (pp. 92–117). Beverly Hills, CA: Sage.

Deaux, K., & LaFrance, M. (1998). Gender. In D. T. Gilbert, S. T. Fiske, & G. Lindzey (Eds.), *Handbook of social psychology* (4th ed., vol. 1, pp. 788–827). Boston: McGraw-Hill.

Deaux, K., & Lewis, L. L. (1984). Structure of gender stereotypes: Interrelationships among components and gender label. *Journal of Personality and Social Psychology, 46,* 991–1004.

Deaux, K., & Major, B. (1987). Putting gender into context: An interactive model of gender-related behavior. *Psychological Review, 94,* 369–389.

Deaux, K., Winton, W., Crowley, M., & Lewis, L. L. (1985). Level of categorization and content of gender stereotypes. *Social Cognition, 3,* 145–167.

Deckers, L. H. (2005). *Motivation: Biological, psychological, and environmental* (2nd ed.). Boston: Allyn and Bacon.

de Dreu, C. K. W. (2003). Time pressure and the closing of the mind in negotiation. *Organizational Behavior and Human Decision Processes, 91,* 280–295.

de Dreu, C. K. W., Koole, S. L., & Oldersma, F. L. (1999). On the seizing and freezing of negotiator inferences: Need for cognitive closure moderates the use of heuristics in negotiation. *Personality and Social Psychology Bulletin, 25,* 348–362.

Deitch, E. A., Barsky, A., Butz, R. M., Chan, S., Brief, A. P., & Bradley, J. C. (2003). Subtle yet significant: The existence and impact of everyday racial discrimination in the workplace. *Human Relations, 56,* 1299–1324.

DeJong, W. (1980). The stigma of obesity: The consequences of naive assumptions concerning the causes of physical deviance. *Journal of Health and Social Behavior, 21,* 75–87.

Desforges, D. M., Lord, C. G., Ramsey, S. L., Mason, J. A., Van Leeuwen, M. D., West, S. C., & Lepper, M. R. (1991). Effects of structured cooperative contact on changing negative attitudes toward stigmatized social group. *Journal of Personality and Social Psychology, 60,* 531–544.

Deutsch, F. M., Zalenski, C. M., & Clark, M. E. (1986). Is there a double standard of aging? *Journal of Applied Social Psychology, 16,* 771–785.

Deutsch, M., & Krauss, R. M. (1965). *Theories in social psychology.* New York: Basic Books.

Devine, P. G. (1989). Stereotypes and prejudice: Their automatic and controlled components. *Journal of Personality and Social Psychology, 56,* 5–18.

Devine, P. G., & Baker, S. M. (1991). Measurement of racial stereotype subtyping. *Personality and Social Psychology Bulletin, 17,* 44–50.

Devine, P. G., & Elliot, A. J. (1995). Are racial stereotypes really fading? The Princeton trilogy revisited. *Personality and Social Psychology Bulletin, 21,* 1139–1150.

Devine, P. G., & Monteith, M. J. (1999). Automaticity and control in stereotyping. In S. Chaiken & Y. Trope (Eds.), *Dual-process theories in social psychology* (pp. 339–360). New York: Guilford.

Devine, P. G., Monteith, M. J., Zuwerink, J. R., & Elliot, A. J. (1991). Prejudice with and without compunction. *Journal of Personality and Social Psychology, 60,* 817–830.

Devine, P. G., Plant, E. A., Amodio, D. M., Harmon-Jones, E., & Vance, S. L. (2002). The regulation of explicit and implicit race bias: The role of motivations to respond without prejudice. *Journal of Personality and Social Psychology, 82,* 835–848.

Devine, P. G., Plant, E. A., & Buswell, B. N. (2000). Breaking the prejudice habit: Progress and obstacles. In S. Oskamp (Ed.), *Reducing prejudice and discrimination* (pp. 185–208). Mahwah, NJ: Erlbaum.

Dew, M. A. (1985). The effects of attitudes on inferences of homosexuality and perceived physical attractiveness in women. *Sex Roles, 12,* 143–155.

de Waal, F. B. M. (2002). Evolutionary psychology: The wheat and the chaff. *Current Directions in Psychological Science, 11,* 187–191.

Dibble, U. (1981). Socially shared deprivation and the approval of violence: Another look at the experience of American Blacks during the 1960s. *Ethnicity, 8,* 149–168.

Diekman, A. B. (2004). Learning to be little women and little men: The inequitable gender equality of nonsexist children's literature. *Sex Roles, 50,* 373–385.

Diekman, A. B., & Eagly, A. H. (2000). Stereotypes as dynamic constructs: Women and men of the past, present, and future. *Personality and Social Psychology Bulletin, 26,* 1171–1188.

Diener, E., Sandvik, E., & Larsen, R. J. (1985). Age and sex effects for emotional intensity. *Developmental Psychology, 21,* 542–546.

Dijker, A. J., & Koomen, W. (2003). Extending Weiner's attribution-emotion model of stigmatization of ill persons. *Basic and Applied Social Psychology, 25,* 51–68.

Dijksterhuis, A., & van Knippenberg, A. (1996). The knife cuts both ways: Facilitated and inhibited access to traits as a result of stereotype activation. *Journal of Experimental Social Psychology, 37,* 271–388.

Dijksterhuis, A., van Knippenberg, A., Kruglanski, A. W., & Schaper, C. (1996). Motivated social cognition: Need for closure effects on memory and judgment. *Journal of Experimental Social Psychology, 32,* 254–270.

Dirks, N. B. (2001). *Castes of mind: Colonialism and the making of modern India.* Princeton, NJ: Princeton University Press.

Dixon, T. L., & Linz, D. (2000). Race and the misrepresentation of victimization on local television news. *Communication Research, 27,* 547–573.

Dobratz, B. A. (2001). The role of religion in the collective identity of the White racialist movement. *Journal for the Scientific Study of Religion, 40,* 287–301.

Dobratz, B. A., & Shanks-Meile, S. L. (2000). *The White separatist movement in the United States.* Baltimore: Johns Hopkins University Press.

Dodge, K. A., Gilroy, F. D., & Fenzel, L. M. (1995). Requisite management characteristics revisited: Two decades later. *Journal of Social Behavior and Personality, 10*(6), 253–264.

Dollard, J., Doob, L. W., Miller, N. E., Mowrer, O. W., & Sears, R. R. (1939). *Frustration and aggression.* New Haven, CT: Yale University Press.

Donnerstein, E., & Donnerstein, M. (1976). Research on the control of interracial aggression. In R. G. Green & E. C. O'Neal (Eds.), *Perspectives on aggression* (pp. 133–168). New York: Academic Press.

Dovidio, J. F. (2001). On the nature of contemporary prejudice: The third wave. *Journal of Social Issues, 57,* 829–849.

Dovidio, J. F., Brigham, J. C., Johnson, B. T., & Gaertner, S. L. (1996). Stereotyping, prejudice, and discrimination: Another look. In C. N. Macrae, C. Stagnor, & M. Hewstone (Eds.), *Stereotypes and stereotyping* (pp. 276–319). New York: Guilford.

Dovidio, J. F., Evans, N., & Tyler, R. B. (1984). Racial stereotypes: The contents of their cognitive representations. *Journal of Experimental Social Psychology, 22*, 22–37.

Dovidio, J. F., & Gaertner, S. L. (1981). The effects of race, status, and ability on helping behavior. *Social Psychology Quarterly, 44*, 192–203.

Dovidio, J. F., & Gaertner, S. L. (1991). Changes in the expression and assessment of racial prejudice. In H. J. Knopke, R. J. Norrell, & R. W. Rogers (Eds.), *Opening doors: Perspectives on race relations in contemporary America* (pp. 119–148). Tuscaloosa: University of Alabama Press.

Dovidio, J. F., & Gaertner, S. L. (1998). On the nature of contemporary prejudice: The causes, consequences, and challenges of aversive racism. In J. L. Eberhardt & S. T. Fiske (Eds.), *Confronting racism: The problem and the response* (pp. 3–32). Thousand Oaks, CA: Sage.

Dovidio, J. F., & Gaertner, S. L. (2000). Aversive racism and selection decisions: 1989 and 1999. *Psychological Science, 11*, 315–319.

Dovidio, J. F., & Gaertner, S. L. (2004). Aversive racism. *Advances in Experimental Social Psychology, 36*, 1–52.

Dovidio, J. F., Gaertner, S. L., Isen, A. M., & Lowrance, R. (1995). Group representations and intergroup bias: Positive affect, similarity, and group size. *Personality and Social Psychology Bulletin, 21*, 856–865.

Dovidio, J. F., Gaertner, S. L., & Validzic, A. (1998). Intergroup bias: Status, differentiation, and a common in-group identity. *Journal of Personality and Social Psychology, 75*, 109–120.

Dovidio, J. F., Gaertner, S. L., Validzic, A., Matoka, K., Johnson, B., & Frazier, S. (1997). Extending the benefits of recategorization: Evaluations, self-disclosure, and helping. *Journal of Experimental Social Psychology, 33*, 401–420.

Dovidio, J. F., Kawakami, K., & Beach, K. R. (2001). Implicit and explicit attitudes: Examination of the relationship between measures of intergroup bias. In R. Brown & S. Gaertner (Eds.), *Blackwell handbook of social psychology: Intergroup processes* (pp. 175–197). Malden, MA: Blackwell.

Dovidio, J. F., Kawakami, K., & Gaertner, S. L. (2000). Reducing contemporary prejudice: Combating explicit and implicit bias at the individual and intergroup level. In S. Oskamp (Ed.), *Reducing prejudice and discrimination* (pp. 117–163). Mahwah, NJ: Erlbaum.

Dovidio, J. F., Kawakami, K., & Gaertner, S. L. (2002). Implicit and explicit prejudice and interracial interaction. *Journal of Personality and Social Psychology, 82*, 62–68.

Dovidio, J. F., Kawakami, K., Johnson, C., Johnson, B., & Howard, A. (1997). On the nature of prejudice: Automatic and controlled processes. *Journal of Experimental Social Psychology, 33*, 510–540.

Dovidio, J. F., Major, B., & Crocker, J. (2000). Stigma: Introduction and overview. In T. F. Heatherton, R. E. Kleck, M. R. Hebl, & J. G. Hull (Eds.), *The social psychology of stigma* (pp. 1–28). New York: Guilford.

Dovidio, J. F., Smith, J. K., Donnella, A. G., & Gaertner, S. L. (1997). Racial attitudes and the death penalty. *Journal of Applied Social Psychology, 27*, 1468–1487.

Doyle, A. B., & Aboud, F. E. (1995). A longitudinal study of White children's racial prejudice as a social-cognitive development. *Merrill Palmer Quarterly, 41*, 209–228.

Dreher, G. F., & Cox, T. H., Jr. (1996). Race, gender, and opportunity: A study of compensation attainment and the establishment of mentoring relationships. *Journal of Applied Psychology, 81*, 297–308.

Dube, K. (2004, June 18). What feminism means to today's undergraduates. *The Chronicle Review, 50*, B5.

Duck, R. J., & Hunsberger, B. (1999). Religious orientation and prejudice: The role of religious proscription, right-wing authoritarianism, and social desirability. *International Journal for the Psychology of Religion, 9*, 157–179.

Duckitt, J. (1994). *The social psychology of prejudice.* Westport, CT: Praeger.

Duckitt, J. (2001). A dual-process cognitive-motivational theory of ideology and prejudice. *Advances in Experimental Social Psychology, 33*, 41–113.

Duckitt, J., & Mphuthing, T. (2002). Relative deprivation and intergroup attitudes: South Africa before and after the transition. In I. Walker & H. J. Smith (Eds.), *Relative deprivation: Specification, development, and integration* (pp. 69–90). New York: Cambridge University Press.

Duckitt, J., Wagner, C., du Plessis, I., & Birum, I. (2002). The psychological bases of ideology and prejudice: Testing a dual process mode. *Journal of Personality and Social Psychology, 83*, 75–93.

Duncan, B. L. (1976). Differential social perception and attribution of intergroup violence: Testing the lower limits of stereotyping of Blacks. *Journal of Personality and Social Psychology, 34*, 590–598.

Duncan, L. E., Peterson, B. E., & Winter, D. G. (1997). Authoritarianism and gender roles: Toward a psychological analysis of hegemonic relationships. *Personality and Social Psychology Bulletin, 23*, 41–49.

Dunning, D., & Sherman, D. A. (1997). Stereotypes and tacit inference. *Journal of Personality and Social Psychology, 73*, 459–471.

Dunton, B. C., & Fazio, R. H. (1997). An individual difference measure of motivation to control prejudiced reactions. *Personality and Social Psychology Bulletin, 23*, 316–326.

Dutton, D. G., & Lake, R. A. (1973). Threat of own prejudice and reverse discrimination in interracial situations. *Journal of Personality and Social Psychology, 28*, 94–100.

Duriez, B., & Van Hiel, A. (2002). The march of modern fascism: A comparison of social dominance orientation and authoritarianism. *Personality and Individual Differences, 32*, 1199–1213.

Eagly, A. H. (1987). *Sex differences in social behavior: A social-role interpretation.* Hillsdale, NJ: Erlbaum.

Eagly, A. H., Ashmore, R. D., Makhijani, M. G., & Longo, L. C. (1991). What is beautiful is good, but . . . : A meta-analytic review of research on the physical attractiveness stereotype. *Psychological Bulletin, 110*, 109–128.

Eagly, A. H., & Chaiken, S. (1993). *The psychology of attitudes.* Fort Worth, TX: Harcourt.

Eagly, A. H., & Chaikin, S. (1998). Attitude structure and function. In D. T. Gilbert, S. T. Fiske, & G. Lindzey (Eds.), *Handbook of social psychology* (4th ed., vol. 1, pp. 269–322). Boston: McGraw-Hill.

Eagly, A. H., & Karau, S. J. (1991). Gender and the emergence of leaders: A meta-analysis. *Journal of Personality and Social Psychology, 60*, 685–710.

Eagly, A. H., & Karau, S. J. (2002). Role congruity theory of prejudice toward female leaders. *Psychological Review, 109,* 573–598.

Eagly, A. H., Makhijani, M. G., & Klonsky, B. G. (1992). Gender and the evaluation of leaders: A meta-analysis. *Psychological Bulletin, 117,* 125–145.

Eagly, A. H., & Mladinic, A. (1994). Are people prejudiced against women? Some answers from research on attitudes, gender stereotypes and judgments of competence. In W. Stroebe & M. Hewstone (Eds.), *European review of social psychology* (vol. 5, pp. 1–35). New York: Wiley.

Eagly, A. H., Mladinic, A., & Otto, S. (1991). Are women evaluated more favorably than men? An analysis of attitudes, beliefs, and emotions. *Psychology of Women Quarterly, 15,* 203–216.

Eagly, A. H., Mladinic, A., & Otto, S. (1994). Cognitive and affective bases of attitudes toward social groups and social policies. *Journal of Experimental Social Psychology, 30,* 113–137.

Eagly, A. H., Wood, W., & Diekman, A. B. (2000). Social role theory of sex differences and similarities: A current appraisal. In T. Eckes (Ed.), *The developmental social psychology of gender* (pp. 123–174). Mahwah, NJ: Erlbaum.

Eberhardt, J. L., & Fiske, S. T. (1994). Affirmative action in theory and practice: Issues of power, ambiguity, and gender versus race. *Basic and Applied Social Psychology, 15,* 201–220.

Eckes, T. (1994). Features of men, features of women: Assessing stereotypic beliefs about gender subtypes. *British Journal of Social Psychology, 33,* 107–123.

Eckes, T. (2002). Paternalistic and envious gender stereotypes: Testing predictions from the stereotype content model. *Sex Roles, 47,* 99–114.

Edwards, J. A., Weary, G., & Reich, D. A. (1998). Causal uncertainty: Factor structure and relation to the Big Five factors. *Personality and Social Psychology Bulletin, 24,* 451–462.

Effects of segregation and the consequences of desegregation; a social science statement. Appendix to appellant's briefs: *Brown v. Board of Education of Topeka, Kansas.* (1953). *Minnesota Law Review, 37,* 427–439.

Ehrlich, H. J. (1999). Campus ethnoviolence. In F. L. Pincus & H. J. Ehrlich (Eds.), *Race and ethnic conflict: Contending views on prejudice, discrimination, and ethnoviolence* (2nd ed., pp. 277–290). Boulder, CO: Westview.

Ehrlich, H. J., Larcom, B. E. K., & Purvis, R. D. (1995). The traumatic impact of ethnoviolence. In L. J. Lederer & R. Delgado (Eds.), *The price we pay: The case against racist speech, hate propaganda, and pornography* (pp. 62–79). New York: Hill and Wang.

Eliason, M. J. (1997). The prevalence and nature of biphobia in heterosexual undergraduate students. *Archives of Sexual Behavior, 26,* 317–326.

Eliason, M. J., Donelan, C., & Randall, C. (1992). Lesbian stereotypes. *Health Care for Women International, 13,* 131–144.

Eller, A., & Abrams, D. (2003). "Gringos" in Mexico: Cross-sectional and longitudinal effects of language school-promoted contact on intergroup bias. *Group Processes & Intergroup Relations, 6,* 55–75.

Eller, A., & Abrams, D. (2004). Come together: Longitudinal comparisons of Pettigrew's reformulated intergroup contact model and the Common Ingroup Identity Model in Anglo-French and Mexican-American contexts. *European Journal of Social Psychology, 34,* 229–256.

Ellison, C. G., & Powers, D. A. (1994). The contact hypothesis and racial attitudes among Black Americans. *Social Science Quarterly, 75,* 385–400.

Ensari, N. (2001). How can managers reduce intergroup conflict in the workplace? Social psychological approaches to addressing prejudice in organizations. *Psychologist-Manager Journal, 5*(2), 83–93.

Ensari, N., & Miller, N. (2002). The out-group must not be so bad after all: The effects of disclosure, typicality, and salience on intergroup bias. *Journal of Personality and Social Psychology, 83,* 313–329.

Erber, J. T. (1989). Young and older adults' appraisal of memory failures in young and older adult target persons. *Journal of Gerontology: Psychological Sciences, 44,* P170–P175.

Erber, J. T. (2005). *Aging and older adulthood.* Belmont, CA: Wadsworth.

Erber, J. T., & Danker, D. C. (1995). Forgetting in the workplace: Attributions and recommendations for young and older employees. *Psychology and Aging, 10,* 565–569.

Erber, J. T., Etheart, M. E., & Szuchman, L. T. (1992). Age and forgetfulness: Perceivers' impressions of targets' capability. *Psychology and Aging, 7,* 479–483.

Erber, J. T., & Rothberg, S. T. (1991). Here's looking at you: The relative effect of age and attractiveness on judgments about memory failure. *Journal of Gerontology: Psychological Sciences, 46,* P116–P123.

Erber, J. T., Szuchman, L. T., & Etheart, M. E. (1993). Age and forgetfulness: Young perceivers' impressions of young and older neighbors. *International Journal of Aging and Human Development, 37*(2), 91–103.

Erber, J. T., Szuchman, L. T., & Rothberg, S. T. (1990). Everyday memory failure: Age differences in appraisal and attribution. *Psychology and Aging, 5,* 236–241.

Ernulf, K. E., Innala, S. M., & Whitam, F. L. (1989). Biological explanation, psychological explanation, and tolerance of homosexuals: A cross-national analysis of beliefs and attitudes. *Psychological Reports, 65,* 1003–1010.

Eschholz, S., Bufkin, J., & Long, J. (2002). Symbolic reality bites: Women and racial/ethnic minorities in modern film. *Sociological Spectrum, 22,* 299–335.

Essed, P. (1991). *Understanding everyday racism: An interdisciplinary theory.* Newbury Park, CA: Sage.

Esses, V. M., & Dovidio, J. F. (2003). The role of emotions in determining willingness to engage in intergroup contact. *Personality and Social Psychology Bulletin, 28,* 1202–1214.

Esses, V. M., Haddock, G., & Zanna, M. P. (1993). Values, stereotypes, and emotions as determinants of intergroup attitudes. In D. M. Mackie & D. L. Hamilton (Eds.), *Affect, cognition, and stereotyping: Interactive processes in group perception* (pp. 137–166). San Diego: Academic Press.

Esses, V. M., Jackson, L. M., & Armstrong, T. L. (1998). Intergroup competition and attitudes toward immigrants and immigration: An instrumental model of group conflict. *Journal of Social Issues, 54,* 699–724.

Esses, V. M., & Zanna, M. P. (1995). Mood and the expression of ethnic stereotypes. *Journal of Personality and Social Psychology, 69,* 1052–1068.

Ezekiel, R. S. (1995). *The racist mind: Portraits of American neo-Nazis and Klansmen.* New York: Penguin.

Ezekiel, R. S. (2002). An ethnographer looks at neo-Nazi and Klan groups: *The Racist Mind* revisited. *American Behavioral Scientist, 46,* 51–71.

Fagan, J. F., & Singer, L. T. (1979). The role of simple feature differences in infants' recognition of faces. *Infant Behavior and Development, 2*, 39–45.

Fagot, B. I. (1985). Beyond the reinforcement principle: Another step toward understanding sex role development. *Developmental Psychology, 21*, 1097–1104.

Fassinger, R. E. (2001). Women in nontraditional occupational fields. In J. Worell (Ed.), *The encyclopedia of women and gender: Sex similarities and the impact of society on gender* (Vol. 2, pp. 1169–1180). New York: Academic Press.

Fazio, R. H. (2001). On the automatic activation of associated evaluations: An overview. *Cognition and Emotion, 15*, 115–141.

Fazio, R. H., & Dunton, B. C. (1997). Categorization by race: The impact of automatic and controlled components of racial prejudice. *Journal of Experimental Social Psychology, 33*, 451–470.

Fazio, R. H., & Hilden, L. E. (2001). Emotional reactions to a seemingly prejudiced response: The role of automatically activated racial attitudes and motivation to control prejudice. *Personality and Social Psychology Bulletin, 27*, 538–549.

Fazio, R. H., Jackson, J. R., Dunton, B. C., & Williams, C. J. (1995). Variability in automatic activation as an unobtrusive measure of racial attitudes: A bona fide pipeline? *Journal of Personality and Social Psychology, 69*, 1013–1027.

Fazio, R. H., & Olson, M. A. (2003). Implicit measures in social cognition research: Their meaning and use. *Annual Review of Psychology, 54*, 297–327.

Fazio, R. H., & Towles-Schwen, T. (1999). The MODE model of attitude-behavior processes. In S. Chaiken & Y. Trope (Eds.), *Dual process theories in social psychology* (pp. 97–116). New York: Guilford.

Feagin, J. R. (1991). The continuing significance of race: Antiblack discrimination in public places. *American Sociological Review, 56*, 101–116.

Feagin, J. R., & McKinney, K. D. (2003). *The many costs of racism.* Lanham, MD: Rowman & Littlefield.

Feagin, J. R., & Sikes, M. P. (1994). *Living with racism: The Black middle-class experience.* Boston: Beacon.

Feagin, J. R., & Vera, H. (1995). *White racism: The basics.* New York: Routledge.

Federico, C. M., & Sidanius, J. (2002). Racism, ideology, and affirmative action revisited: The antecedents and consequences of "principled objections" to affirmative action. *Journal of Personality and Social Psychology, 82*, 488–502.

Fein, S., Hoshino-Browne, E., Davies, P. G., & Spencer, S. J. (2003). Self-image maintenance goals and sociocultural norms in motivated social perception. In S. J. Spencer, S. Fein, M. P. Zanna, & J. M. Olson (Eds.), *Motivated social perception* (pp. 21–44). Mahwah, NJ: Erlbaum.

Fein, S., & Spencer, S. J. (1997). Prejudice as self-image maintenance: Affirming the self through derogating others. *Journal of Personality and Social Psychology, 73*, 31–44.

Festinger, L. (1957). *A theory of cognitive dissonance.* Stanford, CA: Stanford University Press.

Fichten, C. S., & Amsel, R. (1986). Trait attributions about physically disabled college students: Circumplex analyses and methodological issues. *Journal of Applied Social Psychology, 16*, 410–427.

Filardi, J. (Writer), & A. Shankman (Director) (2003). *Bringing down the house.* In D. Hoberman, A. Amritraj, & T. Liberman (Producer), Buena Vista Pictures.

Fine, M., & Asch, A. (1993). Disability beyond stigma: Social interaction, discrimination, and activism. In M. Nagler (Ed.), *Perspectives on disability* (2nd ed., pp. 49–62). Palo Alto, CA: Health Markets Research.

Finkelstein, L. M., Burke, M. J., & Raju, N. S. (1995). Age discrimination in simulated employment contexts: An integrative analysis. *Journal of Applied Psychology, 80,* 652–663.

Finkelstein, N. W., & Haskins, R. (1983). Kindergarten children prefer same-color peers. *Child Development, 54,* 502–508.

Finlay, K. A., & Stephan, W. G. (2000). Improving intergroup relations: The effects of empathy on racial attitudes. *Journal of Applied Social Psychology, 30,* 1720–1737.

Finn, G. P. T. (1997). Qualitative analysis of murals in Northern Ireland: Paramilitary justifications for political violence. In N. Hayes (Ed.), *Doing qualitative analysis in psychology* (pp. 143–178). Hove, England: Psychology Press.

Fischer, A. R., & Good, G. E. (1998). New directions for the study of gender role attitudes: A cluster analytic investigation of masculinity ideologies. *Psychology of Women Quarterly, 22,* 371–384.

Fischer, A. R., & Shaw, C. M. (1999). African Americans' mental health and perceptions of racist discrimination: The moderating effects of racial socialization experiences and self-esteem. *Journal of Counseling Psychology, 46,* 395–407.

Fischer, A. R., Tokar, D. M., Good, G. E., & Snell, A. F. (1998). More on the structure of male role norms. *Psychology of Women Quarterly, 22,* 135–155.

Fishbein, H. D. (2002). *Peer prejudice and discrimination: The origins of prejudice* (2nd ed.). Mahwah, NJ: Lawrence Erlbaum Associates.

Fishbein, H. D., & Imai, S. (1993). Preschoolers select playmates on the basis of gender and race. *Journal of Applied Developmental Psychology, 14,* 303–316.

Fisher, R. D., Derison, D., Polley, C. F. III, Cadman, J., & Johnston, D. (1998). Religiousness, religious orientation, and attitudes toward gays and lesbians. *Journal of Applied Social Psychology, 24,* 614–630.

Fiske, A. P., Kitayama, S., Markus, H. R., & Nisbett, R. E. (1998). The cultural matrix of social psychology. In D. T. Gilbert, S. T. Fiske, & G. Lindzey (Eds.), *The handbook of social psychology* (4th ed., vol. 2, pp. 915–981). Boston: McGraw-Hill.

Fiske, S. T. (1980). Attention and weight in person perception: The impact of negative and extreme behavior. *Journal of Personality and Social Psychology, 38,* 889–906.

Fiske, S. T. (1993). Controlling other people: The impact of power on stereotyping. *American Psychologist, 48,* 621–628.

Fiske, S. T. (1998). Stereotyping, prejudice, and discrimination. In D. T. Gilbert, S. T. Fiske, & G. Lindzey (Eds.), *The handbook of social psychology* (4th ed., vol. 2, pp. 357–411). Boston: McGraw-Hill.

Fiske, S. T. (2003). Five core social motives, plus or minus five. In S. J. Spencer, S. Fein, M. P. Zanna, & J. M. Olson (Eds.), *Motivated social perception* (pp. 233–246). Mahwah, NJ: Erlbaum.

Fiske, S. T., Cuddy, A. J. C., Glick, P., & Xu, J. (2002). A model of (often mixed) stereotype content: Competence and warmth respectively follow from perceived status and competition. *Journal of Personality and Social Psychology, 82,* 878–902.

Fiske, S. T., Lin, M., & Neuberg, S. L. (1999). The continuum model: Ten years later. In S. Chaiken & Y. Trope (Eds.), *Dual-process theories in social psychology* (pp. 231–254). New York: Guilford.

Fiske, S. T., & Neuberg, S. L. (1990). A continuum model of impression formation: From category-based to individuating processes as a function of information, motivation, and attention. *Advances in Experimental Social Psychology, 23,* 1–108.

Fiske, S. T., & Ruscher, J. B. (1993). Negative interdependence and prejudice: Whence the affect? In D. M. Mackie & D. L. Hamilton (Eds.), *Affect, cognition, and stereotyping: Interactive processes in group perception* (pp. 239–268). New York: Academic Press.

Fiske, S. T., & Taylor, S. E. (1984). *Social cognition.* New York: Random House.

Fiske, S. T., & Taylor, S. E. (1991). *Social cognition* (2nd ed.). New York: McGraw-Hill.

Fiske, S. T., Xu, J., Cuddy, A. C., & Glick, P. (1999). (Dis)respecting versus (dis)liking: Status and interdependence predict ambivalent stereotypes of competence and warmth. *Journal of Personality and Social Psychology, 55,* 473–489.

Florack, A., Scarabis, M., & Bless, H. (2001). When do associations matter? The use of automatic associations toward ethnic groups in person judgments. *Journal of Experimental Social Psychology, 37,* 518–524.

Folger, R. (1987). Reformulating the preconditions of resentment: A referent cognition model. In J. C. Masters & W. P. Smith (Eds.), *Social comparison, social justice, and relative deprivation* (pp. 183–215). Mahwah, NJ: Erlbaum.

Forbes, H. D. (1985). *Nationalism, ethnocentrism, and personality: Social science and critical theory.* Chicago: University of Chicago Press.

Ford, T. E., & Ferguson, M. A. (2004). Social consequences of disparagement humor: A prejudiced norm theory. *Personality and Social Psychology Review, 8,* 79–94.

Forsyth, D. R. (2006). *Group dynamics* (4th ed.). Pacific Grove, CA: Brooks/Cole.

Forteza, J. A., & Prieto, J. M. (1994). Aging and work behavior. In H. C. Triandis, M. D. Dunnette, & I. M. Hough (Eds.), *Handbook of industrial and organizational psychology* (Vol. 4, pp. 447–483). Palo Alto, CA: Consulting Psychology Press.

Fox, D. J., & Jordan, V. D. (1973). Racial preference and identification of Black, American Chinese, and White children. *Genetic Psychology Monographs, 88,* 229–286.

Franco, F., & Maass, A. (1999). Intentional control over prejudice: When the choice of measure matters. *European Journal of Social Psychology, 29,* 469–477.

Frank, M. G., & Gilovich, T. (1988). The dark side of self- and social perception: Black uniforms and aggression in professional sports. *Journal of Personality and Social Psychology, 54,* 74–85.

Franklin, A. J. (2004). *From brotherhood to manhood: How black men rescue their relationships and dreams from the invisibility syndrome.* New York: Wiley.

Franklin, K. (1998). Unassuming motivations: Contextualizing the narratives of antigay assailants. In G. M. Herek (Ed.), *Stigma and sexual orientation: Understanding prejudice against lesbians, gay men, and bisexuals* (pp. 1–23). Thousand Oaks, CA: Sage.

Franklin, K. (2000). Antigay behaviors among young adults: Prevalence, patterns, and motivators in a noncriminal population. *Journal of Interpersonal Violence, 15,* 339–362.

Frederickson, G. M. (1999). Models of American ethnic relations: A historical perspective. In D. A. Prentice & D. T. Miller (Eds.), *Cultural divides: Understanding and overcoming group conflict* (pp. 23–34). New York: Russell Sage Foundation.

Fried, C. B. (1996). Bad rap for rap: Bias in reactions to music lyrics. *Journal of Applied Social Psychology, 26,* 2135–2146.

Fried, C. B. (1999). Who's afraid of rap? Differential reactions to music lyrics. *Journal of Applied Social Psychology, 29,* 705–721.

Friedman, D., Putnam, L., Hamberger, M., & Berman, S. (1992). Mini-longitudinal study of the cognitive ERPs during picture-matching in children, adolescents and adults: A replication. *Journal of Psychophysiology, 6,* 29–46.

Friedman, H., & Zebrowitz, L. A. (1992). The contribution of typical sex differences in facial maturity to sex-role stereotypes. *Personality and Social Psychology Bulletin, 18,* 430–438.

Fuegen, K., & Biernat, M. (2000). Defining discrimination in the personal/group discrimination discrepancy. *Sex Roles, 43,* 285–310.

Fullilove, R. E., & Treisman, P. U. (1990). Mathematics achievement among African American undergraduates at the University of California, Berkeley: An evaluation of the Mathematics Workshop Program. *Journal of Negro Education, 59,* 463–478.

Fulton, A. S., Gorsuch, R. L., & Maynard, E. A. (1999). Religious orientation, antihomosexual sentiment, and fundamentalism among Christians. *Journal for the Scientific Study of Religion, 38,* 14–22.

Furnham, A. (1990). *The Protestant work ethic: The psychology of work-related beliefs and behaviours.* New York: Routledge.

Furnham, A., & Mak, T. (1999). Sex-role stereotyping in television commercials: A review and comparison of fourteen studies done on five continents over 25 years. *Sex Roles, 41,* 413–437.

Gaertner, S. L., & Dovidio, J. F. (2000). *Reducing intergroup bias: The common ingroup identity model.* Philadelphia: Psychology Press.

Gaertner, S. L., Dovidio, J. F., Anastasio, P. A., Bachman, B. A., & Rust, M. C. (1993). The common ingroup identity model: Recategorization and the reduction of intergroup bias. In W. Stroebe & M. Hewstone (Eds.), *European review of social psychology* (vol. 4, pp. 1–26). Chichester, UK: Wiley.

Gaertner, S. L., Dovidio, J. F., & Bachman, B. A. (1996). Revisiting the contact hypothesis: The induction of a common ingroup identity. *International Journal of Intercultural Relations, 20,* 271–296.

Gaertner, S. L., Dovidio, J. F., Banker, B., Houlette, M., Johnson, K. M., & McGlynn, E. A. (2000). Reducing intergroup conflict: From superordinate goals to decategorization, recategorization, and mutual differentiation. *Group Dynamics, 4,* 98–114.

Gaertner, S. L., Dovidio, J. F., Banker, B. S., Rust, M. C., Nier, J. A., Mottola, G. R., & Ward, C. M. (1997). Does White racism necessarily mean antiblackness? Aversive racism and prowhiteness. In M. Fein, L. Weis, L. C. Powell, & L. M. Wong (Eds.), *Off White: Readings on race, power, and society* (pp. 167–178). New York: Routledge.

Gaertner, S. L., Dovidio, J. F., Rust, M. C., Nier, J. A., Banker, B. S., Ward, C. M., Mottola, G. R., & Houlette, M. (1999). Reducing intergroup bias: Elements of intergroup cooperation. *Journal of Personality and Social Psychology, 76,* 388–402.

Gaertner, S. L., Mann, J. A., Murrell, A. J., & Dovidio, J. F. (1989). Reducing intergroup bias: The benefits of recategorization. *Journal of Personality and Social Psychology, 57,* 239–249.

Gaertner, S. L., Rust, M. C., Dovidio, J. F., Bachman, B. A., & Anastasio, P. A. (1996). The contact hypothesis: The role of a common ingroup identity on reducing intergroup bias among majority and minority group members. In J. L. Nye & A. M. Bower (Eds.),

What's social about social cognition: Research on socially shared cognition in small groups (pp. 230–260). Thousand Oaks, CA: Sage.

Galinsky, A. D., & Moskowitz, G. B. (2000). Perspective-taking: Decreasing stereotype expression, stereotype accessibility, and in-group favoritism. *Journal of Personality and Social Psychology, 78,* 708–724.

Gallup Organization (2002). *Effects of Sept. 11 on immigration attitudes fading, but still evident.* Retrieved May 5, 2003, from www.gallup.com.

Gallup, G., Jr. (2002). *The Gallup poll: Public opinion 2001.* Wilmington, DE: Scholarly Resources.

Game, F., Carchon, I., & Vital Durand, F. (2003). The effect of stimulus attractiveness of visual tracking in 2- and 6-month-old infants. *Infant Behavior and Development, 26,* 135–150.

Garrison, C. Z., Schoenbach, V. J., Schluchter, M. D., & Kaplan, B. H. (1987). Life events in early adolescence. *Journal of the American Academy of Child and Adolescent Psychiatry, 26,* 865–872.

Geis, F. L., Brown, V., Jennings (Walstedt), J., & Porter, N. (1984). TV commercials as achievement scripts for women. *Sex Roles, 7/8,* 513–525.

Gekoski, W. L., & Knox, V. J. (1990). Ageism or healthism? Perceptions based on age and health status. *Journal of Aging and Health, 2(1),* 15–27.

George, D. M., & Hoppe, R. A. (1979). Racial identification, preference, and self-concept. *Journal of Cross-Cultural Psychology, 10,* 85–100.

Gerbner, G. (1997). Gender and age in prime-time television. In S. Kirschner & D. A. Kirschner (Eds.), *Perspectives on psychology and the media* (pp. 69–94). Washington: American Psychological Association.

Gibbons, F. X., Gerrard, M., Cleveland, M. J., Wills, T. A., & Bordy, G. H. (2004). Perceived discrimination and substance abuse in African American parents and their children: A panel study. *Journal of Personality and Social Psychology, 86,* 1048–1061.

Gilbert, D. T., & Hixon, J. G. (1991). The trouble of thinking: Activation and application of stereotypic beliefs. *Journal of Personality and Social Psychology, 60,* 509–517.

Gilens, M. (1996). Race and poverty in America: Public misperceptions and the American news media. *Public Opinion Quarterly, 60,* 515–541.

Gilman, S. L. (1985). *Difference and pathology: Stereotypes of sexuality, race, and madness.* Ithaca, NY: Cornell University Press.

Glascock, J., & Preston-Schreck, C. (2004). Gender and racial stereotypes in daily newspaper comics: A time-honored tradition? *Sex Roles, 51,* 423–431.

Glick, P. (2002). Sacrificial lambs dressed in wolves' clothing: Envious prejudice, ideology, and the scapegoating of Jews. In L. S. Newman & R. Erber (Eds.), *Understanding genocide: The social psychology of the Holocaust* (pp. 113–142). New York: Oxford University Press.

Glick, P., & Fiske, S. T. (1996). The Ambivalent Sexism Inventory: Differentiating hostile and benevolent sexism. *Journal of Personality and Social Psychology, 70,* 491–512.

Glick, P., & Fiske, S. T. (1997). Hostile and benevolent sexism: Measuring ambivalent sexist attitudes toward women. *Psychology of Women Quarterly, 23,* 519–536.

Glick, P., & Fiske, S. T. (1999). The Ambivalence Toward Men Inventory: Differentiating hostile and benevolent beliefs about men. *Psychology of Women Quarterly, 23,* 519–536.

Glick, P., & Fiske, S. T. (2001a). An ambivalent alliance: Hostile and benevolent sexism as complementary justifications for gender inequality. *American Psychologist, 56,* 109–118.

Glick, P., & Fiske, S. T. (2001b). Ambivalent sexism. *Advances in Experimental Social Psychology, 33,* 115–188.

Glick, P., & Fiske, S. T. (2001c). Ambivalent stereotypes as legitimizing ideologies: Differentiating paternalistic and envious prejudice. In J. T. Jost & B. Major (Eds.), *The psychology of legitimacy* (pp. 278–306). New York: Cambridge University Press.

Glick, P., Fiske, S. T., Mladinic, A., Saiz, J. L., Abrams, D., & Masser, B. (2000). Beyond prejudice as simply antipathy: Hostile and benevolent sexism across cultures. *Journal of Personality and Social Psychology, 79,* 763–775.

Goffman, E. (1963). *Stigma: Notes on the management of a spoiled identity.* Englewood Cliffs, NJ: Prentice-Hall.

Goldfried, J., & Miner, M. (2002). Quest religion and the problem of limited compassion. *Journal for the Scientific Study of Religion, 41,* 685–695.

Goldhagen, D. J. (1996). *Hitler's willing executioners: Ordinary Germans and the Holocaust.* New York: Knopf.

Goldstein, N. (1992). *The Associated Press stylebook and libel manual.* Reading, MA: Addison-Wesley.

Goldstein, S. B., & Johnson, V. A. (1997). Stigma by association: Perceptions of the dating partners of college students with physical disabilities. *Basic and Applied Social Psychology, 19,* 495–504.

Goodman, D. J. (2001). *Promoting diversity and social justice: Educating people from privileged groups.* Thousand Oaks, CA: Sage.

Goodwin, S. A., & Fiske, S. T. (1996). Judge not lest . . . : The ethics of power holders' decision making and standards for social judgment. In D. M. Messick & A. E. Tenbrunsel (Eds.), *Codes of conduct: Behavioral research into business ethics* (pp. 117–142). New York: Russell Sage Foundation.

Goodwin, S. A., Gubin, A., Fiske, S. T., & Yzerbyt, V. Y. (2000). Power can bias impression processes: Stereotyping subordinates by default and by design. *Group Processes and Intergroup Relations, 3,* 227–256.

Gordijn, E. H., Hindriks, I., Koomen, W., Dijksterhuis, A., & Van Knippenberg, A. (2004). Consequences of stereotype suppression and internal suppression motivation: A self-regulation approach. *Personality and Social Psychology Bulletin, 30,* 212–224.

Gordon, P. A., Feldman, D., & Tantillo, J. (2003). *Helping children with disabilities develop and maintain friendships.* Unpublished manuscript, Muncie, IN: Ball State University.

Gore, K. Y., Tobiason, M. A., & Kayson, W. A. (1997). Effects of sex of caller, implied sexual orientation, and urgency on altruistic response using the wrong number technique. *Psychological Reports, 80,* 927–930.

Goto, S. (1999). Asian Americans and developmental relationships. In A. J. Murrell, F. J. Crosby, & R. J. Ely (Eds.), *Mentoring dilemmas: Developmental relationships within multicultural organizations* (pp. 47–62). Mahwah, NJ: Lawrence Erlbaum.

Govorun, O., & Payne, B. K. (2004, January). *Ego depletion and prejudice: Separating automatic and controlled components.* Paper presented at the meeting of the Society for Personality and Social Psychology, Austin, TX.

Graham, L. O. (1995). *Member of the club: Reflections on life in a racially polarized world.* New York: HarperCollins.

Grant, L. (1996). Effect of ageism on individual and health care providers' responses to healthy aging. *Health and Social Work, 21*(1), 9–15.

Grant, P. R., & Brown, R. (1995). From ethnocentrism to collective protest: Responses to relative deprivation and threats to social identity. *Social Psychology Quarterly, 58,* 195–211.

Gray-Little, B., & Hafdahl, A. R. (2000). Factors influencing racial comparisons of self-esteem: A quantitative review. *Psychological Bulletin, 126,* 26–54.

Green, D. P., Glaser, J., & Rich, A. (1998). From lynching to gay bashing: The elusive connection between economic conditions and hate crime. *Journal of Personality and Social Psychology, 75,* 82–92.

Green, D. P., Strolovitch, D. Z., & Wong, J. S. (1998). Defended neighborhoods, integration, and racially motivated crime. *American Journal of Sociology, 104,* 372–403.

Greenberg, J. (1996). *The quest for justice on the job.* Thousand Oaks, CA: Sage.

Greenberg, J., Pyszczynski, T., Solomon, S., Rosenblatt, A., Veeder, M., Kirkland, S., & Lyon, D. (1990). Evidence for terror management theory II: The effects of mortality salience on reactions to those who threaten or bolster the cultural worldview. *Journal of Personality and Social Psychology, 58,* 308–318.

Greenberg, J., Schimel, J., & Martens, A. (2002). Ageism: Denying the face of the future. In T. D. Nelson (Ed.), *Ageism: Stereotyping and prejudice against older persons* (pp. 27–48). Cambridge, MA: MIT Press.

Greenberg, J., Schimel, J., Martens, A., Solomon, S., & Pyszczynski, T. (2001). Sympathy for the devil: Evidence that reminding Whites of their mortality promotes more favorable reactions to White racists. *Motivation and Emotion, 25,* 113–133.

Greenberg, J., Solomon, S., & Pyszczynski, T. (1997). Terror management theory of self-esteem and cultural worldviews: Empirical assessments and conceptual refinements. *Advances in Experimental Social Psychology, 29,* 61–139.

Greene, M. G., Adelman, R., Charon, R., & Hoffman, S. (1986). Ageism in the medical encounter: An exploratory study of the doctor-elderly patient relationship. *Language and Communication, 6,* 113–124.

Greenfield, T. A. (1975). Race and passive voice at Monticello. *The Crisis, 82,* 146–147.

Greenhaus, J. H., Parasuramen, S., & Wormley, W. M. (1990). Effects of race on organizational experiences, job performance evaluations, and career outcome. *Academy of Management Journal, 33,* 64–86.

Greenhouse, S., & Hays, C. L. (2004, June 23). Wal-Mart sex-bias suit given class-action status. *New York Times,* p. 1.

Greenland, K., & Brown, R. (1999). Categorization and intergroup anxiety in contact between British and Japanese nationals. *European Journal of Social Psychology, 29,* 520–521.

Greenwald, A. G., & Banaji, M. R. (1995). Implicit social cognition: Attitudes, self-esteem, and stereotypes. *Psychological Review, 102,* 4–27.

Greenwald, A. G., McGhee, D. E., & Schwartz, J. L. K. (1998). Measuring individual differences in implicit cognition: The Implicit Association Test. *Journal of Personality and Social Psychology, 74,* 1464–1480.

Greenwald, A. G., Oaks, M. A., & Hoffman, H. G. (2003). Targets of discrimination: Effects of race on responses to weapons holders. *Journal of Experimental Social Psychology, 39*, 399–405.

Grieve, P. G., & Hogg, M. A. (1999). Subjective uncertainty and intergroup discrimination in the minimal group situation. *Personality and Social Psychology Bulletin, 25*, 926–940.

Grimmett, M. A. S., Bliss, J. R., & Davis, M. R. (1998). Assessing Federal TRIO McNair Program participants' expectations and satisfaction with project services: A preliminary study. *Journal of Negro Education, 67*, 404–415.

Grofman, B. N., & Muller, E. N. (1973). The strange case of relative gratification and potential for political violence: The V-curve hypothesis. *American Political Science Review, 67*, 514–539.

Grosch, J. W., Roberts, R. K., & Grubb, P. L. (2004, August). *Workplace discrimination after 25 years: A report on national trends.* Paper presented at the American Psychological Association, Honolulu, HI.

Guglielmi, R. S. (1999). Psychophysiological assessment of prejudice: Past research, current status, and future directions. *Personality and Social Psychology Review, 3*, 123–157.

Guimond, S., & Dambrun, M. (2002). When prosperity breeds intergroup hostility: The effects of relative deprivation and relative gratification on prejudice. *Personality and Social Psychology Bulletin, 28*, 900–912.

Guimond, S., Dambrun, M., Michinov, N., & Duarte, S. (2003). Does social dominance generate prejudice? Integrating individual and contextual determinants of intergroup cognitions. *Journal of Personality and Social Psychology, 84*, 697–721.

Gurr, T. R. (1970). *Why men rebel.* Princeton, NJ: Princeton University Press.

Gutek, B. (2001). Working environments. In J. Worell (Ed.), *Encyclopedia of women and gender: Sex similarities and the impact of society on gender* (vol. 2, pp. 1191–1204). San Diego: Academic Press.

Haddock, G., & Zanna, M. P. (1994). Preferring "housewives" to "feminists." *Psychology of Women Quarterly, 18*, 25–52.

Haddock, G., Zanna, M. P., & Esses, V. M. (1993). Assessing the structure of prejudicial attitudes: The case of attitudes toward homosexuals. *Journal of Personality and Social Psychology, 65*, 1105–1118.

Hall, R. E. (1998). Skin color bias: A new perspective on an old social problem. *Journal of Psychology, 132*, 238–240.

Hall, R. E. (2002). A descriptive methodology of color bias in Puerto Rico: Manifestations of discrimination in the new millennium. *Journal of Applied Social Psychology, 32*, 1527–1537.

Hamilton, D. L. (1979). A cognitive-attributional analysis of stereotyping. *Advances in Experimental Social Psychology, 2*, 53–81.

Hamilton, D. L. (1981). Illusory correlation as a basis for stereotyping. In D. L. Hamilton (Ed.), *Cognitive processes in stereotyping and intergroup behavior* (pp. 115–144). Hillsdale, NJ: Erlbaum.

Hamilton, D. L., & Gifford, R. K. (1976). Illusory correlation in interpersonal perception: A cognitive basis of stereotypic judgments. *Journal of Experimental Social Psychology, 12*, 392–407.

Hamilton, D. L., & Rose, T. L. (1980). Illusory correlation and the maintenance of stereotypic beliefs. *Journal of Personality and Social Psychology, 39,* 832–845.

Harber, K. D. (1998). Feedback to minorities: Evidence of a positive bias. *Journal of Personality and Social Psychology, 74,* 622–628.

Harkness, S., & Super, C. M. (1985). The cultural context of gender segregation in children's peer groups. *Child Development, 56,* 219–224.

Harmon-Jones, E., & Mills, J. S. (Eds.). (1999). *Cognitive dissonance: Progress on a pivotal theory in social psychology.* Washington, DC: American Psychological Association.

Harris, A. C. (1994). Ethnicity as a determinant of sex role identity: A replication study of item selection for the Bem Sex Role Inventory. *Sex Roles, 31,* 241–273.

Harris, D. A. (1999). *Driving while black: Racial profiling on our nation's highways.* Retrieved May 5, 2003, from archive.aclu.org/profiling/report.

Harris, M. B. (1994). Growing old gracefully: Age concealment and gender. *Journal of Gerontology: Psychological Sciences, 49,* P149–P158.

Harris, M. B., & Vanderhoof, J. (1995). Attitudes toward gays and lesbians serving in the military. *Journal of Gay and Lesbian Social Services, 3,* 23–51.

Harris, M. J., & Perkins, R. (1995). Effects of distraction on interpersonal expectancy effects: A social interaction test of the cognitive busyness hypothesis. *Social Cognition, 13,* 163–182.

Hartstone, M., & Augoustinos, M. (1995). The minimal group paradigm: Categorization into two versus three groups. *European Journal of Social Psychology, 25,* 179–193.

Harwood, J., Giles, H., & Ryan, E. B. (1995). Aging, communication, and intergroup theory: Social identity and intergenerational communication. In J. F. Nussbaum & J. Coupland (Eds.), *Handbook of communication and aging research* (pp. 133–159). Mahwah, NJ: Erlbaum.

Haslam, N., Rothschild, L., & Ernst, D. (2000). Essentialist beliefs about social categories. *British Journal of Social Psychology, 39,* 113–127.

Haslam, N., Rothschild, L., & Ernst, D. (2002). Are essentialist beliefs associated with prejudice? *British Journal of Social Psychology, 41,* 87–100.

Hass, R. G., Katz, I., Rizzo, N., Bailey, J., & Eisenstadt, D. (1991). Cross-racial appraisal as related to attitude ambivalence and cognitive complexity. *Personality and Social Psychology Bulletin, 17,* 83–92.

Hass, R. G., Katz, I., Rizzo, N., Bailey, J., & Moore, L. (1992). When racial ambivalence evokes negative affect, using a disguised measure of mood. *Personality and Social Psychology Bulletin, 18,* 786–797.

Hastie, R. (1984). Causes and effects of causal attribution. *Journal of Personality and Social Psychology, 46,* 44–56.

Hausdorff, J. M., Levy, B. R., & Wei, J. Y. (1999). The power of ageism on physical function of older persons: Reversibility of age-related gait changes. *Journal of the American Geriatrics Society, 47,* 1346–1349.

Hayden-Thomson, L., Rubin, K. H., & Hymel, S. (1987). Sex preferences in sociometric choices. *Developmental Psychology, 23,* 558–562.

Heaven, P. C. L., & Bucci, S. (2001). Right-wing authoritarianism, social dominance orientation and personality: An analysis using the IPIP measure. *European Journal of Personality, 15,* 49–56.

Heaven, P. C. L., & Oxman, L. N. (1999). Human values, conservatism, and stereotypes of homosexuals. *Personality and Individual Differences, 27,* 109–118.

Heaven, P. C. L., & St. Quintin, D. (2003). Personality factors predict racial prejudice. *Personality and Individual Differences, 34,* 625–634.

Hebl, M. R., Foster, J. B., Mannix, L. M., & Dovidio, J. F. (2002). Formal and interpersonal discrimination: A field study of bias toward homosexual applicants. *Personality and Social Psychology Bulletin, 28,* 815–825.

Hebl, M. R., & Mannix, L. M. (2003). The weight of obesity in evaluating others: A mere proximity effect. *Personality and Social Psychology Bulletin, 29,* 28–38.

Heckman, J. J. (1998). Detecting discrimination. *Journal of Economic Perspectives, 12*(2), 101–116.

Heilman, M. E. (1983). Sex bias in work settings: The lack of fit model. *Research in Organizational Behavior, 5,* 269–298.

Heilman, M. E. (2001). Description and prescription: How gender stereotypes prevent women's ascent up the organizational ladder. *Journal of Social Issues, 57,* 657–674.

Heilman, M. E., Block, C. J., & Martell, R. F. (1995). Sex stereotypes: Do they influence perceptions of managers? *Journal of Social Behavior and Personality, 10*(6), 237–252.

Heilman, M. E., Wallen, A. S., Fuchs, D., & Tamkins, M. M. (2004). Penalties for success: Reactions to women who succeed at male gender-typed tasks. *Journal of Applied Psychology, 89,* 416–427.

Henderson-King, E. I., & Nisbett, R. E. (1996). Anti-black prejudice as a function of exposure to the negative behavior of a single black person. *Journal of Personality and Social Psychology, 71,* 654–664.

Henry, P. J., & Sears, D. O. (2002). The Symbolic Racism 2000 Scale. *Political Psychology, 23,* 253–283.

Herek, G. M. (1986a). The instrumentality of attitudes: Toward a neofunctional theory. *Journal of Social Issues, 42*(2), 99–114.

Herek, G. M. (1986b). On heterosexual masculinity. *American Behavioral Scientist, 29,* 563–577.

Herek, G. M. (1987). Religious orientation and prejudice: A comparison of racial and sexual attitudes. *Personality and Social Psychology Bulletin, 13,* 34–44.

Herek, G. M. (1988). Heterosexuals' attitudes toward lesbians and gay men: Correlations and gender differences. *Journal of Sex Research, 25,* 451–477.

Herek, G. M. (1990). The context of anti-gay prejudice: Notes on cultural and psychological heterosexism. *Journal of Interpersonal Violence, 5,* 316–333.

Herek, G. M. (2000). The psychology of sexual prejudice. *Current Directions in Psychological Science, 9,* 19–22.

Herek, G. M. (2002). Gender gaps in public opinion about lesbians and gay men. *Public Opinion Quarterly, 66,* 40–66.

Herek, G. M. (2003). Why tell if you're not asked? In L. D. Garnets & D. C. Kimmel (Eds.), *Psychological perspectives on lesbian, gay, and bisexual experiences* (2nd ed., pp. 270–298). New York: Columbia University Press.

Herek, G. M. (2004). Beyond "homophobia": Thinking about sexual prejudice and stigma in the twenty-first century. *Sexuality Research and Social Policy, 1,* 6–24.

Herek, G. M., & Berrill, K. T. (1992). *Hate crimes: Confronting violence against lesbians and gay men*. Newbury Park, CA: Sage.

Herek, G. M., & Capitanio, J. P. (1995). Black heterosexuals' attitudes toward lesbians and gay men in the United States. *Journal of Sex Research, 32,* 95–105.

Herek, G. M., & Capitanio, J. P. (1996). "Some of my best friends": Intergroup contact, concealable stigma, and heterosexuals' attitudes toward gay men and lesbians. *Personality and Social Psychology Bulletin, 22,* 412–424.

Herek, G. M., Cogan, J. C., & Gillis, J. R. (2002). Victim experiences in hate crimes based on sexual orientation. *Journal of Social Issues, 58,* 319–339.

Herek, G. M., Gillis, J. R., & Cogan, J. C. (1999). Psychological sequelae of hate-crime victimization among lesbian, gay, and bisexual adults. *Journal of Consulting and Clinical Psychology, 67,* 945–951.

Hergenhahn, B. R. (2005). *An introduction to the history of psychology* (5h ed.). Belmont, CA: Wadsworth.

Herrnstein, R. J., & Murray, C. (1994). *The bell curve: Intelligence and class structure in American life*. New York: Free Press.

Hertzog, C., Lineweaver, T. T., & McGuire, C. L. (1999). Beliefs about memory and aging. In T. M. Hess & F. Blanchard-Fields (Eds.), *Social cognition and aging* (pp. 43–68). San Diego: Academic Press.

Hewstone, M. (1990). The "ultimate attribution error"? A review of the literature on intergroup causal attribution. *European Journal of Social Psychology, 20,* 311–335.

Hewstone, M. (1996). Contact and categorization: Social psychological interventions to change intergroup relations. In C. N. Macrae, C. Stangor, & M. Hewstone (Eds.), *Stereotypes and stereotyping* (pp. 323–368). New York: Guilford.

Hewstone, M., & Brown, R. (1986). Contact is not enough: An intergroup perspective on the "contact hypothesis." In M. Hewstone & R. Brown (Eds.), *Contact and conflict in intergroup encounters* (pp. 1–44). New York: Blackwell.

Hill, J. H. (1995). *Mock Spanish: A site for the indexical reproduction of racism in American English*. Retrieved October 14, 1998, from www.cs.uchicago.edu/archives/subs/hill-jane.

Hill, M. E. (2000). Color differences in the socioeconomic status of African American men: Results of a longitudinal study. *Social Forces, 78,* 1437–1460.

Hill, M. E. (2002). Skin color and the perception of attractiveness among African Americans: Does gender make a difference? *Social Psychology Quarterly, 65,* 77–91.

Hillerbrand, E. T., & Shaw, D. (1990). Age bias in a general hospital: Is there ageism in psychiatric consultation? *Clinical Gerontologist, 9,* 3–13.

Hilton, J. L., & von Hippel, W. (1996). Stereotypes. *Annual Review of Psychology, 47,* 237–271.

Hirschfeld, L. A. (1996). *Race in the making: Cognition, culture, and the child's construction of human kinds*. Cambridge, MA: MIT Press.

Hochschild, A. (1998). *King Leopold's ghost: A story of greed, terror, and heroism in colonial Africa*. Boston: Houghton Mifflin.

Hodson, G., & Dovidio, J. F. (2001). Racial prejudice as a moderator of stereotype rebound: A conceptual replication. *Representative Research in Social Psychology, 25,* 1–8.

Hodson, G., Dovidio, J. F., & Gaertner, S. L. (2002). Processes in racial discrimination: Weighting of conflicting information. *Personality and Social Psychology Bulletin, 28,* 460–471.

Hodson, G., & Esses, V. M. (2002). Distancing oneself from negative attributes and the personal/group discrimination discrepancy. *Journal of Experimental Social Psychology, 38,* 500–507.

Hoffman, C., & Hurst, N. (1990). Gender stereotypes: Perception or rationalization. *Journal of Personality and Social Psychology, 58,* 197–208.

Hogg, M. A., & Abrams, D. (1988). *Social identifications.* London: Routledge.

Hogg, M. A., & Abrams, D. (1990). Social motivation, self-esteem, and social identity. In D. Abrams & M. A. Hogg (Eds.), *Social identity theory; Constructive and critical advances* (pp. 28–47). New York: Harvester Wheatsheaf.

Hogg, M. A., & Mullin, B.-A. (1999). Joining groups to reduce uncertainty: Subjective uncertainty reduction and group identification. In D. Abrams & M. A. Hogg (Eds.), *Social identity and social cognition* (pp. 249–279). Malden, MA: Blackwell.

Holzer, H. J. (1996). *What employers want: Job prospects for less-educated workers.* New York: Russell Sage Foundation.

Hopf, C. (1993). Authoritarians and their families: Qualitative studies on the origins of authoritarian dispositions. In W. F. Stone, G. Lederer, & R. Christie (Eds.), *Strength and weakness: The authoritarian personality today* (pp. 119–143). New York: Springer-Verlag.

Hornsey, M. J., & Hogg, M. A. (2000). Assimilation and diversity: An integrated model of subgroup relations. *Personality and Social Psychology Review, 4,* 143–156.

Hort, B. E., Fagot, B. I., & Leinbach, M. D. (1990). Are people's notions of maleness more stereotypically framed than their notions of femaleness? *Sex Roles, 23,* 197–212.

Hovland, C. I., & Sears, R. R. (1940). Minor studies of aggression: VI. Correlations of lynchings with economic indices. *The Journal of Psychology, 9,* 301–310.

Howard, J. A., & Hollander, J. (1997). *Gendered situations, gendered selves.* Thousand Oakes, CA: Sage.

Hsu, M.-H., & Waters, J. A. (2001, August). *Filial piety and sexual orientation prejudice in Chinese culture.* Poster presented at the annual meeting of the American Psychological Association, San Francisco, CA.

Huddy, L., & Virtanen, S. (1995). Subgroup differentiation and subgroup bias among Latinos as a function of familiarity and positive distinctiveness. *Journal of Personality and Social Psychology, 68,* 97–108.

Huffcutt, A. I., & Roth, P. L. (1998). Racial group differences in employment interview evaluations. *Journal of Applied Psychology, 83,* 179–189.

Hugenberg, K., & Bodenhausen, G. V. (2003). Facing prejudice: Implicit prejudice and the perception of facial threat. *Psychological Science, 14,* 640–643.

Hugenberg, K., & Bodenhausen, G. V. (2004). Ambiguity and social categorization: The role of prejudice and facial affect in race categorization. *Psychological Science, 15,* 342–345.

Hughes, M. (1997). Symbolic racism, old-fashioned racism, and Whites' opposition to affirmative action. In S. A. Tuch & J. K. Martin (Eds.), *Racial attitudes in the 1990s: Continuity and change* (pp. 45–75). Westport, CT: Praeger.

Hughes, M., & Tuch, S. A. (2003). Gender differences in Whites' racial attitudes: Are women's attitudes really more favorable? *Social Psychology Quarterly, 66,* 384–401.

Human Rights Watch (2002). *"We are not the enemy": Hate crimes against Arabs, Muslims, and those perceived to be Arab or Muslim after September 11*. Retrieved May 5, 2003, from www.hrw.org.

Hummert, M. L. (1990). Multiple stereotypes of elderly and young adults: A comparison of structure and evaluations. *Psychology and Aging, 5*, 182–193.

Hummert, M. L. (1993). Age and typicality judgments of stereotypes of the elderly: Perceptions of elderly vs. young adults. *International Journal of Aging and Human Development, 37*, 217–226.

Hummert, M. L. (1994). Physiognomic cues to age and the activation of stereotypes of the elderly in interaction. *International Journal of Aging and Human Development, 39*(1), 5–19.

Hummert, M. L. (1999). A social cognitive perspective on age stereotypes. In T. M. Hess & F. Blanchard-Fields (Ed.), *Social cognition and aging* (pp. 175–196). San Diego, CA: Academic Press.

Hummert, M. L., Garstka, T. A., & Shaner, J. L. (1995). Beliefs about language performance: Adults' perceptions about self and elderly targets. *Journal of Language and Social Psychology, 14*, 235–259.

Hummert, M. L., Garstka, T. A., & Shaner, J. L. (1997). Stereotyping of older adults: The role of target facial cues and perceiver characteristics. *Psychology and Aging, 12*, 107–114.

Hummert, M. L., Garstka, T. A., Shaner, J. L., & Strahm, S. (1994). Stereotypes of the elderly held by young, middle-aged, and elderly adults. *Journal of Gerontology: Psychological Sciences, 49*, P240–P249.

Hummert, M. L., Garstka, T. A., Shaner, J. L., & Strahm, S. (1995). Judgments about stereotypes of the elderly: Attitudes, age associations, and typicality ratings of young, middle-aged, and elderly adults. *Research on Aging, 17*(2), 168–189.

Hummert, M. L., & Ryan, E. B. (1996). Toward understanding variations in patronizing talk addressed to older adults: Psycholinguistic features of care and control. *International Journal of Psycholinguistics, 12*, 149–169.

Hunsberger, B. (1978). Racial awareness and preference of White and Indian Canadian children. *Canadian Journal of Behavioral Science, 10*, 176–179.

Hunsberger, B. (1995). Religion and prejudice: The role of religious fundamentalism, quest, and right-wing authoritarianism. *Journal of Social Issues, 51*(2), 113–129.

Huston-Comeauz, S. L., & Kelly, J. R. (2002). Gender stereotypes of emotional reactions: How we judge an emotion as valid. *Sex Roles, 47*, 1–10.

Ilgen, D. R., & Youtz, M. A. (1986). Factors affecting the evaluation and development of minorities in organizations. *Research in Personnel and Human Resources Management, 4*, 307–337.

Insko, C. A., & Schopler, J. (1987). Categorization, competition and collectivity. In C. Hendrick (Ed.), *Group processes* (pp. 213–251). Beverly Hills, CA: Sage.

Inzlicht, M., & Ben-Zeev, T. (2003). Do high-achieving female students underperform in private? The implications of threatening environments on intellectual processing. *Journal of Educational Psychology, 95*, 796–805.

Islam, M. R., & Hewstone, M. (1993). Dimensions of contact as predictors of intergroup anxiety, perceived out-group variability, and out-group attitude: An integrative model. *Personality and Social Psychology Bulletin, 19*, 700–710.

Ito, T. A., & Urland, G. R. (2003). Race and gender on the brain: Electrocortical measures of attention to the race and gender of multiply categorizable individuals. *Journal of Personality and Social Psychology, 85,* 616–626.

Jacklin, C. N., & Maccoby, E. E. (1978). Social behavior at thirty-three months in same-sex and mixed-sex dyads. *Child Development, 49,* 557–569.

Jackman, M. R. (1994). *The velvet glove: Paternalism and conflict in gender, class, and race relations.* Berkeley: University of California Press.

Jackman, M. R., & Crane, M. (1986). "Some of my best friends are Black . . . ": Interracial friendship and Whites' racial attitudes. *Public Opinion Quarterly, 50,* 459–486.

Jackson, J. W. (2002). The relationship between group identity and intergroup prejudice is moderated by sociostructural variation. *Journal of Applied Social Psychology, 32,* 908–933.

Jackson, L. M., Esses, V. M., & Burris, C. T. (2001). Contemporary sexism and discrimination: The importance of respect for men and women. *Personality and Social Psychology Bulletin, 27,* 48–61.

Jacobs, B. A. (1999). *Race manners: Navigating the minefield between Black and White Americans.* New York: Arcade.

James, E. H. (2000). Race-related differences in promotions and support: Underlying effects of human and social capital. *Organization Science, 11,* 493–508.

James, E. H., Brief, A. P., Dietz, J., & Cohen, R. R. (2001). Prejudice matters: Understanding the reactions of Whites to affirmative action programs targeted to benefit Blacks. *Journal of Applied Psychology, 86,* 1120–1128.

Jang, K. L., McCrae, R. R., Angleitner, A., Riemann, R., & Livesley, W. J. (1998). Heritability of facet-level traits in a cross-cultural twin sample: Support for a hierarchical model of personality. *Journal of Personality and Social Psychology, 74,* 1556–1565.

Jarrett, O. S., & Quay, L. C. (1984). Crossracial acceptance and best friend choice. *Urban Education, 19,* 215–225.

Johnson, A. G. (2006). *Privilege, power, and difference* (2nd ed.). Boston: McGraw-Hill.

Johnson, D. F., & Pittenger, J. B. (1984). Attribution, the attractiveness stereotype, and the elderly. *Developmental Psychology, 20,* 1168–1172.

Johnson, D. J. (1992). Racial preference and biculturality in biracial preschoolers. *Merrill-Palmer Quarterly, 38,* 233–244.

Johnson, D. W., & Johnson, R. T. (2000). The three Cs of reducing prejudice and discrimination. In S. Oskamp (Ed.), *Reducing prejudice and discrimination* (pp. 239–268). Mahwah, NJ: Erlbaum.

Johnson, E. H., & Greene, A. (1991). The relationship between suppressed anger and psychosocial distress in African American male adolescents. *The Journal of Black Psychology, 18,* 47–65.

Johnson, G. R. (2001). The roots of ethnic conflict: An evolutionary perspective. In P. James & D. Goetze (Eds.), *Evolutionary theory and ethnic conflict* (pp. 19–38). Westport, CT: Praeger.

Johnson, M. E., Brems, C., & Alford-Keating, P. (1997). Personality correlates of homophobia. *Journal of Homosexuality, 34*(1), 57–69.

Johnson, O. E. (2001). "The content of our character": Another look at racial differences in Navy officer fitness reports. *Military Psychology, 13,* 41–54.

Johnson, R. S. (1998, August 3). The 50 best companies for Asians, Blacks, and Hispanics. *Fortune,* 94–122.

Johnston, L., & Hewstone, M. (1992). Cognitive models of stereotype change: 3. Subtyping and the perceived typicality of disconfirming group members. *Journal of Experimental Social Psychology, 28,* 360–386.

Jones, E. E. (1998). Major developments in five decades of social psychology. In D. T. Gilbert, S. T. Fiske, & G. Lindzey (Eds.), *The handbook of social psychology* (4th ed., vol. 1, pp. 3–57). Boston: McGraw-Hill.

Jones, E. E., Farina, A., Hastorf, A. H., Markus, H., Miller, T., & Scott, R. (1984). *Social stigma: The psychology of marked relationships.* New York: W. H. Freeman.

Jones, J. M. (1997). *Prejudice and racism* (2nd ed.). New York: McGraw-Hill.

Jones, M. (2002). *Social psychology of prejudice.* Upper Saddle River, NJ: Prentice Hall.

Jordan, C. H., Spencer, S. J., Zanna, M. P., Hoshino-Browne, E., & Correll, J. (2003). Secure and defensive high self-esteem. *Journal of Personality and Social Psychology, 85,* 969–978.

Joseph, J. M. (2001). *Warning: When I am an old woman I shall wear purple.* London: Souvenir.

Jost, J. T. (1995). Negative illusions: Conceptual clarification and psychological evidence concerning false consciousness. *Political Psychology, 16,* 397–424.

Jost, J. T., Glaser, J., Kruglanski, A. W., & Sulloway, F. J. (2003). Political conservatism as motivated social cognition. *Psychological Bulletin, 129,* 339–375.

Jost, J. T., & Thompson, E. P. (2000). Group-based dominance and opposition to equality as independent predictors of self-esteem, ethnocentrism, and social policy attitudes among African Americans and European Americans. *Journal of Experimental Social Psychology, 36,* 209–232.

Joyce, A. (2004, June 24). Wal-Mart suit may force wider look at pay gap between the sexes. *Washington Post,* p. 01.

Judd, C. M., Blair, I. V., & Chapleau, K. M. (2004). Automatic stereotypes vs. automatic prejudice: Sorting out the possibilities in the Payne (2001) weapon paradigm. *Journal of Experimental Social Psychology, 40,* 75–81.

Judd, C. M., Park, B., Ryan, C. S., Brauer, M., & Kraus, S. (1995). Stereotypes and ethnocentrism: Diverging interethnic perceptions of African American and White American youth. *Journal of Personality and Social Psychology, 69,* 468–481.

Judge, T. A., Thoresen, C. J., Bono, J. E., & Patton, G. K. (2001). The job satisfaction–job performance relationship: A qualitative and quantitative review. *Psychological Bulletin, 127,* 376–407.

Jussim, L. J., Clark, C. R., & Lee, Y.-T. (1995). Why study stereotype accuracy and inaccuracy? In Y.-T. Lee, L. J. Jussim, & C. R. McCauley (Eds.), *Stereotype accuracy: Toward appreciating group differences* (pp. 3–27). Washington, DC: American Psychological Association.

Kaiser, C. R., & Miller, C. T. (2001a). Stop complaining! The social costs of making attributions of discrimination. *Personality and Social Psychology Bulletin, 27,* 254–263.

Kaiser, C. R., & Miller, C. T. (2001b). Reacting to impending discrimination: Compensation for prejudice and attributions to discrimination. *Personality and Social Psychology Bulletin, 27,* 1357–1367.

Kalin, R. (1979). Ethnic and multicultural attitudes among children in a Canadian city. *Canadian Ethnic Studies, 11,* 69–81.

Kanter, R. M. (1977). *Men and women of the corporation.* New York: Basic Books.

Karlins, M., Coffman, T. L., & Walters, G. (1969). On the fading of social stereotypes: Studies in three generations of college students. *Journal of Personality and Social Psychology, 13,* 1–16.

Katz, D. (1960). The functional approach to the study of attitudes. *Public Opinion Quarterly, 24,* 163–204.

Katz, D., & Braly, K. (1933). Racial stereotypes in one hundred college students. *Journal of Abnormal and Social Psychology, 28,* 280–290.

Katz, I. (1981). *Stigma: A social psychological analysis.* Hillsdale, NJ: Erlbaum.

Katz, I., & Hass, R. G. (1988). Racial ambivalence and American value conflict: Correlational and priming studies of dual cognitive structures. *Journal of Personality and Social Psychology, 55,* 893–905.

Katz, I., Hass, R. G., & Bailey, J. (1988). Attitudinal ambivalence and behavior toward people with disabilities. In H. E. Yuker (Ed.), *Attitudes toward persons with disabilities* (pp. 47–57). New York: Springer.

Katz, I., Wackenhut, J., & Hass, R. G. (1986). Racial ambivalence, value duality, and behavior. In J. F. Dovidio & S. L. Gaertner (Eds.), *Prejudice, discrimination, and racism* (pp. 35–60). New York: Academic Press.

Katz, I. R., Curlick, S., & Nemetz, P. (1988). Functional psychiatric disorders in the elderly. In L. W. Lazarus (Ed.), *Essentials of geriatric psychiatry* (pp. 113–137). New York: Springer.

Katz, P. A. (1987). Variations in family constellation: Effects on gender schemata. In L. S. Liben & M. L. Signorella (Eds.), *Children's gender schemata* (pp. 39–56). San Francisco: Jossey-Bass.

Katz, P. A. (2003). Racists or tolerant multiculturalists? How do they begin? *American Psychologist, 58,* 897–909.

Katz, P. A., & Kofkin, J. A. (1997). Race, gender, and young children. In S. S. Luthar, J. A. Burack, D. Cicchetti, & J. Weisz (Eds.), *Developmental psychopathology: Perspectives on adjustment, risk, and disorder* (pp. 51–74). New York: Cambridge University Press.

Kawakami, K., Dion, K. L., & Dovidio, J. F. (1998). Racial prejudice and stereotype activation. *Personality and Social Psychology Bulletin, 24,* 407–416.

Kawakami, K., Dovidio, J. F., Moll, J., Hermsen, S., & Russin, A. (2000). Just say no (to stereotyping): Effects of training in the negation of stereotypic associations on stereotype activation. *Journal of Personality and Social Psychology, 78,* 871–888.

Kemper, S., & Harden, T. (1999). Experimentally disentangling what's beneficial about elderspeak from what's not. *Psychology and Aging, 14,* 656–670.

Kemper, S., & Kemtes, K. (2000). Aging and message production and comprehension. In N. Schwartz & D. Park (Eds.). *Cognitive aging: A primer* (pp. 197–213). Philadelphia: Psychology Press.

Kennedy, R. (2002). *Nigger: The strange career of a troublesome word.* New York: Vintage.

Kenyon, C., & Hewitt, J. (1989). Reaction to positive and negative behavior in same-sex vs. opposite-sex others. *Perceptual and Motor Skills, 69,* 931–934.

Kessler, T., & Mummendey, A. (2001). Is there any scapegoat around? Determinants of intergroup conflict at different categorization levels. *Journal of Personality and Social Psychology, 81,* 1090–1102.

Khmelkov, V. T., & Hallinan, M. T. (1999). Organizational effects on race relations in schools. *Journal of Social Issues, 55,* 627–645.

Kierstead, D., D'Agostino, P., & Dill, H. (1988). Sex role stereotyping of college professors: Bias in students' ratings of instructors. *Journal of Educational Psychology, 80,* 342–344.

Kilbourne, J. (2000). *Can't buy me love: How advertising changes the way we think and feel.* New York: Simon & Schuster.

Kim, H.-S., & Baron, R. S. (1988). Exercise and the illusory correlation: Does arousal heighten stereotypic processing? *Journal of Experimental Social Psychology, 24,* 366–380.

Kimball, M. M. (1995). *Feminist visions of gender similarities and differences.* Binghamton, NY: Haworth.

Kimmel, M. (2002, February 8). Gender, class, and terrorism. *The Chronicle of Higher Education,* pp. B11–B12.

Kinder, D. R., & Mendelberg, T. (2000). Individualism reconsidered: Principles and prejudice in contemporary American opinion. In D. O. Sears, J. Sidanius, & L. Bobo (Eds.), *Racialized politics: The debate about racism in America* (pp. 44–74). Chicago: University of Chicago Press.

Kinder, D. R., & Sanders, L. M. (1996). *Divided by color: Racial politics and democratic ideals.* Chicago: University of Chicago Press.

King, M. L., Jr. (1968, August 28). *I have a dream.* Address presented at the March on Washington for Jobs and Freedom, Washington, DC.

Kipling, R. (1899). The White man's burden: A poem. *McClure's Magazine, 12,* 290.

Kirkpatrick, L. A. (1993). Fundamentalism, Christian orthodoxy, and intrinsic religious orientation as predictors of discriminatory attitudes. *Journal for the Scientific Study of Religion, 32,* 256–268.

Kirkpatrick, L. A., Hood, R. W., Jr., & Hartz, G. (1991). Fundamentalist religion conceptualized in terms of Rokeach's theory of the open and closed mind: New perspectives on some old ideas. *Research in the Social Scientific Study of Religion, 3,* 157–179.

Kirschenman, J., & Neckerman, K. M. (1990). "We'd love to hire them, but . . . ": The meaning of race for employers. In C. Jenks & E. Peterson (Eds.), *The urban underclass* (pp. 203–232). Washington, DC: Brookings Institution.

Kite, M. E. (1996). Age, gender, and occupational label: A test of social role theory. *Psychology of Women Quarterly, 20,* 361–374.

Kite, M E. (2001). Gender stereotypes. In J. Worrell (Ed.). *Encyclopedia of gender: Sex similarities and differences and the impact of society on gender* (vol. 1, pp. 561–570). San Diego: Academic Press.

Kite, M. E., & Balogh, D. W. (1997). Warming trends: Improving the chilly campus climate. In N. V. Benokraitis (Ed.), *Subtle sexism: Current practice and prospects for change* (pp. 264–278). Thousand Oaks, CA: Sage.

Kite, M. E., & Branscombe, N. R. (1998). *Evaluations of subtypes of women and men.* Unpublished manuscript, Ball State University, Muncie, IN.

Kite, M. E., & Deaux, K. (1986). Attitudes toward homosexuality: Assessment and behavioral consequences. *Basic and Applied Social Psychology, 7,* 137–162.

Kite, M. E., & Deaux, K. (1987). Gender belief systems: Homosexuality and the implicit inversion theory. *Psychology of Women Quarterly, 11,* 83–96.

Kite, M. E., Deaux, K., & Miele, M. (1991). Stereotypes of young and old: Does age outweigh gender? *Psychology and Aging, 6*(1), 19–27.

Kite, M. E., Stockdale, G. M., & Whitley, B. E., Jr. (2002, August). *Perceived age differences in agency: A meta-analytic review.* Paper presented at the American Psychological Association, Chicago.

Kite, M. E., Stockdale, G. M., & Whitley, B. E., Jr. (2004). *Perceived communion of older and younger adults.* Unpublished manuscript, Muncie, IN.

Kite, M. E., Stockdale, G. M., Whitley, B. E., Jr., & Johnson, B. T. (2005). Attitudes toward older and younger adults: An updated meta-analytic review. *Journal of Social Issues, 61,* 241–266.

Kite, M. E., & Wagner, L. S. (2002). Attitudes toward older adults. In T. D. Nelson (Ed.), *Ageism: Stereotyping and prejudice against older person* (pp. 129–161). Cambridge, MA: MIT Press.

Kite, M. E., & Whitley, B. E., Jr. (1996). Sex differences in attitudes toward homosexual persons, behavior, and civil rights. *Personality and Social Psychology Bulletin, 22,* 336–353.

Kite, M. E., & Whitley, B. E., Jr. (1998). Do heterosexual women and men differ in their attitudes toward homosexuality? A conceptual and methodological analysis. In G. M. Herek (Ed.), *Stigma and sexual orientation: Understanding prejudice against lesbians, gay men, and bisexuals* (pp. 39–61). Thousand Oaks, CA: Sage.

Klein, F. (1978). *The bisexual option: A concept of one hundred percent intimacy.* New York: Arbor House.

Klein, O., & Snyder, M. (2003). Stereotypes and behavioral confirmation: From interpersonal to intergroup perspectives. *Advances in Experimental Social Psychology, 35,* 153–234.

Klein, R. D., & Naccarato, S. (2003). Broadcast news portrayal of minorities: Accuracy in reporting. *American Behavioral Scientist, 46,* 1611–1616.

Kleinpenning, G., & Hagendoorn, L. (1993). Forms of racism and the cumulative dimension of ethnic attitudes. *Social Psychology Quarterly, 56,* 21–36.

Klonoff, E. A., & Landrine, H. (2000). Is skin color a marker for racial discrimination? Explaining the skin color-hypertension relationship. *Journal of Behavioral Medicine, 23,* 329–338.

Knauper, B. & Sudman, S. (Eds.). (1998). *Cognition, aging, and self-reports* (pp. 230–244). Philadelphia: Taylor and Francis.

Knight, J. L., & Giuliano, T. A. (2002). He's a Laker; She's a "looker": The consequences of gender-stereotypical portrayals of male and female athletes by the print media. *Sex Roles, 45,* 217–229.

Knight, J. L., Hebl, M. R., Foster, J. B., & Mannix, L. M. (2002, June). *The influence of race, status, and performance record on appraisals.* Paper presented at the annual meeting of the American Psychological Society, New Orleans, LA.

Knight, K. (1999). Liberalism and conservatism. In J. P. Robinson, P. R. Shaver, & L. S. Wrightsman (Eds.), *Measures of political attitudes* (pp. 59–158). San Diego, CA: Academic Press.

Kobrynowicz, D., & Branscombe, N. R. (1997). Who considers themselves victims of discrimination? Individual difference predictors of gender discrimination in women. *Psychology of Women Quarterly, 21,* 347–363.

Kogan, N. (1979). A study of age categorization. *Journal of Gerontology, 34,* 358–367.

Koss, M. P., Gidycz, C. A., & Wisniewski, N. (1987). The scope of rape: Incidence and prevalence of sexual aggression and victimization in a national sample of higher education students. *Journal of Consulting and Clinical Psychology, 55,* 162–170.

Kovel, J. (1970). *White racism: A psychohistory.* New York: Pantheon.

Kowalski, K. (2003). The emergence of ethnic and racial attitudes in preschool-aged children. *The Journal of Social Psychology, 143,* 677–690.

Kraus, S. J. (1995). Attitudes and the prediction of behavior: A meta-analysis of the empirical literature. *Personality and Social Psychology Bulletin, 21,* 58–75.

Krauth-Gruber, S., & Ric, F. (2000). Affect and stereotypic thinking: A test of the mood-and-general-knowledge model. *Personality and Social Psychology Bulletin, 26,* 1587–1597.

Krieger, N., & Sidney, S. (1996). Racial discrimination and blood pressure: The CARDIA study of young Black and White adults. *American Journal of Public Health, 86,* 1370–1378.

Krosnick, J. A. (1999). Maximizing questionnaire quality. In J. P. Robinson, P. R. Shaver, & L. S. Wrightsman (Eds.), *Measures of political attitudes* (pp. 37–57). San Diego, CA: Academic Press.

Kruglanski, A. W., & Freund, T. (1983). The freezing and unfreezing of lay-inferences: Effects on impressional primacy, ethnic stereotyping, and numerical anchoring. *Journal of Experimental Social Psychology, 19,* 448–468.

Kruglanski, A. W., & Webster, D. M. (1996). Motivated closing of the mind: "Seizing" and "freezing." *Psychological Review, 103,* 263–283.

Krulewitz, J. E., & Nash, J. E. (1980). Effects of sex role attitudes and similarity on men's rejection of male homosexuals. *Journal of Personality and Social Psychology, 38,* 67–74.

Kunda, Z. (1999). *Social cognition: Making sense of people.* Cambridge, MA: MIT Press.

Kunda, Z., Davies, P. G., Adams, B. D., & Spencer, S. J. (2002). The dynamic time course of stereotype activation: Activation, dissipation, and resurrection. *Journal of Personality and Social Psychology, 82,* 283–299.

Kunda, Z., Davies, P. G., Hoshino-Browne, E., & Jordan, C. H. (2003). The impact of comprehension goals on the ebb and flow of stereotype activation during interaction. In S. J. Spencer, S. Fein, M. P. Zanna, & J. M. Olson (Eds.), *Motivated social perception* (pp. 1–20). Mahwah, NJ: Erlbaum.

Kunda, Z., & Sherman-Williams, B. (1993). Stereotypes and the construal of individuating information. *Personality and Social Psychology Bulletin, 19,* 90–99.

Kunda, Z., Sinclair, L., & Griffin, D. (1997). Equal ratings but separate meanings: Stereotypes and the construal of traits. *Journal of Personality and Social Psychology, 72,* 720–734.

Kunda, Z., & Spencer, S. J. (2003). When do stereotypes come to mind and when do they color judgment? A goal-based theoretical framework for stereotype activation and application. *Psychological Bulletin, 129,* 522–544.

Kunda, Z., & Thagard, P. (1996). Forming impressions from stereotypes, traits, and behaviors: A parallel-constraint-satisfaction model. *Psychological Review, 103,* 284–308.

Kurzban, R., & Leary, M. R. (2001). Evolutionary origins of stigmatization: The functions of social exclusion. *Psychological Bulletin, 127,* 187–208.

Lacquer, W. (1996). Postmodern terrorism. *Foreign Affairs, 75*(5) 24–36.

LaFreniere, P., Strayer, F. F., & Gauthier, R. (1984). The emergence of same-sex preferences among preschool peers: A developmental ethological perspective. *Child Development, 55,* 1958–1965.

LaMar, L., & Kite, M. E. (1996). Sex differences in attitudes toward gay men and lesbians: A multi-dimensional perspective. *The Journal of Sex Research, 35,* 189–196.

Lambert, A. J., & Chasteen, A. L. (1997). Perceptions of disadvantage versus conventionality: Political values and attitudes toward the elderly versus Blacks. *Personality and Social Psychology Bulletin, 23,* 469–481.

Lambert, M. J., & Bergin, A. E. (1994). The effectiveness of psychotherapy. In A. E. Bergin & S. L. Garfield (Eds.), *Handbook of psychotherapy and behavior change* (4th ed., pp. 143–189). New York: Wiley.

Lamberth, J. (1998, August 16). Driving while black: A statistician proves the prejudice still rules the road. *Washington Post,* p. 01.

Lamis, A. P. (1984). *The two-party South.* New York: Oxford University Press.

Landau, J. (1995). The relationship of race and gender to managers' ratings of promotion potential. *Journal of Organizational Behavior, 16,* 391–400.

Landau, M. J., Solomon, S., Greenberg, J., Cohen, F., Pyszczynski, T., Arndt, J., Miller, C. H., Ogilvie, D. M., & Cook, A. (2004). Deliver us from evil: The effects of mortality salience and reminders of 9/11 on support for President George W. Bush. *Personality and Social Psychology Bulletin, 30,* 1136–1150.

Landrine, H. (1985). Race x class stereotypes of women. *Sex Roles, 13,* 65–75.

Landy, F. J. (1996). *Mandatory retirement and chronological age in public safety workers.* Testimony before the U.S. Senate Committee on Labor and Human Resources (March 8, 1996). Washington, DC: American Psychological Association.

Laner, M. R., & Laner, R. H. (1979). Personal style or sexual preference: Why gay men are disliked. *International Review of Modern Sociology, 9,* 215–228.

Langlois, J. H., Kalakanis, L., Rubenstein, A. J., Larson, A., Hallam, M., & Smoot, M. (2000). Maxims or myths of beauty? A meta-analytic and theoretical review. *Psychological Bulletin, 126,* 390–423.

Langlois, J. H., Ritter, J. M., Roggman, L. A., & Vaughn, L. S. (1991). Facial diversity and infant preferences for attractive faces. *Developmental Psychology, 27,* 79–84.

Langlois, J. H., & Roggman, L. A. (1990). Attractive faces are only average. *Psychological Science, 1,* 115–121.

Langlois, J. H., Roggman, L. A., Casey, R. J., Ritter, J. M., Rieser-Danner, L. A., & Jenkins, V. Y. (1987). Infant preferences for attractive faces: Rudiments of a stereotype? *Developmental Psychology, 23,* 363–369.

Laramie Project Archives. (2002). Retrieved April 29, 2004, from http://www.nytimes.com/ads/marketing/laramie/.

Larsen, R. J., & Buss, D. M. (2002). *Personality psychology: Domains of knowledge about human nature.* Boston: McGraw-Hill.

Law and Civil Rights (2004). Retrieved October 8, 2004 from www.pollingreport.com/civil.htm.

Lawrence v. Texas, 539 U.S. 538 (2003).

Lawton, C. A., Blakemore, J. E. O., & Vartanian, L. R. (2003). The new meaning of Ms.: Single, but too old for Miss. *Psychology of Women Quarterly, 27,* 215–220.

Lawton, M. P., Kleban, M. H., Rajagopal, D., & Dean, J. (1992). The dimensions of affective experience in three age groups. *Psychology and Aging, 7,* 171–184.

Layng, J. M. (1998). Uncovering the layers of diversity: A semiotic analysis of the corporate training video series "Valuing Diversity." *Semiotica, 119,* 251–267.

Lazarus, R. S. (1993). From psychological stress to the emotions: A history of changing outlooks. *Annual Review of Psychology, 44,* 1–21.

Lee, S. J. (1996). *Unraveling the "model minority" stereotype: Listening to Asian American youth.* New York: Teachers College Press.

Lee, Y.-T., Jussim, L. J., & McCauley, C. R. (Eds.). (1995). *Stereotype accuracy: Toward appreciating group differences.* Washington, DC: American Psychological Association.

Lefkowitz, J. (1994). Race as a factor in job placement: Serendipitous findings of "ethnic drift." *Personnel Psychology, 47,* 497–513.

Leippe, M. R., & Eisenstadt, D. (1999). A self-accountability model of dissonance reduction: Multiple modes on a continuum of elaboration. In E. Harmon-Jones & J. Mills (Eds.), *Cognitive dissonance: Progress on a pivotal theory in social psychology* (pp. 201–222). Washington, DC: American Psychological Association.

Lepore, L., & Brown, R. (1997). Category and stereotype activation: Is prejudice inevitable? *Journal of Personality and Social Psychology, 72,* 275–287.

Lepore, L., & Brown, R. (1999). Exploring automatic stereotype activation: A challenge to the inevitability of prejudice. In M. A. Hogg & D. Abrams (Eds.), *Social identity and social cognition* (pp. 141–163). Malden, MA: Blackwell.

Lerner, J. S., & Tetlock, P. E. (1999). Accounting for the effects of accountability. *Psychological Bulletin, 125,* 255–275.

Levin, J., & McDevitt, J. (2002). *Hate crimes revisited: America's war against those who are different.* Boulder, CO: Westview.

Levin, S., & Sidanius, J. (1999). Social dominance and social identity in the United States and Israel: Ingroup favoritism or outgroup derogation? *Political Psychology, 20,* 99–126.

Levin, S., van Laar, C., & Sidanius, J. (2003). The effects of ingroup and outgroup friendships on ethnic attitudes in college: A longitudinal study. *Group Processes & Intergroup Relations, 6,* 76–92.

Levine, J. M., & McBurney, D. H. (1977). Causes and consequences of effluvia: Body odor awareness and controllability as determinants of interpersonal evaluation. *Personality and Social Psychology Bulletin, 3,* 442–445.

LeVine, R. A., & Campbell, D. T. (1972). *Ethnocentrism: Theories of conflict, ethnic attitudes, and group behavior.* New York: Wiley.

Levy, B. R. (1996). Improving memory in old age through implicit self-stereotyping. *Journal of Personality and Social Psychology, 71,* 1092–1107.

Levy, B. R. (2003). Mind matters: Cognitive and physical effects of aging self-stereotypes. *Journal of Gerontology: Psychological Sciences, 58B,* P203–P211.

Levy, B. R., & Banaji, M. R. (2002). Implicit ageism. In T. D. Nelson (Ed.), *Ageism: Stereotyping and prejudice against older adults* (pp. 49–75). Cambridge, MA: MIT Press.

Levy, B. R., Slade, M. D., Kunkel, S. R., & Kasl, S. V. (2002). Longevity increased by positive self-perceptions of aging. *Journal of Personality and Social Psychology, 83,* 261–270.

Levy, G. D., & Fivush, R. (1993). Scripts and gender: A new approach for examining gender-role development. *Developmental Review, 13,* 126–146.

Levy, S. (2004, January). Introduction. In S. Levy (Chair). *Integrating developmental and social psychological research on prejudice processes.* Symposium conducted at the meeting of the Society for Personality and Social Psychology, Austin, TX.

Leyens, J.-P., & Yzerbyt, V. Y. (1992). The ingroup overexclusion effect: Impact of valence and confirmation on stereotypical information search. *European Journal of Social Psychology, 22,* 549–569.

Lieberman, J. D., Arndt, J., Personius, J., & Cook, A. (2001). Vicarious annihilation: The effect of mortality salience on perceptions of hate crimes. *Law and Human Behavior, 25,* 547–566.

Liberman, N., & Förster, J. (2000). Expression after suppression: A motivational explanation of postsuppressional rebound. *Journal of Personality and Social Psychology, 79,* 190–203.

Life Span Institute. (2004). *Guidelines for reporting and writing about people with disabilities.* Retrieved August 27, 2004, from www.lsi.ku.edu/lsi/internal/guidelines.html.

Limbaugh, R. (2004). *What we want our women to be.* Retrieved July 14, 2004, from www.rushlimbaugh.com.

Lin, M. H., Kwan, V. S. Y., Cheung, A., & Fiske, S. T. (2005). Stereotype content model explains prejudice for an envied outgroup: Scale of anti-Asian American stereotypes. *Personality and Social Psychology Bulletin, 31,* 34–47.

Linville, P. W., Fischer, G. W., & Salovey, P. (1989). Perceived distributions of the characteristics of in-group and out-group members: Empirical evidence and a computer simulation. *Journal of Personality and Social Psychology, 57,* 165–188.

Linville, P. W., & Jones, E. E. (1980). Polarized appraisals of out-group members. *Journal of Personality and Social Psychology, 38,* 689–703.

Lippa, R. A. (2005). *Gender, nature, and nurture* (2nd ed.). Mahwah, NJ: Lawrence Erlbaum.

Lippi-Green, R. (1997). *English with an accent: Language, ideology, and discrimination in the United States.* London: Routledge.

Lippman, W. (1922). *Pubic opinion.* New York: Harcourt.

Lite, J. (2001, July 16). Please ask me who, not "what," I am. *Newsweek, 138,* 9.

Little, B. L., Murry, W. D., & Wimbusch, J. C. (1998). Perceptions of workplace affirmative action plans: A psychological perspective. *Group & Organization Management, 23,* 27–47.

Livingston, R. W., & Brewer, M. B. (2002). What are we really priming? Cue-based versus category-based processing of facial stimuli. *Journal of Personality and Social Psychology, 82,* 5–18.

Lobel, T. E., Bempechat, J., Gewirtz, J. C., Shoken-Topaz, T., & Bashe, E. (1993). The role of gender-related information and self-endorsement traits in preadolescents' inferences and judgements. *Child Development, 64,* 1285–1294.

Lööw, H. (1998). White power rock 'n roll: A growing industry. In J. Kaplan & T. Bjørgo (Eds.), *Nation and race: The developing Euro-American racist subculture* (pp. 126–147). Boston: Northeastern University Press.

Lord, C. G., Lepper, M. R., & Mackie, D. (1980). Attitude prototypes as determinants of attitude-behavior consistency. *Journal of Personality and Social Psychology, 46,* 1254–1266.

Lott, B., & Maluso, D. (2001). Gender development: Social learning. In J. Worrell (Ed.), *Encyclopedia of women and gender, volume one.* (pp. 537–549). San Diego, CA: Academic Press.

Lowery, B. S., Hardin, C. D., & Sinclair, S. (2001). Social influence effects on automatic racial prejudice. *Journal of Personality and Social Psychology, 81,* 842–855.

Lueptow, L. B., Garovich, L., & Lueptow, M. B. (1995). The persistence of gender stereotypes in the face of changing sex roles: Evidence contrary to the sociocultural model. *Ethnology and Sociobiology, 16,* 509–530.

Lyness, K. S., & Judiesch, M. K. (1999). Are women more likely to be hired or promoted into management positions? *Journal of Vocational Behavior, 54,* 158–173.

Lyons, A., & Kashima, Y. (2001). The reproduction of culture: Communication processes tend to maintain cultural stereotypes. *Social Cognition, 19,* 372–394.

Maass, A., & Arcuri, L. (1996). Language and stereotyping. In C. N. Macrae, C. Stangor, & M. Hewstone (Eds.), *Stereotypes and stereotyping* (pp. 193–226). New York: Guilford.

Maass, A., Castelli, L., & Arcuri, L. (2000). Measuring prejudice: Implicit versus explicit techniques. In D. Capozza & R. Brown (Eds.), *Social identity processes: Trends in theory and research* (pp. 96–116). Thousand Oaks, CA: Sage.

Maass, A., Salvi, D., Arcuri, L., & Semin, G. R. (1989). Language use in intergroup contexts: The linguistic intergroup bias. *Journal of Personality and Social Psychology, 57,* 981–993.

Maccoby, E. E., & Jacklin, C. N. (1987). Gender segregation in childhood. In E. H. Reese (Ed.), *Advances in child development and behavior* (vol. 20, pp. 239–287). New York: Academic Press.

MacDonald, A. P. (1981). A little bit of lavender goes a long way: A critique of research on sexual orientation. *The Journal of Sex Research, 19,* 94–100.

MacDonald, T. K., & Zanna, M. P. (1998). Cross-dimension ambivalence toward social groups: Can ambivalence affect intentions to hire feminists? *Personality and Social Psychology Bulletin, 24,* 427–441.

Mackie, D. M., & Smith, E. R. (2002). Beyond prejudice: Moving from positive and negative evaluations to differentiated reactions to social groups. In D. M. Mackie & E. R. Smith (Eds.), *From prejudice to intergroup emotions: Differentiated reactions in social groups* (pp. 1–12). New York: Psychology Press.

MacNeil, R. D., Hawkins, D. L., Barber, E. H., & Winslow, R. (1990). The effect of client's age upon the employment preferences of therapeutic recreation majors. *Journal of Leisure Research, 22,* 329–340.

Macrae, C. N., & Bodenhausen, G. V. (2000). Social cognition: Thinking categorically about others. *Annual Review of Psychology, 51,* 93–120.

Macrae, C. N., Bodenhausen, G. V., & Milne, A. B. (1995). The dissection of selection in person perception: Inhibitory processes in social stereotypes. *Journal of Personality and Social Psychology, 69,* 397–407.

Macrae, C. N., Bodenhausen, G. V., & Milne, A. B. (1998). Saying no to unwanted thoughts: Self-focus and the regulation of mental life. *Journal of Personality and Social Psychology, 74,* 578–589.

Macrae, C. N., Bodenhausen, G. V., Milne, A. B., & Jetten, J. (1994). Out of mind but back in sight: Stereotypes on the rebound. *Journal of Personality and Social Psychology, 67,* 808–817.

Macrae, C. N., Bodenhausen, G. V., Milne, A. B., & Wheeler, V. (1996). On resisting the temptation for simplification: Counterintentional effects of stereotype suppression on social memory. *Social Cognition, 14,* 1–20.

Macrae, C. N., Hewstone, M., & Griffiths, R. J. (1993). Processing load and memory for stereotype-based information. *European Journal of Social Psychology, 23,* 77–87.

Maddox, K. B., & Gray, S. A. (2002). Cognitive representations of Black Americans: Reexploring the role of skin tone. *Personality and Social Psychology Bulletin, 28,* 250–259.

Madon, S., Guyll, M., Aboufadel, K., Montiel, E., Smith, A., Palumbo, P., & Jussim, L. (2001). Ethnic and national stereotypes: The Princeton trilogy revisited. *Personality and Social Psychology Bulletin, 27,* 996–1010.

Maio, G. R., & Esses, V. M. (1998). The social consequences of affirmative action: Deleterious effects on perceptions of groups. *Personality and Social Psychology Bulletin, 24,* 65–74.

Major, B. (1994). From social inequality to personal entitlement: The role of social comparisons, legitimacy appraisals, and group memberships. *Advances in Experimental Social Psychology, 26,* 293–355.

Major, B., Carrington, P. I., & Carnevale, P. (1984). Physical attractiveness and self-esteem: Attributions for praise from an other-sex evaluator. *Personality and Social Psychology Bulletin, 10,* 43–50.

Major, B., Spencer, S. J., Schmader, T., Wolfe, C., & Crocker, J. (1998). Coping with negative stereotypes about intellectual performance: The role of psychological disengagement. *Personality and Social Psychology Bulletin, 24,* 34–50.

Mangan, K. E. (2003, October 24). An Irish pilgrim to Mecca. *The Chronicle of Higher Education,* pp. A7–A8.

Markus, H., & Zajonc, R. B. (1985). The cognitive perspective in social psychology. In G. Lindzey & E. Aronson (Eds.), *Handbook of social psychology* (3rd ed., vol. 1, pp. 137–230). New York: Random House.

Martell, R. F., Lane, D. M., & Emrich, C. (1996). Male-female differences: A computer simulation. *American Psychologist, 51,* 157–158.

Martell, R. F., Parker, C., Emrich, C. G., & Crawford, M. S. (1998). Sex stereotyping in the executive suite: "Much ado about something." *Journal of Social Behavior and Personality, 13,* 127–138.

Martin, C. L. (1987). A ratio measure of sex stereotyping. *Journal of Personality and Social Psychology, 52,* 489–499.

Martin, C. L. (1989). Children's use of gender-related information in making social judgments. *Developmental Psychology, 25,* 80–88.

Martin, C. L. (1990). Attitudes and expectations about children with nontraditional and traditional gender roles. *Sex Roles, 22,* 151–165.

Martin, C. L. (2000). Cognitive theories of gender development. In T. Eckes & H. M. Trautner (Eds.), *The developmental social psychology of gender* (pp. 91–121). Mahwah, NJ: Erlbaum.

Martin, C. L., Eisenbud, L., & Rose, H. (1995). Children's gender-based reasoning about toys. *Child Development, 66,* 1453–1471.

Martin, M. R., Grande, A. H., & Crabb, B. T. (2004, May). *Watch the war, hate Muslims more? Media exposure predicts implicit prejudice.* Paper presented at the meeting of the American Psychological Society, Chicago.

Matchinsky, D. J., & Iverson, T. G. (1996). Homophobia in heterosexual female undergraduates. *Journal of Homosexuality, 31*(4), 123–128.

Matlin, M. (2002). *Cognition* (3rd ed.). Fort Worth: Harcourt.

Matlin, M. (2004). *The psychology of women* (5th ed.). Belmont, CA: Wadsworth.

Matyi, C. L., & Drevenstedt, J. (1989). Judgments of elderly and young clients as functions of gender and interview behaviors: Implications for counselors. *Journal of Counseling Psychology, 36,* 451–455.

Maume, D. J., Jr. (1999). Glass ceilings and glass escalators: Occupational segregation and sex differences in managerial promotions. *Work and Occupations, 26,* 483–509.

McCann, R., & Giles, H. (2002). Ageism in the workplace. In T. D. Nelson (Ed.), *Ageism: Stereotyping and prejudice against older persons* (pp. 163–199). Cambridge, MA: MIT Press.

McCauley, C., & Stitt, C. L. (1978). An individual and quantitative measure of stereotypes. *Journal of Personality and Social Psychology, 52,* 489–499.

McClam, E. (2004, July 13). Morgan Stanley settles discrimination case. *The Boston Globe,* D2.

McConahay, J. B. (1983). Modern racism and modern discrimination: The effects of race, racial attitudes, and context on simulated hiring decisions. *Personality and Social Psychology Bulletin, 9,* 551–558.

McConahay, J. B. (1986). Modern racism, ambivalence, and the Modern Racism Scale. In J. F. Dovidio & S. L. Gaertner (Eds.), *Prejudice, discrimination, and racism* (pp. 91–125). Orlando, FL: Academic Press.

McConahay, J. B., & Hough, J. C., Jr. (1976). Symbolic racism. *Journal of Social Issues, 32*(2), 23–45.

McConahay, J. B., Hardee, B. B., & Batts, V. (1981). Has racism declined in America? It depends on who is asking and what is asked. *Journal of Conflict Resolution, 25,* 563–579.

McConnell, A. R., & Leibold, J. M. (2001). Relations among the Implicit Association Test, discriminatory behavior, and explicit measures of racial attitudes. *Journal of Experimental Social Psychology, 37,* 435–442.

McCrae, R. R. (1996). Social consequences of experiential openness. *Psychological Bulletin, 120,* 323–337.

McCreary, D. R. (1994). The male role and avoiding femininity. *Sex Roles, 31,* 527–531.

McDevitt, J., Balboni, J., Garcia, L., & Gu, J. (2001). Consequences for victims: A comparison of bias- and non-bias-motivated assaults. *American Behavioral Scientist, 45,* 697–713.

McDevitt, J., Levin, J., & Bennett, S. (2002). Hate crime offenders: An expanded typology. *Journal of Social Issues, 58,* 303–317.

McDonald, M. (1999). Cyberhate: Extending persuasive techniques of low credibility sources to the World Wide Web. In D. W. Schumann & E. Thorson (Eds.), *Advertising and the World Wide Web* (pp. 149–157). Mahwah, NJ: Erlbaum.

McFarland, S. G. (1989). Religious orientations and the targets of discrimination. *Journal for the Scientific Study of Religion, 28,* 324–336.

McFarland, S. G. (2001, February). *Prejudiced people: Individual differences in explicit prejudice.* Paper presented at the annual meeting of the Society for Personality and Social Psychology, San Antonio, TX.

McFarland, S. G., Ageyev, V. S., & Djintcharadze, N. (1996). Russian authoritarianism two years after communism. *Personality and Social Psychology Bulletin, 22,* 210–217.

McGregor, J. (1993). Effectiveness of role playing and antiracist teaching in reducing student prejudice. *Journal of Educational Research, 86,* 215–226.

McGuire, L. C., Morian, A., Codding, R., & Smyer, M. A. (2002). Older adults' memory for medical information: Influence of elderspeak and note taking. *International Journal of Rehabilitation and Health, 5,* 117–128.

McGuire, W. J., & McGuire, C. V. (1988). Content and process in the experience of the self. *Advances in Experimental Social Psychology, 21,* 97–144.

McIntosh, P. (1989, July/August). White privilege: Unpacking the invisible knapsack. *Peace and Freedom,* 10–12.

McIntyre, R. B., Paulson, R. M., & Lord, C. G. (2003). Alleviating women's mathematics stereotype threat through salience of group achievements. *Journal of Experimental Social Psychology, 39,* 83–90.

McLeod, A., & Crawford, I. (1998). The postmodern family: An examination of the psychological and legal perspectives of gay and lesbian parenting. In G.M. Herek (Ed.), *Stigma and sexual orientation: Understanding prejudice against lesbians, gay men, and bisexuals* (pp. 211–222). Thousand Oaks, CA: Sage.

Meertens, R. W., & Pettigrew, T. F. (1997). Is subtle prejudice really prejudice? *Public Opinion Quarterly, 61,* 54–71.

Mellor, D. (2003). Contemporary racism in Australia: The experiences of Aborigines. *Personality and Social Psychology Bulletin, 29,* 474–486.

Meloen, J. D. (1993). The F Scale as a predictor of fascism: An overview of 40 years of authoritarianism research. In W. F. Stone, G. Lederer, & R. Christie (Eds.), *Strength and weakness: The authoritarian personality today* (pp. 47–69). New York: Springer-Verlag.

Mendes, W. B., Blascovich, J., Lickel, B., & Hunter, S. (2002). Challenge and threat during social interactions with White and Black men. *Personality and Social Psychology Bulletin, 28,* 939–952.

Messner, M. (1988). Sports and male domination: The female athlete as contested ideological terrain. *Sport Sociology Journal, 5,* 197–211.

Meyer, I. H. (2003). Minority stress and mental health in gay men. In L. D. Garnets & D. C. Kimmel (Eds.), *Psychological perspectives on lesbian, gay, and bisexual experiences* (2nd ed., pp. 699–731). New York: Columbia University Press.

Miller, C. T., & Myers, A. M. (1998). Compensating for prejudice: How heavyweight people (and others) control outcomes despite prejudice. In J. K. Swim & C. Stangor (Eds.), *Prejudice: The target's perspective* (pp. 191–218). San Diego: Academic Press.

Miller, C. T., Rothblum, E. D., Felicio, D., & Brand, P. (1995). Compensating for stigma: Obese and nonobese women's reactions to being visible. *Personality and Social Psychology Bulletin, 21,* 1093–1106.

Miller, D. T., & Prentice, D. A. (1999). Some consequences of a belief in group essence: The category divide hypothesis. In D. A. Prentice & D. T. Miller (Eds.), *Cultural divides: Understanding and resolving group conflict* (pp. 213–238). New York: Russell Sage Foundation.

Miller, N. (2002). Personalization and the promise of contact theory. *Journal of Social Issues, 58,* 387–410.

Miller, N. E., & Bugelski, R. (1948). Minor studies of aggression II: The influence of frustrations imposed by the in-group on attitudes expressed toward out-groups. *Journal of Psychology, 25,* 437–422.

Miller, P. N., Miller, D. W., McKibbin, E. M., & Pettys, G. L. (1999). Stereotypes of the elderly in magazine advertisements 1956–1996. *International Journal of Aging and Human Development, 49,* 319–337.

Milner, D. (1981). Racial prejudice. In J. Turner & H. Giles (Eds.), *Intergroup behaviour* (pp. 102–143). Oxford, England: Blackwell.

Mirvis, P. (1993). *Building the competitive workforce: Investing in human capital for corporate success.* New York: Wiley.

Mitchell, J. P., Nosek, B. A., & Banaji, M. R. (2003). Contextual variations in implicit evaluation. *Journal of Experimental Psychology: General, 132,* 455–469.

Mobley, M., & Payne, T. (1992). Backlash! The challenge to diversity training. *Training & Development, 46*(12), 45–52.

Moghaddam, F. M., Stolkin, A. J., & Hutcheson, L. S. (1997). A generalized personal/group discrepancy: Testing the domain specificity of a perceived higher effect of events on one's group than on oneself. *Personality and Social Psychology Bulletin, 23,* 743–750.

Mohr, J. J., & Rochlen, A. B. (1999, August). *Measuring attitudes regarding bisexuality in lesbian, gay male, and heterosexual populations.* Paper presented at the meeting of the American Psychological Association, Boston.

Monin, B., & Miller, D. T. (2001). Moral credentials and the expression of prejudice. *Journal of Personality and Social Psychology, 81,* 33–43.

Monteith, M. J. (1993). Self-regulation of prejudiced responses: Implications for progress in prejudice-reduction efforts. *Journal of Personality and Social Psychology, 65,* 469–485.

Monteith, M. J. (1996). Contemporary forms of prejudice-related conflict: In search of a nutshell. *Personality and Social Psychology Bulletin, 22,* 461–473.

Monteith, M. J., Ashburn-Nardo, L., Voils, C. I., & Czopp, A, M. (2002). Putting the brakes on prejudice: On the development and operation of cues for control. *Journal of Personality and Social Psychology, 83,* 1029–1050.

Monteith, M. J., Deneen, N. E., & Tooman, G. D. (1996). The effect of social norm activation on expression of opinions concerning gay men and Blacks. *Basic and Applied Social Psychology, 18,* 267–283.

Monteith, M. J., Devine, P. G., & Zuwerink, J. R. (1993). Self-directed versus other-directed affect as a consequence of prejudice-related discrepancies. *Journal of Personality and Social Psychology, 64,* 198–210.

Monteith, M. J., Sherman, J. W., & Devine, P. G. (1998). Suppression as a stereotype control strategy. *Personality and Social Psychology Review, 2,* 63–82.

Monteith, M. J., & Spicer, C. V. (2000). Contents and correlates of Whites' and Blacks' racial attitudes. *Journal of Experimental Social Psychology, 36,* 125–154.

Monteith, M. J., Spicer, C. V., & Tooman, G. D. (1998). Consequences of stereotype suppression: Stereotypes on AND not on the rebound. *Journal of Experimental Social Psychology, 34,* 355–377.

Monteith, M. J., & Voils, C. I. (1998). Proneness to prejudiced responses: Toward understanding the authenticity of self-reported discrepancies. *Journal of Personality and Social Psychology, 73,* 901–916.

Monteith, M. J., & Walters, G. L. (1998). Egalitarianism, moral obligation, and prejudice-related personal standards. *Personality and Social Psychology Bulletin, 24,* 186–199.

Montepare, J. M., & Lachman, M. E. (1989). "You're only as old as you feel": Self-perceptions of age, fears of aging, and life satisfaction from adolescence to old age. *Psychology and Aging, 4,* 73–78.

Montepare, J. M., Steinberg, J., & Rosenberg, B. (1992). Characteristics of vocal communication between young adults and their parents and grandparents. *Communication Research, 19*, 479–492.

Montepare, J. M., & Zebrowitz-McArthur, L. A. (1988). Impressions of people created by age-related qualities of their gaits. *Journal of Personality and Social Psychology, 55*, 547–556.

Mooney, K. M., Cohn. E. S., & Swift, M. B. (1992). Physical distance and AIDS: Too close for comfort? *Journal of Applied Social Psychology, 22*, 1442–1452.

Morgan, J. N. (1992). Health, work, economic status and happiness. In N. E. Cutler, D. W. Gregg, & M. P. Lawton (Eds.), *Aging, money, and life satisfaction: Aspects of financial gerontology* (pp. 101–125). New York: Springer.

Morland, J. K., & Hwang, C. H. (1981). Racial/ethnic identity of preschool children: Comparing Taiwan, Hong Kong, and the United States. *Journal of Cross Cultural Psychology, 12*, 409–424.

Morland, J. K., & Suthers, E. (1980). Racial attitudes of children: Perspectives on the structural-normative theory of prejudice. *Phylon*, 267–275.

Morrison, M., & Morrison, T. (2002). Development and validation of a scale measuring modern prejudice toward gay men and lesbian women. *Journal of Homosexuality, 43*(2), 15–37.

Moses, Y. T. (1989). *Black women in academe: Issues and strategies.* Washington, DC: Association of American Colleges, Project on the Status and Education of Women.

Moskalenko, S., McCauley, C., & Rozin, P. (2004, January). *Group identification under conditions of threat: U.S. students' attachment to country, family, ethnicity, religion, and university before and after September 11th, 2001.* Poster presented at the meeting of the Society for Personality and Social Psychology, Austin, TX.

Moskowitz, G. B., Gollwitzer, P. M., Wasel, W., & Schaal, B. (1999). Preconscious control of stereotype activation through chronic egalitarian goals. *Journal of Personality and Social Psychology, 77,* 167–184.

Moskowitz, G. B., Salomon, A. R., & Taylor, C. M. (2000). Preconsciously controlling stereotyping: Implicitly activated egalitarian goals prevent the activation of stereotypes. *Social Cognition, 18,* 151–177.

Motown melee (2004). Retrieved November 22, 2004, from sportsillustrated.cnn.com/2004/basketball/nba/11/20/bc.bkn.pacers.pistonsbr.ap/.

Muir, D. E. (1991). "White" fraternity and sorority attitudes toward "Blacks" on a deep-South campus. *Sociological Spectrum, 11*, 93–103.

Mullen, B., Brown, R., & Smith, C. (1992). Ingroup bias as a function of salience, relevance and status: An integration. *European Journal of Social Psychology, 22*, 103–122.

Mullen, B., & Johnson, C. (1995). Cognitive representation in ethnophaulisms and illusory correlation in stereotyping. *Personality and Social Psychology Bulletin, 21*, 420–433.

Mummendey, A., Kessler, T., Klink, A., & Mielke, R. (1999). Strategies to cope with negative social identity: Predictions by social identity theory and relative deprivation theory. *Journal of Personality and Social Psychology, 76*, 229–245.

Mummendey, A., & Wenzel, M. (1999). Social discrimination and tolerance in intergroup relations: Reactions to intergroup difference. *Personality and Social Psychology Review, 3*, 158–174.

Munk, N. (1999). Finished at forty. *Fortune, 139,* 50–66.

Muraven, M., & Baumeister, R. F. (2000). Self-regulation and depletion of limited resources: Does self-control resemble a muscle? *Psychological Bulletin, 126,* 247–259.

Murphy, K. R., & Cleveland, J. N. (1995). *Understanding performance appraisal: Social, organizational, and group-based perspectives.* Thousand Oaks, CA: Sage.

Murray, S. B. (1997). It's safer this way: The subtle and not-so-subtle exclusion of men in child care. In N. V. Benokraitis (Ed.), *Subtle sexism: Current practice and prospects for change* (pp. 136–153). Thousand Oaks, CA: Sage.

Myers, D. G. (2002). *Social psychology* (7th ed.). Boston: McGraw-Hill.

Myrdal, G. (1944). *An American dilemma: The Negro problem and modern democracy.* New York: Harper.

Nail, P. R., Harton, H. C., & Decker, B. P. (2003). Political orientation and modern versus aversive racism: Tests of Dovidio and Gaertner's (1998) integrated model. *Journal of Personality and Social Psychology, 84,* 754–770.

National Basketball Association. (2003). *Official site of the Los Angeles Lakers.* Retrieved November 16, 2003, from http://www.nba.com/lakers.

National Committee on Pay Equity. (2004). *Women of color in the workplace.* Retrieved July 13, 2004, from www.pay-equity.org/info-race.html.

National Opinion Research Center. (2003). *Doctorate recipients from United States universities: Summary report 2002.* Chicago: Author.

National Organization of Women. (2004). Retrieved July 21, 2004, from www.now.org.

National Science Foundation. (2002). *Women, Minorities, and Persons with Disabilities in Science and Engineering: 2002* (No. NSF 03-312). Arlington, VA: National Science Foundation, Division of Resource Statistics.

Neisser, U. (1967). *Cognitive psychology.* New York: Appleton-Century-Crofts.

Nelson, L. J., & Miller, D. T. (1995). The distinctiveness effect in social categorization: You are what makes you unusual. *Psychological Science, 6,* 246–249.

Nelson, L. J., Moore, D. L., Olivetti, J., & Scott, T. (1997). General and personal mortality salience and nationalistic bias. *Personality and Social Psychology Bulletin, 23,* 884–892.

Nelson, T. E., Acker, M., & Manis, M. (1996). Irrepressible stereotypes. *Journal of Experimental Social Psychology, 32,* 13–38.

Nelson, T. E., Biernat, M. R., & Manis, M. (1990). Everyday base rates (sex stereotypes): Potent and resilient. *Journal of Personality and Social Psychology, 59,* 664–675.

Neuberg, S. L. (1989). The goal of forming accurate impressions during social interactions: Attenuating the impact of negative expectancies. *Journal of Personality and Social Psychology, 56,* 374–386.

Neuberg, S. L. (1994). Expectancy-confirmation processes in stereotype-tinged social encounters: The moderating role of social goals. In M. P. Zanna & J. M. Olson (Eds.), *The psychology of prejudice* (pp. 103–130). Hillsdale, NJ: Erlbaum.

Neuberg, S. L., & Fiske, S. T. (1987). Motivational influences on impression formation: Outcome dependency, accuracy-driven intention, and individuating processes. *Journal of Personality and Social Psychology, 53,* 431–444.

Neuberg, S. L., & Newsom, J. T. (1993). Personal need for structure: Individual differences in the desire for simple structure. *Journal of Personality and Social Psychology, 65,* 113–131.

Neuberg, S. L., Smith, D. M., Hoffman, J. C., & Russell, F. J. (1994). When we observe stigmatized and "normal" individuals interacting: Stigma by association. *Personality and Social Psychology Bulletin, 20,* 196–209.

Neugarten, B. L. (1975). The future and the young-old. *Gerontologist, 15*(1, Pt 2), 4–9.

Neville. H. A., Lilly, R. L., Duran, G., Lee, R. M., & Browne, L. (2000). Construction and validation of the Color-Blind Racial Attitudes Scale (CoBRAS). *Journal of Counseling Psychology, 47,* 59–70.

Newman, M. A., Liss, M. B., & Sherman, R. (1983). Ethnic awareness in children: Not a unitary concept. *Journal of Genetic Psychology, 143,* 103–112.

Nieman, Y. F., & Dovidio, J. F. (1998). Relationship of solo status, academic rank, and perceived distinctiveness to job satisfaction of racial/ethnic minorities. *Journal of Applied Psychology, 83,* 55–71.

Niemann, Y. F., Jennings, L., Rozelle, R. M., Baxter, J. C., & Sullivan, E. (1994). Use of free responses and cluster analysis to determine stereotypes of eight groups. *Personality and Social Psychology Bulletin, 20,* 379–390.

Nierenberg, D. (2002). *Correcting gender myopia: Gender equity, women's welfare, and the environment.* Washington, DC: Worldwatch.

Norton, J. R., & Fox, R. E. (1997). *The change equation: Capitalizing on diversity for effective organizational change.* Washington, DC: American Psychological Association.

Nussbaum, M. C. (2004, August 6). Danger to human dignity: The revival of disgust and shame in the law. *The Chronicle Review, 50,* B6.

Oakes, J. (1996). Two cities' tracking and within-school segregation. In E. C. Lagemann & L. P. Miller (Eds.), *Brown v. Board of Education: The challenge for today's schools* (pp. 81–90). New York: Teachers College Press.

Oakes, P. J., Haslam, S. A., & Turner, J. C. (1994). *Stereotyping and social reality.* Cambridge, MA: Blackwell.

Ochs, R. (1996). It goes two ways. In B. A. Firestein (Ed.), *Bisexuality.* London: Sage.

O'Connell, A. N., & Rotter, N. G. (1979). The influence of stimulus age and sex on person perception. *Journal of Gerontology, 34*(2), 220–228.

O'Connor, B. P., & St. Pierre, E. S. (2004). Older persons' perceptions of the frequency and meaning of elderspeak from family, friends, and service workers. *International Journal of Aging and Human Development, 58*(3), 197–221.

O'Connor, L. A., Brooks-Gunn, J., & Graber, J. (2000). Black and White girls' racial preferences in media and peer choices and the role of socialization for black girls. *Journal of Family Psychology, 14,* 510–521.

Olian, J. D., Schwab, D. P., & Haberfeld, Y. (1988). The impact of applicant gender compared to qualifications on hiring recommendations: A meta-analysis of experimental studies. *Organizational Behavior and Human Decision Processes, 41,* 180–195.

Oliver, M. B., & Hyde, J. S. (1993). Gender differences in sexuality: A meta-analysis. *Psychological Bulletin, 114,* 29–51.

Olson, J. M., Roese, N. J., Meen, J., & Robertson, D. J. (1995). The preconditions and consequences of relative deprivation: Two field studies. *Journal of Applied Social Psychology, 25,* 944–964.

Operario, D., & Fiske, S. T. (1998). Racism equals power plus prejudice: A social psychological equation for racial oppression. In J. L. Eberhardt & S. T. Fiske (Eds.), *Confronting racism: The problem and the response* (pp. 33–53). Thousand Oaks, CA: Sage.

Operario, D., & Fiske, S. T. (2001). Ethnic identity moderates perceptions of prejudice: Judgments of personal versus group discrimination and subtle versus blatant bias. *Personality and Social Psychology Bulletin, 27,* 550–561.

Opotow, S. (1995). Drawing the line: Social categorization, moral exclusion, and the scope of justice. In B. B. Bunker & J. Z. Rubin (Eds.), *Conflict, cooperation, and justice: Essays inspired by the work of Morton Deutsch* (pp. 347–369). San Francisco: Jossey-Bass.

Osborne, J. W. (1995). Academics, self-esteem, and race: A look at the underlying assumptions of the disidentification hypothesis. *Personality and Social Psychology Bulletin, 21,* 449–455.

Ostrom, T. M., & Sedikides, C. (1992). Out-group homogeneity effects in minimal and natural groups. *Psychological Bulletin, 112,* 536–552.

Overbeck, J. R., & Park, B. (2001). When power does not corrupt: Superior individuation processes among powerful perceivers. *Journal of Personality and Social Psychology, 81,* 549–565.

Oyserman, D., Coon, H. M., & Kemmelmeier, M. (2002). Rethinking individualism and collectivism: Evaluation of theoretical assumptions and meta-analyses. *Psychological Bulletin, 128,* 3–72.

Oyserman, D., & Sakamoto, I. (1997). Being Asian American: Identity, cultural constructs, and stereotype perception. *Journal of Applied Behavioral Science, 33,* 435–453.

Palmore, E. B. (1979). Advantages of aging. *The Gerontologist, 19,* 220.

Palmore, E. B. (1999). *Ageism: Negative and positive.* New York: Springer.

Paolini, S., Hewstone, M., Cairns, E., & Voci, A. (2004). Effects of direct and indirect cross-group friendships on judgments of Catholics and Protestants in Northern Ireland: The mediating role of an anxiety-reduction mechanism. *Personality and Social Psychology Bulletin, 30,* 770–786.

Park, B., & Judd, C. M. (1990). Measures and models of perceived group variability. *Journal of Personality and Social Psychology, 59,* 173–191.

Park, J., & Banaji, M. R. (2000). Mood and heuristics: The influence of happy and sad states on sensitivity and bias in stereotyping. *Journal of Personality and Social Psychology, 78,* 1005–1023.

Parker, C. P., Baltes, B. B., & Christiansen, N. D. (1997). Support for affirmative action, justice perceptions, and work attitudes: A study of gender and racial-ethnic group differences. *Journal of Applied Psychology, 82,* 376–389.

Paskoff, S. M. (1996). Ending the diversity wars. *Training, 33*(8), 42–50.

Pasupathi, M., & Löckenhoff, C. E. (2002). Ageist behavior. In T. D. Nelson (Ed.), *Ageism: Stereotyping and prejudice against older adults* (pp. 201–246). Cambridge, MA: MIT Press.

Patchen, M. (1982). *Black-White contact in schools.* West Lafayette, IN: Purdue University Press.

Paulhus, D. L. (1991). Measurement and control of response bias. In J. P. Robinson, P. R. Shaver, & L. S. Wrightsman (Ed.), *Measures of personality and social psychological attitudes* (pp. 17–59). San Diego: Academic Press.

Paulhus, D. L., Martin, C. L., & Murphy, G. K. (1992). Some effects of arousal on sex stereotyping. *Personality and Social Psychology Bulletin, 18*, 325–330.

Payne, B. K. (2001). Prejudice and perception: The role of automatic and controlled processes in misperceiving a weapon. *Journal of Personality and Social Psychology, 81*, 181–192.

Payne, B. K., Lambert, A. J., & Jacoby, L. L. (2002). Best laid plans: Effects of goals on accessibility bias and cognitive control in race-based misperceptions of weapons. *Journal of Experimental Social Psychology, 38*, 384–396.

Peabody, D. (1985). *National characteristics*. Cambridge: Cambridge University Press.

Peffley, M., Hurwitz, J., & Sniderman, P. M. (1997). Racial stereotypes and Whites' political views of Blacks in the context of welfare and crime. *American Journal of Political Science, 41*, 30–60.

Pendry, L. F., & Macrae, C. N. (1994). Stereotypes and mental life: The case of the motivated but thwarted tactician. *Journal of Experimental Social Psychology, 30*, 303–325.

Pendry, L. F., & Macrae, C. N. (1996). What the disinterested observer overlooks: Goal-directed social categorization. *Personality and Social Psychology Bulletin, 22*, 249–256.

Perreault, S., & Bourhis, R. Y. (1999). Ethnocentrism, social identification, and discrimination. *Personality and Social Psychology Bulletin, 25*, 92–103.

Peters, W. (Producer/Writer/Director). (1970). The eye of the storm. ABC News television program NOW.

Peters, W. (Producer/Director/Writer), & Cobb, C. (Writer/Correspondent). (1985, March 26). Frontline's a class divided [Television broadcast]. Public Broadcasting Service.

Petersen, L.-E., & Dietz, J. (2000). Social discrimination in a personnel selection context: The effects of an authority's instructions to discriminate and followers' authoritarianism. *Journal of Applied Social Psychology, 30*, 206–220.

Peterson, B. E., Duncan, L. E., & Pang, J. S. (2002). Authoritarianism and political impoverishment: Deficits in knowledge and civic disinterest. *Political Psychology, 23*, 97–112.

Peterson, K. (2004). 50-state rundown on gay marriage laws. *Stateline.org: Politics and policy news state by state*. Retrieved November 5, 2004, from www.stateline.org/stateline.

Pettigrew, T. F. (1979). The ultimate attribution error: Extending Allport's cognitive analysis of prejudice. *Personality and Social Psychology Bulletin, 5*, 461–476.

Pettigrew, T. F. (1988). Integration and pluralism. In P. A. Katz & D. A. Taylor (Eds.), *Eliminating racism: Profiles in controversy* (pp. 19–30). New York: Plenum.

Pettigrew, T. F. (1997). Generalized intergroup contact effects on prejudice. *Personality and Social Psychology Bulletin, 23*, 173–185.

Pettigrew, T. F. (1998a). Intergroup contact theory. *Annual Review of Psychology, 49*, 65–85.

Pettigrew, T. F. (1998b). Prejudice and discrimination on the college campus. In J. L. Eberhardt & S. T. Fiske (Eds.), *Confronting racism: The problem and the response* (pp. 263–279). Thousand Oaks, CA: Sage.

Pettigrew, T. F., & Meertens, R. W. (1995). Subtle and blatant racism in Western Europe. *European Journal of Social Psychology, 25*, 57–75.

Pettigrew, T. F., & Tropp, L. R. (2000). Does intergroup contact reduce prejudice? Recent meta-analytic findings. In S. Oskamp (Ed.), *Reducing prejudice and discrimination* (pp. 93–114). Mahwah, NJ: Erlbaum.

Petty, R. E., & Cacioppo, J. T. (1979). Issue involvement can increase or decrease persuasion by enhancing message relevant cognitive responses. *Journal of Personality and Social Psychology, 37,* 1915–1926.

Phelps, E. A., O'Connor, K. J., Cunningham, W. A., Funayama, E. S., Gatenby, J. C., Gore, J. C., & Banaji, M. R. (2000). Performance on indirect measures of race evaluation predicts amygdala activation. *Journal of Cognitive Neuroscience, 12,* 729–738.

Phillips, S. T., & Ziller, R. C. (1997). Toward a theory and measure of the nature of nonprejudice. *Journal of Personality and Social Psychology, 72,* 420–434.

Piaget, J. (1932). *The moral judgement of the child.* London: Kegan Paul.

Piaget, J., & Weil, A. M. (1951). The development in children of the idea of homeland and of relations to other countries. *International Social Science Journal, 3,* 561–578.

Piercy, M. (2003). *Colors passing through us: Poems.* New York: Alfred Knopf.

Pilkington, D. (2002). *Rabbit proof fence: The true story of one of the greatest escapes of all time.* New York: Miramax.

Pilkington, N. W., & D'Augelli, A. R. (1995). Victimization of lesbian, gay, and bisexual youth in community settings. *Journal of Community Psychology, 23,* 34–57.

Pilkington, N. W., & Lydon, J. E. (1997). The relative effect of attitude similarity and attitude dissimilarity on interpersonal attraction: Investigating the moderating roles of prejudice and group membership. *Personality and Social Psychology Bulletin, 23,* 107–122.

Pinel, E. C. (2002). Stigma consciousness in intergroup contexts. *Journal of Experimental Social Psychology, 38,* 178–185.

Pinker, S. (2002). *The blank slate: The modern denial of human nature.* New York: Viking.

Piskur, J., & Degelman, D. (1992). Effect of reading a summary of research about biological bases of homosexual orientation on attitudes toward homosexuals. *Psychological Reports, 71,* 1219–1225.

Plaks, J. E., Stroessner, S. J., Dweck, C. S., & Sherman, J. W. (2001). Person theories and attention allocation: Preferences for stereotypic versus counterstereotypic information. *Journal of Personality and Social Psychology, 80,* 876–893.

Plant, E. A., & Devine, P. G. (1998). Internal and external motivation to respond without prejudice. *Journal of Personality and Social Psychology, 75,* 811–832.

Plant, E. A., & Devine, P. G. (2001). Responses to other-imposed pro-Black pressure: Acceptance or backlash? *Journal of Experimental Social Psychology, 37,* 486–501.

Plant, E. A., & Devine, P. G. (2003). The antecedents and implications of interracial anxiety. *Personality and Social Psychology Bulletin, 29,* 790–801.

Plant, E. A., Devine, P. G., & Brazy, P. C. (2003). The bogus pipeline and motivations to respond without prejudice: Revisiting the fading and faking of racial prejudice. *Group Processes and Intergroup Relations, 6,* 187–200.

Plant, E. A., Hyde, J. S., Keltner, D., & Devine, P. G. (2000). The gender stereotyping of emotions. *Psychology of Women Quarterly, 24,* 81–92.

Pleck, J. H., Sonenstein, F. L., & Ku, L. C. (1993). Masculine ideology: Its impact on adolescent males' heterosexual relationships. *Journal of Social Issues, 49,* 11–29.

Pleck, J. H., Sonenstein, F. L., & Ku, L. C. (1994). Attitudes toward male roles among adolescent males: A discriminant validity analysis. *Sex Roles, 30,* 481–501.

Pratto, F., Liu, J. H., Levin, S., Sidanius, J., Shih, M., Bachrach, H., & Hegarty, P. (2000). Social dominance orientation and the legitimization of inequality across cultures. *Journal of Cross-Cultural Psychology, 31,* 369–409.

Pratto, F., Sidanius, J., Stallworth, L. M., & Malle, B. F. (1994). Social dominance orientation: A personality variable predicting social and political attitudes. *Journal of Personality and Social Psychology, 67,* 741–763.

Pratto, F., Stallworth, L. M., Sidanius, J., & Siers, B. (1997). The gender gap in occupational role attainment: A social dominance approach. *Journal of Personality and Social Psychology, 72,* 37–53.

Preston, K., & Stanley, K. (1987). "What's the worst thing . . . ?" Gender-directed insults. *Sex Roles, 17,* 209–219.

Price Waterhouse v. Hopkins, 490 U.S. 228 (1989).

Pyszczynski, T., Solomon, S., & Greenberg, J. (2003). *In the wake of 9/11: The psychology of terror.* Washington, DC: American Psychological Association.

Quanty, M. B., Keats, J. A., & Harkins, S. G. (1975). Prejudice and criteria for identification of ethnic photographs. *Journal of Personality and Social Psychology, 32,* 449–454.

Quillian, L., & Campbell, M. E. (2003). Beyond Black and White: The present and future of multiracial friendship segregation. *American Sociological Review, 68,* 540–566.

Quinn, D. M., Roese, N. J., Pennington, G. L., & Olson, J. M. (1999). The personal/group discrimination discrepancy: The role of informational complexity. *Personality and Social Psychology Bulletin, 25,* 1430–1440.

Quinton, W. J., Cowan, G., & Watson, B. D. (1996). Personality and attitudinal predictors of support of proposition 187—California's anti-illegal immigrant initiative. *Journal of Applied Social Psychology, 26,* 2204–2223.

Ragins, B. R., & Cornwell, J. M. (2001). Pink triangles: Antecedents and consequences of perceived workplace discrimination. *Journal of Applied Psychology, 86,* 1244–1261.

Ragins, B. R., Cornwell, J. M., & Miller, J. S. (2003). Heterosexism in the workplace: Do race and gender matter? *Group and Organization Management, 28,* 45–74.

Ramsey, S. L., Lord, C. G., Wallace, D. S., & Pugh, M. A. (1994). The role of subtypes in attitudes toward superordinate social categories. *British Journal of Social Psychology, 33,* 387–403.

Rasmussen, J. L., & Moely, B. E. (1986). Impression formation as a function of the sex role appropriateness of linguistic behavior. *Sex Roles, 14,* 149–161.

Reekie, L.-J., & Hansen, F. J. (1992). The influence of client age on clinical judgements of male and female social workers. *Journal of Gerontological Social Work, 19,* 67–82.

Reid, P. T. (1979). Racial stereotyping on television: A comparison of the behavior of both Black and White television characters. *Journal of Applied Psychology, 64,* 465–471.

Reskin, B. F. (1998). *The realities of affirmative action.* Washington, DC: American Sociological Association.

Reuben, D. B., Fullerton, J. T., Tschann, J. M., & Croughan-Minihane, M. (1995). Attitudes of beginning medical students toward older persons: A five-campus study. *Journal of the American Geriatrics Society, 43,* 1430–1436.

Revenson, T. A. (1989). Compassionate stereotyping of elderly patients by physicians: Revising the social contact hypothesis. *Psychology and Aging, 4*, 230–234.

Reyna, C., Henry, P. J., Korfmacher, W., & Tucker, A. (2004, January). *Attributional stereotypes as cues for deservingness: Examining the role of principled conservatism in racial policy decisions.* Poster presented at the meeting of the Society for Personality and Social Psychology, Austin, TX.

Rice, A. S., Ruiz, R. A., Padilla, A. M. (1974). Person perception, self-identity, and ethnic group preference in Anglo, Black, and Chicano preschool and third-grade children. *Journal of Cross-Cultural Psychology, 5*, 100–108.

Richard, O. C. (2000). Racial diversity, business strategy, and firm performance: A resource-based view. *Academy of Management Journal, 43*, 164–177.

Richards, G. (1997). *"Race," racism, and psychology: Towards a reflexive history.* New York: Routledge.

Richards, Z., & Hewstone, M. (2001). Subtyping and subgrouping: Processes for the prevention and promotion of stereotype change. *Personality and Social Psychology Review, 5*, 52–73.

Richeson, J. A., & Ambady, N. (2003). Effects of situational power on automatic racial prejudice. *Journal of Experimental Social Psychology, 39*, 177–183.

Richeson, J. A., Baird, A. A., Gordon, H. L., Heatherton, T. F., Wyland, C., Trawalter, S., & Shelton, J. N. (2003). An fMRI investigation of the impact of interracial contact on executive function. *Nature Neuroscience, 6*, 1323–1328.

Richeson, J. A., & Nussbaum, R. J. (2004). The impact of multiculturalism versus color-blindness on racial bias. *Journal of Experimental Social Psychology, 40*, 417–423.

Richeson, J. A., & Shelton, J. N. (2003). When prejudice does not pay: Effects of interracial contact on executive function. *Psychological Science, 14*, 287–290.

Ridge, R. D., & Reber, J. S. (2002). "I think she is attracted to me": The effect of men's beliefs on women's behavior in a job interview. *Basic and Applied Social Psychology, 24*, 1–14.

Rist, R. C. (1974). Race, policy, and schooling. *Society, 12*(1), 59–63.

Ritter, B. A., & Yoder, J. D. (2004). Gender differences in leader emergence persist even for dominant women: An updated confirmation of Role Congruity Theory. *Psychology of Women Quarterly, 28*, 187–193.

Roberson, L., & Block, C. J. (2001). Racioethnicity and job performance: A review and critique of theoretical perspectives on the causes of group differences. *Research in Organizational Behavior, 23*, 247–325.

Roberson, L., Deitch, E. A., Brief, A. P., & Block, C. J. (2003). Stereotype threat and feedback seeking in the workplace. *Journal of Vocational Behavior, 62*, 176–188.

Robinson, J. D., & Skill, T. (1995). The invisible generation: Portrayals of the elderly on prime-time television. *Communication Reports, 8*, 111–119.

Roccas, S., & Brewer, M. B. (2002). Social identity complexity. *Personality and Social Psychology Review, 6*, 88–106.

Rochlin, M. (1977). *The Heterosexual Questionnaire.* Retrieved October 10, 2004 from www.pinkpractice.co.uk/quaire.htm.

Roderick, T., McCammon, S. L., Long, T. E., & Allred, L. J. (1998). Behavioral aspects of homonegativity. *Journal of Homosexuality, 36*(1), 79–88.

Roese, N. J., & Jamieson, D. W. (1993). Twenty years of bogus pipeline research: A critical review and meta-analysis. *Psychological Bulletin, 114*, 363–375.

Rogers, R. W., & Prentice-Dunn, S. (1981). Deindividuation and anger–mediated interracial aggression: Unmasking regressive racism. *Journal of Personality and Social Psychology, 41,* 63–73.

Rokeach, M. (1960). *The open and closed mind.* New York: Basic Books.

Rokeach, M. (1972). *Beliefs, attitudes, and values.* San Francisco: Jossey-Bass.

Rokeach, M. (1973). *The nature of human values.* New York: Free Press.

Rosenberg, M. (1965). *Society and the adolescent self-image.* Princeton, NJ: Princeton University Press.

Rosenkrantz, P. S., Vogel, H., Bee, I., Broverman, I., & Broverman, D. V. (1968). Sex-role stereotypes and self-concepts in college students. *Journal of Consulting and Clinical Psychology, 32,* 286–295.

Ross, D. F., Dunning, D., Toglia, M. P., & Ceci, S. J. (1990). The child in the eyes of the jury: Assessing mock jurors' perceptions of the child witness. *Law and Human Behavior, 14,* 5–23.

Ross, L. (1977). The intuitive psychologist and his shortcomings: Distortions in the attribution process. *Advances in Experimental Social Psychology, 10,* 174–221.

Roth, P. L., Huffcutt, A. I., & Bobko, P. (2003). Ethnic group differences in measures of job performance: A new meta-analysis. *Journal of Applied Psychology, 88,* 694–706.

Rothbart, M., Evans, M., & Fulero, S. (1979). Recall for confirming events: Memory processes and the maintenance of social stereotyping. *Journal of Experimental Social Psychology, 15,* 343–355.

Rothbart, M., & Mauro, R. (1996). Social categories and decision making: How much discrimination do we need? In D. M. Messick & A. E. Tenbrunsel (Eds.), *Codes of conduct: Behavioral research into business ethics* (pp. 143–159). New York: Russell Sage Foundation.

Rotheram-Borus, M. J., & Fernandez, M. I. (1995). Sexual orientation and developmental challenges experienced by gay and lesbian youth. *Suicide and Life-threatening Behavior, 25,* 26–34.

Rowatt, W. C., & Franklin, L. M. (2004). Christian orthodoxy, religious fundamentalism, and right-wing authoritarianism as predictors of implicit racial prejudice. *International Journal for the Psychology of Religion, 14,* 125–138.

Rowley, C. D. (1970). *The destruction of aboriginal society: Aborginal policy and practice* (vol. 1). Canberra: Australian National University Press.

Roy, A., & Harwood, J. (1997). Underrepresented, positively portrayed: Older adults in television commercials. *Journal of Applied Communication Research, 25,* 39–56.

Rozin, P., Lowery, L., Imada, S., & Haidt, J. (1999). The CAD triad hypothesis: A mapping of three moral emotions (contempt, anger, disgust) and three moral codes (community, autonomy, divinity). *Journal of Personality and Social Psychology, 76,* 574–586.

Rubin, K. H., & Brown, I. D. (1975). A life-span look at person perception and its relationship to communicative interaction. *Journal of Gerontology, 30,* 461–468.

Rubin, L. (1998). Is this a white country, or what? In P. S. Rothenberg (Ed.), *Race, class, and gender in the United States: An integrated study* (4th ed., pp. 92–99). New York: St. Martin's.

Rubin, M., & Hewstone, M. (1998). Social identity theory's self-esteem hypothesis: A review and some suggestions for clarification. *Personality and Social Psychology Review, 2,* 40–62.

Rudman, L. A., & Goodwin, S. A. (2004). Gender differences in automatic in-group bias: Why do women like women more than men like men? *Journal of Personality and Social Psychology, 87*, 494–509.

Rudman, L. A., Greenwald, A. G., & McGhee, D. E. (2001). Implicit self-concept and evaluative gender stereotypes: Self and ingroup share desirable traits. *Personality and Social Psychology Bulletin, 27*, 1164–1178.

Rudman, L. A., & Kilianski, S. E. (2000). Implicit and explicit attitudes toward female authority. *Personality and Social Psychology Bulletin, 26*, 1315–1328.

Runciman, W. G. (1966). *Relative derivation and social justice.* Berkeley: University of California Press.

Ruscher, J. B. (2001). *Prejudiced communication: A social psychological perspective.* New York: Guilford.

Russell, K., Wilson, M., & Hall, R. (1992). *The color complex: The politics of skin color among African Americans.* New York: Harcourt.

Rust, P. C. (1995). *Bisexuality and the challenge to lesbian politics: Sex, loyalty, and revolution.* New York: New York University Press.

Ryan, C. S., Park, B., & Judd, C. M. (1996). Assessing stereotype accuracy: Implications for understanding the stereotyping process. In C. N. Macrae, C. Stangor, & M. Hewstone (Eds.), *Stereotypes and stereotyping* (pp. 121–157). New York: Guilford.

Ryan, E. B. (1992). Beliefs about memory changes across the adult life span. *Journal of Gerontology, 47*, 41–46.

Ryan, E. B., Bieman-Copland, S., Kwong See, S. T., Ellis, C. H., & Anas, A. P. (2002). Age excuses: Conversational management of memory failures in older adults. *Journal of Gerontology: Psychological Sciences, 57B*, P256–P267.

Ryan, E. B., Giles, H., Bartolucci, G., & Henwood, K. (1986). Psycholinguistic and social psychological components of communication by and with the elderly. *Language and Communication, 6*, 442–450.

Ryan, E. B., Meredith, S. D., & Shantz, G. B. (1994). Evaluative perceptions of patronizing speech addressed to institutionalized elders in contrasting conversational contexts. *Canadian Journal on Aging, 13*, 236–248.

Sagar, H. A., & Schofield, J. W. (1980). Racial and behavior cues in Black and White children's perception of ambiguously aggressive acts. *Journal of Personality and Social Psychology, 39*, 590–598.

Sagiv, L., & Schwartz, S. H. (1995). Value priorities and readiness for out-group social contact. *Journal of Personality and Social Psychology, 69*, 437–448.

Sampson, E. E. (1999). *Dealing with differences: An introduction to the social psychology of prejudice.* Fort Worth: Harcourt.

Sandler, B. R., & Hall, R. M. (1986). *The campus climate revisited: Chilly for women faculty, administrators, and graduate students.* Washington, DC: Association of American Colleges, Project on the Status of and Education of Women.

Scarberry, N. C., Ratcliff, C. D., Lord, C. G., Lanicek, D. L., & Desforges, D. M. (1997). Effects of individuating information on the generalization part of Allport's contact hypothesis. *Personality and Social Psychology Bulletin, 23*, 1291–1299.

Schaller, M., Conway, L. G., & Tanchuk, T. L. (2002). Selective pressures on the once and future contents of ethnic stereotypes: Effects of the communicability of traits. *Journal of Personality and Social Psychology, 82*, 861–877.

Schencker, L., & Brenner, J. (2002, February 27). Part 1: Driving while black? *The Daily Illini.* Retrieved March 14, 2003 from www.dailyillini.com/feb02/feb27/news/stories.

Schimel, J., Simon, L., Greenberg, J., Pyszczynski, T., Solomon, S., Waxmonsky, J., & Arndt, J. (1999). Stereotypes and terror management: Evidence that mortality salience enhances stereotypic thinking and preferences. *Journal of Personality and Social Psychology, 77,* 905–926.

Schmader, T. (2002). Gender identification moderates stereotype threat effects on women's math performance. *Journal of Experimental Social Psychology, 38,* 194–201.

Schmader, T., & Johns, M. (2003). Converging evidence that stereotype threat reduces working memory capacity. *Journal of Personality and Social Psychology, 85,* 440–452.

Schmader, T., Major, B., & Gramzow, R. H. (2001). Coping with ethnic stereotypes in the academic domain: Perceived injustice and psychological disengagement. *Journal of Social Issues, 57,* 93–111.

Schmidt, D. F., & Boland, S. M. (1986). Structure of perceptions of older adults: Evidence for multiple stereotypes. *Psychology and Aging, 1,* 255–260.

Schmitt, M. T., Branscombe, N. R., & Kappen, D. M. (2003). Attitudes toward group-based inequality: Social dominance or social identity? *British Journal of Social Psychology, 42,* 161–186.

Schneider, B. W. (1987). Coming out at work: Bridging the private/public gap. *Work and Occupations, 13,* 463–487.

Schneider, D. J. (2004). *The psychology of stereotyping.* New York: Guilford.

Schofield, J. W. (1986). Causes and consequences of the colorblind perspective. In J. F. Dovidio & S. L. Gaertner (Eds.), *Prejudice, discrimination, and racism* (pp. 231–253). Orlando, FL: Academic Press.

Schofield, J. W. (1989). *Black and White in school: Trust, tension, or tolerance?* New York: Teachers College Press.

Schofield, J. W. (1991). School desegregation and intergroup relations: A review of the literature. *Review of Educational Research, 17,* 335–409.

Schofield, J. W. (2001a). Improving intergroup relations among students. In J. A. Banks & C. A. M. Banks (Eds.), *Handbook of research on multicultural education* (pp. 635–646). San Francisco: Jossey-Bass.

Schofield, J. W. (2001b). Review of research on school desegregation's impact on elementary and secondary school students. In J. A. Banks & C. A. M. Banks (Eds.), *Handbook of research on multicultural education* (pp. 597–616). San Francisco: Jossey-Bass.

Schofield, J. W., & Eurich-Fulcer, R. (2001). When and how school desegregation improves intergroup relations. In R. Brown & S. L. Gaertner (Eds.), *Blackwell handbook of social psychology: Intergroup processes* (pp. 475–494). Malden, MA: Blackwell.

Schofield, J. W., & Francis, W. D. (1982). An observational study of peer interaction in racially mixed "accelerated" classrooms. *Journal of Educational Psychology, 74,* 722–732.

Schofield, J. W., & Sagar, H. A. (1977). Peer interaction patterns in an integrated middle school. *Sociometry, 40,* 130–138.

Schuerger, J. M., Zarella, K. L., & Hotz, A. S. (1989). Factors that influence the temporal stability of personality by questionnaire. *Journal of Personality and Social Psychology, 56,* 777–783.

Schultz, P. W., Stone, W. F., & Christie, R. (1997). Authoritarianism and mental rigidity: The *Einstellung* problem revisited. *Personality and Social Psychology Bulletin, 23,* 3–9.

Schuman, H. (2000). The perils of correlation, the lure of labels, and the beauty of negative results. In D. O. Sears, J. Sidanius, & L. Bobo (Eds.), *Racialized politics: The debate about racism in America* (pp. 302–323). Chicago: University of Chicago Press.

Schuman, H., Steeh, C., Bobo, L., & Krysan, M. (1997). *Racial attitudes in America: Trends and interpretations* (rev. ed.). Cambridge, MA: Harvard University Press.

Schuster, R. (1993, February 8). Arthur Ashe: 1943–1993; Ashe legacy goes beyond sports, race. *USA Today,* p. 1 C.

Schwartz, S. H. (1996). Value priorities and behavior: Applying a theory of integrated value systems. In C. Seligman, J. M. Olson, & M. P. Zanna (Eds.), *The psychology of values* (pp. 1–24). Mahwah, NJ: Erlbaum.

Schwarzenegger, A. (2004). *Arnold's "girlie men" goad grates.* Retrieved August 30, 2004, from www.cbsnews.com/stories/2004.

Sears, D. O. (1988). Symbolic racism. In P. A. Katz & D. A. Taylor (Eds.), *Eliminating racism: Profiles in controversy* (pp. 53–84). New York: Plenum.

Sears, D. O. (1994). Ideological bias in political psychology: The view from scientific hell. *Political Psychology, 15,* 547–556.

Sears, D. O., & Henry, P. J. (2003). The origins of symbolic racism. *Journal of Personality and Social Psychology, 85,* 259–275.

Sears, D. O., Henry, P. J., & Kosterman, R. (2000). Egalitarian values and contemporary racial politics. In D. O. Sears, J. Sidanius, & L. Bobo (Eds.), *Racialized politics: The debate about racism in America* (pp. 75–117). Chicago: University of Chicago Press.

Sears, D. O., Hetts, J. J., Sidanius, J., & Bobo, L. (2000). Race in American politics: Framing the debates. In D. O. Sears, J. Sidanius, & L. Bobo (Eds.), *Racialized politics: The debate about racism in America* (pp. 1–43). Chicago: University of Chicago Press.

Sears, D. O., & Kinder, D. R. (1971). Racial tensions and voting in Los Angeles. In W. Hirsch (Ed.), *Los Angeles: Viability and prospects for metropolitan leadership* (pp. 51–88). New York: Praeger.

Sears, D. O., & McConahay, J. B. (1973). *The politics of violence: The new urban Blacks and the Watts riot.* Boston: Houghton-Mifflin.

Sears, D. O., Sidanius, J., & Bobo, L. (Eds.). (2000). *Racialized politics: The debate about Racism in America.* Chicago: University of Chicago Press.

Sears, D. O., & Vallentino, N. A. (1997). Politics matter: Political events as catalysts for preadult socialization. *American Political Review, 91,* 45–65.

Sears, D. O., van Laar, C., Carillo, M., & Kosterman, R. (1997). Is it really racism? The origin of White Americans' opposition to race-targeted policies. *Public Opinion Quarterly, 61,* 16–53.

Seccombe, K., & Ishii Kuntz, M. (1991). Perceptions of problems associated with aging: Comparisons among four older age cohorts. *Gerontologist, 31,* 527–533.

Sechrist, G. B., & Stangor, C. (2001). Perceived consensus influences intergroup behavior and stereotype accessibility. *Journal of Personality and Social Psychology, 880,* 645–654.

Sekaquaptewa, D., Espinoza, P., Thompson, M., Vargas, P., & von Hippel, W. (2003). Stereotypic explanatory bias: Implicit stereotyping as a predictor of discrimination. *Journal of Experimental Social Psychology, 39,* 75–82.

Serbin, L. A., Poulin-Dubois, D., Colburne, K. A., Sen, M. G., & Eichstedt, J. A. (2001). Gender stereotyping in infancy: Visual preference for and knowledge of gender-stereotyped toys in the second year. *International Journal of Behavioral Development, 25,* 7–15.

Shaffer, D. R., & Wallace, A. (1990). Belief congruence and evaluator homophobia as determinants of the attractiveness of competent homosexual and heterosexual males. *Journal of Psychology & Human Sexuality, 3*(1), 67–87.

Shaheen, J. G. (2003). Reel bad Arabs: How Hollywood vilifies a people. *Annals of the American Academy of Political and Social Science, 588,* 171–193.

Shelton, J. N. (2000). A reconceptualization of how we study issues of racial prejudice. *Personality and Social Psychology Review, 4,* 374–390.

Shelton, J. N. (2003). Interpersonal concerns in social encounters between majority and minority group members. *Group Processes & Intergroup Relations, 6,* 171–185.

Shelton, J. N., & Richeson, J. A. (2005). Intergroup contact and pluralistic ignorance. *Journal of Personality and Social Psychology, 88,* 91–107.

Shelton, J. N., & Stewart, R. E. (2004). Confronting perpetrators of prejudice: The inhibitory effects of social costs. *Psychology of Women Quarterly, 2,* 215–223.

Shen, F., Longo, J., Ernst, J. M., Reeder, G. D., & Pryor, J. B. (2004, June). *Threats to masculinity lead to endorsing anti-gay attitudes in men.* Paper presented at the American Psychological Society, Chicago.

Sherif, M. (1966). *In common predicament: Social psychology of intergroup conflict and cooperation.* Boston: Houghton Mifflin.

Sherman, J. W., & Bessenoff, G. R. (1999). Stereotypes as source-monitoring cues: On the interaction between episodic and semantic memory. *Psychological Science, 10,* 106–110.

Sherman, J. W., Groom, C. J., Ehrenberg, K., & Klauer, K. C. (2003), Bearing false witness under pressure: Implicit and explicit components of stereotype-driven memory distortions. *Social Cognition, 21,* 213–246.

Sherman, J. W., Stroesser, S. J., Loftus, S. T., & Deguzman, G. (1997). Stereotype suppression and recognition memory for stereotypical and nonstereotypical information. *Social Cognition, 15,* 205–215.

Sherman, S. J., & Gorkin, L. (1980). Attitude bolstering when behavior is inconsistent with central attitudes. *Journal of Experimental Social Psychology, 16,* 388–403.

Sherman, S. J., Hamilton, D. L., & Lewis, A. C. (1999). Perceived entitivity and the social identity value of group memberships. In D. Abrams & M. A. Hogg (Eds.), *Social identity and social cognition* (pp. 80–110). Malden, MA: Blackwell.

Sherrill, K. (1996). The political power of lesbians, gays, and bisexuals. *PS: Political Science and Politics, 29,* 469–473.

Shields, S. A., & Eyssell, K .M. (2001). History of the study of gender psychology. In J. Worell (Ed.). *Encyclopedia of women and gender: Sex similarities and differences and the impact of society on gender* (vol. 1, pp. 593–600). San Diego: Academic Press.

Shore, T. H. (1992). Subtle gender bias in the assessment of managerial potential. *Sex Roles, 27,* 499–515.

Shrum, W., & Cheek, N. H., Jr. (1987). Social structure during the school years: Onset of the degrouping process. *American Sociological Review, 52,* 218–223.

Shrum, W., Cheek, N. H., Jr., & Hunter, S. M. (1988). Friendship in school: Gender and racial homophily. *Sociology of Education, 61,* 227–239.

Sibicky, M., & Dovidio, J. (1986). Stigma of psychological therapy: Stereotypes, interpersonal reactions, and the self-fulfilling prophecy. *Journal of Counseling Psychology, 33,* 148–154.

Sidanius, J., & Pratto, F. (1999). *Social dominance: An intergroup theory of social hierarchy and oppression.* New York: Cambridge University Press.

Sidanius, J., Pratto, F., & Bobo, L. (1996). Racism, conservatism, affirmative action, and intellectual sophistication: A matter of principled conservatism or group dominance? *Journal of Personality and Social Psychology, 70,* 476–490.

Sidanius, J., Pratto, F., & Mitchell, M. (1994). Ingroup identification, social dominance orientation, and differential intergroup social allocation. *Journal of Social Psychology, 134,* 151–167.

Sidanius, J., Singh, P., Hetts, J. J., & Federico, C. (2000). It's not affirmative action, it's the Blacks: The continuing relevance of race in American politics. In D. O. Sears, J. Sidanius, & L. Bobo (Eds.), *Racialized politics: The debate about racism in America* (pp. 191–235). Chicago: University of Chicago Press.

Signorielli, N. (1993). Television, the portrayal of women, and children's attitudes. In G. L. Berry & J. K. Asamen (Eds.), *Children and television: Images in a changing sociocultural world* (pp. 229–242). Newbury Park, CA: Sage.

Simon, A. (1998). The relationship between stereotypes of and attitudes toward lesbians and gays. In G. M. Herek (Ed.), *Stigma and sexual orientation: Understanding prejudice against lesbians, gay men, and bisexuals* (pp. 62–81). Thousand Oaks, CA: Sage.

Simon, L., & Greenberg, J. (1996). Further progress in understanding the effects of derogatory ethnic labels: The role of preexisting attitudes toward the targeted group. *Personality and Social Psychology Bulletin, 22,* 1195–1204.

Simoni, J. M. (1996). Pathways to prejudice: Predicting students' heterosexist attitudes with demographics, self-esteem, and contact with lesbians and gay men. *Journal of College Student Development, 37,* 68–78.

Sinclair, L., & Kunda, Z. (1999). Reactions to a Black professional: Motivated inhibition and activation of conflicting stereotypes. *Journal of Personality and Social Psychology, 77,* 885–904.

Sinclair, L., & Kunda, Z. (2000). Motivated stereotyping of women: She's fine if she praised me but incompetent if she criticized me. *Personality and Social Psychology Bulletin, 26,* 1329–1342.

Singleton, L. C., & Asher, S. R. (1977). Peer preferences and social interaction among third-grade children in an integrated school district. *Journal of Educational Psychology, 69,* 330–336.

Singleton, L. C., & Asher, S. R. (1979). Race integration and children's peer preferences: An investigation of developmental and cohort differences. *Child Development, 50,* 936–941.

Skitka, L. J., Mullen, E., Griffin, T., Hutchinson, S., & Chamberlin, B. (2002). Dispositions, scripts, or motivated correction? Understanding ideological differences in explanations for social problems. *Journal of Personality and Social Psychology, 83,* 470–487.

Skrypnek, B. J., & Snyder, M. (1982). On the self-perpetuating nature of stereotypes about women and men. *Journal of Experimental Social Psychology, 18,* 277–291.

Slaby, R. G., & Frey, K. S. (1975). Development of gender constancy and selective attention to same-sex models. *Child Development, 46*, 849–856.

Slater, A., Von der Schulenburg, C., Brown, E., Badenoch, M., Butterworth, G., Parsons, S., & Samuels, C. (1998). Newborn infants prefer attractive faces. *Infant Behavior and Development, 21*, 345–354.

Slavin, R. E. (2001). Cooperative learning and intergroup relations. In J. A. Banks & C. A. M. Banks (Eds.), *Handbook of research on multicultural education* (pp. 628–634). San Francisco: Jossey-Bass.

Slotterback, C. A., & Saarnio, D. A. (1996). Attitudes towards older adults reported by young adults: Variation based on attitudinal task and attribute categories. *Psychology and Aging, 11*, 563–571.

Smetana, J. G. (1986). Preschool children's conceptions of sex-role transgressions. *Child Development, 57*, 862–871.

Smedley, A. (1999). *Race in North America: Origin and evolution of a worldview* (2nd ed.) Boulder, CO: Westview.

Smith, E. R. (1993). Social identity and social emotions: Toward new conceptualizations of prejudice. In D. Mackie & D. L. Hamilton (Eds.). *Affect, cognition, and stereotyping: Interactive processes in group perception* (pp. 297–315). San Diego: Academic Press.

Smith, E. R. (1999). Affective and cognitive implications of a group becoming part of the self: New models of prejudice and of the self-concept. In D. Abrams & M. A. Hogg (Eds.), *Social identity and social cognition* (pp. 183–196). Malden, MA: Blackwell.

Smith, R. A. (1997). Race, income, and authority at work: A cross-temporal analysis of Black and White men (1972–1994). *Social Problems, 44*, 19–37.

Smith, R. A., & Elliott, J. R. (2002). Does ethnic concentration influence employees' access to authority? An examination of contemporary urban labor markets. *Social Forces, 81*, 255–279.

Sniderman, P. M., Crosby, G. C., & Howell, W. G. (2000). The politics of race. In D. O. Sears, J. Sidanius, & L. Bobo (Eds.), *Racialized politics: The debate about racism in America* (pp. 236–279). Chicago: University of Chicago Press.

Sniderman, P. M., & Tetlock, P. E. (1986a). Reflections on American racism. *Journal of Social Issues, 42*(2), 173–187.

Sniderman, P. M., & Tetlock, P. E. (1986b). Symbolic racism: Problems of motive attribution in political analysis. *Journal of Social Issues, 42*(2), 129–150.

Snowden, F. M., Jr. (1983). *Before color prejudice: The ancient view of Blacks.* Cambridge, MA: Harvard University Press.

Snyder, M. (2001). Self-fulfilling prophecies. In J. Worrell (Ed.), *Encyclopedia of women and gender: Sex similarities and differences and the impact of society on gender* (pp. 945–953). San Diego: Academic Press.

Snyder, M., & Haugen, J. A. (1994). Why does behavioral confirmation occur? A functional perspective on the role of the perceiver. *Journal of Experimental Social Psychology, 30*, 218–246.

Snyder, M., & Miene, P. (1994). On the functions of stereotypes and prejudice. In M. P. Zanna & J. M. Olson (Eds.), *The psychology of prejudice* (pp. 33–54). Hillsdale, NJ: Erlbaum.

Snyder, M., & Swann, W. B., Jr. (1978). Hypothesis testing in social interaction. *Journal of Personality and Social Psychology, 14*, 148–162.

Snyder, M., Tanke, E. D., & Berscheid, E. (1977). Social perception and interpersonal behavior: On the self-fulfilling nature of social stereotypes. *Journal of Personality and Social Psychology, 35,* 656–666.

Soder, M. (1990). Prejudice or ambivalence? Attitudes toward persons with disabilities. *Disability, Handicap, and Society, 5,* 227–241.

Solomon, S., Greenberg, J., & Pyszczynski, T. (2000). Pride and prejudice: Fear of death and social behavior. *Current Directions in Psychological Science, 9,* 200–204.

Son Hing, L. S., Bobocel, D. R., & Zanna, M. P. (2002). Meritocracy and opposition to affirmative action: Making concessions in the face of discrimination. *Journal of Personality and Social Psychology, 83,* 493–509.

Son Hing, L. S., Li, W., & Zanna, M. P. (2002). Inducing hypocrisy to reduce prejudicial responses among aversive racists. *Journal of Experimental Social Psychology, 38,* 71–78.

Sontag, S. (1979). The double standard of aging. In J. Williams (Ed.), *Psychology of women* (pp. 462–278). New York: Academic Press.

Spalding, L., & Peplau, L. A. (1997). The unfaithful lover: Heterosexuals' perceptions of bisexuals and their relationships. *Psychology of Women Quarterly, 21,* 611–625.

Spence, J. T., & Hahn, E. D. (1997). The Attitudes Toward Women Scale and attitude change in college students. *Psychology of Women Quarterly, 21,* 17–34.

Spence, J. T., & Helmreich, R. (1972). The Attitudes Toward Women Scale: An objective instrument to measure attitudes toward the rights and roles of women in contemporary society. *JSAS Catalog of Selected Documents in Psychology, 2,* 66.

Spencer, M. B. (1982). Personal and group identity of black children: An alternative synthesis. *Genetic Psychology Monographs, 106,* 59–84.

Spencer, S. J., Fein, S., Wolfe, C. T., Fong, C., & Dunn, M. A. (1998). Automatic activation of stereotypes: The role of self-image threat. *Personality and Social Psychology Bulletin, 24,* 1139–1152.

Spencer, S. J., Steele, C. M., & Quinn, D. M. (2001). Stereotype threat and women's math performance. *Journal of Experimental Social Psychology, 35,* 4–28.

Spielman, D. A. (2000). Young children, minimal groups, and dichotomous categorization. *Personality and Social Psychology Bulletin, 26,* 1433–1441.

Spilka, B., Hood, R. W., Jr., Hunsberger, B., & Gorsuch, R. (2003). *The psychology of religion: An empirical approach* (3rd ed.). New York: Guilford.

Stafford, W. (1998). *The way it is: New and selected poems.* St. Paul, MN: Graywolf.

Stangor, C. (1995). Content and application inaccuracy in social stereotyping. In Y.-T. Lee, L. J. Jussim & C. R. McCauley (Eds.), *Stereotype accuracy: Toward appreciating group differences* (pp. 275–292). Washington, DC: American Psychological Association.

Stangor, C., Lynch, L., Duan, C., & Glass, B. (1992). Categorization of individuals on the basis of multiple features. *Journal of Personality and Social Psychology, 62,* 207–218.

Stangor, C., & McMillan, D. (1992). Memory for expectancy-congruent and expectancy-incongruent information: A review of the social and social developmental literatures. *Psychological Bulletin, 111,* 42–61

Stangor, C., Sechrist, G. B., & Jost, J. T. (2001). Changing racial beliefs by providing consensus information. *Personality and Social Psychology Bulletin, 27,* 486–496.

Stangor, C., Sullivan, L. A., & Ford, T. E. (1991). Affective and cognitive determinants of prejudice. *Social Cognition, 9,* 359–380.

Stangor, C., Swim, J. K., Van Allen, K. L., & Sechrist, G. B. (2002). Reporting discrimination in public and private contexts. *Journal of Personality and Social Psychology, 82,* 69–74.

Stake, J. E. (2003). Understanding male bias against girls and women in science. *Journal of Applied Social Psychology, 33,* 667–682.

Statham, A., Richardson, L., & Cook, J. A. (1991). *Gender and university teaching: A negotiated difference.* Albany, NY: State University of New York Press.

Staub, E. (2002). The psychology of bystanders, perpetrators, and heroic helpers. In L. S. Newman & R. Erber (Eds.), *Understanding genocide: The social psychology of the Holocaust* (pp. 11–42). New York: Oxford University Press.

Steele, C. (1988). The psychology of self-affirmation: Sustaining the integrity of the self. *Advances in Experimental Social Psychology, 21,* 261–346.

Steele, C. (1992, April). Race and the schooling of Black Americans. *Atlantic Monthly, 269*(4), 68–78.

Steele, C. (1997). A threat in the air: How stereotypes shape intellectual identity and performance. *American Psychologist, 52,* 613–629.

Steele, C., & Aronson, J. (1995). Stereotype threat and the intellectual test performance of African Americans. *Journal of Personality and Social Psychology, 69,* 797–811.

Steele, C., Spencer, S. J., & Aronson, J. (2003). Contending with group image: The psychology of stereotype and social identity threat. *Advances in Experimental Social Psychology, 34,* 379–440.

Steele, J., & Ambady, N. (2004, January), *Unintended discrimination and preferential treatment through category activation in a mock job interview.* Paper presented at the meeting of the Society for Personality and Social Psychology, Austin, TX.

Steele, J., James, J. B., & Barnett, R. C. (2002). Learning in a man's world: Examining the perceptions of undergraduate women in male-dominated academic areas. *Psychology of Women Quarterly, 46,* 46–50.

Steinhorn, L., & Diggs-Brown, B. (1999). *By the color of our skin: The illusion of integration and the reality of race.* New York: Dutton.

Stephan, C. W., Stephan, W. G., Demitrakis, K. M., Yamada, A. M., & Clason, D. L. (2000). Women's attitudes toward men: An integrated threat theory approach. *Psychology of Women Quarterly, 24,* 63–73.

Stephan, W. G. (1985). Intergroup relations. In G. Lindzey & E. Aronson (Eds.), *Handbook of social psychology* (3rd ed., vol. 2, pp. 599–658). New York: Random House.

Stephan, W. G. (1986). The effects of school desegregation: An evaluation 30 years after *Brown.* In M. J. Saks & L. Saxe (Eds.), *Advances in applied social psychology* (vol. 3, pp. 181–206). Mahwah, NJ: Erlbaum.

Stephan, W. G., Boniecki, K. A., Ybarra, O., Bettencourt, A., Ervin, K. S., Jackson, L. A., McNatt, P. S., & Renfro, C. L. (2002). The role of threats in racial attitudes of Blacks and Whites. *Personality and Social Psychology Bulletin, 28,* 1242–1254.

Stephan, W. G., Diaz-Loving, R., & Duran, A. (2000). Integrated threat theory and intercultural attitudes: Mexico and the United States. *Journal of Cross-Cultural Psychology, 31,* 240–249.

Stephan, W. G., & Finlay, K. (1999). The role of empathy in improving intergroup relations. *Journal of Social Issues, 55,* 729–743.

Stephan, W. G., & Stephan, C. W. (1984). The role of ignorance in intergroup relations. In N. Miller & M. B. Brewer (Eds.), *Groups in contact: The psychology of desegregation* (pp. 229–255). Orlando, FL: Academic Press.

Stephan, W. G., & Stephan, C. W. (1985). Intergroup anxiety. *Journal of Social Issues, 41*(3), 157–175.

Stephan, W. G., & Stephan, C. W. (1989). Antecedents of intergroup anxiety in Asian-Americans and Hispanic-Americans. *International Journal of Intercultural Relations, 13,* 203–219.

Stephan, W. G., & Stephan, C. W. (2000). An integrated threat theory of prejudice. In S. Oskamp (Ed.), *Reducing prejudice and discrimination* (pp. 23–45). Mahwah, NJ: Erlbaum.

Stephan, W. G., & Stephan, C. W. (2001). *Improving intergroup relations.* Mahwah, NJ: Erlbaum.

Stephan, W. G., Ybarra, O., & Bachman, G. (1999). Prejudice toward immigrants. *Journal of Applied Social Psychology, 29,* 2221–2237.

Stephan, W. G., Ybarra, O., Martínez, C. M., Schwarzwald, J., & Tur-Kaspa, M. (1998). Prejudice toward immigrants to Spain and Israel: An integrated threat theory analysis. *Journal of Cross-Cultural Psychology, 29,* 559–576.

Stern, P. C., & Kalof, L. (1996). *Evaluating social science research* (2nd ed.). New York: Oxford University Press.

Stevens, L. E., & Fiske, S. T. (2000). Motivated impressions of a powerholder: Accuracy under task dependency and misperception under evaluation dependency. *Personality and Social Psychology Bulletin, 26,* 907–922.

Stoker, L. (1998). Understanding Whites' resistance to affirmative action: The role of principled commitments and racial prejudice. In J. Hurwitz & M. Peffley (Eds.), *Perception and prejudice: Race and politics in the United States* (pp. 135–170). New Haven, CT: Yale University Press.

Stone, A. A., Turkkan, J. S., Bachrach, C. A., Jobe, J. B., Kurtzman, H. S., & Cain, V. S. (Eds.). (2000). *The science of self-report: Implications for research and practice.* Mahwah, NJ: Erlbaum.

Stone, J., Lynch, C. I., Sjomeling, M., & Darley, J. M. (1999). Stereotype threat effects on Black and White athletic performance. *Journal of Personality and Social Psychology, 77,* 1213–1227.

Stone, W. F., Lederer, G., & Christie, R. (Eds.). (1993). *Strength and weakness: The authoritarian personality today.* New York: Springer-Verlag.

Stone, W. F., & Smith, L. D. (1993). Authoritarianism: Left and right. In W. F. Stone, G. Lederer, & R. Christie (Eds.), *Strength and weakness: The authoritarian personality today* (pp. 144–156). New York: Springer-Verlag.

Stouffer, S. A., Suchman, E. A., DeVinney, L. C., Star, S. A., & Williams, R. A., Jr. (1949). *The American soldier: Adjustments during army life.* Princeton, NJ: Princeton University Press.

Strom, K. J. (2001). *Hate crimes reported in NIBRS, 1997–99* (U.S. Department of Justice, Bureau of Justice Statistics Report No. NCJ 186765). Retrieved June 6, 2004, from http://www.ojp.usdoj.gov/bjs/pub/pdf/hnrc99.pdf.

Strong, B., DeVault, C., Sayad, B. W., & Yarber, W. L. (2005). *Human sexuality: Diversity in contemporary America.* Boston: McGraw-Hill.

Sue, D. W. (2003). *Overcoming our racism: The journey to liberation.* San Francisco: Jossey-Bass.

Sumner, W. (1906). *Folkways.* Boston: Ginn.

Swan, S., & Wyer, R. S., Jr. (1997). Gender stereotypes and social identity: How being in the minority affects judgments of self and others. *Personality and Social Psychology Bulletin, 23,* 1265–1276.

Swim, J. K. (1994). Perceived versus meta-analytic effect sizes: An assessment of the accuracy of gender stereotypes. *Journal of Personality and Social Psychology, 23,* 601–631.

Swim, J. K., Aikin, K. J., Hall, W. S., & Hunter, B. A. (1995). Sexism and racism: Old-fashioned and modern prejudices. *Journal of Personality and Social Psychology, 68,* 199–214.

Swim, J. K., Ferguson, M. L., & Hyers, L. L. (1999). Avoiding stigma by association: Subtle prejudice against lesbians in the form of social distancing. *Basic and Applied Social Psychology, 21,* 61–68.

Swim, J. K., Hyers, L. L., Cohen, L. L., & Ferguson, M. J. (2001). Everyday sexism: Evidence for its incidence, nature, and psychological impact from three diary studies. *Journal of Social Issues, 57,* 31–53.

Swim, J. K., Hyers, L. L., Cohen, L. L., Fitzgerald, D. C., & Bylsma, W. H. (2003). African American college students' experiences with everyday racism: Characteristics of and responses to these incidents. *Journal of Black Psychology, 29,* 38–67.

Syverson, P. D. (2003). Data sources. *Council of Graduate Schools Communicator, 36,* 5–10.

Tajfel, H. (1969). Cognitive aspects of prejudice. *Journal of Social Issues, 25*(4), 79–97.

Tajfel, H. (1978). The achievement of group differentiation. In H. Tajfel (Ed.), *Differentiation between social groups* (pp. 77–98). London: Academic Press.

Tajfel, H., Billig, M. G., Bundy, R. P., & Flament, C. (1971). Social categorization and intergroup behaviour. *European Journal of Social Psychology, 1,* 149–178.

Tajfel, H., & Turner, J. C. (1986). The social identity theory of intergroup behavior. In W. G. Austin & S. Worchel (Eds.), *Psychology of intergroup relations* (2nd ed., pp. 7–27). Chicago: Nelson-Hall.

Takaki, R. (1993). *A different mirror: A history of multicultural America.* Boston: Little, Brown.

Tatum, B. D. (1997). *Why are all the Black kids sitting together in the cafeteria? And other conversations about race.* New York: Basic Books.

Taylor, D. M., & Lambert, W. E. (1996). The meaning of multiculturalism in a culturally diverse urban American area. *Journal of Social Psychology, 136,* 727–740.

Taylor, D. M., & Moghaddam, F. M. (1994). *Theories of intergroup relations: International social psychological perspectives* (2nd ed.). Westport, CT: Praeger.

Taylor, D. M., Wright, S. C., Moghaddam, F. M., & Lalonde, R. N. (1990). The personal/group discrimination discrepancy: Perceiving my group, but not myself, to be a target for discrimination. *Personality and Social Psychology Bulletin, 16,* 254–262.

Taylor, D. M., Wright, S. C., & Porter, L. E. (1994). Dimensions of perceived discrimination: The personal/group discrimination discrepancy. In M. P. Zanna & J. M. Olson (Eds.), *The psychology of prejudice* (pp. 233–255). Hillsdale, NJ: Erlbaum.

Taylor. M. C. (1995). White backlash to workplace affirmative action: Peril or myth? *Social Forces, 73,* 1385–1414.

Taylor, M. C. (1998). How White attitudes vary with the racial composition of local populations: Numbers count. *American Sociological Review, 63,* 512–535.

Taylor, M. C. (2002). Fraternal deprivation, collective threat, and social resentment: Perspectives on White racism. In I. Walker & H. J. Smith (Eds.), *Relative deprivation: Specification, development, and integration* (pp. 13–43). New York: Cambridge University Press.

Taylor, S. E. (1981). A categorization approach to stereotyping. In D. L. Hamilton (Ed.), *Cognitive processes in stereotyping and intergroup behavior.* Hillsdale, NJ: Erlbaum.

Taylor, S. E. (1998). The social being in social psychology. In D. T. Gilbert, S. T. Fiske, & G. Lindzey (Eds.), *The handbook of social psychology* (4th ed., vol. 1, pp. 58–95). Boston, MA: McGraw-Hill.

Teitelbaum, S., & Geiselman, R. E. (1997). Observer mood and cross-racial recognition. *Journal of Cross Cultural Psychology, 28,* 93–106.

Test makers to revise national merit exam to address gender bias. (1996). Retrieved January 15, 2004, from www.fairtest.org/examarts/fall96/natmerit.htm.

Tetlock, P. E. (1994). Political psychology or politicized psychology: Is the road to scientific hell paved with good moral intentions? *Political Psychology, 15,* 509–529.

Texas NAACP. (1999). *James Byrd, Jr.* Retrieved April 29, 2004, from http://www.texasnaacp.org/jasper.htm.

Thimm, C., Rademacher, U., & Kruse, L. (1998). Age stereotypes and patronizing messages: Features of age-adapted speech in technical instructions to the elderly. *Journal of Applied Communication Research, 26,* 66–82.

Thomas, K. M. (2005). *Diversity dynamics in the workplace.* Belmont, CA: Wadsworth.

Thomas, P. J., Edwards, J. E., Perry, Z. A., & David, K. M. (1998). Racial differences in male Navy officer fitness reports. *Military Psychology, 10,* 127–143.

Thomas, R. R., Jr. (1991). *Beyond race and gender: Unleashing the power of your total work force by managing diversity.* New York: AMACOM.

Thomas, R. R., Jr. (1996). *Redefining diversity.* New York: American Management Association.

Thomas, W. I., & Thomas, D. S. (1928). *The child in America: Behavior problems and programs.* New York: Alfred A. Knopf.

Thompson, S. K. (1975). Gender labels and early sex-role development. *Child Development, 46,* 339–347.

Thompson, T. L., Judd, C. M., & Park, B. (2000). The consequences of communication social stereotypes. *Journal of Experimental Social Psychology, 36,* 567–599.

Thompson, T. L., & Zerbinos, E. (1997). Television cartoons: Do children notice it's a boy's world? *Sex Roles, 37,* 415–432.

Tiedens, L. Z., & Linton, S. (2001). Judgment under emotional certainty and uncertainty: The effects of specific emotions on information processing. *Journal of Personality and Social Psychology, 81,* 973–988.

Tilby, P. J., & Kalin, R. (1980). Effects of sex-role deviant lifestyles in otherwise normal persons on the perceptions of maladjustment. *Sex Roles, 6,* 581–592.

Tomkiewicz, J., Brenner, O. C., & Adeyemi-Bello, T. (1998). The impact of perceptions and stereotypes on the managerial mobility of African Americans. *Journal of Social Psychology, 138,* 88–92.

Topolski, R., Boyd-Bowman, K. A., & Ferguson, H. (2003). Grapes of wrath: Discrimination in the produce aisle. *Analyses of Social Issues and Public Policy, 3,* 111–119.

Tougas, F., Brown, R., Beaton, A. M., & Joly, S. (1995). Neosexism: Plus ça change, plus c'est pareil. *Personality and Social Psychology Bulletin, 21,* 842–850.

Towles-Schwen, T., & Fazio, R. H. (2001). On the origins of racial attitudes: Correlates of childhood experiences. *Personality and Social Psychology Bulletin, 27,* 162–175.

Towles-Schwen, T., & Fazio, R. H. (2003). Choosing social situations: the relation between automatically activated racial attitudes and anticipated comfort interacting with African Americans. *Personality and Social Psychology Bulletin, 29,* 170–182.

Trafimow, D., & Finlay, K. A. (1996). The importance of subjective norms for a minority of people: Between-subjects and within-subjects analyses. *Personality and Social Psychology Bulletin, 22,* 820–828.

Triplet, R. G., & Sugarman, D. B. (1987). Reactions to AIDS victims: Ambiguity breeds contempt. *Personality and Social Psychology Bulletin, 13,* 265–274.

Trope, Y., & Thompson, E. P. (1997). Looking for truth in all the wrong places? Asymmetric search of individuating information about stereotyped group members. *Journal of Personality and Social Psychology, 73,* 229–241.

Tropp, L. R., & Anderson, R. A. (2004, January). *Assessing interest in cross-group interactions: Minority and majority perspectives.* Paper presented at the meeting of the Society for Personality and Social Psychology, Austin, TX.

Tropp, L. R., & Wright, S. C. (1999). Ingroup identification and relative deprivation: An examination of multiple social comparisons. *European Journal of Social Psychology, 29,* 707–724.

Tropp, L. R. (2003). The psychological impact of prejudice: Implications for intergroup contact. *Group Processes & Intergroup Relations, 6,* 131–149.

Tsui, A. S., Egan, T. D., & O'Reilly, C. A. III. (1992). Being different: Relational demography and organizational attachment. *Administrative Science Quarterly, 37,* 549–579.

Tucker, W. H. (1994). *The science and politics of racial research.* Urbana: University of Illinois Press.

Tuckman, J., & Lorge, I. (1953a). The effect of changed directions on the attitudes about old people and the older worker. *Educational and Psychological Measurement, 13,* 607–613.

Tuckman, J., & Lorge, I. (1953b). "When aging begins" and stereotypes about aging. *Journal of Gerontology, 8,* 489–492.

Turner, J. C. (1996). Henri Tajfel: An introduction. In W. P. Robinson (Ed.), *Social groups and identities: Developing the legacy of Henri Tajfel* (pp. 1–23). Oxford, England: Butterworth-Heinemann.

Turner, J. C., & Oakes, P. J. (1989). Self-categorization theory and social influence. In P. B. Paulus (Ed.), *The psychology of group influence* (pp. 233–275). Hillsdale, NJ: Erlbaum.

Turpin-Petrosino, C. (2002). Hateful sirens . . . Who hears their song? An examination of student attitudes toward hate groups and affiliation potential. *Journal of Social Issues, 58,* 281–301.

Twenge, J. M. (1997a). Changes in masculine and feminine traits over time: A meta-analysis. *Sex Roles, 35,* 461–488.

Twenge, J. M. (1997b). Attitudes toward women, 1970–1995: A meta-analysis. *Psychology of Women Quarterly, 21,* 35–51.

Twenge, J. M., & Crocker, J. (2002). Race and self-esteem: Meta-analyses comparing Whites, Blacks, Hispanics, Asians, and American Indians and comment on Gray-Little and Hafdahl (2000). *Psychological Bulletin, 128,* 371–408.

Twenge, J. M., & Zucker, A. N. (1999). What is a feminist? Evaluations and stereotypes in closed- and open-ended responses. *Psychology of Women Quarterly, 23,* 591–605.

Tyler, T. R., & Smith, H. J. (1998). Social justice and social movements. In D. T. Gilbert, S. T. Fiske, & G. Lindzey (Eds.), *Handbook of social psychology* (4th ed., vol. 2, pp. 595–629). Boston: McGraw-Hill.

U.S. Bureau of Labor Statistics (2002a). *Employment status of the civilian noninstitutional population 16 years and over by sex* (Table 2). Retrieved September 24, 2004, from www.bls.gov.

U.S. Bureau of Labor Statistics (2002b). *Employed persons by major occupation and sex, 1983 and 2002 annual averages* (Table 10). Retrieved September 27, 2004, from www.bls.gov.

U.S. Bureau of the Census. (2003, October 21). *Educational attainment—People 25 years old and over, by total money earnings in 2002, work experience in 2002, age, race, Hispanic origin, and sex.* Retrieved May 7, 2004, from http://www.ferret.bls.census.gov/macro/032003/perinc/new03_000.htm.

U.S. Department of Education (2003). *Enrollment in degree granting institutions.* Washington, DC: Author.

U.S. Equal Employment Opportunity Commission. (2004, March 17). *Occupational employment in private industry by race/ethnic group/sex, and by industry, United States, 2002.* Retrieved May 6, 2004, from http://www.eeoc.gov/stats/jobpat/2002/us.html.

U.S. Federal Bureau of Investigation, (1999). *Hate crimes data collection guidelines.* Retrieved June 7, 2004, from http://www.fbi.gov/ucr/hatecrime.pdf.

U. S. Senate Special Committee on Aging (1986). *Developments in aging: 1985* (vol. 1). Washington, DC: U.S. Government Printing Office.

Urban Alliance on Race Relations. (1995). *Policeman ad.* Retrieved September 28, 2003, from http://www.urban alliance.ca/uarr/policeman.html.

Utsey, S. O., McCarthy, E., Eubanks, R., & Adrian, G. (2002). White racism and suboptimal psychological functioning among White Americans: Implications for counseling and prejudice prevention. *Journal of Multicultural Counseling and Development, 30,* 81–95.

Valentine, S. (1998). Self-esteem and men's negative stereotypes of women who work. *Psychological Reports, 83,* 920–922.

Van Biema, D. (2001, October 1). As American as . . . *Time,* 72–74.

van den Berghe, P. L. (1967). *Race and racism: A comparative perspective.* New York: Wiley.

van der Meide, W. (2000). *Legislating equality: A review of laws affecting gay, lesbian, bisexual, and transgendered people in the United States.* New York: Policy Institute of the National Gay and Lesbian Task Force.

van Dick, R., Wagner, U., Pettigrew, T. F., Christ, O., Wolf, C., Petzel, T., Smith Castro, V., & Jackson, J. S. (2004). Role of perceived importance in intergroup contact. *Journal of Personality and Social Psychology, 87,* 211–227.

Van Hiel, A., & Mervielde, I. (2002). Explaining conservative beliefs and political preferences: A comparison of social dominance orientation and authoritarianism. *Journal of Applied Social Psychology, 32,* 965–976.

Van Hiel, A., Pandelaere, M., & Duriez, B. (2004). The impact of need for closure on conservative beliefs and racism: Differential mediation by authoritarian submission and authoritarian dominance. *Personality and Social Psychology Bulletin, 30,* 824–837.

Vanman, E. J., Paul, B. Y., Ito, T. A., & Miller, N. (1997). The modern face of prejudice and structural features that moderate the effect of cooperation on affect. *Journal of Personality and Social Psychology, 73,* 941–959.

Vanneman, R. D., & Pettigrew, T. F. (1972). Race and relative deprivation in the urban United States. *Race, 13,* 461–486.

van Oudenhoven, J. P., Groenewoud, J. T., & Hewstone, M. (1996). Cooperation, ethnic salience, and generalization of interethnic attitudes. *European Journal of Social Psychology, 26,* 649–661.

van Oudenhoven, J. P., Prins, K. S., & Buunk, B. P. (1998). Attitudes of minority and majority members towards adaptation of immigrant. *European Journal of Social Psychology, 28,* 995–1013.

Van Vianen, A. E. M., & Willemsen, T. M. (1992). The employment interview: The role of sex stereotypes in the evaluation of male and female job applicants in the Netherlands. *Journal of Applied Social Psychology, 22,* 471–491.

Vasil, L., & Wass, H. (1993). Portrayal of the elderly in the media: A literature review and implications for educational gerontologists. *Educational Gerontology, 19,* 71–85.

Verkuyten, M. (1996). Personal self-esteem and prejudice among ethnic majority and minority youth. *Journal of Research in Personality, 30,* 248–263.

Verkuyten, M. (2001). "Abnormalization" of ethnic minorities in conversation. *British Journal of Social Psychology, 40,* 257–278.

Verkuyten, M., & Hagendoorn, L. (1998). Prejudice and self-categorization: The variable role of authoritarianism and in-group stereotypes. *Personality and Social Psychology Bulletin, 24,* 99–110.

Verkuyten, M., & Nekuee, S. (2001). Self-esteem, discrimination, and coping among refugees: The moderating role of self-categorization. *Journal of Applied Social Psychology, 31,* 1058–1075.

Vescio, T. K., & Biernat, M. (2003). Family values and antipathy toward gay men. *Journal of Applied Social Psychology, 33,* 833–847.

Vescio, T. K., Sechrist, G. B., & Paolucci, M. P. (2003). Perspective taking and prejudice reduction: The mediational role of empathy arousal and situational attributions. *European Journal of Social Psychology, 33,* 455–472.

Vescio, T. K., Snyder, M., & Butz, D. A. (2003). Power in stereotypically masculine domains: A social influence x stereotype match model. *Journal of Personality and Social Psychology, 85,* 1062–1078.

Vitello, P. (2004). When bias hits golf, all eyes on Tiger. In P. S. Rothenberg (Ed.), *Race, class and gender in the United States* (6th ed., pp. 252–253). New York: Worth.

Voci, A., & Hewstone, M. (2003). Intergroup contact and prejudice toward immigrants in Italy: The mediational role of anxiety and the moderational role of group salience. *Group Processes & Intergroup Relations, 6,* 37–54.

Voils, C. I., Ashburn-Nardo, L., & Monteith, M. J. (2002). Evidence of prejudice-related conflict and associated affect beyond the college setting. *Group Processes & Intergroup Relations, 5,* 19–33.

Vonk, R., & Ashmore, R. D. (2003). Thinking about gender types: Cognitive organization of female and male types. *British Journal of Social Psychology, 42,* 257–280.

Wagner, U., & Zick, A. (1995). The relation of formal education to ethnic prejudice: Its reliability, validity, and explanation. *European Journal of Social Psychology, 25,* 41–56.

Waldus, S., & Mummendey, A. (2004). Inclusion in a superordinate category, in-group prototypicality, and attitudes towards out-groups. *Journal of Experimental Social Psychology, 40,* 466–477.

Walker, I., & Crogan, M. (1998). Academic performance, prejudice, and the jigsaw classroom: New pieces to the puzzle. *Journal of Community & Applied Social Psychology, 8,* 381–393.

Walker, I., & Smith, H. J. (2002). Fifty years of relative deprivation research. In I. Walker & H. J. Smith (Eds.), *Relative deprivation: Specification, development, and integration* (pp. 1–9). New York: Cambridge University Press.

Wallace, G. C. (1963, January 14). *The 1963 Inaugural Address of Governor George C. Wallace,* Montgomery, Alabama. Retrieved July 7, 2003, from www.archives.state.al.us/govs_list/Inauguralspeech.html.

Waller, D. (2002, December 30). Lott: The fallout. *Time,* 21.

Walton, G. M., & Cohen, G. L. (2003). Stereotype lift. *Journal of Experimental Social Psychology, 39,* 456–467.

Watkins, S. (1993, October 18). Racism du jour at Shoney's. *The Nation,* pp. 424–428.

Weakland, M., & Kite, M. E. (1999, August). *Sexual orientation and the implicit inversion model.* Paper presented at the American Psychological Association, Boston.

Weary, G., & Edwards, J. A. (1994). Individual differences in causal uncertainty. *Journal of Personality and Social Psychology, 67,* 308–318.

Weary, G., Jacobson, J. A., Edwards, J. A., & Tobin, S. J. (2001). Chronic and temporarily activated causal uncertainty beliefs and stereotype usage. *Journal of Personality and Social Psychology, 81,* 206–219.

Weber, R., & Crocker, J. (1983). Cognitive processes in the revision of stereotypic beliefs. *Journal of Personality and Social Psychology, 45,* 961–977.

Webster, R. J., & Coon, H. (2004, January). *Social dominance orientation, right-wing authoritarianism, and gender as predictors of heterosexuals' attitudes toward homosexuality, Blacks, and Arabs.* Paper presented at the meeting of the Society for Personality and Social Psychology, Austin, TX.

Wegener, D. T., Petty, R. E., Smoak, N. D., & Fabrigar, L. R. (2004). Multiple routes to resisting attitude change. In E. S. Knowles & J. A. Linn (Eds.), *Resistance and persuasion* (pp. 13–38). Mahwah, NJ: Erlbaum.

Wegner, D. M. (1994). Ironic processes of mental control. *Psychological Review, 101,* 34–52.

Wegner, D. M., & Gold, D. B. (1995). Fanning old flames: Emotional and cognitive effects of suppressing thoughts of a past relationship. *Journal of Personality and Social Psychology, 68,* 782–792.

Wegner, D. M., Schneider, D. J., Carter, S. R. III, & White, T. L. (1987). Paradoxical effects of thought suppression. *Journal of Personality and Social Psychology, 53,* 5–13.

Weiland, A., & Coughlin, R. (1979). Self-identification and preferences: A comparison of White and Mexican-American first and third graders. *Journal of Cross-Cultural Psychology, 10,* 356–365.

Weinberg, G. (1972). *Society and the healthy homosexual.* New York: St. Martin's.

Weiner, B. (1995). *Judgments of responsibility: A foundation for a theory of social conduct.* New York: Guilford.

Weiner, B., Perry, R. P., & Magnusson, J. (1988). An attributional analysis of reactions to stigmas. *Journal of Personality and Social Psychology, 55,* 738–748.

Wernick, M., & Manaster, G. J. (1984). Age and the perception of age and attractiveness. *The Gerontologist, 24,* 408–414.

Wheeler, S. C., Jarvis, W. B. G., & Petty, R. E. (2001). Think unto others: The self-destructive impact of negative racial stereotypes. *Journal of Experimental Social Psychology, 37,* 173–180.

Whitbourne, S. K., & Hulicka, I. M. (1990). Ageism in undergraduate psychology texts. *American Psychologist, 45,* 1127–1136.

White, J. A. (2001). Political eschatology: A theology of antigovernment extremism. *American Behavioral Scientist, 44,* 937–956.

Whitley, B. E., Jr. (1990). The relationship of heterosexuals' attributions for the causes of homosexuality to attitudes toward lesbians and gay men. *Personality and Social Psychology Bulletin, 16,* 369–377.

Whitley, B. E., Jr. (1999). Right-wing authoritarianism, social dominance orientation, and prejudice. *Journal of Personality and Social Psychology, 77,* 126–134.

Whitley, B. E., Jr. (2001a). Gender-role variables and attitudes toward homosexuality. *Sex Roles, 45,* 691–722.

Whitley, B. E., Jr. (2001b, August). *Group-based dominance, opposition to equality, and prejudice.* Poster presented at the meeting of the American Psychological Association, San Francisco.

Whitley, B. E., Jr. (2002). *Principles of research in behavioral science* (2nd ed.). New York: McGraw-Hill.

Whitley, B. E., Jr., & Lee, S. E. (2000). The relationship of authoritarianism and related constructs to attitudes toward homosexuality. *Journal of Applied Social Psychology, 30,* 144–170.

Whitley, B. E., Jr., & Wilkinson, W. W. (2002, June). *Authoritarianism, social dominance orientation, empathy, and prejudice: A test of three models.* Poster presented at the meeting of the American Psychological Society, New Orleans.

Wilder, D. A. (1984). Intergroup contact: The typical member and the exception to the rule. *Journal of Experimental Social Psychology, 20,* 177–194.

Wilder, D. A. (Ed.). (1986). *Social categorization: Implications for creation and reduction of intergroup bias.* New York: Academic Press.

Wilder, D. A., & Simon, A. F. (2001). Affect as a cause of intergroup bias. In R. Brown & S. Gaertner (Eds.), *Blackwell handbook of social psychology: Intergroup processes* (pp. 153–172). Malden, MA: Blackwell.

Wilder, D. A., Simon, A. F., & Faith, M. (1996). Enhancing the impact of counterstereotypic information: Dispositional attributions for deviance. *Journal of Personality and Social Psychology, 71*, 276–287.

Wilkinson, W. W. (2004). Religiosity, authoritarianism, and homophobia: A multidimensional approach. *International Journal for the Psychology of Religion, 14*, 55–67.

Williams, J., & Best, D. L. (1990). *Measuring sex stereotypes: A thirty-nation study*. Newbury Park, CA: Sage.

Williams, J. E., & Morland, J. K. (1976). *Race, color, and the young child*. Chapel Hill, NC: The University of North Carolina Press.

Williams, K., Kemper, S., & Hummert, M. L. (2003). Improving nursing home communication: An intervention to reduce elderspeak. *Gerontologist, 43*, 242–247.

Williams, K. Y., & O'Reilly, C. A. III. (1998). Demography and diversity in organizations: A review of 40 years of research. *Research in Organizational Behavior, 20*, 77–140.

Williams, L. (2000). *It's the little things*. New York: Harcourt.

Williams, P. J. (1997, December 29). Of race and risk. *Nation*, 10.

Wilson, M. S., & Liu, J. H. (2003). Social dominance orientation and gender: The moderating role of gender identity. *British Journal of Social Psychology, 42*, 187–198.

Wilson, T. C. (1996a). Cohort and prejudice: Whites' attitudes toward Blacks, Hispanics, Jews and Asians. *Public Opinion Quarterly, 53*, 174–183.

Wilson, T. C. (1996b). Compliments will get you nowhere: Benign stereotypes, prejudice, and anti-Semitism. *The Sociological Quarterly, 37*, 465–479.

Wilson, T. D., Lindsey, S., & Schooler, T. Y. (2000). A model of dual attitudes. *Psychological Review, 107*, 101–126.

Winkler, J. D., & Taylor, S. E. (1979). Preference, expectations, and attributional bias: Two field studies. *Journal of Applied Social Psychology, 9*, 183–197.

Winocur, S., Schoen, L. G., & Sirowatka, A. H. (1989). Perceptions of male and female academics within a teaching context. *Research in Higher Education, 30*, 317–329.

Wisby, G. (2001, October 2). Merits of ethnic, race stops disputed by experts. *Chicago Sun Times*, 14.

Wittenbrink, B., Judd, C. M., & Park, B. (1997). Evidence for racial prejudice at the implicit level and its relation to questionnaire measures. *Journal of Personality and Social Psychology, 72*, 262–274.

Wittenbrink, B., Judd, C. M., & Park, B. (2001). Spontaneous prejudice in context: Variability in automatically activated attitudes. *Journal of Personality and Social Psychology, 81*, 815–827.

Wittig, M. A., & Molina, L. (2000). Moderators and mediators of prejudice reduction in multicultural education. In S. Oskamp (Ed.), *Reducing prejudice and discrimination* (pp. 295–318). Mahwah, NJ: Erlbaum.

Wolff, C. (1989, September 29). New York sues job agencies in bias case. *New York Times*, p. B1.

Wolin, R. (2003, October 24). Are suicide bombings morally defensible? *The Chronicle of Higher Education*, p. B12–B14.

Wolsko, C., Park, B., Judd, C. M., & Wittenbrink, B. (2000). Framing interethnic ideology: Effects of multicultural and color-blind perspectives on judgments of groups and individuals. *Journal of Personality and Social Psychology, 78*, 635–654.

Wood, P. B., & Bartkowski, J. P. (2004). Attribution style and public policy attitudes toward gay rights. *Social Science Quarterly, 85,* 58–74.

Wood, P. B., & Sonleitner, N. (1996). The effect of childhood interracial contact on adult antiblack prejudice. *International Journal of Intercultural Relations, 20,* 1–17.

Worchel, S. (1999). *Written in blood: Ethnic identity and the struggle for human harmony.* New York: Worth.

Word, C. O., Zanna, M. P., & Cooper, J. (1974). The nonverbal mediation of self-fulfilling prophecies in interracial interaction. *Journal of Experimental Social Psychology, 10,* 109–120.

Wormser, R. (2003). *The rise and fall of Jim Crow.* New York: St. Martin's.

Wright, P., Ferris, S. P., Hiller, J. S., & Kroll, M. (1995). Competitiveness through management of diversity: Effects on stock price valuation. *Academy of Management Journal, 38,* 272–287.

Wright, S. C., Aron, A., McLaughlin-Volpe, T., & Ropp, S. A. (1997). The extended contact effect: Knowledge of cross-group friendships and prejudice. *Journal of Personality and Social Psychology, 73,* 73–90.

Wyer, N. A., Sherman, J. W., & Stroesser, S. J. (1998). The spontaneous suppression of racial stereotypes. *Social Cognition, 16,* 340–352.

Wyer, N. A., Sherman, J. W., & Stroesser, S. J. (2000). The roles of motivation and ability in controlling the consequences of stereotype suppression. *Personality and Social Psychology Bulletin, 26,* 13–25.

Yang, A. S. (1997). Trends: Attitudes toward homosexuality. *Public Opinion Quarterly, 61,* 477–507.

Ybarra, O., Stephan, W. G., Schaberg, L., & Lawrence, J. S. (2003). Beliefs about the disconfirmability of stereotypes: The stereotype disconfirmability effect. *Journal of Applied Social Psychology, 33,* 2630–2646.

Yee, M. D., & Brown, R. (1994). The development of gender differentiation in young children. *British Journal of Social Psychology, 33,* 183–196.

Yoder, J. D. (1985). An academic woman as a token: A case study. *Journal of Social Issues, 41,* 61–72.

Yoder, J. D. (1991). Rethinking tokenism: Looking beyond the numbers. *Gender and Society, 5,* 178–192.

Yoder, J. D. (1997). "Outsider within" the firehouse. Subordination and difference in the social interactions of African American women firefighters. *Gender and Society, 11,* 324–341.

Yoder, J. D. (2002). Context matters: Understanding tokenism processes and their impact on women's work. *Psychology of Women Quarterly, 26,* 1–8.

Young-Bruehl, E. (1996). *The anatomy of prejudices.* Cambridge, MA: Harvard University Press.

Yzerbyt, V. Y., Schadron, G., Leyens, J., & Rocher, S. (1994). Social judgeability: The impact of meta-informational cues on the use of stereotypes. *Journal of Personality and Social Psychology, 66,* 48–55.

Zajonc, R. B. (2002). The zoomorphism of human collective violence. In L. S. Newman & R. Erber (Eds.), *Understanding genocide: The social psychology of the Holocaust* (pp. 222–238). New York: Oxford University Press.

Zalk, S. R., & Katz, P. A. (1978). Gender attitudes in children. *Sex Roles, 4*, 349–357.

Zargarpour, S. (2002). Individual differences in children's group perceptions and peer preferences as a function of prejudice level. *Dissertation Abstracts International (Section B): The Sciences and Engineering, 62* (11–B), 5436.

Zebrowitz, L. A. (1996). Physical appearance as a basis of stereotyping. In C. N. Macrae, C. Stangor & M. Hewstone (Eds.), *Stereotypes and stereotyping* (pp. 79–120). New York: Guilford.

Zebrowitz-McArthur, L. A. (1981). What grabs you? The role of attention in impression formation and causal attribution. In E. T. Higgins, C. P. Herman, & M. P. Zanna (Eds.), *Social cognition* (pp. 201–246). Hillsdale, NJ: Erlbaum.

Zepelin, H., Sills, R. A., & Heath, M. W. (1986). Is age becoming irrelevant? An exploratory study of perceived age norms. *International Journal of Aging and Human Development, 24*(4), 241–256.

Zimmerman, B. J. (2002). Differences in children's implicit gender knowledge and explicit gender beliefs as a function of age and gender schematicity. *Dissertation Abstracts International (Section B): The Sciences and Engineering, 63,* (5-B), 2628.

Zucker, K. J., Wilson-Smith, D. N., Kurita, J. A., & Stern, A. (1995). Children's appraisals of sex-typed behavior in their peers. *Sex Roles, 33*, 703–725.

Zuckerman, M. (1990). Some dubious premises in research and theory on racial differences: Scientific, social, and ethical issues. *American Psychologist, 45*, 1297–1303.

Zuwerink, J. R., Devine, P. G., Monteith, M. J., & Cook, D. A. (1996). Prejudice toward Blacks: With and without compunction? *Basic and Applied Social Psychology, 18,* 131–150.

Name Index

Subject Index

Boldface page numbers indicate key terms.